Earlier

Contemporary Social Problems

FOURTH EDITION

AUTHORS

JOHN A. CLAUSEN
 University of California, Berkeley
ALBERT K. COHEN
 University of Connecticut
JAMES S. COLEMAN
 University of Chicago
KINGSLEY DAVIS
 University of California, Berkeley
CYNTHIA FUCHS EPSTEIN
 Queens College
AMITAI ETZIONI
 Columbia University
WILLIAM J. GOODE
 Columbia University
EDWIN HARWOOD
 New College
SEYMOUR MARTIN LIPSET
 Stanford University
DAVID MATZA
 University of California, Berkeley
ROBERT K. MERTON
 Columbia University
HENRY MILLER
 University of California, Berkeley
ROBERT NISBET
 Columbia University
THOMAS FRASER PETTIGREW
 Harvard University
DAVID RIESMAN
 Harvard University
MATILDA WHITE RILEY
 Bowdoin College
JAMES F. SHORT, JR.
 Stanford University
ROBERT STRAUS
 University of Kentucky
JOAN WARING
 Russell Sage Foundation
ROBERT S. WEISS
 Harvard Medical School

Contemporary Social Problems

FOURTH EDITION

Edited by

ROBERT K. MERTON
Columbia University

and

ROBERT NISBET
Columbia University

HARCOURT BRACE JOVANOVICH, INC.
New York   Chicago   San Francisco   Atlanta

ISBN: 0-15-513793-X

Library of Congress Catalog Card Number: 76-4690

Printed in the United States of America

Picture Credits

Russell Abraham/Jeroboam, Inc.: p. 229
James Andanson/Sygma: p. 705
Paul Conklin/Monkmeyer Press Photo: p. 444
George W. Gardner: pp. 264, 304, 326, 327, 602, 638, 716, 726
Charles Gatewood: pp. 46, 58, 92, 102, 140, 158, 180, 365, 380, 510,
    556, 562, 650
Ingbert Grüttner/Peter Arnold Photo Archives: p. 281
Ellis Herwig/Stock, Boston: p. 458
James H. Karales/Peter Arnold Photo Archives: pp. 174, 475, 516
J. P. Laffont/Sygma: p. 674
Andy Mercado/Jeroboam, Inc.: pp. 421, 625
Lida Moser/DPI: p. 218
Werner H. Müller/Peter Arnold Photo Archives: p. 354
National Institute on Alcohol and Alcohol Abuse: p. 191
Nikolais Dance Theatre, photo by Susan Schiff Faludi: p. 2
Bill Ray/Time/Life Picture Agency: p. 412
Kent Reno/Jeroboam, Inc.: p. 294
Sybil Shelton/Monkmeyer Press Photo: p. 133
Harvey Stein: p. 663
Hap Stewart/Jeroboam, Inc.: p. 248
Erika Stone/Peter Arnold Photo Archives: p. 213
United Press International: pp. 119, 497, 574
Peter Vilms/Jeroboam, Inc.: p. 617

PREFACE

This Fourth Edition is the most thorough revision of *Contemporary Social Problems* in the book's history. It includes four entirely new chapters, and the other chapters have been rewritten or greatly revised in content, organization, and style. And of course every chapter is abreast of the current state of knowledge in the field.

The modifications in this edition reflect changes in the social reality and in the sociological understanding of social problems. But neither our society nor our knowledge of it has been wholly transformed in a few years. Along with change, there are basic continuities. That is why the fundamental character of this book has remained constant through all editions.

Above all else, we retain the conviction that no one mind, nor any two or three minds, can deal authoritatively with the wide range of social problems treated in this book. We therefore continue to have each problem examined by a scholar-specialist who knows it in great depth and can distill its essentials for the student. Now, as before, there are two main divisions in the book —"Deviant Behavior" and "Social Disorganization." We have intensified our effort to integrate the materials in the book, partly by having both editors and authors refer to related discussions in other chapters.

A short review of the principal changes will orient previous users of the book and new readers alike.

1. The Introduction (in previous editions, the Epilogue) by Robert K. Merton sets out the structure of the book, with ample illustrative materials drawn from the following chapters. It emphasizes that although there is no one comprehensive and uniformly accepted theory, the various "schools of sociology" do agree on certain fundamental ideas, and it specifically indicates how current theories of deviance complement one another as they deal with different aspects of the same problems. Largely rewritten and shortened, the chapter is designed to help the reader acquire a theoretical orientation to social problems before turning to the problems themselves.

2. The Epilogue is new to this edition. In place of his Introduction to the three earlier editions, Robert Nisbet has written this final chapter dealing with social problems in their relationship not only to discernible historical trends, but also to possible futures confronting humanity. The chapter looks at the future as a perennial object of interest and study, as a context for social problems, and as an influence on human behavior. It focuses on the distinctive character of today's Western societies by way of illustration and prediction.

3. As we have said, the new chapters reflect both social changes and an enlarged understanding of some of those changes. Thus Chapter 7, "Equality and Inequality," by Seymour Martin Lipset, examines the processes leading

to various forms of social inequality together with their human consequences. It puts these matters in perspective by systematically comparing social inequalities in the United States and the Soviet Union.

Inequalities of the sort found in class stratification and in race and ethnic relations have long been recognized as related to social problems. These inequalities receive careful attention in this edition as in past ones. But an intensified social awareness of other inequalities has brought with it new research and new understanding. Chapter 8, "Age and Aging," by Matilda White Riley and Joan Waring, provides an analysis of the social problems attending age inequalities, age conflict, and age segregation at every phase in the life course of human beings. We know of no comparable analysis of how the process of growing older (not merely growing old) leads to problems for people at all stages of life and for society as a whole.

A growing sense of sex inequalities has been fostered by women's social movements of recent years. Cynthia Fuchs Epstein examines these inequalities in the new Chapter 9, "Sex Roles," which centers on the social problems raised for both women and men by various forms of sex-typing of social roles and by the cumulative disadvantages that often go with them.

4. Just as changes in society and in knowledge have inspired the new chapters, so they have resulted, in the revised chapters, in the consideration of new topics. These are too numerous to be itemized in full, but they include: professional crime, white-collar crime, and corruption, as well as evolving theories of crime, in Chapter 1, "Crime and Juvenile Delinquency," by Albert K. Cohen and James F. Short, Jr.; developing patterns of drug use and abuse in Chapter 3 by John A. Clausen; a much fuller examination of the problems of world shortages of energy and other resources in Chapter 6, "The World's Population Crisis," by Kingsley Davis; Chicano-Anglo relations in Chapter 10, "Race and Intergroup Relations," by Thomas Fraser Pettigrew; a reworked analysis of marital stability in different segments of the U.S. population and a consideration of "no-fault" divorce in a historical classification of divorce complaints in Chapter 11, "Family Disorganization," by William J. Goode; increased coverage of urban problems in James S. Coleman's Chapter 12, "Community Disorganization"; school violence, political terror, and guerrilla tactics in Amitai Etzioni's Chapter 15, "Collective Violence."

These substantial changes, which have their counterparts in the other chapters, serve, among other things, to deepen our understanding of the interplay between social disorganization and deviant behavior—a theme that runs throughout the book.

The foregoing refers to changes in the *substance* of the book. Beyond these are changes in format, organization, and style.

5. The text of this edition is shorter than that of any of its predecessors and the chapters are more nearly uniform in length. This curtailment, we believe, has not been at the expense of essentials. The writing is more student-oriented, it is less technical, and, we like to think, it is livelier and clearer.

6. For the first time, each chapter is preceded by an outline of its contents

and followed by a compact, point-by-point summary. The purpose of these devices is not to simplify but to sharpen understanding by providing useful check-points for major perspectives and themes. The authors have also appended brief bibliographies of recommended reading for students interested in pursuing their subjects further.

These are the changes. We should note once again that along with change there is continuity. We have retained the basic structure and orientation of this collaborative effort that, over the years, have given *Contemporary Social Problems* an identifiable place in the continuing and far-from-completed development of a comprehensive understanding of social problems.

ROBERT K. MERTON   ROBERT NISBET
Columbia University   Columbia University

Preparation of this book has been informed throughout by the responses of readers of past editions, to whom we gratefully acknowledge our debt. Further, the editors have been greatly aided by the tireless assistance of Mary Wilson Miles and Thomas F. Gieryn of Columbia University. All collaborators in this book have benefited from the often inventive aid provided by members of the staff of Harcourt Brace Jovanovich, most notably Judith Greissman, Claire T. Rubin, Anna Kopczynski, Kay Reinhart Ziff, and Kenzi Sugihara.

RKM   RN

CONTENTS

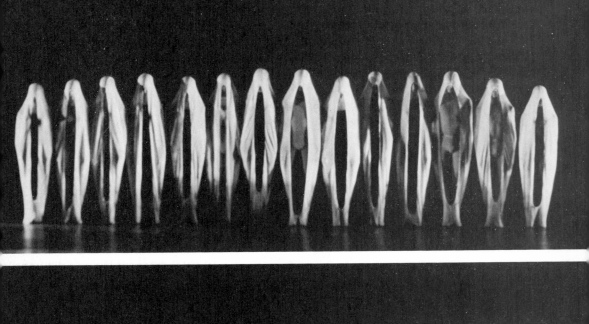

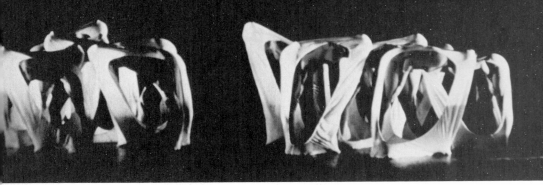

Introduction

The Sociology of Social Problems

ROBERT K. MERTON

How do social problems arise? What kinds of problems are there and how do they affect people's lives? What do we know about ways of coping with them, once they have surfaced? And what do we know about the further social consequences of our coping strategies?

These are a few of the many questions considered in the body of sociological theory that focuses on social problems. That the answers to these difficult questions are far from clear is evident from the conspicuous problems that afflict societies everywhere. All the same, these problems would probably be even worse without the knowledge we do have to draw upon in our collective efforts to deal with them.

The sociological theory of social problems consists of developing sets of ideas designed to help us understand the kinds, sources, persistence, and consequences of major troubles in society. That theory gets fairly complicated at times, the complexity being one sign of its comparative immaturity. We can therefore benefit from having some guides through the maze. Two sociological parables may be helpful. By a sociological parable I mean a short tale that teaches a sociological lesson or truth. Two such stories may help us remember some basic ideas that run through this chapter and through the entire book.

Let us call the first of these "the Monsieur Jourdain parable." It is based upon the chief character in the famous seventeenth-century play by Molière, *Le Bourgeois Gentilhomme* (best translated as *The Would-Be Gentleman*). Jourdain is a newly-rich, upwardly-mobile fellow who, having made his pile, is eager to acquire the manners and skills suitable to what he hopes will be his new station in life. He hires a few tutors who undertake, for ample fees, to teach him fencing, dancing, and, not least, the proper use of the French language. In his most memorable absurdity, Jourdain is greatly pleased to learn that along with poetry there is something called *prose,* and he is absolutely delighted to discover that he himself has actually been *speaking* prose all his life, *without even knowing it!*

Once encountered, the story of Monsieur Jourdain is not easily forgotten. Apart from lampooning the parvenu, it immortalizes the idea that people engage in patterns of behavior without realizing that they do so, just as a child speaks understandable sentences before learning the rules of grammar and syntax. Applied to our subject, the parable helps us remember that whenever people talk about social problems, they speak, *whether they know it or not,* the prose of sociological theory. If we are not to be as naive as Monsieur Jourdain, therefore, we had better bring the ideas we use out into the open and examine them as we try to understand the character, sources, and human consequences of social problems. It is the purpose of this chapter to do precisely that, in preparation for the more detailed analyses of specific social problems in the chapters that follow.

A companion to the Monsieur Jourdain parable can be described as "the Benjamin Rush parable." It too helps us keep in mind something we might be inclined to forget in our search for a sociological understanding of social problems. A signer of the Declaration of Independence and often called the father of American psychiatry, Rush was a many-sided man. He himself, however, mistakenly regarded one theory as his major contribution to medicine: his theory that all disease had the same single cause, a condition of excessive "excitability in the blood vessels," and could therefore be cured by the practice of bleeding and purging. This theory of *the single universal cause of disease* was influential for a time, but could not withstand the results of empirical research and the alternative theories proposing different causes for different diseases. Rush's theory dropped out of sight and is dredged up here, not as an historical curiosity, but as a story with a sociological moral.

The Benjamin Rush parable serves to remind us of the fallacy of assuming that any one theory can account for the whole wide range of social problems. Just as Rush mistakenly took the term "disease" to imply that there must be a single disorder with a single cause, rather than many diseases often with distinctive causes, so we risk being mistaken in assuming that the term "social problem" must refer to a single entity with its universal cause. The parable warns against any doctrine of a single cause of social problems, whether it be original sin, human nature, economic structure, genetic deficiencies, or environmental deficits. It warns us off the sociological version of the extreme view that everything we dislike in the social world results from somebody's deliberate evil-doing, or that only good can beget good and only evil can beget evil. Doctrines of this sort confuse purposes with actual outcomes; they leave no place for an important social phenomenon—the unintended consequences of purposive social action.[1]

This does not mean that there is only a chaos of conflicting theories. As in many disciplines, in place of one all-encompassing theory we find a condition of theoretical pluralism, with differing theories often complementing each other rather than being inevitably opposed. The theories of social disorganization and deviant behavior examined briefly in this chapter and variously utilized throughout the book typically deal with different aspects of the same social problem, or with different problems altogether. Thus, the theory of anomie tries to account for the social *origins* of deviant behavior, while labeling theory focuses rather on the ways in which deviant behavior is perpetuated by having stigmatizing labels affixed to people judged to have engaged in that behavior. As we shall see in detail, the important point is that such theoretical orientations need not be in conflict precisely because they typically deal with different aspects of social problems.

The Monsieur Jourdain parable, then, reminds us that in examining social problems we inescapably use *some* theory, whether we know it or not, while the Benjamin Rush parable reminds us that no single theory accounts for every aspect of the wide range of social problems although complementary theories can, in principle, be consolidated into an enlarged sociological understanding.

---

[1] Maria Ossowska, *Social Determinants of Moral Ideas* (Philadelphia: University of Pennsylvania Press, 1970), pp. 108–109; Robert K. Merton, "The Unanticipated Consequences of Purposive Social Action," *American Sociological Review*, Vol. 1 (1936), pp. 894–904.

THE SOCIOLOGICAL DIAGNOSIS OF SOCIAL PROBLEMS

Since everyone lives in society and encounters troubles in doing so, just about everyone has some conception of "social problems." Crime, disease that goes uncured though it is curable, violence, group conflicts and public confusions, the victimizing of people by social institutions—all these and more are what most of us ordinarily mean by "social problems." This popular meaning is not far removed from the sociological sense of the term. But there are differences, and it is useful to see what we learn by looking at social problems from a sociological perspective.

We can move toward such an understanding by examining (1) the criteria for a social problem; (2) the social origins of social problems; (3) the conflicts between social groups and strata in defining social problems; (4) the important difference between manifest (readily identifiable) and latent (obscure) social problems; (5) people's perception of social problems; and finally, (6) the ways in which the belief that unwanted social situations can or cannot be changed enters into the public definition of social problems.

Criteria: Social Realities and Social Norms

Basically, *a social problem exists when there is a sizeable discrepancy between what is and what people think ought to be.* It is difficult to estimate the extent of the disparity between the actual conditions of social life and social norms. It varies among societies and it varies in the same society among social groups and from time to time, since both the social realities and the social norms differ and change. All sociologists agree that current social statistics about troubles in society—crime and juvenile delinquency, mental illness, alcohol and drug abuse, and community disorganization, to take only a few examples—are seriously defective. In order to have unbiased statistics it is necessary to obtain a systematic count of comparable units, and there are many unsolved difficulties in accomplishing this in the case of social problems. (It is ironic that the most nearly satisfactory social statistics available in American society deal with performance in professional sports; among statistics dealing with social troubles, the ones on traffic accidents and casualties are perhaps the most reliable.) Beyond such technical shortcomings are further theoretical and methodological problems of measuring the discrepancy between actual and preferred conditions.

In dealing with relatively clear-cut forms of socially defined deviant behavior, simple measures serve—but only up to a point. For example, a full record of the number of homicides in a society would seem to indicate the extent of the gap between the rule forbidding murder and actual behavior in this respect. But even this seemingly simple case contains ambiguities. Many moralities hold every human life to be sacred. For people subscribing to this value, each homicide violates it and so the absolute number occurring in a society would be sufficient to indicate the extent to which homicide constitutes a social problem. But for other observers, who want to compare the scale of this problem among different societies in order to understand how it comes about and what might be done about it, the absolute number of homicides will not serve. Standardized rates must be employed—say, homicides per 100,000 of the population or per 100,000 of subgroups in the population. (On the limitations of crime statistics, see Chapter 1, "Crime and Juvenile Delinquency.")

What holds for homicide holds for all other social problems. For people holding fast to a norm, the *absolute numbers* of departures from it register the scale of a problem; for the sociological researcher, intent on ferreting out the causes and effects of that problem, it will ordinarily be the *relative numbers,* the rates or proportions, that are most useful.

Gauging the magnitude of social problems has further complexities. The mere frequency of acts defined as socially deviant—whether counted in absolute or in relative numbers—does not measure the social significance of the gap between norms and actual conditions. Social values and their associated norms are not all of a kind. They vary greatly in the importance people assign to them. Everyone knows that petty larceny is seen as far less significant morally and socially than homicide; for one thing, very different punishments are meted out to the two classes of offenders.[2] But how are we to compare these two classes of behavior in terms of their magnitude as social problems? Is one homicide to be equated with 10 petty thefts? with 100? with 1,000? Or how are we to compare a case of rape and a large-scale corporate crime involving the swindling of tens of millions of dollars? We sense that these actions are incommensurable and so *feel* that the question of comparing their magnitudes is nonsensical. This feeling requires us to recognize the more general point: *that we have no strict common denominator for comparing the magnitudes of social problems,* even when the comparison is greatly simplified by dealing, as in this example, with various kinds of acts defined as criminal.[3]

The difficulty, of course, is even greater when we try to compare the magnitudes of different *kinds* of social problems. Do the approximately 20,000 homicides in 1974 represent about two-fifths as great a social problem in the United States as the approximately 50,000 deaths from vehicle accidents in that year? How are both problems to be compared with the more than 8 million unemployed Americans in 1975, the nearly quarter of a million patients resident in mental hospitals, or the unnumbered millions who are seriously alienated from their jobs, who find little joy and small purpose in them and at best resign

[2] It was not always so. What is now defined as petty larceny and subject to mild punishment was in other times and places defined as a capital offense. In sixteenth- and seventeenth-century England, for example, thieves were savagely punished. Many were included among the 72,000 offenders estimated to have been executed during the reign of Henry VIII alone. The reasons for such differences over time and space in punishment for the same kinds of actions are one of the largely unsolved problems of sociology. See Jerome Hall, *Theft, Law, and Society* (Boston: Little, Brown, 1935), pp. 84–85.

[3] Jerome G. Manis, "Assessing the Seriousness of Social Problems," *Social Problems,* Vol. 22 (1974), pp. 1–15.

themselves to using only a small part of their capacities in work that is for them little more than a necessary evil?

In the end, it is the values held by people in society that provide crude bases for the relative importance assigned to social problems. As we shall see later in the chapter, this circumstance leads to badly distorted impressions of the social consequences of various problems, even when they are being judged in the light of widespread values.

Social Origins of Social Problems

It is sometimes said that social problems must have social origins. This may seem to mean simply what we have just seen—that the concept of a social problem involves a discrepancy, widely judged as unacceptable, between social norms and social reality. It means more than that, however.

An important claim of sociological theory is that the very *structure* of society—not just its rules concerning behavior—is a substantive source of social problems. In ways that the chapters of this book will examine in detail, social problems such as ethnic, age, and gender discrimination; crime; poverty; and violence result from identifiable social circumstances. Sociologists usually focus on the social, rather than other, sources of major problems in society.

This does not mean that only socially caused difficulties qualify as social problems. Obviously, earthquakes, tornadoes, floods, epidemics, and other natural catastrophes greatly affect people's lives. These are cases of nonsocial events resulting in social disruption. No satisfactory case has yet been made for considering as problems of society only those resulting from the society itself. For whatever forces produce these discrepancies between social standards and social realities, members of the society must respond to them. And the nature of that collective response is greatly affected by the structure of the society, its institutions, and its values.

Someday we may discover that societies develop distinct patterns of coping with social problems according to their origins. This would be an important step forward in practical sociological understanding. But even that discovery would not negate the basic idea that *whatever their origins, social problems are defined by their social consequences.*

One Group's Problem, Another Group's Solution

We now come to a third component in the diagnosis of social problems, one that must be confronted by every school of sociological thought on the subject: Who are the people that define the norms and judge that there is a significant discrepancy between those norms and the social actualities? And what leads these judgments to be either conflicting or generally agreed upon?

Sociologists of every theoretical persuasion often say that "people" or "many people" or "a functionally significant set of people" or even "a majority of people" in a society must regard a social situation as departing from their standards in order for it to qualify as a social problem. When social norms are a matter of overwhelming consensus, as in the cases of laws prohibiting murder, rape, and kidnapping, a more exacting formulation is not required. But many other kinds of cases are far less clear.

Social definitions of social problems have much in common with other normative definitions in society. It is a mistaken notion that each member of society sets about to define social problems in a wholly personal way and that the sum of these independent judgments determines whether behaviors are defined as legitimate or not and institutions as desirable or not. People occupying positions of authority and power, of course, carry more weight than others in deciding social policy and in identifying what are to be taken as significant departures from social norms. Once again, otherwise differing schools of sociological thought are agreed on this general point. All societies have a variety of structurally connected social positions, although the degree of such structural differentiation varies. People occupying different positions in these social structures tend to have different and sometimes strongly conflicting interests and values, even while they also share other interests and values. As a result, they will not have the same ideas about what issues are important problems and require concerted social action.

As a case in point, the widespread acceptance of things as they are in society registers for some the social problem of public apathy, while for others it is organized social protest that is the problem. Or again, the ancient ethical concept of "distributive justice" directs our attention to "the way in which the major social institutions distribute fundamental rights and duties"[4] among those in the society. In terms of distributive justice, a basic problem of societies lies in the fact that the advantages gained by banding together cooperatively for the common good are distributed unevenly among people in different parts of the social structure.

For these structural reasons, *one group's social problem tends to be another group's social solution, just as, sequentially, one group's solution becomes defined as another group's problem.*

The cases of alcohol and marijuana   More than half a century ago many Americans were persuaded that easy access to alcoholic drink led to widespread alcoholism. As a result, such access was prohibited by the Eighteenth Amendment to the Constitution. A good many other Americans considered the cure worse than the disease. They felt that Prohibition violated their values and created other problems. They felt that government was intruding into their private lives to make decisions that should remain altogether personal. For them, it was the legalized "solution" that constituted the new social problem.

---

[4] John Rawls, *A Theory of Justice* (Cambridge, Mass.: Harvard University Press, 1972), p. 4.

After 13 tempestuous years of social conflict over the issue, the Prohibition amendment was repealed. (For further context and analysis, see Chapter 4, "Alcoholism and Problem Drinking.")

Much the same pattern is found today with regard to the legal prohibition of marijuana and certain other drugs. As is observed and elucidated by John Clausen in Chapter 3, "Drug Use":

> Few events in American history did more to undermine the authority of the law and to encourage the development of organized crime than the passing, 50 years ago, of a Constitutional amendment to prohibit the manufacture, sale, and transport of alcohol as a beverage. To some observers of American society, our efforts to deal with drug use have produced a similar problem, one far greater than drugs themselves have brought about.

The case of abortion Abortion provides a particularly instructive example of how social practices defined as problems by people in one part of the social structure may be regarded as solutions by people elsewhere in that structure. The practice of abortion can be examined from both the microscopic standpoint of individuals concerned with solving their personal problems and the macroscopic standpoint of the society concerned with solving its social problems.

Prospective parents may perceive abortion as a way to avoid having an unwanted child. The child may be unwanted for a variety of reasons, some emerging only after the time of conception and others before. For example, the child may have been conceived by intent, and become unwanted only after it was discovered that the pregnancy endangered the woman's life or health, or that the child would probably be born with serious biological defects. Or conception may have occurred by error or ignorance, thus being an unanticipated and undesired consequence of a decidedly purposive action. In the latter case, the child may be unwanted because it will be born out of marriage (a response to a norm varying greatly among societies and over time, as Chapter 11, "Family Disorganization," indicates), or because it is perceived as an economic or social burden interfering with other goals and values such as "moving up" in the world. Whatever the specific reasons, it is the expected birth of the unwanted child, not its abortion, that constitutes the personal problem.

But for other individuals in the society with differing social affiliations and value commitments, abortion constitutes the problem, not the solution. Members of the "Right to Life" social movement, for example, maintain that human life is sacred, that it begins with fertilization, and that killing a fetus is a form of murder. For them, the solution, not the problem, resides in allowing the child, whether wanted or not, to be born, thus upholding the sanctity of human life.

Seen from the macroscopic perspective of the society, abortion exhibits the same pattern. Thus, proponents of certain population policies see the legalized practice of abortion as one way to deal with the problem of massive overpopulation. They advocate institutionalized arrangements and incentives for the use of abortion and other techniques of birth control. But, as Kingsley Davis observes in Chapter 6, "The World's Population Crisis," even the "family planning movement," committed to the furnishing of contraceptives as the prime legitimate means of population control, for a time "opposed legalizing abortion" and even went on to justify "contraception as a way of meeting 'the abortion problem.'"

The case of social welfare   Medicaid is a federal-state program to provide medical care for people who cannot pay for it. Medicare is a federal program to finance medical care for people over the age of 65 and the physically disabled. Both are now familiar parts of the American structure of social welfare. A couple of generations ago, this sort of institutional arrangement was defined as a *social remedy* by Walter Reuther and his followers in the Congress of Industrial Organizations (CIO) just as it was defined as a dangerous *social problem* ("socialized medicine") by a succession of American Medical Association presidents and their followers. So, too, in the eyes of some, unemployment benefits help solve a problem by providing financial aid to people for their work in the past and for willingness to work in the present. (See Chapters 13 and 14, "The World of Work" and "Poverty and Proletariat.") For others, whose comparatively secure positions in society help them sustain the belief, these benefits are at best a dole, morally suspect and socially undesirable.

The case of race and gender discrimination   In recent years, the U.S. government has instituted programs of "affirmative action" requiring employers to compensate for past discrimination against ethnic minorities and women by giving them preference insofar as possible in hiring new personnel. (See Chapter 9, "Sex Roles," and Chapter 10, "Race and Intergroup Relations.")

Once again, social developments are clarified by the sociological idea that one group's solution is often another group's problem. We find just what the sociological principle leads us to expect. What many minority members and many women see as a long-delayed effort to end job and educational inequities, many whites and many men see as a new social problem of "reverse discrimination." They contend that such programs as affirmative action favor minorities over others and therefore discriminates in reverse. In 1975, for example, an organization of some 15,000 supervisory employees of the New York Telephone Company charged that the new employment policy designed to redress the results of past discrimination has resulted in the company's having

> taken women and minorities whom it has itself rated as unqualified and promoted them over those whom it has rated as outstanding. . . .[5]

---

[5] Tom Schug, president of Federation of First Line Telephone Management, Inc., quoted in *The New York Times,* October 19, 1975, p. 26.

This case and others like it on the docket of the Supreme Court clearly show once again how people differently situated in the social structure tend to define social problems and would-be social solutions in conflicting ways.

Manifest and Latent Social Problems

Social problems have both subjective and objective aspects. Their subjective aspect appears in the perceptions and evaluations of social conditions by people in the society and their objective aspect in the social conditions themselves. It has sometimes been proposed that sociologists should confine their attention to the conditions generally regarded as undesirable. But this policy would lead them to exclude study of all manner of other conditions that are accepted by people *even though those conditions are in fact at odds with their declared interests and values.* It would result in sociologists' adopting the subjective judgments of the groups and individuals under study—say, managers of large corporations or managers of small street gangs—while believing that they maintained the objectivity of the scientific observer. The basic point is that people themselves do not always identify the conditions and processes of society that have consequences opposed to their self-defined interests and values. It is therefore a function of sociologists to study not only manifest social problems—those widely identified in the society—but also latent social problems—the conditions that are also at odds with current interests and values but are not generally recognized as being so.[6] In undertaking to supply knowledge about latent social problems, sociologists do not impose their own values upon others, although, as we shall see later in this chapter, their values do affect their choice of problems to investigate.

To identify latent problems is to alert people to pending difficulties and to provide a basis for judging the efficacy of various social policies. For example, in Chapter 6, when the demographer Kingsley Davis identifies the social, economic, and cultural consequences of rapid population growth in diverse societies, he in effect calls the advocates of alternative population policies to account. They can no longer evade responsibility for certain social consequences of policy by claiming these to be unforeseeable. So, too, the sociologists who demonstrate the waste of socially prized talent that results from great inequalities of opportunity bring to a focus what was diffusely experienced by many as involving only personal troubles rather than constituting a problem of society. Again, as our knowledge of the consequences of racial or sex discrimination is enlarged, advocates of alternative policies use that knowledge in their arguments, as the great debates on women's liberation testify. See, for example, the ingenious experiments by Bem and Bem on sex bias in advertising practices reported in Chapter 9, "Sex Roles." The development of "tech-

[6] For critical discussions of this orientation to the study of social problems, see John I. Kitsuse and Malcolm L. Spector, "Toward a Sociology of Social Problems," *Social Problems,* Vol. 20 (1973), pp. 407–419; Jerome G. Manis, "The Concept of Social Problems: *Vox Populi* and Sociological Analysis," *Social Problems,* Vol. 21 (1974), pp. 305–315.

nology assessment"[7]—a sort of early-warning system for anticipating major social and ecological consequences of proposed technological innovations—is another recent thrust toward accountability in what were once regarded as decisions to be made exclusively by entrepreneurs rather than recognized as the socially consequential decisions they are. In these ways, sociological knowledge can be used to press policy makers to justify their social policies to their constituencies, or to modify them.

A major function of the sociologist, then, is to make latent social problems manifest. By discovering unwanted consequences of institutionalized arrangements, the sociologist inevitably becomes a social critic, as leaders in totalitarian societies that limit or reject sociological inquiry evidently realize. This sociological stance has certain advantages. It avoids the opposite and equal errors of assuming that "whatever is, is right" or "whatever is, is wrong." It allows us to examine social conditions in terms of their consequences for people diversely located in the society, including the consequences that relate to values variously held in the society. In following this path, sociologists avoid claims to knowledge that, in the remote future, human society is bound to move toward either cumulative improvement or cumulative decline. (See the Epilogue by Robert Nisbet.) Not least, this sociological perspective provides a substantial place for the idea that people can make their own history while avoiding the Utopianism that beguiles. But this perspective also recognizes that the degrees of freedom people have in making their history are limited, sometimes severely limited, by the objective constraints set by nature, society, and culture.

We have no reason to expect, however, that knowledge of the consequences stemming from established social beliefs and practices will promptly lead people to modify or abandon them, even if those consequences have been shown to frustrate some of their own basic interests and values. The sociological truth does not instantly make men and women free. For one thing, people are not so rational as that. They cling to familiar institutional arrangements that are reinforced by tradition and sentiment. For another thing, arrangements demonstrably dysfunctional for many in society are frequently not rejected, if only because they often benefit people in powerful social strata and groups. Still, as we have seen, by uncovering latent social problems and clarifying manifest ones, sociological inquiry helps make people accountable for the outcomes of their individual, collective, and institutionalized actions. Some of those outcomes are short-run and immediately demonstrable; others are long-run and largely speculative. It might be asked why we should be interested in possible long-run consequences of current policy decisions since, as John Maynard Keynes reminded us, in the long run we are all dead. The reply is as evident

---

[7] See the penetrating paper by one of the chief architects of the basic report to Congress on technology assessment, a paper which can serve as a root reference to the rapidly growing library on the subject: Laurence H. Tribe, "Technology Assessment and the Fourth Discontinuity: The Limits of Instrumental Rationality," *Southern California Law Review*, Vol. 46 (1970), pp. 617–660.

as the question: because, contrary to our egoistic faith, the world does not die *with* us.

The distinction between manifest and latent social problems thus serves several purposes. It crystallizes ideas governing the range of problems selected for sociological investigation and the ways in which they are investigated. It signals us that to confine the study of social problems to *only* those circumstances popularly defined as social problems is arbitrarily to ignore other, widely unnoticed conditions that are also dysfunctional for designated groups or strata in the society. To adopt such a limited course is to hamstring inquiry into the kinds of conditions that would be socially defined as problems were their consequences made evident. By adopting the ideas central to the distinction between manifest and latent social problems, sociologists neither abdicate their human responsibilities as social scientists nor assume the position of sitting in perpetual moral judgment on their fellows.

Social Perception of Social Problems

Our consideration of manifest and latent social problems leads us directly to a further question: How correctly do people perceive situations identified as social problems? For reasons we are only beginning to understand, the public imagery even of manifest social problems is often distorted. Some, such as mental illness, are walled off and, as far as possible, denied. Others, such as "crime waves" and drug abuse, are often exaggerated far beyond their actual extent. If public misperceptions often occur with respect to the scale and distribution of social problems, they are all the more apt to occur with respect to the more obscure questions of their causes and consequences.

An ingenious sociological study reminds us that in large, complex societies we generally know about deviant behavior and social disorganization through *mediated perception:* not firsthand, but primarily through the media of mass communication: newspapers, radio, and television. The study found that the amount of crime *news* reported in four Colorado newspapers was not significantly correlated with the amount of *crime* officially recorded. The newspapers were selective in the crime news they thought fit to print. Furthermore, a survey found that public estimates of the amount of violent crime and theft reflected the trends in the amount of crime *news* rather than in recorded crime *rates.* Here, misperception of the extent of crime resulted from the filtering of experience by journalists concerned with "human-interest stories."[8]

A familiar kind of episode demonstrates how socio-psychological processes make for disparity between the actual magnitude of collective events and

---

[8] F. James Davis, "Crime News in Colorado Newspapers," *American Journal of Sociology,* Vol. 57 (1952), pp. 325–330; see also Bernard Roshco, *Newsmaking* (Chicago: University of Chicago Press, 1975). On the general subject of public misperceptions, see Gerald Gurin et al., *Americans View Their Mental Health* (New York: Basic Books, 1960) and Daniel Bell, "The Myth of Crime Waves," in his *The End of Ideology* (New York: Free Press, 1960), Ch. 8.

social perceptions of them. Many more people are killed each year in the United States by automobile accidents than by airplane accidents. In 1974, for example, about 50,000 Americans were put to death by automobiles and about 1,300 by airplanes. When measured in terms of fatalities per million miles traveled, airplanes continue to be less deadly than cars. Yet many people feel that air travel is more risky than automobile travel, and the intensity of attention accorded a dramatic airplane accident in the mass media makes a far greater impression than the diffuse coverage of the many fatal accidents on the road.

Popular perceptions, then, are no safe guide to the magnitude of social problems. Impressions that people receive in the course of their everyday lives do affect their attitudes toward social problems, but these impressions cannot afford a sound basis for diagnosing social problems or for dealing with them. The processes of social perception[9] are only partly understood, and involve the patterned emphasizing, omitting, supplementing, and organizing of what is selectively perceived as the social reality. The dramatic airplane disaster is perceived as a single event that evokes public attention. In contrast, the hundreds of automobile accidents occurring on the same day are largely lost to view in the cold, impersonal, aggregative numbers.

There is another reason why the sociologist does not necessarily order the importance of social problems in the same way as the man-and-woman-on-the-street. Some pervasive social problems, such as poverty or job discrimination, have little visibility for large sectors of the population. They are apt to arouse mild public interest compared to less serious problems that erupt dramatically in the public spotlight. Sensing that their problems are invisible to many in the society, chronic victims of collective suffering occasionally take dramatic steps to call public attention to their conditions. Riots, violence in the streets, rent strikes, sit-ins, and all manner of less organized forms of collective protest are often designed to increase the visibility of problems that, being chronic and widespread, tend to be taken as part of the usual scheme of things. These consciousness-raising devices serve roughly the same function of providing high visibility as the nearly instantaneous mass communication of dramatic large-scale disasters.[10] Whatever their other purposes and consequences, such col-

---

[9] For a comprehensive overview, see Henri Tajfel, "Social and Cultural Factors in Perception," in Gardner Lindzey and Elliot Aronson, *The Handbook of Social Psychology*, 2d ed., Vol. 3 (Reading, Mass.: Addison-Wesley, 1969), Ch. 22; Harry C. Triandis et al., *The Analysis of Subjective Culture* (New York: Wiley, 1972).

[10] For more on this important difference in social response to chronic suffering and to sudden, acute episodes of collective stress, see Allen Barton, *Communities in Disaster: A Sociological Analysis of Collective Stress Situations* (New York: Doubleday, 1969), pp. 208, 232–238. For a general formulation of how both visibility and observability enter into social processes, see Robert K. Merton, *Social Theory and Social Structure*, enlarged ed. (New York: Free Press, 1968), pp. 373–376, 390–411. On the functions of violence and mass demonstrations in focussing public attention on chronic suffering, see Lewis A. Coser, *Continuities in the Study of Social Conflict* (New York: Free Press, 1967), Ch. 4. For historical analysis of the changing functions of collective violence, see Charles Tilly, "Collective Violence in European Perspective," in Hugh D. Graham and Ted R. Gurr (eds.), *Violence in America* (New York: American Library, 1969), pp. 4–42.

lective bids for attention help to shake people loose from the tacit conviction that whatever is, is inevitable, and so might as well be accepted.

Related to the misperceptions of social problems is the apparent gap between people's concern with public and private problems. The disparity has been depicted by the scientist and civil servant C. P. Snow in his novel *The New Men*.[11] It is the morning after the earth-shaking bomb has been dropped on Hiroshima:

> I went straight off to sleep, woke before four, and did not get to sleep again. It was not a bad test of how public and private worries compare in depth, I thought, when I remembered the nights I had lain awake because of private trouble. *Public* trouble—how many such nights of insomnia had *that* given me? The answer was, just one. On the night after Munich, I had lain sleepless—and perhaps as I went through the early hours of August 7th [1945], I could fairly count another half.

What the novelist Snow had his fictional hero report, the sociologist Stouffer found to be generally true for Americans: public troubles take a poor second place to private troubles. Stouffer's study[12] was conducted during the summer of 1954, when the Army–Joseph McCarthy hearings were in full swing and avidly watched on television by millions of Americans. During this time of deep-seated public troubles, less than 1 percent in each of the two matched national samples of Americans reported that "they were worried either about the threat of Communists in the United States or about civil liberties." No more than 8 percent had anything to say about the danger of war or other forms of international conflict as a source of anxiety. Even when interviewers drew attention to public concerns by asking whether there were "other problems you worry about or are concerned about, especially political or world problems," more than half had nothing to add to their roster of worries. In this period of McCarthyism, the number referring to threats to civil liberties rose from the unimpressive total of 1 percent to the no more impressive total of 2 percent. When asked about the kinds of problems they had discussed with friends during the preceding week or so, one-half of these representative Americans said they had talked only about personal or family problems. Even the most demanding public troubles of the time seemed comparatively remote, crowded out by routine personal problems at home and at work. The Stouffer research thus is further evidence that the aggregated individual judgments by members of the society afford no secure guide for assessing the magnitude of social problems. The connections between public and private troubles are far from conspicuous, and most people make no effort to detect them.

[11] C. P. Snow, *The New Men* (London: Macmillan, 1954), p. 188.

[12] Samuel A. Stouffer, *Communism, Conformity and Civil Liberties* (New York: Doubleday, 1955), pp. 59–74, reports the findings we have adapted to our purposes here; much of the study has been replicated in James A. Davis, "Communism, Conformity, Cohorts, and Categories: American Tolerance in 1954 and 1972–73," *American Journal of Sociology,* Vol. 81 (1975), pp. 491–513.

Fatalism, Activism, and Collective Action

Broadly speaking, societies differ in their belief systems about social problems. At one extreme are those appreciably committed to fatalism, a belief that everything has its appointed outcome, which cannot be avoided or modified by foreknowledge or effort. Anyone seriously committed to fatalism will of course have little sense of social problems; rampant disease, high death rates, widespread poverty, and all the other items in the catalogue of social troubles are regarded as simply inevitable. In a society so oriented to resignation and quietism, social problems tend to remain latent although pervasive.

At the other extreme are societies largely committed to an activist philosophy of life and regarding just about everything as subject to human control. Such a society, full of people trying to cope with its problems—reducing death rates, curbing disease, reducing acute poverty, fighting crime—may have many manifest social problems but comparatively fewer problems altogether. Its members are more apt to focus on certain discrepancies between what they have and what they want and try to do something about them. The fatalistic society, in contrast, may have a greater complement of social problems altogether, since people in it regard what exists as inevitable and are not disposed to do much about it.

Fatalism and social problems tend to reinforce one another. Once again, observers of quite different theoretical schools agree that fatalism tends to develop in fact if not in philosophy among people living under conditions of extreme stress, deprivation, or arbitrary rule. People tend to think fatalistically under severely depressed conditions, and those conditions tend to persist because people think fatalistically. The passive acceptance of institutional things as they are develops among those at the bottom of the social structure, described by Karl Marx as the *Lumpenproletariat* ("the thieves and criminals of all kinds, living on the crumbs of society, people without a hearth or a home"), by Lloyd Warner as the lower-lower class, and by many recent observers as the underclass.[13] And what the most severely deprived social stratum cannot do for itself, some in the more privileged social strata will not do. The fatalism of the depressed provides the privileged with an escape from responsive change.[14]

The contrast between fatalist and activist value systems and the societies or social strata in which they thrive has been deliberately exaggerated here in order to point up the theoretical idea. In reality, few groups have maintained a wholly passive and fatalistic outlook on all their conditions of life, just as few have succeeded in maintaining a wholly active outlook on all their unapproved conditions of life. Strands of active rebellion against fate are found in dominantly fatalistic collectivities, just as strands of apathy and retreatism

---

[13] H. Draper, "The Concept of the *Lumpenproletariat* in Marx and Engels," *Economie et Société* (December 1972), cited in David McLellan, *Karl Marx: His Life and Thought* (New York: Harper & Row, 1973), p. 182; see the classic paper by Genevieve Knupfer, "Portrait of the Underdog," *Public Opinion Quarterly*, Vol. 11 (1947), pp. 103–114.

[14] See A. Eustace, "Fatalism," *Encyclopedia of the Social Sciences*, Vol. 6 (New York: Macmillan, 1931), p. 147. And see Chapter 14, "Poverty and Proletariat," in this volume.

are found in dominantly activistic collectivities. But if the extremes are seldom encountered in detailed and sharp contrast, they have nevertheless been approximated in the form of social apathy and social revolution.

Max Weber and Karl Mannheim,[15] among others, have noted that the *ethic of fatalism* has sometimes been replaced by the *ethic of responsibility*, in which discovering the sources of problems and attempting to control them becomes a moral obligation. In such a context, collective apathy about social problems becomes defined as a social problem itself.

To the extent that the activist ethic of responsibility obtains in a society, social problems tend to become manifest. But even in such a society countervailing processes cause some problems to remain latent. Chief among these processes is what the German jurist, Georg Jellinek, has described as "the normative force of the actual." By this he means that, whatever their origins, existing social practices tend to be converted into normatively prescribed practices.

Connected with the tendency to *legitimatize what exists* is the tendency toward *tacit acceptance of what exists*, without necessarily regarding it as legitimate. For example, people who are opposed in principle to discrimination have long accepted *de facto* (unintended but real) discrimination against ethnic minorities and women in access to jobs and education. Unintended social conditions that are by-products of the socially structured ways of doing things are generally ignored. Even when they do become a focus of attention, moral sentiments are not greatly offended by them since the problems are not intended by those whose actions in the aggregate lead to them. Widespread states of anxiety in a population, the waste of abilities resulting from economic inequities in opportunity, the pollution of air and water, the choking of transportation in tangled traffic—these are only a few of the problems long considered the inevitable costs of a complex society even by many who pay these costs, partly because, obnoxious as they are, the conditions are not the result of deliberate intent. In contrast, purposive behavior that violates socially shared norms is at once defined as a problem of society. Violent crime is generally regarded as a social problem; widespread alienation from the job is not. As we shall see, in a society such as ours, *people are less apt to experience social disorganization than deviant behavior as a social problem.*

This does not mean, of course, that the public is not concerned with the costs of social problems. After all, much organized effort is devoted to the replacing of slum housing by public housing; increasing effort is being mounted to enlarge educational opportunity for minority groups; the new conservationists known as the "ecology movement" are working to curb the pollutions that derive from largely uncontrolled industrial development. But this concern itself represents a major social change. It results in part from an

[15] See Max Weber, *Essays in Sociology,* trans. and ed. by H. H. Gerth and C. W. Mills (New York: Oxford University Press, 1946), pp. 120–125; Karl Mannheim, *Ideology and Utopia,* trans. by L. Wirth and E. A. Shils (New York: Harcourt Brace Jovanovich, 1936), pp. 170–171.

accumulating *social* knowledge and technology, just as other social changes result in part from more rapidly accumulating *physical* technology. Social scientists and social critics alert increasing numbers of people to the costs of living complacently under unacceptable conditions that might be brought under at least partial control. By design or not, the findings of social science raise the public awareness of social problems.

It may appear paradoxical that complex, industrial societies, with comparatively high standards of living and education, are sometimes considered more problem-ridden than societies of much less material wealth and education. But it is not actually a paradox, since social problems involve important discrepancies between what exists in a society and what a significant number of people in that society seriously want to exist. The extent of such discrepancies can widen through a great rise in social demands or through a deterioration of social conditions, or both. That is why, as the political philosopher Alexis de Tocqueville noted more than a century ago, public satisfaction may decline even while social conditions improve.

It was precisely in those parts of France [during the reign of Louis XVI] where there had been most improvements that popular discontent ran highest. . . . For it is not always when things are going from bad to worse that revolutions break out. On the contrary, it oftener happens that when a people which has put up with an oppressive rule over a long period without protest suddenly finds the government relaxing its pressure, it takes up arms against it. Thus the social order overthrown by a revolution is almost always better than the one immediately preceding it, and experience teaches us that, generally speaking, the most perilous moment for a bad government is one when it seeks to mend its ways. For the mere fact that certain abuses have been remedied draws attention to the others and they now appear more galling; people may suffer less, but their sensibility is exacerbated.[16]

In short, as the "tide of expectations" advances more than the achieving of shared objectives, there tends to develop a sense of collective "relative deprivation," a widespread feeling that people "are deprived of some desired state or thing, in comparison with some standard, or with the real or imagined condition of other people."[17] Thus, a careful study found that the urban racial dis-

---

[16] Alexis de Tocqueville, *The Old Régime and the French Revolution,* trans. by Stuart Gilbert from the French ed. of 1858 (Garden City, N.Y.: Doubleday, 1955), pp. 176–177; for a close analysis of Tocqueville's seminal ideas, see Robert A. Nisbet, *The Sociological Tradition* (New York: Basic Books, 1966), Ch. 1, *passim.*

[17] The concept of relative deprivation introduced by Samuel Stouffer can be thought of as a counterpart to the concept of rising expectations implied by Tocqueville. For the most penetrating analysis of the concept, see Robin M. Williams, Jr., "Relative Deprivation," in Lewis A. Coser (ed.), *The Idea of Social Structure* (New York: Harcourt Brace Jovanovich, 1975), pp. 355–378, quoted at p. 355. See also Herbert H. Hyman and Eleanor Singer (eds.), *Readings in Reference Group Theory and Research* (New York: Free Press, 1968); W. G. Runciman, *Relative Deprivation and Social Justice* (London: Routledge & Kegan Paul, 1966); Thomas J. Crawford and Murray Naditch, "Relative Deprivation, Powerlessness, and Militancy: The Psychology of Social Protest," *Psychiatry,* Vol. 33 (1970), pp. 208–223.

turbances of the 1960s were less a matter of responses to conditions in the local community than one of responses to "multiple deprivations and frustrations" suffered by blacks throughout the society.[18] (See further Chapter 10, "Race and Intergroup Relations, by Thomas Pettigrew.)

This observation reminds us once again of that major premise in sociology: *The discrepancies between social standards and actual social conditions that are defined as social problems have both subjective and objective components.*

PITFALLS IN SOCIOLOGICAL THEORIZING

As the Monsieur Jourdain parable reminds us, and as the preceding pages illustrate, in diagnosing social problems we inevitably use the prose of sociological theory. But that theory is not uniformly cogent or adequate and much of it is controversial. Two such controversial issues bear directly upon our understanding of social problems. One of them bears upon a matter we have examined in some detail: the subjective components in the definition of social problems. And the other bears upon the important question whether the values of social scientists keep them from analyzing social problems objectively.

The Hazards of Subjectivism

Variations in the social perception of social problems and the principle that one group's solution is often another group's problem might at first seem to imply that social problems exist *only* if many people declare them to exist.[19] But this, of course, is not the case. It represents a deep misunderstanding of the basic idea that all human action has a subjective component. This idea was unforgettably formulated by W. I. Thomas in what is probably the single most consequential sentence ever written by an American sociologist:

> If men define situations as real, they are real in their consequences.[20]

Now, it is one thing to maintain, with Max Weber, Thomas, and the other giants of sociology, that to understand human action we must take note of its subjective components: what people perceive, feel, believe, and want. Were sociologists to ignore the personal and public definitions of social problems, they could not begin to understand them. But it is quite another thing to exaggerate this sound idea by holding that human action generally and social

---

[18] Seymour Spilerman, "The Causes of Racial Disturbances: A Comparison of Alternative Explanations," *American Sociological Review,* Vol. 35 (1970), pp. 627–649; Williams, *op. cit.,* p. 372.

[19] This section draws largely upon Robert K. Merton, "Social Knowledge and Public Policy," in Mirra Komarovsky (ed.), *Sociology and Public Policy* (New York: Elsevier, 1975), pp. 153–177, esp. pp. 173–176.

[20] W. I. Thomas and Dorothy Swaine (Thomas) Thomas, *The Child in America* (New York: Knopf, 1928), p. 572.

problems specifically are nothing but matters of subjective definition. Total subjectivism—"social problems are *only* what people think they are"—leads us astray by neglecting social, demographic, economic, technological, ecological, and other objective constraints upon human beings. To ignore those constraints is to imply, mistakenly, that they do not significantly affect both the choices people make and the personal and social consequences of those choices. It is to pave the road to Utopianism with bad assumptions. In the pithy phrasing of the sociologist Arthur Stinchcombe, which tempers the subjective emphasis of W. I. Thomas with the objective emphasis of Karl Marx, "People define situations, but do not define them as they please."[21]

Sociological theory can take account of how people perceive and define situations without falling into the error of total subjectivism. An example is the concept of the self-fulfilling prophecy. According to this concept, social definitions popular in groups and collectivities make up an important, dynamic part of the process through which anticipations help to create the anticipated social reality. Thus, when schoolteachers decide in advance that children from certain ethnic or economic origins are apt to be of substandard intelligence *and treat them accordingly*, they help bring about the retarded learning they anticipated.[22] Subjective definitions of the situation therefore matter, and can matter greatly. But they do not alone matter.

To correct the imbalance that comes with total subjectivism and to restore the objective components of social situations to their indispensable place, we plainly need this counterpart to the Thomas Theorem:

> And if people do *not* define *real* situations as real, they are nevertheless real in their consequences.

Despite the idiomatic expression to the contrary, in society, as in other domains, what you don't know (or don't notice) *can* hurt you. Indeed, it is precisely what you do not know that will often hurt you most, since you cannot take appropriate measures against the unknown. Whether their causes were socially defined as real or not, tuberculosis and Asiatic cholera managed to decimate many populations before Robert Koch discovered their pathogenic agents and laid the basis for their control.

In the same way, as Chapter 6, "The World's Population Crisis," makes clear, runaway population growth has its objective consequences, even though *its* causes are not part of people's general understanding, with many being ideologically motivated to ignore both causes and consequences.

It is a major function of sociological research to promote better understanding of socially induced situations that are *not* popularly defined as real, because of (sometimes motivated) ignorance. The geneticist Joshua Lederberg

---

[21] See Arthur L. Stinchcombe, "Merton's Theory of Social Structure," in Coser, *The Idea of Social Structure*, pp. 15–16.

[22] Robert K. Merton, "The Self-Fulfilling Prophecy," *The Antioch Review* (Summer 1948), pp. 193–210, reprinted as Ch. 13 in Merton, *Social Theory and Social Structure*.

made this observation regarding new and unwelcome knowledge about the effects of radiation. It holds also for new and often unwelcome knowledge about such problems as excessive population growth, mental illness, racism, and sexism:

> [There are] some who wish we did not know that radiation is mutagenic and carcinogenic. We could then use our atmosphere and other resources as sinks for our waste in that sphere, and get at least a short-term advantage of the economic utility of the procedures. Unfortunately, you cannot play those kinds of games with nature for very long. Those costs will be incurred to the extent that they are real . . . to the extent that there are actual health hazards . . . connected with them *whether you know about them or not*. Merely to be ignorant of them is simply to defer your recognition of them into the future—in no way to blunt . . . the actual impact.[23]

"Value-free Sociology": Unmuddling a Muddle

The distinction we have drawn between manifest and latent social problems helps to clarify the question whether sociology is or is not "value-free," and the related question whether it is possible to achieve objective knowledge about social phenomena. Much of that debate has succeeded only in noisily obscuring the central theoretical issues formulated by Max Weber as early as the first decades of this century.[24]

Of course, Weber argued, scientists, like everyone else, have values. And, of course, those values influence their selection of problems for investigation. In that sense, science in general and sociology in particular are *not* value-free. Far from it; with or without intent, the choice of problems has "value-relevance" (*Wertbeziehung*). Their values may lead scientists to refuse to work on certain scientific problems—for example, research that will lead to still more catastrophic weapons systems—or may lead them to focus on certain other scientific problems—for example, research on the origins of cancer, or on the social mechanisms that perpetuate racial discrimination.

How do values enter into sociological inquiry? The question is important not merely for sociologists—an inconsiderable tribe, at best—but also for the considerable rest of society. Sociological research is increasingly employed as one basis for forming or justifying social policy. For example, the Coleman Report on Educational Opportunity (see Chapter 10, "Race and Intergroup

[23] Joshua Lederberg, *Remarks on the Tenth Anniversary of the National Institute of General Medical Sciences* (Washington, D.C.: U.S. Department of Health, Education and Welfare Publication # (NIH) 74–274, 1974), p. 16.

[24] No student of sociology should fail to read the classical essays of Max Weber on the subjects of "ethical neutrality" and "objectivity in social science" rather than rely upon second-hand, often distorted versions of them. Written in the first two decades of the century, they appear in English translation in Max Weber, *On the Methodology of the Social Sciences*, trans. by E. A. Shils and H. A. Finch (New York: Free Press, 1949), pp. 1–112. For more on Weber's notion of value-relevance, see Lewis A. Coser, *Masters of Sociological Thought* (New York: Harcourt Brace Jovanovich, 1971), pp. 219–222.

Relations") has often been invoked to justify the practice of bussing pupils in order to decrease racial segregation in public schools and to improve the quality of education provided to children of the ethnic minorities.

The important question of how values affect sociological inquiry is often obscured, not clarified, by polemics. For that reason, it may be useful to look at a further example of how *moral issues inhere in the very formulation of problems for sociological research*.

A social scientist claiming to have no traffic with values may nonetheless have designed his or her research problems in such a way that the results will be useful to one group and not to another. For example, a "value-free" sociologist investigating the use of propaganda for mass persuasion proceeds with his study and states his findings: If certain techniques of persuasion are used, a given proportion of people will be induced to take the desired action. The investigator does not take a stand; he merely reports his findings. But his solution of a moral problem by abdicating moral responsibility is no solution at all. It overlooks the crux of the problem: his *first formulation* of the question was conditioned by his implied values. Had he been influenced by democratic values like the dignity of the individual, he would have framed his problem in terms not only of the immediate result of propaganda but also of its more remote effects on the individual personality and the society. A society under a constant barrage of "effective" half-truths and exploitation of its mass anxieties may soon lose the mutual confidence and trust that a stable society needs. An investigation based in democratic values would be more likely than a "morally neutral" one to address such questions. Moreover, because of the way his investigation was formulated, the results he obtains are more likely to be of use to one group—the potential users of propaganda—than to others in the society at large.[25]

The interplay between values and sociological research moves beyond the formulation of problems. For once the investigation has begun, the modes of assessing the evidence for knowledge claims are again value-connected. The institution of science, like all other social institutions, has its values, specified in the form of norms. One of those norms, described as "organized skepticism," calls for critical surveillance of public claims to scientific knowledge by competent peers. The vigorous debates over the question of "value-free" science themselves exemplify organized skepticism in action, action carried out by some of the same scientists who deny that there are norms in science. But, of course, passionate criticism of others' work only exhibits in practice what the norm of organized skepticism calls for in principle.

It is no paradox, therefore, to say that values and norms help to produce objectivity in scientific inquiry. Both tacit and explicit norms govern what kinds of evidence will be judged acceptable by the pertinent community of scientists, requiring individual scientists to approximate objectivity in their

[25] This paragraph is drawn from a fuller statement first published in Robert K. Merton, *Mass Persuasion* (New York: Harper & Row, 1946), and reprinted in Robert K. Merton, *The Sociology of Science* (Chicago: University of Chicago Press, 1973), pp. 86–87.

scientific work. Once again, as throughout this chapter, we find that otherwise differing orientations in sociology share ideas, including this decisive one that science is more than a value-determined set of opinions. It is an idea central to structural and functional sociology, as we have seen, just as it is an idea central to symbolic interactionism, sometimes described as a conflicting orientation. Thus Howard Becker, a leading exponent of symbolic interactionism, writes:

> I take it that all social scientists agree that, given a question and a method of reaching an answer, any scientist, whatever his political or other values, should arrive at much the same answer, an answer given by the world of recalcitrant fact that is "out there" whatever we think about it. Insofar as a Left Wing sociologist proposes to base political action on his own or others' research findings, he had better strive for this and hope that it can be done. Otherwise, his actions may fail because of what his values prevented him from seeing.[26]

It is misleading, then, to formulate the issue of a "value-free sociology" in terms of the false alternatives of a science *entirely unrelated* to values and one that is *entirely determined* by values. From the early work of Max Weber to the recent formulations by the scientist-philosopher Michael Polanyi and the philosopher of science Karl Popper, there has developed the understanding that objectivity in science is in part possible because a framework of institutionalized values and norms provides the basis for it.

To recapitulate the ways in which values and norms enter into scientific work, including the sociological analysis of social problems, without converting that work into collections of merely subjective opinion:

1. The values of scientists affect their selection and formulation of problems.
2. Differently formulated problems have differing potentials of utility for differing sectors of the society.
3. Moral choices are thus involved in the selection and formulation of problems.
4. Science itself, as a social institution, has its own set of values and norms.
5. That normative framework (for example, the norm of organized skepticism) makes for objectivity in science.

To describe this array of ideas as expressing the view that science in general and sociology in particular is "value-free" because it rejects the notion of science as merely subjective sets of opinions would only be to play fast and loose with language.

SOCIAL DISORGANIZATION

Central to the plan of this book is the idea that social problems can be usefully thought of in two broad classes: social disorganization and deviant behavior.

---

[26] Howard S. Becker, *Outsiders,* rev. ed. (New York: Free Press, 1973), p. 198.

Even without examining the theoretical basis of these two concepts, we can be sure that they focus not on totally different phenomena but on different aspects of the same ones. That is why we shall find in each of the concrete social problems examined in this book evidence of both social disorganization and deviant behavior, though in differing compound. The distinction between matters of disorganization and matters of deviant behavior is useful if we note that the two interact and, under certain conditions, reinforce each other.

No single concept of social disorganization is employed by sociologists today, any more than yesterday. But there is much agreement. "Social disorganization" refers to inadequacies in a social system that keep people's collective and individual purposes from being as fully realized as they could be. Social disorganization is relative. It is not tied to any absolute standard, which would be Utopian, but to a standard of what, so far as we know, could be accomplished under attainable conditions. When we say that a group or organization or community or society is disorganized, we mean that its structure of statuses and roles is not working as effectively as it might to achieve valued purposes. Whatever the theoretical persuasion of the observer—functional sociologist, symbolic interactionist, or social critic—this type of statement amounts to a *technical judgment about the workings of social systems.*

Sources of Social Disorganization

We can identify four major sources of social disorganization: conflicting interests and values, conflicting status and role obligations, faulty socialization, and faulty social communication.

Conflicting interests and values The potential for social disorganization comes partly from the basic structural fact that social groups and social strata have some interests and values in common and also some different, sometimes conflicting, interests and values. As can be seen in Chapter 12, "Community Disorganization and Urban Problems," *people may work at cross-purposes precisely because they are living up to the norms of their respective positions in society.* When the social organization of an economy, for example, does not provide ways of settling clashes between workers, management, and stockholders, the result is an unstable condition in which interest groups cannot even estimate soundly what actions would be in their own interest. Such poorly regulated conflicts of interest, then, both reflect social disorganization and contribute to it.

Conflicting status and role obligations People inevitably occupy a variety of statuses in society—say, as parent, Catholic, Democrat, carpenter, and labor-union member. These statuses can pull in different directions by calling for opposed modes of behavior. When the social system fails to provide a widely shared set of priorities among these competing obligations, the individuals subject to them experience strains. Their behavior becomes unpredictable and socially disruptive, which may be judged "good" or "bad," but in either case remains disorganizing. Competition between obligations of home and work, of local mores and national law, of religion and state, of friendship and "the organization" make for potential conflicts. When they do flare up and further disorganization results, the fault—not in a moral sense but in an objective, almost geological, one—lies in the inept structuring of the potential conflicts, not in the ineptitude of the people confronted with them.

Faulty socialization   Socialization is the acquisition of the attitudes, values, skills, and knowledge needed to fulfill social roles or to modify them effectively. Defects in this process are a prominent source of disorganization. For example, rapid social mobility for the individual or rapid social change in the social system often occur without adequate resocialization of individuals involved in these processes. People simply do not know how to behave in their newly acquired statuses or in radically changed social situations. Not knowing the informal limits on his formally prescribed authority, the new boss may "throw his weight around," making demands on workers that, though well within the scope of his formal authority, are far beyond the limits of the group's normative expectations. Or, not socialized to recognize significant changes in racial, ethnic, and gender roles, the boss or fellow workers continue to act in terms of obsolete images of what blacks or women "can do." The effectiveness of organized social effort declines in such cases, and problems of disorganization ensue.

Faulty social communication   Disorganization results also from structural inadequacies or partial breakdowns in channels of communication between people in a social system. The people in a purposive association, local community, or national society must be able to communicate since they depend on one another for doing what they are socially expected to do and what they individually want to do. Many studies have shown that faulty communication in an organization, even without opposed interests and values, leads to disorganization.

Disorganization and Unorganization

Seen in time perspective, some social situations can be better thought of as cases of unorganization rather than of disorganization. In unorganization a system of social relations has not yet evolved, while in disorganization acute or chronic disruptions occur in a more or less established system of social relations. The difference is a little like the difference between an apartment about to be occupied by new tenants, with furniture still scattered almost at random, lacking structural arrangement and functional utility, and an apartment long lived in but now a shambles after a knockdown, dragout fight. The first is a case of no array; the second, one of disarray. Corresponding social instances are a situation where the rules and the status structure are vague or still unevolved, as when people find themselves in a previously unexperienced kind of catastrophe, versus a situation where there is a complex of ill-assorted, incompatible, or badly linked statuses so that individual and collective purposes are frustrated.

DEVIANT BEHAVIOR

Social disorganization is one type of social problem; deviant behavior, another. Whereas social disorganization involves the defective arrangement or breakdown of systems of statuses and roles, deviant behavior involves significant departures from norms socially assigned to various statuses and roles. What constitutes deviant behavior in any one case is not unequivocally clear for, as we have repeatedly noted, people sometimes differ widely on social norms. The amount of agreement depends on what the norms are: Americans are in far more accord on rules against murder, kidnapping, and rape than on those against gambling, prostitution, and drunkenness. The variation also depends upon the extent of structural differentiation in the society with its differing subcultures.

All the same, empirical studies find much more agreement on the seriousness of violating various kinds of legal rules than many sociologists had conjectured would prove to be the case. In a pioneering work with theoretical implications that extend well beyond the field of criminal behavior, Sellin and Wolfgang[27] developed a scale to measure social evaluations of the seriousness of crimes and found these to be ranked in much the same way by their samples of judges, police, and college students. Since then, a series of comparable studies tapping broader cross-sections of American and other societies have consistently found a wide consensus on the seriousness of acts traditionally defined as criminal. A survey of some 3,300 adults in Virginia, for example, found a "high level of agreement" on ranking 17 offenses, assigning "consistently harsh sanctions" to crimes of violence against persons and "moderate to lenient treatment" to property offenders, and having "a particularly tolerant attitude toward those involved in victimless crimes."[28] One of the most skillfully analyzed studies of this kind concluded that:

> the norms defining how serious various crimes are considered to be, are quite widely distributed among blacks and white, males and females, high and low socio-economic levels, and among levels of educational attainment.[29]

[27] Thorsten Sellin and Marvin Wolfgang, *The Measurement of Delinquency* (New York: Wiley, 1964).

[28] Charles W. Thomas et al., "Public Opinion on Criminal Law and Legal Sanctions." Paper presented to the American Society of Criminology, November 4, 1974, p. 16 and Tables 1 and 2.

[29] Peter H. Rossi et al., "The Seriousness of Crimes: Normative Structure and Individual Differences," *American Sociological Review,* Vol. 39 (1974), p. 237.

A comprehensive review of the now considerable literature on the normative evaluation of crime summarizes the general finding that "a clear social consensus exists concerning 'traditional crime.' "[30] To supplement these consistent empirical findings on norms that reflect *shared* values and interests, further research is needed to find out whether consensus gives way to dissensus when it comes to norms that reflect *conflicting* values and interests.[31]

Nonconforming Behavior and Aberrant Behavior

"Deviant behavior" is a morally neutral term. As it has entered into everyday idiom, however, it has become swollen with the connotation of moral censure. In that idiom, all deviant behavior is "bad." Yet frequently departures from established social norms do not work against the interests and values of significant groups or even of the society at large. In order for deviant behavior to remain a useful concept rather than merely a moralizing phrase, we must distinguish two major kinds. The first can be called "nonconforming behavior"; the second, "aberrant behavior." Both concepts are sociological; they do not smuggle in moral judgments through the back door. They refer to forms of deviant behavior that differ systematically in their makeup and in their social consequences.

Five differences mark off nonconforming from aberrant behavior:

1. Nonconformers announce their dissent publicly; aberrants try to hide their departures from social norms. Political or religious dissenters insist on making their dissent known to as many as will look or listen; the aberrant criminal tries to avoid the limelight of public scrutiny. Contrast the behavior of those who announced their conscientious objection to the war in Vietnam with that of the unconscientious draft-dodgers of the 1940s, who tried to remain hidden in obscurity from the start.

2. Nonconformers challenge the legitimacy of the social norms they reject or at least challenge their applicability to certain situations. Organized sit-in campaigns designed to attack local norms of racial segregation in schools, restaurants, and other organizations afford an example of this aspect of nonconforming behavior. Aberrants, in contrast, acknowledge the legitimacy of the norms they violate. It is only that they find it expedient or expressive of their states of mind to violate them. They may try to justify their behavior, but they do not argue that theft is right and murder virtuous.

3. Nonconformers aim to change the norms they deny in practice. They

---

[30] Graeme R. Newman and Carol Trilling, "Public Perceptions of Criminal Behavior: A Review of the Literature," *Criminal Justice and Behavior,* Vol. 2 (1975), p. 232; for cross-cultural studies, see Graeme R. Newman, "Toward a Transnational Classification of Crime and Deviance," *Journal of Cross-Cultural Psychology,* Vol. 6 (1975), pp. 297–315.

[31] For example, lower social strata are the least likely to perceive mental illness as deviant; see Bruce Dohrenwend and E. Chin-Shong, "Social Status and Attitudes toward Psychological Disorder: The Problem of Tolerance of Deviance," *American Sociological Review,* Vol. 32 (1967), pp. 417–433.

want to replace norms they believe to be morally repugnant with ones having a firm moral basis. Aberrants, in contrast, are simply concerned with escaping the sanctions that go with the existing norms, rather than with proposing substitutes for them. When subjected to social sanctions, nonconformers typically appeal to a higher morality; aberrants do not, appealing at most to extenuating circumstances.

4. Possibly in response to the preceding components of their behavior, nonconformers are acknowledged, however reluctantly, by conventional members of the social system to be breaking rules for disinterested, valued purposes rather than for personal gain. Aberrants are generally regarded as deviating from the norms in order to serve their own interests. The law of the land may not distinguish between nonconformers and aberrants, but many members of the society do. Both types of deviant behavior involve rule breaking, but they are widely acknowledged to have far different social meaning and consequences. Those courageous highwaymen of seventeenth-century England, John Nevinson and his much advertised successor, Dick Turpin, were thus not of a sociological kind with that courageous nonconformist of the same time, Oliver Cromwell. And if one's political or religious sympathies as well as the detachment made easy by historical distance serve to make this observation self-evident, one should re-examine those judgments that once made Trotsky or Nehru out to be little more than criminals heading up sizable gangs of followers.

5. Finally, nonconformers, with their appeal to an allegedly higher morality, can lay claim to legitimacy by drawing upon the society's ultimate values, rather than its particular rules. They see themselves as trying to make justice a social reality rather than an institutionalized fiction, as asking for authentic freedom of speech rather than its everyday pretense. They argue for changing the social structure to provide actual equality of opportunity rather than allow its mere appearance to be mistaken for the real thing. By thus emphasizing discrepancies between socially prized values and the established social reality, nonconformers can play a major catalytic role in institutional change. When they do, it is by obtaining the assent of other members of society who were less critical and venturesome at first, but whose ambivalence toward the social structure can be drawn upon for support. Nonconformity is not a private dereliction but a thrust toward a new morality or restoration of a morality that has become ignored in social practice. In this respect nonconformers are far removed from aberrants, who have nothing new to propose and nothing old to restore, but seek to express their private interests or to satisfy their private cravings.

Sociologists of social problems tend to lavish more attention on aberrant behavior, but they have greatly accelerated systematic study of nonconforming behavior. As a result, this book can examine the modes of nonconformity found in race, ethnic, and gender liberation movements as well as other forms of collective social protest, while also discovering the principal kinds of aberrant behavior, such as crime, alcoholism, and drug abuse.

Theories of Deviance

As the Benjamin Rush parable leads us to expect, there is no single theory of deviance that is both exhaustive and exclusive. An *exhaustive theory* would explain every aspect of deviance. It would explain the formation of social rules and differing rates of rule breaking in various groups, the processes leading people to enter upon careers as deviants, and the consequences of all this for different individuals and groups. An *exclusive theory* would have no rivals in accounting for the aspects of deviance it deals with. In place of an exhaustive and exclusive theory of deviance, there is, and will no doubt continue to be, a plurality of theories.

The principal theories of deviance—the theories known as differential association, anomie-and-opportunity-structure, labeling, and social conflict—are set forth and repeatedly utilized in this book, particularly in Chapter 1, "Crime and Juvenile Delinquency," and Chapter 3, "Drug Use." We therefore have no need to examine them in detail here. By way of introduction, however, we can identify what they have in common, what distinguishes them from each other, how they become extended or consolidated, how they become vulgarized as they are widely adopted for a time, and, most of all, how the focus on key questions in each theory leaves largely untouched the questions central to the other theories.

Theories and theoretical orientations   To begin with, we should recognize that when sociologists speak of "theories" of deviance, they only adopt a convenient abbreviation. Strictly speaking, none is a theory in the exacting sense— a set of logically connected assumptions giving rise to a continuing flow of hypotheses that can be confirmed or falsified by empirical research. Rather, they are general theoretical orientations that indicate *kinds of sociological variables* to be taken into account in trying to understand deviance. They do not state definite relationships between sets of *specific variables*.[32] Thus, it has been noted that anomie theory identifies types of deviant behavior without specifying the conditions under which each will occur, and that "the labeling approach (with its lack of clear-cut definition, failure so far to produce a coherent set of interrelated propositions, testable hypotheses, and so on) ought not, at least at this stage, to be considered a theory in any formal sense." This critic rightly adds: "Formal theoretical status, however, should not be the major criterion in assessing its value.[33] These sets of ideas are therefore sometimes

---

[32] On the differences between theory and general theoretical orientations, see Merton, *Social Theory and Social Structure*, pp. 141–155. Erich Goode incisively examines such differences in the case of one approach to deviant behavior: "On Behalf of Labeling Theory," *Social Problems*, Vol. 22 (1975), pp. 570–583.

[33] Edwin M. Schur, *Labeling Deviant Behavior* (New York: Random House, 1971), p. 35.

described not as theories but as theoretical perspectives, conceptual schemes, or paradigms. Nevertheless, we shall follow general practice by using the convenient abbreviation "theory" as we proceed to note its uses in raising significant questions about deviance and in proposing the forms which answers to those questions should take.

The key questions In connection with the Benjamin Rush parable we observed that the existence of many theories need not mean that they are in conflict and that we need to choose among them. Often they are complementary, not contradictory.[34] And so it is with sociological theories of deviance. Each has its own theoretical thrust. Each has its own key questions, focused on selected aspects of the complex social phenomena of deviance. Furthermore, each theory typically neglects other questions. For as the brilliant philosopher of literature, Kenneth Burke, put it: "A way of seeing is also a way of not seeing—a focus upon object A involves a neglect of object B."[35]

The theory of *differential association,* set forth by the criminologist, E. H. Sutherland, states that individuals become deviants by associating with others, principally in face-to-face groups, who prefer and practice various forms of deviant behavior. This theory centers on the problem of the cultural transmission of deviant behavior. Its key question therefore inquires into the modes of socialization, the ways in which patterns of deviant behavior are learned from others. How does one learn to become a professional thief, for example, as compared with learning to become a professional lawyer or physician? With its focus on this key question, the theory has little to say about how those patterns of behavior developed in the first place.

The theory of *anomie-and-opportunity-structures,* set forth by Robert K. Merton, states that rates of various kinds of deviant behavior (not merely crime) are highest where people have little access to socially legitimate means for achieving culturally induced goals; for example, the culture affirms that all members of the society have a right to climb whatever is defined as the ladder of success, but many are excluded from acceptable means for doing so.[36] Since the key question directs us to the socially structured *sources* of deviant behavior, the theory has next to nothing to say about how such patterns of behavior are transmitted or how these initial departures from the rules sometimes crystallize into careers as deviants.

Labeling theory, or, as it is sometimes called, the societal reaction approach to deviance, was originally set forth by Edwin M. Lemert and Howard S. Becker and advanced by Kai T. Erikson, Aaron V. Cicourel, and John I.

---

[34] On the complementary relations in a plurality of paradigms, see Robert K. Merton, "Structural Analysis in Sociology," in Peter M. Blau (ed.), *Approaches to the Study of Social Structure* (New York: Free Press, 1975), pp. 47–52.

[35] Kenneth Burke, *Permanence and Change* (New York: New Republic, 1935), pp. 50ff.

[36] For a brief comparative application of this theoretical orientation to American and Soviet societies, see the concluding section, "Pressures toward Deviation," in Chapter 7.

Kitsuse.[37] Becker states the theory crisply: "Social groups create deviance by making rules whose infraction constitutes deviance, and by applying those rules to particular people and labeling them as outsiders." The theory thus centers on the question: What are the processes through which people are assigned a social identity as deviants by others and enter upon ongoing careers as deviants? Lemert distinguishes between "primary" and "secondary" deviance. Primary deviance is the initial rule-breaking behavior that sometimes leads to the affixing of a stigmatizing label—like "delinquent," "criminal," or psychotic"—to the rule breaker by such rule enforcers as the police and the courts. Secondary deviance refers to the responses stigmatized people make to such societal reactions to their deviance.

Labeling theory, with its focus on the key question of the formation of deviant careers, has little to say about the sources of primary deviance or of differing rates of deviant behavior in various groups, the very questions which are central to theories of differential association and anomie. As one of the founders of labeling theory perceptively notes, "when attention is turned to the rise and fall of moral ideas and the transformation of definitions of deviance, labeling theory and ethnomethodology do little to enlighten the process."[38]

It is precisely this sort of matter that *conflict theory* takes as its key question. The main thrust of this theory, as set forth in variant versions by Austin Turk and Richard Quinney, is that a more or less homogeneous power elite incorporates its interests in the making and imposing of legal rules.[39] It centers on the question: How do legal rules and other norms get formulated and administered? Focusing on this question means neglecting the other questions about deviant behavior that are central to the preceding theories we have touched upon. For that reason, the several theories have a *potential* for being complementary.

The various theoretical perspectives can be brought together in a more comprehensive theory, of course, only if they adopt mutually consistent assumptions and give rise to compatible hypotheses. This is far from the case. Exponents of one perspective often question the assumptions or empirical claims of others. To take only one example, the labeling theorist Lemert states, in opposition to the conflict theorists, that the empirical evidence now available makes it "doubtful that the emergence of new morality and procedures

[37] Edwin M. Lemert, *Social Pathology* (New York: McGraw-Hill, 1951); *Human Deviance, Social Problems and Social Control* (Englewood Cliffs, N.J.: Prentice-Hall, 1972); "Beyond Mead: The Societal Reaction to Deviance," *Social Problems*, Vol. 21 (1973), pp. 457–468; Howard S. Becker, *Outsiders*, rev. ed. (New York: Free Press, 1973); Howard S. Becker (ed.), *The Other Side: Perspectives on Deviance* (New York: Free Press, 1964) which includes the seminal paper by Kai T. Erikson, "Notes on the Sociology of Deviance," pp. 9–21 and another by John I. Kitsuse, "Societal Reaction to Deviant Behavior," pp. 87–102; John I. Kitsuse and Aaron V. Cicourel, "A Note on the Uses of Official Statistics," *Social Problems*, Vol. 11 (1963), pp. 131–139; Aaron V. Cicourel, *The Social Organization of Juvenile Justice* (New York: Wiley, 1968).

[38] Lemert, "Beyond Mead," p. 462.

[39] Austin Turk, *Criminality and the Legal Order* (Chicago: Rand McNally, 1969); Richard Quinney, *The Social Reality of Crime* (Boston: Little, Brown, 1970).

for defining deviance can be laid to the creations of any one group, class, or elite. Rather they are the products of the interaction of groups."[40]

Extensions and fusions of theory   Occasionally theories of deviance focusing on distinct key questions have been extended or consolidated. Richard Cloward and Lloyd Ohlin,[41] for example, consolidated Sutherland's differential association theory and Merton's theory of anomie-and-opportunity-structures. They did so by introducing the idea that some people have better access than others not only to the *legitimate* opportunity structure but also to the *illegitimate* one. For instance, in order to enter upon a sustained career of deviance in crime, drugs, and the like, one needs to learn the ropes from an accessible subculture. This theoretical development was extended further by Richard Jessor and his associates in an exacting field study of deviant behavior, especially the heavy use of alcohol, which combined the Merton and Cloward-and-Ohlin conceptions with the social learning theory of the psychologist Julian B. Rotter.[42] Another example, examined in the following chapter, is provided by the work of Albert K. Cohen, which fuses anomie and interactionist perspectives to arrive at a way of explaining collective responses to problems of adapting to anomic conditions.

Apart from explicit efforts to consolidate theories of deviance, sometimes particular ideas are used by theorists of differing perspectives. Labeling theorists, for example, have instructively adopted the concept of "the self-fulfilling prophecy." As we have seen, that concept refers to the process through which widespread beliefs about some people, even though false, create a social environment that so limits their range of options that their subsequent behavior seems to confirm those beliefs.[43] Becker, Erikson, and other labeling theorists have usefully applied the concept to the formation of deviant careers:

> Treating a person as though he were generally rather than specifically deviant produces a self-fulfilling prophecy. It sets in motion several mechanisms which conspire to shape the person in the image people have of him. One tends to be cut off, after being identified as deviant, from participation in more conventional groups. . . . When caught, one is treated in accordance with the popular diagnosis

---

[40] Lemert, "Beyond Mead," p. 462.

[41] See Richard A. Cloward and Lloyd E. Ohlin, *Delinquency and Opportunity* (New York: Free Press, 1960); Richard A. Cloward, "Illegitimate Means, Anomie, and Deviant Behavior," *American Sociological Review*, Vol. 24 (1959), pp. 164–176; Robert K. Merton, "Social Conformity, Deviation and Opportunity Structures," *American Sociological Review*, Vol. 24 (1959), pp. 177–189; E. H. Mizruchi, *Success and Opportunity: Class Values and Anomie in American Life* (New York: Free Press, 1964).

[42] Richard Jessor et al., *Society, Personality, and Deviant Behavior* (New York: Holt, 1968); Julian B. Rotter, *Social Learning and Clinical Psychology* (Englewood Cliffs, N.J.: Prentice-Hall, 1954). See also the important paper by Lucien Laforest, "Force et Faiblesse de la Théorie de l'Anomie comme Source Explicative de la Déviance Alcoolique," *Toxicomanies*, Vol. 8 (1975), pp. 219–238.

[43] The concept of the self-fulfilling prophecy is set forth in Merton, *Social Theory and Social Structure*, Ch. 13.

of why one is that way, and the treatment itself may likewise produce increasing deviance.[44]

Popular distortions of theories   As sociological ideas spread into the society, they undergo changes, and not always for the better. One such change is their oversimplification into proverbs, which invariably fail to state the conditions under which they hold true. Thus differential-association theory can be vulgarized into the proverbial "evil companions corrupt"; anomie theory into the biblical statement that "many are called, but few are chosen"; labeling theory into the proverb "give a dog a bad name and hang him" as well as Hamlet's "there is nothing good or bad, but thinking makes it so"; and conflict theory into the proverbial "he who pays the piper calls the tune."

Along with simplifications of these theories are self-interested, made-to-order distortions of them, one of which has lately found its way into history. We can be reasonably confident that Richard Nixon was not given to reading treatises on the societal reaction perspective. But he invented a crude version of it by attacking the press and other mass media for *producing* the Watergate episode. For, in Nixon's opinion, it was not the *actions* of breaking into Democratic party headquarters, forging letters ascribed to opposing candidates for the presidency, pressuring corporations to contribute illegal funds to his election campaign, or repeatedly committing perjury that constituted the deviance. It was rather, he said, the pernicious societal labeling of the people engaged in these actions as thieves, forgers, bagmen, and liars-under-oath that created the deviance, with all of its personal and social consequences.

The defensive Nixon doctrine surely has no connection with any sociological theory. But it shows how readily the important, widely recognized element of *truth* in a theoretical orientation can be distorted in practice. Much more in point, the Watergate episode exhibits the fallacy that arises when the labeling or societal-reaction theory is exaggerated into the *exclusive* explanation of repeated deviant behavior. Neither Nixon nor his powerful delinquent associates had been led into their career of continuing deviance by responding to stigmatizing labels applied to them. On the contrary, it could be said that being apprehended and labeled as criminal offenders by the courts and as unethical offenders by public opinion seems to have brought their deviant careers to a halt.

The Watergate episode is further relevant to the observation made by various sociologists about an assumption basic to labeling theory:

> If deviant behavior is defined only in terms of reactions to it, then Becker cannot speak properly of "secret deviance" [as he emphatically and usefully does]. . . . To be consistent, Becker, Kitsuse, and Erikson would have to insist that behavior

[44] Becker, *Outsiders,* p. 34. See also Kai T. Erikson, *Wayward Puritans: A Study in the Sociology of Deviance* (New York: Wiley, 1966), p. 17ff.; Erikson, "Notes on the Sociology of Deviance," p. 17; William D. Payne, "Negative Labels: Passageways and Prisons," *Crime and Delinquency* (1973), pp. 39–40.

which is contrary to a norm is not deviant unless it is discovered and there is a particular kind of reaction to it.[45]

Theory shifts and problem shifts Although they coexist, the four theories touched upon here were first formulated at different times: the differential-association and anomie theories in the late 1930s, labeling theory in the 1950s, and conflict theory in the 1960s. This does not mean that each theory has replaced the ones that emerged before. As we have seen, the theories all focus on distinctive questions, so that they tend to complement rather than contradict one another.

One theory, then, does not simply replace another. Rather, shifts of attention occur in the focus of attention among workers in the sociological vineyard.[46] As a newly formulated theory elicits interest, the key questions in it are investigated and become somewhat better understood. But it will be remembered that a focus on A means a neglect of B. After a period of use, the new theory is subjected to intensive criticism.[47] New areas of ignorance are identified and new theoretical orientations develop to specify that ignorance. By contrast with aspects of the subject that have been long worked over, the neglected aspects take on even greater interest. A new focus of theory develops, and new research is done. In this way, more often gradually than suddenly, some of the gaps in our understanding of deviance have been filled in.

Identified by sociologists of science since the 1930s and deeply analyzed in recent years by the historical philosopher of science, Imre Lakatos,[48] this process of shifts in foci of scientific attention is often misunderstood. It is especially

---

[45] Jack P. Gibbs, "Conceptions of Deviant Behavior: The Old and the New," *Pacific Sociological Review*, Vol. 9 (1966), p. 13. Other pointed formulations indicate that a theory of deviance must deal with *both* the sources of deviant acts and societal responses to them: Milton Mankoff, "Societal Reaction and Career Deviance," *The Sociological Quarterly*, Vol. 12 (1971), pp. 204–218; Ronald L. Akers, "Problems in the Sociology of Deviance: Social Definitions and Behavior," *Social Forces*, Vol. 46 (1968), pp. 455–465. Charles R. Tittle, "Deterrents or Labeling?" *Social Forces*, Vol. 53 (1975), pp. 399–410 examines the research evidence and concludes that deterrence as well as secondary deviance results from the use of sanctions, with the actual outcome depending upon some known and some unknown specifiable conditions.

[46] For a detailed analysis of such shifts, see Stephen Cole, "The Growth of Scientific Knowledge: Theories of Deviance as a Case Study," in Coser, *The Idea of Social Structure*, pp. 175–220.

[47] The older theories of differential association and anomie-and-opportunity-structures have long been subject to intensive criticism, in accord with the norm of science described as "organized skepticism." In due course, this is now the case for labeling theory. Note the observation by Goode (*op. cit.*, p. 570): "by the early 1970s the antilabeling stance became almost as fashionable as labeling had been a decade earlier." See also J. W. Rogers and M. D. Buffalo, "Fighting Back: Nine Modes of Adaptation to a Deviant Label," *Social Problems*, Vol. 22 (1974), p. 101.

[48] Imre Lakatos's formulation of problem-shifts and "scientific research programmes" contributes greatly to our understanding of how scientific thought develops. See his "History of Science and Its Rational Reconstruction," *Boston Studies in the Philosophy of Science*, Vol. 8 (1971), pp. 91–136, 174–182 and his "Falsification and the Methodology of Scientific Research Programmes," in Imre Lakatos and Alan Musgrave (eds.), *Criticism and the Growth of Knowledge* (Cambridge: Cambridge University Press, 1970), pp. 91–195.

apt to become obscured when enthusiastic exponents of some theoretical perspective come to regard that perspective as both exhaustive and exclusive, even though it is equipped to deal only with certain aspects of complex phenomena (such as deviance). There then ensue those noisy disagreements which, upon inspection, are found not to express contradictory ideas or conflicting empirical findings, but only to represent different interests and rival bids for support of work on different problems.[49]

SOCIAL DYSFUNCTIONS

The study of social problems requires sociologists to consider the dysfunctions of patterns of behavior, belief, and organization rather than focusing primarily on their functions. A social dysfunction is any process that undermines the stability or survival of a social system. The presence of this concept in sociology curbs any tendency toward the doctrine that everything in society works for "harmony" and "the good."

We can briefly state the theoretical connection of social dysfunctions to social disorganization. *Social disorganization*, as we have seen, refers to the whole composite of defects in the operation of a social system. A *social dysfunction* is a specific inadequacy of a particular part of the system for meeting a particular functional requirement. Social disorganization can thus be thought of as the composite resultant of various social dysfunctions.

Four general points will serve to keep our thinking straight about the concept of social dysfunction as a tool for analyzing social problems.

Specifying dysfunctions Social dysfunctions need to be specified. A full analysis of a social dysfunction provides a *designated* set of consequences of a *designated* pattern of behavior, belief, or organization that interferes with a *designated* functional requirement of a *designated* social system. Otherwise, the term becomes little more than an epithet of disparagement or a vacuous expression of attitude. To say, for example, that a high rate of social mobility is "dysfunctional" (or, for that matter, "functional") without specifying its consequences for a social system is to say little. But it is quite another thing to propose, as such ideologically contrasting theorists as Karl Marx and Vilfredo Pareto did propose, that a high rate of upward social mobility from the working class is dysfunctional for maintaining its solidarity and attaining its goals, since such mobility exports talent from the class and depletes its potential leadership.[50] More recently, a related ambivalence toward upward mobility

---

[49] Since the theoretical perspectives are not altogether mutually exclusive, they do sometimes lead to conflicting hypotheses or predictions (for example, on the question of whether sanctions for deviant behavior deter from renewed deviance or only help bring it about).

[50] For essentially the same hypothesis about the dysfunctions of rapid, large-scale mobility see Karl Marx, *Capital* (Chicago: Kerr, 1906), pp. 648–649 and Vilfredo Pareto, *The Mind and Society* (New York: Harcourt Brace Jovanovich, 1935), Vol. 3, pp. 1419–1432; Vol. 4, pp. 1836–1846. For analysis of the pattern of "cognitive agreement and value disagreement" evident in this case, see Merton, *The Sociology of Science*, pp. 65–66.

has been observed among "the masses of lower-class Negroes [who] regard this movement up the ladder with mixed feelings, both proud and resentful of the success of 'one of their own.' "[51] In the same ambivalent fashion, the collective efforts to have many more black scholars appointed to the faculties of major universities and colleges has been described as "the black brain drain to white colleges."

Composite functions-and-dysfunctions: different groups   The same social pattern can be dysfunctional for some segments of a social system and functional for others. This arises from a basic characteristic of social structure that we have emphasized: *In a differentiated society, the consequences of social patterns tend to differ for individuals, groups, and social strata variously located in the structure.*

If a social pattern persists, it is unlikely that it is uniformly dysfunctional for all groups. Thus, comparatively free access to higher education, irrespective of racial, ethnic, or other status, is dysfunctional for maintaining a relatively fixed system of caste. At the same time, it is functional for the attainment of higher education, a culturally induced goal, by people formerly excluded from it.

As we have noted, various groups and strata in the structure of a society have *conflicting* interests and values as well as *shared* interests and values, and this means that one group's problem sometimes becomes another group's solution. This structural condition is one reason why the periodically popular notion of a society in which everything works together for good is literally utopian. (See the Epilogue of this book, "The Future and Social Problems.") But abandoning this image of a perfect society does not mean that nothing can be done to reduce social disorganization. Quite the contrary: it is by discovering and disclosing dysfunctional social formations that sociology links up with critical morality as opposed to conventional reality.[52]

Composite functions-and-dysfunctions: same group   Not only is the same pattern sometimes functional for some groups and dysfunctional for others, it can also serve some and defeat other functional requirements of the *same* group. The reason for this resembles the reason why a pattern has different consequences for different groups. A group has diverse functional requirements.

One example of composite function-and-dysfunction aptly illustrates the general idea. A group requires enough social cohesion to provide a sense of group identity, but prime attention to this need can conflict with the need to work effectively toward collective goals. Activities functional for one require-

[51] Kenneth B. Clark, *Dark Ghetto: Dilemmas of Social Power* (New York: Harper & Row, 1965), pp. 57–58.

[52] Ralph Ross, *Obligation: A Social Theory* (Ann Arbor: University of Michigan Press, 1970), esp. Ch. 5, "Critical Morality," and Chs. 8 and 9.

ment can become dysfunctional for the other.[53] Sociologists have found that up to a certain point, social cohesion facilitates the productivity of a group. People feel at one with each other and so are more willing to work together for joint objectives. But this mutually reinforcing relation between the two sets of activities holds only within certain limits. Beyond those limits, a dysfunctional imbalance develops between activity that serves chiefly to maintain social cohesion and activity that results chiefly in getting work done. There can be too much of a good thing. Members of an exceedingly cohesive group become reciprocally indulgent and fail to hold one another to effective standards of performance; or they devote too much of their social interaction to expressing solidarity, at the expense of time and energy for getting the job done. Correlatively, a group may become so exacting in its demands for instrumental activity that it fails to maintain a sufficient degree of cohesion.

This is a prototype of the functional decisions that must be made in social systems of all kinds. Morale and productivity, compassion and efficiency, personal ties and impersonal tasks—these are familiar enough pairs of values not simultaneously realizable to the fullest extent. This way of thinking is a sociological equivalent to the economist's concept of opportunity costs, which means, in effect, that under certain conditions one commitment reduces the opportunities for making other commitments. By recognizing the composite pattern of function-and-dysfunction, we guard ourselves against the utopian thinking that neglects the social constraints that result from prior commitment to other objectives. Neglecting these constraints leads to the false assumption that all values can be totally fulfilled simultaneously in society. But as the following chapters variously testify, cost-free social action is a sociological fantasy.

A sociological, not moral, concept   Above all else, it must be emphasized that the concept of social dysfunction does not harbor a concealed moral judgment.[54] Social dysfunction is not equivalent to immorality, unethical practice, or social disrepute. It is a concept referring to an objective state of affairs. Whether one judges a particular social dysfunction as *ethically* good or bad, as desirable or undesirable, depends upon an entirely individual judgment of the moral worth of that system, not upon sociological analysis. When we observed, for example, that extending opportunities for higher education to all is dysfunctional for the maintenance of a caste system, we surely were not suggesting that this dysfunction was undesirable or evil. Or when it is observed that the extremely authoritarian character of the Nazi bureaucracy was dysfunctional for its effective operation by excessively restricting lines of communication among its several echelons, this is surely not to deplore the break-

---

[53] The classic experimental work on instrumental and expressive interaction in groups is Robert F. Bales, *Interaction Process Analysis* (Reading, Mass.: Addison-Wesley, 1951).

[54] Dorothy Emmet, *Function, Purpose, and Powers* (London: Macmillan, 1958), pp. 78–82.

down of Nazism. Correlatively, when sociologists specify the functions of social conflict in general and of racial conflict in particular, they are engaged in sociological analysis, not in making moral judgments.[55] Sociological analyses of function and dysfunction are in a different universe of discourse from that of moral judgments; they are not merely different expressions of the same thing.

All this would not require emphasis except for the widespread assumption that nonconforming behavior is necessarily dysfunctional to a social system and that social dysfunctions, in turn, necessarily violate ethical codes. Yet frequently the nonconforming minority in a society represents its ultimate values and interests more fully than the conforming majority. This is not a moral but a functional judgment, not a statement in ethical theory but a statement in sociological theory. In the history of many societies, one supposes, some of its culture heroes became heroes partly because they had the courage and vision to challenge the beliefs and routines of their society. The rebel, revolutionary, nonconformist, heretic, or renegade of an earlier day is often the culture hero of today. The distinction we have drawn between nonconforming and aberrant behavior is designed to capture basic *functional* differences in forms of deviant behavior. For the accumulation of dysfunctions in a social system is often the prelude to concerted social change toward a system that better serves the ultimate values of the society.

SUMMARY

1   We all use some sociological theory when we think about social problems, whether we are aware of it or not. No single theory can account for all social problems; instead, various theories often complement each other.

2   A social problem is a perceived discrepancy between what is and what people think out to be—between actual conditions and social values and norms—which is regarded as remediable.

3   There is no strict common denominator for comparing the magnitude of social problems and for indicating which are "most important." For people holding fast to a norm, the absolute number of violations indicates the scale of a problem; for researchers concerned with causes and effects, relative numbers are more informative.

4   Social problems result from identifiable social circumstances, so it can be said that the very structure of society is a source of social problems. It is their social *consequences*, however, that define social problems, whatever their origins.

5   Although they share some interests and values, people located in different parts of the social structure typically have different and sometimes conflicting interests and values. A situation seen by one group as a problem may therefore constitute a solution in the eyes of another group.

[55] Lewis A. Coser, *The Functions of Social Conflict* (New York: Free Press, 1956) and *Continuities in the Study of Social Conflict* (New York: Free Press, 1967); Jonathan H. Turner, *The Structure of Sociological Theory* (Homewood, Ill.: Dorsey Press, 1974), esp. Ch. 6 ("Dialectical Conflict Theory: Ralf Dahrendorf") and Ch. 7 ("Conflict Functionalism: Lewis A. Coser"); Robert A. Dentler and Kai T. Erikson, "The Functions of Racial Conflict," *Social Problems,* Vol. 7 (1959), pp. 98–107.

6 *Manifest social problems* are those generally recognized as problems. *Latent social problems* are conditions not widely identified as problems even though in fact they are at odds with people's interests and values. By making evident the consequences of such conditions, sociologists can bring about greater accountability in public policy making, thus adopting the attitude of social critics without sitting in moral judgment of people.

7 The popular perception of even manifest social problems is often inaccurate, with public and private troubles only remotely connected in people's minds. Two reasons for this are that we generally have a *mediated perception* of social problems, learning about them through the media of mass communication, and that some of the most pervasive forms of social disorganization, like poverty, have little visibility to most of the public.

8 Groups that are largely fatalistic in their outlook tend to legitimatize or at least to accept things as they are. In contrast, groups with an activist value system generally feel obliged to bring about responsive change. In such an activist society, social problems are more apt to become manifest or even to be exaggerated, as rising expectations create a sense of "relative deprivation." Even here, there is a tendency for existing conditions to be regarded as legitimate.

9 In diagnosing social problems, then, we are constantly reminded that they have both subjective and objective components.

10 While recognizing the subjective aspect of social problems, it is important to keep in mind that they are defined by their *consequences*. Even if people do not recognize a social problem as real, it is nonetheless a problem if its consequences are real.

11 Are sociologists influenced by their own values in defining and examining social problems? They are, in the sense that their values influence the choice of problems for study. The way in which a question is formulated will affect, for example, the usefulness of the answers to people variously located in the social structure. Moreover, science has its own values and social controls making for objectivity in assessing the evidence for these answers, so that values can actually help produce objectivity. The two extremes, purely subjective opinion and "value-free" sociology, are false alternatives.

12 It is useful to categorize social problems as either *social disorganization* or *deviant behavior,* although elements of both appear in most problems. Social disorganization is some condition that keeps the social structure from working as well as it might to fulfill collective purposes and values. Deviant behavior involves significant departures from norms socially assigned to various statuses and roles.

13 Social disorganization occurs because (1) people have conflicting and not only complementary interests and values by virtue of occupying different statuses and roles in the society, (2) each person inevitably occupies several statuses or roles that can impose conflicting obligations, (3) through faulty socialization, people do not learn how to fulfill their social roles, and (4) people fail to communicate what they want to do and what they expect of others, even when these expectations do not conflict.

14 Distinct from social disorganization is *unorganization,* the case where an effective system of social relations has not yet evolved to meet new conditions.

15 Although people sometimes differ widely on social norms, more agreement on

what constitutes violations of them, or deviant behavior, has been demonstrated than many sociologists had expected.

16 Among types of deviant behavior it is important to distinguish *nonconforming behavior* from *aberrant behavior*. Nonconformers are public dissenters who challenge the legitimacy of the norms they violate and aim to change them, and are generally acknowledged as having disinterested, valued purposes; they appeal to the society's highest values rather than its particular rules. Aberrants try to hide their violations, acknowledge that they are wrong, and wish merely to escape the sanctions rather than to change the rules. In contrast to nonconformers, they are identified by most people, if not by the law, as self-interested and concerned only with satisfying their private cravings.

17 The principal theories of deviance are differential association, anomie-and-opportunity-structures, labeling, and social conflict. They tend to be complementary, since each focuses on different key questions. These theories are subject to popular distortions and over-simplifications, but contribute to our understanding of social problems, particularly as they are consolidated in more extended theories.

18 Sociologists with diverse theoretical commitments focus, in their study of social problems, on the dysfunctions rather than on the functions of social behavior, values, and organization. A *social dysfunction* is a specific inadequacy that works against the persistence or survival of a specified social system. The accumulation of dysfunctions makes for social change.

19 In thinking about social dysfunctions it is necessary to (1) specify the social system, the functional requirement, the organizational or behavioral pattern, and the consequences under study, (2) recognize that the same social pattern is often functional for some parts of the system and dysfunctional for others, (3) recognize also that a given pattern may serve some and defeat other needs of the *same* group, and (4) avoid attaching moral judgments to the concept of dysfunction.

RECOMMENDED READING

The recommended readings appended to the following chapters provide guidance to works dealing with the varieties of social disorganization and deviant behavior. Here, we consider the more general, theoretical works that supplement references found in the chapter itself.

Instructively enough, there is no single authoritative treatise on the current state of theoretical knowledge about social problems. In his paper, "Looking Back: A 25-Year Review and Appraisal of Social Problems Research" (*Social Problems*, Vol. 24 [1976], in press), Melvin L. Kohn provides the most searching and informative overview of the field available in short compass. A crisp introduction to the general subject in little more than a hundred pages is the paperback by Richard L. Henshel and Anne-Marie Henshel, *Perspectives on Social Problems* (1973). The most comprehensive, quite detailed volume is the many-authored *Handbook on the Study of Social Problems* (1971), edited by Erwin O. Smigel. Distinctively useful are the chapters on methods of doing research in this field, such as Chapter 4 by Allen H. Barton on "The Use of Surveys in the Study of Social Problems." Along the same lines, Edward R. Tufte has imaginatively assembled a paperback anthology, *The Quantitative Analysis of Social Problems* (1970).

Students will want to develop the useful practice of keeping in touch with developments in the field published in the major sociological journals and, in particular, *Social Problems*. Wider, ready access to pertinent articles is afforded by scanning the weekly publication, *Current Contents*, which lists the titles of articles in more than a thousand journals in the social and behavioral sciences.

As we have noted in this chapter, much of the work on social problems focuses on deviant behavior rather than on social disorganization. This emphasis is reflected in the abundance of anthologies on theories of deviance which, interestingly enough for a field as controversial as this, have assumed a fairly standard cast of articles. Among the best and most accessible of these are the paperbacks, Ronald A. Farrell and Victoria Lynn Swigert (eds.), *Social Deviance* (1975), Stuart H. Traub and Craig B. Little (eds.), *Theories of Deviance* (1975), Mark Lefton, James K. Skipper, and Charles H. McCaghy (eds.), *Approaches to Deviance* (1968), and Paul Rock and Mary McIntosh (eds.), *Deviance and Social Control* (1974).

In a book better described by its subtitle—*For a Social Theory of Deviance*—than by its more limiting title, *The New Criminology* (1973), Ian Taylor, Paul Walton, and Jock Young provide a penetrating, critical exposition of the major theoretical orientations to deviance, linking these with their often classical antecedents in sociological theory. Highly critical of theoretical perspectives other than his own, Edward Sagarin raises basic questions of theory and method in his *Deviants and Deviance* (1975). A classic theoretical essay on processes leading to deviance, which has yet to receive the critical analysis it deserves, is David Matza's *Becoming Deviant* (1969).

Recently, sociology became the twentieth scientific discipline in the authoritative series on recent research and theory published in the distinguished *Annual Reviews*. The first *Annual Review of Sociology* (1975) includes an incisive paper by Jack P. Gibbs and Maynard L. Erickson, "Major Developments in the Sociological Study of Deviance." Students will often find articles of collateral interest in the *Annual Review*. In this one, they will profit from reading the chapters by Robin M. Williams, Jr., "Race and Ethnic Relations," Joseph Ben-David and Teresa A. Sullivan, "The Sociology of Science," Claude S. Fischer, "The Study of Urban Community and Personality," and Gary T. Marx and James L. Wood, "Strands of Theory and Research in Collective Behavior."

Part One

Deviant Behavior

1

Crime and Juvenile Delinquency

ALBERT K. COHEN
JAMES F. SHORT, JR.

I t would be difficult to find a public official or private citizen, a police officer or convict who believes that we are handling the problems of crime and juvenile delinquency correctly—or one who believes nothing can be done. To some segments of the population, the need to suppress certain kinds of criminal behavior is the problem; to others, the criminality is a minor problem, and the conduct of the police or the puritanical zeal of the legislature is the problem. Debates rage about whether some form of behavior should be made criminal or some criminal behavior should be legalized; about which laws should be enforced more vigorously and which less; about the proper penalty for, say, murder or drug abuse; about the techniques of law enforcement (e.g., "police brutality" vs. "shackling the police"). Crusades against specific "evils" erupt and subside, without any substantial change in behavior patterns. (Witchcraft and alcoholic beverages are obvious examples.) Old laws fall into disuse and new laws are written—because the values we use to assess behavior change, because a value consensus that once prevailed has broken down, or because a group that did not actively participate in the political process has acquired a voice in law making and law enforcement. Taking all this into account, the study of the social problems relating to crime and juvenile delinquency goes well beyond the study of crime itself.

We begin this chapter by explaining what sociologists mean when they say that crime and juvenile delinquency are creations of the law. The difference between the way our society defines and handles adults who commit crimes and juvenile offenders illustrates this clearly. We then turn to the question of how the criminal- and juvenile-justice systems relate to society as a whole, with particular emphasis on extralegal pressures on the agencies and individuals who are authorized to apply the law. It is a well-known fact that crime rates among different segments of the population vary. We describe trends and the distribution of crime and juvenile delinquency in the next section. However, statistics do not *explain* crime. Why does a particular individual commit a particular crime? Do social structures and processes account for varying crime rates and in some sense promote violation of the law? How is crime itself organized? The answers to these questions lay the foundation for our analysis of the issues surrounding social policy on crime and juvenile delinquency in the final section of the chapter.

THE CONCEPTS OF CRIME AND DELINQUENCY

Crime and delinquency are special cases of a more general phenomenon. Wherever people do business with one another—in offices, schools, families, or gangs—they develop rules, break the rules, and do something about people who break the rules. In this chapter, we take the perspective of a particular social system, the "state," and the system of rules, the "law," that is backed by the authority of the state. One subdivision of the law is the criminal law. This is a body of rules specifying, with greater or less precision, certain kinds of acts as "crimes" and prescribing for those acts certain punishments to be administered by agents of the state in the name and on behalf of the politically organized community. The law distinguishes between crimes, offenses against the community, and torts, offenses against private individuals, which are settled in civil courts.

Crime is, in a very real sense, a creation of the law. What crimes have in common is not that they are regarded as wrong or wicked (some are not), but that people who commit them are liable to be arrested, tried, pronounced guilty in a solemn public ceremony, and then punished and degraded by being deprived of their lives, liberty, or property; they are liable, in short, to be caught up in the elaborate social machinery called the criminal-justice system. It makes a consequential difference whether a person is "sued" by a private citizen in a civil court and ordered to pay damages, or convicted by a jury for willfully and with malice aforethought committing a crime against the peace and dignity of the state and led away in handcuffs.

Just as crime is a creation of the criminal law, so juvenile delinquency is a creation of the statutes establishing the juvenile courts. Until the end of the nineteenth century, young offenders in the United States were either placed beyond the reach of the law or treated as criminals. Children under 7 were "irrebuttably presumed" to be incapable of having "criminal intent." If not capable of criminal intent, a child was not capable of crime. His misconduct might be a matter for his parents or kinsmen, master or priest, but it was not a matter for the criminal courts. Unless shown to be immature, children from 7 to 14 were presumed to be capable of criminal intent and were subject to the same law, the same courts, the same procedures, and the same penalties as adults.

During the late nineteenth century courts in several countries began developing quite different procedures for dealing with young offenders. By the end of the century, practically every state in this country had established juvenile courts or their equivalent. The new laws created a new kind of machinery for handling young offenders (under 18) outside the criminal law, and therefore a new category of persons, young people subject to handling by this machinery. The *delinquent child*—the legal term for a child subject to the jurisdiction of the juvenile court—was thus a nineteenth-century invention.[1]

The acknowledged and intended functions of the criminal courts are to administer "justice," to see that offenders pay for their crimes. A crime is defined in relatively precise language. The crime of burglary, for example, might be defined legally as: breaking and entering a dwelling-house at night with the intent to commit a felony. An act must fit every part of this definition to qualify as the crime of burglary, and the court must be satisfied by competent evidence

---

[1] Anthony M. Platt, *The Child Savers: The Invention of Delinquency* (Chicago: University of Chicago Press, 1969). Creation of the juvenile court culminated nearly a century of effort by groups representing a variety of religious, class, professional, and other interests to "save" wayward children. See, also, Sanford L. Fox, "Juvenile Justice Reform—An Historical Perspective," *Stanford Law Review*, Vol. 22, No. 6 (June 1970): pp. 1187–1239.

on each point. Minimal and maximal penalties are prescribed (leaving the court some discretion). Furthermore, the procedures of the criminal court are designed to provide the defendant an opportunity to confront accusers, challenge their interpretation of the law, and rebut their testimony.

In contrast, juvenile courts are designed to "help children in trouble," to "do what is in the child's best interests," to "rehabilitate." The official language of the juvenile court carefully avoids the terminology of the criminal process; it speaks of "petition on behalf of the child" rather than "indictment," of "hearing" rather than "trial," of "disposition" rather than "sentence," of "training school" rather than "prison," and so on.

The juvenile court statutes generally start out by defining a delinquent child as one who has committed any act which, if it were committed by an adult, would be a crime. In addition, most states prohibit other actions and patterns of conduct that would not be crimes if performed by adults—including such vague offenses as "incorrigibility." Historically, juvenile statutes have *not* prescribed procedures to be followed in the courtroom in order to insure "due process of law." The net—and intended—effect is to give the judge great discretion with respect to the conduct of juvenile proceedings and to the determination of whether a child falls under the definition of "delinquent child." This is consistent with what has come to be known as the juvenile court philosophy: the idea that the juvenile court, unlike the criminal court, is not concerned with exacting payment for a crime; that its job, like that of a loving parent or a physician, is to help the child; and that it must be free to take into consideration anything about the child's personality and the circumstances it considers relevant, and must not be hamstrung by minutely detailed rules of procedure. By the same logic, the statutes do not prescribe, as the criminal law does, that certain offenses shall be dealt with in specified ways—for example, "three to ten years in a state prison." The presumption is that the needs of the child, not the seriousness of offensive behavior, should determine disposition.

In point of fact, the dispositions of the juvenile court, ranging from probation to institutionalization, are deprivations of freedom that a child experiences as punishment. Furthermore, neither the court nor anyone else knows enough about the causes and treatment of delinquent behavior to "diagnose" and "prescribe treatment" with confidence that it will in fact prove rehabilitative. Regardless of rhetoric or intentions, the juvenile court administers punishment. But unlike the criminal court, it has not been constrained by procedural rules to insure justice to the child until quite recently. In the 1967 Gault decision, the U.S. Supreme Court ruled that children in juvenile courts, like defendants in criminal courts, are entitled to representation by counsel, timely notice of the charges against them, and the rights to confront and cross-examine witnesses against them and to refuse to testify against themselves. While we do not know the full impact of Gault and other appellate court decisions on the juvenile-justice system, juveniles clearly are armed with rights previously denied them. Studies find much variation from one jurisdiction to another in compliance with Supreme Court decisions, and the ferment which culminated in the Gault decision continues in the form of widespread modification of juvenile statutes in nearly all states.[2]

THE CRIMINAL-JUSTICE SYSTEM AND THE EXTRALEGAL ORDER

The criminal- and juvenile-justice systems we have described do not operate in a vacuum. They are part of the larger social system, and affect and respond to other sectors of society in various ways.

First, the justice system shares responsibility for regulating behavior with other institutions: the police, courts, and prisons do not stand alone. Indeed, prior to the early nineteenth century, police forces as we know them in the United States and England did not exist. People depended on other institutions, such as the family and church, for social control. The magnitude and effectiveness of government agencies of social control does not determine the crime rate. Social conditions that create the incentives to crime and delinquency and informal mechanisms of social control operating in the community at large must also be taken into account. And these factors affect the system of justice.

For example, the impact the law has upon behavior depends upon what we shall call the *moral status* of the law and the agencies of justice. By this we mean the extent to which the rules of the legal system agree or disagree with the values and norms of the people to whom they apply, and the respect and legitimacy the people accord to the police, the courts, and other agencies of justice. Public sentiment firmly supports the use of the criminal law to control such behaviors as forcible rape and mugging. With respect to other behaviors, this support may be weak, divided, or variable over time. Some laws may be regarded by some segments of the public as intolerable infringements on liberty or privacy. Consider, for example, laws regulating or prohibiting abortion, drunkenness, the use of marijuana, and homosexual relations among consenting adults, and changes in these laws in response to changing public sentiment. Furthermore, the criminal justice system may itself be viewed by some as the disinterested guardian of the public weal, by others as instruments of oppression. Laws that run counter to public opinion are difficult, if not impossible, to enforce.

Sometimes laws have effects extending beyond the behavior they directly proscribe. For example, they may be used to control or punish behavior that is not in fact illegal but is offensive to the law-enforcement agencies or to some influential segment of the public. There are few people who could not be arrested for violating *some* building code, licensing ordinance, or curfew, or for

---

[2] See W. Vaughan Stapleton and Lee E. Teitelbaum, *In Defense of Youth* (New York: Russell Sage Foundation, 1972). The Gault case decision is reprinted in "The President's Commission on Law Enforcement and Administration of Justice," *Task Force Report: Juvenile Delinquency and Youth Crime* (Washington, D.C.: U.S. Government Printing Office, 1967). See, also, Mark M. Levin and Rosemary C. Sarri, *Juvenile Delinquency: A Comparative Analysis of Legal Codes in the United States* (Ann Arbor: National Assessment of Juvenile Corrections, 1974).

vagrancy or disturbing the peace. But few people are; the police tend to enforce such laws selectively, and sometimes capriciously. Of course, misuse of the law in this manner may have the side effects of undermining belief in the disinterestedness and impartiality of the law and of increasing hostility to the agencies of law enforcement.

Furthermore, attempts to regulate behavior—especially the so-called vices—may generate other forms of crime to satisfy the demand for a forbidden activity. The Volstead Act made alcoholic beverages illegal, but it did not extinguish the demand for these products. Instead a vast industry sprang up outside the law to satisfy the demand. It is common knowledge that the criminalization of narcotics has made this traffic disreputable and hazardous; tended to drive the trade into the hands of professional criminals; and created an intricate black market in which many different individuals get their "cut" (including compensation for unusual risks). This has made narcotic drugs enormously expensive for the ultimate consumers.

Finally, the penalties and deprivations that the court directly inflicts may be only part, and often the lesser part, of the punishment that the offender experiences. The words *criminal* and *delinquent* are also terms for social roles of everyday life. People may attribute a whole bundle of deviant attributes to someone who bears such a label, and organize their behavior toward that person on the basis of these imputed attributes. The criminal or delinquent role may so narrow opportunities for the rewards and gratifications of conventional behavior that illegal alternatives may become more rather than less attractive. However, an individual does not automatically acquire the social role of criminal or delinquent by virtue of an adjudication. People who have been convicted of tax irregularities or of *white-collar crimes*—that is, violations of criminal statutes regulating the conduct of business and trade—are not likely to be labeled "criminal" in their everyday world. By contrast, people who have been arrested, even if not convicted, for "ordinary" crimes such as automobile theft are much more likely to be saddled with at least some of the burden of a criminal identity.

The Effects of Crime on the Criminal-Justice System

How laws are written and administered is responsive to how they are broken and on what scale. Crime, like law enforcement, is intelligent, motivated behavior in which people may have high stakes. It is not extinguished readily and sometimes grows in the face of efforts to suppress it, sometimes in consequence of those efforts. Some kinds of crime are invisible except to the participants, some obvious; some easy to prove in a court of law, some hard; some easily discouraged, some—to use the language of the economists—inelastic. The criminal-justice system, like any set of social arrangements, is shaped by the material it works on. When the material is obdurate and resistant, it may respond in various ways. (Which way the system should respond often becomes a social problem, a subject of social controversy and political conflict.)

Laws may be sharpened, loopholes eliminated, penalties increased. Additional resources may be pumped into the system, or existing ones diverted from efforts to control some other crime that does not, at the moment, enjoy as high a priority. If the pressure to suppress certain behavior is great, law-enforcement people may try to increase their efficiency by violating laws that restrict their freedom of operation—for example, those relating to illegal search and seizure. On the other hand, if the costs of enforcement become increasingly burdensome and the forbidden behavior continues to thrive, efforts to enforce the law may simply be abandoned or, as sometimes happens, the law may be changed and the behavior legalized. Instead of the law extinguishing the crime, the crime extinguishes the law and, in the process, ceases to be a crime.

The criminal law, the machinery of criminal justice, processes of social control outside the legal system, and criminal behavior—each influences and is in turn influenced by each of the others. Criminologists are just beginning to grope for theoretical approaches that can deal simultaneously with all these sectors and their interaction.[3]

Pressures on Criminal-Justice Systems

Even the most rationally designed organization is much more than a mechanism for accomplishing a preconceived purpose. Police departments, courts, and prisons consist of people working at more or less full-time jobs. With these jobs they make their livings, establish their social identities, have fun, accumulate worries, and grow gray. Like people in any organization, they seek to simplify their lives and to get along with the people with whom they have to work—especially those who can make trouble for them. They tend over time to develop a subculture that will serve these ends. This includes understandings about lines of authority, the distribution of responsibility, what constitutes a fair day's work, mutual aid, and solidarity vis-à-vis "outsiders." What people actually do and what they produce is partly shaped by these understandings. But people do not have complete freedom to tailor their work to their own comfort and convenience. The organization as a whole is evaluated by those on whom it depends for legitimacy, resources, and cooperation. Criticism may lead to withdrawal of support and threaten the interests of its members. Therefore the organization also tends to adapt to the outside demands; to produce, or appear to produce, what the environment demands; to call upon the members to promote a favorable public image (perhaps by concealing what is publicly discreditable); and to persuade its publics that they are getting what they are paying for.

This means that a host of considerations over and above the manifest content of the criminal law and the official purpose of each agency shape the

---

[3] See, for example, William J. Chambliss, "The State, the Law, and the Definition of Behavior as Criminal or Delinquent," in Daniel Glaser (ed.), *Handbook of Criminology* (Chicago: Rand McNally, 1974), pp. 7–43, and Malcolm Spector and John Kitsuse, *Constructing Social Problems* (Menlo Park: Cummings, forthcoming).

actual activities of policemen, prosecutors, judges, probation officers, and corrections personnel. In addition, limited resources make it impossible for an
agency to do everything it is in principle supposed to do. It must somehow
develop priorities, deliberately or otherwise. Furthermore, no matter how detailed, an organization's mandate always leaves wide room for the exercise of
judgment and discretion.

For example, the way the police and courts allocate their resources will
depend in part on the feedback they get from different publics, which are
likely to have different interests in the suppression of different kinds of crime.
These different publics will also have different power to help or hurt the various agencies, so that each agency will be more sensitive to the feedback from
some than from others. The relative power of the different publics may itself
change over time, and the agency alter its policy in response. And even for
the same public, concern and alarm over a particular offense may vary over
time, and with it the pressure on the agency to do something about that particular offense. Lois B. DeFleur's research suggests, for example, that police
activity with respect to drugs may be a response to public pressure and to
organizational and policy changes rather than to objective factors related to
drug use or law violation.

> . . . [O]fficers also consistently mentioned pressures from the community, organiza-
> tions, parents, etc. Thus, during the late 1960s, they were bringing in pot and pills,
> while earlier they had largely ignored these drugs. "We always worked out south
> before—with the Mau Mau's (blacks in general)—it was mostly heroin and coke
> . . . the pot and stuff went down the stool (toilet) since nobody gave a damn about
> it and we didn't want to inventory the stuff. . . . [T]he first time we came across
> a LSD factory we didn't know what it was. . . . [N]ow we bring in every seed and
> joint." In recent years, the officers have felt that arrests for these drugs were
> acceptable and that the courts would convict at least some of the offenders. Thus,
> community pressures and police perception of public demand influenced their
> enforcement activities. Specifically, they changed who was arrested, where, for
> what, and in what manner.[4]

Prosecutors may consent to waive or reduce charges against the defendant
in return for a guilty plea to a lesser charge in order to obtain convictions with
the least expenditure of time and manpower. Farther up the line, in the parole
and probation systems and in jails, prisons, and juvenile training schools, what
is actually done in the name of prevention, punishment, or rehabilitation is
shaped by a variety of considerations, only some of which are related to these
ends. Measures of success in accomplishing these goals are poor at best, and
where we do have useful measures, we know very little about how to achieve
the desired results (except in the case of punishment, about which we know a
good deal). The tendency, then, is to be guided on the one hand by intuitive

---

[4] Lois B. DeFleur, "Biasing Influence on Drug Arrest Records: Implications for Deviance
Research," *American Sociological Review*, Vol. 40 (February 1975), pp. 88–103.

but unsubstantiated ideas about "what works," and on the other by considerations of administrative convenience, harmony among the staff, and the avoidance of public scandal and outrage. For example, in most prisons the most important single consideration in determining everything from the design of the physical plant to staff–inmate relations is the prevention of escape. This has little to do with crime prevention, punishment, or rehabilitation, but a great deal to do with avoiding bad publicity, public alarm, and legislative investigations. Although the number of inmates who will attempt escape may be small, the effort to contain that number shapes the prison experience for the staff and the body of inmates as a whole. To take a very different sort of example, efforts to experiment with new programs in a correctional institution may entail a redistribution of power, changes in the value placed on various kinds of knowledge and skills, and new kinds of relationships among staff members and between staff and inmates. These changes may be threatening to the staff, who may effectively thwart the attempt at innovation.

TRENDS AND DISTRIBUTION OF CRIME AND DELINQUENCY

It is impossible to state unequivocally how much crime and delinquency there is in the United States or whether such behavior has been increasing or decreasing over the past several decades. One reason is that the officials who compile data on crime and delinquency are subject to all of the influences we have been describing.

The Meanings and Limitations of Official Statistics

Official statistics are the bookkeeping records of business transacted by the numerous agencies of the criminal- and juvenile-justice systems. These agencies compile data for a variety of purposes: for internal use, for the preparation of budget requests, and for presentation to such audiences as "city hall," the mass media, and taxpayers' groups. Their statistics tell us something about complaints received, crimes known to the police, the numbers of persons arrested and prosecuted for various crimes, the outcomes in court, and the size of institutional populations. They are direct descriptions of the behavior of officials, not of offenders. As such, they are clearly useful for the study of agency activities and the ways in which citizens who are caught up in the criminal-justice systems are processed.

They may also be useful as indicators of criminal behavior, because such behavior is one of the influences on official behavior. However, official statistics are neither a census nor a scientific sampling of the universe of crime. Much crime and delinquency is not discovered; if discovered, not reported; if reported, not recorded. Different kinds of offenders and offenses have different but largely unknown probabilities of becoming officially known. Furthermore, officials do not routinely compile statistics for all crimes, and great secrecy surrounds some of the information they collect (for example, data on white-collar and syndicated crime). Many crimes committed by persons of upper-socioeconomic status in the course of business are handled by quasi-judicial bodies, such as the Federal Trade Commission, and do not appear in the records of the criminal-justice system. Syndicated criminal activities that cross municipal and state boundaries are beyond the jurisdiction of local police departments; the legal technicalities of local business regulations require expertise beyond the resources available to police. As a result, systematic information about crime and delinquency is generated by widely scattered and sometimes overlapping agencies, and a good deal of crime goes unrecorded by any agency. Coverage of different types of offenses varies enormously, as does the extent to which such information is publicly available.

To compensate for the limitations of official statistics, students of crime and delinquency have experimented with many other sources of data and methods of study. These include large numbers of clinical reports and intensive case studies, surveys of self-reported behavior and of victimization, "participant observation" and other types of field observation, and the use of various kinds of nonpublic data.[5] The methodological ingenuity of researchers into crime and delinquency has been considerable, but information continues to be uneven, sketchy, and, in many instances, of unknown representativeness and relevance to particular aspects of "the crime problem." However, imaginative attempts to refine and supplement data from official sources and systematic surveys of criminal victimization show promise of improving measures of crime related activity.[6]

Trends in Crime and Deliquency

Both the Children's Bureau data on alleged delinquents known to the juvenile courts and the FBI statistics on crimes known to the police and persons arrested show startling rises beginning immediately after World War II, and

[5] For a clinical report see Lester E. Hewitt and Richard L. Jenkins, *Fundamental Patterns of Maladjustment: The Dynamics of Their Origin* (Springfield: State of Illinois, 1947); for an intensive case study, Clifford R. Shaw, *The Jack-Roller A Delinquent Boy's Own Story* (Chicago: University of Chicago Press, 1966). Self-reported behavior is the basis for Robert H. Hardt and George E. Bodine, *Development of Self-Reporting Instruments in Delinquency Research: A Conference Report* (Syracuse University Press, 1965). For a survey of victimization, see Phillip H. Ennis, "Crime, Victims, and the Police," *Trans-Action* (June 1967), pp. 36–44. For a sharp critique of most other methods of studying criminals and delinquents and a defense of field observation, see Ned Polsky, "Research Method, Morality, and Criminology," Chap. 3 in *Hustlers, Beats and Others* (Chicago: Aldine, 1967). The use of records of department-store detectives is illustrated in by Mary Owen Cameron, *The Booster and the Snitch* (New York: Free Press, 1965).

[6] As, for example, surveys to determine perceived seriousness of various criminal acts, and the careful use of police descriptions of delinquency events to study delinquency. See Thorsten Sellin and Marvin E. Wolfgang (eds.), *Delinquency: Selected Studies* (New York: Wiley, 1969). More recently the U.S. Department of Justice and the Bureau of the Census have cooperated in studying criminal victimization among a carefully selected National Crime Survey Panel.

People who have been arrested, even if not convicted, for "ordinary" crimes such as automobile theft are much more likely than those convicted of tax irregularities or of white-collar crimes to be saddled with at least some of the burden of a criminal identity.

all-time highs in the mid-1970s. As suggested above, these statistics may reflect the actual volume of serious crimes of a public nature, but we have no reliable measures of such phenomena as white-collar crime, gang delinquency, syndicated crime, and the vast amount of less serious "ordinary" crime that is hidden from official view. We may note, however, that more than 2.5 percent of all children aged 10 to 17 are involved in court cases each year, compared to approximately 1 percent in the pre-World War II period. The risk that a citizen will be the victim of a serious crime, as reported by police agencies to the FBI, rose to more than 4 per 100 persons by the mid-1970s. Victimization studies find even higher rates of serious crimes.[7]

All agree that these rates are high, but it is not at all clear that they represent real increases in crimes over time. There is some evidence that citizens

[7] A. D. Biederman and A. J. Reiss, Jr., "On Exploring the Dark Figure of Crime," *Annals of the American Academy of Political and Social Science*, Vol. 374.

may be reporting higher proportions of crimes than they did in previous years. A study in Portland, Oregon found that the rate of burglaries reported to the police increased by 22 percent between 1971–72 and 1973–74, while the rate of burglaries as determined by surveys of victims declined by 13 percent.[8] The discrepancy was accounted for by the fact that the proportion of burglaries reported to the police increased from 50 percent in 1971–72 to 71 percent in 1973–74. The largest increase occurred among participants in an anti-burglary program, suggesting that public sensitivity to crime issues and willingness to report victimization are quite changeable.

Rates of crime and delinquency may be "very high" today only when compared to the "very low" rates of the 1930s (when national statistics began to be collected). This hypothesis is supported by a survey of delinquency in Cuyahoga County (Cleveland), Ohio for the years 1918–57, another for Cook County, Illinois for the years 1900–1959, and studies of crime in individual urban areas extending in one case (Boston) as far back as the early years of the nineteenth century.[9] Studies of past historical eras, in the United States and other countries, chronicle the existence of a great deal of violence, theft, and other crimes. Although systematic records are virtually nonexistent, such studies provide strong evidence that present levels of crime and public concern have been equaled and exceeded in other countries and in our own past.

The Distribution of Crime and Delinquency

The relative size of groups with differing rates of involvement in crime in any population has such an important bearing on crime rates that trends may reflect changes in population composition, rather than changes in crime-related activity among these components. The most important of these population components, or *categoric risks,* as Walter Reckless called them, are discussed below.

Variation by age Statistical evidence of so many kinds, from so many jurisdictions, over so many years, is so consistent on this score, that it may be reasonably assumed that older adolescents and young adults have higher crime rates than other age groups. Relevant data are presented in Table 1-1. Statistics are likely to exaggerate offense rates of these age groups as compared with rates of other age groups. (Children and younger adolescents are less likely to be arrested and more likely to be turned over to their parents than are older adolescents, and older people are more likely to possess either the skills or the "clout" necessary to avoid arrest.) Nevertheless, there appear to be real dif-

---

[8] See Anne L. Schneider, *Crime and Victimization in Portland: Analysis of Trends, 1971–74* (Eugene: Oregon Research Institute, 1975).

[9] Negley K. Teeters and David Matza, "The Extent of Delinquency in the United States," *The Journal of Negro Education,* Vol. 28 (Summer 1959), pp. 210–211 and unpublished data collected by Henry McKay of the Institute of Juvenile Research, Chicago, Illinois. Data and references for Boston are discussed in Roger Lane, "Urbanization and Criminal Violence in the 19th Century: Massachusetts as a Test Case," Chap. 12 in Hugh Davis Graham and Ted Robert Gurr (eds.), *Violence in America: Historical and Comparative Perspectives* (Washington, D.C.: U.S. Government Printing Office, 1969), pp. 359–370.

Table 1–1   Arrests for Major Crimes in the United States, 1974,
by Age and Sex

Offense charged	Number of persons arrested	Percentage of those arrested	
		Under 18	Male
Class I Offenses			
Larceny—theft	729,661	48.9	69.3
Burglary—breaking or entering	340,697	53.3	94.6
Auto theft	107,226	55.2	93.5
Aggravated assault	154,514	17.0	86.6
Robbery	108,481	32.6	93.2
Forcible rape	17,804	19.4	100.0
Criminal homicide:			
(a) Murder and nonnegligent manslaughter	13,818	10.1	85.4
(b) Manslaughter by negligence	2,226	10.0	87.6
Class II Offenses			
Drunkenness	911,837	3.1	92.8
All other offenses (except traffic)	757,040	26.3	84.2
Driving under the influence of alcohol	616,549	1.4	92.0
Disorderly conduct	544,321	20.1	79.5
Narcotic-drug-laws	454,948	26.0	85.8
Other assaults	269,643	20.1	86.1
Liquor-law violations	191,213	41.5	84.9
Runaways	154,653	100.0	43.3
Vandalism	146,261	68.7	92.1
Weapons: carrying, possessing, etc.	119,189	15.9	91.8
Fraud	91,176	5.2	67.4
Stolen property: buying, receiving, possessing	76,943	34.3	89.9
Curfew-and-loitering-law violations	70,167	100.0	76.7
Prostitution and commercialized vice	53,309	4.0	24.4
Gambling	45,900	4.1	91.4
Sex offenses (except forcible rape and prostitution)	44,375	22.4	92.2
Forgery and counterfeiting	39,741	13.3	71.4
Offenses against family and children	34,902	10.6	88.1
Suspicion	33,363	32.0	86.0
Vagrancy	32,802	14.1	87.5
Arson	10,756	58.7	89.5
Embezzlement	5,891	7.7	73.7

Source: Federal Bureau of Investigation, *Crime in the United States, 1974, Uniform Crime Reports* (Washington, D.C.: Government Printing Office, 1975), adapted from pp. 188–189.

ferences. In recent years, persons 16 years of age have comprised the largest number of persons arrested for all categories of crime combined, with 15-, 17-, and 18-year-olds close behind. It also appears that rates of serious crimes committed by young people have risen more rapidly than have those for older persons in the last decade.

Young people are not as likely as older persons to be involved in white-collar crime, professional theft, or syndicated crime. They come to the attention of the police primarily for property crimes, vandalism, and specifically juvenile offenses, such as running away and curfew violation. With the exception of embezzlement, fraud, forgery, and counterfeiting, which require greater finesse and higher social position, juveniles account for a large percentage of all property-offense arrests.

Variation by sex   If an investigator were asked to use a single trait to predict which persons in any given town would become criminals, he would make the fewest mistakes if he simply chose sex and predicted criminality for the males and noncriminality for the females. Most of the males, to be sure, would not become criminals, and some of the females would, but he would be wrong in more cases if he used any other single trait, such as age, race, family background, or a personality characteristic.

Crime and delinquency rates for males greatly exceed rates for females—in all nations, all communities within a nation, all age groups, all periods of history for which organized statistics are available, and for all types of crime (except for a few peculiar to women, such as prostitution). Ratios vary by offense, however, as is clear from Table 1-1. While self-report studies indicate that girls engage in much the same *types* of delinquency as boys,[10] they are brought before the court far more often than boys for such offenses as "incorrigibility" and "delinquent tendencies," which often are euphemisms for problems related to sexual behavior.

In recent years the ratio of boys to girls appearing before juvenile courts in the United States has dropped to about 4 to 1, probably the lowest ratio of any country. The figure represents a considerable decrease from the 50 and 60 to 1 ratios which obtained in this country around the turn of the century. The ratio in England and Wales is about 8 to 1, also a declining figure in recent years. Adult ratios tend to be higher than juvenile ratios, though they too have dropped. In 1973, for example, male arrests reported to the FBI outnumbered female arrests by almost 6 to 1.[11] But females accounted for 19 percent of arrests for serious crimes, and when age and sex are combined it is clear that male "dominance" in crime-related activity is waning. Arrests of females under 18 for serious crimes over the five-year period of 1968–1973 rose 52 percent, compared with a 10 percent rise among young males.

The extent to which crime rates for males exceed those for females varies greatly from one cultural setting to another. In some traditional societies, such as those of Ceylon, Algeria, Tunis, and Japan before World War II, male criminals and delinquents came to official attention 3,000 to 4,000 times as frequently as females.[12] However, in contemporary Japan and Turkey, where women have become more nearly equal to men, marked increases in the proportion of female offenders have been noted.

[10] See recent reports of the Illinois Institute for Juvenile Research survey of the youthful population of that state. Our thanks to Patricia Miller for information on this point.

[11] Federal Bureau of Investigation, *Crime in the United States, 1973* (Washington, D.C.: U.S. Government Printing Office, 1974), p. 34.

[12] E. Hacker, *Kriminalstatistische and Kriminalaetiologische Berichte* (Miskolc, Hungary: Ludwig, 1941).

Men are involved to a greater extent than women in most types of professional and syndicated crime, and in white-collar crime. This, too, may change as women have more opportunities to commit crimes in illegitimate as well as legitimate business.[13]

Race and ethnicity There are no easy generalizations about the relationship of race and ethnicity to rates of crime and delinquency; the rates vary too greatly within each group at any given time and they change too much over time. Present-day crime and delinquency rates are the cumulative product of the cultures ethnic groups brought with them to this country, the circumstances under which they arrived, the problems they faced, the transformations they underwent in consequence of their experiences in the new land, and their present economic and social situation. Groups once feared as part of a "criminal class," such as the early Irish immigrants to U.S. cities, have long since acquired respectability.[14] Some groups, such as the Chinese and Southern Italians, came with traditional patterns of behavior and social organization, including ways of relating to governmental authority, that were *ipso facto* criminal in the new cultural context or which encouraged modes of adjustment that were defined as criminal in this country.[15] For some groups, Old World traits speeded assimilation into the new world; for others, the traditional culture and a persistent sense of national or ethnic identity provided the basis for isolated but in the main law-abiding enclaves. Still others, for example, Native Americans and blacks, were the early victims of conquest or slavery, in the course of which their history and ancestral cultures were largely destroyed. For them, the problems of survival within and accommodations to the larger society were very different and far more difficult.

Groups in the United States that have the highest rates of crime and delinquency today are those that are either the newest arrivals (many from Puerto Rico and Latin American countries) or those with the longest history of cultural conflict and deprivation (for example, Native Americans and blacks). Some groups with especially low crime rates, for example, American Jews, once had fairly high rates. Conversely, American Orientals, long noted for low rates of crime and delinquency, in some places now evidence higher rates, in response to declining cultural isolation, changed economic conditions, and deterioration of established patterns of community social control.[16]

---

[13] Ianni reports that ethnic succession in organized crime involves more women today than in the past because of differing historical roles of women in Italian and black families and culture in the U.S. Francis A. J. Ianni, *Black Mafia: Ethnic Succession in Organized Crime* (New York: Simon and Schuster, 1974).

[14] See, e.g., Roger Lane, *op. cit.*

[15] See, e.g., Stanford Lyman, *Chinese Americans* (New York: Random House, 1974), and Francis A. J. Ianni, *A Family Business: Kinship and Social Control in Organized Crime* (New York: Russell Sage Foundation, 1972).

[16] See, e.g., Ivan Light and Charles Choy Wong, "Protest or Work: Dilemmas of the Tourist Industry in American Chinatowns," *American Journal of Sociology* (May 1975), pp. 1342–1368. Mass media reports have described increased delinquencies among Chinese-American youth, e.g., "The Gangs of Chinatown," *Newsweek* (July 2, 1973), p. 22.

The rates we speak of refer to official data, with all their limitations. Earlier studies reported that black children, for example, were committed at younger ages, for less serious crimes, and with fewer prior court appearances and institutional commitments than were white children—inflating the black delinquency rate.[17] More recent studies are inconsistent with respect to these and other aspects of law enforcement and judicial processes.[18] In part, these inconsistencies reflect varying customs and practices of different agencies, courts, and localities; in part, they reflect problems of measurement, analysis, and research design. Such problems aside, the studies suggest that, in most jurisdictions, relatively little of the variation in rates of serious crime and delinquency among racial and ethnic groups can be accounted for by *prejudicial* discretion on the part of police, probation officers, and judges. Much of the variation is based not on race or ethnicity *per se,* but on factors associated with socioeconomic status, and blacks and other groups are disproportionately concentrated in the lower economic strata. Thus some of the variation in disposition of young offenders is entirely consistent with the juvenile court philosophy which stresses state intervention based on "need" rather than seriousness of offense, and this "need" (as interpreted by the courts) is greatest where economic resources are least. At the adult level, demonstration that convicted black rapists whose victims were whites are more often sentenced to death "than defendants in any other racial combination of defendant and victim" has been an important factor in U.S. Supreme Court deliberations concerning the constitutionality of the death penalty.[19]

Social class and delinquency   Many studies indicate that lower-class individuals run greater risks of being officially defined as criminals or delinquent than middle- or upper-class persons. Studies based on self-reported behavior and victimization, however, reveal a great deal of "hidden" crime and delinquency on the part of persons of all social classes.[20]

Victimization studies and observational data suggest that the incidence of serious "ordinary" crime (e.g., the seven FBI index offenses) is higher in lower-class neighborhoods in big cities than in middle-class neighborhoods or in

[17] Sidney Axelrad, "Negro and White Male Institutionalized Delinquents," *American Journal of Sociology* (May 1952), pp. 569–574. See also Don C. Gibbons and Manzer J. Griswold, "Sex Differences Among Juvenile Court Referrals," *Sociology and Social Research* (November–December 1957), pp. 106–110.

[18] C. Thomas and C. Sieverdes, "Juvenile Court Intake: An Analysis of Discretionary Decision-Making," *Criminology* (February 1975), pp. 413–431.

[19] Marvin E. Wolfgang, "The Social Scientist in Court," *The Journal of Criminal Law and Criminology,* Vol. 65, No. 2 (1944), p. 242. See also Wolfgang and Marc Riedel, "Race, Judicial Discretion, and the Death Penalty," *Annals of the American Academy of Political and Social Science,* Vol. 407 (1973), pp. 119–133.

[20] See, e.g., Austin Porterfield, "Delinquency and Its Outcome in Court and College," *American Journal of Sociology,* Vol. 49 (1943), pp. 199–204; J. S. Wallerstein and C. J. Wyle, "Our Law-abiding Lawbreakers," *Probation,* Vol. 25 (March–April 1947), pp. 107–112.

smaller cities and rural areas.[21] The data are inconsistent, however. The only state-wide ethnographic study of delinquent behavior (in Illinois) found that adolescents from different socioeconomic backgrounds were much the same. A companion survey of 3,000 adolescents concurs with this judgment, adding that the major exception to the overall "delinquent similarity" of adolescents across social classes, races, and communities, are the "significantly higher rates of violence and theft, among inner-city nonwhites."[22] Although the probability of arrest and court referral increases with frequency and seriousness of behavior, the differences by race, class, and sex in arrest, and especially court statistics, greatly exaggerate the differences in behavior, sometimes show differences where none exist, and sometimes even reverse them.[23]

Ecological differences Probably the best-established patterns of variation in official crime and delinquency statistics are of an ecological nature. Data from many countries and many different times indicate that urban areas have higher rates of crime and delinquency than do rural areas and that, in the United States at least, suburban and "semiurban" areas fall between these extremes. The chief caution in interpreting these findings concerns differences in resources for handling cases. It seems likely that in rural areas less serious offenses tend to be handled outside the court, by parents, neighbors, ministers, and others. In urban areas, where official resources are more fully developed and people rely more on legal controls, similar offenses are more likely to find their way into the courts. The difference between urban and rural crime rates holds for more serious offenses as well, so it cannot be accounted for solely in these terms. But serious crimes known to the police have been increasing more rapidly in suburban and rural areas than in core cities, perhaps reflecting the spread of urban influences and a national culture to which crime and delinquency are responsive.

The classic works of Clifford R. Shaw and Henry McKay and more recent studies reveal wide variations in the spatial concentration of crime and delinquency within cities.[24] Though the details vary in different cities, the general

[21] Cf. Robert H. Hardt, "Delinquency and Social Class: Bad Kids or Good Cops," in Irwin Deutscher and Elizabeth J. Thompson (eds.), *Among the People: Encounters with the Poor* (New York: Basic Books, 1968), pp. 132–145. James F. Short, Jr. and Fred L. Strodtbeck, *Group Process and Gang Delinquency* (Chicago: University of Chicago Press, 1965), Chaps. 4, 5, and 7; Walter B. Miller, Hildred S. Geertz, and Henry S. C. Cutter, "Aggression in a Boys' Street-Corner Group," *Psychiatry*, Vol. 24 (1961), pp. 283–289.

[22] William Simon, Joseph E. Puntil, and Emil Peluso, "Continuities in Delinquency Research," in James F. Short, Jr. (ed.), *Crime, Delinquency and Society* (Chicago: University of Chicago Press, forthcoming).

[23] J. R. Williams and M. Gold, "From Delinquent Behavior to Official Delinquency," *Social Problems*, Vol. 20, No. 2 (Fall 1972), pp. 209–229.

[24] Clifford R. Shaw et al., *Delinquency Areas* (Chicago: University of Chicago Press, 1929); Clifford Shaw and Henry McKay, *Juvenile Delinquency and Urban Areas*, rev. ed., (Chicago: University of Chicago Press, 1969); and Robert A. Gordon, "Issues in the Ecological Study of Delinquency," *American Sociological Review* (December 1967), pp. 927–944. Cf. Lois B. DeFleur, "Ecological Variables in the Cross-Cultural Study of Delinquency," *Social Forces* (June 1967), pp. 556–570.

pattern in American cities at least is remarkably consistent. Rates of crime and delinquency and of recidivism are highest in the inner-city areas characterized by physical deterioration and the concentration of other social ills, such as poverty, suicide, mental illness, and certain diseases. As one moves away from these *delinquency areas,* rates go down fairly regularly. When studied over time these ecological distributions change little, despite changes in the racial and ethnic composition of the areas studied.

Sellin, Figlio, and Wolfgang, for example, found that of approximately 10,000 boys born in 1945 and residing in Philadelphia from age 10 through 17, 35 percent had at least one officially recorded police contact during this 8-year period; of these, 55 percent had more than one police contact; a smaller group of 627 "chronic offenders" (five or more recorded offenses)—6.3 percent of the entire cohort—accounted for more than half of all delinquencies recorded, including 53 percent of the personal attacks, 62 percent of the property offenses, and 71 percent of the robberies attributed to the cohort.[25] Delinquency tended to be concentrated in the blighted slum areas of the city. These delinquency areas not only have higher overall rates of delinquent behavior and higher rates of serious delinquency, but also larger numbers of more frequently and seriously involved delinquents.

While trends in delinquency rates suggest that most communities are remarkably stable in this respect, rapid increases are found in a few communities and rapid decreases in others. McKay's analysis of trends in Chicago communities revealed that communities with the most pronounced upward trends in delinquency rates are areas that were most recently settled by blacks, while communities with the most pronounced downward trends had been predominantly black since the beginning of the period studied.[26] These findings are consistent with those concerning other racial and ethnic groups. Under the disorganizing impact of residential shift from an "invading" socially and economically disadvantaged population, communities lose their ability to control behavior defined as delinquent. Conventional institutions break down and social problems in great variety increase. In time, however, these institutions become reestablished and other forms of social control also become more effective.

Crime rates and demographic change   We cannot infer from increasing overall crime rates that the crime rates for the constituent categories of the population or for people living under particular sets of conditions have increased correspondingly, if at all. The overall increases could result from changes in the proportions that these subpopulations constitute of the larger population. For example, Theodore N. Ferdinand has demonstrated that when migration from rural areas to cities is taken into account, approximately one-fifth of the increase in serious crime (FBI Class I offenses; see Table 1) in this

[25] Marvin E. Wolfgang, Robert M. Figlio, and Thorsten Sellin, *Delinquency in a Birth Cohort* (Chicago: University of Chicago Press, 1972).

[26] See Henry McKay's discussion of these findings in Shaw and McKay, *op. cit.*

country between 1950 and 1965 can be attributed to urbanization.[27] In addition, more than one-tenth of the arrests for these crimes in 1965 represented changes in the age structure during this period (that is, expansion of the 10 to 24 age group). The influence of such demographic shifts varies for different offenses, with fully one-fourth of the recorded rise in robberies and auto thefts, but only 8 percent of criminal homicides, attributable to increased urbanization. Forty-seven percent of the increase in arrests for forcible rape, but much smaller percentages of other serious crimes, may be attributed to the increased proportion of the population in the 10 to 24 age group. More recently, 99 percent of the rise in arrests for serious crimes from 1967 to 1972 in Pittsburgh has been attributed to changes in the age, sex, and racial composition of the population of that city. No change in arrests for specific population groups was found, with one exception, *viz.*, an "increased criminality of arrest vulnerability among young women."[28]

CRIMINOLOGICAL THEORY

We saw in the preceding section that crime and delinquency are statistically associated with many different conditions. It is tempting to conclude that such associations signify causation, the importance of each factor depending upon the strength of the association. However, a statistical association means only that some factor occurs in connection with some phenomenon more frequently than would be expected by chance. It does not necessarily mean one causes the other—that trousers, for example, cause maleness, or that maleness causes crime; or, to round out the absurdity, that trousers cause crime. No single circumstance is in itself a push in the direction of crime. Criminal events are the product of the interaction of some set of circumstances, not their mere summation. Poverty in combination with one set of circumstances may indeed promote crime; in combination with another set of circumstances, it may promote honest toil.

When we explain something—falling bodies, the price of corn, or a criminal act—we show that the event fits and follows from some *general rule* that applies not only to this event but to all events of that class. Such a general rule (or, more often, set of rules) provides a language—a set of abstract categories or "variables"—into which we can translate the outcomes to be explained and the concrete circumstances or "factors" that may affect these outcomes. It also tells us how the outcomes depend upon *the relationships among* the values of the remaining variables. The explanation, then, lies not in this or that factor, or in the sum of several factors, but in demonstration that observed relationships among factors and outcomes can be accounted for by a general rule. We call these rules *theories*. They are hard to come by. The best theories are those

---

[27] Theodore N. Ferdinand, "Demographic Shifts and Criminality: An Inquiry," *British Journal of Criminology* (April 1970), pp. 169–175.

[28] Alfred Blumstein and Daniel S. Nagin, *Analysis of Arrest Rates for Trends in Criminality* (Pittsburgh: Carnegie Mellon University School of Urban and Public Affairs, 1974).

that make sense out of the most facts and leave the fewest threads dangling. Statistical relationships are not theories; they are descriptive statements of observed tendencies of the joint occurrence of certain events. They do not explain; they require explanation. Such explanation is the office of theory.

Sociologists approach the task of explaining crime and delinquency by asking three kinds of questions. Perhaps the question most commonly asked is: Why did *this* individual commit *this* crime? It should be clear that no list of personality characteristics, no compilation of background information about the individual actor can of itself predict criminal behavior. It is reasonable to ask, however, whether we can identify kinds of persons who have a high probability of involvement in certain kinds of criminal actions, how they became that way, and in what ways their personal characteristics facilitate such involvement. These are what are ordinarily called "psychological" questions.

Criminal events are located not only in the biographies of individuals, but in social systems as well. Rates of criminal events can be enumerated and their characteristic distributions in social systems and over time studied. Some forms of criminal organization—for example, syndicated crime as we know it in the United States—may be characteristic of some societies and absent in others. We may therefore ask: What are the properties of social systems—their organization, their cultures, their technologies, their economies, and so forth—that account for differences within and between systems? This is the perspective of *macrosociology*.

Finally, if we view a criminal event as the product of interaction among offenders, victims, and perhaps others, over time and in varying circumstances, we may ask: Why did it "run off" as it did? How did interaction among these participants shape the outcome or event? Put another way: What general propositions can we formulate about the structure and the development of interactive processes that produce criminal actions? This is the *microsociological* perspective on crime. As we shall see, these questions have not been asked as often as the others, and the least is known about them.

When we approach crime and delinquency from these different perspectives, we arrive at different, but not necessarily competing or conflicting, explanations. They are different because they are answers to different questions. Therefore, arguments to the effect that "psychological" explanations are superior to "sociological" explanations (or vice versa) are largely pointless. They are explaining different things.

The Individual Level of Explanation

We have a long history of theories that attempt to explain crime and delinquency in terms of observable or hypothetical processes or conditions "characteristic of the organism, rather than its present environment."[29] However, our

[29] Saleem A. Shah and Loren E. Roth, "Biological and Psychophysiological Factors in Criminality," in Daniel Glaser (ed.), *Handbook of Criminology* (Chicago: Rand McNally, 1974), p. 104. This chapter (pp. 101–173) presents an excellent survey and bibliography of research and theory on this topic.

knowledge of specific relationships between these variables remains, for the most part, crude, speculative, and uncertain.

Biological and psychophysiological theories   One of the earliest, and most famous, of the theories emphasizing *organic* processes and conditions was Cesare Lombroso's theory of the "born criminal." Though sharply criticized when presented and later qualified by Lombroso himself, the general idea of a criminal type, recognizable by bestial or otherwise unlovely stigmata, has attracted many scholars.[30] Most of this work, like Lombroso's has been found wanting on methodological grounds.[31]

The most sophisticated of these efforts relates body type, temperament, and behavior. William H. Sheldon found delinquents to be predominantly mesomorphic (sturdy, muscular, and athletic), rather than endomorphic (corpulent, slow of foot) or ectomorphic (tall, scrawny, and fragile).[32] He hypothesized that mesomorphy and its attendant temperament, somatotonia (characterized by assertiveness of posture and movement, love of physical adventure, restless energy, need for and enjoyment of exercise), produce aggressive, daring types of people; it is the stuff of which generals, athletes, and politicians, as well as delinquents, are often made.

Sheldon's work has been subject to devastating criticism (although some investigations claim to support his findings).[33] Methodological problems aside, it is clear that social reactions to persons of different body types may influence both temperament and behavior. For example, youngsters with outstanding physical endowment may receive special attention from delinquent peers as well as from athletic directors. Regrettably, there has been little research into the ways in which the *interaction* of biological endowment and social experience might affect crime and delinquency.

The evidence is stronger for some kind of relationship between certain specific organic disorders and crime. Tumors and other forms of brain pathology are sometimes followed by assaultive and predatory behavior in individuals with no prior history of such behavior.[34] But these disorders are relatively infrequent, they are not uniformly followed by criminal behavior, and they could

---

[30] See the introduction to Gina Lomroso-Ferrero, *Criminal Man According to the Classifications of Cesare Lombroso* (New York: Putnam, 1911), pp. xiv–xv. Lombroso's *L'uomo Delinquente* was first published in 1876.

[31] See, e.g., E. A. Hooton, *Crime and the Man* (Cambridge, Mass.): Harvard University Press, 1939); and Robert K. Merton and M. F. Ashley-Montagu, "Crime and the Anthropologist," *American Anthropologist,* Vol. 42 (1940), pp. 384–468.

[32] William R. Sheldon, *Varieties of Delinquent Youth* (New York: Harper, 1949).

[33] Cf. Albert K. Cohen, Alfred R. Lindesmith, and Karl F. Schessler (eds.), *The Sutherland Papers* (Bloomington: Indiana University Press, 1956), pp. 279–290; Sheldon and Eleanor Glueck, *Physique and Crime: A Biopsychosocial Approach* (New York: Seminar Press, 1972). Additional references may be found in Shah and Roth, *op. cit.*

[34] N. Malamud, "Psychiatric Disorder with Intracranial Tumors of Limbic System," *Archives of Neurology,* Vol. 17 (1965), pp. 113–123, cited in Shah and Roth, *op. cit.,* p. 116. See also, H. Brill, "Postencephalitic Psychiatric Conditions," in S. Arieti (ed.), *American Handbook of Psychiatry,* Vol. 2 (New York: Basic Books, 1959).

not possibly contribute to more than a small fraction of the bulk of crime and delinquency.[35]

Other, more common, biological conditions have also been linked to crime and delinquency, but again the reasons for the linkage are not fully understood. Saleem A. Shah and Loren E. Roth note that a number of disorders that are associated with crime and delinquency are known to result in part from birth trauma and from inadequate nutrition, and pre- and postnatal care. These, in turn, are found most often among socially and economically disadvantaged groups.[36] However, the precise nature of these interrelationships is far from clear. More generally, we know that the physiology, neurology, and chemistry of the body may affect learning, mood, energy, and rhythms, and these in turn are likely to have some effect on other aspects of behavior, including criminal behavior. With possible rare exceptions, however, the linkage will be mediated by both past experience and present situation, and especially by the way in which others define and interact with the person affected. An adequate theory of human behavior, including criminal and delinquent behavior, requires a much better understanding than we now have of all these interrelationships.

Psychometric approaches Immediately before and after World War I, when intelligence testing came into vogue, feeble-mindedness came to be regarded as an important cause of crime. By 1920, H. H. Goddard claimed that "nearly all" criminals and delinquents were of low-grade mentality.[37] Such claims are no longer made. It is now the general view that the feeble-minded do not show rates of crime and delinquency very different from those of the general population.[38]

Psychologists and others have used dozens of tests, rating scales, and other measuring devices to study the relationship between crime and delinquency and a host of psychological traits such as mechanical aptitude, aggressiveness, speed of decision, emotional instability, caution, self-assurance, excitability, and motor inhibition. Generally speaking, the work in this area has been fragmentary in character, in the sense that studies are made without reference to a systematically developed theory of crime.

Although individual studies do show correlations between personality traits and crime and delinquency, the correlations tend to be weak and the results of different studies to be inconsistent.[39] Certainly there is no criminal or delin-

---

[35] L. Berkowitz and J. Macaulay, "The Contagion of Criminal Violence," *Sociometry* (June 1971), pp. 238–260; see also, Albert Bandura, *Social Learning Theory* (New York: General Learning Press, 1971).

[36] Shah and Roth, *op. cit.*

[37] Henry H. Goddard, *Feeblemindedness, Its Causes and Consequences* (New York: Macmillan, 1912); Henry H. Goddard, *Human Efficiency and Levels of Intelligence* (New Jersey: Princeton University Press, 1920), pp. 73–74.

[38] Carl Murchison, *Criminal Intelligence* (Worcester, Mass.: Clark University Press, 1926), and Samuel H. Tulchin, *Intelligence and Crime* (Chicago: University of Chicago Press, 1939).

[39] Karl F. Schuessler and Donald R. Cressey, "Personality Characteristics of Criminals," *American Journal of Sociology*, Vol. 55 (March 1950), pp. 476–484.

quent personality type, if by this we mean a distinguishable pattern of measurable personality characteristics that always or even usually results in criminal or delinquent behavior.

Psychiatric theories　Psychiatric perspectives on crime and delinquency rest heavily on conceptions of motivation and personality derived from psychoanalytic theory. According to this theory, behavior is motivated by impulses and "drive energy" of a fundamentally biological nature (the *Id*), and modified by socialization experiences, which provide the individual with the capacity for thought and rational assessment (the *Ego*), and internal restraints in the form of conscience (the *Superego*).[40]

In the classic statement of this position, delinquent behavior results when the restraining forces are too weak to curb inherent aggressive and destructive tendencies. Such tendencies are universal to the species. We are all, in this view, born criminals. We do not learn to become criminals; rather some of us learn to control the criminality with which all are afflicted, while some do not. However, modern psychiatry has moved considerably beyond the simple determinism implied in this earlier model. Seymour Halleck observes that "While some aggressive and some sexual activity is often correlated with a weakening of control mechanisms . . . the act of law violation is often a deliberate, planned and complicated operation which may require a great deal of ego strength."[41]

Halleck and many other psychiatrists see behavior as adaptive problem-solving. Specifically, they see crime as "an adaptation to stress . . . best understood in terms of the manner in which the individual experiences the biological, psychological, and socially determined situations of his existence."[42]

Psychiatric perspectives on crime and delinquency lean heavily on assumptions concerning unconscious mental and emotional processes that do not easily admit to empirical inquiry. Psychiatric writing usually takes the form of detailed case histories of patients in treatment, not systematic research aimed at generalized knowledge. Consisting largely of interpretations based on theory and on the author's clinical intuition, such writing does not often yield propositions of a testable character. Investigators often probe psychic processes until an emotional problem is located, whereupon they announce that the problem is responsible for the delinquency, with little attempt to connect the two in a logical or empirical way. One cannot easily quarrel with the notion that human behavior is concerned with solving problems, whether these problems are conceived in biological, psychiatric, or sociological terms. However, all theories that attempt to account for crime or delinquency as

---

[40] For a review of this position and its modification, see Franz Alexander and Hugo Staub, *The Criminal, the Judge, and the Public* (New York: Free Press, 1956).

[41] Seymour Halleck, *Psychiatry and the Dilemmas of Crime* (New York: Harper, 1967), p. 61.

[42] *Ibid.,* p. 63.

ways of coping with problems must explain why some people solve their problems in illegal ways while others do not. Psychiatric theories often fail this test, but the failing is not peculiar to them.

Role theory   What people do, they do as participants in an interaction process. From the sociological perspective, the circumstances that shape individuals' actions are those that affect the manner of their participation in interaction processes.

Human beings do not participate in interaction simply as representatives of a species. We are all continually trying to convince others that we are a certain sort of person. This is what we mean by the self, or more precisely, *self-demands:* how we must appear (to ourselves and others) in order to be acceptable to ourselves. In any interaction, we are likely to select, from the possibilities open to us, that course of action that appears most likely to contribute to the establishment of an image of ourselves that is consistent with our self-demands. Thus our *behavior is oriented to the creation, maintenance, and enhancement of self under conditions of interaction.*

The self is largely defined in role terms. In order to do business with one another, to know what to expect of one another, to pass judgment on one another, we must decide what position or *role* others occupy in the activity or organization in which we are interacting. To these roles there attach socially standardized expectations, which we may fittingly call *role demands,* and these demands provide the standards by which we judge one another. If the selves that we present to others are to make sense, they must be formulated largely in terms of generally understood roles. Therefore, the selves that we create and claim for ourselves consist largely of roles to which we aspire and their corresponding demands ("tough guy," "law-abiding citizen," "friend," "member of the Golden Dragons," "good soldier," "radical," "devoted wife," "liberated woman," etc.).

In an effort to establish or validate a self or identity, an individual may act in a certain way because it directly fulfills role demands, because the behavior is role-expressive. For example, being aggressive, daring, or defiant may get a boy in trouble, but such characteristics are "all boy," according to the traditional conception of the male role; they are expressive of that role. Such behavior is not expressive of the traditional conception of the female role. For those who define their "girlishness" in traditional terms, validation of identity comes from being physically attractive, having winsome, feminine ways, and being identified with popular boys. In all likelihood, if such a girl steals, it is not "for the hell of it" (to demonstrate daring and prowess), but to acquire clothing, cosmetics, and accessories that will enable her to play the traditional female role more successfully. Although stealing *as such* is not expressive of the female role, *this kind* of stealing may be supportive of that role. By extension, the boy who breaks windows and steals hubcaps may, a few years later, abandon such behavior because it is defined as "kids' stuff." It is not expressive of the new, adult identity he is creating for himself.[43]

The value and meaning of the self are influenced by a person's reference groups. Insofar as we have any choice in the matter, what kinds of identities or selves will we try to construct? Self-demands are not given in the nature of things. The value and meanings we attach to different roles depend upon their value and meanings for others with whom we live, work, play. But these "others" may disagree in small ways and large, and for each individual the judgments of some groups carry more weight than those of others. We call those groups that carry weight *reference groups*. They are influential in two ways. First, they provide the standards against which we check the validity of our own thinking. "Is it true that anybody with a conscience and whose eyes are open has just got to be radical?" "Is being a shoplifter shameful and degrading, or is it just another way of making a living?" "If I, as a physician, know that one of my colleagues is engaged in illegal fee-splitting, do I have an obligation to make this public?" Our answers to questions like these depend very much on how they are answered by our reference groups.

Reference groups also provide acceptance or rejection. For example, whether the prospect of public exposure will deter us from throwing rocks at policemen, shoplifting, or illegal price-rigging depends partly on whom we look to for affection, recognition, and acceptance, and how such exposure will affect us in *their* eyes. Most reference groups are influential in both ways, but some (normative reference groups) may be more important as authoritative criteria of validity and others (status reference groups) as groups from which we seek social acceptance.

In general, role theory emphasizes that most of what we do, we do with other people and with an eye to what it will mean to them and how it will affect our relationships. Role theory tends to account for behavior that is criminal and behavior that is not in terms of the same underlying processes, whereas the other theories we have discussed tend to seek their explanations in terms of personal qualities and characteristics that differentiate criminals from non-criminals.

Differential association   Most sociologists take the position that the values and beliefs that favor delinquent and criminal behavior are originally part of our cultural milieus and that they are taken over in the same way that anti-delinquent and anti-criminal values and beliefs are taken over—through cultural transmission. The most systematic statement of this view is Edwin H. Sutherland's theory of *differential association*.[44]

Differential-association theory emphasizes that criminal behavior is learned

---

[43] The role-expressive and role-supportive distinction is from George Grosser, *Juvenile Delinquency and Contemporary American Sex Roles* (Unpublished Ph.D. dissertation, Harvard University, 1952).

[44] Edwin H. Sutherland and Donald R. Cressey, *Criminology*, 8th ed. (Philadelphia: Lippincott, 1970).

in interaction with other persons in a process of communication. Such learning includes the specific direction of values, attitudes, motives, drives, and rationalizations of criminality, as well as techniques of committing crime. Most importantly, however, a person acquires definitions of criminal actions that are favorable and unfavorable to violation of law. In Sutherland's view, "a person becomes delinquent because of an excess of definitions favorable to violation of law over definitions unfavorable to violation of law."

No criminological theory successfully integrates everything that is relevant to the nature and acquisition of criminal motivation. However, the theory of differential association probably comes closer than any other single theory to making sense of the greatest range of facts about crime. As a theory of learning, its power is enhanced if we add to it a central theme of identity theory: The impact of exposure to a definition depends upon its relevance to the kind of self we are trying to construct or maintain. Things that will help us in accomplishing our projects—and building a self is a most important project—are most quickly perceived and leave the deepest and most lasting impression.[45]

Macrosociological Theories

Macrosociological theories emphasize those properties of social systems that account for variations in the crime rate both within and between societies, as indicated above.

Anomie theory The theory of anomie, formulated by Robert Merton,[46] is based on the idea that people's aspirations, and therefore their definitions of success and failure, are to a large extent determined by goals set for them by their culture. Success in American society, for example, is defined largely in terms of material success. This definition of success is more or less the same for all groups. However, different racial, class, and ethnic groupings are radically unequal in their ability to realize their aspirations by those means that the culture defines as legitimate. Where the disjunction between "culture goals" and "institutionalized means" for their achievement is great, a condition of *anomie* develops—that is, a breakdown of the regulative norms—and people turn to whatever means will "work." Where anomie prevails, we are likely to find high rates of crime and delinquency. In societies where different classes of people are indoctrinated with aspirations more in keeping with the means available to them, the sense of deprivation is not so acute, anomie is less likely to occur, and rates of deviant behavior are not so high.

Anomie theory treats variations in rates of deviance both within and be-

[45] Differential association has also been integrated with modern psychological theories of reinforcement and social learning theory. See Ronald L. Akers, *Deviant Behavior: A Social Learning Approach* (Belmont, California: Wadsworth, 1973). For a review and synthesis of psychological theories in this area see Albert Bandura, *Aggression: A Social Learning Analysis* (Englewood Cliffs, N.J.: Prentice-Hall, 1973).

[46] Robert K. Merton, *Social Theory and Social Structure*, rev. ed. (New York: Free Press, 1968).

tween societies as products of culture and social structure. It identifies several different possible responses to a disjunction between goals and means, including steadfastness in conforming behavior even though it is not rewarded. But it does not specify the conditions that determine choices among the possible responses. Note also that a great deal of crime and delinquency does not readily make sense as alternative, albeit illegal, means to the acquisition of worldly goods. Examples would be gang violence and juvenile vandalism, on the one hand, and the illegal tactics employed at one time or another by students, militant minorities, and other groups as part of "confrontation politics," on the other. Whatever may be its limitations, anomie theory is squarely based on the sociological principle that human actions represent choices "between socially structured alternatives." Not only law breaking but law making and law enforcement as well consist of selecting goals and the means for pursuing them from a range of possibilities provided by the culture and the social structure, and these possibilities will be different at different locations in the social system. The basic point that individuals and groups make choices "between socially structured alternatives," and that these choices have consequences for law making and its enforcement, and for law breaking, has broad application beyond the particular elements of the theory.[47]

Differential social organization   The theory of differential association states that the chances of an individual engaging in criminal behavior depend on the balance between his pro-criminal and anti-criminal associations. From this it follows that the rate of criminal behavior in a given social category or group depends on whether society is organized to promote or prevent exposure of members of that group to pro-criminal and anti-criminal associations.[48] For example, to the extent that the family and occupational systems restrict freedom of movement of females as compared with males, and consequently reduce the likelihood that they will be exposed to association with pro-criminal patterns, we would expect the female crime rate to be lower than the male. Starting from the premise that conflicting cultural definitions of criminal conduct exist in all societies, the concept of differential social organization adds the important idea that the organization of social relationships affects the chances of association with these different definitions. Note that this theory does not try to explain why variant cultural definitions exist; it deals only with the structural determinants of differential exposure and transmission.

Subcultural theories   A number of influential theorists treat crime and delinquency as ways of conforming to the expectations of subcultures that differ from the dominant middle-class culture of American society, and relate the nature and distribution of these subcultures to the structure of the larger society.

[47] See Arthur L. Stinchcombe, "Merton's Theory of Social Structure," in Lewis A. Coser (ed.), *The Idea of Social Structure: Papers in Honor of Robert K. Merton* (New York: Harcourt, 1975), p. 12.

[48] Cohen et al., *op. cit.*

Albert K. Cohen, for example, focuses on male, working-class delinquency.[49] Like Merton, he assumes that delinquency is related to a discrepancy between culture goals and the availability of legitimate means for achieving them. Cohen assumes that in American society males of all social levels are judged by the same set of standards, especially when they move out of the home and compete with other youth in school and occupational settings. These middle-class criteria of status include such things as a high level of ambition, middle-class speech and manners, the possession of skills of potential academic, occupational, and economic value, and so on. Children growing up in working-class homes are less likely to learn to perform well in terms of these criteria than others are. Thus, working-class children are systematically disadvantaged in the competitive pursuit of status and may find themselves "at the bottom of the heap," with their self-respect damaged.

One way of coping with this problem is to draw together with others who have the same problems, to reject the middle-class culture and the middle-class reference world, and, through sympathetic interaction, collectively develop a new subculture, in which virtue consists of defying middle-class morality. Those who participate in this subculture take one another as reference objects and reward one another with status and acceptance for behavior that is condemned by the representatives of middle-class morality. The emergence of such a subculture depends upon the availability of and sympathetic interaction among a plurality of individuals with like problems. Cohen thus emphasizes the critical role of such interaction in shaping a collective solution to problems of adjustment—a consideration lacking in the earlier formulations of anomie theory.

Richard A. Cloward and Lloyd E. Ohlin, like Cohen, assume that delinquent subcultures are jointly contrived solutions to problems arising out of thwarted aspirations or, in Merton's terms, to disjunctions between culture goals and the structure of legitimate opportunities.[50] However, they add an important element to these theories. Not only does the social structure provide differential access to legitimate opportunities; it also provides differential access to *illegitimate* opportunities, and the availability of illegitimate opportunities is an important determinant of the solutions people adopt. For example, some social areas are characterized by the presence of professional crime, which provides attractive role models and opportunities to learn, practice, and perform certain kinds of delinquent roles, but which does *not* encourage violence, bloodshed, or other kinds of behavior that are likely to "bring on the heat" and are therefore frowned on by professional criminals. Other areas do not have such a "criminal opportunity structure," but there are few effective controls from the adult population on the expression of violence. In the first type of area we are likely to see the formation of juvenile "criminal" subcul-

---

[49] Albert K. Cohen, *Delinquent Boys* (New York: Free Press, 1955).

[50] Richard A. Cloward and Lloyd E. Ohlin, *Delinquency and Opportunity* (New York: Free Press, 1960).

tures; in the second, the formation of violent gangs, or "conflict subcultures." Then there are those individuals who do not have access to either type of illegitimate opportunity structure; these tend to form their own "retreatist" subcultures, centering around the use of drugs, alcohol, or some other "kick."

To date, neither of these theories has found convincing support in research. However, the general idea of subcultures as collective solutions to problems characteristic of certain locations in the social system and the concept of legitimate and illegitimate opportunity structures have implications that extend well beyond these two theories, and recur as elements of many other interpretations of crime and delinquency.

Walter B. Miller also sees delinquent behavior as conformity to a culture pattern, but rejects the notion that delinquents create the culture themselves.[51] It is the lower-class culture itself, acquired through socialization in lower-class settings, that generates delinquent behavior. The culture attaches value to "trouble, toughness, smartness, excitement, fate or luck, and autonomy." These *focal concerns*, as Miller calls them, are not inherently and necessarily delinquent. However, their pursuit is highly conducive to delinquent behavior. The argument can easily be extended to provide an explanation of lower-class adult crime. Miller's description of the focal concerns is generally regarded as an excellent statement of the main concerns of lower-class street corner gangs. His theory has been criticized on a number of grounds, however, especially for his assumption that these focal concerns are attributes of a very widespread "lower-class culture" that stands, so to speak, on its own feet and is unaffected by contact with middle-class culture.

Conflict theories   A very different sort of theory is premised on the assumption that crime and delinquency (and all other societal phenomena) are products of unceasing conflict between different sectors of society.[52]

In every society, the mode of governance, the division of labor, the system of production, the structure of authority, and the distribution of wealth and other rewards are organized in a characteristic way—what we call the institutions of that society. In all known societies these institutions work to the relative advantage of some segments of the society compared to others. Some reap the lion's share of the rewards; others do most of the work and get little in return. Every institutional order, then, generates opposing interests among major segments (classes, sexes, ethnic and racial groups) of society. Furthermore, segments of society have differential access to resources and opportunities, suffer or prosper in characteristic ways, live under importantly different

[51] Walter B. Miller, "Lower-Class Culture as a Generating Milieu of Gang Delinquency," *Journal of Social Issues,* Vol. 14, No. 3 (1958), pp. 5–19.

[52] See, e.g., William Chambliss, "The State, the Law, and the Definition of Behavior as Criminal or Delinquent," in Glaser, *op. cit.,* pp. 7–43; Richard Quinney, *The Social Reality of Crime* (Boston: Little, Brown, 1970); Austin T. Turk, *Criminality and the Legal Order* (Chicago: Rand McNally, 1969).

life-conditions, and develop characteristic problems. In consequence, different life-styles, value systems, conceptions of justice, priorities, and critiques of society develop within a society. Division and conflict, rather than harmony and consensus, are the natural state of society.

Every institutional order places the power to regulate, maintain, and modify that institutional order in the hands of some minority. This minority— the *ruling class*—is the beneficiary of the existing system. Its members tend to see that system as fair and just; to view inequality as inherent in the nature of society and their own privileges as legitimate; and to use power, derived from strategic advantage in government and the economy, to protect their privileges and to preserve and strengthen the established order.

The legal system, including the system of criminal justice, is one of the institutions the powerful manipulate to secure their own interests and to foster their own values. The reach of the substantive criminal law extends beyond crimes *malum in se* ("wrong in themselves") to forms of behavior that are offensive to the morality of the powerful; that directly threaten *their* persons, property, or dignity; or that tend to undermine the institutional order from which they derive power and privileges. The creation of crime, according to this view, is a political act.

Some criminal laws are more consistently and severely enforced than others. For example, the functionaries of the criminal-justice system, who are themselves at the service of the power elite, ignore or punish lightly the crimes that are characteristically committed by politicians and businessmen. The same crimes may be treated differently when committed by the powerful and by the weak. The greatly disproportionate number of blacks and lower-class persons in our criminal statistics do not reflect entirely correspondingly disproportionate involvement in criminal behavior. The data also reflect their powerlessness and vulnerability to arrest and conviction. Here, then, is another sense in which the creation of crime is a political act. Finally, behavior that does not violate the criminal law may be repressed by the agencies of criminal justice if it threatens the interests or cherished policies of the ruling elite. An example would be the wholesale arrests of militant protestors against our involvement in the Viet Nam War, even when they had broken no laws—when, in fact, they were exercising constitutionally-guaranteed rights.

It is difficult in a brief space to evaluate this school of thought (of which there are many variants) because it is not a matter simply of deciding "truth" or "falsity." There is obviously a substantial element of truth in every proposition of this position. A very large and growing body of research data documents the ways in which the making and administration of the criminal law respond to the interests of the powerful. However, several kinds of questions can be raised concerning the claims of at least the more extreme versions of conflict theories.

First, granted that the various segments of society have conflicting interests and that the conflicts are typically resolved through power politics, does it follow that they do not also have common interests, loyalties, and identities that sometimes transcend their differences and that also make their impress on the legal system?

In a sense it is obvious, even tautological, that the powerful make and administer the laws. If anything gets done, it is because somebody had the power to do it. The less obvious question is: Where does this power come from and what are its limits? How is power in the political and legal sphere related to power and participation in other institutional sectors?

Those who are supposed to be oppressed by a system of laws imposed upon them by a ruling minority often seem unaware of their oppression. Indeed, they are frequently among the strongest partisans of the existing legal order, accepting the criminal law in its main outlines and clamoring for more stern and efficient enforcement of the laws. It can be argued that they have been brainwashed by the ruling establishment, who have used their power to confuse them as to their true interests. But this requires that we distinguish between what people define as their interests and their "true" interests, a distinction that has given rise to a great deal of complex, subtle, and inconclusive polemic.

Finally, when farmers, workers, or even racial and ethnic minorities organize to promote what they conceive to be their interests, they often have a large and important impact on the making and enforcement of laws. Doesn't this mean that they, too, are part of the power structure? And if they are, doesn't this mean that the distribution of power in society is more widespread and complicated than is suggested by writers who speak of a simple division of society into "the powerful" and "the powerless"?

The Microsociological Perspective

The central concern of microsociological inquiry is the interactive processes that produce criminal actions, rather than the biographies or social structures that produce criminal offenders. What do we mean by "interactive processes"? Every social action—a bunt in a baseball game, a joke at a cocktail party, a shot fired in anger during a domestic quarrel—is an episode in some ongoing activity. Different individuals make different contributions to this activity at various stages of its evolution. One picks up where another left off; one takes advantage of a situation prepared by another; one provokes, invites, challenges, threatens, or reassures another; one provides or denies to another information or facilities or rewards; one does one part of a task because he or she is confident that other parties are doing or will do their part. We continually adjust our own actions to the changed situations created by other people's responses to what we have done. The history of any particular event, then—criminal events included—is the history of the interaction process in which that event is embedded. Individuals do not make things happen by themselves (even when they are alone). Therefore, to understand or explain an event one must view it as the product of its history, and that involves interaction with others.

The literature of the microsociology of crime is modest, consisting largely of empirical studies that are rich with implications for theory. One line of investigation shifts the spotlight from the offender—that is, the individual who eventually becomes socially or legally defined as the offender—to the relationships between offenders, victims, and various situational contexts. Lynn A. Curtis' studies of criminal violence, for example, indicate that criminal homicides and assaults in the United States (and in many other countries) most often involve "trivial altercations with little premeditation."[53] Statistical evidence from numerous surveys is consistent with participant observational studies and reports of experienced law enforcement officers:

"Murders result from little ol' arguments over nothing at all," noted a veteran Dallas homicide detective. "Tempers flare, a fight starts, and somebody gets stabbed or shot. I've worked on cases where the principals had been arguing over a 10¢ record on a juke box, or over a one dollar gambling debt from a dice game."[54]

William J. Goode observes that "When a conflict between intimates issues in assault or homicide . . . one or both are surprised"; for the most part, interaction in such instances begins very "like any other interaction."[55] Why does violence or some other criminal act occur in one situation and not another? It is to this question that microsociological theory addresses itself.

The sequence of events that may eventuate in criminal or delinquent actions entails a series of decisions on the part of the participants.[56] These decisions are determined in large part by the payoffs and costs of the available courses of action. The results of a particular decision in turn alter the situation for the actor as well as the other participants, often in ways that none of them expect—posing new threats and challenges to their identities, opening up new avenues of action and closing off others, and changing the payoffs and costs that attach to particular courses of action. These, in turn, are influenced by such considerations as, What is the possibility of "leaving the field" if one is confronted by a painful choice?[57] (In a prison, for example, one may not be so

[53] Lynn A. Curtis, *Violence, Race and Culture* (Lexington, Mass.: Heath, 1975), p. 54.

[54] The evidence from several studies is summarized in Lynn A. Curtis, *Criminal Violence: National Patterns and Behavior* (Lexington, Mass.: Heath, 1974), esp. p. 78. The quotation is from the *Dallas Morning News* (October 27, 1968), p. 18A, in Curtis, p. 66.

[55] William J. Goode, "Violence Among Intimates," in Donald Mulvihill and Melvin Tumin, with the assistance of Lynn C. Curtis, *Violent Crime: A Task Force Report to the National Commission on the Causes and Prevention of Violence* (Washington, D.C.: U.S. Government Printing Office, 1970), p. 955.

[56] The calculus of decision making has been studied in such widely varying social systems as gangs [see M. W. Klein and L. Y. Crawford, "Groups, Gangs, and Cohesiveness," *Journal of Research in Crime and Delinquency*, Vol. 4 (1967), pp. 63–75]; crowds [see Richard A. Berk, "A Gaming Approach to Crowd Behavior," *American Sociological Review* (June 1974), pp. 355–373]; and among lovers, families, and friends [see Goode, "Violence Among Intimates"; and Suzanne K. Steinmetz and Murray A. Straus (eds.), *Violence in the Family* (New York: Dodd, Mead, 1973)].

[57] A variety of terms and models have been applied to decision making. See, e.g., R. Duncan Luce, *Individual Choice Behavior* (New York: Wiley, 1959); Thomas C. Schelling, *The Strategy of Conflict* (New York: Oxford Press, 1963); and Howard Raiffa, *Decision Analysis* (Reading, Mass.: Addison-Wesley, 1970).

free to avoid a confrontation as in the outside world.) Who, by virtue of his role and status in the group, has the most to lose by not rising to a particular challenge? How does the activity in progress affect social rewards for a particular decision? (For example, is the group planning a dance or recouping their reputation as a fighting gang? Entire groups may alternate between "gang" and "club" phases, with important implications for their relationships to other groups and the institutions of the larger society and for the demands they make upon their members.[58]) What are the status relationships within a gang and between gangs, and how are these threatened by some incident, remark, or confrontation?[59] What kinds of interactions within and between gangs and with agents and agencies of the larger society amount to "burning one's bridges," so that options previously present are no longer available?[60]

Questions like these identify issues that are relevant to interaction processes in a very broad range of settings. Further research on these issues is a precondition to a more fully developed microsociology of crime and delinquency. Always, however, the ways in which interaction processes unfold are conditioned upon the framework of social organization within which they occur, and it is to this subject that we now turn.

CRIMINAL ORGANIZATION[61]

The interactional framework emphasizes that no event stands by itself. It happens because other events provide pressures, temptations, information, illusions, diversions, threats, resources and opportunities, cooperation and resistance. These other events shape the conception, course, and outcome of any human project. When we analyze the ways in which events interlock, stimulate, and facilitate one another—in other words, form a structure of interacting events—we are engaged in the study of social organization. From this point of view, all criminal behavior is organized, even though the law may single out some particular person (for example, an embezzler), and say, "*He* did it." Unfortunately, the study of criminal organization has been retarded by a preoccupation with certain kinds of large-scale, spectacular criminal enterprises commonly known as "organized crime," to the neglect of the larger and infinitely more complex subject of criminal organization generally.

---

[58] Leon Jansyn, "Solidarity and Delinquency in a Street Corner Group," *American Sociological Review* (October 1967), pp. 600–614.

[59] Fred L. Strodtbeck and James F. Short, Jr., "Aleatory Risks versus Short-Run Hedonism in Explanation of Gang Action," *Social Problems* (Fall 1964), pp. 127–140.

[60] See, e.g., Lawrence W. Sherman, *Youth Workers, Police and the Gangs,* published Master's Thesis, University of Chicago, 1970; R. Lincoln Keiser, *The Vice Lords: Warriors of the Streets* (New York: Holt, 1969); James F. Short, Jr., "Youth, Gangs and Society: Micro- and Macrosociological Process," *The Sociological Quarterly* (Winter 1974), pp. 3–19.

[61] This section is based in part on A. K. Cohen, "The Concept of Criminal Organization," a paper read at the Institute of Criminology, Cambridge, England, July 5, 1973. To be published in a forthcoming issue of the *British Journal of Criminology*.

The Structure of Criminal Activities and Relations

Most stealing for economic gain is done with a view to disposing of the merchandise—whether jewels, cigarettes, or trade secrets—at a profit. This influences the conception of the crime, the size of the working group, the choice of victim and "loot," and the arrangements for transporting, storing, and selling it—in short, practically every phase of the activity. Suppose you were suddenly in possession of a truckload of beef, an enormous and world-famous diamond, or, for that matter, three dozen ten-dollar watches—all stolen. What would you do with them? *Fencing*, or criminal receiving of stolen goods, clearly plays a critical role in thefts. It is a complex subject. There are many kinds of fences and the problems of disposal are different for different kinds of merchandise. Remarkably, however, the study of fencing and its relation to stealing is only in its infancy.[62]

If we consider the subject of disposal further, we see that the study of criminal organization entails more than the study of criminals and criminal activities. The disposal of securities involves financial institutions and the securities market. Unique objects of great value—say, a Rembrandt painting—are almost impossible to sell, but may be ransomed. In many cases insurance companies pay the ransom because it is cheaper than paying off the insurance. If not for the modern insurance industry, the theft of such objects would often be pointless. Many objects are fenced through wholesalers who maintain legitimate businesses, which makes it possible for them to mingle the stolen goods with their legitimate stock. Regular customers provide them with ready and unwitting markets. Thus routine, "normal," respectable, and even essential features of the social organization of lawful activity are involved in the social organization of crime.

We have been talking about organization in the sense of structures of activities. We may also speak of organization in the sense of structures of association, or relational structures—that is, temporary or enduring patterns of social relationships among the parties who are, in one way or another (and often unwittingly), involved in these criminal actions. (A ball game is a structure of activity; a ball team is a relational structure.) Relational structures in crime are as varied as those in business, education, or the professions. They may consist of networks of individuals who are linked by relations of contract, kinship, friendship, neighborhood, fealty (personal loyalty in exchange for sponsorship and protection), coercion ("offers you can't refuse"), competition in the same market, mutual recognition and respect as practitioners of the same profession, and so on. They may, on the other hand, consist of associations—groups of individuals who think of themselves as members of some superindividual entity and act together in its behalf. Such are robber bands, boys' gangs, pickpocket mobs, and teams of safecrackers. The internal structure of these associations varies greatly; some are linked to other associations and individuals through networks or matrices, some not.

[62] See, e.g., Carl B. Klockars, *The Professional Fence* (New York: Free Press, 1974).

Associations also differ with respect to the *centrality* of crime or delinquency to the goals of the association. For example, it is probable that most boys' gangs that engage in delinquent behavior are not organized for and held together primarily by their interest in the pursuit of delinquent behavior. Current research seems to indicate that people come together and stick together in delinquent gangs primarily for relational satisfactions—affection, friendship, acceptance, mutual aid, and so on.[63] The relationships among the members and the structure of the group are unconsciously designed to serve these needs; the delinquent conduct of these groups does not so much shape the organization of the group as reflect it. At the other extreme, we have criminal associations ranging from shoplifting teams to gambling syndicates that are in the business of crime to make a living. The organization of such groups is rationally designed to serve this end, just as an automobile factory or a supermarket is rationally designed to make money by producing a particular kind of goods or service.

We may also distinguish among associations on the basis of duration. Mary McIntosh has distinguished between craft crime and project crime.[64] *Craft crime,* which is very ancient, consists of small, relatively permanent groups (of pickpockets, burglars, and the like) who work together, day after day, within some circumscribed area, committing crimes that entail little planning and yield relatively small but regular returns. *Project crime,* on the other hand, is a response to distinctively modern conditions: the concentration of potential "loot" of great value in one place, heavily guarded by security personnel and technological gadgetry. Successful theft requires technical sophistication and expertise, careful planning that varies with the circumstances of each theft, fine coordination, a quick getaway and dispersal of the members of the group to evade concerted and determined pursuit by highly professional security forces, public and private. Such criminal projects are usually carried out by "task forces" of individuals who are highly specialized in the particular operations required by the project at hand and carefully selected over a period of time. After the proceeds have been distributed, the group dissolves and may never be reconstituted.

Crime Within Legitimate Associations

Virtually *any* association, organized for whatever purpose, whose prestige, security, or continued viability depend upon its success in accomplishing certain goals, will experience pressure to violate the law, civil and criminal. Laws frequently get in the way of accomplishing goals, and so are frequently violated. The first associations that come to mind are business firms, which operate openly, with the blessing of the state, for the purpose of making money for

---

[63] Klein and Crawford, *op. cit.;* Jansyn, *op. cit.;* J. F. Short, Jr. and F. L. Strodtbeck, *Group Process and Gang Delinquency* (Chicago: University of Chicago Press, 1965).

[64] Mary McIntosh, "Changes in the Organization of Thievery," in Stanley Cohen (ed.), *Images of Deviance* (Middlesex, England: Penguin, 1971), pp. 98–133.

their owners. Government imposes many restrictions on business, however. Federal and state statutes prohibit "combinations and conspiracies in restraint of trade," regulate labor practices, set standards for products and services, forbid frauds and misrepresentation, require health and safety measures to protect employees, and so on. Most, and perhaps all, large corporations violate some of these laws occasionally; many of them do so regularly, systematically, and on a large scale. This is one kind of white-collar crime.[65] The criminal acts of corporations are seldom prosecuted in the criminal courts, however, and when they are, usually result in penalties that are small or even trivial relative to the costs they inflict on their victims. Although the biggest organizations are the biggest offenders, these sorts of crimes are also extremely common among smaller firms of every kind, right down to the neighborhood shoe store and restaurant.[66]

Another major class of criminal offenders is government agencies, especially those that regulate, police, and protect the public. Again, we are speaking of offenses committed with a view to accomplishing the objectives of the agency, as these are interpreted by the agency. Police agencies on every level are rewarded on the basis of results; they have powerful incentives to employ all means necessary to achieve these results.[67] They are also regulated and restricted in order to insure that innocent persons do not suffer loss of privacy, property, liberty, and their good names. Police tend to see themselves as experts, skilled and knowledgeable in their craft, and to view restrictions as shackles that prevent them from using their expertise for the benefit of the citizenry. They tend to develop subcultures that support violations and evasions of restrictive laws regulating arrests, searches, wiretapping, detention and interrogation of suspects, and so on.[68] By and large, the general public is not overly concerned with these violations and the police are seldom charged, much less prosecuted or punished for them. In short, the watchdogs and guardians of the community are seldom watched and poorly guarded, and they are among the most prolific producers of criminal behavior. Much the same can be said of intelligence and military establishments in all countries.

Organizations with strong incentives to accomplish certain results have strong incentives to commit crime, but like most criminal offenders seldom see their crimes as serious, reprehensible, or even as "real" crimes.[69] Labor unions engage in illegal strikes, boycotts, and other coercive actions in order to obtain

---

[65] Edwin H. Sutherland, *White Collar Crime* (New York: Dryden, 1949).

[66] See, e.g., Herbert Edelhertz, *The Nature, Impact and Prosecution of White-Collar Crime* (Washington, D.C.: U.S. Government Printing Office, 1970); Gilbert Geis, "Avocational Crime," in Glaser, *op. cit.,* pp. 273–298.

[67] See, e.g., Albert J. Reiss, Jr., *The Police and the Public* (New Haven: Yale University Press, 1971).

[68] See, e.g., Jerome H. Skolnick, *Justice Without Trial*, 2nd ed. (New York: Wiley, 1975).

[69] See Donald R. Cressey, "Restraint of Trade, Recidivism, and Delinquent Neighborhoods," in James F. Short, Jr., *Crime, Delinquency and Society* (Chicago: University of Chicago Press, forthcoming).

justice, as they see it, for the working man. In their eyes, the ends justify the means, even if this does not make them legal. Indeed, most of those activities of organized labor that are legal and generally accepted as necessary and proper today were once illegal. This is but one instance of illegal practices achieving acceptance and even respectability.

Another and final example is the criminal behavior of associations dedicated to political change—or resistance to change—by legally unacceptable means, including assassination, highjacking and kidnapping, robbery to obtain funds for the cause, and a wide spectrum of nonviolent methods of protest and civil disobedience. These are examples of what Merton has called *nonconformity,* as contrasted to *aberrance* (see the Introduction). The participants see themselves not as lawless and self-interested, but as selfless and dedicated people whose actions are legitimated or even demanded by a "higher law," overriding the demands of the criminal law. Such acts are generally called *political crimes.*[70] They are political acts and they are crimes. How they should be dealt with depends on whether or not one sympathizes with the ostensible objectives of the behavior and feels that they justify and ennoble the behavior, even if it is technically criminal.

We have been speaking of criminal acts committed by individuals in behalf of an association or its goals. If committed, authorized, or directed by responsible officers of the association, they are usually regarded as acts of the association rather than of the individuals in their personal capacity, "in their own right" so to speak. These are to be distinguished from crimes committed by individuals or groups within an association that are structured by the fact that they are members of the association, but are not committed in its behalf. Such crimes are motivated by the interests of the individuals severally or of other associations to which these individuals also belong, external to the association in question.

It is a fundamental principle of criminology that every position in every organization provides incentives and opportunities to commit criminal actions. To accomplish their goals, associations give individuals a job to do, and the authority, resources, and discretion to enable them to do it. This provides legitimate means for accomplishing legitimate ends (the legitimate opportunity structure). But all legitimate opportunities—money, information, control over the actions of others, and so on—can be turned to unauthorized ends. That is, they are illegitimate opportunities, as well. They may be used, not to further the goals of the association, but to exploit it or persons outside the association. This is another way in which the lawful, institutionalized structure of society helps to shape criminal behavior.

For example, consider some of the things governmental agencies do. They pass laws or formulate administrative rules and regulations to carry out the intent of the laws; issue licenses and permits; provide protection from fire,

[70] See Marshall B. Clinard and Richard Quinney, *Criminal Behavior Systems* (New York: Holt, 1973), Chap. 6, and Stephen Schafer, *The Political Criminal* (New York: Free Press, 1974).

crime, and unsanitary conditions; buy and sell real estate; let contracts; hunt down people who commit crimes and punish them; collect taxes; and so on and on. To do these things, numerous functionaries are given resources and discretion in making decisions. Depending on how these decisions are made, some people are benefitted, some inconvenienced, and some hurt. There are always some people who are willing to pay a price for favorable decisions. In short, by virtue of the discretion and resources placed at their disposal for the accomplishment of the legitimate aims of the organization, all governmental officials and functionaries are in a position and under some temptation and pressure to enter into private deals—to act or refrain from acting, to decide one way rather than another, to provide or withhold a service—in exchange for bribes, kickbacks, or some other personal advantage. Or they may use privileged information, which is necessary to the proper performance of their responsibilities, to exploit the general public or the organization itself. Policemen, patrolling the dark streets at night, are ideally situated to commit burglary without arousing suspicion; public employees in charge of agencies' moneys and books are in a position to falsify records and pocket funds. Immediate material gain is not the only illicit end to which legitimate opportunities may be converted. Personal power and security, advancement to positions of prestige, or illicit favors for friends or relatives may be sought. That tangled web of crime, malfeasance, and betrayal of trust that we call Watergate was more than a "conspiracy of wicked men." No collection of ordinary citizens, regardless of how unscrupulous they might have been, could have perpetrated this encyclopedic collection of crimes and improprieties. In a very important sense, the cause of Watergate was the legitimate and hallowed institutions of the American system of government, which provided on the one hand, the temptation and on the other hand, the access to money, information, and other resources (including power over government agencies and officials, vast discretion, and immunity from observation and accountability) without which Watergate would have been impossible.

This is not to indict the American form of government, but to point out a dilemma inherent in any form of government and, indeed, in any set of institutional arrangements, governmental or otherwise. Every organization is a structure of legitimate opportunities that may be converted to illegitimate opportunities. One way to prevent crime within organizations is to limit discretion, authority over others, and access to resources so severely and to subject individuals to such close and unremitting surveillance that there are few opportunities to betray their trust. However, their ability to act swiftly and efficiently, to exercise judgment in the face of changing or unforeseen circumstances, to make the best use of their intelligence and experience will be circumscribed as well. The interrelations between legitimate and illegitimate opportunity, and the question of why legitimate opportunities are not more widely abused and exploited than they are, are among the central but neglected issues of criminological theory.

Professional Crime

Students sometimes steal books from bookstores or the college library; house-wives sometimes "lift" food or clothes for their families; factory workers some-times help themselves to tools. Most people commit crimes for economic gain at least occasionally, many of us quite frequently. But although in the aggre-gate they may entail huge costs to their victims, the kinds of crimes that we have just mentioned are typically peripheral to the identities and livelihoods of those who commit them. There are other people who regularly pursue a lawful occupation, but who engage in one or another variety of theft as a kind of secondary occupation.[71] Stealing represents a major source of their income; they sell what they steal, do business with other thieves and with fences, and have some reputation and standing in the world of thieves. Still others engage in crime for profit on a more or less full-time basis. They think of themselves as burglars, con men, or some other kind of thief. This self-conception is central to their identity. Their life style and career are largely built around this identity; their associates and reference groups are drawn largely from the criminal underworld; they take pride in their skills and their "good name" as thieves; they speak the esoteric lingo of their trade easily so that other prac-titioners can quickly determine that they are authentic insiders. They are, in short, full-fledged *professional criminals.*

When we speak of professional crime, then, we are not speaking of, say, robbing banks as contrasted to stealing books. Either of these may be done on a professional or nonprofessional basis. It is a matter of how the criminal activity is *organized,* where it fits in the offender's general life scheme, and how it is linked to the activities, criminal and noncriminal, of other people. In speaking of craft and project crime, we have already said something about the social organization of professional crime. Some professional crime is com-mitted by independent entrepreneurs; most, by groups who work together. Details of social organization vary greatly, being adapted to the special re-quirements of the task at hand, the nature of the competition, the problems of training competent colleagues, and so on. In this general sense, the sources of variability in criminal organization are very much the same as they are in the world of lawful enterprise. However, criminal trades have certain problems in common. All must contend with the special hazards growing out of the fact that they are criminal and so vulnerable to the repressions and punishments of the criminal-justice system. Professional criminals cannot avail themselves of the "equal protection under the law" enjoyed by legitimate businessmen. Their organization must, at every point, be designed to evade, neutralize, or somehow reduce the costs of arrest, prosecution, and imprisonment. They must find ways of locating one another, advertising for workers, learning about promising op-portunities to ply their particular trades, avoiding the law, buying it off, obtaining and paying for legal counsel, and so on. These are common, shared problems. To a large extent, solutions must be found within the community

---

[71] The distinction with respect to shoplifting is documented in Cameron, *op. cit.*

of professional criminals. This entails a certain sense of identification with professional criminals generally, the reduction of interaction with "straight" people, the development of codes and understandings concerning secrecy, mutual protection, mutual aid, and the development of "grapevines" through which vital news and messages can travel quickly.

We must not, however, give the impression of a tightly knit, highly disciplined brotherhood of crime. Professional crime is a hazardous occupation. It is marked by many conflicting interests and much anxiety, suspicion, and distrust. There are those who honor their obligations and those who cheat and betray their fellows. A community of interest generates a community of sentiment and solidarity but, like most human communities, it is loose, imperfect, and vulnerable.[72]

Syndicated Crime

In the world of business there is an inveterate tendency for small, independent firms to become absorbed into larger ones. This happens for several reasons. One is that increasing size usually, although not always, brings economies of scale. For example, the larger firm, geared to a greater output, can make fuller use of expensive equipment and highly specialized personnel, thereby reducing production costs. A second reason is that in order to compete with one another, smaller, independent firms have to keep their prices down, thereby reducing profits below the level they would reach if they did not have to compete. Any arrangement whereby formerly competing firms act as one for purposes of setting prices enables them to charge more for their products. Such arrangements range from full mergers to agreements to reduce competition by fixing prices, restricting output, or dividing up markets. All involve a loss or voluntary surrender of freedom to act independently. A third reason for merger is that firms that have, for whatever reason, prospered and have capital to invest, may purchase a controlling interest in or buy out smaller firms. Finally, when several firms are dependent upon a single firm for some essential resource or service, that single firm is in a powerful position to demand a voice in setting the policies of the other firms. Whatever the reason, and whatever the resulting structure, the outcome is the removal of control, to a greater or lesser degree, from the independent firm to some superordinate level of decision-making.

All these processes tending to the creation of a hierarchical system of control operate in the world of criminal enterprise as well. There is, however, an important difference. Legitimate businesses are subject to various governmental limitations on their freedom to merge, to act in union, and to exercise con-

---

[72] Classic descriptions are found in Chic Conwell, *The Professional Thief*, annotated and interpreted by Edwin H. Sutherland (Chicago: University of Chicago Press, 1937), and in David W. Maurer, *The Big Con* (Indianapolis: Bobbs-Merrill, 1940). More recent treatments are found in James A. Inciardi, "Vocational Crime," in Glaser, *op. cit.*, pp. 299–401, and in Andrew Walker, "Sociology and Professional Crime," in Abraham S. Blumberg (ed.), *Current Perspectives on Criminal Behavior* (New York: Knopf, 1974), pp. 87–113.

trol over other businesses. These laws are neither vigorously enforced nor scrupulously observed, but they have been a significant restraint on the rate of concentration of economic power. Furthermore, certain methods of persuading or coercing other firms—especially violence and the threat of violence—are legally unacceptable and not much used. Criminal enterprises, on the other hand, are already outside the law. To engage in illegal "combinations and conspiracies in restraint of trade" does not make them any more illegal than they already are. When cheating or violence occur within criminal enterprise, neither party is in a position to go running to the law for protection. They are not registered with the Securities and Exchange Commission and their books are not open to public inspection. In short, the legal constraints that provide some check on concentration of power in the world of legitimate business do not operate in the world of crime. It is no more remarkable that we have bigness, centralization, and monopoly in the field of crime than in the field of legitimate business enterprise.

In this chapter we shall use the term *syndicated crime* to refer to a structure of criminal association in which a number of operating units are coordinated by a hierarchically superior center of decision-making. This is what distinguishes it from the small groups characteristic of traditional craft and project crime and from independent professionals. We prefer the term *syndicated crime* to the more popular term organized crime, because the use of the latter term tends to obscure the fact that all crime is organized. Our definition identifies only the distinguishing characteristic of syndicated crime. Many other attributes are associated with syndicated crime but, apart from their defining characteristics, the forms of syndicated crime are exceedingly variable. These variables include the number of hierarchical levels, the size of the organization, the area over which it is effective, the degree to which it exercises a monopoly, the variety of criminal activities it embraces, the thoroughness and effectiveness of centralized control, and the mechanisms through which that control is exercised (including violence).

The popular terms *organized crime, Mafia,* and *Cosa Nostra* evoke an image of large, tightly-knit, highly-disciplined structures, organized on military or bureaucratic lines, subject to the autocratic control of a boss. Sets of such organizations are in turn dominated by a single "boss of all bosses." These bosses, each all-powerful in the region under his command, are in turn linked together through a national conspiracy which, through an efficient chain of command that radiates to all parts of the country, can issue orders that will be quickly obeyed all down the line. All the key positions in this structure are occupied by persons of Italian extraction who are bound to one another in a secret brotherhood. There is some substance to this image—and much myth. How much there is of each is uncertain because serious scholarly research on syndicated crime is still in its infancy, but it is certain from the returns now in that the picture is infinitely more complex.[73]

---

[73] See Donald R. Cressey, *Theft of the Nation* (New York: Harper, 1969).

The extent to which crime is centrally coordinated depends on a number of factors. One of the most critical is the extent to which a number of operating units depend on some central agency for essential goods and services. This might be capital, information, merchandise from wholesalers, or the fix—that is, the corruption of law enforcement officials so that criminal activities may proceed without unacceptable risk. Numbers rackets and similar gambling activities may be subject to devastating losses if there happens to be heavy betting on winning numbers. To carry on they need ready access to large loans. The "bankers" who provide these loans can in turn demand a large share of control as well as of the profits of the local gambling operations. Therefore these gambling activities lend themselves to syndication. Another example: illicit importation of drugs in large batches entails great expense. As a result, the supply of such drugs in a given area is likely to be controlled by a relatively few persons with large financial resources. These persons, the ultimate wholesalers with something approaching a monopoly of the commodity, are in a position to exercise considerable control over the drug trade in their area. On the other hand, literally thousands of enterprising individuals are in a position to cross the border into Mexico and pick up small batches of marijuana to resell in the States at a profit large enough to compensate for the risk. It is very difficult for any person or organization to corner the wholesale market in marijuana. A detailed consideration of the factors that affect the degree of vertical integration in a particular line of illicit trade is beyond the scope of this chapter, but these examples suggest how variable they may be from one criminal business to another.

The precise nature of the forms of association—of the links between participants in syndicated crime—is also highly variable. Sometimes it approximates the military or bureaucratic model, with a table of organization, a chain of command, and a salaried work force. Sometimes it is more like that of a holding company, where one group has financial interests in and therefore some measure of control over a number of operating firms. Sometimes it resembles the franchise system, where the central office advances capital and sets people up in business, who then run the business with a greater or lesser degree of independence, sharing the profits on an agreed-upon basis with "the company." In other cases, it is more a matter of interlocking directorates or of a cluster of family businesses with feudal overtones.[74] (We will not try to make this list exhaustive or to discuss the ways in which several different types of relationships may coexist within the same structure.)

In the world of legitimate business large companies, identified with one line of business, often buy up or invest in companies engaged in very different lines of business. They do this for very good economic reasons: to diversify their holdings, so that they will not be wholly dependent on the market for a

---

[74] See, e.g., Ianni, *A Family Business: Kinship and Social Control in Organized Crime* and *Black Mafia: Ethnic Succession in Organized Crime.* The latter book focusses on yet another controversy concerning "organized crime," *viz.,* the importance of racial and ethnic relationships.

single commodity, and to reinvest their profits wherever they are likely to bring in a good return. Criminal businesses do the same, and for the same reasons. And some of the firms in which they reinvest earnings are legitimate businesses. Whether this changes the character of legitimate businesses and converts them into objects of exploitation or merely puts the earnings of syndicated crime to work in the legitimate sector is a matter of some controversy.

The subject of syndicated crime is large and complex and should not be identified with the popular stereotypes of "organized crime." It is also a subject where further research is bound to yield better understanding of crime and the relationships between criminal and noncriminal activity.

Illicit Trades and Social Policy

Syndicated crime is generally regarded as a major social problem, and we spend a lot of money trying to stamp it out. These efforts have not generally been very successful, a fact that is commonly attributed to the inefficiency or corruption of law-enforcers. A different approach to a solution begins with a recognition that most syndicated (and much nonsyndicated) crime is related to the production and sale of illegal goods and services in response to consumer demand—drugs, prostitution, gambling, and the like. Those who make the law regard these goods and services as immoral; catering to these appetites and interests is therefore stigmatized and punished as criminal. The legal prohibition, however, never seems to eliminate the trade. It does make it more dangerous and costly to carry on; the cost is passed on to the consumer in the form of higher prices than the products would ordinarily command; the profits go to the sorts of people who are willing to live by breaking the law (and to law-enforcement people who ignore or protect the illicit trade); and the government loses the taxes that would otherwise be paid on the forbidden fruits. This suggests that one solution to the problem would be to make the activity lawful, bring it out into the open, and perhaps regulate it, as we do the sale of tobacco and liquor. Many people advocate this: those who believe that there is nothing wrong with the activities in question; those who disapprove but believe gambling or prostitution are matters of personal taste and morality and not the law's business; and those who would like to see these activities curbed, but believe the criminal law merely creates new problems without solving the original problem.

In recent years the trend, although fitful and uneven, has been in the direction of decriminalization.[75] However, there are still those who hold that such "vices" as heroin use and prostitution are contrary to the public interest and elementary morality. According to this view, to legalize them is in effect to condone and encourage them. By making them criminal we may not stamp them out but at least we publicly proclaim, as a body corporate, our values

---

[75] See Herbert L. Packer, *The Limits of the Criminal Sanction.* (Stanford, Calif.: Stanford University Press, 1968).

and our principles. Moreover, it is not a foregone conclusion that vigorous efforts at law enforcement may not substantially curtail, even if they do not eliminate, the offending behavior.

SOCIAL CONTROL

What should we *do* about crime and delinquency? The conflicting answers to this question and conflicting efforts to get various answers translated into social action are the essence of the *social problem* of crime and delinquency. A social problem is never merely a dispute over the facts. Obviously, any policy position takes into account knowledge and notions, sound and unsound, about what in fact is happening and what will happen if we do this or that. However, whenever we deal with questions of policy we also consciously and unconsciously take into account notions about what is worth doing, what price is worth paying, who should pay the price, and what objectives are worth slighting in order to achieve other objectives. For example, a policy that might be more effective than another in terms of seeing that all offenders "get their just desserts" might be less effective in terms of preventing crime or rehabilitating offenders. Which of these is more important? Strict control of crime entails restraint on our mobility, surveillance by police, undercover investigation of private lives, and police power to detain, interrogate, and embarrass people, some of whom turn out to be innocent. How much are we willing to pay in these terms for a given reduction of crime? Suppose it were established that the liberal use of the death penalty has no significant effect upon the murder rate. Some of us might infer from this that we should abolish the dealth penalty. But what shall we say to those who insist that, whether the death penalty is an effective deterrent or not, someone who wantonly takes another's life ought to pay for it with his own? After "all the facts are in," there are still questions that cannot be resolved by appeal to the facts alone. They are settled (if at all) by persuasion, by appeals to sentiment and interest, and by superior power.

Analysis of social problems relating to crime and delinquency is further complicated by the fact that the rhetoric in which the debate is carried on is a poor indicator of the values, interests, and passions that really move the participants. At any given time certain slogans and formulae are more respectable than others; whatever our underlying sentiments, we will be inclined to defend our policy recommendations in terms of those rhetorics. For example, it is not respectable to call for "an eye for an eye, a tooth for a tooth" nowadays. We may be moved by a desire for vengeance, but we are more likely to frame our arguments in terms of "rehabilitation" or possibly "deterrence." This need not be with an intention to deceive; we may be reluctant to acknowledge our underlying sentiments even to ourselves.

The objectives that we seek to promote through the criminal-justice system are too numerous to list. Those that have figured most in open debate are retribution, incapacitation, deterrence, and rehabilitation. By *retribution* we mean

the infliction of pain or deprivation for reasons of vengeance or satisfaction of the sense of justice. By *incapacitation* we mean confining the offender so that he is not in a position to commit further crimes. By *deterrence* we mean discouraging the offender from repeated offenses or discouraging others by the example of what happens to offenders. By *rehabilitation* we mean efforts to retrain the offender or somehow alter his person or situation so that he will no longer commit offenses. (This list is only a beginning.)

The things that we do in the name of social control seldom succeed in accomplishing their alleged objectives. One reason is that they are often contradictory and cancel one another out. This is not necessarily a declaration of human stupidity. It is a comment on the fact that different people make different demands on the criminal-justice system, and most people want to see a number of things done at the same time—for example, that no criminal should go free and, at the same time, that no innocent person should be punished; or that the wicked should be made to suffer for their sins and, at the same time, that they should be humanely and compassionately transformed into upright citizens who abhor wrongdoing. But the methods that are likely to promote one objective are likely to prevent the accomplishment of the other. In trying to respond to the conflicting demands of its various publics, the criminal-justice system apparently does none of the things it is supposed to do well, and manages to do some things that few want it to do.

Current Trends

In the face of mounting crime rates, in spite of increasing investments in manpower and hardware, faith in our traditional assumptions about crime and criminal justice has been badly shaken. This is reflected in new emphases in theory and research, in critical scientific evaluation of the results of different control policies and procedures, and in a willingness, on the part of citizens and public authorities, to experiment with new methods. Yet there is massive resistance to change, and so the scene is one of great confusion. We shall briefly identify some of the main movements, intellectual and practical, that seem to be emerging from this confusion.

Deterrence Deterrence through punishment has always been one of the main objectives of the criminal-justice system. However, the rhetoric of control and the theories of students of crime and delinquency have tended to downgrade deterrence in favor of other objectives, especially treatment and rehabilitation. In recent years, however, a growing body of research provides evidence that the swiftness and certainty of punishment—and, to a lesser extent, its severity—have a tangible deterrent effect on crime rates.[76] The implications of this research for policy, however, are not so clear. For one thing, the deterrent effects that have been demonstrated are not generally very large. Furthermore, to accomplish a significant increase in the swiftness and certainty of punishment is very costly, especially if our enforcement methods are tempered with careful regard for civil rights. There is a question, then, of what price we are willing to pay in terms of material costs, civil rights, and the risk of jailing the innocent and individuals who are guilty but whose likelihood of repeating would be no greater if they were not incarcerated. And research suggests that a very large proportion, possibly the majority, of offenders fall in the latter category.

Treatment and rehabilitation Probably the most prevalent conception of people who commit crimes is that they are special kinds of people: that they suffer from some illness or personality defect, or that they are committed to a culture that removes their moral inhibitions on certain kinds of criminal or delinquent behavior. This suggests that we should seek to change their behavior by trying to provide them with experiences that will correct the defect or

[76] Charles R. Tittle, "Deterrence of Labelling?" *Social Forces*, Vol. 53 (March 1975), 399–419; Johannes Andenaes, *Punishment and Deterrence* (New York: Elsevier, 1975).

change their values. Programs intended to accomplish this are of many kinds. Some emphasize individualized psychiatric treatment and counseling; others various forms of group therapy or "guided group interaction"; and still others self-help groups, in which people with similar problems take collective responsibility for effecting change by monitoring one another, encouraging and supporting one another, providing examples to one another, and rewarding one another for progress toward the group goal of personality reconstruction or cultural change. For many decades this has been the dominant rhetoric of social control in the correctional system. On a greater or lesser scale, such programs have been operated in most of our correctional institutions.

There is a considerable body of research evaluating such programs, and it is becoming increasingly apparent that they have not been effective in accomplishing their goals. In study after study, differences in outcome between groups subject to these treatments and control groups have turned out to be nonexistent or negligible.[77] This applies not only to treatment in the clinical sense but also to programs emphasizing education and vocational training. There is growing disillusionment with the treatment rhetoric and treatment programs, although there is not yet any mass movement toward the abandonment of these programs.

Diversion   There is, however, a real and visible movement toward finding alternatives to incarceration and even to formal processing within the criminal- and juvenile-justice systems.[78] This grows out of several considerations. First, there is growing disillusionment about treatment within an institutional setting, as noted. Second, current research indicates that alternatives to incarceration—such as probation or early release on parole—produce results not greatly different from incarceration or continued incarceration. Third, many believe that incarceration or merely being processed by law-enforcement agencies results in stigmatization, discrimination, the denial of opportunity for lawful employment and conventional associations, increased interaction with other offenders, and the transformation of the casual or episodic offender into a more confirmed and habitual criminal. Finally, judicial processing and especially incarceration are enormously costly, and the tax-paying public is interested in finding cheaper solutions to the problem of crime. It may well be that the latter is the dominant motivation to the search for alternatives; it is certainly the argument that is most heavily emphasized in public discussion.

"Diversion" from the criminal justice system takes many forms. It can occur before official charges are brought, after charges have been filed but before

[77] Robert Martinson, "What Works? Questions and Answers About Prison Reform," *The Public Interest,* Vol. 35 (Spring 1974), pp. 22–54. Detailed data from this study are presented in Douglas Lipton, Robert Martinson, and Judith Wilks, *The Effectiveness of Correctional Treatment: A Survey of Evaluation Treatment Studies* (New York: Praeger, 1975).

[78] See, e.g., Edwin M. Lemert, *Instead of Court: Diversion in Juvenile Justice* (National Institute of Mental Health, Center for Studies of Crime and Delinquency; Washington, D.C.: U.S. Government Printing Office, 1971).

trial or hearing, after trial in the form of probation rather than incarceration, or after incarceration in the form of early release. The alternative dispositions are many, including referral to community-based treatment agencies, counseling, training, and employment assistance, halfway houses, and work-release (confinement to an institution only at night or on weekends, so that offenders are free to work and to live a more normal life at other times). It is too early to assess the results of diversion; they will no doubt be different for its many different forms.

"The justice model" Prisons are sure to be with us for a long time to come. But ideas about the proper function and administration of prisons and other institutions are changing. The view is growing that we should frankly recognize that we send people to prison primarily for punishment, not for treatment; that, in any case, treatment is largely ineffective; that compelling people to undergo treatment with a view to changing their personalities is morally questionable; and that releasing people from institutions on the basis of supposed changes under treatment rather than the nature and gravity of their crimes offends the sense of justice of the inmates themselves and aggravates problems of institutional management. There is increasing convergence on the view that sentences should be carefully fixed in advance of incarceration and not altered at the discretion of institutional authorities or parole boards; that sentences are too long and should be reduced, but in proportion to the seriousness of the offense; that institutions should make treatment services available to inmates, but not require them to make use of them or reward inmates for doing so; that within the institution, inmates should have as many of the privileges of people on the outside as is compatible with reasonable security and the protection of inmates from one another. In short, the view that institutions should be designed to satisfy the sense of justice of the larger society and of the inmate community within the walls is gaining support.[79]

Civil rights There is an unmistakable trend, despite the furor over "law and order" and "coddling criminals," toward granting alleged and convicted offenders the full panoply of legal rights and privileges enjoyed by other citizens.[80] It is, in a sense, the generalization of the justice model to all aspects of the criminal-justice system: police, courts, detention, probation, imprisonment, and parole. The general principle is that any incursion on the freedom and dignity of a citizen—whatever his alleged or proven offense, regardless of his social position, power, or reputation—is a very serious matter and must be

---

[79] For an articulate statement of this position, and a "model" prison for repetitively violent offenders, see Norval Morris, *The Future of Imprisonment* (Chicago: University of Chicago Press, 1973).

[80] See Ronald Goldfarb and Linda Singer, "Redressing Prisoners' Grievances," *George Washington Law Review*, Vol. 39 (December 1970), pp. 175–320; more recent information, and an evaluation of a legal aid to prisoners project, may be found in Goeffrey P. Alpert, *Legal Problems of Prison Inmates: A Review and Analysis,* unpublished Ph.D. Dissertation, Washington State University, 1975.

justified by strict interpretation of the laws. More specifically, advocates of full civil rights for prisoners argue that people caught up in the criminal-justice system not only must be treated equally; the system has an *obligation* to provide these people with the resources to defend their interests if they do not possess them. Thus the state should provide poor people with competent counsel and make it easy for prisoners to seek redress against alleged denial of their rights within the institution; detention of persons accused but not convicted of crimes should be reduced to a minimum. By denying convicted offenders freedom to move outside the prison walls, prisons have already achieved the punitive objective of incarceration. Any further indignity or deprivation is unnecessary, inhumane, and unjust. According to this view, any restrictions on how the inmate spends his time within the institution, on his right to correspond freely and with whomever he wants as much as he wants, or on his right to complain (through the mass media if he wishes) about the institution must be justified, not on the grounds that he has forfeited those rights by committing a crime, but on the same kinds of grounds that free citizens in the open community accept restrictions on their own liberty.

It is doubtful that, in a society where people have grossly unequal resources, substantial equality before the law can ever be achieved or that members of the captive society of prisoners can ever successfully claim all the rights that the law might assign them. However, the civil rights movement within the criminal-justice system is finding increasing support in the appellate courts and public opinion. It has already had tangible effects on all levels of the system, including our prisons.

Decriminalization We spoke earlier of a trend toward reducing the amount of crime the justice system must handle by changing the laws so that some behavior now so classified ceases to be criminal. This trend is largely confined to so-called *victimless crimes*—that is, to voluntary transactions, exchanges, and relationships in which none of the parties directly involved feels himself or herself to be a victim. These include a variety of sexual relationships between consenting adults, such as prostitution and homosexuality, the trade in pornography, gambling, and the sale and use of drugs. The reasons for the trend include increasing tolerance or acceptance of the behavior itself, but also the high cost and the meager results of efforts at enforcement.[81]

Structural Change

The criminal-justice system is primarily concerned with making criminal behavior more costly to the offender, with finding and judging accused offenders, and with treating or punishing them. It has little to say about the broad structural conditions in society that generate criminal opportunities, or about the strains, tensions, and human problems that produce personalities, subcultures,

[81] See Packer, *op. cit.*

needs, and wants that make people inclined to use criminal opportunities. These broad structural conditions—the distribution of power, wealth, and dignity in our society; the availability of meaningful and rewarding employment or of employment of any kind; the conditions that affect the degree of control people have over their own lives; the control and discipline that people exercise over one another by virtue of their interrelationships at home, in the neighborhood, and the workplace—these have not been carefully studied in relation to either the production or control of crime. Changes in the criminal-justice system may be justified on many grounds, but it is unlikely that any of them will produce massive change in criminal behavior. This is not to say that we know with confidence what structural changes will produce such changes in criminal behavior, or that if we did know that we would eagerly embrace them. Most of us have many attachments to and investments in the existing social order, but some of us much more so than others. We are fearful of changes that might threaten those attachments and investments; indeed, *any* massive change is likely to be threatening and will certainly be resisted. We would not be likely to welcome sweeping reforms merely because they held out some uncertain promise of reducing crime. This may be the main reason why there is so little interest in and so little serious study of the relationship between the structure of the larger society and criminal behavior. It may be that we would rather not know because we prefer solutions that will not require radical readjustments in our way of life.

SUMMARY

1   Crime and delinquency are special cases of rule-making and -breaking, from the perspective of the "state" and the "law" (the system of rules backed by the authority of the state).

2   Crime is a creation of the law; delinquency, of statutes applying to juveniles. Whereas the manifest function of the criminal courts is to administer "justice," that of juvenile courts is to "help children" (although in effect juvenile courts, too, punish offenders, and until recently young people were virtually denied due process).

3   Most of the behavior regulated by the legal system is subject to regulation by other institutions as well. The impact of the law and the effectiveness of legal agents and institutions depend on the moral status of the law. Laws sometimes have effects extending beyond legislative intent, and may generate other forms of crime to satisfy the demand for such illegal goods and services as drugs or gambling.

4   The labels *criminal* and *delinquent* become social roles as well as indications of legal status. Both the social roles and legal status are applied differentially with respect to social position and type of activity. Violation of statutes regulating business is less stigmatizing, for example, than are street crimes.

5   Laws and law enforcement interact with behavior in a variety of ways. Widespread violation of laws may lead to lack of enforcement; pressures on law-enforcement agencies may lead to violation of laws regulating law enforcement.

Who is arrested, for what, and in what manner depend in part upon police perceptions of public demand and on pressures within the community.

6   Despite volumes of official statistics of crime (the bookkeeping records of official agencies), reporting is uneven and it is impossible to determine with certainty how much crime there is in the United States, or how current levels compare with those in the past.

7   All sources of data agree that older adolescents and young adults have higher rates of street crime than other age groups, and that crime and delinquency rates for males greatly exceed rates for females (although the gap is closing). Crime rates for racial and ethnic groups reflect indigenous cultural characteristics, and the historical and contemporary circumstances under which they live. Lower-class neighborhoods and individuals have higher official crime rates than do other communities and individuals, but these rates may be exaggerated. Statistics from many countries and over different periods of time find that urban areas have higher rates of crime than do rural areas. Demographic changes, such as changing age and sex composition of the population and urbanization, must be taken into account when seeking to determine crime trends.

8   Criminological theory seeks general propositions concerning three types of questions.

9   Why do certain individuals commit certain crimes? (the individual approach) Biological and psychometric answers have only limited application. Psychiatry emphasizes the point that every individual is capable of anti-social behavior, particularly in adapting to stress.

10   Sociological perspectives on motivation emphasize that most of what we do—criminal and noncriminal—we do with other people, with an eye to what our behavior will mean to them and how it will affect our relationships to them.

11   What properties of social systems are related to crime? (the macrosociological approach) The organization of social relationships, and the opportunities to learn and pressures to perform criminal or noncriminal acts vary greatly among groups in a society. Different subcultures emerge from different conditions. In any society, the extent to which conflicting interests are recognized, reconciled, oppressed, or acceded to in matters of law and law enforcement varies.

12   What is the nature and structure of the development of interactional processes that lead to criminal acts? (the microsociological approach) All behavioral sequences, including those that result in crime, entail decisions on the part of participants in ongoing action. These decisions are determined in large part by perceived costs and payoffs of available courses of action. These, in turn, are related to such matters as group role relationships, the relative status of groups in interaction, and perceived threats to personal and group status.

13   The organization of crime, as of any type of behavior, involves *structures of activities* (e.g., a gang fight) and *relational structures* (e.g., a street gang). Organizations differ in the extent to which crime is a central object or goal of both activities and relations.

14   Rules, including laws, frequently impede goal accomplishment, and so generate pressures to deviate. In addition, every position in every organization provides opportunities and incentives to commit criminal, or at least deviant, acts.

15   Professional crime, white-collar crime and corruption, and syndicated crime may be understood in terms of these general organizational principles, as well as in terms of specific subcultural and organizational characteristics.

16   Failure of the criminal law to regulate goods and services for which there is widespread demand, corruption related to such regulation, the widely held belief that the law should not be used to regulate personal behavior which does not injure others, and recent court decisions have led to decriminalization of some activities previously considered serious crimes (e.g., use of marijuana or homosexual behavior).

17   The objectives sought under the rubric of social control of crime are varied, often contradictory, and impossible to resolve by appeal to facts alone. They include, at a minimum, retribution, incapacitation, deterrence, and rehabilitation.

18   The deterrent value of punishment is the subject of continued controversy and increasing research. Swiftness and certainty of punishment appear to be more important deterrents than is severity, but may be costly in terms of economics and civil rights. Forced treatment and rehabilitation programs generally have proven ineffective in accomplishing their goals. As a result, the search is on for effective alternatives to incarceration and to formal processing in the criminal- and juvenile-justice systems. Increasingly, incarceration is viewed as punishing rather than rehabilitative. Other punishments within institutions are under attack, however, and prisoners have gained some of the civil rights long denied them.

19   The structural conditions associated with crime are not under the control of the criminal-justice system. Uncertainties as to the effects on crime of structural changes, fear of such changes, and attachments and investments in the present structure render large-scale changes unlikely.

RECOMMENDED READING

The literature of criminology is enormous and growing. The latest compendium—definitely not for a quiet evening's relaxed reading, but excellent for reference and for treatment of most traditional topics and issues of the field—is the *Handbook of Criminology*, edited by Daniel Glaser (1974). A less comprehensive and technical, but hard headed, practical, and entertaining treatment is found in Norval Morris and Gordon Hawkins' *The Honest Politician's Guide to Crime Control* (1970). Those interested in the new directions in criminology will find the *Crime and Justice Annual*, first published in 1974, informative and interesting.

The evolution and functioning of the criminal- and juvenile-justice systems are dealt with in innumerable legal, historical, and sociological treatises. Among those we have found most helpful are: Jerome Hall, *Theft, Law, and Society* (1935); Anthony M. Platt, *The Child Savers* (1969); and John Kaplan, *Criminal Justice* (1973). Problems with official data likewise are discussed in many places. Among the most intelligent and innovative is Thorsten Sellin and Marvin E. Wolfgang's *The Measurement of Delinquency* (1964). This same research group (joined by Robert M. Figlio) reports the results of a longitudinal study of *Delinquency in a Birth Cohort* (1972). The book offers the most comprehensive picture of the social distribution of delinquency (regrettably only of males) as reflected in police contacts in Philadelphia.

Aside from references in the *Handbook* (above), the psychological literature abounds in studies of crime and delinquency at the individual level of explanation. We have found Seymour Halleck's *Psychiatry and the Dilemmas of Crime* (1971) especially thoughtful and sound. At the macrosociological level, the major theoretical advances in recent years have dealt with delinquency rather than with crime. Among the most important of these, in terms of impact on the field, are the following: Clifford R. Shaw and Henry D. McKay's classic, *Juvenile Delinquency and Urban Areas* (1942, rev. ed., 1969); Albert K. Cohen's *Delinquent Boys* (1955); and Richard A. Cloward and Lloyd E. Ohlin's *Delinquency and Opportunity* (1960). The conflict perspective is well represented by *The Social Reality of Crime*, by Richard Quinney (1970) and *The New Criminology*, by Ian Taylor, Paul Walton, and Jock Young (1973). The microsociology of crime and delinquency is poorly developed, represented chiefly in scattered chapters and articles. The most extensive statement of the perspective is found in James F. Short, Jr. and Fred L. Strodtbeck, *Group Process and Gang Delinquency* (1965, new paperback edition, 1974).

Criminal organization is most extensively discussed in Donald R. Cressey, *Criminal Organization: Its Elementary Forms* (1972), and in books which treat particular aspects of organization among criminals, e.g., syndicated crime. Examples are Cressey's *Theft of the Nation* (1969) and two books by Francis A. J. Ianni: *A Family Business: Kinship and Social Control in Organized Crime* (1972), and *Black Mafia: Ethnic Succession in Organized Crime* (1974). The topic of professional crime is most often treated in terms of specific manifestations of the genre. Informative and entertaining paperbacks include: David W. Maurer, *The Big Con* (1940) and Edwin H. Sutherland's edited and interpreted story of Chic Conwell, *The Professional Thief* (1937).

Social control is experiencing a revival of scholarly and societal interest, perhaps as a result of present high rates of crime and political violence and the failure of past policies to control these phenomena. Recent books which examine these issues include: Norval Morris, *The Future of Imprisonment* (1974); Douglas Lipton, Robert Martinson, and Judith Wilks, *The Effectiveness of Correctional Treatment* (1975); and Jack P. Gibbs, *Crime, Punishment and Deterrence* (1975).

Finally, it should be noted that reports of recent national commissions speak to many of the questions discussed in this chapter. In general, staff reports are more scholarly and critical than are final commission reports, in part because the latter are directed to somewhat broader audiences. Commissions of greatest interest are The President's Commission on Law Enforcement and Administration of Justice (the most recent "crime commission" with reports published in 1967), the National Advisory Commission on Civil Disorders (the "Kerner" commission, 1968), and the National Commission on the Causes and Prevention of Violence (1969).

2

Mental Disorders

JOHN A. CLAUSEN

llness, whether physical or mental, is not only a misfortune but a source of deviance. The ill person cannot meet normal expectations. In preliterate societies, much illness is ascribed to causes that we regard as irrational or unnatural, such as witchcraft or displeasure of the gods. In our society, we view disease as a consequence of natural biological processes such as the body's response to harmful germs and viruses, unregulated cell growth, and the breakdown of organ systems, or as a consequence of wear and tear associated with aging, improper diet, life stress, and so on. We do not in general regard people who are ill to be at fault for their illness. Family and friends may be concerned and annoyed if a person practices poor personal hygiene, smokes and drinks a lot, gets little sleep, or otherwise risks infection or injury unnecessarily. When such people become ill, we may even feel that they brought it on themselves, but no serious blame is likely to be attached unless the illness happens to be a stigmatized condition such as venereal disease or mental disorder.

HEALTH CARE AS A SOCIAL PROBLEM

In contemporary society we respond to illness by providing health services and establishing roles for those who are to use such services. A person who is seriously ill is not expected to participate in normal activities, but to seek care and follow the therapeutic regime prescribed by a physician. It is generally assumed that the medical profession will bring knowledge and technical skills to bear in order either to cure the disease or to limit impairment. This assumption is not always justified. Until the last century it was hardly justified at all, for physicians were as likely to shorten life as to lengthen it. Nevertheless, modern medicine has made remarkable advances. Increasingly effective medical care, coupled with public health measures (which have had even greater effect) have almost doubled life expectancy for the average person in developed nations over the past 200 years.

As long as medicine was relatively ineffective, the distribution and provision of medical services was not of wide concern. But now that suffering, impairment, and death from acute diseases can be markedly reduced by adequate care, its availability to the general population has become a social issue.

In this chapter we shall be dealing with one very special kind of health problem. Mental disorders constitute a major source of anguish and disablement in our society as in all societies. Only in relatively recent times, however, have they been dealt with as health problems. One could, in fact, argue that even today the general public does not regard mental illness in this way. And to a considerable degree, mental illness differs from other illnesses. The manifestations of mental disorder are varied, but they frequently are disruptive of the individual's closest ties. As we shall see, persons whom physicians would classify as suffering from a mental disorder are often not seen by their close associates as ill but as difficult and intentionally unpleasant. We have already mentioned that mental disorder tends to be stigmatized. The mentally ill are often rejected; even the seeking of psychiatric help tends to be devalued. We shall examine mental disorders both as a social problem dealt with within a medical context and as a source of deviance that tends to disrupt the social order.

Certain of the problematic aspects of mental disorder are best illustrated by a case description. This one is from a long-term study of the impact of mental illness on one family.

> Lorraine B. was 40 years old when she was first admitted to a mental hospital. Married for seven years to Fred B., a meagerly educated but hard-working and steady laborer, she was the mother of a five-year-old daughter and a three-year-old son. She had been married previously and had had two children who died in infancy. Her mother had been hospitalized with the diagnosis "schizophrenia" in 1943, staying in the hospital about six months.
>
> Mrs. B. was committed to the hospital on certification by two physicians that she was insane. Questioned by the admitting psychiatrist as to why she was sent to the hospital, she blamed her husband. She said he was frequently drunk, was sexually demanding, and ran around with other women. Further, her family didn't want her to read the Bible and preach. On questioning, she acknowledged that she had seen God in the clouds and had been hearing noises which she was unable to identify. The provisional diagnosis was *schizophrenia, paranoid type.*
>
> Mr. B. was interviewed at home soon after his wife's admission to the hospital. What had happened prior to her admission? When had he first felt that something might be wrong? Fred B. was not a highly verbal person. His education went only to the fifth grade in rural North Carolina. His answers were brief, direct, concrete —and, the interviewer felt, sincere. His wife had become violently distrustful of him, especially in the past 18 months, but the first indication had come nearly five years ago. He recalled: "It was when Sue [the daughter] was about three months old. My wife was jealous if I played with the baby. She resented it."
>
> From this time, Mr. B. thought of his wife as having "a nasty streak in her that made her act jealous." He was frequently angry with her, especially when she falsely accused him of running around with other women. Still, she was a good mother to the children and when she flew off the handle, he would go out for a walk to avoid further conflict.
>
> When had he first thought that the problem might be serious? [We did not use the term "mental illness," since we wanted his words.] It was the night, about three months before she went to the hospital, when she said someone had "done something" to the alarm clock to change its shape. Her husband had tried to reason with her, but it wasn't any more possible to get her to listen than it had been when he tried to convince her he wasn't running around with other women. "Then," he said, "I thought she wasn't right in the head."
>
> She began to restrict the children's play. When a neighbor came to see how Mrs. B. was, she ordered her former friend out of the house, waving a butcher knife. Lorraine B. moved out of her husband's bed, but frequently kept him awake much of the night while she prowled the house to "protect her papers and books."
>
> A neighbor spoke to Mr. B., suggesting that his wife needed to see a doctor. Fred went to see the family doctor and asked him to drop by the apartment to see Mrs. B. The doctor did so. He prescribed some "nerve pills," which she threw away.

During the final week before hospitalization, Lorraine smashed the radio because it was "making sounds" even when it was turned off. When the children were invited to a friend's birthday party and went without their mother's consent, she went after them, denounced the neighbor who had invited them, and screamed obscenities that aroused the whole neighborhood. Then she became mute and completely withdrawn.

Mr. B. went back to the doctor, who said that he had expected that something of this sort would happen (though he had not told Mr. B. at the time). The doctor filled out commitment papers and told Mr. B. to go to the county seat to arrange for getting his wife to the hospital. He was advised to swear out a warrant so that the police could transport Mrs. B. to the hospital. But the police placed her in the county jail overnight and did not drive her to the state hospital until the next day. Confused and enraged, she felt that she had been betrayed by her husband and rejected by everyone else.

When Mr. B. first went to visit his wife at the hospital, she refused to see him; she was alternately withdrawn and hostile toward others. After a few days, she was started on a course of treatment using a strong tranquilizing drug. In a few weeks she was reported to have become "cooperative" and she began to help other patients and to participate in cleaning and kitchen work. She reported no more delusions. At the end of approximately three months, Mrs. B. was permitted to return to her family.

When she returned home, her husband said that his wife had not been "so easy to live with" for years. But five years after her return home, she again became suspicious and fearful. One day she reported that the house was filling up with poison gas, and she smashed all the windows to let in fresh air. Then she chased her children with a club. She was again hospitalized.

As of 15 years after her initial breakdown, Mrs. B. had been rehospitalized several times but was back with her family. She seemed to be able to manage reasonably well as long as she took her medication (a phenothiazine).

The case of Mrs. B. illustrates several respects in which mental disorder differs from physical illness. The difficulty that her husband had in assessing what was wrong and what could be done about the problem attests to the difficulty of recognizing mental disorder and to the lack of well organized patterns for dealing with it. The tension and conflict generated by the symptoms were quite different from anything found with physical illness. The indignity of Mrs. B.'s being taken to jail on the way to the hospital affords further testimony to a persisting difference between mental illnesses and other illnesses. For patient and family, then, and for the community as a whole, mental illness is a puzzling, disruptive phenomenon, a problem whose social aspects are not adequately encompassed within the medical context.

The case of Mrs. B. also serves to highlight the extent to which our ways of dealing with mental illness have changed in the past 20 years. Mrs. B. was first hospitalized in the 1950s. Her three-month stay in the hospital was then about average for patients with a diagnosis of schizophrenia. At the present time, in most states, a patient presenting similar symptoms would be returned home in about three weeks rather than three months. On the other hand, 20 years earlier she might have been retained in a state hospital for the rest of her life.

At the time Mrs. B. was first hospitalized, a patient could be "committed" to a hospital indefinitely on the basis of a certificate signed by two physicians. At present, the state in which she lives permits initial commitment for a maximum of five days, at which time the patient must be released unless he or she chooses to remain, or clear evidence is presented at a court hearing that the patient constitutes a serious danger to self and others.

Response to mental disorder in Western society is very much in transition. Many difficulties remain. The very nature of the problem presented is often unclear; it emerges in continuing social interaction, often unrecognized for months or even years. Recognized or not, mental disorder threatens or spoils intimate relationships. Living with mental illness can be torture not only for the patient but for loved ones as well. Moreover, mental disorder still carries a stigma, though perhaps less than in the past, for patient and family alike.

We do not know how to prevent most forms of mental disorder, nor do we have effective means of fully curing them. Treatment may be helpful, but the consequences of labeling as mentally ill a person who is merely upset and of sending him to a mental hospital may be devastating. There are many dilemmas to be resolved, and they affect millions of lives. In any given year, more than a million Americans receive care in mental hospitals and perhaps 2 million receive outpatient care for mental disorder. From many perspectives, then, mental disorder is a social problem of major magnitude.

THE NATURE AND VARIETIES OF MENTAL DISORDER

Mental disorders vary in type and severity just as physical illnesses do. And just as it is difficult to draw a sharp line between physical health and mild illness, it is difficult to distinguish clearly between mental health and mild deviations from it. When we speak of mental disorder we mean to denote significant departures from normal cognitive and emotional functioning, so that the individual is impaired. The impaired person may not see himself as ill, even though he may be desperately miserable. Ironically, the more serious the mental illness, the less likely the patient is to recognize that he is ill. Perhaps it is this aspect of mental illness—the patient's inability to realize that he is sick and needs help—along with the fact that mental illness disrupts interpersonal relationships, that has set apart mental patients not as ill persons, but as insane, "crazy," alienated.

Alternative Perspectives

Mental disorder is manifest in behavior, including thoughts and feelings that are reported or displayed to others. Regardless of the causes of the disorder, the behavior will express not only distortions in thought processes or emotional upset but also something of the normal personality and concerns of the person.

In this respect mental disorder is quite different from physical illness. Organisms differ little in their functioning and in the contributions that each particular organ makes to the total system. Personalities differ enormously. A person's response to any given psychological stress or pathogen may be influenced by genetic makeup, but it will also be influenced by life experience. This makes it much more difficult to discern specific diseases except in instances of clear organic causation.

The norms of one's culture, social position, and unique experiences all influence how one learns to respond to hurt and to feelings of tension and upset. Further, we all cherish some false beliefs and impossible dreams. Under difficult circumstances we may temporarily "go to pieces." Whether one calls such episodes "illness" or "disorder" is a matter of semantics; they are certainly different from most physical diseases.

When we are confronted by a friend who "goes to pieces" or who feels betrayed and plotted against, it is difficult to know whether the friend is "just upset" or whether there is something more serious involved. Some psychiatrists and social scientists believe that there is never anything more serious involved *unless we call the person mentally ill.* That is, they believe that there is no such thing as mental disease, but rather that there exists a set of beliefs about mental disease that can lead a person to act crazy.[1] We shall examine this position in greater detail later in the chapter, for it constitutes a theory to explain mental illness. For the moment, however, we shall confine ourselves to a general statement before examining the psychiatric view of mental disorder.

The term *mental disorder* embraces a wide variety of behaviors and mental and emotional states. Some are consequences of organic disease, some are reflections of stress, some are a result of maladaptive strategies, and some are reflections of cultural emphases different from those dominant in the society. Certain of these types can be considered illnesses or diseases. Others, though they entail discomfort or even suffering, may be viewed more fruitfully as inappropriate learning. But all give rise to reactions or responses from others. Annoying or crippling behaviors are bound to be categorized, whether by associates or psychiatrists. We must, then, be aware that there are very different perspectives toward the behaviors and mental states that psychiatrists call mental disorder, and we should also know the consequences of the reactions of others to the behaviors in question.

Psychiatric Classification

In the past two decades, through the efforts of the World Health Organization, a high degree of consensus has been achieved in the classification of major mental disorders by psychiatrists in Western nations. While some national and cultural variations exist, there is general agreement on the major types and

---

[1] Many of the writings of Thomas Szasz (e.g., *The Myth of Mental Illness*) and of Ronald Laing maintain this position.

principal categories. There is less agreement on specific criteria for classifying individual instances of mental disorder.[2]

As a starting point, we may note the breakdown of mental disorders into three major classes: the *psychoses,* which entail a gross derangement of mental processes and problems in the evaluation of external reality; the *neuroses,* which entail emotional discomfort and impairment of functioning (usually in limited realms of behavior) but no sharp break with reality; and *psychosomatic* or *psychophysiological disorders,* which entail very real organic symptoms and malfunctions caused at least in part by psychological processes.

The psychoses   A number of psychoses have clearly organic causes; they are referred to as *organic brain syndromes.* Far more prevalent, except among the aged, are the *functional* psychoses. They are called "functional" because they are without clearly defined organic cause or identifiable structural change in the nervous system. They are assumed to be psychological in origin, at least to some degree, although there is increasingly strong evidence that genetic vulnerability is entailed in schizophrenia and perhaps also in manic-depressive psychoses.

Schizophrenia is the most common diagnosis of young adults who exhibit severe thought disorders—delusions, hallucinations, flights of ideas. Two-thirds of those patients who are diagnosed as schizophrenic come into treatment for the first time between the ages of 15 and 35.[3] Roughly three-fifths of all patients under 65 years of age occupying beds in mental hospitals in the United States are diagnosed as schizophrenic. Most are now hospitalized briefly and returned to the community.

Most schizophrenics have periodic or perennial difficulty relating to others and tend to be withdrawn. A generation ago schizophrenia was regarded by most psychiatrists as a deteriorating disease. It is no longer so regarded and, indeed, is thought by many to be a family of disorders of varying intensity.

From studies of various populations where psychiatric care is available, it has been estimated that roughly one person in a hundred will experience this disorder between adolescence and the later years.

Included with schizophrenia among the functional psychotic disorders are *manic-depressive reactions* and *involutional melancholia,* both of which tend to occur in middle life. The manic-depressive patient shows alternations of periods of extreme excitement and elation with periods of extreme depression and despair. Manic-depressive psychosis tends to be episodic; patients given this diagnosis may be perfectly normal for years and then have recurrences of

---

[2] In the United States, the detailed classification scheme along with differentiating criteria are published in the *Diagnostic and Statistical Manual of Mental Disorders* by the American Psychiatric Association, most recently revised in 1968. Efforts to achieve sharper definitions of criteria through cross-national studies are described in *The International Pilot Study of Schizophrenia* (Geneva, Switzerland: World Health Organization, 1973).

[3] This estimate and others below are from H. M. Babegian, "Schizophrenia: Epidemiology," in Alfred M. Freedman et al., *Comprehensive Textbook of Psychiatry,* Vol. 2 (Baltimore: Williams and Wilkins, 1975).

either manic or depressive symptoms. The diagnosis of *involutional melancholia* tends to be given by psychiatrists to depressed patients who are near the phase of physical change of life. The symptoms are very difficult to distinguish from those of the depressed type of manic-depressive patient.

Paranoid symptoms such as delusions of grandeur or of persecution may be found in manic-depressive and involutional states and in the mental disorders of old age, as well as in schizophrenia. Paranoia is a relatively rare condition in which an elaborate set of ideas and beliefs is built up around a faulty premise without markedly affecting other thought processes or personality. Paranoia used to be considered a specific mental disease; now it is more generally regarded as a common type of symptom occurring in a number of different disorders.

The mental disorders of old age—primarily *senile dementia* and *psychosis with cerebral arteriosclerosis*—have become both more prevalent and more difficult to cope with, as the bulk of the population has shifted from farms and small rural communities to the cities, and as life expectancy has increased. These disorders involve a variety of symptoms, such as confusion, suspiciousness, loss of memory, lack of concern for amenities, and sometimes loss of control of bodily functions. To a considerable degree, the symptoms are accentuations of characteristics widely found among older persons, especially those who feel that they no longer have any real purpose or function in life. The causes appear to be partly organic and partly related to social role and life situation.

The mental disorders of old age must not be thought of as representing a steady or inevitable decline in the organism. Although it is true that many older patients go to mental hospitals and die there, a substantial number may be able to function with reasonable adequacy in a somewhat sheltered environment where they feel they have a secure place and some degree of usefulness. Moreover, symptoms often fluctuate with life circumstances, so that persons who are markedly impaired one month may be much more effective the next.[4]

The psychoneuroses and psychosomatic disorders   The terms "neurosis" and "neurotic" have achieved a wide currency in contemporary life. We all have our hang-ups, things that worry us and make us anxious. Anxiety is the chief characteristic of neuroses. When the intensity of anxiety is so great that it produces symptoms that markedly impair the individual's ability to interact with others or carry out normal activities, it is appropriate to label the resulting state a neurosis. Closely akin to neuroses, in which anxiety finds expression in behavior and thought, are the psychosomatic or psychophysiological disorders, in which anxiety has a direct effect upon the physiological functioning of the organism.

The forms that a neurosis takes—that is, the kinds of symptoms manifested—

[4] An excellent study that also gives a review of earlier work is that of Marjorie Lowenthal et al., *Aging and Mental Disorder in San Francisco* (San Francisco: Jossey-Bass, 1967).

will depend on the way the person has learned, whether consciously or not, to handle anxiety. The anxiety may be diffuse and uncontrolled, may come out in partial paralyses, tics, etc., or may be expressed symbolically in fears of specific ideas, objects, or situations. In some forms of neurosis the anxiety is associated with the persistence of unwanted ideas and repetitive impulses to perform acts that may be considered morbid or unreasonable. Depressive reactions, often associated with a feeling of guilt for past failures or deeds, are also common. Thus in certain forms, severe neuroses are somewhat akin to psychoses and may be difficult to distinguish from the latter.

Estimates of the prevalence of psychoneurosis obviously depend upon where one draws the dividing line between the normal and the pathological. During World War II, more than a half million men were rejected by the Selective Service because of psychoneurotic tendencies; more than 300,000 others were discharged from the military services for psychoneurosis. To a degree, all of us have psychoneurotic tendencies, but most of us are not noticeably impaired by them. We are simply less pleasant or less effective than we might otherwise be. Intensive interviews with persons in both urban and rural settings suggest that more than half have experienced distress from psychoneurotic symptoms.[5]

At times of considerable tension or worry about some difficult situation we have to face, many of us experience headaches, occasional attacks of diarrhea, or unexplained skin rashes. More than three-fourths of persons interviewed in systematic studies report that they have experienced such symptoms to a significant degree at one time or another. Freud considered them part of the cost we pay for civilization. Perhaps they are rather part of the cost of being self-aware.

The more severe forms of psychosomatic disorder can at times produce structural changes that threaten life itself. Among those forms are severe asthma, ulcerative colitis, hypertension, and a good many disorders that we think of as primarily physical. Body and mind are not separable; they are aspects of a functioning person. How the body responds to various demands placed upon it will depend on the particular genetic material that goes into the developing person, the specifics of personality development, and the kinds of demands that are encountered. Thus, while the psychosomatic disorders are readily defined as belonging in the medical context, personality and social situations must be considered in dealing with them.

Other diagnostic groups   The present psychiatric classification also includes several other broad categories of mental disorder, of which the most important are the personality disorders and the behavior disorders of childhood and adolescence. The former are characterized by "deeply ingrained maladaptive patterns of behavior" and may be marked by difficulties in interpersonal

---

[5] See Thomas Langner and Stanley Michael, *Life Stress and Mental Health* (New York. McGraw-Hill, 1963) and Dorothea Leighton et al., *The Character of Danger* (New York: Basic Books, 1964).

relationships or by various forms of deviance, such as sexual deviation, alcoholism, and drug dependence. Since most of these forms of deviance are dealt with elsewhere in this book, we shall not discuss this category further in the present chapter.

The term "insane"—which has legal meaning but no technical status in psychiatry—is most often applicable to persons suffering from the acute or chronic phases of psychosis. However, a recurrent legal problem is posed by the fact that the boundary between sane and insane is not always the same as that between psychotic and nonpsychotic.

THE FREQUENCY AND DISTRIBUTION OF TREATED MENTAL DISORDERS

Until recent decades, estimates of the amount of mental disorder were based almost entirely on the number of persons coming into treatment. Now, thanks to systematic population surveys and the use of psychological tests with large samples of the population, we have a much better idea of the prevalence of psychological turmoil, psychophysiological symptoms, and other indicators of possible mental disorder. From these surveys we know that treated cases constitute only a small part of the total problem of mental disorder. Well-educated persons, sophisticated in the use of medical care services, may seek psychiatric consultation for relatively minor discomforts, but people in large segments of the population, who may be much more seriously distressed or impaired, will not think of seeking psychiatric help. Nevertheless, data on treated mental disorder do give us some idea of the magnitude of serious mental disorder, especially of the psychoses, as well as an indication of the demand for treatment.

Moreover, our knowledge of the prevalence of each of the various categories of mental illness is limited to cases that come into treatment. Surveys of the prevalence of various types of symptoms in the general population simply do not afford sufficient information to permit a psychiatrist to arrive at minimally defensible diagnoses, even in those instances where survey respondents are markedly symptomatic.

Psychiatric diagnoses tend to be unreliable classifications except under the most ideal of circumstances. Within many hospitals and clinics, the psychiatrists who are responsible for diagnoses have only brief contact with patients. Many psychiatrists have little training in research methodology and are not greatly concerned with problems of classification. As a consequence, diagnoses given in the course of normal institutional operation are far less reliable than if they were made by research-trained psychiatrists. Further, psychiatrists are oriented toward looking for pathology, not for health. When they assess persons from working-class or minority-group backgrounds grossly divergent from their own middle-class backgrounds, psychiatrists often mistake differing life styles for pathology.

Nevertheless, for all of its inadequacies, the system of classification and diagnosis incorporates the experience and codified knowledge of people who have studied mental disorder intensively. Increasingly, it incorporates research evidence regarding the correlates and courses of the various disorders that have been distinguished. As specific causes of particular mental disorders have been established, it has become possible to distinguish these disorders from others with similar symptomatology (e.g., to distinguish *paresis* or syphilis of the central nervous system from schizophrenia). Ideally, a classification system should be based upon causation. Where the cause is unknown, however, the classification of mental disorder is likely to depend upon manifest symptoms, life-history features, and the age and sex of the patient.

Let us now examine some of the data compiled on treated mental disorders in the United States in a recent year.[6] Table 2-1 gives an idea of the relative

Table 2-1 Number of Patient Care Episodes in Inpatient and Outpatient Psychiatric Services, United States, 1971

Diagnostic group	Inpatient services	Outpatient services
Total	1,692,752	2,316,754
Organic brain syndromes	157,691	58,462
Schizophrenia	537,174	363,945
Depressive disorders	321,708	293,553
Other psychoses	27,810	34,041
Alcohol disorders	227,626	125,394
Drug disorders	68,162	48,907
All other	352,581	1,392,452

Source: Adapted from National Institute of Mental Health, "Patient Care Episodes in Psychiatric Services," *Statistical Note 92*, 1973, Table 5.

frequency of inpatient and outpatient treatment for various mental disorders. It shows "episodes of treatment" rather than individuals treated, because some persons are treated in several different facilities in a given year. In compiling statistics there is no way of avoiding such duplication at present. It is difficult to know how much duplication occurs, but unless more than half of those hospitalized were admitted more than once, which is unlikely, the number of persons hospitalized for psychiatric disorders during the year in question was probably over 1 million.

It will be noted that persons who were diagnosed as having organic brain syndromes were much more likely to be hospitalized than were those presenting other types of psychotic symptomatology. The "all other" category in Table 2-1 includes primarily psychoneuroses, personality disorders, and mild situa-

---

[6] Data on the number and characteristics of patients and of mental health facilities and their staffs are published annually by the Survey and Reports Section, Biometry Branch, National Institute of Mental Health, U.S. Department of Health, Education and Welfare. In addition, many special reports and analyses of current use and of trends in the use of services are periodically issued. Data in this section are largely drawn from recent Statistical Notes from the NIMH.

Figure 2-1   Number of Patient Care Episodes per 100,000 Population in Psychiatric Facilities by Type of Facility, by Age, United States, 1971

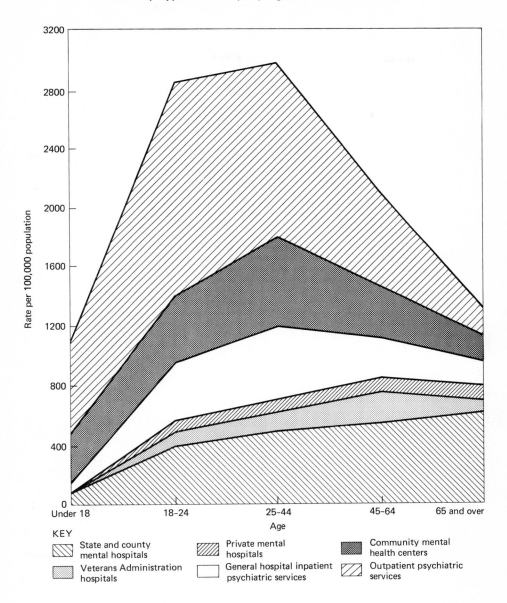

KEY

State and county mental hospitals	Private mental hospitals	Community mental health centers
Veterans Administration hospitals	General hospital inpatient psychiatric services	Outpatient psychiatric services

Source: National Institute of Mental Health, "Patient Care Episodes in Psychiatric Services," *Statistical Note 92*, 1973, p. 7, Figure 1.

tional upsets, the great bulk of which are treated in outpatient services, plus cases of mental retardation (less than 10 percent of the category).

Figure 2-1 shows for the same group of patients as Table 2-1 the rates of patient care episodes per 100,000 population by age. Rates of diagnosed mental disorder as treated in all types of facilities are highest in the age groups 18–24 and 25–44, as can readily be seen. If, however, we consider persons who are hospitalized in state and county mental hospitals, the rates are highest in the "65 and over" age group, where organic brain syndromes prevail. Outpatient services provide most of the treatment given to patients under 18.

Men and women are equally likely to come into treatment for mental disorder, but both the services used and the diagnoses given tend to vary by sex.[7] Males are somewhat more likely to be hospitalized, especially in state and county mental hospitals, and females to receive outpatient treatment. The two sexes differ little in rates of diagnosed schizophrenia, but women are twice as likely as men to be treated for depressive disorders. Women are also more likely to be treated for psychoneurosis. Men, on the other hand, are four times as likely to be treated for alcoholic disorders.

There may be real differences in the frequency of occurrence of certain disorders among men and women, but the major determinants of rates of coming into treatment are undoubtedly cultural norms relating to the use of psychiatric services and to the circumstances under which problems are defined as "psychiatric."

Marital status also has considerable bearing on the likelihood of treatment for mental disorder. In general, married men and women have low rates of treatment (and low rates of symptoms of psychological impairment). Those who are separated, divorced, or widowed tend to have much higher rates of both hospitalization and outpatient treatment. Rates of mental disorder are also high among men who remain unmarried, but are only slightly higher among unmarried women than among their married sisters. With rapidly changing patterns of marriage and divorce, however, these findings from past research may not continue to be valid.[8]

For both men and women, the likelihood of being admitted to a state or county mental hospital is inversely related to the level of education completed. Men and women who have not graduated from grade school are more than six times as likely as college graduates to be admitted to a state or county hospital at any given age level beyond 20.[9]

Differences in rates of hospitalization or outpatient treatment for mental disorder reflect two independent sets of forces: (1) causal factors, which make for differences in the occurrence of mental disorder, and (2) selective factors or social contingencies that influence the ways in which mental disorder is recognized and responded to. We can hardly evaluate efforts to study the

[7] Summarized from National Institute of Mental Health, "Differential Utilization of Psychiatric Facilities by Men and Women," *Statistical Note 81, 1972.*

[8] For an interpretation of such findings, see Leona Bachrach, "Marital Status and Mental Disorder: An Analytical Review," (Washington, D.C.: National Institute of Mental Health, 1975).

[9] National Institute of Mental Health, *Statistical Note 104, 1974.*

causation of mental disorder without understanding something about the way in which mental disorder is responded to, so we shall address the latter topic first.

RECOGNITION AND RESPONSE TO MENTAL DISORDER

When should a person seek help for an emotional problem or mental disorder? What determines whether others will regard someone as "mentally ill" or in need of psychiatric care? Mrs. B., the schizophrenic woman described at the start of this chapter, did not express any wish for help. She was fearful, she heard noises, "saw God in a cloud," and thought that others were trying to steal her children's love. Her neighbors were afraid of her and thought that she needed to be "put away." Her husband first thought that she had a jealous streak, then came to feel that she was "off," but did nothing because she could still care for the children. Then the threat of violence precipitated action.

Studies of the process of defining serious mental illness suggest that the problem is most often recognized by family members or others who are in a position to see the person in the full range of his or her activities.[10] The onset is often hard to pinpoint, but the individual's behaviors become difficult to understand and/or to accept. Alternative explanations are tried out—explanations in terms of physical illness, stresses on the job, character flaws, and the like. Often the symptoms fluctuate and so does the definition of what is wrong. The troubled person may be alternately rational and irrational, withdrawn or excitable, elated or deeply depressed. Often it is only when all other explanations have failed as a basis for action that the interpretation of mental illness comes to the fore.

Despite educational programs to the effect that mental illness is like other illnesses, it is not so viewed by most members of the public.[11] Initially, at least, most people regard mental illness as something that could not happen to them or their loved ones. Most people will make a distinction between an emotional upset or "nervous breakdown" and a *mental disorder*. The latter is far more stigmatized. Seeking psychiatric care is itself regarded as leading to devaluation and, as a consequence, many persons faced with mental disorders in a family member will put off consulting a psychiatrist.

Pathways into treatment are varied. Where family members have come to the conclusion that medical help is needed (regardless of what they call the problem), they may be able to persuade the disturbed person to seek help. If the patient and the family do not come to a definition, outsiders may. Social

---

[10] John A. Clausen and Marian R. Yarrow (eds.), "The Impact of Mental Illness on the Family," *Journal of Social Issues,* Vol. 11, No. 4 (1955) (entire issue).

[11] For a more detailed discussion, see John A. Clausen and Carol Huffine, "Sociocultural and Social-Psychological Factors Affecting Social Responses to Mental Disorder," *Journal of Health and Social Behavior,* Vol. 16 (December 1975).

agencies and the police are frequently involved in the hospitalization of lower-status persons, who are more often committed than voluntarily admitted to a hospital. Middle-class patients more often enter treatment by virtue of the recommendation of the family doctor or of family and friends.

Hospitalization may be precipitated by an increase in the disruptiveness and threatening character of symptoms, by a change in the family's ability to accommodate to a disturbed patient, or by the inability of the patient to perform roles crucial to family functioning. The more resources the family has, the greater the possibility of alternatives to hospitalization, but also the greater the probability that some form of treatment will be undertaken.

THE SEARCH FOR CAUSES OF MENTAL DISORDER

What accounts for the frequency of mental disorder in modern society? Are there particular features of society or particular kinds of life experiences that are associated with a high frequency of mental disorder? More than a century ago, it was widely believed that the pursuit of success and the increasing complexity and lack of cohesion in contemporary society had greatly increased the prevalence of insanity.[12] Yet by present-day standards, the society of a hundred years ago appears to have been relatively simple and cohesive.

Theories to explain mental disorder may focus on the broad features of cultural norms and social processes, on specific life situations or sources of stress that impinge on certain individuals or groups within society, or on the history of individual personality development. We cannot, in the compass of this chapter, examine these formulations in detail, but we shall briefly consider the evidence available for some of the more promising or persistent theories.

Mental Illness and Modern Urban Society

From the building of the first state hospitals early in the nineteenth century until 1955, the number of mental patients hospitalized increased more rapidly than the rate of growth of the total population. The more hospital beds there were, the more patients were put in them. A careful study of records of jails, almshouses, and other places where mentally ill persons were confined in Massachusetts between 1840 and 1850 revealed, however, that the rate of psychosis among persons in the prime of life at that time must have been at least as high as in 1950.[13]

Massachusetts was a highly urbanized state even in 1840. It is likely that many of the disorganizing effects of urbanization and industrialization had already taken place. The existence of value conflicts, the segmentalization of

---

[12] See, for example, David J. Rothman, *The Discovery of the Asylum* (Boston: Little, Brown, 1971).

[13] Herbert Goldhamer and Andrew Marshall, *Psychosis and Civilization* (New York: Free Press, 1953).

relationships, and the lack of stable occupational expectations—all concomitants of social change and of urbanization—might be expected to contribute stresses leading to an increase in mental breakdown. One might ask, then, whether a proportionally lower amount of mental illness would be expected in a population with high consensus as to values, a relatively homogeneous set of occupational and familial expectations, and close integration of the individual into the network of community relations. The Hutterite communities of Montana and the Dakotas, settled in the latter half of the nineteenth century by Anabaptist immigrants from central Europe, approximate this ideal type of homogeneous and highly integrated community. These rural villages have managed to maintain a surprising degree of resistance against the encroachments of the competitive, hedonistic emphasis in American life. Yet a careful check of Hutterite communities to locate mentally ill persons by a research team that included a psychiatrist, a psychologist, and a sociologist disclosed that the occurrence of episodes of severe mental illness among the Hutterites was roughly comparable to the occurrence of hospitalization for mental illness in New York State.[14] Among the Hutterites, however, patients were cared for at home rather than in mental hospitals. Moreover, both the duration and patterning of the symptoms manifested by members of the Hutterite communities differed somewhat from those of patients from the larger American society.

From time to time, anthropologists, travelers, and workers in nonliterate cultures have proclaimed the people of a particular society to be essentially without mental disorder. In every instance in which more thorough study has been undertaken, the original reports have been found to be untrue. No one person's experience is likely to be an adequate basis for an estimate of the frequency of mental disorder unless systematic observations have been recorded for defined populations. Few of those who have made pronouncements in this area have been adequately trained in either psychiatry or statistics, and almost none have been adequately trained in both. The major forms of mental disorder are almost certainly found among all peoples, regardless of their way of life.[15]

Social Status and Mental Health

The social status of one's family influences to a considerable degree the relative ease or discomfort of one's physical existence, the values that one learns early in life, the opportunities that become available, and the attitudes that are expressed toward one by other persons. Social status influences personality development but does not *determine* it. Many persons move up the status ladder, and some move down. To what extent do mental disorders vary by social status? In seeking to answer this question, investigators have used a number of indexes of social status as well as a variety of indexes of mental disorder.

One of the most influential studies of the distribution of mental disorder was Faris and Dunham's *Mental Disorders in Urban Areas*.[16] These researchers plotted the residential distribution of all patients from the city of Chicago admitted to public and private mental hospitals, and computed rates of hospital admission for the various diagnostic categories of illness by area. The study conclusively demonstrated that hospitalized mental illness was not randomly distributed through the city. The highest rates were found near the center of the city in areas of high population mobility and heterogeneity and low socio-

---

[14] Joseph W. Eaton and Robert J. Weil, *Culture and Mental Disorders* (New York: Free Press, 1955).

[15] For a thorough analysis of the intricate relationships between the patternings of mental disorder and cultural orientations, see Marvin Opler, *Culture and Social Psychiatry*, rev. ed. (New York: Atherton, 1967).

[16] Robert E. L. Faris and H. Warren Dunham, *Mental Disorders in Urban Areas* (Chicago: University of Chicago Press, 1939).

economic status. Conversely, the lowest rates were found in the stable residential areas of higher socioeconomic status.

Nearly two decades after the study by Faris and Dunham, Hollingshead and Redlich[17] set out to establish whether there were significant differences in the prevalence and incidence of mental illness among the social classes in New Haven. Data were secured not only from hospitals and clinics but from private psychiatrists as well. For hospitalized mental illness, Hollingshead and Redlich found the same general pattern that Faris and Dunham had found, with highest rates in the lower social strata and substantially lower rates in the upper strata. The New Haven study contributed further evidence that schizophrenia, insofar as it results in psychiatric treatment, tends to be more prevalent in the lower social strata. On the other hand, most of the differential between classes resulted from the much greater duration of hospitalization for lower-class patients. Once they came into treatment or care, they were more likely to remain there, but the frequency with which they initially became ill was only slightly greater than that of higher-status patients.

The New Haven study for the first time presented evidence on the distribution of persons receiving outpatient treatment, either in clinics or from private psychiatrists. Here the picture tended to be almost the reverse of that shown for hospitalized patients—the highest rates were in the upper social strata. Hollingshead and Redlich were able to demonstrate conclusively that the way in which persons came into treatment, the kind of treatment received, and the duration of treatment all varied greatly by social class. Their study was exceedingly valuable in giving an understanding of the way in which treatment services operate; by the same token it clearly demonstrated that data on treated cases of mental illness could not be used as a basis for estimating the true prevalence of illness within the population.

The most conclusive study to date of the actual distribution of symptoms in an urban population is the Midtown Manhattan study. Its psychiatric classifications were based upon interviews of a cross section of nearly 1,700 persons in an area of New York City. The interview was designed to get at such matters as the respondent's having had a "nervous breakdown" or having sought psychotherapy; the presence of somatic disorders that frequently have a psychogenic basis; acknowledgment of nervousness, restlessness, and other psychophysiological manifestations of emotional disturbance; indications of memory difficulties; acknowledgment of difficulties in interpersonal relations; and indications of emotional disturbance given by the respondent's behavior in the interview situation.[18] Information from each of these areas of the interview was abstracted and given to a team of psychiatrists who rated the respondent as to the degree of psychiatric symptomatology, if any, and the apparent amount of impairment of functioning as a result of such symptomatology.

---

[17] A. B. Hollingshead and F. Redlich, *Social Class and Mental Illness* (New York: Wiley, 1958).

[18] For a full description of the methodology see Leo Srole et al., *Mental Health in the Metropolis* (New York: McGraw-Hill, 1962), Ch. 3.

Perhaps the most startling finding of the Midtown study was the very high proportion of the population rated "impaired" by psychiatric symptoms—23.4 percent. This proportion varied considerably by socioeconomic status. In the lowest economic stratum, nearly one-half of all those interviewed were rated "impaired," while in the highest stratum, only about one person in eight was so rated. Also striking was the finding that at the upper status levels, fully one-fifth of those persons who had been rated "impaired" were currently receiving outpatient therapy and more than one-half had at one time or another been psychiatric patients, mostly outpatients.[19] At the lower status levels, on the other hand, only one percent of the persons rated "impaired" were currently receiving psychiatric treatment and another 20 percent had previously been patients (almost all in mental hospitals). Thus more of the poor had serious symptoms, yet fewer of those with symptoms ever received treatment.

Receiving a rating of "impaired" as a result of one's responses to an intensive interview is not, of course, the same thing as being diagnosed as mentally ill. The surveys used in epidemiological studies of mental illness have focused upon symptoms and have tended to ignore strengths. Moreover, many of the symptoms may be primarily reflections of physical illness or of objective problems of living. Nevertheless, an examination of the interview responses of persons classified as "impaired" leaves one with little doubt that most of them have emotional problems quite comparable to those of many persons who seek psychiatric help. Indeed, the finding that more than half of the upper-status impaired group had sought such help indicates something of the potential demand for psychiatric service if everyone with emotional problems were to seek it.

Both treated mental disorder and symptoms of emotional distress are, then, found more often among the deprived than among the privileged. A recent study of mental illness and the economy also finds that hospitalization for mental disorder is very significantly related to economic conditions generally. Using data in admissions to New York State mental hospitals from 1842 to 1967, Brenner has found that when employment has gone down, mental hospital admissions, especially first admissions, have tended to go up.[20] The closest relationship between employment and admissions is found among higher status groups—in income, education, occupation, and ethnic background—which suggests an indirect relationship. That is, it is not the direct threat of unemployment, which is less serious among groups of high status than among those of low status, but perhaps something in the general social climate that accounts for increasing hospitalizations. Further research is needed to delineate the mechanisms involved, but Brenner's findings demand explanation and extension. At the same time, it should be noted that few students of mental health and illness believe that increasing unemployment causes widespread

---

[19] *Ibid.*, p. 246.
[20] M. Harvey Brenner, *Mental Illness and the Economy* (Cambridge, Mass.: Harvard University Press, 1973).

mental illness. In the great depression of the 1930s, for example, there was no indication of a major increase in rates of mental disorder.

Social Stress and Mental Disorder

We noted earlier some of the reasons why rates of mental disorder might be expected to vary by social status. Life in the working class, especially at the lowest levels of education, occupational skill, and income, entails not only economic insecurity but the experience of conditions, relationships, and events that are more often punishing than rewarding. Such conditions and events are stressors, imposing demands for adaptation. There is a folk saying to the effect that every person has a "breaking point"; stresses cannot be piled on indefinitely without threatening the organism or the person's emotional balance.

Stress is a convenient concept and a sensible one. We all know that we feel uncomfortable or anxious in certain situations that we call stressful. But one person's stressor can be another's zestful challenge. Some students dread having to give a report in class or to take an exam; others seem to enjoy such situations. The psychological stressfulness of any situation depends largely on the meaning that a person has learned to attach to that kind of situation in the course of development. Situations that threaten our self-respect or our self-image and personal values are experienced as stressful. On the other hand, physical discomfort or danger may or may not be so experienced, depending in part on whether one feels trapped and defenseless or feels competent to handle the discomfort or danger in the pursuit of some goal.

Studies of the effects of various types of stress on mental health and illness have taken two major approaches. One is to ask what conditions or events are experienced as stressful by almost everyone (the death of a spouse, for instance), and then to study the frequency of occurrence of such events in the general population and among persons who come into treatment for mental disorders or who report symptoms of emotional upset, psychophysiological discomfort, and the like. The second approach, which has been widely used in recent years, is to look for the occurrence in one's life of any kinds of events or changes—favorable or unfavorable—that call for adaptation. We do not normally think of getting married or of being promoted on a job as stressors, yet they pose great demands for adaptation. Much recent research has examined the effect of "life events" on the physical and mental health of samples of the population.[21]

There is a good deal of evidence that persons who come into treatment with a mental disorder are likely to have experienced more unfavorable events or losses in the weeks or months prior to breakdown than one finds in the general population. In some instances (for example, in the case of schizophrenics), it appears that there has been a piling up of stressful events during

---

[21] For examples of such research see Barbara Dohrenwend and Bruce Dohrenwend (eds.), *Stressful Life Events: Their Nature and Effects* (New York: Wiley, 1974).

the weeks prior to entry into treatment but that these stresses merely precipitated a breakdown that was likely to occur sooner or later anyway. In other instances, such as certain forms of depression, it appears that those who became mentally ill had experienced more severe stresses or losses than those who did not break down. Stress appeared, in other words, to be a direct cause, not merely a precipitant.

Several studies have shown stress and an excess of unfavorable life events to be more frequent in lower-class than in middle-class life. Moreover, it appears that resources for coping with comparable levels of stress are far less adequate among persons of low social status. As a consequence, when stress level is held constant, persons at lower status levels show more symptoms of discomfort and impairment than do those at higher levels.[22]

Social Relations, Genetics, and Schizophrenia

The prevalence of the disorder or group of disorders called schizophrenia and the early age at which schizophrenia tends to occur make it the most devastating of mental disorders. Schizophrenia is diagnosed more often in the United States than in most other Western nations. Nevertheless, when criteria for diagnosis are systematically specified, similar groups of schizophrenics can be identified in cross-national research and a substantial level of diagnostic consensus can be achieved in any given research center.[23]

Members of several scientific disciplines have laid claim to being able to explain the causes of schizophrenia, but such claims tend to be unconvincing to outsiders. Sociologists have proposed first social isolation and more recently the effects of low social status as causes of schizophrenia. Geneticists have presented evidence of hereditary linkages in the transmission of schizophrenia. Psychoanalysts have advanced theories of failure of ego differentiation, largely as a result of deficient mothering. Communication patterns in the family have also been implicated. Biochemists, neuropathologists, and other scientists studying the nervous system have postulated but not yet demonstrated biochemical or neurophysical differences between schizophrenics and samples of the normal population.

At present, the most convincing evidence of causation comes from research on genetic linkages.[24] One approach has been to study schizophrenia in twins, and specifically the probability that schizophrenia will be found in both twins if it is found in one. That probability is much higher among identical twins, who share the same genes because they were produced by the splitting of a single egg, than it is among fraternal twins, who are genetically comparable

---

[22] See Thomas Langner and Stanley Michael, *Life Stress and Mental Health* (New York: McGraw-Hill, 1963).

[23] *The International Pilot Study of Schizophrenia* (Geneva, Switzerland: World Health Organization, 1973).

[24] An overview is contained in David Rosenthal and Seymour Kety (eds.), *The Transmission of Schizophrenia* (London: Pergamon, 1969), esp. Part 2, "Genetic Studies."

to non-twin brothers and sisters. Another approach has been to compare the life experiences of two groups of individuals adopted very early in life by normal parents—one group born to women hospitalized for schizophrenia and the other to nonschizophrenic mothers. Such studies have consistently shown that although the adoptive families differed little, schizophrenia and a variety of problematic behaviors were found far more often among those individuals whose mothers had been schizophrenic.

The evidence for a genetic component in the etiology of schizophrenia does not rule out the possibility that social and psychological influences are also involved. Only about 10 percent of children having one schizophrenic parent and 40 to 50 percent of children with two schizophrenic parents develop schizophrenia. Many studies are now being conducted among these so-called "high-risk" groups to try to establish what features of development or experience seem to be associated with the subsequent development of schizophrenia.[25]

Another consistent finding in research on schizophrenia is its overrepresentation among the lower-status segments of the population. Schizophrenia is less frequent among professionals and highly educated people than it is among those in unskilled or semi-skilled occupations and those with relatively meager education.[26] This finding appears to be due in part to the tendency of persons rendered ineffective by schizophrenia to drift downward or at least to fail to advance in occupational status. Childhood social status is somewhat related to schizophrenia but not nearly so strongly as adult status. Therefore, although the greater stresses and personal devaluation that are encountered at lower-class status levels cannot be ruled out as a causal influence, the evidence is not nearly as convincing as is that for a genetic effect.

Family socialization and communication patterns may also have some effect in precipitating schizophrenia in vulnerable persons. In recent years, intensive psychiatric studies of the families of schizophrenic children have suggested that the dynamics of family relationships in those families differ significantly from the patterns found in "normal" families.[27] The parents often seem impervious to the needs of the child for autonomy and self-respect. Their behavior toward the schizophrenic may communicate the opposite message from that conveyed verbally, thereby putting him in a "double bind." Intergenerational boundaries may be so obscured that the child is confused as to what his own role should be. The net effect of most of the family patterns noted is that they make it difficult for the child to achieve an identity of his own and to develop competence and self-reliance.

A major limitation on the inferences that can be drawn from such research, however, derives from the fact that the families can be identified and studied

[25] For a detailed discussion of the conceptual models proposed to account for the occurrence of schizophrenia, see Norman Garmezy, "Children at Risk: The Search for the Antecedents of Schizophrenia," *Schizophrenia Bulletin*, Nos. 8 and 9 (Spring and Summer 1974).

[26] For a thorough discussion, see Melvin L. Kohn, "Social Class and Schizophrenia: A Critical Review and a Reformulation," *Schizophrenia Bulletin*, No. 7 (Winter 1973), pp. 60–79.

[27] Here again, an overview is afforded in Rosenthal and Kety, *op. cit.*, pp. 175–266.

only after the schizophrenia has become manifest. In living with a schizophrenic child, the families are confronting one of the most devastating stresses that can be imagined, and parents may well develop behavioral patterns different from those that had characterized the family before.

Certainly the most tenable hypothesis about the etiology of schizophrenia today is that various combinations of hereditary vulnerability and environmental stress (either in early childhood or in later life) may lead to overt manifestation of the disorder.

Mental Illness as a Social Role—Labeling Theory

Many students of deviance have stressed that deviants come to official attention not so much because of specific acts as because they have been formally "labeled" deviant by others. Deviance is, then, a status conferred upon a person. In particular, it is noted that once labeling takes place, the deviant is expected to conform to the prescriptions for the role in which he has been cast. Once one has been labeled a "madman," for example, others expect him to behave nonrationally and do not give him a chance to behave like a normal person.

This "labeling theory" of deviance has been applied to mental disorder by Thomas Scheff. Scheff is critical of the whole concept of mental illness and specifically rejects the idea that there is any such thing as schizophrenia except in the minds of psychiatrists. Scheff has suggested that many persons may unconsciously take on the stereotyped role of the insane once someone has suggested that they are mentally ill. He observes that a great many people deviate from social norms without necessarily receiving any particular label thereby. If, however, this "residual deviance" is challenged and labeled mental illness by others, the disturbed individual may tend to let himself go and behave according to a stereotyped notion of mental illness. In Scheff's words: "If, however, labeling occurs, the rule breaking . . . may be stabilized; thus the offender through the agency of labeling is launched on a career of 'chronic mental illness.' "[28]

This argument has been voiced less forcefully and explicitly by a number of sociologists who have been impressed by the coercive consequences of psychiatric diagnoses and by the impact of hospitalization upon an already upset person. Most of us know people who occasionally "lose their heads" when they get frustrated, frightened, or upset. If they are hospitalized because of complaints brought against them at such times, they have doubly lost control of themselves.

Being labeled "mentally ill" is undoubtedly a devastating blow. So is being jailed for a crime, or being rejected by a loved one. But most of the patients who are hospitalized with a diagnosis of schizophrenia have not merely been

---

[28] Thomas Scheff, *Labeling Madness* (Englewood Cliffs, N.J.: Prentice-Hall, 1975), p. 10. Scheff's earlier work, *Becoming Mentally Ill, A Sociological Theory* (Chicago: Aldine, 1966), is a fuller statement of this theory.

upset or irrational in one or two situations. Hospitalization frequently is preceded by months or even years of difficulties that include disordered thought
and emotion. Labeling people mentally ill tends, as we have seen, to come as
a last resort, when all other hypotheses have proven inadequate to explain their
behavior. Labeling cannot be said to stabilize behavior that has long been
problematically patterned.

Moreover, labeling leads to treatment, and treatment now usually leads to
a decline in symptoms and early release from the hospital. Most persons admitted for the first time with a diagnosis of schizophrenia are returned home
in less than a month. Moreover, when we follow former patients for up to 20
years, we find that feelings of stigmatization diminish and that many former
patients live quite normal lives. It is probably true that in the past we launched
many acutely disturbed persons on careers of chronic mental illness by keeping
them in mental hospitals until every spark of motivation and zest for life had
been snuffed out. But mental illness existed long before psychiatry and mental
hospitals, and it simply will not do to blame psychosis on labeling.

The Etiology of Neuroses

There is much greater agreement as to the crucial role of psychosocial factors
in the etiology of neuroses than in that of the functional psychoses. In the
United States, at least, the psychoanalytic theory of the neuroses, or some
variant of it, is held by most psychiatrists. Without attempting to present this
theory in detailed or technical terms, we may say that it rests upon the concept
of unconscious motivation and upon the needs, vulnerabilities, and conflicts
that are unconsciously internalized as a result of life experience, especially in
early childhood. The biological organism, with its drives for physical gratification and its needs for nurturing, is entirely dependent upon others for security
in the satisfaction of those needs. But for a variety of reasons, such security
may not be achieved. Biological needs are channeled and "disciplined"; infant
strivings are often frustrated. In attempting to ward off anxiety stemming from
inevitable frustrations and frightening experiences, the child evolves various
modes of psychological defense. These "defense mechanisms," which everyone
uses to some extent, may permit the channeling of anxiety in relatively harmless forms. Unfortunately, they may also lead to stereotyped ways of meeting
situations, often quite inappropriate to the requirements of the situation. Being
unaware of the reason for his stereotyped behavior, the potential neurotic is
unable to modify it. When defenses patently lead to inappropriate responses
or when for some reason they break down, full-blown neurosis, in one form
or another, results.

Classical psychoanalytic theory placed the roots of neurosis in psychosexual
development in childhood. Freud postulated an inevitable conflict between
man's biological nature and the demands placed on that nature by civilization.[29] Neo-Freudians, such as Erich Fromm, Karen Horney, and Harry Stack

[29] The classic statement was, of course, that of Freud in *Civilization and Its Discontents*.

Sullivan, however, have pointed out that Freud mistook the characteristics of middle-class Austria in the late nineteenth century for the immutable characteristics of "civilization." As a consequence, he was unaware of the enormous role played by culture in patterning interaction within the family and in setting life goals. He seems also to have underestimated the importance of later childhood and subsequent experiences in generating neurotic conflicts.

Whereas Freud emphasized the frustration of libidinal (essentially sexual) needs by civilization, many psychoanalysts now emphasize conflicts contained in Western culture itself that are internalized by its bearers: the conflict between competitive striving and brotherly love; the conflict between materialistic aspirations and the possibility of their fulfillment; and the conflict between the ideal of individual freedom and the reality of regimentation.[30]

There seems to be little question that the sociocultural heritage is implicated in neurotic conflicts and in psychophysiological disorders. We cannot, however, assume that the elimination of specific cultural themes (if this were possible) would automatically reduce pathology, any more than we can predict the psychological stress value of a specific situation without knowing the whole context in which it is embedded.

SOCIAL POLICY AND MENTAL DISORDER

Before the National Mental Health Act was passed in 1946, mental health was not considered a legitimate concern of the federal government. The Constitution had left the states responsible for the indigent and the unfortunate, and the states varied considerably in their allocation of priorities to this end. There was one dominant mode of dealing with recognized mental disorder: incarceration in a so-called mental hospital or asylum. Our mental hospitals were much like prisons and most patients were there against their wishes. Who would voluntarily choose to go to such a place?

We have made great progress in dealing with mental illness in contemporary Western society, but many issues and some real dilemmas remain. It may be useful to examine briefly the trends in U.S. social policy toward mental disorder before addressing the core issues that have emerged in the formulation of public policy today.

Major Trends in U.S. Policy

The building of state mental hospitals began early in the nineteenth century.[31] The impetus came from several sources. In the early years of our nation, a person with a mental disorder might be kept at home if the family had ade-

---

[30] Karen Horney, *The Neurotic Personality of Our Time* (New York: Norton, 1937).

[31] The history of the care of the mentally ill in America is ably described by Albert Deutsch, *The Mentally Ill in America* (New York: Columbia University Press, 1949); Gerald M. Grob, *The State and the Mentally Ill* (Chapel Hill, N.C.: University of North Carolina Press, 1966); and Rothman, *op. cit.*

quate resources, but was more likely to be lodged in a jail or poorhouse if it did not. Such persons were often cruelly mistreated. Following the French Revolution, physician-reformers such as Pinel in France and the Quaker William Tuke in England demonstrated that many mental patients who had been imprisoned for long periods responded to humanitarian treatment and could be returned home. American reformers called for the establishment of asylums where such treatment could be given. At the same time, there was a strong conviction that modern (early-nineteenth-century) society, with its chaotic life styles, had caused a great increase in mental illness. Therefore society should provide places for the mentally ill where a planned (regimented) existence might restore sanity.

As we noted earlier, each year from the building of the first state asylums to 1955 saw an increase in the number of persons hospitalized. By 1955, nearly 600,000 were confined in state and county hospitals for the long-term care of the mentally ill. There were more people in mental hospitals than in all other hospitals combined. Many state hospitals were in remote areas. They were poorly staffed with very few qualified physicians, and those who worked most closely with patients were almost totally unskilled attendants.

With the passage of the National Mental Health Act, the federal government made funds available for three major types of programs: (1) research into the causes and treatment of mental illness; (2) training of professionals for both research and patient care; and (3) state development of community outpatient services for the treatment of the mentally ill. Although many professionals in the field of mental health argued that funds should have been provided to the states for improving mental hospitals, the focus on other approaches proved to be much more strategic. The states were forced to look more closely at their mental hospitals and to examine the role that they played in the care of the mentally ill. Within a very short time, research demonstrated that long-term stays in such hospitals were a primary cause of mental and physical deterioration of patients.

The training of greatly increased numbers of psychiatrists, clinical psychologists, psychiatric nurses, and social workers soon permitted more adequate staffing of state hospitals. The development of the first effective "tranquilizers," coupled with a move toward open wards, made it feasible to use the mental hospital more flexibly for shorter-term stays. Once it became apparent that mental hospital populations could be reduced, a still greater federal investment was made when Congress enacted the Community Mental Health Centers Act of 1963, which authorized funds for the construction of comprehensive community mental health centers throughout the nation. Two years later, the Act was amended to fund the staffing of the centers. Although the objectives of this program are still far from realization, they stand as a clear enunciation of public policy.

By the mid-1960s, more mental patients were being seen in outpatient settings—clinics, mental health centers, and private psychiatrists' offices—than in mental hospitals. By 1974, the number of resident patients in long-term mental hospitals had declined to substantially less than half that in 1955, despite a substantial increase in the population in the intervening years. Mental patients who need short-term hospitalization now tend to go to the psychiatric wards at general hospitals in their home communities rather than to remote state hospitals.

In the past 25 years, the mentally ill have thus been brought much more into the sphere of health care services rather than set aside in state hospitals where most received neither treatment nor loving care. This does not mean that most mental illness is now being cured, or that we do not need any state mental hospitals, but there has been a marked improvement for most patients and their families. As we shall see, however, some new problems have emerged. Before discussing these problems, we should examine the mental hospital and the tasks with which it is charged.

The Mental Hospital

Mental hospitals tend to be quite different from the hospitals in which patients with serious physical ailments are treated. Many older state mental hospitals are extremely large institutions designed for the custodial care of a great many patients at low per-person cost. Some resemble prisons far more than hospitals. Although more and more hospitals are managing to unlock many of their wards and buildings, in most public mental hospitals in the United States some locked wards are considered a virtual necessity.

Most mental patients do not need to be in bed except for normal sleep requirements. In some hospitals patients have an opportunity for meaningful activities; in others they are simply regimented, like prisoners, for certain activities and left alone at other times.

As a social organization designed to help mentally ill or emotionally disturbed persons achieve mental health and take up normal social roles in the community, the traditional mental hospital has many defects. Limited staff and resources, coupled with large size and isolation from the community, make many mental hospitals little more than repositories for custodial care. From the standpoint of the patient, herded as a member of a collectivity with little attention to personal needs or desires, such hospitals are not very different from prisons and concentration camps. Goffman has characterized them as "total institutions" and has noted the ways in which staff and inmates interact and work out adjustments.[32] Although supervision of the wards and decisions relating to patient care and release from the hospital are technically the re-

---

[32] See Erving Goffman, *Asylums* (New York: Doubleday, 1961). Other influential studies of mental hospitals include the following: Ivan Belknap, *Human Problems of a State Mental Hospital* (New York: McGraw-Hill, 1956); William Caudill, *The Mental Hospital as a Small Society* (Cambridge, Mass.: Harvard University Press, 1958); H. Warren Dunham and S. K. Weinberg, *The Culture of a State Mental Hospital* (Detroit: Wayne State University Press, 1960); and Alfred Stanton and Morris Schwartz, *The Mental Hospital* (New York: Basic Books, 1954).

sponsibilities of medical personnel, the limited number of psychiatrists and other physicians available in most public hospitals precludes any substantial amount of contact between doctor and patient. Attendants or aides, who have the most direct contact with patients (though even here it may be limited to only a few minutes per day outside their glass-enclosed "stations"), can readily control the flow of information to psychiatric staff so as to influence the prescription of treatments such as shock and hydrotherapy.

Patients are to be fitted to the demands of the system, not the system to the needs of patients. The patient, distressed and often disoriented, is usually relieved of his personal possessions, denied the privileges that self-respecting adults take for granted, and, in short, treated in such a way as to be deprived of all of the trappings of self-respect. Despite efforts at hospital reform and, indeed, very real improvements in our mental hospitals, the mental hospital is still, by and large, consonant not with the medical model of mental illness, but with a model of social control. Patients are often powerless; they are treated as non-persons.

A few years ago, Rosenhan made front-page news with a systematic investigation of the experience of eight normal persons who were hospitalized after they reported that they thought that they were hearing voices.[33] These volunteer patients simulated symptoms to gain admission to 12 different hospitals. They were hospitalized from a minimum of seven to a maximum of 52 days *even though they behaved perfectly normally once they entered the hospital.* Other patients voiced the suspicion that the pseudo patients were journalists or professors or someone else "checking on the hospital." Hospital staff regarded their note taking as simply further evidence of pathology. The typical response of psychiatrists, nurses, and other staff to questions from these patients was to move on, head averted, so as not to make eye contact or otherwise acknowledge the existence of a human relationship.

From our own research on mental patients and their families we are convinced that there will always be a need for confining, at least briefly, mentally disordered persons whose delusions, hallucinations, or obsessions make them a danger to themselves or to others. At very least, the hospital can afford a temporary refuge and a moratorium for such persons. The sleepless, panic-stricken patient can often find rest. The person fearful of harming a loved one can feel secure in the knowledge that he will now do no harm. In general, however, hospitalization also has connotations of defeat and of extreme devaluation. To be hospitalized involuntarily must be one of the most devastating blows that a person can suffer. Ironically, this blow will fall most heavily on the persons who are least seriously disturbed, for they will be best able to appreciate what is being done to them. The problem of commitment requires at least brief discussion.

[33] See David Rosenhan, "On Being Sane in Insane Places," *Science,* Vol. 179 (1973), pp. 250–258.

The Problem of Commitment

Involuntary commitment to a mental hospital may be necessary for patients who might harm themselves or others as a result of a mental disorder. Unfortunately, commitment tends to be utilized also in instances where the patient is simply a problem or annoyance to his family or others in the community. There is an ever-present danger that the nonconformist or the person with extreme idiosyncracies will be committed unjustly, especially if he lacks power. Recent studies indicate that patients committed after formal hearings often do not manifest any behaviors that would legally justify hospitalization; rather, they are committed on the basis of hearsay and summary judgments that are based on complaints by family members, co-workers, and so on.[34] Such commitments occur infrequently, however, where the person being examined is represented by counsel. Of those represented at commitment proceedings by their own lawyers, most are released; among those equally symptomatic but not represented by counsel, most are committed. One recent study found, for example, that among persons appearing at sanity hearings but not exhibiting behaviors that met legal criteria for commitment, none of those having legal counsel were committed to the hospital but two-thirds of those without counsel were ordered hospitalized.[35]

Two recent court actions dramatize the commitment issue. The most important was the action of the Supreme Court in 1975, in behalf of Kenneth Donaldson, a former patient who had been imprisoned involuntarily in a Florida mental hospital for nearly 15 years.[36] Throughout his confinement he received no treatment and his petitions for release were repeatedly refused by the courts. When finally released from the hospital in 1971, he filed a damage suit against hospital officials. He was awarded damages by a jury and the verdict was upheld both by the Federal Court of Appeals and by the Supreme Court. The Court's written opinion emphasized that "Mere public intolerance or animosity cannot constitutionally justify the deprivation of a person's physical liberty." Many questions remain unresolved, but it appears that authority to commit a person will now entail responsibility for seeing that that person receives treatment.

In another recent case, a middle-aged man who was employed as an expert typist but who had an obsession that he needed more money was arrested for begging. He promised not to beg again and noted that he did not really need to beg. To prove it, he opened the attaché case that he was carrying and revealed nearly $25,000 in small bills. He was immediately hauled into court, where the judge suggested a psychiatric examination. He was diagnosed as a

---

[34] See Thomas Scheff, "The Societal Reaction to Deviance: Ascriptive Elements in the Psychiatric Screening of Mental Patients in a Mid-Western State," *Social Problems,* Vol. 11 (Spring 1964), pp. 401–413.

[35] See Dennis L. Wenger and C. R. Fletcher, "The Effect of Legal Counsel on Admissions to a Mental Hospital: A Confrontation of Professions," *Health and Social Behavior,* Vol. 10 (March 1969), pp. 66–72.

[36] Reported in *Newsweek,* July 7, 1975, p. 45.

This community mental health center provides an opportunity for relaxed sociability as well as formal therapy.

paranoid schizophrenic. His family questioned the man's ability to take care of himself. He was thereupon committed by a county judge to an indefinite stay in a mental hospital. Despite his having been committed, he has been asked to pay all of his hospital bills out of his savings. Heavily drugged while in the hospital, he has lost his skill as a typist. Although now released from the hospital by court order, commitment converted an eccentric who was competent into a disillusioned man who has lost his competence.

As mental health services have improved, the proportion of persons who enter treatment voluntarily has steadily increased. Nevertheless, it is still primarily the poor, the deprived, and others lacking power who are most often committed, and the rights of patients will continue to be an issue in mental health care for some time.

Maintaining Patients in the Community

The basic tenet in recent social policy regarding mental disorder has been that patients should be treated in the community. A major objective in the development of community mental health centers has been to provide comprehensive services at the local level so that patients can be maintained in their normal social roles in family and community to the maximum degree possible. Five essential elements of service were specified in the design of community mental health centers: (1) inpatient services providing 24-hour care for the treatment of acute disorders; (2) outpatient services; (3) partial hospitalization services, such as day care, night care, or weekend care; (4) emergency services available around the clock; and (5) consultation and educational services available to community agencies and professional personnel. Ideally, a substantial number of mental health centers should also serve as places of training and should actively carry out research on mental disorder and evaluation of the services provided.

The availability of inpatient services within community mental health centers and the increasing number of psychiatric wards in general hospitals has made it feasible to use the hospital much more flexibly in the course of treatment. In addition, the use of psychoactive drugs has made it possible to maintain many psychotic patients at home by relieving their acute anxiety and making them less likely to act aggressive or disruptively. Experimental studies have demonstrated that as many as three-fourths of patients scheduled for hospital admission could be maintained in the community if they received medication and supportive visits from public health nurses.[37] Since hospital care is extremely expensive, keeping patients at home can result in substantial savings, in addition to sparing patients the trauma of hospitalization.

There are, however, other factors to be considered. A patient may be maintained in the home at the expense of the emotional well-being of other family members, or other family members may be required to stay away from work or school to care for him. Psychotic mothers are often unable to care properly for their children, even after a period of hospital treatment. When they remain in the home throughout a psychotic episode, there is a serious risk of disturbance in the children. There is also a higher risk of additional births as a consequence of poor contraceptive practices.

Moreover, follow-up studies of schizophrenic patients treated in the community and comparable groups treated in hospitals suggest that patients who have been hospitalized may actually function somewhat more effectively. Even a year or two after the initial upset, families have been found much less likely to be confronted with problems if the patient has been hospitalized for a period.[38] And certain forms of treatment—electroconvulsive therapy and lithium treatment for depressed patients, for example—are much more appropriately given in the hospital than in outpatient settings.

Except in the case of severe psychoses, however, most mental disorder can

[37] See Benjamin Passamanick et al., *Schizophrenics in the Community: An Experimental Study in the Prevention of Hospitalization* (New York: Appleton, 1967).

[38] See Jacqueline Grad, "A Two-Year Follow-Up," in Richard H. Williams and Lucy D. Ozarin, *Community Mental Health: An International Perspective* (San Francisco: Jossey-Bass, 1968), pp. 429–454.

be handled in the community, especially if recognized in the early stages of distress. Recognition of the need to do something to relieve severe anxiety, inability to sleep, depression, or other symptoms may be more important than the particular action taken. Often the emotional support of family and friends, coupled with situational adjustments, can relieve the immediate pressures and stave off breakdown. Where such informal action is taken, no record of outcome is available, yet there is reason to believe that the immediate social milieu can be and often is as therapeutic as a psychiatrically staffed milieu. In the many instances where the patient's symptoms are primarily a manifestation of tensions or impossible demands in the home milieu, a professional assessment is clearly needed. By the same token, a resolution of the problem entails something more than individual therapy.

Treatment modalities   The varieties and potentialities of psychiatric treatment have been greatly augmented in the past two decades. The broad classes include: organic therapies for psychosis (electroconvulsive therapy, drug therapies, etc.); behavior therapies; individual and group psychotherapy; and milieu therapies.[39] Organic therapies have tended to be looked down on by psychodynamically oriented psychiatrists, but a wealth of research documents that for both schizophrenic and manic-depressive or depressed patients, drugs contribute more to maintaining the individual in normal social functions than any form of psychotherapy that has been studied.

Different types of drugs, acting on different biochemical systems in the brain, serve to diminish the symptoms of schizophrenia on the one hand and depression on the other. The drugs most effective in controlling symptoms also tend to produce side effects that may themselves be quite serious or even life-threatening. This is especially true of certain of the antidepressant drugs. For depression, electroconvulsive therapy still appears to be the most effective treatment.[40] It has saved thousands of lives of patients who in earlier days would have committed suicide, and in controlled studies has been found to speed up the patient's recovery markedly. Yet it meets vehement opposition from well-meaning crusaders who see it as a form of torture or punishment. Without doubt this form of treatment lends itself to misuse, especially in understaffed state hospitals, but it is equally true that it is often a very effective means of relieving acute suffering.

The psychotherapies or talk therapies have long been the treatment of choice for psychoneuroses and personality disorders in middle-class patients. Psychotherapy provides a supportive, empathic relationship in which the patient can feel accepted and free to express and examine facets of his behavior

---

[39] For detailed discussions of various therapies by outstanding authorities, see Alfred M. Fredman et al., *Comprehensive Textbook of Psychiatry*, Volume 2, "Psychotherapies" (pp. 1799–1920), "Organic Therapies" (pp. 1921–1989) and "Milieu Therapy" (pp. 1990–2009).
[40] *Ibid.*, pp. 1951–1952; 1973–1974.

and development. It thus becomes a means of achieving awareness of feelings and reactions toward self and others.

Group therapy has been used increasingly in both hospitals and clinics to involve patients who may have difficulty in expressing themselves in individual psychotherapy. It also serves, of course, to stretch therapeutic resources. To be effective, group therapy (or any psychotherapy) must involve a real commitment on the part of the patient. It has been the experience of community mental health centers in poverty areas that such commitments are frequently not sustained. Therefore, crisis intervention efforts, entailing a single session on an individual basis, are somewhat more typical of therapeutic work with deprived groups.

Some Unresolved Issues

There is no question that symptoms of psychological discomfort and of greater impairment are more prevalent among deprived population groups, but there is a very real question as to whether these symptoms are to be taken as evidence of the need for some form of medical treatment. It may be that other forms of help—perhaps training programs in interpersonal relations—would have greater payoff in furthering competence and, through it, self-confidence.[41]

An issue that must be explored further is whether mental disorders do belong almost exclusively within the realm of the medical profession or whether there are facets that need to be dealt with by other approaches. Many psychiatrists are convinced that the "medical model" of disease and treatment cannot adequately encompass the field of mental disorders. Others are interested in extending the scope of psychiatry both in the community and in various institutional settings.

A more circumscribed issue concerns the use of psychoactive drugs for both inpatients and outpatients. There has been a tendency to prescribe certain drugs (especially phenothiazines) in heavy dosage despite some research evidence that patients experiencing acute "reactive" psychotic episodes may actually recover more quickly when less potent drugs are used. Too many patients have been tranquilized to the point of psychological and social ineffectiveness even after they have passed the period of acute upset.

A great many patients now never receive psychiatric services because they are maintained on drugs by general practitioners. Many family doctors and some psychiatrists have only the most rudimentary knowledge of the effects of the drugs they are prescribing. In more than a few instances the physician has heaped one drug prescription on another, keeping the patient drugged but not in any way dealing with the underlying problem.

Despite the great expansion of psychiatric services in recent years, very little attention and almost no direct help is being given to families struggling

---

[41] For a fuller discussion of this approach see David Mechanic, *Mental Health and Social Policy* (Englewood Cliffs, N.J.: Prentice-Hall, 1969), pp. 108–116.

to deal with a seriously disturbed patient. A model of community mental health centers has been developed and sold with very little solid research evidence that it is adequate for dealing with the full range of mental disorder and the human problems generally subsumed under that term.

We have corrected some of our past errors in attempting to cope with mental illness. We still have a long way to go if all segments of the population are to have an equal opportunity for mental health.

SUMMARY

1 As medical care has become more effective, the provision of adequate care to all members of the population has become a social issue. Mental health care has long been a responsibility of the states, but has left much to be desired.

2 Mental disorders are manifest in behavioral deviance and disrupt relationships. Thus they entail problems of control and care not found in physical illness.

3 Mental disorders vary in symptomatology, duration, and severity, just as physical illnesses do. Some mental disorders result from organic malfunctions and some from stressful psychological experiences (often coupled with personality vulnerabilities), and some primarily reflect faulty strategies that have been learned earlier in life.

4 Schizophrenia accounts for the largest single category of persons hospitalized for psychosis. Most psychiatrists and biologists agree that it is a disease that is transmitted at least in part by genetic mechanisms, but some sociologists argue that schizophrenia is a myth and that the most serious and persistent manifestations of what is called schizophrenia derive from the social labeling of the deviant.

5 Surveys of psychological functioning of cross-sectional samples of the population suggest a high level of psychological discomfort and impairment, largely untreated, but such surveys do not permit estimates of the frequency of specific mental disorders.

6 Rates of treated mental illness are highest for both men and women in the middle years. Most episodes of treatment take place in outpatient settings. Men are relatively more likely than women to be hospitalized, while women are more likely to be treated as outpatients.

7 Mental illness is often not recognized as such; alternative interpretations are entertained to explain the disturbed person's behavior. Medical help may not be sought until all other possibilities are exhausted, partly, at least, because of the stigma that still attaches to mental disorder.

8 Neither the pace nor the complexity of modern life seems to have appreciably altered the amount of severe mental illness from what it was a century or more ago.

9 Symptoms of psychological discomfort (and impairment) and cases of severe mental illness seen in treatment facilities are both more prevalent among lower status persons than among those of higher socioeconomic status. Higher status also makes for better quality treatment.

10 Although stresses—like war and famine—that impinge upon whole populations do not appear to cause increases in the amount of mental illness, stressful life events that call for individual adaptation trigger emotional breakdowns.

11 At least some forms of schizophrenia appear to entail genetic vulnerability. It is

hypothesized that schizophrenia results from an interaction between such vulnerability and certain types of life experience, especially in the family.

12   In the past 20 years, as clinics and community mental health centers have provided outpatient treatment in many communities, the number of mental patients confined in state and county mental hospitals has declined by more than 50 percent.

13   The typical mental hospital has many defects, but it nevertheless still has a function in the short-term treatment of acutely disturbed persons who constitute a severe burden on their families if maintained at home.

14   New therapeutic techniques have enabled modern psychiatry to be more effective in the treatment of mental disorders. There are, however, facets of the mental health problem, especially relating to psychological discomfort and impairment, that may be dealt with more appropriately through nonmedical approaches. Consideration needs to be given to the overall design of a model to cope more adequately with the full range of mental disorders and the problems of living that affect mental health.

RECOMMENDED READING

The meaning of mental illness and the treatment of the mentally ill in past eras have been described in vivid historical perspective by George Rosen in *Madness and Society* (1968). A highly interpretive but fascinating analysis of power relations in the care of the mentally ill during the Enlightenment is philosopher Michel Foucault's *Madness and Civilization: A History of Insanity in the Age of Reason* (1973). Albert Deutsch's *The Mentally Ill in America*, 2nd edition (1949) is still the best overall history of the care of the mentally ill from Colonial days to World War II, but David Rothman's *The Discovery of the Asylum* (1971) gives a more sociologically sophisticated analysis of the forces behind the building of mental hospitals and other asylums.

A reissuing, in paperback, of *Mental Health in the Metropolis: The Midtown Manhattan Study* (1975) by Leo Srole and others makes this classic study of the distribution of symptoms of mental disorder readily available. The earlier work of A. B. Hollingshead and F. Redlich, *Social Class and Mental Illness* (1958), which deals with treated mental illness rather than symptoms, affords a comparison of research approaches.

There are several useful collections of papers on sociological aspects of mental disorder. All aspects of the patient career from the prepatient stage to the return from hospital to community and epidemiological studies are dealt with in Spitzer and Denzin's *The Mental Patient* (1968). Somewhat less comprehensive is Thomas Scheff's *Mental Illness and Social Processes* (1967). The student who wants a more vivid feel for the experience of mental illness will find it in Bert Kaplan's *The Inner World of Mental Illness* (1964). The perspective that schizophrenia is a mode of living adapted to particular family circumstances rather than an illness is illustrated with family histories in R. D. Laing and A. Esterson's *Sanity, Madness and the Family* (1970).

The most provocative and influential sociological study of a mental hospital (really of a class of institutions) is Erving Goffman's *Asylums* (1961). A more recent hospital study is Robert Perrucci's *Circle of Madness* (1974), which proceeds from the premise that mental disease is a myth, and strongly reflects the author's negative attitudes toward the hospital.

For a well-rounded yet critical assessment of policy issues from a sociological perspective, David Mechanic's *Mental Health and Social Policy* (1969) is by all odds the book to read. And for the student who wishes detail on any aspect of mental disorder and the modes of dealing with it, *The Comprehensive Textbook of Psychiatry, II,* 2nd ed. (1975) is a two-volume encyclopedia (2,600 pages) that belongs in every college library.

3

Drug
Use

JOHN A. CLAUSEN

D rug use illustrates, perhaps better than any other form of deviance, the extent to which the existence of a social problem depends on definitions made within a given society at a given time. The use of drugs to achieve relaxation and pleasurable states of mind is as ancient as their use to treat illness. Until the start of this century, the most widely used drugs in Western medicine were opium and its derivatives, which are potently addictive. Yet drug addiction has not been regarded as a major social problem in most countries and was not so regarded even in Western society until a century or so ago. The opiates were commonly dispensed in patent medicines until shortly before World War I, and the number of persons in the United States physically addicted to them was much larger at the turn of the century than it is now. After the problem of addiction had been widely publicized, however, control over drug distribution was instituted by state and federal governments, and for half a century drug addiction has been a matter of great public concern.

In recent decades a number of drugs—some new, some ancient—other than opiates have been widely used for pleasure. These too have become sources of concern and of new legislation. In the 1960s marijuana went from being a common feature of the lives of jazz musicians to being a common object in the jeans pockets of many middle-class high school and college students. LSD and other psychedelics were sought as "mind expanders" by others. As patterns of drug use changed, so did the characteristics of the users. Marijuana users had been considered deviants in most high schools in 1950; by the 1970s they were often members of the "in" crowds.

Prior to 1950, most research on drug use was research on drug addiction. Most research on addiction, moreover, was limited to atypical samples of addicts who had been arrested and incarcerated or who were in treatment. Now knowledge of drug use and its social and psychological correlates is expanding rapidly. It is important to be alert, then, to both the changing nature of drug use and the changing social response to it.

Our task in this chapter will be to examine the various facets of drug use and dependence in American society and the changing attitudes and policies that have marked efforts to deal with these problems. First we shall consider the respects in which drug use is believed to be a social problem. Then we shall turn to what is known and what is popularly believed about various drugs now proscribed by law except when medically prescribed. We shall touch upon the physiological and psychological effects of certain of these drugs. A knowledge of drug effects tells us very little about how drugs will be used, but is a necessary step toward analysis of use. Next we shall consider the nature and amount of illegal drug use and its historical and social patterns. Since drug use is learned within social contexts and cannot be understood without consideration of its meanings in particular groups and relationships, we shall be dealing with a variety of practices among a variety of groups and not with a single phenomenon. We shall examine, for certain groups, the symbolic significance of drugs, how drug use begins and is sustained, and, insofar as they are known, the psychological and social consequences of using various drugs in various ways. Social policy toward drug use will then be reviewed in historical perspective and in the light of comparative data from other societies. Finally, we shall examine some of the assumptions underlying our legal definitions of drug use and the practical problems of implementing our drug laws.

DRUG USE AS A SOCIAL PROBLEM

In what ways is drug use a social problem? The answer depends on one's point of view and personal experience. Our society has generally regarded certain drugs as a problem because they are said to impair people's ability to mobilize themselves and direct their lives. Some drugs are believed to undermine moral restraints and lead to criminality and violence. Perhaps the most feared drugs are the opiates, because of the physiological dependence and consequent psychological dependence attaching to opiate use.

We are just emerging from a period in which the image of the "drug fiend" was foisted upon the American people in order to secure public support for enforcement of narcotics laws.[1] If most members of the public are now somewhat less ready than their parents were to believe horror stories about drugs—largely because alternative evidence is available—the consensus of opinion remains that drug use entails dangers and negative effects for many users. In any event, persons who use mind-altering drugs for pleasure, escape, or mystical experience (and especially those who are "dependent" on drugs) are stigmatized in most segments of American society.

Drug use is regarded as a social problem by some members of our society because certain drugs have become part of a life style that flouts such conventional middle-class values as the pursuit of wealth and occupational success. Drug use, like long hair and unconventional dress, is interpreted as a symbol of an ominous threat to the American way of life. Even if the drugs are not seriously harmful, their use is opposed by those who feel it tends to threaten basic moral values.

Recently, an increasing number of people have taken a very different perspective, maintaining that it is not so much the use of drugs but the laws against such use that create the primary social problem at the present time. Early in this century, according to the best estimates available, there were between 200,000 and 500,000 opiate addicts in the United States, most of them addicted to patent medicines that were available at any drugstore.[2] Their addiction was basically a medical problem, and in many instances it did not

---

[1] See, for example, the annual reports of the Commissioner, Bureau of Narcotics, U.S. Treasury Department, during the 1930s, 1940s, and 1950s, and Harry J. Anslinger and William S. Tompkins, *The Traffic in Narcotics* (New York: Funk and Wagnalls, 1953).

[2] See Charles E. Terry and Mildred Pellens, *The Opium Problem* (New York: Committee on Drug Addiction, 1928), for a thorough analysis of the nature and extent of drug use in the United States prior to federal control of opium and its derivatives.

seriously interfere with their personal effectiveness. But by legislation that made opiates unavailable except through illegal channels, and by subsequent vilification of the drug user, addicts were transformed into criminals.

The laws against marijuana use have been especially problematical. Millions of Americans, most of them under 30 years of age, use marijuana at least occasionally. In many states, these individuals may be defined as felons if they are arrested with marijuana in their possession. The penalties for violation of drug laws are more severe in some states than those for armed robbery or attempted murder.[3] Widespread use of marijuana in the face of current drug laws has accentuated lack of respect for the law and has resulted in nonenforcement or differential enforcement of the law, depending upon the whims of law-enforcement officers.

Few events in American history did more to undermine the authority of the law and to encourage the development of organized crime than the passing, 50 years ago, of a Constitutional amendment to prohibit the manufacture, sale, and transport of alcohol as a beverage. To some observers of American society, our efforts to deal with drug use have produced a similar problem, one far greater than drugs themselves have brought about. When drug laws *are* enforced, both addicts and casual users pile up in our prisons.

Drug use may also be viewed as an aspect or manifestation of a much more general social problem. If substantial numbers of people find it necessary to use drugs in order to feel comfortable, or if their lives are lacking in meaning and they therefore turn to drugs to provide it, the problem is less in the drugs than in the way of life that has been offered them. Although drugs can serve many functions, they can also undermine the individual's motivation to deal effectively with his or her problems and to work for social reforms that will attack the causes of those problems.

There are, then, several senses in which drugs pose a problem in contemporary society. Experts are not unanimous on what our public policy should be, but almost all informed persons except enforcement personnel seem to agree that our current punitive laws make little sense.

DRUGS AND THEIR EFFECTS

Social definitions are, as we have noted, of crucial importance in understanding the "problem" of drug use. It may be helpful, then, to start by examining our terms of reference. First of all, what is a "drug"? A standard textbook on therapeutic pharmacology defines a drug as "any chemical agent which affects living protoplasm," and goes on to note that few substances would escape this defini-

---

[3] See Neil L. Chayet, "Legal Aspects of Drug Abuse," in J. R. Wittenborn et al. (eds.), *Drugs and Youth* (Springfield, Ill.: Charles C. Thomas, 1969), pp. 236–249. Some state legislatures are now acting to soften these unreasonable penalties.

tion.[4] A substance may be known as a food in one century and a drug in the next, or vice versa. Drugs may be used to fight disease; to avoid or minimize pain, fatigue, or anxiety; or to achieve a level of euphoria. In most societies there is approval of at least occasional use of stimulants, narcotics, or other drugs to help achieve these objectives. When such use is not *disapproved,* the substances are most often no longer referred to as drugs. Thus, in contemporary America as in much of the world, alcohol is the drug most widely used to produce pleasurable states of mind, and most drinkers do not regard their indulgence as drug use.

Similarly, tobacco and coffee are widely used for their drug effects (those of nicotine and caffeine), and there was a time when both were proscribed drugs. It is rather startling to read treatises written by leading physicians and lawmakers just a century or two ago, describing the moral depravity and physical debilitation that followed the use of coffee or of tobacco.[5] The smoking of tobacco was at one time or another punishable by death in Russia, Persia, Turkey, and parts of Germany. In England, a little more than two centuries ago, efforts to stamp out the use of tobacco included penalties as extreme as splitting or cutting off the nose of the offender. Ironically, tobacco use became respectable, and ultimately the most common form of it was in cigarettes. Today we know that heavy use of cigarettes starting early in adolescence can reduce life expectancy by as much as eight years, yet tobacco use is not yet markedly devalued in the United States. Smokers are not called drug users or drug addicts, despite the fact that many heavy smokers meet all of the criteria that would define "classical" addiction (see below). Few people would brand cigarette advertisers as "merchants of death," in spite of the warning that appears in their ads and on their packages, yet those who sell *illegal* drugs that may have less serious consequences for health have been so branded.

When we talk of drug use as a social problem, then, we shall be talking primarily about legally forbidden or socially devalued forms of drug use. Custom and law, not science or logic, are the definers. We shall be concerned primarily with the use of opiates, the hallucinogens, the barbiturates, and the amphetamines, but we shall occasionally touch on other forms of drug use, including prescription drugs, since attitudes toward one form of drug use may influence attitudes toward other forms, and customs and laws are subject to change as a consequence of such influence.

Drug Addiction and Related Concepts

The term "drug addiction" has been variously defined. Some definitions stress uncontrollable psychological craving on the part of the user, and others stress

[4] Louis S. Goodman and Alfred Gilman (eds.), *The Pharmacological Basis of Therapeutics,* 3rd ed. (New York: Macmillan, 1965), p. 1.

[5] Louis Lewin, *Phantastica: Narcotics and Stimulating Drugs, Their Use and Abuse,* trans. from 2nd German ed. by P. H. A. Wirth (New York: Dutton, 1964).

phsysiological dependency on a particular drug. We shall use the term only when both features are present, as in very heavy, continued use of alcohol, opiates, and barbiturates. Expert committees of the World Health Organization and various national organizations have struggled to differentiate forms of drug "abuse," but ultimately it has become clear that values, not scientific criteria, most strongly influence the pronouncements of such groups. Terms like "habituation," "craving," "detrimental drug effects," and "psychological dependency" cannot be defined in operational terms that produce agreement among experts.[6]

There are, however, certain features of drug action that differentiate drugs and make some drugs more likely than others to be widely used for nontherapeutic purposes. Most obviously, different classes of drugs have different actions on the nervous system: Some produce stimulation and feelings of excitement; some serve as pain killers and often produce tranquility and drowsiness; some induce sensations of altered perception. We shall consider such effects shortly, but here we are concerned with *tolerance* and *physical dependence*. Many drugs produce a much stronger effect when first used than when taken for some time. The body accommodates to the drug—develops *tolerance*—so that much larger doses are required to produce the effect originally produced by a small amount. Alcohol, opiates, amphetamines, and barbiturates all fall into the category of drugs that produce tolerance. In the case of many such drugs, as dosages are increased to give a desired level of effect (intoxication, relaxation, stimulation) the body becomes *dependent* on the drug for normal functioning. If the drug is *not* taken regularly, the user who is physiologically dependent will suffer withdrawal symptoms, often called the *abstinence syndrome* (e.g., *delirium tremens* or the D.T.'s with alcohol). When we speak of addiction, then, we shall be referring to physiological dependence on a drug that is used as a source of pleasure. As we shall see, warding off the abstinence syndrome becomes a potent force making for continued use of those drugs that produce physiological dependence.

Certain types of drugs induce tolerance and physical dependence as well as psychological craving; others produce tolerance without physical dependence or craving without tolerance; and still others produce neither physical dependence nor craving, yet may be sought for their psychic effects. The characteristics of drug action depend on the chemical structure of the drug, on the amount administered (and sometimes on the route of administration—e.g., oral, subcutaneous, or intravenous), and on the social definitions and the circumstances of the situation in which the drug is used. In large enough doses, chemical effects tend to override the influence of social circumstances. Even for relatively modest doses, drugs differ in their effects, but the differences are often quite subtle.

[6] See Reginald G. Smart, "Addiction, Dependency, Abuse or Use: Which Are We Studying with Epidemiology?" in Eric Josephson and Eleanor E. Carroll (eds.), *Drug Use: Epidemiological and Sociological Approaches* (New York: Wiley, 1974), pp. 23–42.

The Opiates

The opium poppy has been the source of sleep-inducing drugs and soothing beverages since antiquity. Eventually it was learned that the ingredients responsible for the soporific properties were contained in the juice that exudes from the ripe poppy head when it is lanced. This juice, collected and dried, is opium. Early in the nineteenth century, the two major components (alkaloids) of opium, morphine and codeine, were first identified. They are distinct though related in drug action. From morphine are derived heroin, dilaudid, and a number of other drugs that produce similar effects. Comparable drugs such as methadone are produced synthetically.

Opium and its derivatives were inexpensive drugs and were used with almost no limitations for a wide variety of human ills until the early twentieth century. The bold use of opium appears to have been the basis for the reputations of a number of famous physicians of earlier times. If the drug was used intermittently, tolerance was not built up and addiction was not recognized. The regular user developed tolerance, but as long as he had a steady, inexpensive supply available, he was unlikely to recognize the extent of his physical dependence. Indeed, it was not until the 1830s that the phenomenon of physical dependency was described in medical literature and physicians began to warn against the dangers of opiate addiction.

When a person has been taking one of the opiates steadily for a period of a week or so (orally, subcutaneously, or intravenously), his body comes to require the drug in order to feel normal. If he is then deprived of the drug he will experience a train of symptoms of *withdrawal*, varying somewhat in intensity and course depending upon the particular drug, the length of time he has used it, and the amount he has been taking. For example, about six hours after morphine or heroin is suddenly and completely withdrawn, an addict begins to feel tense. A little later his eyes begin to water, his nose runs, and he sweats and yawns. Restlessness and nervousness become progressively worse as the hours go by. Within 24 hours of the last dose of the drug, most patients are acutely miserable, complaining of chilly sensations and cramps in the muscles of the back and extremities. Recurring waves of goose flesh appear. Restlessness is accompanied by almost constant twitching of the arms, legs, and feet.

Perhaps the most startling aspect of the bodily reaction of an addict deprived of an opiate is that at any time during the acute abstinence period, a single dose of the drug (or any closely related opiate or synthetic) will produce prompt and pronounced relief. The drug becomes, then, both a source of euphoria and the means of avoiding the acute illness of withdrawal. Lindesmith has postulated that the essential feature of addiction is the addict's recognition that the tortures of abstinence can be warded off by the drug.[7]

Although it does not explain craving for the drug long beyond the period of abstinence symptoms, the process of labeling oneself as dependent has important consequences for identity. The addict knows the extent to which his

[7] Alfred R. Lindesmith, *Opiate Addiction* (Evanston, Ill.: Principia Press, 1947).

future comfort depends on the drug; he knows he is hooked. Before he has experienced the abstinence syndrome, he may assume that he can stop using the drug at any time, though he may not choose to do so. Once he is hooked, only inability to get the drug will induce him to stop using it. Consequently, when he realizes he is hooked, he is ripe for assimilation into the culture of the addict, where assurance of drug supply becomes a primary goal in life.

Marijuana

Marijuana is a crude preparation of the flowering tops, leaves, seeds, and stems of female plants of Indian hemp (*Cannabis sativa*). In the United States it is usually smoked in cigarettes ("joints" or "reefers") rolled by the user. The active drug ingredient is found in the sticky resin exuded by the tops of the plants. When the tops and leaves are used, the resin is not highly concentrated. The resin itself may be used for smoking or eating; it is best known as hashish.

There are few topics on which opinions are as sharply divided as are those on marijuana and its effects. Moreover, the divergency of opinions is unlikely to be resolved by scientific evidence; it is based on ideological commitments and grossly differing premises as to what is good, right, or desirable. The short-term effects of marijuana have been studied in the laboratory, and of course both short- and longer-range effects have been observed by millions of users. Therefore it is hardly correct to say, as some writers do, that we know almost nothing about the effects of marijuana. We know a good deal, but what we make of this knowledge depends on what we choose to emphasize.

During the 1930s, the head of the Federal Bureau of Narcotics became committed to the proposition that marijuana was a major menace to the nation. He asserted, in official publications of his agency and in appearances before Congress, that marijuana destroys the will power, releases moral restraints, and leads to violence and debauchery. Congress was impressed, and it included marijuana in the same category as the opiates in federal drug legislation.

Careful studies of the effects of marijuana give little support to the extreme charges against the drug. Pharmacological and psychological studies reveal changes in perception and in the flow of ideas but no increased tendency to violence. The most carefully controlled study of the effects of marijuana smoking revealed that its effects depend very largely on one's prior experience with it.[8] Young adult males who had not previously used marijuana did not achieve "highs" but did show some impairment of performance on simple intellectual and psychomotor tests. By contrast, regular users of marijuana felt high but showed no impairment of performance; indeed, some showed slight improvement. The conclusion of the research team, based on all the evidence of their very carefully conducted laboratory study, is that "Marihuana appears to be a relatively mild intoxicant." This conclusion has been borne out overwhelmingly in other recent studies.

[8] Andrew T. Weil et al., "Clinical Psychological Effects of Marihuana in Man," *Science*, December 13, 1968, pp. 1235–1238.

LSD and Other Hallucinogens

LSD—lysergic acid diethylamide—was first synthesized in 1938.[9] Its capacity to produce hallucinations and emotional changes was not discovered until five years later. It was used only for experimental studies and limited therapeutic trials until well into the 1950s. Some psychiatrists used it to gain access to chronically withdrawn patients and found that it enabled them to verbalize suppressed components of their conflicts. Others used it, in small quantities, as an aid to psychotherapy, especially with neurotic and alcoholic patients. Discovery of the intensity and depth of perceptual and emotional experience released by the drug made it attractive to many persons interested in esthetic and mystical experience as well as to those seeking to transcend the normal range of consciousness.

The psychic effects of LSD—the "trip"—begin approximately 30 minutes after the ingestion of a tiny quantity (150 micrograms), and are often preceded by transitory physical symptoms such as nausea, headache, chills, and sweating. Emotions are markedly heightened, but whether the individual will be happy or miserable is likely to depend on the social situation. Sensitivity to sensory input is enormously enhanced. Tactile and visual distortions and "hallucinations" occur, flooding the senses. The altered subjective experience presents a startling contrast to ordinary reality.

The dangers of LSD and related hallucinogens appear to be of three types: (1) those associated with "bad trips" or panic states, especially when the drug is used without proper safeguards and by persons who have severe neuroses or "hang-ups"; (2) the tendency of many users to become so preoccupied with subjective experiences and sensations as to become disengaged from normal social roles and activities; and (3) the danger that such drugs may cause damage to the organism, either with respect to brain function or in effects on the genetic apparatus (chromosome breakage). Research findings regarding organic damage are conflicting; early reports of damage have not been confirmed.

There are markedly conflicting reports on the frequency of "flashbacks"—hallucinatory images in the absence of the drug—in the case of heavy LSD users and also on the frequency of suicide among users who have had bad trips. On the basis of a follow-up study of adults who had taken LSD 10 to 15 years earlier, McGlothlin concluded that the measurable lasting effects among adults who took the drug under medical supervision are minimal, but that LSD can be a potent means of facilitating rapid modification of beliefs and values.[10] In a therapeutic situation such modification may be desirable; in other situations and settings it may not.

---

[9] The pharmacological properties of LSD and its behavioral effects, as well as many aspects of LSD use, are discussed in Richard C. DeBold and R. C. Leaf, *LSD, Man and Society* (Middletown, Conn.: Wesleyan University Press, 1967).

[10] W. H. McGlothlin, "The Epidemiology of Hallucinogenic Drug Use," in Josephson and Carroll, *op. cit.*, pp. 292–293.

Stimulants: Cocaine and the Amphetamines

Cocaine, a natural derivative of the coca leaf, has long been used by natives of the Andes to combat fatigue. In the last century it was regarded as an attractive local anesthetic, and was widely used by physicians, who regarded it as nonaddicting. In the 1890s, however, it became recognized that cocaine was an extremely dangerous drug because of its long-term effects upon the nervous system. A cocaine "high" produces extreme euphoria. In early use it enhances alertness and creativity, and the user may begin to develop feelings of omnipotence. Unfortunately, however, continued use leads first to poor judgment and then, very frequently, to paranoid delusions and to auditory, visual, and tactile hallucinations. Although its use had declined markedly after the advent of the amphetamines, in recent years cocaine has again become the favored stimulant of a substantial number of popular entertainers and others who are able to afford this very expensive smuggled drug.

The amphetamines are synthetic stimulant drugs that have been widely prescribed in recent decades for weight control (through reduction of appetite) and to offset fatigue and feelings of depression. Performance on a wide variety of tasks that require alertness is improved by low doses of the amphetamines, which have long been popular with students cramming for examinations, truck drivers plagued by sleepiness, and other persons having difficulty getting going. Like cocaine, however, with increasing dosage levels the amphetamines have a deleterious effect upon the nervous system. They produce insomnia, tension, and a loss of reflective judgment.

Paranoid symptoms also occur frequently among heavy users of amphetamines, particularly those who inject methamphetamine (known as "crystal" or "speed").[11] Even in groups where multiple drugs are used, the consequences of injecting methamphetamine are summed up in the saying, "speed kills." Physical debilitation is severe, and at the end of a "run" the user may be in a state of total collapse. Apathy and feelings of depression may persist for weeks or months thereafter.

Depressants: Barbiturates and Hypnotics

The barbiturates and hypnotics (nembutal, seconal, and the like) are drugs used medically for calming and slowing down the patient, helping him to sleep soundly, and so forth. They have a disinhibiting effect not unlike that of alcohol and hence can be used to attain "highs" as well as relaxation. Barbiturates are sometimes used by opiate addicts as a substitute for an opiate, but they are more commonly paired with other drugs to enhance or offset their effects, depending on circumstances. Because of easy availability, they are widely used by youth experimenting with drug effects.

Barbiturates are characterized by tolerance and physical dependence. The

---

[11] See J. T. Carey and J. Mandel, "A San Francisco Bay Area 'Speed' Scene," *Journal of Health and Social Behavior*, Vol. 9 (June 1968), pp. 164–174.

abstinence syndrome following heavy barbiturate use is extremely severe, often involving convulsions. Barbiturate action is in several respects similar to that of alcohol, and the latter may be used to attenuate withdrawal effects of barbiturates.

EXTENT AND DISTRIBUTION OF DRUG USE

American society, as exemplified by its middle class of northwestern European origins, was long characterized by a valuing of asceticism and rational practicality. The use of drugs for pleasure or for the reduction of minor discomfort is not consonant with such values. Since males were supposed to be strong and to bear pain without complaint, while females were long regarded as weak, it is not surprising that prior to drug control the primary users of narcotics in the United States were middle-class women whose "female disorders" served as an excuse for their reliance on patent medicines. Apart from such members of conventional society, heavy drug use was, until recent decades, largely confined to members of subgroups whose behaviors were seriously deviant in other respects. Criminals and prostitutes, who by and large have lived dreary lives, full of anxiety and misery, have long tended to use opiates and other proscribed drugs. This is one reason for the belief that drugs cause crime; there has been an undeniable association between the two.

In recent years, the ethic against drug use has grown less strong. Esthetic and mystical experiences have been increasingly valued among American intellectuals, especially in the past decade or two. In the same period, many new drugs have been discovered for treating both physical and mental ailments. Sales of medically prescribed psychoactive drugs now account for nearly one-third of domestic sales of drug manufacturers in the United States.[12]

Legal Use of Psychotropic Drugs

A fifth of all women interviewed in a national cross-sectional survey reported use of physician-prescribed tranquilizers or sedatives in the previous year, while one woman in twelve had used a stimulant drug such as amphetamines.[13] Women were more than twice as likely as men to report use of one or the other of these two classes of drugs in the year prior to the survey. For both men and women, stimulants are more often taken by the young and middle-aged, while tranquilizers and sedatives are more often taken by persons in the middle years or older. As might be expected, use of drugs is most frequent among those who report that they have experienced a high degree of psychological distress.

[12] See Charlotte Muller, "The Overmedicated Society," *Science,* Vol. 176 (May 5, 1972), pp. 488–492.

[13] See Glen D. Mellinger et al., "An Overview of Psychotherapeutic Drug Use in the United States," in Josephson and Carroll, *op. cit.,* pp. 333–336.

Among such persons, 25 percent of men and 35 percent of women had turned to prescription drugs in the year previous to the interview.

Amphetamines have been widely used by adults in countries such as Japan, Sweden, and the United States where there is a strong emphasis on productivity and personal achievement.[14] Usage is high among those in positions where they are consistently challenged to come up to greater and greater levels of productivity or creativity. While middle-class adults secure their amphetamines by prescription (and sometimes by injection) from physicians, young people seeking highs obtain their drugs through illegal channels. Before turning to consideration of the frequency of illegal use of these and other drugs, we should note that prescription drugs are most readily available to middle-class persons who have a relationship with a private physician. More generally available are a number of widely advertised "over-the-counter" drugs that purportedly help the nervous, tense, or apathetic person to get through the day without losing his temper or falling asleep. Such drug use is neither illegal nor devalued to any significant degree by most adults; it is extremely widespread.

Availability of psychoactive drugs to combat serious feelings of depression or to reduce tension and permit sleeping when one has been under extreme stress is clearly a significant medical and social resource. For some persons, however, the resource appears to become a habitual mode of coping, thus substituting for analysis of one's situation and a search for ways of changing the situation. Tranquilized mothers tend to be inattentive to the needs of their children, for example. We do not know how many users are "overly dependent" on psychoactive drugs; assessing over-dependence rests on value judgments. There are dangers, however, and they need to be explored further.[15]

Illegal Drug Use

Estimates of the extent of illegal drug use are crude at best. In general, a user becomes known to agencies that compile statistics on drug use and addiction only if he or she is arrested or seeks treatment. Most persons who are arrested for drug possession are users, but drug possession as such tells nothing about the extent of the individual's drug use.

In recent years, survey research has been utilized to assess the frequency of drug use in the population at large and among students and other institutional populations. Drug use varies with characteristics of personality, demography, social structure, and culture. Willingness to admit drug use to an unknown interviewer likewise varies. If most of his associates and the members of various groups to which he belongs are also drug users, and if this fact is widely

[14] See E. H. Ellingwood, "The Epidemiology of Stimulant Abuse" in Josephson and Carroll, *op. cit.*, pp. 303–329.

[15] For a discussion of some of the hazards implicit in widespread dependence on psychoactive drugs, see Henry L. Lennard et al., *Mystification and Drug Misuse* (San Francisco: Jossey-Bass, 1971).

known, an individual is much more likely to be willing to acknowledge his drug use than if very few of his associates are users. Even in the former instance, however, acknowledgment of drug use will certainly depend upon the kind of agency conducting the survey and the characteristics of the interviewer himself. In general, we would expect surveys to understate the amount of drug use except in groups where drug use is valued as a sign of sophistication and maturity (as would seem to be the case among some adolescents).

Estimates of the number of persons who have used or are using any given drug reveal little about the nature of drug use; they give no basis, for example, for determining the significance of drug use in the life of the individual. On the other hand, prevalence of use is clearly evidence of relative acceptability in any group and very frequent use is likely to connote preoccupation with a drug. Any adequate analysis of drug use as a social phenomenon requires knowledge of the distribution of various forms of drug use in different parts of the population. We shall therefore briefly review available statistical data before turning to a more detailed examination of patterns of drug use.

The prevalence of recreational drug use   Marijuana is undoubtedly the most frequently used illegal drug and has been for some time. Its use increased enormously in the late 1960s and early 1970s, especially among middle-class adolescents and young adults. For example, successive Gallup polls conducted between 1967 and 1974 indicated that the percentage of college students who had tried marijuana increased from 5 percent in 1967 to 55 percent in 1974. Other studies of marijuana use in high schools and colleges around the country show considerable regional variation but suggest that from one-half to three-fourths of students in many colleges have tried marijuana a few times and that most of those who have tried it continue to use it at least occasionally. In the general population, marijuana use is most prevalent among persons under 25 years of age and relatively infrequent in persons over 40. In 1972 the National Commission on Marihuana and Drug Abuse estimated that 24 million Americans had tried marijuana and that about 10 million were using it at least two or three times a month. Three percent of adults 18 and over and 5 percent of youth 12 to 17 were reported as using it every day.[16] Among younger persons, males and females are equally likely to smoke marijuana. Use is slightly higher among upper middle-class youth than among lower status youth.

No other illegal drug comes close to marijuana in prevalence of usage, though hashish is becoming increasingly popular in college populations in particular. The relative prevalence of various forms of drug use depends on a number of factors, including ease of obtaining supplies, cost, general life styles of the users, age, sex, socioeconomic status, and ethnic background. To provide a general overview of the prevalence of various forms of drug use, we have summarized in Table 3-1 results of three surveys conducted among student

---

[16] National Commission on Marihuana and Drug Abuse, *Marihuana: A Signal for Misunderstanding* (Washington, D.C.: Government Printing Office, 1972), p. 34.

populations in the early 1970s: the first is of a cross-section of public high school students in New York State (drawn from 18 high schools), the second a cross-sectional survey of American college students (involving a total of 48 colleges and universities), and the third a more recent longitudinal study of students in a large state university.[17] The figures given for the high school students and the cross-section of college students are for the total population, while those for the large state university show rates for the same students sampled at two points in time, early in the freshman year and midway through the junior year.

Table 3-1   Reported Prevalence of Recreational Use of Various Drugs in Several Major Surveys*

	New York State high schools 1971	Cross-section of American colleges 1971	Large state university Freshmen 1970–71	Large state university Juniors 1972–73
Marijuana	29	42	59	77
Hashish	21	28	a	a
Amphetamines	15	7[b]	13	30
Barbiturates, sedatives	12	22[b]	6	15
Tranquilizers	8	19[b]	a	a
LSD, other psychodelics	11	10	21	36
Opium	a	5	6	14
Heroin	3	1	—	2
Other opiates	a	a	2	7
Cocaine	4	4	2	19

Source: See text and footnote 17 for description of samples.
a Not separately ascertained.
b Includes both prescribed use and recreational use.

Drug use is obviously lower among freshmen than it is among juniors and seniors, both in high schools and in colleges. For example, in the New York State high school sample 17 percent of the freshmen and 41 percent of the seniors reported having used marijuana. The data reported in Table 3-1 relate to drug use up to the time of the survey; they thus markedly understate the level of drug use by the end of the high school or college years. The large state university for which drug use is reported is one that has been in the front ranks of student activism and undoubtedly has long had rates of drug use higher than most other schools. It may perhaps approach the ceiling for expected prevalence of various forms of drug experimentation.

Several studies, among them the college study represented in Table 3-1,

[17] The data on high school students have been derived from Denise Kandel et al., "The Epidemiology of Drug Use in Rates of Use," *American Journal of Public Health* (January 1976). The data from the national survey of colleges are reported in W. E. Groves, "Patterns of College Student Drug Use and Life Styles," in Josephson and Carroll, *op. cit.*, p. 243. The data from the large state university study are reported in Susan Davidson et al., "Changing Patterns of Drug Use Among University Men," (Berkeley: Institute for Research in Social Behavior, December 1974).

have followed the same group of students over time. The probability of having ever tried a given drug obviously increases over time. Some who have tried a drug will continue at least occasional use and some will become regular users, but others will discontinue use. With alcohol and marijuana, the proportion who are current users at any given time tends to rise until well into the adult years, since the number of new recruits each year is greater than the number who discontinue. On the other hand, use of tobacco stabilizes much earlier, with as many users among college students discontinuing in a given year as there are new smokers in the same age group. Discontinuation of use also tends to be high for LSD and other hallucinogens, for amphetamines, and for barbiturate and sedative drugs, so that fewer of those who have ever tried the drug become regular, long-term users than is the case with alcohol and marijuana.

In general, the use of any drug for nonmedical reasons increases the likelihood of using other drugs. There is an even stronger tendency for those who use any *illegal* drug to use other illegal drugs. It has often been suggested that use of marijuana is a first step toward using heroin, and indeed, most heroin users have first used marijuana. But most marijuana users among high school and college students do not go on to use heroin. Morever, adolescent drug use tends to begin not with marijuana but with tobacco and alcohol. Those students who smoke cigarettes or drink alcoholic beverages are much more likely than nonsmokers and nondrinkers to use marijuana and other illegal drugs. There is a tendency for drug use to entail a progression of severity, from the most widely used legal drugs to the least widely used illegal drugs, cocaine and heroin.[18] If a person uses the latter drugs, he or she has probably used a wide variety of other legal and illegal drugs. Although use of marijuana is likely to have preceded use of hallucinogens or amphetamines as well as use of heroin, there are many individual and subcultural variations. For example, white youth who are heavy marijuana users are more likely to use hallucinogens or amphetamines; black youth are twice as likely to use cocaine or heroin.

The opiates and cocaine   Because of the problems attendant on their use, the opiates and cocaine require special discussion. Neither is widely used in the student populations reported on in Table 3-1, but their use among students in some slum schools is appreciable. In general, students who report having tried either drug do not persist in doing so, but cocaine use appears to be very much on the increase in some schools and may come to constitute a severe problem if this trend continues.

The most frequent form of opiate use, intravenous injection of heroin, is most heavily concentrated in slum areas of the largest metropolitan centers. Roughly 40 percent of the nation's heroin addicts are believed to live in New York City. Estimates of the size of the addict population are derived in large

---

[18] See Eric Single et al., "Patterns of Multiple Drug Use in High School," *Journal of Health and Social Behavior,* Vol. 15, No. 4 (December 1974).

part from "registers" or lists of known addicts that are maintained by a number of cities and states and by the Federal Bureau of Narcotics and Dangerous Drugs. Registers do not permit an accurate estimate of the number of current addicts, since they are subject to several forms of error and bias. On the one hand, names of individuals who cease to use narcotics are not removed, and duplication occurs from one register to another. On the other hand, persons who are addicted are not listed on a register unless they have been arrested or treated for opiate use. But an attempt can be made to assess the effects of these sources of error, using other fragmentary evidence, and rough estimates can be achieved.

A recent estimate puts the number of addicts in New York City at about 150,000 and the number in the nation as a whole at about 375,000.[19] This is substantially higher than the estimated number of addicts a decade ago, but we cannot be certain whether the higher estimate derives from more adequate data or from a real increase.

When we consider that there are an estimated 5 million alcoholics in the United States (see Chapter 4), the prevalence of heroin addiction is not great. On the other hand, no other Western nation has anywhere near this number of addicts. Despite an eightfold increase in heroin addiction in Great Britain during the late 1960s, the number of addicts there in the early 1970s has almost certainly not exceeded 4 thousand, and recent reports suggest that the number is again declining.

Heroin users in the United States tend to be young, are more often male than female (though rates of addiction for women have gone up faster than those for men in the past decade), and reside mostly in the areas of New York and other metropolitan centers where various forms of crime and other social problems are most prevalent, areas inhabited by the poorest and most disadvantaged groups in the population.

EXPLANATIONS OF DRUG USE

How does one explain the high prevalence of drug use in American society at the present time? One view, now largely discredited, is that smugglers and peddlers of drugs, out to make fortunes at the expense of ruined lives, push drugs upon young, innocent, and weak members of the larger society. Another is that persons who are maladjusted or unable to face up to the realities of life seek escape in drug use. A third view, more widely accepted by social scientists, is that various forms of drug use are patterns of learned behavior that are congenial to people sharing certain values and views of society and of themselves; in this view, group memberships and identifications are more important as explanations of drug use than personality factors or the mere availability of drugs.

---

[19] W. H. McGlothlin, et al., "Alternative Approaches to Opiate Addiction Control: Costs, Benefits and Potential" (Washington, D.C.: U.S. Department of Justice, 1972).

Let us first emphasize a point made previously: the term "drug use" stands for many different behaviors. Drug use is overwhelmingly *social* behavior; it is a group activity. Like any other form of social behavior, drug use means different things to different individuals. Its functions for the individual depend upon both his personal history and the way that drug use is defined behaviorally in those groups that mean most to him. Knowledge of such meanings is difficult to assess unless one can freely observe the drug user among his friends or at least come to know thoroughly how members of the group think and feel about drug use for themselves and their peers. Different drugs may be used, or the same drug may have very different meanings, in different social worlds. One frequently hears the term "the drug scene," but there are many drug scenes and they are played to different scenarios.

It may sometimes be more significant to ask why some persons do *not* use a drug than why others do. When use of a particular drug is strongly disapproved, the user is by definition of most members of the larger society a deviant, though he or she may not be a serious deviant within a given sociocultural milieu. When the drug is widely accepted, a user is seen as a relaxed person, a sophisticate, etc. The changing meaning of marijuana use in the past two decades is a good illustration of this.

In the early 1950s, the widespread use of marijuana in the street-corner society of adolescents living in urban slums was viewed with horror by many members of the middle class. Marijuana use was frequently associated with delinquency and with the general search for "kicks" on the part of minority youth deprived of opportunities for rewarding experience in conventional society. Moreover, there was in the same areas an epidemic of heroin use among adolescents and young adults, almost all of whom had been marijuana users previously. Marijuana was then seen as a step on the road to heroin.

As long as marijuana was markedly devalued and feared in conventional society, its use there was minimal. It was, however, tried by musicians, artists, and other *avant garde* groups who were less bound by conventional moral and social controls. Once it became apparent that marijuana did not produce the horrible consequences ascribed to it, its use spread, especially among younger persons of an inquiring mind. As marijuana use became much more popular, the personal and social correlates of marijuana use changed very quickly. Now, in the 1970s, it appears that marijuana use is somewhat more prevalent among children of upper-middle-class parents than among the deprived groups in which it was used two decades ago.

We may note that where social correlates change, psychological correlates are also likely to change. That is, when a drug is strongly devalued, those who use it are likely to belong to very unconventional groups or to have personal problems that are quite different from those of their peers. As use becomes more widely accepted, the cost to one's reputation of experimenting with a drug is cut down. Traditional norms against it are eroded or undermined. Ultimately, behavior once deemed deviant can become not only accepted but even expected within relatively conventional circles.

Use of recreational drugs is almost always part of a complex of attitudes, personal preferences, and practices that characterize a type of life style or a distinctive subculture. Marijuana use tends to be an important element of life styles in several quite different subcultures, while heroin use appears to constitute the basis for a much more sharply delimited subculture. Before examining the specific features of these life styles and subcultures, it will be useful to consider the larger social context within which they are embedded.

Changing Values, Peer Relations, and Drug Use

The great increase in recreational drug use by young people is obviously part of a much broader trend in recent social change. Whether or not it is valid to talk of a "generation gap," there has been a significant disjunction between certain of the values held by older members of our society and their adolescent offspring. There is an indication that this disjunction is becoming less acute in the 1970s than it was in the 1960s. This is not so much because the young have listened more intently to their elders as because children have been teaching their parents that they had been misinformed or had limited perspectives on a number of topics.

Within American society the role of the adolescent has been ill-defined, beyond the expectation of remaining a student. An "adolescent society" or youth culture has come into being, based upon student status and a reordering of priorities regarding a number of the norms and values of the dominant adult culture. Among the major emphases of this adolescent society are a strong orientation to other members of one's age group, the concentration of intimate psychic bonds among one's peers, a press toward autonomy from adult authority, concern for the underdog, and an interest in change from the status quo.[20] Social controls enforced within the peer group tend to be far more effective than social controls that emanate from the older members of the society.

Several recent studies have indicated that continuities in value transmission from one generation to the next appear to be less dependent on direct adolescent-parent resemblance in values than upon the sharing of more general perspectives by virtue of early socialization, the mass media, peer interaction, and shared reference groups. Attitudes toward drug use and actual use among youth are far more strongly influenced by the beliefs and practices of intimate friends than by parental beliefs and practices. In a study of high school students that involved not only a random sample of students but also their best friends and their parents, Kandel found that the attitudes and drug use of best friends were highly similar. Indeed, in no other respects except age, sex, and race did best friends resemble one another so closely as in illegal drug use.[21] Use of alcohol and psychoactive drugs on the part of parents increases the likelihood that an adolescent will use marijuana *if his or her friends do,* but does not affect the probability of the adolescent's using if friends do *not* use.

Drug use is learned with and from one's friends just as any other interest of activity is learned. To the degree that he or she has fears about the possible consequences of drug use, the prospective user will require reassurance and evidence from others that dangers have been exaggerated. As Howard Becker noted at a time when marijuana use was relatively infrequent and strongly devalued in conventional society, becoming a regular marijuana user entailed learning to disengage oneself from the controls exerted by conventional beliefs and attitudes as well as learning the proper circumstances, techniques, and labeling of effects to insure pleasure from the experience of smoking.[22]

Marijuana use is now so widespread and has received so much publicity that much of the mythology that previously served to deter persons from trying a "joint" has been dispelled. Nevertheless, becoming a regular marijuana user still entails learning to enjoy the drug, to arrange for supplies, and the like. Becker noted that the novice does not ordinarily get high the first time he smokes marijuana. To get maximum effect, one must first learn to inhale deeply and hold the smoke in his lungs long enough to allow for absorption of the drug into the blood stream. Even with training in the technique of inhaling, one must learn to recognize and label the effects, which are quite subtle.

[20] See *Youth: Transition to Adulthood,* Report of the Panel on Youth of the President's Science Advisory Committee (Chicago: University of Chicago Press, 1974).

[21] See Denise Kandel, "Adolescent Marihuana Use: Role of Parents and Peers," *Science,* Vol. 181 (September 14, 1973), pp. 1067–1070. The importance of peer relations is also documented in Bruce D. Johnson, *Marihuana Users and Drug Subcultures* (New York: Wiley, 1973).

[22] Howard S. Becker, "Becoming a Marihuana User," *American Journal of Sociology,* Vol. 59 (November 1953), pp. 235–242. See also "Marihuana Use and Social Control," *Social Problems,* Vol. 3 (July 1955), pp. 35–44. Both papers are contained in Becker's book, *Outsiders* (New York: Free Press, 1963).

As we have noted, marijuana is most often first experienced by an individual because it has been made available either by a close friend or, in a group setting, by a member who has access to a source of supply. In fact, the use of marijuana tends at first to be primarily a function of availability; the occasional user can become a regular user only by finding a stable source. He must get to know sellers, but this is not usually difficult, since many regular users become sellers at one time or another.

People who find pleasure in smoking marijuana at social occasions have an added bond, and those who are uncomfortable in such situations tend to steer clear of them. Whether or not one uses a wide variety of other drugs along with marijuana is likely to depend both upon personality and upon the dominant values, interest, and activities of the group in which one has his primary identification.[23] The greater the proportion of a person's friends who are regular marijuana smokers, the greater is the likelihood that he or she smokes marijuana frequently and has tried drugs other than marijuana.

Goode found the relationship between levels of use and whether or not one has bought or sold marijuana to be nicely in accord with Becker's earlier formulation. The great majority of those who used marijuana more than once a month had bought marijuana, but less than one-third of occasional users had purchased their marijuana directly. Moreover, among those who smoked several times a week, the vast majority had themselves dealt in marijuana. Those who had bought or sold marijuana were very likely to have tried a number of other drugs. Persons assimilated to groups in which regular drug use is the rule are by that assimilation inducted into practices that sustain and enlarge their use of drugs.

Drug Use, Life Styles, and Subcultural Patterns

Closely linked with peer relationships are group memberships and attitudes toward conventional norms. Surveys of college populations reveal that almost all forms of drug usage are lowest in religiously controlled institutions that are not highly selective of their student bodies. In general, drug users tend to be less religious, more radical politically, more likely to engage in premarital sex, and more disapproving of the distribution and use of power in American society and in our international dealings than are their nondrug-using age mates. As Suchman and others have noted, the regular marijuana user tends to favor a "hang-loose" ethic and to reject as "uptight" the traditional Protestant ethic.[24]

In the hippie movement of the 1960s, drug use symbolized the rejection of

---

[23] This has been dramatically documented by Erich Goode, "Multiple Drug Use among Marijuana Smokers," *Social Problems,* Vol. 17 (Summers 1969), pp. 48–64.

[24] See Edward A. Suchman, "The Hang-Loose Ethic and the Spirit of Drug Use," *Journal of Health and Social Behavior,* Vol. 9 (June 1968), and Charles W. Thomas et al. "Student Drug Use: A Re-examination of the Hang-Loose Ethic," *Journal of Health and Social Behavior,* Vol. 16 (March 1975).

many of the values of the larger society. Use of marijuana and psychedelics in the search for subjective experience served as a highly visible expression of counter-cultural values. The hippie movement no longer exists as such, but the counter-cultural themes are widely in evidence not only in communes and literature, but in enclaves within many institutions.

While students with a strong counter-cultural orientation are more likely to be drug users than are their peers, it would hardly be appropriate to characterize most marijuana users in high school and college populations as being strongly counter-culture. As the proportion of users has increased, it would appear that peer orientations and personal tastes are the primary determinants of whether a student uses marijuana or not. *How much* he or she uses is strongly tied to life style, subculture, and personality.

In the street-corner society of the urban slums, marijuana and sometimes heroin and other drugs are incorporated into peer-group activity that occasionally involves delinquency but is especially directed towards the search for and the exploitation of "kicks." The norms and values of street-corner society tend to be inconsistent with those of the larger society. Yet they are norms and values; consequently, they constrain or encourage certain types of behavior, help bind the peer group together, and enhance feelings of adequacy and power in the face of dismal living conditions and family relationships.

In a group seeking kicks, prestige comes from willingness to experiment and let oneself go, whether in delinquent acts, in the use of intoxicants or stimulants, or in other forms of behavior that are intrinsically exhilarating, involve an element of risk, or defy convention and conformity.[25] In street-corner society the pursuit of kicks is much more widespread than the use of narcotics. Even in the areas of highest drug use, it appears that only a minority of young people experiment with heroin or other opiates, though most use marijuana. In general, youth growing up in these areas learn both the norms and the values of street-corner society and those of the conventional society. Patterns of association and the extent to which the traditional norms turn out to have payoff value will determine to a large extent whether or not a given youth participates in the subculture of heroin use.

Even within street-corner society, the largest number of marijuana users limit their smoking to occasions when it enhances sociability, music, or sex. "Mellow dudes" do not maintain large supplies of marijuana or deal in it. Grass is a fine addition to partying but not an end in itself. More preoccupied with marijuana are the "pot-heads" whose lives rotate around the drug. But mellow dudes and pot-heads both seek to be "cool"; in this they differ sharply from the "rowdy dudes," whose drug use is indiscriminate. The rowdy dudes are likely to use alcohol heavily and turn to heroin much more readily than do their peers.

[25] See Harold Finestone, "Cats, Kicks, and Color," *Social Problems,* Vol. 5 (July 1957), pp. 3–13. For a more recent but consonant description, see Harvey W. Feldman, "Ideological Supports to Becoming and Remaining a Heroin Addict," *Health and Social Behavior,* Vol. 9 (June 1968), pp. 131–139.

In college drug scenes, similar types are found, though drug orientations are less colorfully labeled. Carey contrasts the experimenters, who tried marijuana but did not proceed to regular use; the recreational users, who find marijuana a pleasant adjunct to many social situations but who use it with discretion and are concerned not to become overly dependent on it; and the "heads," whose use is more open, frequent, and central to their life styles.[26] Very similar is Keniston's characterization of "tasters," "seekers," and "heads" among college users.[27] Keniston's seekers are occasional users who "seek in drug use some way of intensifying experience, expanding awareness, breaking out of deadness and flatness or overcoming depression." The heads, whether pot-heads or acid-heads, are the committed users, who share the "turned-on" ideology of the hippie subculture even though they retain at least some relationship to the campus community.

Recreational users or seekers in the college scene are often average or better-than-average students, intellectually curious, and not vocationally oriented in their studies. They are more often found among students in the humanities and social sciences than among students in the "hard" sciences or in professional schools. They often have good work habits and a genuine interest in academic work but are not overly grade conscious. They may or may not be alienated from American society, but most are critical of the materialistic, militaristic, and racist tendencies they see in American life.

Heads, on the other hand, tend to be disengaged from conventional ties and much more sharply alienated from most of the dominant values in American society. Perhaps most alienated are those heads who become members of hippie enclaves or communes. Here one's whole way of life expresses estrangement from the institutions and fashions of conventional society. Shoulder-length hair and flowing beards for men, striking clothes (most of which may be shared communally), and manifest contempt for amenities and material comforts serve both as disclaimers of membership in the larger society and as elements in a new identity.[28]

The characterization of types is more defensible as a descriptive aid than as a model of reality. While it is useful to know what distinctions are being made within groups of drug users themselves, most individuals do not conform to the stereotypes. Tasters may become seekers and seekers may become heads. And even long-term heads may decide that the drug scene is a bad trip. In addition to the flux across type lines, there is considerable variation in the combination of backgrounds, motives, and activities of users, as well as in the mixture of drugs used. Unhappy, unstable, and amoral individuals tend to gravitate into drug scenes. One cannot explain most drug use on the basis of

---

[26] James J. Carey, *The College Drug Scene* (Englewood Cliffs, N.J.: Prentice-Hall, 1968).
[27] Kenneth Keniston, "Heads and Seekers: Drugs on Campus, Counter Cultures and American Society," *The American Scholar*, Vol. 38 (Winter 1968–69), p. 100.
[28] This is not to suggest that such attributes are all there is (or once was) to hippie life. For a description of positive themes in the hippie way of life, see Fred Davis, "Why All of Us May be Hippies Someday," *Trans-action*, Vol. 5 (December 1967), pp. 10–18.

motives, but it would be absurd to suggest that the personality of the user is irrelevant to an understanding of his use of drugs.

Personality Characteristics and Drug Use

Psychiatrists who have specialized in the treatment of drug addicts are in substantial agreement that most opiate addicts are not "normal" personalities. Few would make the same assertion about recreational drug users. Social scientists are more inclined to hold the view that both addicts and nonaddicted drug users are products of particular types of environments and occupants of particular social roles—that is, that the patterns of behavior and attitude characteristic of drug subcultures are learned by a high proportion of persons who share a given milieu. They are learned from role models, just as skills in sports are learned from older youth by boys growing up in middle-class suburbs.

There is not necessarily any conflict between the view of the addict as a deviant personality and the view of the addict as a social type. Undoubtedly the addiction of some persons is to be understood primarily as the expression of personal unhappiness or even severe psychopathology. The addiction of others has come about as a result of subjection to environmental pressures too strong to resist—as is the case, for example, with children whose older siblings or peers made drugs available to them. But personality is not independent of environmental influences, and, by and large, the influences that permit heroin to be available to a teen-ager and permit a high proportion of adolescents to become members of street-corner society also create psychological needs and vulnerabilities that enhance the value of narcotics to the individual.

Psychopathology is both more frequent and more severe among young drug users than among nonusers growing up in the same environment. Chein and his associates provide convincing evidence that the personality attributes of young male heroin users are not merely a reflection of their deviance and social role but derive from family experiences that have been found generally to contribute to the development of psychopathology. As compared with nonusers from the same neighborhoods, drug users far more often came from homes characterized by the absence of a positive relationship between the boy and an adult male role model.[29]

We may say, then, that among the younger group of addicts whose early life was spent in the milieu of drug use, family relationships, psychodynamics, and prevailing social attitudes all played a part in leading the adolescent or young adult to experimentation with drugs and incorporation into the culture of narcotics use.

Marijuana users and users of what have come to be called "soft" (nonaddicting) drugs do not present a comparable picture of psychopathology. Nevertheless, many heavy users began to experiment with drugs during periods of stress or upset that made them less responsive to relationships and controls that

[29] Isidor Chein et al., *The Road to H* (New York: Basic Books, 1964), pp. 273–274.

had previously been influential. Thus in New York, among members of the East Village drug scene who were asked about their life circumstances at the time they began to use drugs, nearly half reported emotional problems, and almost as many reported that they were in conflict with their families (41%) or felt at odds with society (38%).[30] Detachment from society, purposelessness, and lack of direction in life were almost universally felt in substantial degrees in this group. It would appear, then, that persons who become most fully committed to heavy use of any sort are likely to have had personal problems that led them to be deeply alienated and to find in drugs a sense of solidarity with others.

Personality needs and life problems can also be a basis for *giving up* drug use. Many heavy users decide, after a time, that drugs are unduly complicating their lives. Some give up drugs for the same social reasons that led to turning on in the first place. That is, they become attached to new groups where drug use is not in vogue, or they fall in love with someone who has strong feelings against drug use. Others find that life crises are more difficult to handle with drugs than without them. To date, we have just the beginnings of research on this topic, but much more attention needs to be addressed to it. It is, of course, easiest for the occasional or recreational user to turn his back on drugs. For "heads" to do so, particularly when their drug use has been part of a quest for meaning, there must typically be both a crisis that precipitates the decision and an alternative code for governing their lives.[31]

Opiate Addiction as a Special Problem

Opium is an inexpensive drug on the world market and its derivative forms are cheaply produced. Of those forms, heroin, with its high potency and ease of dilution with lactose (sugar of milk) for injection, has long been regarded as the ideal opiate for illicit use. Once heroin was outlawed, however, its cost skyrocketed. The penalties for dealing made for an enormous mark-up in the price from producer to smuggler to dealer to peddler. As a consequence, only the wealthy can sustain a heroin addiction without recourse to crime.

The opiates, as we noted earlier, are great relaxants, sleep inducers, and pain killers. When Marx referred to religion as "the opiate of the masses" he had in mind the action of opiates that makes one accept one's situation, even if it is objectively miserable. The opiates are an escape—as long as one can maintain a sufficient level of dosage. Tolerance does not increase indefinitely, but an addict requires, to prevent withdrawal, sufficient heroin to kill a person who has not been using the drug. Yet even this amount of heroin will not produce the high that a small amount originally produced.

[30] Douglas Holmes, "Selected Characteristics of 'Hippies' in New York City: An Overview," paper presented at the Conference on Drug Use and Drug Subcultures, Asilomar, California, February 12, 1970.

[31] Patrick Biernacki and Fred Davis, "Turning Off: A Study of Ex-Marihuana Users," paper presented at the Conference on Drug Use and Drug Subcultures, Asilomar, California, February 12, 1970.

To achieve a real high, therefore, the addict needs a very large amount of heroin. Given that large dosage, he or she can experience not only the "bang" that is sought but a period of relaxation and relief from other concerns. Addiction requires moving back and forth between scheming to get money for drugs and being "on the nod," not driven by inner tensions.

Not everyone who experiments with heroin becomes addicted. Since most of those who try it realize that addiction requires substantial regular use, a number remain occasional users or "chippers" for considerable periods of time. They may hold down use to weekends or special occasions. At some point, however, the appeal of the drug will usually become so strong that frequency of use is increased and the individual becomes dependent. In the early period of heavy use, the addict is frequently so enthusiastic that he or she tries to recruit others to use. In areas where heroin use has not hitherto been widespread, it frequently develops that a small number of enthusiastic new addicts recruit enough of their peers to lead to a veritable epidemic of heroin use.[32]

Recent research reveals, however, that even after physical dependency occurs, there are real differences among the life styles of heroin addicts. Addicts know that the more they use, the more they will need merely to feel normal. Therefore each one potentially faces a policy decision: whether to go for euphoria every time or at least every day, or to hold down use to the level needed to ward off the discomforts of abstinence and seek a euphoric "bang" only part of the time, perhaps on weekends. McAuliffe and Gordon have characterized as "hard-core addicts" those who go for a high every day.[33] These addicts spend more per week for drugs (averaging $349), are more likely to be dealers themselves, and tend to be engaged almost exclusively in illegal activities to make money. "Weekenders," addicts who seek euphoria only on special occasions (even though they must have heroin every day to ward off abstinence distress) are more likely to be committed to maintaining relationships with conventional society. Half of McAuliffe and Gordon's sample held jobs. Weekenders spend substantially less for heroin than hard-core addicts (averaging $227 per week) and seem also to rely more often on methadone for avoiding withdrawal. Methadone does not produce euphoria but wards off abstinence distress and is more readily available both in treatment programs and on the black market.

In attempting to estimate the total costs of opium addiction to the society, McGlothlin and his associates estimated the value of property stolen by addicts to finance drug purchases at close to 3 billion dollars.[34] Heroin addiction is undoubtedly a major factor in various forms of theft. We may note, however, that contrary to popular belief, violent offenses against the person are much

---

[32] The dynamics of such an epidemic in England are described by R. de Alarcon, "The Spread of Heroin Abuse in the Community," *Bulletin on Narcotics,* Vol. 21, No. 3 (1969).

[33] See William E. McAuliffe and R. A. Gordon, "A Test of Lindesmith's Theory of Addiction: The Frequency of Euphoria Among Long Term Addicts," *American Journal of Sociology,* Vol. 79 (January 1974), pp. 795–840.

[34] McGlothin et al., *op. cit.*

less frequent among addicts than among other criminal offenders. Further, studies of the behavior of adolescent gangs in which a substantial number of members begin to use heroin reveals a corresponding decrease in such activity as gang fights and assaults.

Intravenous "mainlining" of heroin greatly increases euphoria and provides a kind of psychological reinforcement to the drug-taking addict that is peculiarly difficult to overcome. There has been a widespread belief, even among addicts, that "once a junkie, always a junkie." There is abundant evidence that this is another drug myth, but it dies hard. It is true that most addicts who go through detoxification programs and those who have gone to federal narcotics hospitals or who have been off heroin by virtue of imprisonment revert to the use of drugs once they are returned to the community. Almost always they are returned to the setting in which they became addicted and they seldom receive supervision or help. Nevertheless, when former addicts are followed up for a period of a decade or more, a significant proportion of them manage to remain abstinent.[35]

One aspect of heroin addiction that must be mentioned is the high mortality of addicts. In Vaillant's 12-year follow-up of an addict group, the number who had died was five times the number expected for that age group. Deaths due to overdose are frequent. In New York City alone, drug overdose deaths were running roughly 80 per month during 1970, prior to major new efforts to curtail the drug traffic. More recently, uninformed young addicts have injected large quantities of methadone in order to seek a high, and an increasing number of deaths from this drug have been reported. Hepatitis is, of course, a frequent disease among addicts who use the intravenous technique (as it is among users of "speed").

The costs of opium addiction to the addict are totally different from those of the moderate use of recreational drugs. Many addicts experience extreme debilitation due to poor nutrition and self-neglect. While a small proportion of addicts manage to maintain normal functioning and to look after themselves while remaining addicted, the weight of evidence indicates that most become ineffective performers.

PUBLIC POLICY AND DRUGS

In the Introduction to its second report, *Drug Use in America: Problem in Perspective*, the National Commission on Marihuana and Drug Abuse likened its experiences to those of Alice in Wonderland, in that:

> our two year examination of drug use, misuse and "abuse" has given us a constantly reinforced perception that all is not as it seems and that beliefs and realities

---

[35] See George E. Vaillant, "Twelve Year Follow-Up of New York Narcotic Addicts: II, The Natural History of a Chronic Disease," *New England Journal of Medicine*, Vol. 275 (December 8, 1966), pp. 1282–1288.

are not always equal. All too often, familiar guideposts and landmarks, which we assumed could give us direction and purpose, faded, changed shape or simply disappeared when carefully scrutinized. All too often, plans and policies conceived in good will and high hopes had unanticipated negative aspects which created as many problems as they did solutions.[36]

For more than half a century our public policy has been to stamp out the traffic in drugs and to imprison not only drug smugglers and peddlers but users as well. The addict has been maligned as a matter of policy by federal officials. Until recently, expenditures to try to help addicts have been miniscule in comparison with expenditures to enforce drug laws and keep violators in prison. Until recently there has been little effort to understand the difference between recreational drug use and opiate use. Our laws—federal, state, and local—have been an ill-conceived patchwork based on myths that came to be accepted as truth. Their premises have been faulty—medically, psychologically, and sociologically. Before considering alternative perspectives, it may be useful to review briefly the history of attempts to deal with the drug problem in the United States.

Federal Legislation on Drug Abuse

Federal legislation restricting the availability of opiates in the United States began with the Harrison Act in 1914. It provided for close control of the distribution of addicting drugs and prohibited possession except for "legitimate medical purposes." The mechanism used was registration and taxation; hence enforcement was lodged in the Treasury Department.

Prior to passage of the Harrison Act, the 200,000 or more persons addicted to opiates could apply to any member of the medical profession for help in cutting down their drug use, or they could purchase drugs directly from any supplier at moderate prices. The Act cut off sources of drug supply and left the question of medical dosage open to legal interpretation. Before the Supreme Court could render a judgment on the scope of the Act, the officials of the Narcotics Division of the Treasury Department declared that doctors were no longer free to administer opiates to addicted persons. Addicts were characterized by federal officials as moral degenerates and criminals who should be locked up. Although the Supreme Court in 1925 rejected the interpretation that physicians were prohibited by the Harrison Act from treating addicts by prescribing drugs, the medical profession had by this time abandoned the field to the illicit drug peddler.

In 1937, marijuana was added to the list of drugs controlled under the Harrison Act. States were urged to pass similar legislation and all of them subsequently did, often without any more adequate knowledge of what they

---

[36] National Commission on Marihuana and Drug Abuse, *Drug Use in America: Problem in Perspective* (Washington, D.C.: Government Printing Office, 1973), p. 1.

were legislating against than the assertions of personnel from the Federal Bureau of Narcotics. Marijuana was characterized as leading inevitably to moral degeneracy; legislators hurried to express their aversion to degeneracy by increasing penalties for those found to have marijuana in their possession as well as for those trafficking in it.

In the 1960s it became apparent that many drugs other than marijuana and heroin were being obtained and used without prescription, especially by young people. Congress reacted by passing new laws aimed at preventing the abuse of stimulant and depressant drugs. This time responsibility was delegated to the Federal Drug Administration, for many of the drugs in question were widely used pharmaceuticals. In recognition of the need for medical and professional judgment, Congress left to the head of the FDA the designation of specific drugs to be controlled. Subsequently, LSD and other psychedelic drugs were readily brought under control without additional legislation. For the first time, those charged with doing something about problems of drug abuse in the United States had an interest in understanding the nature of the problem and not merely in confiscating illegal drugs.

Within a few years, however, the Bureau of Dangerous Drugs within the FDA and the Bureau of Narcotics within the Department of the Treasury were merged and lodged in the Department of Justice. In the Nixon administration, under Attorney General Mitchell, new comprehensive legislation was introduced dealing with addictive and dangerous drugs. It harkened back to the punitive approach almost exclusively; no provision was made for treatment of drug offenders but only for their imprisonment. Enforcement officials were given extraordinary power to violate civil rights. Concerted opposition to the Nixon administration's proposed law brought about a number of significant modifications, among them provision for federally supported community treatment facilities and for continuing research on a much larger scale than hitherto. Subsequently the National Institute of Drug Abuse was established within the Department of HEW, thereby guarding against total domination of the program by the perspective of law enforcement personnel.

The new law also provided for the establishment of the National Commission on Marihuana and Drug Use, made up equally of experts in drug research and members of the Congress. The publication of the first of the Commission's reports, issued in 1972, may have marked the end of the punitive approach, at least so far as marijuana is concerned. While the Commission opposed the legalization of marijuana, it strongly recommended that possession of marijuana for personal use no longer be a basis for arrest.

Where heroin is concerned, our federal laws have changed little in recent years, except to provide assistance to the states and funding for research and experimental control programs. Concern with the level of heroin addiction in New York State led to even more severe penalties for drug dealing there. At the same time, several states, among them New York and California, which together contain more than half the nation's addicts, have developed alternatives to imprisonment for the addict who is not a major dealer. Before turning to consideration of these alternatives, we might note some of the consequences of the punitive approach.

Consequences of the Punitive Approach

During the period when laws against drug use multiplied and penalties became more severe, drug use increased enormously. Increased funding of law-enforcement units concentrating on drug offenses had little effect on the drug traffic, but an enormous effect on the number of addict prisoners.

More arrests and fewer convictions   The decade of the 1950s saw the piling up of drug offenders in federal prisons. Between 1950 and the early 1960s, the number and proportion of drug offenders in such prisons had more than doubled and the average length of sentences served by these prisoners increased roughly fourfold. Addicts received no treatment in federal or state prisons. They were discharged to the settings and circumstances in which their drug use had been learned and sustained. For the most part they received no help in finding jobs and no supervision after release. Those who had previously had little contact with crime had in prison received a thorough orientation to the perspectives of professional criminals. Even if they were not tempted to become criminals themselves, they emerged from prison bitter and stigmatized. The consequences for marijuana users were even more dismal, for few of them had been involved in criminal acts apart from their use of marijuana. We earlier noted the great increase in marijuana use in school and college populations between the mid-1960s and the early 1970s. Figure 3-1 documents the corresponding increase in the number of arrests for marijuana possession in this period, as derived from the first report of the National Commission on Marihuana and Drug Abuse. In just five years, the number of arrests at the state level went from under 19,000 to nearly 190,000. During this period, marijuana possession was a felony in a great majority of states, and in some of them even a first offense could lead to life imprisonment. As the number of arrests increased, it became obvious to more and more judges and juries that the state laws made no sense. Convictions dropped markedly, especially in states where prison sentences were mandatory.

Drug laws and the creation of victims   Laws against drug use, like laws pertaining to sexual relations between consenting adults, are designed not so much to protect persons against victimization by other persons as to enforce morality. If the moral norms underlying a law are widely shared, enforcement of the law is likely to be much more even than if there exists wide divergency in acceptance of the norms within the larger society. To the extent that a norm has relatively little force apart from its legal embodiment—as in the case of the current legal prohibition of marijuana—enforcement of the law will depend on

Figure 3-1 State and Federal Marijuana Arrests, 1965–1970

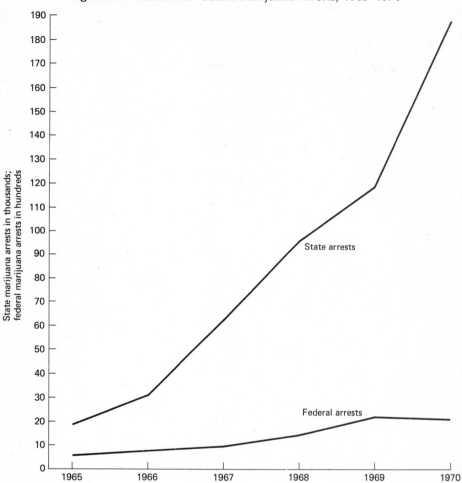

Source: Data compiled from National Commission on Marihuana and Drug Abuse, *Marihuana: A Signal of Misunderstanding* (Washington, D.C.: Government Printing Office, 1972), pp. 106–107.

contingencies having little to do with the specific norm violation. A marijuana user is likely to be arrested because of other attributes or characteristics that call him or her to the attention of police, such as race, appearance, disrespectful behavior toward the police, and powerlessness. Thus the laws serve not so much to control marijuana use as to create victims of law enforcement.[37]

[37] This problem is nicely described by Erich Goode, "Notes on the Enforcement of Moral Crimes," in H. A. Farberman and E. Goode (eds.), *Social Reality* (Englewood Cliffs, N.J.: Prentice·Hall, 1973), pp. 254–264.

Towards a Rational Policy on Drugs

A rational public policy relating to the use of drugs in American society requires a systematic analysis of the risks and consequences of taking any particular drug at specified levels and frequency of dosage and of the probable risks and consequences of specific laws and control activities. With the appointment of the National Commission on Marihuana and Drug Abuse and the establishment of broadly based research programs through the National Institute of Drug Abuse, we are at least moving toward basing national policy on rational grounds rather than on fear and ignorance.

There are a number of questions that must be answered or at least addressed before attempting to outlaw any drug that is used for its psychological effects:

1. What are the dangers or potential consequences of widespread occasional use of a particular drug? How likely are occasional users to become heavy users? What are the consequences of heavy, prolonged use?

2. How can seriously detrimental drug consequences best be avoided? How feasible is it to prohibit completely the use of a particular substance? What are the costs of enforcing such prohibition, relative to the costs of other possible forms of regulation? If criminal penalties are attached to drug possession, how many persons would be subject to prosecution if the laws were fully enforced? Would the weight of legislation and enforcement fall unevenly on certain sectors of the population who are not otherwise involved in law violation? Would other forms of regulation, such as licensing of sources of supply at free market prices, offer a measure of control at lesser cost in dollars and in human terms?

3. What should be the approach to public education about drugs? Can educational programs provide guidance in appropriate use of various drugs and thereby cut down the frequency of inappropriate use? How can knowledge of the real dangers inherent in the use of certain drugs be imparted without being discounted because of the myths previously purveyed in much public education?

4. How can persons now heavily dependent on drug use be assisted to learn more effective modes of coping? In the case of addicted individuals, what are the pros and cons of providing drugs at cost in order to sustain the addict in the community without recourse to crime? How do social, cultural, and personality attributes of the addict influence the effectiveness of various forms of treatment or assistance?

5. When drug use is closely tied with other problem behaviors or is primarily a symptom of serious problems in the lives of individuals or of groups within the society, what more basic reforms or programs might serve to eliminate or mitigate the primary underlying problems?

Space does not permit more than cursory comment on some of the issues of drug policy and control. There are some drugs that possess obvious dangers if widely available. Tobacco and alcohol are among them. We are apparently committed to allowing individual choice in the use of these drugs not only to adults but even to young adolescents. There is little attempt to prevent cigarette smoking by high school students, and in many states alcoholic beverages are readily available as well.

The danger of addiction to opiates and its consequences suggest that control of such drugs is highly desirable. This is true of many drugs that can be secured legally only through prescription. Heavy expenditures for drug-control enforcement measures have not markedly reduced the availability of heroin to street addicts except for relatively short periods. What alternatives exist?

In England, heroin addiction has been a much less serious problem, for a variety of reasons. Undoubtedly the primary reasons lie in the cultural values and social controls of British society. But another important reason is that there has been no real basis for a major illegal traffic in heroin. An addict in England can be prescribed heroin by a physician, thereby avoiding the need to steal the price of illegal heroin.[38] In the late 1960s some physicians were careless in their prescribing, and the British have turned to clinics for meeting the needs of addicts. It appears that the "epidemic" of the late 1960s has abated without giving rise to large-scale smuggling of heroin.

Within the United States a number of facilities and programs have been developed in recent years to aid the opiate addict: detoxification programs, designed to reduce tolerance gradually and return the addict to a drug-free state without undue suffering; methadone maintenance programs, designed to keep the addict functioning in the community without having to steal for heroin; civil commitment programs that offer treatment during incarceration; and therapeutic communities, such as Synanon. Table 3-2 indicates the esti-

Table 3–2   Estimated Status of the Population of Opiate Addicts, December 1971

	Number of Addicts	Percent
Total	375,000	100
Methadone maintenance	40,000	11
Therapeutic communities	8,000	2
Detoxification (in-patient)	2,500	1
Civil commitment (nonmethadone)	18,400	5
Antagonist programs	200	
In prisons, jails	37,500	10
On the street	268,400	72
Temporarily abstinent 40,000		
Addicted 228,400		

Source: Adapted from W. H. McGlothlin et al., "Alternative Approaches to Opiate Addiction Control: Costs, Benefits and Potential" (Washington, D.C.: U.S. Department of Justice, 1972).

[38] See Eric Josephson, "The British Response to Drug Addiction," in *Technical Papers of the Second Report of the National Commission on Marihuana and Drug Abuse*, Appendix Vol. 4 (Washington, D.C.: Government Printing Office, 1973), pp. 173–197.

Methadone can be taken orally and hence is easily dispensed in clinic settings.

mated status of American opiate addicts as of late 1971. Since then there has been at least a doubling in the number of addicts in methadone maintenance programs.

The major development in recent years has been "methadone maintenance." Participants are usually volunteers, though they may be under court order in some jurisdictions. Methadone can be taken orally and hence is easily dispensed in clinic settings. In high dosage it not only meets the body's needs for opiate but blocks the euphoric effects of heroin. In low dosage it merely wards off withdrawal, so that the addict who wishes the euphoric effects of heroin can still obtain them.

Methadone maintenance does not do away with addiction; it maintains addiction, but, unless taken in small amounts, denies the addict the "bang" of heroin. Its advocates are convinced that it markedly reduces the amount of crime committed by addicts. The evidence for this is reasonably good, but it is possible that a substantial portion of the gain comes from close supervision of the addicts in maintenance programs.

Recognition of the hopelessness of solving the addiction problem by locking addicts in state and federal prisons led many states, in the early 1960s, to develop "civil commitment" programs. In essence, civil commitment laws provide for suspension of criminal proceedings against addicts who have committed crimes in order to supply their drug habit. These addicts are then committed not to prisons but to rehabilitation programs where they presumably receive therapy and useful training, following which they are returned to the community and receive close supervision for a substantial period.

Civil commitment programs are not a panacea. Civil commitment sometimes represents little more than a change of name for imprisonment; the rights of the individual to due process of the law may actually be infringed. Although "civil" commitment technically avoids the label of "criminal," the individuals may in fact be as strongly stigmatized as if they had been imprisoned for a criminal charge, especially if committed to facilities that also house convicted felons, as is the case in California. On the other hand, the development of specialized programs for drug users and the provision of close supervision in the community offer some promise that more effective rehabilitation methods will be developed. In any case, the New York and California programs have produced some valuable information about the addict after his return to the community.

Therapeutic communities, like Synanon in California and its counterparts elsewhere, afford the addict a structured, drug-free environment in which there are strong bonds of mutual acceptance and commitment. Most such programs entail strong, even authoritarian controls over the members, and most addicts are not attracted to them. For those who are, therapeutic communities seem often to become a permanent home.

A dilemma facing programs aimed at helping or rehabilitating addicts is that in general, incarceration, forced education, and compulsory treatment do not seem to be appropriate ways of dealing with the alienation that frequently underlies drug use; nor are they appropriate responses to levels of recreational drug use that do not interfere with the individual's ability to manage his affairs. So long as the drug user is isolated, rejected, and punished, he is likely to become more alienated and more deviant. There comes a point, of course, where enforced isolation of deviants may be necessary. Too often we seem to push drug users to that point.

Should Marijuana Be Legalized?

It should by now be abundantly clear to readers of this chapter that the dangers of recreational drug use are relatively modest. Only a small proportion of users become dependent on illegal drugs. Far more are dependent on the legal drugs, tobacco, and alcohol. This is not to say that if it were easy to get marijuana and hashish at reasonable prices, and if there were no legal or moral constraints against use, the number of regular users would not greatly increase. Almost certainly there would be a substantial increase in prevalence of use and probably a significant increase in the number of heavy users. Clearly some measure of regulation would seem desirable, but at current levels of marijuana use it seems unrealistic to maintain prohibition, as proposed by the National Commission.

Perhaps it will be useful to consider an action the reverse of legalization of marijuana. Imagine enactment of a bill to make possession of cigarettes a felony. Prior to passage there might be riots by tobacco farmers and workers in the tobacco industry, but compensation to those directly affected economically and retraining programs would be incorporated into the final law. Enactment would require the destruction of all existing supplies of tobacco. Heavy smokers would experience weeks and months of acute discomfort. Some would go abroad to get supplies.

Soon smuggling from the Orient and Latin America would begin. Plane loads and boat loads of cigarettes would cross our borders and land on our shores each night. Big dealers and local peddlers would communicate by code. Many would be caught and would draw long prison terms, but enough cigarettes would get through to satisfy part of the demand. A single cigarette would soon cost a dollar. A pack could be bought in some neighborhoods for 10 dollars, if one knew the right people.

The wealthy might build air-conditioned smoking rooms, from which the scent of tobacco could be erased in a few seconds. The poor would huddle in doorways to take a few quick drags. Within a few months there would be millions of felons. Some enforcement agents would be unable to resist the lure of seized tobacco. They would withhold some cigarettes, and when their children were asleep they might go to the basement or attic and light up.

It is unthinkable to most smokers of tobacco that cigarettes should be outlawed. Legislation to prohibit the possession of cigarettes would have no chance of passage, despite the evidence that cigarette smoking is a major factor in the two leading causes of death.

To legalize a drug that has long been proscribed will probably be easier than prohibiting a drug that is widely used and accepted. Yet the resistance to legalization of marijuana suggests that where traditional moral issues are involved, legislatures will tend to lag behind public opinion and the action of the courts. Although the National Commission on Marihuana and Drug Abuse recommended decriminalizing possession of marijuana, it opposed substituting regulation for prohibition, on the grounds that most members of the general population would be opposed to legalization. Yet the Commission's report indicated that the general population's views were based on myths and distortions, not on accurate knowledge. Further, in the Commission's view (undoubtedly correct) prohibition symbolizes official disapproval and thereby reinforces informal controls.

In the last analysis, legislation will require substantial changes in public opinion. However, in little more than a decade the views of educated Americans toward abortion underwent an almost complete turnabout, and views on marijuana may well change as radically in the next few years, as today's users become an increasingly large proportion of the electorate.

SUMMARY

1   The use of drugs to achieve relaxation and pleasurable states began long before civilization. Whether or not a given form of drug use is regarded as a problem in any society or era depends on the values of that society or era and prevailing beliefs about the consequences of such use more than upon known consequences. Alcohol and tobacco are at present acceptable drugs in American society, while marijuana and the opiates are not acceptable, though opiates were acceptable a century ago and marijuana seems on the verge of becoming acceptable now.

2   Pleasurable drugs that entail physiological dependency once they have been used regularly pose especially difficult problems for the individual who has become habituated to them but wishes to give up drug use. When deprived of the drug, dependent ("addicted") persons develop a severe physiological illness known as the abstinence syndrome.

3   American society was long characterized by a strong ethic against drug use except in connection with illness and pain. More recently, esthetic and mind-expanding experiences have been increasingly sought, especially by young adults, and experimentation with various drugs has been a part of the quest for deeper experiences.

4   Stimulant and tranquilizing drugs are also widely used by members of conventional society as an aid to day-to-day functioning.

5   Marijuana is now smoked at least occasionally by a very substantial proportion of high-school and college students and young adults—by more than half in many otherwise conventional groups. Illegally obtained hallucinogens, stimulants, and barbiturates are used by smaller proportions of young adults.

6   Recreational drug use is learned much as any other cultural pattern is learned, through association with others. To the extent that the pattern is regarded as deviant and unacceptable in some groups and acceptable in others, the neophyte who finds drug use congenial is likely to change his patterns of association.

7   Recreational drug use is part of a larger subculture or life style that entails rejection of the traditional values of the "Protestant ethic," which include hard work, sexual asceticism outside of marriage, participation in organized religion, and priority for "law and order" over human rights. Drug users tend to be more liberal politically and more oriented toward careers that afford opportunity for altruistic or artistic expression.

8   Heroin use and addiction is more heavily concentrated among deprived groups. Majority group members who use heroin are usually severely deviant before they turn to the drug. Nevertheless, heroin use is almost always learned through intimate association with other users; pressures from peers to try the drug are often a stronger force making for drug use than are conventional social controls and fear of becoming addicted.

9   Public policy relating to drugs in the United States has been largely a product of fear and ignorance. Federal laws made criminals first of opiate users and then of marijuana users. Despite federal and state laws, opiate use has flourished and accounts for a very substantial portion of all thefts in urban areas. Marijuana laws, differentially enforced, create gross inequities in the operation of the legal system and often result in the victimization of users.

10 The elimination of drugs from the environment is not possible short of totalitarian

rule. A rational policy of drug control will require continuing research, honesty in the interpretation of the research, and a much greater reliance on informed discussion as a basis for informal social control.

RECOMMENDED READINGS

Although the most widely distributed books on drugs tend to be either alarmist or to defend or sing the praises of drug use, a number of sound discussions are now available in paperback, among them, James Carey's *The College Drug Scene* (1968), *Drugs and Use* by Robert Coles et al. (1970), Erich Goode's *Drugs in American Society* (1974), and Helen Nowlis' *Drugs on the College Campus* (1969). Coles and his collaborators and Nowlis attempt to give a dispassionate analysis to the concerned citizen, while the Carey book is more descriptive of patterns of drug use and Goode affords a more sociological analysis.

A somewhat more technical but nevertheless highly readable volume providing both an overview of problems of drug use and a number of detailed accounts of recent research on the distribution and correlates of drug use is *Drug Use: Epidemiological and Sociological Approaches,* edited by Eric Josephson and Eleanor E. Carroll (1974).

There is a considerable literature on marijuana, including the First Report of the National Commission on Marijuana and Drug Use (*Marihuana: A Signal of Misunderstanding,* 1972) available in paperback from the U.S. Government Printing Office, Erich Goode's *Marijuana* (1969), and John Kaplan's *Marijuana: The New Prohibition* (1975). The latter gives the perspective of a law professor who has campaigned vigorously against marijuana laws.

Popular paperbacks in the field of opiate use tend to be sensational and often grossly misleading. A useful collection of papers from varied perspectives is *Narcotic Addiction* (1966) edited by John O'Donnell and John C. Ball. The most thorough study of the setting and correlates of urban heroin use by young adults is still Isidor Chein's *The Road to H* (1961). A more popular but still useful work is Joel Fort's *The Pleasure Seekers* (1969). A detailed journalistic account of the international drug traffic is contained in *The Heroin Trail,* published as a paperback in 1973 from a series of articles that first appeared in *Newsday.*

Issues of public policy and modes of dealing with the problematic use of drugs are dealt with in considerable detail in the Marihuana Commission's Second Report, *Drug Use in America: Problem in Perspective* (1973) and in William H. McGlothin et al., "Alternative Approaches to Opiate Addiction Control" (1972), published by the U.S. Department of Justice, and R. E. Meyer's *Guide to Drug Rehabilitation: A Public Health Approach* (1972).

4

Alcoholism and Problem Drinking

ROBERT STRAUS

Alcoholism and problem drinking are generally found in association with most other social problems as well as other problems of individual health and well-being. Alcoholics, compared with nonalcoholics, have higher rates of physical and mental illness, are more frequently divorced or alienated from their families, are more apt to be involved in other forms of deviant behavior—crime, drug abuse, accidents, sexual nonfulfillment, suicide— and are more apt to be unemployed or maladjusted to both work and leisure. Alcohol problems illustrate a tendency toward a clustering of many forms of social pathology—a tendency for problems to beget problems.

The customs of drinking and the problems that they generate are also related to several forms of social disorganization. In fact, this chapter suggests that problem drinking both contributes to and is a response to disorganization in major social institutions—religion, government, economics, family, education, work, leisure.

In this chapter, following an identification of the various problems of alcohol, the physiological and psychological effects of alcohol on the human body and mind are considered in relation to social and cultural variables that influence the ways in which people drink. The relationships between drinking and the problems of alcohol are then considered. Alcoholism is defined and differentiated from other forms of problem drinking in terms of different kinds of dependence on alcohol that alcoholics and other problem drinkers exhibit. Various theories of causation are examined, and it is suggested that alcoholism usually results from a combination of social, cultural, psychological, and biological factors. The special problems of alcohol that pertain to youth, the family, employment, and driving are then examined. The chapter concludes with a consideration of social responses to alcohol problems and conflicts between social policies aimed at controlling alcohol problems and the forces of prevailing custom that support problem-producing drinking behavior.

IDENTIFYING THE PROBLEMS OF ALCOHOL

After nearly a decade of national preoccupation with the problems of illicit drug use, "alcohol dependence" was identified in 1973 by a government study as "without question, the most serious drug problem" in the United States.[1] In 1974 the National Institute on Alcohol Abuse and Alcoholism estimated the economic costs associated with the misuse of alcohol in the United States at a "conservative" 25 billion dollars a year.[2] The same agency estimated that there are at least 10 million problem drinkers and that alcohol abuse is increasing in American society.

[1] Drug Use in America: Problem in Perspective, Second Report of the National Commission on Marihuana and Drug Abuse (Washington, D.C.: Government Printing Office, March 1973), p. 143.

[2] Alcohol and Health: New Knowledge, Second Special Report to the U.S. Congress from the Secretary of Health, Education and Welfare [Washington, D.C.: DHEW Publication No. (ADM) 74-124, June 1974], pp. 49–59. This figure is based on rough estimates for 1971.

It is important to recognize that alcohol has been used by human beings since before the beginnings of recorded history. Many societies have tried to suppress or completely prohibit its use because the associated problems are massive and affect almost everyone. Yet the attractions of alcohol have been so compelling that legal prohibitions have invariably been repealed, circumvented, or defied. An essential dilemma in devising social policy to deal with alcohol problems stems from the fact that alcohol is functional as well as dysfunctional. It has great capacity for alleviating pain, relieving tension and worry, and providing a pleasurable sense of well-being, relaxation, conviviality, and good will toward others. For these reasons, the use of alcohol has been highly valued in many societies, and people have clung tenaciously to their right to drink. Alcohol has been invested with positive religious symbolism, used commonly in the sanctification of birth, puberty, marriage, and death, and associated with good health and nutrition. It has been an important element in the economies of many nations, supporting international commerce, creating employment, and providing tax revenues.

A few societies have been able to enjoy the benefits of alcohol and avoid its severe liabilities. However, for most of the world where its use has been common, alcohol has also brought serious negative consequences. Essentially these stem from its intoxicating properties, by which many users become temporarily incapacitated and to which some become addicted. In societies having high rates of alcohol abuse, concerns about drunkenness and alcoholism have increased as urbanization and industrialization have dramatized the threat that an intoxicated person or an alcoholic poses to the well-being of others. There is also increasing concern about the impact of alcoholism in families on the health of wives, husbands, and children, and about the effect of problem drinking at work on the productivity and safety of fellow employees. Today, the recognized problems of alcohol through much of the world include accidents caused by driving vehicles while under the influence of alcohol; industrial accidents, absenteeism, and loss of production attributable to alcohol abuse; the special threat that some societies perceive in drinking by the young and "uninitiated"; alcohol-related poverty, physical and mental illness, family instability, crime, and suicide.

Drinking behavior affects almost every aspect of social life in some way. The nature and severity of alcohol problems found in a particular society or at a particular time depend on the drinking customs that prevail. To understand the relationship between drinking customs and drinking problems, however, we must consider the nature of alcohol and its impact on the human body and human behavior.[3]

---

[3] In a 1967 discussion of the relevance of biological variations to the understanding of deviant behavior, R. L. Means cited the sociological literature on alcoholism as an example of the tendency of sociologists to neglect the consideration of biological factors in their studies and analyses of social problems. Nearly a decade later, this neglect still characterizes most sociological writing on alcoholism. R. L. Means, "Sociology, Biology, and the Analysis of Social Problems," *Social Problems*, Vol. 15 (Fall 1967), pp. 200–212.

THE EFFECTS OF ALCOHOL

Physiological Effects

Alcoholic beverages vary widely in their alcohol content depending on the raw materials and the processes used in producing them. Wines, produced by fermentation of fruit juices, have a natural alcohol content of 9 to 14 percent. Some wines are "fortified" by the addition of alcohol to bring their content up to about 20 percent. Brewed beverages, derived from various cereals, usually have an alcohol content of from 3 to 6 percent, depending on local custom or law. Stronger beverages such as whiskies and brandies are manufactured by distilling fermented or brewed products and recovering liquids with an alcohol content of 35 to 50 percent. The alcohol strength of distilled beverages is usually designated by the term "proof," a value equal to twice the percent of alcohol content. Thus a whisky labeled "100 proof" contains 50 percent alcohol.

The major impact of alcohol on human behavior depends on its action as an anesthetic and a depressant on the central nervous system. The degree of effect depends on the concentration of alcohol in the blood when it reaches the brain. Since alcohol, once absorbed by the blood, is subject to oxidation by which it is eventually reduced to carbon dioxide and water, significant intoxication will be experienced only when the conditions of drinking are such that the rate of absorption is sufficiently greater than the rate of oxidation. Important drinking conditions include the type and alcoholic strength of the beverage, the rate of ingestion, whether or not there is food in the stomach to impede the rate of alcohol absorption, and the body weight of the drinker.

A man of average weight consuming a pint of whisky gradually over a 24-hour period would probably experience no marked effect, while the same man consuming the same amount of whisky in the space of an hour would suffer intoxication. A man weighing 120 pounds will feel a much greater effect than a man weighing 240 pounds from the same amount and rate of drinking. Five ounces of alcohol will usually produce a greater effect when consumed as ten ounces of 50-percent whisky than when drunk as 100 ounces of 5-percent beer. This is because the 5 ounces of alcohol in the whisky can be consumed, and would be absorbed, much more quickly than the same amount of alcohol in the beer. The effect of drinking on an empty stomach greatly exceeds the effect produced by drinking the same amount after a heavy meal.

Roughly speaking, a man of moderate weight (155-165 pounds) who consumes an ounce of whisky or a bottle of beer might achieve an alcohol concentration in the blood of no more than 0.02 percent. However, were he to consume 5 or 6 ounces of whisky rather quickly, he would achieve a concentration of about 0.1 percent. The effect on behavior of a concentration of 0.02 percent is negligible for most people. A concentration of 0.1 percent, however, produces definite depression of sensory and motor functions (slight staggering, fumbling, and tripping of the tongue over even familiar words). Unfortunately, despite functional impairment, many drinkers at this level have the illusion that their reactions, perception, and discrimination are better than normal. A concentration of 0.2 percent of alcohol incapacitates most drinkers both physically and emotionally. At 0.3 percent the drinker is stuporous. A concentration about 0.4 percent leads to coma, and 0.6 or 0.7 percent would affect the ability to breathe and cause death.

Although the concentration of alcohol in the blood that reaches the brain is a critical factor in determining alcohol's effect on behavior, the relationship between alcohol and human behavior can also be influenced by other important variables. As with all drugs, some users may experience an adverse reaction to very small amounts while others may require more than average amounts to experience an average effect. Even for a particular individual, there are variations in response to alcohol that cannot be represented by a simple formula. Persons who have recently been ill or who are fatigued may experience unusual hypersensitivity. That is, they may find that one drink affects their sensations and behavior as they normally would expect two or three drinks to do. A similar reaction occurs for some people who drink when their usual rhythm of sleep and activity is disrupted—for example, when they cross several time zones in jet airplane travel. Some people react differently to alcohol at different times of day or night even without disruption in their normal rhythm. Since alcohol is a mood-altering drug, its effect on a particular drinker can also be influenced by the physical environment, the social setting, and any other factors that contribute to the drinker's psychological status when drinking begins.

Psychological Effects

The psychological effects of alcohol include effects on *overt* behavior, such as perception, reaction time, the performance of motor tasks, the processes of learning, remembering, reasoning, and problem solving, and *emotional* reactions such as fear, anxiety, tension, hostility, or the feelings of being "on edge" or of euphoria.

The effect of alcohol on task performance increases with the complexity of the task, the unfamiliarity of the task to the performer, and the inexperience of the performer with drinking. Even small amounts of alcohol may affect the carrying out of simple tasks if the performer is inexperienced both in drinking and in the task at hand. The inexperienced drinker, moreover, is apt to overreact to the sensations produced by alcohol and may behave as if intoxicated when under the influence of very small amounts. Some experienced drinkers, on the other hand, appear to learn how to compensate psychologically, so that they can appear to be sober and can sometimes even satisfactorily perform complex tasks with which they are familiar, despite the handicap of alcohol's effect.

The effect of alcohol on task performance is sometimes related to its effect on emotional behavior. For those individuals whose ability to perform is seriously limited by their anxiety or inhibitions, alcohol may provide enough re-lief from the anxiety or release from inhibitions to permit performance. In situations that do not demand special skills, such as social gatherings, some alcohol can produce a feeling of well-being and relaxation without liability. Where efficiency is required, however, the relaxing qualities of alcohol can be dangerously misleading, for the very same properties that are conducive to relaxation are not conducive to effective task performance.

Combination with Other Drugs

An additional factor that complicates the physical and psychological effects of alcohol for many people is its use in combination with one or more other sedative drugs. Twenty-five years ago most people who drank to intoxication were using only alcohol. Today, with an estimated 15 million users of pre-scribed antianxiety drugs in the United States and 20 to 25 million users of sedative antihistamines that are contained in most "cold remedies," allergy medications, and over-the-counter sleeping pills, there are literally millions of people who combine these drugs with alcohol and usually experience an ef-fect that is "greater than the sum of the parts." Unfortunately, few people today are aware of the danger of drinking when they are also taking tran-quilizers, antihistamines, or many other kinds of medicines.

The Impact of Drinking Customs

The impact of alcohol on people is also related to differences in customary beliefs and patterns of use. Where it is usual to drink under conditions that favor the rapid absorption of sufficient alcohol to affect behavior, higher rates of intoxication and increased exposure to alcoholism occur. Such conditions are generally found where most drinking occurs on an empty stomach and in-volves beverages with a high alcohol content in relatively undiluted form. The late afternoon cocktail party is a good example. Not only is the buffering effect of food missing, but people tend to drink more rapidly when they are not eat-ing, and when they are standing rather than seated.

Low rates of alcoholism and problem drinking tend to be found where customs favor drinking beers or low-alcohol wines and where the conditions of drinking impede rapid ingestion or absorption. People who consume alcohol primarily because they believe in its medicinal efficacy are apt to space their drinking regularly over time or do it only when a specific need arises. People who consider alcohol a form of food and who customarily drink only with meals rarely achieve a high level of alcohol concentration. Food provides a competing substance for ingestion and impedes the absorption of alcohol through the walls of the stomach. Historically, variations in the types of alco-holic beverages available to a society and in patterns of drinking have been related to geographical factors such as soil, climate, and terrain. For example, these factors have supported the growth of grapes in southern Europe and for many centuries wines derived from grapes have been the principal alcoholic beverages used by the people of southern France and Spain and Italy. In central and northern Europe, on the other hand, geographic factors have favored the growth of various types of grain used in the brewing process and, historically, brewed beers and ales have been the predominant beverages in these areas. With the discovery of distilling processes, the types of distilled spirits used—brandies in the south of Europe and whiskies in the north—also were influenced by geographic factors. However, in the last century technological advances in agriculture, transportation, and manufacturing have reduced the distinctions between drinking customs of different societies. This process is illustrated by the history of drinking in the United States.

AMERICAN DRINKING CUSTOMS IN HISTORICAL PERSPECTIVE

The colonists who came to America from England brought with them well-established habits and attitudes about the use of alcohol. Alcoholic beverages had important religious, medical, and dietary significance that were well integrated into family life and community recreational practices and quickly became a prominent component of commerce and of the colonial economy.

Prior to 1700, drinking appears to have been primarily a family-centered and family-controlled activity. Religious sanctions were directed against drunkenness. The incidence of intoxication grew coincidentally with the immigration of numbers of unattached males whose drinking was unrelated to family sanctions and may have served to compensate for the absence of the gratifications, responsibilities, and stability of family living. The frequent use of alcohol to produce intoxication became particularly characteristic of life on the ever-expanding frontier and among the less stable segments of communities during the several decades following the Revolutionary War.

Perhaps in reaction to the excesses of drinking on the frontier and in its urban counterpart, the practice of family drinking appears to have diminished by the early nineteenth century, when frequent heavy consumption of distilled spirits, much of it by unattached men, became the dominant drinking practice. This type of drinking, which was often accompanied by uninhibited, destructive behavior, became a major social concern. Intoxication was seen as a threat to the personal well-being and property of peaceful citizens, and the loss of productive manpower through drunkenness was seen as a threat to the national economy and vitality.

After about 1820, waves of immigration from many nations introduced great variety into American drinking, particularly increasing the relative significance of beer and wine and reviving the importance of family-centered drinking.

Despite changes in patterns of consumption, from 1850 to 1960 the total annual per capita consumption of pure alcohol in all beverage forms, for persons 15 years of age and over, remained virtually unchanged at about 2 gallons. In recent years, however, an upward trend has been recorded—from 1.98 gallons of absolute alcohol consumed in 1958 to 2.63 gallons in 1972, a rise of 33 percent.[4] During roughly the same period of time, similar or greater increases in absolute alcohol consumption were being recorded in most other countries of the Western world.

The rise in per capita consumption of alcohol in the United States has been accompanied by only a slight rise in the percentage of adults who use alcohol. In annual nationwide surveys since 1939, the American Institute of Public Opinion has included the question: "Do you have occasion to use alcoholic beverages such as liquor, wine or beer, or are you a total abstainer?" Responses have ranged from a low of 55 percent users of alcohol in 1958 to a high of 68 percent in 1974, with relative stability for the last 10 years.[5] When these and several similar estimates of drinking prevalence from other samples are related to census data, it is apparent that at least 90 million American adults are now using alcoholic beverages. Studies of the drinking practices of high school and college age youth report rates of use ranging from 50 to 90 percent with a steadily increasing percentage of users reported for each age level from 16 through 20. When these youth are added to adult drinkers, an estimate of at least 100 million users in the American population seems reasonable.

Overall data on the prevalence of drinking in the total population can be misleading. All studies report greater use by men than by women. Gallup, in 1974, found that 76 percent of men and 61 percent of women used alcohol. Comparisons over time, however, suggest that the prevalence of use among women is rising more rapidly than among men. Drinking is more frequent among persons with college educations, with higher incomes, living in the East or Midwest, and working in professional or higher-echelon business jobs. It is less among those with no more than a grade school education, lower incomes, living in the South, and working in unskilled jobs. By age, the prevalence of use seems to peak at around age 20 for both men and women and drops to about 40 percent for each sex by age 65. Available data suggest similar rates of use and abstention for black and white men but higher rates of use for white than for black women.[6]

WHO ARE THE PROBLEM DRINKERS?

The study of problem drinking and alcoholism has long been severely compromised by the strong reluctance of alcoholics to be studied. When serious sociological attention was first devoted to alcohol problems in the early 1940s, the only data that could be assembled on the characteristics and experiences

[4] Vera Efron et al., *Statistics on Consumption of Alcohol and on Alcoholism* (New Brunswick, N.J.: Rutgers Center of Alcohol Studies, 1974).

[5] George Gallup, syndicated article in the Louisville *Courier-Journal*, July 9, 1974.

[6] For a national study that focused specifically on drinking practices, see D. Cahalan et al., *American Drinking Practices: A National Survey of Drinking Behavior and Attitudes* (New Brunswick, N.J.: Rutgers Center of Alcohol Studies, 1969).

of persons with drinking problems were based on studies of "captive" populations such as skid row habitués or inmates of jails, prisons, or mental hospitals. Reports at that time tended to associate alcoholism with the extreme social and emotional instability that these particular alcoholics displayed. Such characterizations served to stereotype alcoholics as either derelicts or deranged, to intensify the prevailing stigma of alcoholism, and to reinforce the tendency of problem drinkers who were maintaining family, job, and community stability to deny their alcoholism. The emergence in the 1940s and 1950s of treatment programs for alcoholism, including both the self-help programs of Alcoholics Anonymous and the professional help offered through community clinics and hospitals, attracted problem drinkers from all walks of life, many of whom were struggling to maintain family and employment ties. Studies of problem drinkers who were seeking help provided a new but still limited perspective on the social characteristics, personality traits, and drinking experiences of alcoholics. Most of these men and women had experienced long histories of increasing problems with alcohol that culminated in their accepting, out of desperation, the reality of needing help. Most were in middle life and most reported a long progression into alcoholism.

A major breakthrough in the sociological study of alcohol problems occurred in the mid-1960s, when household surveys regarding drinking practices and problems were introduced and a basis was established for studies of drinking behavior that follow the same individuals over long periods of time in order to identify any significant changes in drinking and relate these to changes in other aspects of the drinkers' lives. Such surveys, although they exclude institutionalized problem drinkers, have made it possible to study drinking problems in various stages of development and to include men and women whose experiences with alcohol, while causing difficulties, have not yet resulted in the total disintegration of their life adjustment or progressed to a state of desperation. Key findings of a national survey of problem drinking among American men, ages 21 to 59, included:[7]

(1) The majority (72%) of American men interviewed in their homes had at some time experienced a problem associated with drinking that was of sufficient significance to be recalled and reported. The problems most commonly reported were frequent heavy drinking, quarrels with wives over drinking, the feeling of a psychological need to drink, belligerence when intoxicated, and drinking as a symptom of other difficulties. In reflecting on the high prevalence of drinking problems reported by this sample of American men, it is important to realize that neither the population base nor the criteria of problem drinking are consistent with traditional conceptions of alcoholism based on people who were institutionalized or who referred themselves for treatment. Most of those people had become caught up in a progressive, vicious spiral involving more and more complications of drinking. It is very significant that

---

[7] Don Cahalan, *Problem Drinking* (San Francisco: Jossey-Bass, 1970); Don Cahalan and Robin Room, *Problem Drinking Among American Men* (New Brunswick, N.J.: Rutgers Center of Alcohol Studies, 1974).

The typical alcoholic American

young | old | male | female

black | white | rich | poor

employed | unemployed | executive | laborer

student | doctor | immigrant | native born

There's no such thing as typical.
We have all kinds.
It's our number one drug problem.

NATIONAL INSTITUTE
ON ALCOHOL ABUSE
AND ALCOHOLISM

in the household population study at least half of the men who reported having once had drinking-related problems claimed to have experienced no such problems within the past three years. This indicates a *remission* phenomenon in problem drinkers who have not become caught in an irreversible progression, and it has major significance for the development of preventive intervention.

(2) All types of drinking problems studied in the survey were more prevalent among men aged 20 to 24 than in any other age group. In fact, 40 percent of this young adult age group reported having some problems at a significant level of involvement. Although these findings point to a very rapid decline in the prevalence of drinking problems after age 25, they also suggest that long-term alcohol problems begin early.

(3) Drinking problems having the most serious consequences were reported most frequently by men from the lowest social class and least frequently by men from upper-middle or high social positions. Although the sociological studies of problem drinking based on institutionalized populations tended to emphasize a lower social class weighting, studies based on alcoholics seen in treatment programs and those based on members of Alcoholics Anonymous emphasized a heavier weighting of alcoholics in the middle and upper social strata. Findings from the household sampling indicate that we should re-evaluate our ideas about the distribution of alcoholism among social classes.

More than anything else, recent social-epidemiological studies of drinking point to the need for a clarification of the terms *alcoholism* and *problem drinking*, including both the characteristics of the population that these terms describe and the behavioral dynamics that they encompass.

ALCOHOLISM AND PROBLEM DRINKING

Alcohol problems are generally associated with situations in which people drink what for them is "too much." These can range from incidental episodes of intoxication in persons who usually abstain or drink only moderately, to a devastating combination of organic disease, psychological disorientation, and social dysfunctioning in alcoholics who compulsively seek intoxication at every opportunity.

Often the more knowledge we gain, the more difficult it becomes to communicate precisely what we think we know. The field of alcohol studies is no exception. Until recently, it was common practice to refer to all pathological drinking as "alcoholism." However, as more and more has been understood about the forms and causes of problem drinking, it has become apparent that the term was being used to describe a number of quite distinct disorders. There are many forms of pathological drinking and associated problems to which a variety of descriptive terms are currently being applied. Such widely used terms as "alcoholism," "problem drinking," "addictive drinking," and "alcohol dependence" can be quite confusing unless there is some agreement on behaviorally related definitions.

The term *problem drinker* has been adopted as a broader umbrella that covers individuals suffering from various forms of alcoholism and also others who encounter problems with alcohol. Although changes in measurements, labeling, and perceptions make meaningful comparisons difficult over time, there is evidence to suggest that in the last 15 years more people in the United States have been using more alcohol and that the prevalence of related problems has been rising. In the mid-1970s, various rough estimates suggest that there are at least ten million problem drinkers in the United States, of whom probably six million are alcoholics.

In this chapter, "problem drinker" will be defined as encompassing all individuals who *repeatedly* use alcohol to an extent that exceeds customary dietary use or prevailing socially accepted customs or in amounts that, for them, cause problems of physical health, interfere with interpersonal relations, or disrupt the fulfillment of family, economic, or community expectations. This definition recognizes both social and individual dimensions. Problem drinking exists if either social customs or the individual's capacity to handle alcohol are repeatedly violated.

Among problem drinkers, *alcoholics* can be defined as those whose persistent abuse of alcohol is associated with a state of physical or psychological dependence involving often unbearable stress or discomfort or tension. The origin of the discomfort may be physiological, psychological or social, or a blending of all three. The factors that distinguish alcoholics from other problem drinkers are their degree of dependence and their inability to control their drinking.

The Concept of Dependence

The concept of dependence is useful in considering various forms of drinking behavior and the relationship between drinking problems and other social problems. Most references to dependence in this context emphasize its dysfunctional aspects. Dependence on alcohol or other drugs is usually assumed to be associated with behavior that is damaging to the individual user, adversely affects interpersonal relationships, and has undesirable consequences for other people. "Dependence" also implies necessity, in the sense of requiring alcohol in order to meet some goal or need.

While certain kinds of dependence are destructive, it is important to recognize that dependence is actually a universal phenomenon of human life. Everyone depends on food, air, water, rest, and shelter; these are basic requirements for survival. Because the human newborn is quite incompletely deveoped at birth, all infants are totally dependent on adults in order to survive. Among adults, some kinds of mutual dependence along with role diversification and specialization are universally characteristic of human societies.

Most dependence behavior is functional. It is concerned with seeking a particular activity or object in an amount that brings satisfactions. These can be measured physiologically and experienced psychologically. The acquisition of food, in the amounts and varieties compatible with bodily needs at a particular time, leads to physiological relaxation and a psychological sense of well-being. Similarly with water, sex, rest, exercise, and other basic and derived human needs—we depend on these substances or activities in order to feel comfortable or to survive. Yet in all of these cases, there is a point of satisfaction beyond which we experience physiological stress and tension rather than relaxation, and a sense of anxiety and foreboding rather than a psychological sense of well-being. Thus, with every kind of activity there is a point of overindulgence at which the same behavior that has been functional in preventing stress or sickness becomes excessive, damaging, and dysfunctional. People who feel driven to seek what, for them, is too much food, too much sex, too much exercise, or even too much sleep can be said to have a dysfunctional form of dependence. In this sense, the term *dependence* is comparable to the concept of addiction.

Certainly the drinking of alcohol is less basic than eating or exercise or sexual intercourse. Yet the worldwide use of alcohol to achieve a desired state of mind and body by so many societies over such a long period of time suggests a kind of functional dependence. At the same time, we have evidence that most alcohol-using societies have included some members who used too much alcohol. There are even historical suggestions that the demise or destruction of some societies was preceded by the development of drinking practices in which, on too many occasions, too many people were using too much alcohol. A classical example of this is said to have been the Roman Empire. More recently, alcohol abuse played a significant role in the subjugation of American Indians, and today high rates of alcoholism are associated with the continuing economic and social disorganization that plagues the native American population.

As applied to the misuse of alcohol or other drugs, "dependent" refers to individuals who exhibit a need to use the drug in ways that are dysfunctional. They seem compelled to take amounts that are "too much"—either for their bodies to handle physiologically, or in terms of the intoxicating effects they experience, or because they are unable, under the toxic influence of the drug, to meet social responsibilities or avoid violating social rules or amenities.

Three major categories of dysfunctional dependence on alcohol—physical, psychological, and social—will be discussed in this chapter.

Physical dependence   Physical dependence on alcohol is generally assumed to exist when drinkers either demonstrate characteristic signs of physical distress when alcohol is abruptly withdrawn during a drinking episode or show signs of increased tolerance to alcohol, or both. Withdrawal reactions may include rapid heartbeat, profuse sweating, severe nausea, uncontrollable tremors and, in the more severe form, disorientation, hallucinations, and the classical seizures known as delirium tremens. Withdrawal symptoms usually develop only in persons who have engaged in fairly heavy drinking over a long period of time. However, they have been observed in persons who have been drinking relatively moderately for only a few days. The underlying mechanisms that produce withdrawal distress are not known, but it is thought that they are an expression of physiological changes caused by alcohol itself.

Persons who develop physical dependence on most drugs other than alcohol reach a stage where their drug use seems primarily motivated by the need to avoid the frightening and life-threatening withdrawal experience rather than by the desire for satisfaction. Many alcoholics, on the other hand, report that their compulsive drinking is associated with a craving for some intensive experience or euphoria; they become insatiable—persistently seeking an unattainable peak intensity of intoxication. Such drinkers seem to lose control over their ability to stop drinking, once an episode has commenced.

Associated with physical dependence on alcohol and many other drugs is the ability to tolerate increasing amounts without showing increasing effects. Compared with tolerance to some other drugs like the opiates or barbiturates, which makes it possible for accustomed users to consume amounts that would prove fatal to novice users, the tolerance developed to alcohol is relatively minor. Some alcoholics can achieve a blood alcohol level of, say, 0.15 or 0.2 without seeming as intoxicated as would most drinkers. Also, some alcoholics can consume greater amounts day after day without becoming sick to their stomachs than would be possible for most drinkers. The effect of tolerance on levels of overdose, however, is relatively minor. That is, alcohol levels in the blood of about 0.4 and above would lead to coma and levels of 0.6 or 0.7 would bring death even to most alcoholics. More significant is that people who are physically dependent on alcohol tend to consume amounts that can cause damage to the liver and other body tissues and organs. For this reason, physical dependence on alcohol is commonly associated with other diseases.

Some of the diseases connected with alcoholism are related to alcoholic malnutrition. Alcohol is high in caloric value but provides no other nutritional needs. Heavy drinkers can obtain a large portion of the calories they need from alcohol. Moreover, they often suffer from chronic gastritis. As a result, they frequently do not eat enough food containing essential proteins, vitamins, minerals, and other nutrients. It has been estimated that malnutrition will occur in those who are obtaining more than about 40 percent of their caloric needs through alcohol. While physical dependence is commonly associated with alcohol diseases, it should be stressed that many of the physiological effects of chronic excessive alcohol consumption, such as cirrhosis of the liver or heart disease, can occur in heavy drinkers who do not show the usual signs of physical dependence.

Psychological dependence   Everyone who develops a physical dependence on alcohol is psychologically dependent as well. However, a very significant amount of alcoholism is found in persons who are psychologically dependent without demonstrating a withdrawal syndrome, tolerance, or alcohol-related diseases.

Psychological dependence on alcohol is often characterized by an intense, inner-directed need to drink and by what has been called "loss of control" over drinking. Loss of control is manifested in two ways. One is the inability to stop once drinking has started; the other is inability to refrain from drinking even under circumstances in which it is blatantly inappropriate. Alcoholics who lose the ability to stop have usually been drinking heavily for some time and with increasing frequency. They report a striving for a peak intensity of intoxication and describe an experience that seems analogous to a conditioned response: With any exposure to alcohol they feel impelled to seek its ultimate impact. Because this impulsive response to alcohol tends to remain even after long periods of abstention, it is assumed that the alcoholic cannot ever again drink safely. Alcoholics refer to this phenomenon by saying they lack "terminal facilities."

Inability to refrain from inappropriate drinking may or may not be associated with inability to stop drinking once begun. Those who cannot control the circumstances under which they begin to drink seem dominated by a fear of being without alcohol. Such drinkers have become so dependent on alcohol-induced mood modification that without it they cannot face situations that, for them, pose unbearable anxiety. Sometimes there are situations that involve testing one's capabilities under circumstances where success is crucial and the very drinking that permits the individual to face the test will, at the same time, assure failure. Examples include taking an examination, being interviewed for a job, trying to make a sale, meeting an important stranger, making love, or demonstrating one's worth as a parent. (The alcoholic who would be a good parent may promise to take his child to the circus, but invariably at the appointed time he will get drunk instead.)

Not all psychological dependence on alcohol involves loss of the ability to stop drinking or to refrain from drinking. Nor, as noted earlier, is all psychological dependence destructive or dysfunctional. A relatively mild form of it can be found in drinkers who feel a desire for alcohol and usually seek it in response to or in anticipation of stressful circumstances. They are simply responding to mood discomfort by resorting to one of the most readily available and commonly used mood-modifying drugs. This kind of dependence is often specific to particular situations. The wife who regularly takes a drink in anticipation of her husband's return from work or the husband who mildly fortifies himself at a bar before facing his family for dinner are both demonstrating a situationally specific psychological dependence on alcohol. In these situations, the use of alcohol may be quite functional. The wife may become more relaxed, loving, and attractive, the husband less tense and better able to respond to the emotional needs of his family. Only if the drinking increases to a point where it stops facilitating meeting the needs and expectations of others and begins to interfere with it, or where it damages the health of the drinker, will it be considered a problem.

Social dependence The third type of dependence on alcohol is characterized by needs associated with meeting the expectations of social situations rather than with physical or mood discomfort or compulsion. This is social dependence on alcohol, and it can exist quite apart from physical or psychological dependence. In many societies, custom defines numerous situations in which drinking, sometimes heavy drinking, is considered necessary. For example, many salesmen feel that they must drink with their prospective customers because alcohol is an important factor in preparing the customer for the sale, and because drinking has become an expected part of the selling situation. Many college students feel that they have to drink in order to be accepted by their peer groups. Factory workers may have to stop at a bar for a drink on the way home from work in order to be "one of the boys"; army officers may have to demonstrate their ability to hold their liquor in order to attain desirable assignments or promotions; diplomats may find themselves in situations where drinking is expected or required. Because people vary in their capacity to handle alcohol comfortably and safely, the amount of drinking required in certain social situations may exceed the limits for some individuals. If, as a result, they repeatedly drink what is, for them, "too much" alcohol, they are problem drinkers irrespective of whether psychological and/or physical dependence on alcohol exists or develops. Social dependence, uncomplicated by psychological or physical dependence, can account for the significant amount of persistent problem drinking in persons who would not be classified as alcoholics. It would also account for the remission phenomenon identified by Cahalan and Room,[8] and for persons who report a history of moving "in and out" of problem drinking.[9] Some men and women, for certain significant periods of time in their lives, have repeatedly used alcohol in ways that led to problems, while for significant periods in between they have been able to drink moderately or abstain comfortably. These people are not alcoholics. Their problem drinking is primarily a reflection of social dependence, not psychological or physical dependence. As their work or other situations requiring social drinking have changed, they have been able to modify their drinking patterns accordingly.

Currently, the terms *alcoholism* and *problem drinking* are used interchangeably by the general public and by many professional persons concerned with social policy and social action to combat alcohol abuse. Yet, from the viewpoint of intervention and treatment, a distinction between the alcoholic problem drinker and the not-yet-addicted problem drinker is critical. Alcoholics have learned that a goal of total sobriety is an essential part of their recovery. No currently known therapeutic measures have helped change the factor of "loss of control" over drinking once begun and, until or unless new knowledge is developed, it is in the best interest of alcoholics to suggest that they can never safely engage in "normal" drinking.

[8] Cahalan and Room, *op. cit.*, pp. 45–49.

[9] Kaye M. Fillmore, "Drinking and Problem Drinking in Early Adulthood and Middle Age," *Quarterly Journal of Studies on Alcohol*, Vol. 35 (September 1974), pp. 819–840.

Nonalcoholic or nonaddicted problem drinkers are manifesting different stages or different types of dependence on alcohol. They have not yet developed intensive psychological dependence, physical dependence, or inner-directed compulsions to drink. Because their problem drinking is primarily associated with social dependence, they can be helped to modify their drinking behavior in response to changes in life style and social situations.

Alcohol, Institutional Dependence, and the Plateau Effect

An interesting combination of social and psychological dependence is found in people who use alcohol in social situations where psychological dependency needs are not being met, but who can be quite content without alcohol as long as they are in a setting where they are psychologically comfortable. This particular phenomenon is common among the population of homeless men whose way of life involves the revolving doors of jails, public infirmaries, mental hospitals, live-in menial jobs, and skid-row shelters.[10] Life histories of these men reveal a pattern of deep-seated dependence on institutional settings that is very closely interrelated with their pattern of alcohol use. Most have come from broken families and have experienced some form of institutional living, either in childhood or during adolescent years, or both. In particular, these men have missed the normal transition that most people in our society experience from dependence on a parental family to independence with respect to obtaining the basic necessities of living, developing a value orientation, making decisions, expressing initiative, fulfilling economic roles, and engaging in close interpersonal associations. As a result, they tend to be undersocialized and are often unprepared to cope with even the simplest amenities relating to other people and meeting their own needs in a community setting. A similar problem has been identified for people who spend significant periods of time as adults in prisons, long-term hospitals, or other institutions and have become de-socialized for community living. Drinking, for institutionally dependent individuals, is almost always alternated with institutional living, and dependence on alcohol is manifest when their dependency needs are not being met by institutions. For some, public intoxication is deliberately used as a means to regain the protective custody of an institution. Quite typically, institutionally dependent persons turn to alcohol to help dull the intense feelings of anxiety, inadequacy, helplessness, and degradation that they experience when outside of institutions. For such persons, although manifested in terms of acute psychological stress, the need to drink is specific to a particular kind of social situation. Their dependence on alcohol is primarily associated with the non-institutional setting and they often report that they don't have any particular desire to drink while living within the security of an institutional setting.

Many institutionally dependent problem drinkers, who are relying on alcohol to alter mood discomfort, place less emphasis on the intensity of the effect

---

[10] For a lifelong case history of alcoholism and institutional dependence see Robert Straus, *Escape from Custody* (New York: Harper & Row, 1974).

achieved from alcohol than on its duration. They are seeking a *plateau* rather than a *peak* level of intoxication. Such drinkers can control their drinking and quite often will plan it deliberately in order to attain the most desirable combination of effect and duration within the limits of resources available for drinking.

The plateau effect is also sought by others in whom excessive drinking seems directed toward dulling the experience of unpleasant situations. These include men and women who function quite successfully at work but seek an alcohol-induced escape from their marital responsibilities on evenings and weekends. Increasingly, a plateau form of alcohol misuse has been recognized among women who have failed to fulfill self-expectations in their routine roles as housewives and mothers and use alcohol to obliterate feelings of boredom, meaninglessness, and alienation. Such drinkers may never experience extreme intoxication, but their day-long sipping is sufficient to render them chronically ineffective and inefficient.

THEORIES ABOUT CAUSATION

The understanding of alcoholism and problem drinking has, until quite recently, been clouded by a persistent groping for simple explanations of causation. The evidence today suggests that alcoholism in its various forms is usually related to several underlying stress-producing conditions. It is difficult to identify basic causal factors because the pathological use of alcohol in connection with primary forms of stress invariably generates additional stress-producing conditions, which ultimately become an integral part of the overall syndrome. Harold Kalant has emphasized the problem of sorting out specific processes from the viewpoint of a biological scientist:

> With the expansion of knowledge on functional interrelations, it has become clear that the metabolism of the liver affects the function of the central nervous system, that psychological and peripheral sensory stimuli acting on the central nervous system affect the release of various hormonal factors, that the resulting hormonal imbalances affect the metabolic behavior of the liver and of all other tissues, including the brain and so on and on. Because of this, it has become very difficult indeed to pick out those effects of alcohol which are primary and those which are secondary and nonspecific consequences of the disturbance resulting from alcohol.[11]

The social scientist faces the same kind of dilemma in his effort to understand alcoholism. Most types are found in association with some form or forms of social pathology. Marital discord, job instability, social alienation, economic strain, and chronic ill health can both contribute to and be supported by an

[11] Harold Kalant, "Some Recent Physiological and Biochemical Investigations on Alcohol and Alcoholism," *Quarterly Journal of Studies on Alcohol*, Vol. 23 (March 1962), p. 53.

alcoholic drinking pattern, and each of these problems tends to interact with the others in a complex clustering of social, psychological, and biological pathology.

There are no completely satisfactory theories about the causes of various types of pathological drinking. Although no specific physiological or biochemical factors have yet been positively identified, the evidence indicates that some biological deficiencies or sensitivities will eventually be found to contribute to at least some forms of alcoholism.

A number of psychological traits are common among people who drink excessively, and much has been written about the "alcoholic personality." Alcoholics have been characterized as suffering from extreme feelings of inadequacy and chronic anxiety and as excessively dependent on emotional support from others. Yet similar traits can be found in users of narcotics, individuals with various kinds of psychosomatic diseases, and persons addicted to food, as well as in many men and women who appear to function quite effectively within normal ranges of physical health and socially acceptable behavior. Because alcohol has the psychological effect of alleviating anxiety and providing a sense of well-being, it is easy to see why it is attractive to and functional for persons with deep feelings of emotional insecurity. But why do some of these people become alcoholics while others do not?

Cultural Factors

A number of sociologists have approached the study of alcoholism by examining various drinking customs. Obviously alcoholism occurs only in persons who participate in drinking customs. And differences in the prevalence and typology of pathological drinking have been identified with variations both in drinking customs and in beliefs, attitudes, and values about alcohol.

The Irish   R. F. Bales has suggested three general aspects of culture and social organization that may influence rates of alcoholism.[12] First are factors that operate to create inner tension, such as culturally induced anxiety, guilt, conflict, suppressed hostility, and sexual tension. Second are culturally supported attitudes toward drinking and intoxication—depending on these, drinking may be an acceptable means of relieving inner tension, or the thought of drinking for this purpose may in itself be anxiety-provoking enough to preclude it. Third are the alternate methods provided by the culture for resolving tension.

Bales described how in the nineteenth-century, when many Irish emigrated to the United States, the culture in Ireland supported the development of intensive inner frustration, hostility, and unrelieved sexual tension in the large numbers of males who retained the social status of "boy" throughout their

[12] Robert Freed Bales, "Cultural Differences in Rates of Alcoholism," *Quarterly Journal of Studies on Alcohol,* Vol. 6 (March 1946), pp. 480–499.

adulthood.[13] As a form of social control and a "safe" outlet for the potentially explosive force created by enforced dependency, especially mother-son dependency, and sexual deprivation, the culture permitted the frequent excessive use of alcohol by single males, a kind of institutionalized intoxication. In addition, there was a tendency to substitute drinking for eating, since food was often in short supply. After emigrating to the United States, the Irishmen found themselves at the bottom of the socioeconomic scale, in a situation that perpetuated the anxieties of the old country. Moreover, the expectations of the new culture regarding the independence of the adult male served to deepen their anxiety. Because they brought with them practices and attitudes supporting the heavy use of alcohol to deal with tension, Irish males have experienced a greater exposure to frequent intoxication than most other Americans.

The Jews   C. R. Snyder tested Bales' concepts in an extensive study of the use of alcohol by Jews in the United States.[14] Particularly among the Orthodox Jews, Snyder found that drinking was an integral part of the socialization process, repeatedly experienced as a part of religious ritual and thoroughly compatible with the prevailing norms. Even though alcohol use was extensive, and there were symbolically meaningful situations when intoxication was culturally sanctioned, alcoholism was virtually nonexistent. Snyder found that with decreasing orthodoxy among Jews, the decline of the traditional rites with which drinking had been integrated, the dissociation of drinking experiences from the normal socialization process, and the introduction of alcohol use in social contexts solely for the purpose of its effect, were all associated with an increase in the rates of alcohol pathology.

The Italians   Several studies of the drinking practices of Italians in both Italy and the United States[15] have identified alcohol as an integral part of dietary beliefs and customs. Drinking and eating are inseparable activities. Drinking usually involves wine, which has low alcohol content, and excessive drinking usually occurs in the context of excessive eating. Even when large amounts of alcohol are consumed, they are taken slowly and interspaced with food, which slows the rate of absorption. Intoxication, when it does occur, is in the context of social conviviality and is considered in the same light as indigestion or other results of gluttony. Alcoholism is rare. As in the case of the Jews, marked changes in drinking patterns are found to occur with later generations and greater acculturation in the United States. As alienation from the original Italian culture takes place, drinking occurs apart from the context of meals, involves beverages other than wine or beer, and occurs in settings where Italian group sanctions do not prevail. Under such conditions, drinking for the

---

[13] See the classic study by Conrad M. Arensberg, *The Irish Countryman* (New York: Macmillan, 1947).

[14] Charles R. Snyder, *Alcohol and the Jews* (New York: Free Press, 1958).

[15] See, for example, G. Lolli et al., *Alcohol in Italian Culture* (New York: Free Press, 1958).

sake of drinking becomes more common and intoxication more frequent, and alcoholism begins to appear.

These distinctive patterns of drinking and low rates of alcoholism cannot be attributed to less inner tension or fewer problems of adjustment among traditional Jews or Italians. On the contrary, both groups appear to have their expected share of various forms of mental illness, with Jews perhaps exceeding most other religious groups. And both groups seem to include more than their share of individuals who eat to the point of gross obesity in an apparent effort to deal with stress.

Another relevant study examined varying rates of alcoholism and other forms of deviance among inhabitants of a small triethnic (Anglo-American, Spanish-American, American Indian) community in southwestern Colorado. It was found that rates of pathology were correlated with the degree of culture-conflict with Anglo values.[16]

The studies cited here are among many that have considered the relationship between cultural norms and pathological drinking. They add convincing evidence that cultural factors must be included in a holistic theory of the causes of alcoholism. It has been seen that alcoholism is most apt to become a response to stress in those cultures where drinking customs create exposure to frequent intoxication, where intoxication is sought for its effect on the individual rather than as a means of fulfilling group functions, and where there are no culture-approved alternative modes of dealing with stress such as overeating or using a tranquilizing drug with fewer or less serious adverse effects.

Can Alcoholism Be Inherited?

Numerous studies have revealed a tendency for alcoholism to "run in families." That is, there is a greater statistical probability that a person will become an alcoholic if one or both parents are alcoholic than if neither parent is an alcoholic.[17] These observations have rekindled a long interest in the question of alcoholism and heredity and the search for genetic factors that can cause alcoholism. Although specific factors have not yet been identified to support a free-standing theory of biological causation, there is evidence that individuals differ in sensitivity to alcohol and in vulnerability to alcoholism, whether or not genetic factors contribute to the differences. Actually, whatever its cause, hypersensitivity to alcohol could quite conceivably operate in two directions. For some persons, it might increase vulnerability to alcoholism by producing toxic effects from relatively small amounts of alcohol; for others, the unpleasantness associated with drinking might serve to protect users from ever drinking too much. Similarly, low sensitivity to alcohol could permit some users to drink more than average amounts without encountering problems, while endangering others by delaying the normal warning signs of intoxication.

[16] R. Jessor et al., *Society, Personality and Deviant Behavior* (New York: Holt, 1968).
[17] Donald W. Goodwin, "Is Alcoholism Hereditary?" *Archives of General Psychiatry,* Vol. 25 (December 1971), pp. 545–549.

Apart from the question of biological heredity, there are several factors that can help explain the high frequency of alcoholism among offspring of alcoholic parents. Children who grow up in households with alcoholics are often subjected to inconsistent parental behavior. For example, parents can be unreasonably punitive and rejecting when intoxicated, and guilt-ridden and overindulgent when sober. Factors such as tension and unpredictability in the alcoholic parent, anxiety or resentment in the other parent, and stigmatization by peers can have a profound influence on the physical and emotional health of a child and on childhood personality development. If, as a result, children of alcoholics suffer more than others from feelings of insecurity, inadequacy, or diffuse anxiety they are more prone to find special solace in the tranquilizing properties of alcohol. Furthermore, the alcoholic home provides an environment where resort to alcohol in response to stress is modeled and the example of heavy drinking is established. Although some children of alcoholics totally reject drinking, their resolution to abstain may be more fragile than that of other nondrinkers, and if they ever do drink they may be more apt to drink heavily.

In summary, the high prevalence of alcoholism in families of alcoholics suggests the possibility of a contributing genetic factor, as yet unidentified. It can also quite logically be associated with psychological, social, and cultural factors including the emotional environment of the home and the normative drinking behavior to which children of alcoholics are exposed.

ALCOHOL AND YOUTH

A major social problem associated with alcoholic beverages revolves around drinking by young people. For most people drinking begins before adulthood, and the goal of preventing the use of alcohol by children and youth has received high priority from both temperance societies and lawmakers. The laws of every state in this country require instruction about alcohol in the public schools. There is a tendency to assume that almost any untoward behavior involving young people has resulted from their drinking, even in the face of clear evidence to the contrary. For example, a news item about vandalism that occurred during a college picnic noted in its headline and lead paragraph that the incident was undoubtedly the result of drinking by students, while buried later in the article was a police report that exonerated the students altogether. This tendency to equate disturbing behavior in young people with drinking was overshadowed in the late 1960s and early 1970s by social concern about the use of hallucinogens, marijuana, heroin, and other illicit drugs, as well as by anxiety on the part of adults over the many ways in which young people were expressing their disenchantment with societal values and priorities. In the mid-1970s, alcohol is again high on the list of adult concerns about youthful behavior.

Like many other social concerns, the question of teen-age drinking elicits a wide variety of ineffectual social responses. Some people exaggerate the problem; others deny that it even exists. Parents, schools, and law enforcement agencies tend to place responsibility on each other, and religious institutions frequently blame all three.

Although available data indicate that the majority of high school students who drink at all do not drink very often or consume very much at a time, drinking by high school students is reported to be increasing in the 1970s.[18] In the college-age group of 18 to 21, the prevalence of drinking equals—and the quantity and frequency may exceed—that of the general population. Intoxication is a special problem for teen-agers because their reactions to alcohol are complicated by their lack of experience in coping with its effects and because much of their drinking occurs in public. When adolescents do become intoxicated they are, therefore, likely to get involved in other difficulties and be highly visible. As noted earlier, some adolescents may give the illusion of intoxication when they have consumed only a single drink. Such behavior undoubtedly has contributed to an exaggerated impression among adults of the excesses of teen-age drinking.

Most adolescent drinking reflects the practices and sanctions of family, friends, and other reference groups. For some adolescents, however, drinking involves breaking with family or religious convictions. The mere act of drinking, the effects of drinking, or the behavior of drinking companions may evoke feelings of personal conflict or guilt. Or drinking may be associated with sexual behavior, which evokes similar kinds of conflict. The reaction to these anxieties of students who do drink is complicated by the fact that the pharmacological properties of alcohol actually can provide temporary relief from them. This is a "solace" denied to young people who may be equally anxious because they have decided not to drink despite peer pressures to do so. The dilemma of those who abstain in the face of pressures to drink should not be omitted from an inventory of alcohol-associated problems.

Confusion and conflict about drinking by young people in American society has been compounded by inconsistencies between actual behavior and laws. The realities of drinking by high school and college youth have exhibited widespread disregard of legal sanctions. One study of college drinking patterns actually found that, although colleges with formal prohibitions against drinking had relatively fewer drinkers than "liberal" colleges, those students who broke with regulations against drinking generally drank more frequently and more heavily, and were involved in more drinking-related problems than the student drinkers in schools with only token or no restrictions. As one student expressed the tendency, "When you go to the trouble of driving 50 miles to get a drink, you don't have just two drinks." This tendency to use more alcohol when drinking involves extra effort or the flaunting of authority is not restricted to adolescents. It is reminiscent of adult drinking practices during Prohibition

---

[18] *Alcohol and Health: New Knowledge, op cit.,* pp. 8–12.

and in the "dry" areas of states where the prohibition of alcoholic beverages is a matter of local option.

Until about 1970, only two states, New York and Louisiana, permitted the purchase of all forms of alcoholic beverage at age 18. Most states withheld the legal right to buy any form of alcoholic beverage until age 21. Yet there was evidence that a majority of young people were drinking despite the prohibitions and that illegal drinking tended to involve more effort, more alcohol, and more problems, while legal drinking was more casual, less contrived, and less apt to end in intoxication or problems. Because of this, the Cooperative (United States and Canada) Commission on the Study of Alcoholism recommended in 1967 that the legal age for purchasing and using alcohol be standardized at 18 in the United States and Canada.[19] A trend was started; by the end of 1973, 20 states had set the minimum age for purchasing alcohol at 18 and only 13 still prohibited all alcohol purchases until age 21. This movement coincided with the nationwide enfranchisement of 18-year-olds and a trend to establish other aspects of adult status at age 18.

The lowering of the legal drinking age has not yet produced the reduction in drinking problems that some advocates of this measure anticipated. In at least some states and provinces that have lowered the age limit, rates of automobile accidents involving youthful drivers have risen and there are reported signs of increasing intoxication. There are conflicting interpretations of cause and effect. The fact that there seems to be an increase in problem drinking by young people could simply mean that public attention has shifted from other drugs to alcohol; it could be a factor of increased drinking by the society at large as documented by the recent significant rise in per capita consumption of alcohol; it could, as opponents of the lowered legal drinking age insist, be in part a consequence of giving young people a more liberal license to drink; or it could be part of a youth behavior movement that is quite independent of alcohol laws.

Rapid social change has enlarged the barriers between the roles and values of parents and those of their adolescent children. The greater the rate of change, the less meaningful adults are as role models and the less security they can provide. In the face of conflict, insecurity, and confusion, adolescents have developed a distinctive subculture. They seek a self-identity. They tend to press for rights and to reject symbols of authority as repressive. Even where laws have been liberalized, drinking provides an apt symbol of having achieved adult status and a "red flag" for rejection of authority. Thus, many well-intentioned efforts to control or moderate the drinking of young people have either served to enhance the attractiveness and status of drinking or had no effect. Drinking that is an expression of personal conflict or social rebellion is more likely to involve conditions conducive to intoxication—large amounts of al-

[19] Thomas F. A. Plaut, *Alcohol Problems: A Report to the Nation,* by the Cooperative Commission on the Study of Alcoholism (New York: Oxford, 1967), p. 149.

cohol, distilled spirits rather than beer, quick consumption, no food, and often the specific purpose of becoming drunk.

Assuming that the youth behavior movement of the mid-1970s includes an increasing prevalence of drinking that frequently involves intoxication, it is logical to speculate on the future implications of such drinking since, as noted earlier, Cahalan and Room have recently reported evidence that "the seeds to longer-term serious problems with alcohol are probably usually sown by drinking habits in the early twenties."[20] Kaye Fillmore, reporting on a preliminary 20-year follow-up study of men and women who participated in the college drinking survey of the early 1950s also found evidence that "early problem drinking is significantly related to later problem drinking over a 20-year period."[21]

ALCOHOL AND THE AUTOMOBILE

Alcohol-related automobile and small-aircraft accidents have been described as "one of the most costly aftermaths of the introduction of technology in modern society."[22] Problems resulting from alcohol use in transportation are not really new. Intoxication has been cited as a common factor in accidents involving Roman chariots, clipper ships, and even mule drivers. But the liability of alcohol use in transportation has increased with mechanization and with such factors as traffic density and speed. In just 33 years, from 1940 to 1973, the number of motor vehicles registered in the United States rose by 375 percent, from roughly 33 to 124 million; from 1940 to 1972, the total number of miles traveled annually rose 420 percent, from 302 to 1,268 billion; and the average vehicle speed increased from 33 to 60 miles per hour.[23]

The impact of alcohol on traffic accidents in the United States has been starkly demonstrated by numerous studies based on the blood alcohol levels of drivers and other data from arrest records. It has been estimated that there are at least 800,000 alcohol-related motor vehicle accidents annually in the United States and that these account for about 30,000 deaths, or roughly half of all the highway fatalities in the country, in addition to immeasurable property damage, disabling injuries, loss of wages, and medical and insurance expenses. Accidents involving alcohol tend to be more severe, in terms of both property damage and personal injuries, than those in which alcohol is not present. Alcohol has been cited as the single most significant factor in multiple-vehicle accidents, single-vehicle accidents, and accidents involving pedestrians, who have often been drinking themselves. With the rapid increase in private

[20] Cahalan and Room, *op. cit.*, p. 52.

[21] Fillmore, *op. cit.*, p. 837.

[22] U.S. Dept. of Health, Education and Welfare, *Report of the Secretary's Advisory Committee on Traffic Safety* (Washington, D.C.: Government Printing Office, 1968), p. xi.

[23] U.S. Bureau of the Census, *Statistical Abstract of the United States, 1974* (Washington, D.C.: Government Printing Office, 1974), pp. 556, 562.

flying, reports based on pilot toxicology examinations indicate that alcohol is involved in a significant proportion of fatal accidents with small aircraft.

The relationship between drinking and driving is primarily due to alcohol's depressive action on the central nervous system and its consequent effects on perceptions, motor responses, and emotional states. Tests of actual driving that require the simultaneous coordination of several motor and perceptual responses indicate high sensitivity to the influence of alcohol. In fact, impairment of performance has been demonstrated in drivers when alcohol concentration is as low as 0.05 percent. Since the liabilities of alcohol on driving increase sharply as the task becomes more complex, individual experiences can be dangerously misleading. The drinker who is an experienced driver may be able to handle a car safely as long as driving is routine, but unable to respond to demands for a unique or rapid reaction. Contemporary driving is rarely routine, and the complexity of the task is increased with higher density of traffic, accelerated speed, poor visibility, darkness, bad road conditions, faulty vehicles, or unpredictable dangerous actions of other drivers. An unfortunate effect of alcohol on the drinking driver is that it may give him a heightened illusion of competence or increase his impulsivity and recklessness at the very same time that his actual abilities have been compromised. A disproportionate number of fatal accidents tend to occur at night, especially between 10 P.M. and 6 A.M. These are also the hours when heavy drinkers are most likely to be driving home from drinking situations, thus combining the worst conditions of driving with the highest degree of driver intoxicaton.

Although anyone who drives while under the influence of alcohol increases the risk of having an accident, it has been found that alcoholics contribute more than their share to alcohol-related accidents. This may be simply because alcoholics are intensively intoxicated more often than other drivers, or it could reflect the feeling of omnipotence or false sense of security that many alcoholics display when they are drinking. It could also be related to a high incidence of emotional and social instability, and possibly to suicidal tendencies, which are common in alcoholism.

Studies on the blood alcohol levels that can affect psychosensory and psychomotor responses enough to impair driving ability have led to the development of laws in most states establishing specific levels as legal evidence of intoxication. A number of packaged laboratories are available to police departments for use in obtaining quick measurements of the blood alcohol concentration of drivers at the scene of an accident. There is considerable variation among states, but the level of 0.15 percent is generally accepted as clear evidence of intoxication, and there is a movement in many states to reduce this to 0.10 percent or even 0.08 percent. One problem with establishing legally *dangerous* alcohol levels is that it implies that one can drink and drive safely as long as these levels are not reached. Since even small amounts of alcohol often impair good judgment and since alcoholics, particularly, are prone to rationalize their special need for alcohol, the impression that there are *any* "safe" levels may be dangerous. Even mild sensations produced by alcohol, if experienced at the particular moment when a novice drinker-driver must respond to an unusual traffic crisis, may cause an accident. For both poor-risk drivers and poor-risk drinkers, the implication of a "safe" level may be providing a dangerous "license" for driving when under the influence of alcohol. Furthermore, the concept of safe limits does not account for accidents in which a driver might conceivably have been at a "safe" level when entering a vehicle, reach a peak dangerous level of alcohol before having an accident, and be back at a "safe" level shortly afterwards, when a breath or blood sample would be taken for analysis. Relatively sudden but brief periods of alcohol concentration may be particularly common after drinking moderately but hastily on an empty stomach, as one might do at a late afternoon cocktail party.

In several countries, notably Great Britain and the Scandinavian nations, legislation has been passed imposing both loss of license and imprisonment on persons convicted of driving while intoxicated. Public opinion has seemed to support such sanctions and there have been some modifications of social custom to provide alcohol-free drivers for persons who plan to drink away from home. Yet traffic accident rates remain high and the alcohol factor in such accidents remains significant. Again, the two highest-risk groups, alcoholics and youths, are most visible. The very condition of alcoholism makes alcoholics less likely to be deterred by sanctions, blood tests, or punishment. For some young drivers, severe sanctions seem to offer a special challenge that becomes an incentive for drinking or an attractive way of expressing bravado and rejecting authority.

In the United States, while the interests of public safety clearly support a broad social movement to discourage drinking prior to driving, blood-alcohol tests and penalties for conviction in accident cases have been generally ineffective. Efforts to modify drinking-and-driving customs have met with abysmal failure. Public resistance seems rooted in the strong mores that have protected the "right to drink" against legal prohibitions, and in the equally strong mores that have developed around the "right to drive." Supported perhaps by an illusion of individual omnipotence or invulnerability, public sentiment in the United States has generally been against safety measures that involve stringent controls on the right to drive. There has been resistance to re-examining drivers, to inspecting vehicles, and to imposing penalties on chronic traffic law violators, as well as to efforts to control driving while intoxicated. At this time, prevailing mores in America appear to place a higher value on the rights to drink and to drive than on protecting others from the drinking driver.

Currently, a considerable investment is being made by public national agencies, including the Department of Transportation and the National Institute on Alcohol Abuse and Alcoholism, by numerous state and voluntary alcohol programs, and by the insurance industry, to publicize the extent to which drinking and driving violates the interests of public safety. Thus far, however, despite the dramatic evidence of death and disaster for drinking drivers and for innocent victims, neither laws, punishment, nor appeals to intelligence, reason, or emotion have been effective in reducing the prevalence of driving under the influence of alcohol.

THE PROBLEMS OF ALCOHOL AND MAJOR SOCIAL SYSTEMS

Alcohol problems and the uses of alcohol permeate almost every aspect of society. The national economy reflects the great size of the alcoholic beverage industry as an employer, as a user of natural products, and as a consumer of such major services as transportation, advertising, and retail sales. Personal consumption expenditures for packaged alcoholic beverages in the United States in 1972 amounted to 20.3 billion dollars, or 2.8 percent of all personal expenditures.[24] This equals the amount spent that year on private education and research and religious and welfare activities combined.

The alcoholic beverage industry is a significant source of tax revenue for local, state, and federal governments. Federal and state taxes on alcoholic beverages in 1972 came to 6.8 billion dollars, more than 2 percent of all such revenue.[25] But tax revenues, no matter how large, seem modest when weighed against the estimated economic costs of alcohol-related problems.

The Costs of Problem Drinking

As noted at the beginning of this chapter, the annual economic cost of alcohol-related problems has been roughly estimated at 25 billion dollars.[26] This figure was termed "conservative," and included the costs of lost production of goods and services attributed to male problem drinkers; expenditures for alcohol-related health and medical problems; alcohol's contribution to the costs of motor vehicle accidents; alcohol-related costs of maintaining the criminal justice system and of police, courts, jails, and prisons; expenditures for programs of treatment, rehabilitation, prevention, education, and research on alcohol problems; and alcohol-related costs to social welfare programs. Not included were costs of lost productivity of women or of alcoholics living in institutions or on skid row; costs incurred by victims of alcohol-related crime (although alcohol was cited as an associated factor in a substantial number of murders, assaults, and rapes); welfare payments to offset income loss for alcoholics or their families; the costs of health and mental health services for spouses or children of alcoholics; or alcohol-related costs of the nation's annual losses due to fire.

More than 8 billion dollars was estimated as the annual cost of alcohol-related health and medical problems. This comprised 12 percent of all adult health expenditures and 20 percent of the total adult expenditures for hospitali-

---

[24] *Statistical Abstract of the United States, 1974*, p. 376.
[25] *Ibid.*, p. 248.
[26] *Alcohol and Health: New Knowledge*, pp. 49–57.

zation. Other studies have reported that about a third of the male patients in general hospitals are problem drinkers, although nearly none are being treated for their drinking problems, and that a fourth of all admissions to state and county mental hospitals are problem drinkers. In one general hospital, problem drinkers were found to be much sicker than other patients. Their average hospital stay was 11.2 days compared with 7.7 days, their average utilization of intensive-care facilities was 5.3 days compared with 3.0 days, and their average charges for hospitalization were $1,506 compared with $964.[27]

Great as these estimates of the economic costs of alcohol-related problems may be, they cannot begin to express the magnitude of the problems personally experienced in the family, at work, and in other primary social relationships.

The Family

It is within the family that the effects of drinking and the problems of alcohol are most intimately experienced. Most people are first exposed to the values, beliefs, and customs of drinking or abstaining in the context of their families. Several studies have found that the family is the most frequent setting and family members the most frequent companions at the time of earliest exposure to alcohol, and that about half of those who drink report having had some experiment or taste by the age of 10. The importance of the family in the transmission of drinking customs is further demonstrated by high correlations between young people and their parents in regard to the types of beverages used, frequency of drinking, and amounts consumed. It is within their families that most individuals acquire the sense of security or inadequacy that may influence the psychological meaning of alcohol for them and their future motivations for drinking. The significance of the family for adolescent drinking is also seen in those cases where use of alcohol does not conform to family norms but appears rather as a rebellious reaction to the authority of parents and others.

As noted in the section on causes of alcoholism, the fact that children of alcoholic parents are more prone to alcoholism suggests that the family environment may contribute to its occurrence. Life histories of alcoholics often contain evidence that family stress or unresolved, ambivalent feelings toward parents contributed, notably both in families that generated conflict or guilt about the use of alcohol and in those that provided role models for the use of alcohol as a way of acting out conflict or dealing with stress.

In turn, alcoholism clearly contributes to family stress and instability. Alcoholics are more frequently divorced or separated than nonalcoholics, and the wives, husbands, and children of alcoholics have relatively high rates of physical, emotional, and psychosomatic illness. Alcoholics usually demand a great deal of emotional support from others but provide little or no such support in return. Also, because of their preoccupation with alcohol, because of personality traits associated with alcoholism, or merely because of the impotence

[27] Robert Straus, "Alcohol and Society," *Psychiatric Annals,* Vol. 3 (October 1973), p. 72.

resulting from the sedative impact of alcohol, alcoholics are often unsatisfying sexual partners. Additional stress for families stems from the economic burdens often associated with the relatively high cost of alcohol and the loss of income resulting from alcohol pathology.

Work

Outside of the family, the primary setting that can both contribute to and be affected by problem drinking is the job situation. The costs of problem drinking employees are measured in terms of loss of efficiency, absenteeism, accidents and injuries, extra sick leave, wasted time, faulty decision making, spoiled goods, impaired morale of co-workers, and frequent job turnover. Traditionally, alcoholics have simply been fired when their condition became too great a job liability, but in recent years many large firms have begun to establish programs of education, detection, and treatment for alcoholic employees.

Not yet generally recognized are work-connected factors that contribute to the onset or progression of problem drinking. In contemporary industrial society, there are many jobs that demand more skills, or impose greater responsibilities, than most human beings can comfortably or healthfully maintain on a continuing basis. When men and women are promoted to positions beyond their level of competence or beyond a level of human endurance, they often suffer great physical and emotional discomfort and stress because of the very jobs that symbolize their success. Alcohol provides a convenient, quickly effective, temporary, and often dangerous antidote for their discomfort.

A much larger segment of the working force includes men and women who find themselves at a plateau in their jobs beyond which they can never advance. They may be victims of rapid technological change, corporate policy, or their own incompetence, but they work in a society that places strong moral value on job promotion and advancement as symbols of success. In the face of these prevailing values, many workers experience a kind of anomie. Their jobs become empty, meaningless, and intrinsically unsatisfying; they often feel little identification with the purpose or product of the work, no loyalty, and no sense of pride. For those whose jobs become hateful necessities, alcohol offers a chemical antidote. Still other aspects of work that can contribute to problem drinking are job-associated situations that are perceived to require drinking—such as selling, attending conventions, or demonstrating appropriate conviviality.

Thus far, industrial programs for problem drinking and alcoholism have been aimed primarily at detection and rehabilitation or at modifying the drinker's behavior through education. Although these programs represent a significant change in attitudes and policies toward alcoholic employees, they do not address the more basic questions of identifying what it is about work situations and work experiences that makes it meaningful for employees to drink too much or what programs of preventive intervention might modify these conditions.

SOCIAL RESPONSES TO ALCOHOL PROBLEMS

Up to about 1940, public provision for alcoholics was found only in jails, asylums, public infirmaries, or shelters. Important changes began to take place in the early 1940s. It was then that the first outpatient clinics were established to offer a combination of medical, psychological, and social work therapies for alcoholics. By providing both help and hope, these community-based programs began to attract the formerly hidden alcoholic for treatment, making possible a better understanding of the alcoholic's social assets and liabilities. They brought into visibility patients with relative stability in marriage, employment, and community. This helped to alter the prevailing stereotypes and to reduce stigma. Coincidently, in the 1940s, the organization known as Alcoholics Anonymous emerged into prominence. The Alcoholics Anonymous program is structured around reliance on personal faith and the support and insight gained from others with similar experiences and needs. Its essential therapeutic element appears to be the provision of a meaningful reference group concerned with maintaining sobriety. The social impact of Alcoholics Anonymous includes its contribution to a better understanding of and sympathy for the alcoholic. Along with formal treatment programs, the movement has demonstrated that alcoholics are found in all walks of life and that they can be reclaimed as useful, productive, and respectable members of the community.

Victims of alcoholism and their families have provided much of the drive behind efforts to focus attention and understanding on the long-neglected problems of alcohol, develop effective social mechanisms for coping with these problems, and stimulate the assumption of responsibility by government at all levels. In the United States, a substantial public health movement has developed that encompasses the voluntary National Council on Alcoholism, community-based voluntary health groups in many major cities, state tax-supported programs for education and treatment of alcoholism and, in the 1970s, significant developments at the level of the federal government. The United States Congress has created the National Institute on Alcohol Abuse and Alcoholism within the Department of Health, Education and Welfare and is currently appropriating substantial funds in support of training, education, and treatment programs, and grants to state and regional agencies.

Evaluating Change in Social Responses

In spite of increased activity at various levels of government, there is as yet no consistent social response to alcohol problems in the United States. Many discriminatory or ineffective policies still prevail. Although the laws of many states have relieved the alcoholic of criminal responsibility for drunkenness, chronic public intoxication is still dealt with primarily by police, courts, and jails. The force of public opinion continues to make laws against driving when drinking a mockery. Many hospitals, social agencies, and health and welfare personnel still try to justify refusing to treat people for alcoholism. Many

employers summarily dismiss alcoholic employees upon detection. In relation to the magnitude and severity of these problems, the funds invested in research, education, treatment, and prevention are still pitifully small.

Yet recent years have seen encouraging change. The stigma of alcoholism has been moderated. The alcoholic is less likely to be morally blamed for his problem and more likely to be depicted as the victim of a problem. As a result, he is now more likely also to admit that he has a problem and to seek help. The perception of what behavior constitutes problem drinking has become broader, and there has been a distinct trend for people with drinking problems to seek help at younger ages and sometimes even when they do not have the extreme symptoms of physical or psychological dependence on alcohol.

Several kinds of alcoholism have been identified and concepts of multiple causation have emerged, although there is not yet a generally accepted theory about causes. Numerous treatment resources have been developed and a variety of drugs have been found to help the alcoholic maintain sobriety, although they do not cure his alcoholism. Clinics, specialized hospitals, and specially designated beds in general hospitals have become available to alcoholics. Some physicians are now specializing in the treatment of alcoholism. Alcoholics Anonymous has had a significant, if unmeasurable, impact. Although these growing resources serve only a small portion of the population of problem drinkers and must operate within the limits of available knowledge, they are proving effective. Generally, the approaches that combine medical, psychological, and social intervention have had the greatest degree of success.

Growing awareness of public responsibility for the problems of alcoholism has been reflected in the increasing support provided for governmental programs. Major employers and insurance companies are also beginning to give some attention to these problems, although only after much resistance. But there are still no cures, and no known ways of preventing alcoholism. Nor do the various helping programs appear to have brought about any measurable reduction in the incidence of alcoholism and other problem drinking in the United States.

Social Policy and Normative Behavior

Laws or regulations representing change in social policy often conflict with the way people are accustomed to behaving. This poses a dilemma for many societies today, as it has for generations, with respect to social policy on alcohol. In most societies where a large majority of the adult population attaches some importance to the right to drink, governments have accepted a responsibility to make alcohol available and have capitalized on the opportunity to collect a considerable amount of tax revenue. At the same time, governments have a fundamental responsibility to protect the individual and the society from the many threats posed by alcohol abuse to the public health and well-being.

The most common type of governmental intervention—prohibition—has been invoked for the purpose of protecting the public but at the expense of both accessibility and tax revenue. Moreover, prohibition has generally failed because it has violated prevailing norms that demanded accessibility of alcohol.

In the United States, conflicts between mores and laws continue to characterize many aspects of drinking behavior. The phrase "vote dry and drink wet" is an apt description not merely of attitudes toward prohibition laws, but also of the predominant response to most other legal restrictions associated with drinking customs: drinking-and-driving codes, laws regulating the hours of sale and other aspects of distribution, laws covering manufacturing, and taxation. Many people will strongly support alcohol-control laws in principle but will violate them freely and, unless a violation has involved personal and direct damage to themselves, will condone their violation by others.

Experience in the United States and elsewhere in the world clearly indicates that efforts to cope with problems of alcohol by legislating change will prove ineffective unless laws can be made that reflect normative forces of behavior. In the United States, drinking customs reflect the beliefs and values of many national, regional, ethnic, and social groups. The absence of homogeneity in drinking norms also contributes a difficulty in dealing with alcohol—the problem of conceptualization, which has been a recurring theme of this chapter.

SUMMARY

1   Drinking behavior interacts in some way with almost every aspect of social life and all major social institutions: health, family, religion, economics, government, education, and recreation.

2   The nature and severity of alcohol problems involve a relationship between the drinking customs of the society and the chemical effect of alcohol on the individual's psychological behavior and physiological functioning.

3   Alcohol is both functional and dysfunctional. When used moderately, for many people alcohol can provide relief from tension, worry, or pain, and a pleasurable sense of well-being, relaxation, and conviviality. But when used in circumstances that are socially inappropriate or in amounts that exceed an individual's capacity, the intoxicating properties of alcohol can cause serious problems ranging from incidental drunkenness and its consequences to problem drinking and alcoholism.

4   The impact of alcohol on human behavior depends on the concentration of alcohol in the blood when it reaches the brain. This in turn is influenced by such factors as the type and alcohol content of the beverage, the rate of ingestion, the presence or absence of food in the stomach, and the amount consumed in relation to the body weight of the drinker.

5   As with all drugs, some users of alcohol may experience an adverse reaction to very small amounts, while others may require more than average amounts to experience an average effect. Reaction may be influenced by level of fatigue, health, time of day, social setting, biological rhythm, mood, the use of other drugs, prior drinking experience, and prevailing social expectation regarding alcohol use.

6   The per capita consumption of alcohol in the United States and most other Western countries is rising. About three out of four American men and three out of five women use some kind of alcohol beverage. Together with youthful drinkers, they comprise over 100 million users of alcohol. Of these, at least 10 million are *problem drinkers* and probably about 6 million are *alcoholics.*

7   Problem drinkers are people whose use of alcohol repeatedly exceeds either prevailing social customs or their capacity to handle alcohol.

8   Alcoholics are problem drinkers whose persistent abuse of alcohol is associated with physical or psychological dependence involving an inability to control drinking or intensive unbearable stress, discomfort, or tension when alcohol is not available.

9   Physical dependence on alcohol is evidenced by signs of acute physical distress when alcohol is withdrawn during a drinking episode or by the ability of the drinker to drink more and more before experiencing some of the more common toxic effects.

10   Psychological dependence on alcohol is characterized by an inability to stop drinking once an episode has started, an inability to refrain from drinking in inappropriate situations, or an inability to face, without alcohol, situations that pose anxiety. In alcoholics, psychological dependence is associated with an intensive and compulsive sense of need for alcohol.

11   Social dependence on alcohol occurs in people who drink primarily in order to conform to the drinking expectations of social situations, rather than in response to internal physical or mood discomfort. People who repeatedly drink too much in response to the pressures of social situations are socially dependent problem drinkers.

12   Currently available knowledge suggests that problem drinking and alcoholism are caused by variable combinations of factors including (a) apparent but as yet unidentified factors of physical or biochemical vulnerability, (b) factors of personality that create psychological vulnerability, and (c) drinking customs that repeatedly expose individuals to situations in which they drink too much.

13   Intoxication is a special problem for teen-agers because their reactions to alcohol are complicated by their lack of experience in coping with its effects and because much of their drinking occurs in public.

14   Alcohol-related traffic accidents have increased along with traffic density, speed, and the use of alcohol and other psychoactive substances. Motor vehicle accidents involving alcohol account for about half of all highway fatalities in this country, as well as a high percentage of nonfatal accidents, many accidents involving pedestrians, and a significant proportion of fatal accidents with small aircraft.

15   Because of individual variations in response to alcohol it is dangerous to assume that there are any really "safe" margins for drinking and driving. Despite the overwhelming evidence that drinking drivers bring death and disaster to themselves and to innocent victims, neither laws and punishment nor appeals to intelligence, reason, or emotion have effectively reduced the prevalence of driving under the influence of alcohol.

16   Problem drinking and alcoholism can be both responsive and contributory to family stress and instability, job dissatisfaction and ineffectiveness, sexual and interpersonal incompatibility, physical and emotional illness, and other major social problems.

17   Increasing social concern about alcohol abuse, along with the efforts of recovered alcoholics and their families, has led to the development of governmental and private programs for education, prevention, and treatment. There are still no sure cures and no known ways of preventing alcoholism, nor is there any measurable reduction in problem drinking.

18   Efforts to control alcohol abuse and its consequences through legal controls have generally failed, partly because such laws have been in conflict with the prevailing norms.

RECOMMENDED READING

For readers who want to explore any aspect of knowledge about alcoholism or problem drinking, the most valuable source of continuing information is the *Quarterly Journal of Studies on Alcohol.* This Journal, published since 1940, includes both original articles and abstracts of the world literature. In 1975 it began monthly publication and became the *Journal of Studies on Alcohol*. Up-to-date reports on recent developments are published monthly in newspaper format in *The Journal* of the Addiction Research Foundation of Toronto.

An excellent, thorough but brief, authoritative article by Mark Keller on "Alcohol Consumption" appears in the 15th Edition of the *Encyclopedia Britannica* (1974). A useful summary of current knowledge was assembled by the National Institute on Alcohol Abuse and Alcoholism for reports to the U.S. Congress entitled *Alcohol and Health* (1971) and *Alcohol and Health: New Knowledge* (1974).

Readers who are interested in the personal experiences of alcoholics will want to read the book *Alcoholics Anonymous* (2nd Edition 1955) or other publications of the Alcoholics Anonymous organization, or the recent biography by Robert Thompson of AA's founder, *Bill W.* (1975). The relationship between alcoholism and institutional dependency is explored in the author's study of a 68-year life record, *Escape from Custody* (1974). A many-sided picture of drinking practices and problems among college students can be found in George L. Maddox's *The Domesticated Drug* (1970).

A historical and cross-cultural perspective on drinking behavior and problems, edited by David J. Pittman and Charles R. Snyder, is *Society, Culture and Drinking Patterns* (1962). A new perspective on drinking practices in American Society became available through Don Cahalan, Ira M. Cisin, and H. M. Crossley's *American Drinking Practices* (1969), which is based on interviews with a national probability sample of American households. Further insights on the identity of problem drinkers and the course of problem drinking are found in Don Cahalan's *Problem Drinkers* (1970) and in Cahalan and Robin Room's *Problem Drinking Among American Men* (1974).

Readers who are particularly interested in theories about the causes of alcoholism are referred to E. M. Jellinek's classic *The Disease Concept of Alcoholism* (1960), and to J. B. Roebuck and R. G. Kessler's *The Etiology of Alcoholism* (1972), and to William Madsen's *The American Alcoholic* (1974).

An excellent collection of articles on recent research is in R. J. Gibbins et al., *Recent Advances in Alcohol and Drug Problems*, Volume 2 (1975). Recent efforts to conceptualize the field of drinking behavior and alcohol problems have been edited by William J. Filstead, Jean J. Rossi, and Mark Keller, in a volume entitled *Alcohol and Alcohol Problems: New Thinking and New Directions* (1976).

5 Sexual Behavior

KINGSLEY DAVIS

How much control should society exercise over sexual behavior? Conflicting views range from a purely authoritarian position at one extreme to an utterly individualistic or anarchic position at the other. The extremes are interesting, not because they are persuasive or widely held, but because they bring the logic of the issue into sharp focus.

The extreme authoritarian view is that sexual problems would disappear if the sexual mores were observed. These mores, it explains, have evolved during thousands of years and therefore reflect the wisdom of cumulative human experience. For instance, if the taboos against premarital and adulterous intercourse were observed, there would be no illegitimacy, less venereal disease, and less divorce. Among contemporary nations, Ireland and Communist China seem most nearly to uphold this view.

The extreme permissive view holds that sex is natural and private; hence attempts to regulate it are contrary to nature and an invasion of privacy. Worse yet, according to this view, the effort to suppress and control sexual expression creates hypocrisy, subjects individuals to the risk of public disgrace, and often leads to excessive guilt and neurosis. This view is today most vigorously espoused in Sweden and the United States. In California, for example, a 1975 law repealed all legal constraints on sexual acts between consenting adults.

The authoritarian argument, if taken in an absolute sense, begs the question. If the existing sexual mores are valuable, why are so many of them so frequently violated? If violation is the problem, conformity is a "solution" only in a tautological sense. An effective solution would require a change in the *causes* of violation. The causes of violation may lie in a strain between old mores and new conditions, a clash of ethnic groups, or a breakdown in enforcement mechanisms. But whatever they are, the causes must be dealt with if the problems associated with sexual behavior are to be solved. Admonition to conform is futile.

The anarchic position also begs the question. If sex is purely natural and its regulation harmful, how does it happen that human societies always and everywhere have rules governing sexual conduct? To dismiss the rules as "prejudice" or "superstition" is merely to restate the question, because these are terms for the sentiments or beliefs underlying the mores themselves. There must be some explanation of why people are so widely and similarly prejudiced. Perhaps the rules accomplish something; perhaps their abolition would have undesirable consequences. If rules are "outmoded," new ones, not the abolition of all rules, may be needed.

Few people espouse either of these extremes. Virtually no one maintains that *all* sexual mores should be obeyed or that *none* should be. Some rules are inconsistent, others anachronistic or quixotic; it would be difficult to observe them all. On the other hand, even the most rabid nonconformists tend to take for granted certain regulations—such as those against rape and incest. The debate over sexual regulation thus boils down in practice to a quarrel between "liberal" and "conservative" points of view. The liberal approach is to condemn *certain* of the existing norms and advocate their modification or replacement

221

by "more enlightened" ones. The conservative's reply is to point out that the particular norms being criticized *are* the most enlightened and should be retained and obeyed or at most be only slightly modified. With the debate thus focusing on particular rules and control mechanisms, there is a large area of unspoken, if somewhat nebulous, agreement. It is this common ground that allows liberals and conservatives to coexist in the same society.

Our aim is to deal with causes and consequences of sexual behavior in human societies. A logical first step is to explain why sexual norms exist, and the next is to explain why violations occur. Once these two foundations in sociological theory are laid, the next task is easier—to see how changing conditions in modern society have affected observance and violation of sex norms (including rules about premarital, adulterous, commercial, and homosexual relations), and what the unforeseen consequences have been.

THE THEORY OF SEXUAL NORMS

The basic answer to why sex norms exist is that they do something for human societies. Broadly speaking, what they do is what norms in general do; but beyond that the sex norms make a special contribution arising from the particular characteristics and unique potentialities of sexual behavior. Accordingly, in this section we shall first analyze what norms in general do, then delineate significant features of the sex drive and sexual behavior, and finally describe how these features are utilized in social systems.

Norms in General

Norms exist because human behavior is mainly learned from others by symbolic communication and example. The life of a society is not organized solely by instinct but also by patterns received from and enforced by other members of the society. Competition between societies as well as with other species forces the invention and spread of new patterns. Those that prove advantageous survive, the others die out. Through thousands of years of evolution, man has become so dependent on acquired patterns that he cannot live without them.

Conformity to patterns does not occur automatically. It is induced by rewards and penalties. The very existence of regulation implies that something needs regulating. This something is by no means confined to organic drives or appetites; it is also composed of interests, emotions, and desires generated by social interaction itself. Violations may occur because the individual cannot help himself (as in an acquired drug addiction), because the norms themselves are in conflict, or because the risk is less than the potential gain. A man who successfully embezzles a million dollars reaps a big reward for nonconformity, as a wife does who secretly murders her rich but unloved husband. The factors making for nonconformity are so powerful, and so much a part of society itself, that the battle for social control is never-ending. Understandably, then, the mechanisms by which conformity is induced are complex. Much of the enforcement is informal and personal. If an individual disappoints the expectations of others, they retaliate by disappointing *his* expectations.

People tend often to "explain" behavior by citing the relevant norm and to criticize or justify a particular norm by assuming or citing other norms. Scientific explanation, however, is neither justification nor criticism, and it cannot be satisfied by appeal to norms. It subjects the norms themselves to explanation, and to do this it finds the causes in the dynamics of societies—that is, in the competition of individuals and groups for scarce goods under complex conditions and rules. The rules themselves are only a part of the system.

The Sex Drive as an Object of Regulation

Like other forms of human behavior, sexual activity must be learned, and like other norms, sex norms help get the business of society accomplished. The sex drive itself can be powerful and disruptive, but it can also motivate people to perform in ways that serve the community at large; it has, in fact, more scope for social articulation than most other drives. Although sexual gratification cannot be entirely suppressed after puberty,[1] it is not required for individual survival in the way that alleviation of hunger, thirst, or fatigue is. For this reason, sex taboos can be more absolute than food taboos, for example. Again, because the human sex drive can be stimulated by visual as well as olfactory and tactile pathways, and because it can be released in numerous ways, it is capable of an extraordinary amount of both situational and emotional conditioning. This means there is an amazing variety of sexual behaviors to regulate.

While the capacity for conditioning *allows* the sex drive to be enmeshed in a web of social relations, another feature *forces* it to be so. This is its dependence on intimate contact with another person for gratification. Masturbation can of course occur alone, but it is frequently accompanied by fantasies of partners. The human sexual urge is not simply for orgasm, but also for tactile contact and communication with another person. This desire for contact brings erotic interests into social relations and links eroticism with such interpersonal emotions as affection, trust, esteem, aggression, distrust, and jealousy.

The complexities introduced by the malleability and mutuality of the sex drive are limitless. In satisfying any desire for which the means are scarce, people compete with one another. They compete for land, jobs, shelter, clothes, and the like. An orderly society, by definition, keeps competition from degenerating into force or fraud. In the case of sexual desire, however, the "scarce objects" of gratification are themselves persons. This makes the assignment of

---

[1] See Alfred C. Kinsey et al., *Sexual Behavior in the Human Male* (Philadelphia: Saunders, 1948), pp. 205–213, and *Sexual Behavior in the Human Female* (Philadelphia: Saunders, 1953), pp. 512, 526–527; W. S. Taylor, *A Critique of Sublimation in Males,* Genetic Psychology Monographs, Vol. 13 (1933); and Hugo G. Beigel, "Abstinence," in *Encyclopedia of Sexual Behavior* (New York: Hawthorn Books, 1961).

rights over the means of satisfaction much more difficult than when the scarce objects are, say, land or inventions. Sexual access can be deliberately withheld or made available. Sexual desirability is thus an asset that can be traded for economic and social advantage. Conversely, sexual unattractiveness is a liability that can be overcome by nonsexual means (for example, payment). With these complications, the development and maintenance of a stable competitive order with respect to sex is extremely difficult, because sexual desire itself is inherently variable. Erotic relationships are subject to constant danger—a change of whim, a loss of interest, a third party, a misunderstanding. Competition for the same sexual object may inflame passion and stir conflicts; failure may injure one's self-esteem. The intertwining of sex and society is a fertile ground for joy, happiness, paranoia, homicide, and suicide.[2]

THE PROBLEM OF ENFORCEMENT

In these terms, we can understand why the enforcement of sexual norms is difficult. Not only is the drive strong and yet capable of release in a brief and clandestine encounter, but it is so subject to conditioning and social involvement that the stimuli to prurient arousal are innumerable. Of necessity, sex regulation must be versatile, running the gamut from the most informal mechanisms to the most durable rewards and awesome penalties.

The role of informal and personal enforcement of sexual norms—by gossip, loss of face, resentment, retaliation—is often overlooked. A girl may refrain from suggestive behavior because friends might talk or males might become aggressive. In Java, husbands and wives are suspicious of any outside contact. They interpret minute deviations of behavior as indications of possible infidelity. When asked the meaning of *tjemburu* (jealousy, suspicion), they give examples, showing "an almost paranoid watchfulness between spouses." If violation occurs, anger and reprisal are certain.[3]

In all societies such informal controls probably bear the major share of sex regulation; but supporting them are more formal enforcement mechanisms of both a positive and negative character. One such mechanism is the elevation of the sex mores to the sacred realm, where they are surrounded with mystery and imbued with deep moral significance. For instance, six of the Ten Commandments concern human relationships, and two of these deal directly with sex ("Thou shalt not commit adultery" and "Thou shalt not covet thy neighbour's wife") and one ("Honor thy father and thy mother") deals with the pair whose sexual relationship created the individual addressed. Placing sex control under supernatural auspices makes punishment for transgression seem

---

[2] See Kingsley Davis, "Jealousy and Sexual Property," in *Human Society* (New York: Macmillan, 1948), Ch. 7; Suzanne K. Steinmetz and Murray A. Straus (eds.), *Violence in the Family* (New York: Dodd, Mead, 1974), particularly pp. 3–110, 190–204; George R. Bach and Peter Wyden, *The Intimate Enemy* (New York: Morrow, 1969).

[3] Hildred Geertz, *The Javanese Family* (New York: Free Press), 1961, pp. 128–133.

inescapable: God sees everything. Another mechanism of control is institutionalized ignorance and silence. Protected from "the facts of life," women and children in some societies are often unaware of possible "sins." A third enforcement structure is surveillance and reduction of opportunities for indiscretion through such social conventions as chaperonage and female seclusion. Still another scheme is making material and social benefits depend on conformity to the sexual mores. In Muslim societies, for example, virginity is considered an absolute prerequisite to a girl's marriage, so much so that proof of her virginity is often demanded by the groom or his relatives. Finally, legislation adds its weight to control by enabling individuals to retaliate in court when their sexual interests have been injured or by enabling officials to prosecute when public morals have been offended.

The Gradation of Sex Norms

Sex norms vary in intensity. At the top are the hallowed crystallized statements, often dating from long ago (and often unrelated to current conditions). These presumably embody a society's highest ideals, publicly professed. Below these are secondary norms that often conflict with the official ideals but nevertheless regulate behavior because conformity to them is rewarded and deviation punished. Beneath these are tertiary norms, and so on down the scale of respectability and rightness until one gets to the "counter-mores," which define certain kinds of conduct as good precisely because, in respectable circles, they are defined as bad.

Further, the norms apply differentially to people in different roles. By strict interpretation, absolute celibacy is the highest Catholic ideal; but in practice it applies only to the clergy, lay celibacy being looked at askance. Many practices of the young are disapproved by the general public but nevertheless expected and ignored. People usually favor more license for themselves than for others, however. Much depends on *whose* behavior is being judged, and *who* is doing the judging.

What Sex Regulation Does: Two Keys to Sex Norms

With these features before us, we can answer the question we started with— why sex regulation? The answer lies in two facts: First, sexual intercourse has the potential of creating a new human being. The normative system links coitus with the institutional mechanisms that guarantee the bearing and rearing of children. This causes sexual norms and reproductive norms to become intertwined. Second, a person's desirability as a sex object is a valuable but scarce and perishable good. This being the case, the normative system provides for an orderly distribution of rights in the use of this good, which is integrated with the regulation of rights and obligations with respect to other goods. In sum, then, the sex norms contribute to the replacement of people in society and to the maintenance of an orderly distribution of rights.

This analysis suggests two keys to the nature of sex regulation. The first is that sex rules are subordinate to the family, in the sense that they either support the formation and continuance of families or at least do not interfere with them; the second is that the departures from the familial character of sex norms derive mainly from the system of political and economic differentiation in the society. Let us consider each key in turn.

The Primacy of Marriage and the Family

The primacy of marriage and the family in sex regulation accounts for the relative force and worldwide distribution of certain well-known sex mores. It explains, for instance, the principle of legitimacy (which establishes a family), the incest taboo (which eliminates overt sexual rivalry from the nuclear family), and the rule that coitus is obligatory within marriage (the only universal *positive* sex rule). The primacy of the family also accounts for the widespread preoccupation with premarital relationships and for the universal fact that sex norms are different for men and women. (Women are the ones who become pregnant.) It further enables us to account for the inequality of certain roles, or statuses, within societies. Family roles generally have more prestige than other roles in which sexual relations play a part. For example, for a woman the status of being a wife has more economic and legal security, and more respectability, than any other status involving sexual relations. A concubine has a lower position than a wife even when concubinage is customary. In all societies the single woman—that is, one who has remained unmarried past the customary age of marriage—has done nothing illegal, yet she is punished by her inability to be a "legitimate" mother or by her exclusion from other advantages (economic and social) accruing to wives. She is generally assumed to be single by necessity rather than by choice.

Sex rules that vary from one society to another are those that either interfere least with family formation and continuance or else fit the special features of family structure in different kinds of societies. For example, although the incest taboo, essential for the structure of the nuclear family, is found everywhere and is strongly sanctioned, premarital intercourse is treated quite differently in different societies, being outlawed in some groups, abetted in others. The reason for this variability is that premarital relations do not necessarily interfere with marriage; when controlled in certain ways, they may lead to marriage. Again, incest taboos outside the nuclear family vary from one society to another, because the number and kinds of external kinsmen who are socially important to the individual are different in different societies.

Economic Exchange and Sex Bargaining

The second key to sex norms explains most of the rules not explained by the first principle. Not only must societies biologically engender the next generation; they must also supply the goods and services that the present and next

generation need. These goods must be exchanged as well as produced, hence an incentive system is built into the division of labor that characterizes human societies. Since sexual desirability is itself a good, sexual access can be exchanged for economic or political advantage. The distribution of sexual favors thus gets involved with the distribution of political and economic goods. There are, of course, limits to treating sex as an exchangeable commodity. These limits are precisely the norms already referred to, for they regulate the exchange of sex in favor of the family. Within the limits, rules governing the exchange of sex favors tend to resemble those governing human services in general. The basic principle is that in entering into an agreement, each person be a free agent, not subject to force or fraud. Thus the sex rules generally protect minors against sexual exploitation, bar the use of force in gaining sexual access, protect the public from nuisances and health hazards, condemn sexual blackmail, limit third-party profiting from sexual relations (as in pimping), and hold the individual responsible for the consequences of his or her sexual acts. The tenor of the rules, whether by law or custom, is to guarantee fair bargaining in sexual matters.

It happens that both sexual desirability and economic capacity are age-linked, but the two scales are at variance. Sexual attractiveness is greatest in youth, whereas economic and political advantage (other things equal) are greater in middle or late age. Also, there is a division of labor by sex, the man's sphere being primarily economic and the woman's primarily familial. Hence normally in competing for attractive younger women, older men partially compensate economically and politically for what they may lack in youth and handsomeness.

Conflict Between the Two Principles

Inevitably, some conflict arises between the "exchange" and the "family" side of sexual regulation. Each side tends to limit the other. The particular patterns of accommodation depend on the stage of development and on the class and kinship structure of the society. In the past, in highly stratified societies, males of the upper stratum generally had more access to females (through polygyny and concubinage) than males of the lower strata, but while many of the extra females were from the lower ranks, the first wife usually came from the same stratum as the man. In modern open-class societies, vertical and geographical mobility tends to reduce the durability but not the frequency of sexual bonds, especially those outside the nuclear family.

Whatever the particular mode of accommodation in a society, the two principles of sex regulation seem to be in rough balance. The exchange influence prevents familialism from turning the society into an economically unproductive breeding system, and yet familialism is strong enough to prevent economic domination from subordinating all sex to money, status, and pleasure. There is no perfect solution to the dilemmas of sexual regulation, as can be seen by comparing alternative systems.

ALTERNATIVE SCHEMES OF SEX REGULATION

In comparing societies with respect to sex regulation, one must beware of reverse ethnocentrism—that is, the attitude that some society other than one's own is the standard, and that one's own society must be judged in terms of that standard. For instance, it has often been claimed that the "Judeo-Christian" cultural heritage is unusually strict, and that certain societies regulate sex hardly at all. "There are cultures," says Kinsey, "which more freely accept sexual activities as matters of everyday physiology, while maintaining extensive rituals and establishing taboos around feeding activities."[4] However, the only reference given for this statement is to Bronislaw Malinowski's *The Sexual Life of Savages in Northwestern Melanesia,* an account of the Trobriand Islanders which gives abundant evidence of sexual control. For instance, women of a man's own clan (roughly one-fourth of the women in the society)

---

[4] Alfred C. Kinsey et al., *Sexual Behavior in the Human Male,* p. 4.

are forbidden as sexual objects; adultery by either husband or wife is forbidden; "many things which we regard as natural, proper, and moral are anathema to the Trobriander." Hundreds of millions of Hindus, Muslims, and Buddhists consider the sex morals of Jews and Christians to be scandalously loose. Sociological analysis tries to understand how social systems actually operate. It is not facilitated by an attitude of judging, whether ethnocentric or reverse-ethnocentric. With this in mind, let us look objectively at control and deviance with respect to some significant aspects of sexual behavior.

Who Are the Sex Partners?

Among all the rules controlling sexual behavior, the most important are those defining the proper partners. As we have seen, one of those rules—that coitus is obligatory within marriage—universally links sex regulation to the family. Since that rule is universal the only variation possible concerns partners *outside* of marriage. Here we encounter one of man's major moral dilemmas. Should sexual expression be confined to marriage? If not, to what degree, under what circumstances, and for whom should other partners be permitted?

For the participants, there is no satisfactory solution. Man's instinctive apparatus was evidently formed in primate groups with relatively free access to responsive females. If so, permanent pairing is more a function of social regulation than of biological constitution, and it is undermined by stimulants to sexual interest (novelty, youth, beauty) over which social control has little power. As literature throughout history demonstrates, the tension between marital monopoly and extramarital temptation involves emotional and often tragic conflicts that cannot be reconciled. This is why different societies have different rules about it, and why the rules, whatever they are, are subject to criticism and violation. They vary in what is expected prior to marriage, and in the ease of divorce and remarriage, but they somehow give priority to the marital bond.

Most of the world's people still live in societies that have a "double standard" —double in two ways. Respectable women are held to strict rules, while respectable men are free to philander; and women are divided into two categories, reputable and disreputable, the disreputable being the ones who make male freedom possible. Such a system accentuates the respectable woman's family role and usually supports marital permanence. The man, once married, is responsible for his wife and may be bound to her for life, in return for which he is reasonably assured that the offspring are his own. The wife, chaperoned before marriage and jealously watched afterwards, has little opportunity for sexual experience apart from marriage. In other ways as well, the feminine sphere is sharply demarcated from the masculine, thus reinforcing the double standard.

A survey in Chile illustrates the system.[5] Of married men, 25 percent in

[5] M. Francoise Hall, "Male Use of Contraception and Attitudes toward Abortion, Santiago, Chile, 1968," *Milbank Memorial Fund Quarterly*, Vol. 48 (April 1970), pp. 145–166.

the rural sample, 49 percent of the lower-class urban sample, and 61 percent of the middle- and upper-class urban sample, admitted extramarital intercourse during the three months preceding the interview. Among unmarried men, the proportion reporting intercourse was 84 percent for the rural and 93 percent for the urban sample. No question on extramarital intercourse was asked of married women, but unmarried women were asked about use of contraception. Only 6 percent reported such use, although 45 percent of the unmarried men did so.

In such a system the women available for extramarital coitus (prostitutes, concubines, mistresses, servants, and pickups) come predominantly from the lower classes. The distinction between them and respectable women is sometimes so pronounced that sexual relations for enjoyment are felt to be almost inappropriate for a married couple. Puerto Rican husbands, for instance, "draw a sharp distinction between prostitutes, easy women, and their wives. The former are women to be enjoyed because they are evil. The wife, on the other hand, is like one's mother—holy, pure, and saintly. . . . Husbands seem concerned about the fidelity of their wives and the chastity of the daughters to an almost phobic extent."[6]

Under urban-industrial conditions, the double standard does not disappear but becomes attenuated. As surveillance by neighbors and relatives diminishes, as outside employment gives women economic independence, as contraception separates coitus more surely from pregnancy, women have more opportunity for extramarital sex and less to fear. Within wedlock, sexual love and daily companionship gain greater importance. Marriage comes to depend more on mutual affection; divorce is more by mutual consent and easier to obtain. Inevitably the rules of sexual behavior grow more similar for the two sexes. Adultery becomes less acceptable for husbands, premarital coitus more acceptable for women. The double standard changes from a difference of kind to one of degree.

Admittedly, the tendency to base marriage on mutual affection leads to considerable instability. There are several ways, however, in which marital instability is mitigated. For instance, intimate courtship encourages selection on the basis of compatibility and starts marriages with an already established personal bond. Premarital intercourse—either socially sanctioned, as in Scandinavian countries,[7] or tolerated, as in the United States—allows courtship to approximate a trial marriage. Marital stability is further encouraged by a convergence of male and female interests. Women as well as men study, work,

---

[6] J. Mayone Stycos and Reuben Hill, "The Prospects of Birth Control in Puerto Rico," *Annals of the American Academy of Political and Social Science*, Vol. 285 (January 1953), p. 141.

[7] Harold T. Christensen, "Cultural Relativism and Premarital Sex Norms," *American Sociological Review*, Vol. 25 (February 1960), pp. 31–39; and "Scandinavian and American Sex Norms: Some Comparisons, with Sociological Implications," *Journal of Social Issues*, Vol. 22 (April 1966), pp. 60–75. Thomas D. Eliot and Arthur Hillman (eds.), *Norway's Families* (Philadelphia: University of Pennsylvania Press, 1960).

travel, and pursue interests. Education and birth control help to prevent the wife from being completely absorbed by home and children. Nevertheless, although the lessening of role differentiation makes marriages more companionable, there is less community support for marital permanence.

Social Change and Sex in Industrial Societies

Although it is clear that contemporary industrial societies are shifting away from the old standards, it is not clear where they are headed. While underdeveloped countries have familiar problems, the industrial countries are moving in unprecedented directions and experiencing unparalleled problems. One development is a rising skepticism and dissension concerning the sex rules themselves. Premarital intercourse is viewed by some as an evil, by others as a good. Pornography is widely condemned but yet blatantly promoted by commercial interests. Nudity is regarded by some as obscene and by others as wholesome. Abortion is seen both as the solution of a problem and as a problem in itself. Without consensus on what the problems are, arguments over the means of solving them are as pointless as they are bitter.

In agricultural societies where the old mores were formed, one of the main problems was how to bear enough children to survive high death rates. Sex rules that encouraged marriage and reproduction were supported by supernatural sanctions and small-village surveillance. Now, however, with death rates lowered to an unprecedented level, the old rules tying sex to reproduction seem obsolete. Further, industrial societies have grown to massive size and developed cultural diversity and contrasting views. Cloaked in urban anonymity, people violate sexual rules with relative impunity. Criticism of the rules is hailed as "open-mindedness"; advocacy of enforcement is condemned as "authoritarianism." Hostilities and psychic insecurities are expressed by attacking any rules that restrict freedom.

Sex regulation, however, does not become completely paralyzed. Industrial societies are, after all, societies. Violations bring efforts to restore order; personal injury brings retaliation. Individuals have a stake in sexual bargaining, and the community tries to protect the interests of those who cannot protect themselves. Some consensus on sex regulation exists despite the appearance of chaotic change.

There is majority agreement, for instance, on the desirability of minimizing certain by-products of sexual activity: illegal abortion, venereal disease, illegitimacy, forced marriage, child marriage, and organized procuring. Dispute is mainly confined to means of combatting them. One side argues that a major cause of the evils is illicit coitus. The other side argues that *if* contraception is efficiently practiced, coitus will *not* lead to an abortion or an illegitimate birth; nor will it lead to venereal disease *if* prophylactic precautions are taken. Why not simply teach people contraception and prophylaxis? Why not recognize that problems are often caused by oppressive sex rules themselves? For example, illegal abortion is dangerous *because* it is illegal, not vice versa.[8]

However, as noted earlier, the conflict over sex norms is not simply between a view that sexual pleasure is always sinful and a view that it is always desirable. The issue is more limited. The argument against regulation is generally that a particular behavior does no harm or does less harm than the cost of enforcing it. This argument is hard to refute because the harm is assumed away by unconsciously positing that other elements in the situation are favorable. Prostitution does no harm *if* there is protection against disease, *if* the woman is of age, and *if* she is a free agent; adultery does no harm *if* the spouse approves. This is not always the case. The argument that sex rules themselves do psychological harm is also hard to refute, because any rule, if violated, has the possibility of causing guilt feelings and therefore, presumably, psychological malaise.

Conflict over sex norms for youth is especially intense, because in youth the sex drive reaches its peak simultaneously with emancipation from authority and the making of lifetime decisions. It is the younger generation whose sex problems are most intensified by changing social conditions. The adults mainly responsible for youth—parents, school officials, group leaders—often shirk responsibility and, demoralized by radical criticism, fail to give firm guidance. By default, the operating norms come to be those spontaneously arising among young people themselves. These have counter-moral and egocentric components that may cripple the individual's capacity to perform as an adult. James Coleman writes of the American high school as follows:

> The dichotomy . . . between "life-adjustment" and "academic emphasis" is a false one, for it forgets that most of the teenager's energy is not directed toward either of these goals. Instead the relevant dichotomy is cars and the cruel jungle of rating and dating versus school activities.[9]

To an unusual degree, each young person must fend for himself.

PREMARITAL SEX RELATIONS

Among societies there is considerable variation in rules regarding premarital sex, and in modern industrial societies there is increasing premarital sex freedom. Such variability suggests that the question of chastity or indulgence before marriage, or the question of when, how, and with whom, however important it may be to the individual concerned, is of only minor sociological significance.

[8] In nations that permit and provide facilities for abortion, the operation is no more dangerous than taking the contraceptive pill regularly or wearing an IUD, and less dangerous than childbirth, particularly if performed in the first trimester. However, according to Japanese reports, a higher incidence of sterility may follow induced abortions. Christopher Tietze, "Somatic Consequences of Abortion" in Sidney H. Newman, Mildred B. Beck, and Sarah Lewit (eds.), *Abortion, Obtained and Denied* (New York: Population Council, 1971), and Christopher Tietze and Sarah Lewit, "A National Medical Experience" in Howard J. and Joy D. Osofsky (eds.), *The Abortion Experience* (New York: Harper & Row, 1973).

[9] James S. Coleman, *The Adolescent Society* (New York: Free Press, 1961), p. 51.

The first thing to note is that premarital norms are rules about proper sex partners. Among the negative partner rules, the strongest are those pertaining to pairs *for whom marriage is forbidden* (near kin, already married, too young, same sex, celibate orders, or wrong castes). This rationale, however, does not pertain to premarital relations per se. If a young couple are both of age and free to marry, their coitus does not interfere with marriage but may, under certain rules, facilitate it. This is why premarital intercourse can be permitted in many societies, and why, if not permitted, it is usually punished less severely than other infractions of the partner rules.

Then why is premarital intercourse ever forbidden? The answer is that societies thus seek to avoid illegitimacy. If so, why is premarital intercourse often permitted or only mildly sanctioned? The answer is that the unmarried are generally young and sexually at their peak. A ban on intercourse among them is difficult to enforce. Anyway, there is always a possibility that coitus will not result in childbirth, or that, if it does, the couple will get married.

Variations in Premarital Regulation

Societies have unconsciously evolved quite different solutions to the dilemmas of premarital relations. I have already cited the widespread system that forbids premarital coitus for respectable women but permits it for respectable men and a limited class of disreputable women. In Muslim societies each family bases its "honor" on the sexual purity of its women, and exerts the utmost vigilance to prevent its unmarried daughters from committing any sexual indiscretion. For village boys and girls in Egypt,

> any conversation about sex is taboo. . . . Chastity as a moral and religious ideal implies the avoidance of any stimulating pleasurable influence from the opposite sex. . . . Sexual pleasure of any kind outside the marriage tie is condemned by the Koran, . . . Manifestations of this excessive repression and fear of sex are obvious in the veiling of adolescent girls and women and the hiding of the breast contours with extra pieces of cloth. . . .

> In this community I heard of no cases of adultery or illegitimate children for the last thirty years, though cases of homosexuality and jokes about sexual pleasure from animals are not uncommon among the adolescents and young men.[10]

In contrast, some peasant societies have allowed freedom of intercourse on condition that the couple marry if pregnancy ensues. In pre-industrial Scandinavia, pregnancy demonstrated that the union would be fertile and that therefore marriage was in order. Such a custom, in effect a trial marriage, required a rural society where everybody knew who was "keeping company," and where, accordingly, expected behavior could be enforced even if the male wished to escape. In industrial societies, although the identification of the father is tech-

---

[10] Hamed Ammar. *Growing Up in an Egyptian Village* (London: Routledge, 1954), pp. 185–192. Cf. Carrol McC. Pastner, "Accommodations to Purdah: The Female Perspective," *Journal of Marriage and the Family,* Vol. 36 (May 1974), pp. 408–414.

nologically feasible (with blood tests, lie detectors, monitoring devices, and sworn witnesses), the effort to coerce him is considered too costly and repugnant.

A different kind of arrangement is one that can be called the *promiscuous peer-group system.* It permits intercourse freely among young unmarried people but condemns unmarried reproduction. Obviously requiring abortion or contraception, it is often found in primitive societies that emphasize age classes. Chagga boys, after puberty but prior to marriage, were "instructed to practice interfemoral intercourse or coitus interruptus unless the girl places a pad in the vagina to avoid conception."[11] A somewhat similar pattern was observed among American college students in the 1920s to 1940s. Kinsey found "petting to climax" to be a major "outlet." Among males aged 21, it had occurred in 12.3 percent of those with a grade-school education, 23.7 percent of those with a high-school education, and 50.1 percent of those with college education.[12] By age 20, 10 percent of the women who were born before 1900 had petted to climax, while almost 28 percent of those born between 1920 and 1929 had done so; and by age 25, the two percentages were 14 and 43.[13]

The Increase in Premarital Intercourse

Heavy petting was evidently a transitional stage in the changing sexual pattern. It prevented pregnancy and maintained "technical virginity." As condoms, diaphragms, spermicidal jellies, and steroid pills became increasingly available to teenagers, full coitus became more frequent. A 1960 survey among students at four Peoples' colleges in Sweden found that 40 percent of the girls had experienced intercourse; a 1965 survey of the same colleges found that 64 percent had done so. A later study of 497 students (average age 17) at two schools in Örebro found that 46 percent had had intercourse.[14] In the United States, the percentage of white women having intercourse prior to marriage changed as follows:

	Among women born			
	Before 1900*	1900–1909*	1910–1929*	1952–1956†
By age 15	2%	2%	4%	14%
By age 20	8	18	22	46

* Kinsey et al., *Sexual Behavior in the Human Female,* p. 339. I have combined the data for the cohorts born in 1910–1919 and 1920–1929.

† John F. Kantner and Melvin Zelnik, "Sexual Experience of Young Unmarried Women in the United States," *Family Planning Perspectives,* Vol. 4 (October 1972), p. 10. The 46 percent is for age 19 rather than age 20.

[11] Clellan S. Ford and Frank A. Beach, *Patterns of Sexual Behavior* (New York: Harper & Row, 1951), p. 182. See also Max Gluckman, "Kinship and Marriage among the Lozi of Northern Rhodesia and the Zulu of Natal" in A. R. Radcliffe-Brown and Daryll Forde (eds.), *African Systems of Kinship and Marriage* (London: Oxford University Press, 1950), p. 181.

[12] Kinsey et al., *Sexual Behavior in the Human Male,* p. 56.

[13] Kinsey et al., *Sexual Behavior in the Human Female,* p. 275.

[14] Gustav Johnson, "Sexualvanor hos svensk ungdom," Brigitta Linnér, *Sex and Society in Sweden* (New York: Random House, 1967), pp. 18–20.

Furthermore, among those having premarital coitus, promiscuity seems to be rising.[15] A 1971 survey of 19-year-old unmarried white girls in the United States showed that, of those who had experienced intercourse, the proportion by number of partners was:[16]

One partner only	47.6%
2–5 partners	43.7
6 or more	8.7

Similar trends appear in other industrial countries.[17]

Cohabitation

What is the meaning of such abundant premarital coitus? In itself, it has no meaning. It has meaning only as it has consequences, and these depend on its role in social situations.

One of the easiest ways to make sex a part of a relationship in which other things are shared is to live together. For this reason, the ideal of many young people, particularly college students, is cohabitation. A survey at Pennsylvania State University found 33.4 percent of male students and 32.3 percent of female students were or had been cohabiting. At Arizona State University the male percentage was 28.7 and the female 17.9, and at Cornell University, in a group of 86 junior and senior women at the beginning of the fall term in 1971, the figure was 34 percent.[18] Not only is the cumulative incidence rather high, but the proportion viewing cohabitation as desirable is even higher. At Arizona State, 71.4 percent of the males and 42.6 percent of the females who had never cohabited said that they "would want to." When asked what kind of arrangements they would prefer *after* college, Penn State male cohabitors said they would prefer cohabitation to marriage; female cohabitors preferred marriage by only a narrow margin. For noncohabitors, however, marriage still had a clear edge.

[15] Kinsey et al., *Sexual Behavior in the Human Female*, p. 336.

[16] Melvin Zelnik and John F. Kantner, "Sexuality, Contraception and Pregnancy among Young Unwed Females in the United States," Commission on Population Growth and the American Future, *Research Reports*, Vol. 1 (Washington, D.C.: Government Printing Office, 1972), p. 365. Similar findings are reported by Arthur M. Vener and Cyrus S. Stewart, "Adolescent Sexual Behavior in Middle America Revisited," *Journal of Marriage and the Family*, Vol. 36 (November 1974), pp. 728–735.

[17] Harold T. Christensen and Christina F. Gregg, "Changing Sex Norms in America and Scandinavia," *Journal of Marriage and the Family*, Vol. 32 (November 1970), p. 621; Eleanore B. Luckey and Gilbert D. Nass, "A Comparison of Sexual Attitudes and Behavior in an International Sample," *Journal of Marriage and the Family*, Vol. 31 (May 1969), p. 375.

[18] Dan J. Peterman, Carl A. Ridley, and Scott M. Anderson, "A Comparison of Cohabiting and Noncohabiting College Students," *Journal of Marriage and the Family*, Vol. 36 (May 1974), pp. 344–354; Lura F. Henze and John W. Hudson, "Personal and Family Characteristics of Cohabiting and Noncohabiting College Students," *Journal of Marriage and the Family*, Vol. 36 (November 1974), pp. 722–726; and Eleanor D. Macklin, "Heterosexual Cohabitation among Unmarried College Students," *The Family Coordinator*, Vol. 21 (October 1972), pp. 463–472.

Cohabitation has sometimes been characterized as "trial marriage," but marriage implies a major commitment to long-term economic and household cooperation and generally a willingness to bear and rear children together. College cohabitation generally is not undertaken with that in mind. Of 35 cohabiting females at Cornell, only 4 were contemplating marriage while 14 characterized their relationship as so casual as to permit dating with other men. Furthermore, cohabitation is normally too ephemeral to be characterized as experimental marriage. At Penn State, 62 percent of the male and 41 percent of the female cohabitors said that their longest cohabitation lasted less than a month. A study at Boulder, Colorado, found that cohabiting couples were less committed to marriage than those merely going together, but that sexual satisfaction, especially for males, was greater.[19]

It thus looks as though cohabitation is mainly a matter of convenience. In the college environment where parents and the community at large foot the bills, and where young people can thus concentrate on pleasure, couples can best combine sex and companionship by sharing a room or an apartment. To a lesser degree the same goes for young people not in college but living away from home, but these suffer the constraints of having to work. In either case, the relation lasts only so long as both parties are satisfied. It usually does not involve children, economic commitment, or community responsibility. It is the kind of unburdened sexual arrangement that young males have always preferred but seldom attained in such abundance.

Only if cohabitation became a substitute for marriage could it assume major importance, but the likelihood of that seems remote because among adults the motivation for parenthood has too many institutional supports to be lightly set aside. In so far as cohabitation is prolonged and involves children, it is marriage, whether legal or not. We are familiar with that kind of marriage in the consensual unions of Latin America and the common-law unions of English-speaking countries. Contemporary cohabitation, on the other hand, seems to involve fewer commitments.

Anomie and Conflict in Premarital Sexual Conduct

Contemporary sexual behavior prior to marriage is often ascribed to "a change in moral standards," but such a characterization seems to imply that *new* standards are being substituted for old ones. Since it is difficult to find such new standards, a more accurate designation may be a *breakdown* of standards. Some authors have characterized sex relations among the young as a "jungle" or a "wilderness."[20] Formerly in European society, a respectable woman gave her sexual favors only in return for the promise of a stable relationship and economic support. The man was drawn into the bargain by his sexual interest. If he obtained coitus under false pretenses, he risked retaliation by the girl's

---

[19] Judith L. Lyness et al., "Living Together: An Alternative to Marriage," *Journal of Marriage and the Family,* Vol. 34 (May 1972), pp. 305–314.

[20] Vance Packard, *The Sexual Wilderness* (New York: David McKay, 1968).

relatives and friends. The girl could thus use her relatively short period of maximum attractiveness to settle her future in the best way possible—by marriage. This is still the bargain that many girls in contemporary society would like to make, and some of them do, but their bargaining position has been undermined by the growing loss of family and community controls. As a consequence, girls increasingly give their favors for nothing. This is described, ironically, as female "emancipation." In some circles a girl now feels that she must be willing to indulge in intercourse to enjoy male company. As a student nurse put it,

> Whether you like it or not, you have to go along with them, at least some of the time. Otherwise, you get left out and sitting in the dorm all the time.[21]

Given an absence of sanctions against males and the intense desire of most females to get married, girls are easily exploited.

> One nursing student reported she became acquainted with an intern, . . . became sexually intimate and eventually very serious about him, only to discover he was already married; the whole charade was carried out with the knowledgeable aid of the intern's friends and cohorts.[22]

That disorganization rather than simply a change of sexual standards is occurring is suggested not only by the frequency of fraud but also by the rise of sexual crime and violence. For instance, between 1960 and 1973 the rate for reported rapes in the United States rose 2½ times. According to the age-specific rates found in a 1965 national survey of crime victims, each thousand American women living from age 10 to age 50 would experience 48 rapes; this figure would be approximately doubled in 1975.[23] Many rapes and attempted rapes, however, are not reported to the police, still less other forms of sexual coercion. In a study of 291 girls at Ohio State University, Kirkpatrick and Kanin found that 56 percent had experienced sexual aggression at least once during the preceding academic year.

> 21 percent were offended by forceful attempts at intercourse and 6 percent by . . . attempts . . . in the course of which menacing threats or coercive infliction of physical pain were employed.[24]

[21] James K. Skipper, Jr. and Gilbert Nass, "Dating Behavior: A. Framework for Analysis and an Illustration," *Journal of Marriage and the Family*, Vol. 28 (November 1966), p. 417.

[22] *Ibid.*, p. 419.

[23] Computed from U.S. Bureau of the Census, *Statistical Abstract of the United States, 1972* (Washington, D.C.: Government Printing Office, 1972), p. 145. Even if reported, a rapist's chance of avoiding a penalty is excellent. In American cities in 1972, only 49.4 percent of rapes reported resulted in an arrest, and only 8.9 percent were found guilty. *Ibid.*, 1974, p. 153.

[24] Clifford Kirkpatrick and Eugene Kanin, "Male Sex Aggression on a University Campus," *American Sociological Review*, Vol. 22 (February 1957), p. 53. See also Eugene Kanin, "Male Aggression in Dating-Courtship Relationships," *American Journal of Sociology*, Vol. 62 (September 1957), p. 200.

The girl of today must walk a slender tightrope. Expected to "comply," she is in danger of a bad reputation if she does so frequently and with numerous partners. Males do not wish to marry the females whom they have "passed around,"[25] yet the early age at which intercourse starts and the lack of controls insure that many girls will be passed around.

In quest of a stable relationship, a girl often does more than perform the normal duties of a wife. In many cases, with no legal commitment, she interrupts her own education and takes a dead-end job in order to support the young man while he pursues his education. Even if married, she may find herself later divorced in favor of a younger and more eager competitor. Whereas formerly the man was obligated to practice birth control with the condom or withdrawal, the burden has gradually been shifted to the woman. It is she, not he, who makes intercourse safe by having an intrauterine device inserted, taking a dangerous pill, or having an "unrestricted" abortion performed on her. It is she who bears the responsibility for illegitimate children born of her sexual hospitality. In its rush to "abolish" illegitimacy, contemporary society has abolished only the old custom of holding the male responsible. That is one reason why government aid to dependent children rose thirteen times between 1950 and 1973, faster than nearly any other form of public assistance. In California in 1973 over half the children of unwed mothers were on welfare.[26]

Problems Associated with Premarital Coitus

These observations remind us that unmarried coitus can have one or more of several outcomes. On the favorable side, it can be part of a warm and satisfying relationship, perhaps one leading to marriage. On the unfavorable side, it can spread venereal disease or cause a pregnancy ending in abortion, an unwanted marriage, or a fatherless child. With contraceptive and prophylactic techniques available, it is strange that the undesired sequelae loom so large.

Illicit Pregnancy   Nobody knows exactly the number of illicit impregnations. However, in a state where abortion is legal, an approximation can be made by adding the abortions and the births that occur to unmarried women, and then adding these to the births occurring in marriage but conceived previously. In California, where 73 percent of legal abortions are to unmarried

[25] In the lower class in Britain, premarital intercourse is taken for granted; yet a girl's marriage prospects are injured if she gets a reputation for promiscuity. Mary Morse, *The Unattached* (Baltimore: Penguin Books, 1965), pp. 116, 164–165, 172–173. In the mid-1960s the percentage of male university students saying they would be troubled to marry a girl who had experienced coitus with someone else was 70.2 in the United States, 69 in Canada, 41.6 in England, and 42 in Norway. Luckey and Nass, "A Comparison of Sexual Attitudes and Behavior . . . ," p. 368.

[26] Unpublished study by Kingsley Davis and Susan De Vos, International Population and Urban Research, University of California.

women, in fiscal year 1971–1972 a third of all *known* pregnancies were non-marital.[27]

In the nation as a whole in 1973, the official estimate of illegitimate births was 407,300. Thirteen percent of all births, this represented a birth rate of 24.5 per 1000 unmarried women aged 15 to 44, as compared to a rate of 102.8 for married women. Both the proportion and the rate were three and one-half times as large as they were in 1940. A similar increase has occurred in Australia and in England, and some rise has occurred in virtually all industrial countries, including those where the illegitimacy rate was already high, such as Sweden.

Given sexual intercourse, illegitimate births result from various motives—a willingness to take a chance when intercourse is unexpected, a belief in the "safe period," an inability to acquire an abortion, or perhaps an effort to trap a man or woman into marriage. The idea that illegitimate children are born mainly because of ignorance or unavailability of contraceptives is erroneous. In Melvin Zelnik and John F. Kantner's study of girls 15 to 19, nearly a third of all nonmarital pregnancies were wanted rather than unwanted; nevertheless, the motives reveal immaturity and poor judgment under unfavorable circumstances. Among 1062 unwed mothers studied in California in 1954, only 55 percent claimed that the child was conceived in a friendship or love relationship rather than in an ephemeral contact.[28] Infant mortality among illegitimate children is usually one and one-half to two times that for legitimate children, the birth weight is substantially less, and the proportion of premature births and foetal mortality is much higher.[29] If the child survives and remains with his mother, he normally has no father, is supported by government welfare, and runs a high risk of being abused.[30] If he goes into a foster home, he may be cared for poorly. His best bet is to be adopted, but more and more unwed mothers are keeping their children. In California approximately 38 percent of illegitimate children born in 1966 were legally adopted, but by 1973 the proportion had fallen to 13 percent. For her part, the unwed mother braves the inconveniences and hazards of pregnancy either for nothing (perhaps an adoption fee) or for the onerous task of caring for a child by herself. Her chances of furthering her education, finding a good job, or making a good

[27] Calculated from June Sklar and Beth Berkov, "The Effect of Legal Abortion on Legitimate and Illegitimate Birth Rates: The California Experience," *Studies in Family Planning*, Vol. 4 (November 1973), pp. 290–291. See also Melvin Zelnik and John F. Kantner, "The Resolution of Teenage First Pregnancies," *Family Planning Perspectives*, Vol. 6 (Spring 1974), p. 75.

[28] Zelnik and Kantner, *op. cit*, and Clark Vincent, *Unmarried Mothers* (New York: Free Press, 1961), p. 83.

[29] See National Center for Health Statistics, Series 3, Studies of infant mortality in foreign countries; *Vital statistics of the United States*, issued annually; and *Trends in Illegitimacy in the United States, 1940–1965*, Series 21, No. 15 (February 1968).

[30] A nationwide survey of child abuse in 1967–68 revealed that 30 percent of abused children lived in female-headed households, and nearly 20 percent in stepfather-headed households. David G. Gil, "Violence Against Children," *Journal of Marriage and the Family*, Vol. 33 (November 1971), pp. 638–640.

marriage are reduced—particularly if she is a teen-ager, as many unwed mothers are.

Forced marriages   Illicit pregnancies lead to marriage almost as often as to illegitimate births. The previously cited nationwide survey of girls aged 15 to 19 found that 34.8 percent of those who had a first pregnancy without being married had married before the pregnancy ended. Another 10.4 percent had married after it ended, especially if the pregnancy resulted in a livebirth.[31] In such cases, since the original sex relation is often casual and the couple usually immature, the marriages are often unstable. This is demonstrated by the finding that girls who marry following an illegitimate birth or during an illicit pregnancy are twice as likely to be divorced three years after marriage as those whose first child was born a year or more after marriage.[32]

Abortions   If an illicit pregnancy is unwanted—as about two-thirds of them are in the United States—abortion offers a way out. Although in many countries abortions are still illegal and hence dangerous and expensive, they have been legalized in Japan, several Scandinavian and East European countries, and recently in the United States. Logically, one might expect the legalization of abortion to halt the rise in illegitimacy, but the evidence is that, except in Japan, it has merely dampened the rise. In Norway and Sweden, where abortion laws were liberalized early, the rise in illegitimacy after 1940 was much less than in the United States and Britain, where liberalization was later. In the United States, Colorado led off in 1967, and by 1970 some 14 additional states had liberalized abortion; then in 1972 the Supreme Court made abortion legal during the first two trimesters. Although in 1973 the illegitimacy ratio was 4.9 percent greater than in 1972, this was a third less than the average annual increase between 1960 and 1972. This suggests that the abortion law was having some effect, but in California where legal abortions were common by 1970, and where the illegitimacy ratio fell in 1971, the effect was short-lived, for the ratio started a steep upward climb again in 1972 and 1973.[33] Clearly, then, the sudden availability of abortion may temporarily affect the trend, but neither it nor the availability of contraception stops the social forces and motives leading to unwed pregnancy.

Venereal disease   Another problem associated with sexual freedom—venereal disease—is publicly underestimated because the well-known venereal diseases are underreported and the public is unaware of the others. With respect to syphilis, gonorrhea, and chancroid, physicians often refuse to report cases even though legally required to do so. But although all statistics on VD are undercounts, the reported figures are sizable, and although we have the capac-

---

[31] Zelnik and Kantner, *op. cit.*, p. 76.

[32] John R. Weeks, *A Demographic Analysis of Teenage Marriages in California* (doctoral dissertation, University of California, Berkeley, 1971), Ch. 8.

[33] Sklar and Berkov, *op. cit.*, p. 87.

ity to eliminate or greatly reduce these afflictions, the trends are often upward.

Almost all countries reporting to the World Health Organization showed a high incidence of gonorrhea soon after World War II. There was then a decline that reached a trough in 1951 and 1952 and remained there for three to five years, and next a sharp rise again in most countries.[34] "Viewed globally," says one authority, "we find something of a general paradox, in that the more highly developed countries, with the best arrangements, seem to have the highest incidences." The ratio of male to female cases varies between 2:1 and 6:1, not because males have more gonorrhea than females but because "most females infected are asymptomatic carriers" and are not diagnosed or reported as often.[35] Despite underreporting of VD, gonorrhea is now the most commonly reported infectious disease in industrial countries. In 1972 in the United States it was more frequently reported than all other infectious diseases combined. It overwhelmingly affects young people, and it is by far the most important cause of sterility.[36] In about 10 percent of women who have the disease, inflammation of the Fallopian tubes (salpingitis) occurs, and in approximately 20 percent of such cases the result is permanent infecundity. Sometimes, chronic arthritis also follows the disease, and if the gonococci infect the eyes of a baby at birth, blindness is likely to occur.

The record for syphilis looks better. In the United States, the drop in reported cases between the end of World War II and 1955 was dramatic. Regardless of the number of reported cases, however, the death rate has fallen dramatically and steadily, showing that we have had more success in curing syphilis than in preventing it (see Table 5-1). The Public Health Service believes that about half a million persons in the United States have undetected syphilis and need treatment. For many deaths, syphilis is an underlying but unregistered cause. Antibiotics in the early 1940s led to the belief that VD would be eliminated. "We could eliminate venereal diseases in a couple of years at the cost of one or two battleships, but we are not doing so," said a physician in 1943. He attributed the failure to puritanical attitudes in "middle-class countries."[37] Three decades later, however, VD was epidemic. The gonococcus and spirochete had evolved strains resistant to penicillin and other widely used antibiotics. Rising promiscuity, especially among teen-agers, and the apparently growing contribution of homosexual contacts had increased the

---

[34] R. S. Morton, *Venereal Diseases* (Baltimore: Penguin, 1966), p. 33. In the United States the number of reported civilian cases was 313,363 in 1945, fell to 236,197 in 1955, and rose again to 767,215 in 1972. See U.S. Bureau of the Census, *Statistical Abstract of the United States, 1969* (Washington, D.C.: Government Printing Office, 1969), p. 77, and *Statistical Abstract of the United States, 1974*, p. 86.

[35] R. S. Morton, *op. cit.*, pp. 35, 36.

[36] See U.S. Bureau of the Census, *1960 Census of the Population*, Final Report PC(2)-3A, *Women by Number of Children Ever Born* (Washington, D.C.: Government Printing Office), p. 18, and Wilson H. Grabill and Paul C. Glick, "Demographic and Social Aspects of Childlessness: Census Data," *Milbank Memorial Fund Quarterly*, Vol. 37 (1959), pp. 1–27.

[37] Henry E. Sigerist, *Civilization and Disease* (Ithaca, N.Y.: Cornell University Press, 1943), pp. 78, 238.

Table 5–1   Reported VD Cases and Deaths from Syphilis

	Reported civilian cases Gonorrhea	Syphilis	Deaths from syphilis (per 100,000 population)
1940			14.4
1945	313,363	351,767	10.6
1950	286,746	217,558	5.0
1955	236,197	122,392	2.3
1960	258,933	122,003	1.6
1965	324,925	112,842	1.3
1970	600,072	91,382	0.23
1972	767,215	81,149	0.15

Sources: U.S. National Center for Health Statistics, *Vital Statistics of the United States 1940–1960*, p. 388; U.S. Bureau of the Census, *Statistical Abstract of the United States, 1969* (Washington, D.C.: Government Printing Office, 1969), pp. 58, 77, and *Statistical Abstract of the United States, 1974*, pp. 62, 86.

number of undetected carriers. The popularity of the pill had displaced the prophylactic condom as a contraceptive.

Among all types of bodily contact, sexual intercourse is the most intimate, moist, and prolonged—an ideal means for the transmission of disease. Not surprising, then, is the recent discovery that other diseases are transmitted in this way. One of these, nonspecific urethritis in the male, may be the cause of Reiter's syndrome, involving arthritis and inflammation of the eyes. A common female disease apparently transmitted by coitus is trichomonal vaginitis.[38] But more disturbing is the discovery that cervical cancer is spread venereally. Women who start coitus early and have numerous sex partners, and wives whose husbands are promiscuous, appear more susceptible than others.[39] Also, there is accumulating evidence that infectious hepatitis, apparently a virus disease, is spread by kissing and sexual intercourse.

EXTRAMARITAL SEX RELATIONS

Although rules about *pre*marital sex vary from one society to another, the same cannot be said of *extra*marital relations. All major civilizations prohibit adultery by the wife. Hence it is news when evidence of secret violation is uncovered or when groups openly flout the rule. The very intensity of the rule suggests the strength of temptation to violate it—and also makes it difficult to obtain information on the extent of violation. Kinsey found that 26 percent of married females aged 40 had had extramarital intercourse sometime in their lives, and Robert R. Bell and his associates found the same percentage for a

[38] R. S. Morton, *op. cit.*, pp. 98, 100–107.
[39] *American Journal of Public Health*, Vol. 57 (May 1967), pp. 803–829, 840–847; *Science*, Vol. 178 (October 20, 1972), pp. 319–320.

sample of women with average age of 34.5 in 1971.[40] A more recent study of a hundred American couples in their late forties and fifties found 10 percent of the wives admitting adultery.[41] Their restraint, however, was largely due to lack of opportunity; presented with a hypothetical situation in which the husband was out of town, 56 percent of the women would do things ranging from spending an evening with a man in her or his house to having intercourse with him.[42] The more urbanized the society and the more unsupervised the wives, the more frequent adultery will be; but it does not follow that the rule itself is changing or that it is ineffective. The occurrence of crime does not make crime control a failure, for crime left uncontrolled would be much greater. Most societies are structured so as to minimize opportunities for marital infidelity.

As a result, organized extramarital experiments—swinging groups, sex communes, open marriages, group marriages—arouse sensational attention far beyond their numerical significance, for they represent both a suspension of the rule and provision of opportunities. Swinging, or mate-swapping for purposes of sex, began to attract attention in the fifties. It involves candor and *quid pro quo*, since what one mate does the other does too.

> They [swingers] view the sexual relationship of the marriage as one of love and of emotion and the consensual extramarital relationship as physical. They drop out of swinging if the wife desires to get pregnant in order to insure that the husband is the child's father. Jealousy is avoided by giving the marriage paramount loyalty and by avoiding emotional attachments to others.[43]

The preoccupation of swinging couples with coital variety strikes most people as either humorous or vacuous. Swingers are "conventional in every way save one—they screw at parties."[44] Although some researchers have reported that swinging helps marriages, Duane Denfeld points out that there is a sampling bias, since couples who have swung and quit are not included. Denfeld himself studied the dropouts by querying 2,147 marriage counselors. The problems these couples encountered suggest why swinging is likely to remain rare. The most frequently mentioned reason for dropping out was jealousy.

> A number of husbands became quite concerned over their wives' popularity or sexual performance (for example, endurance capabilities), or feared that their

---

[40] Kinsey et al., *Sexual Behavior in the Human Female*, pp. 416, 440; and Robert R. Bell et al., "A Multivariate Analysis of Female Extramarital Coitus," *Journal of Marriage and the Family*, Vol. 37 (May 1975), p. 380.

[41] Ralph E. Johnson, "Extramarital Sexual Intercourse: A Methodological Note," *Journal of Marriage and the Family*, Vol. 32 (May 1970), pp. 279–282.

[42] Larry L. and Joan M. Constantine, *Group Marriage* (New York: Macmillan, 1973), p. 5.

[43] Duane Denfeld, "Dropouts from Swinging," *The Family Coordinator*, Vol. 23 (January 1974), p. 45.

[44] Constantine and Constantine, *op. cit.*, p. 24.

wives were having more fun than they were. When wives reported jealousy it was more likely related to fear of losing their mate.[45]

Some couples felt guilty and others found the extramarital activity a threat to the marriage. Although the code frowned on swinging twice with the same couple, emotional attachments arose anyway and sometimes led to clandestine arrangements or to divorce. Other couples found the mate exchanges boring, mainly because of the lack of seduction and emotion. The wives were less enthusiastic than the husbands, a finding corroborated by other studies.[46] This suggests that husbands use their wives as a means of attaining sexual variety.

To many advocates of sexual permissiveness, mere *trading* of sexual partners is too hedonistic. More significant to them is the ancient question of whether sex can cement the solidarity of groups wider than the family. Contemporary communes bear on the question, but they are too diverse to give a clear answer. Some are durable, some not; some engulf the individual, some do not; and some involve sexual sharing and some do not. The anarchistic, or hip, commune ideally regulates nothing, least of all sexual behavior. One might expect this to result in free-for-all sex, and perhaps it does in ephemeral crash pads, but in communes with any stability it does not. Bennett M. Berger and colleagues, in a study of rural hip communes,[47] found that pairs tend to form. These are fragile because the ideology is that nobody plans and nobody imposes or accepts obligations; yet few members completely accept the prospect of serial pairings, much less group sex. The women particularly "hope for an ideal lover or a permanent mate" but have little expectation that it will really happen. Actually, the authors found that well-functioning communes and relatively stable pairings go together: "heterosexual couples are the backbone of most communes. . . . They seem more stable and dependable than single people do, if only because their search for partners is ended, even if that ending is temporary." Pairs often break up when children arrive. The mother must perforce take care of her infant, but the father is technically free to "split" and avoid even the semblance of an obligation. Although there are some communes whose members are all expected to have sexual relations with one another, these appear to be so rare as to suggest unsurmountable difficulties in that arrangement.

Another sexual arrangement is "group marriage." We know that many societies have permitted polygyny and that a few have permitted polyandry. These are group marriages, but the modern idea is to have "marriages" in which two or more of *each* sex are involved. Larry L. and Joan M. Constantine were not able to find historical societies that permitted such arrangements, but by dint of extraordinary effort they found some in the United States. All told,

[45] Denfeld, *op. cit.*, p. 46.

[46] Anne-Marie Henshel, "Swinging—A Study of Decision Making in Marriage," *American Journal of Sociology,* Vol. 78 (January 1973), pp. 885–891.

[47] Bennett M. Berger et al., "Child Rearing in Communes," in Louise Kapp Howe (ed.), *The Future of the Family* (New York: Simon and Schuster, 1972), pp. 159–169.

they were able to locate and interview 26 groups, six involving three persons and twenty involving four or more. Only two were in communes, the rest being in ordinary neighborhoods.[48] The Constantines, though sympathetic with the idea, pinpointed specific problems that explain the rarity of group marriage. For one thing, everybody admits the complexity of such marriages. Given an initial pair, the number of relationships increases by three for each person added. With one person added, there are three relationships, with two persons added their are six, and so on. This means that the groups are difficult to form and maintain, because so many relationships have to be worked out simultaneously. The main difficulties lie, according to the Constantines, in the relations between co-wives and co-husbands, especially between the latter. Foursomes must cope with "an almost irresistible tendency to become two parallel dyads."[49] Finally, the majority of participants enter the group as established couples. These tend to be more cohesive than the new relationships, and when the group breaks they remain together. Of the 26 group marriages studied by the Constantines, 21 had broken up. Jealousy was a factor, as were differences over the way children should be reared.[50]

PROSTITUTION

To put sex into a meaningful social context inevitably means to treat it exclusively—to confine it to a durable pair or group. Prostitution, which cements no affectionate or institutional bond, is the opposite of exclusiveness. It requires the female to be *promiscuous*. Also, she *sells* her favors and is *emotionally indifferent*. Although the trading of sexual favors for economic security has long been the basis of marriage (a wife who submits to intercourse dutifully but reluctantly is fulfilling her obligation), this has taken place in a stable relationship. The prostitute's affront is not that she trades but that she trades promiscuously and with emotional indifference.

Both prostitution and the prostitute herself rise in social esteem insofar as one or more of three conditions are present: (1) The promiscuity is lessened by some basis of choice; (2) the earnings of prostitution are used for a goal considered socially desirable; (3) the prostitute combines other roles with that of sexual gratification.

In ancient Greece, the lowest prostitutes were streetwalkers and brothel inmates. Far above both were the *hetairae*, who were distinguished by being educated in the arts, by serving only the wealthy and powerful, and by providing entertainment and intellectual companionship as well as sexual gratification. The *hetairae*, drawn from the alien population, compensated for the fact that respectable wives and daughters (that is, women of Greek citizen families) were not permitted to entertain, go outside the home, or acquire an

[48] Constantine and Constantine, *op. cit.*, pp. 68, 249.
[49] *Ibid.*, Ch. 7, particularly pp. 78, 81.
[50] *Ibid.*, Ch. 19, and p. 249.

education. Often cited in this connection is a statement attributed to Demosthenes: "Man has the *hetairae* for erotic enjoyments, concubines for daily use, and wives to bring up children and to be faithful housewives." Yet the *hetairae* were not respectable. They had a reputation for being faithless, avaricious, vain, and shrewd.[51]

Similarly, Japan until recently had three classes of women outside of respectable family life—the *joro* in brothels; the *jogoku*, or unlicensed prostitutes on the streets or in bath houses; and the *geisha*, or dancing girls. Trained in dancing, singing, samisen playing, and other methods of entertaining guests in tea houses, geisha girls were an indispensable adjunct at every Japanese entertainment. Not all of them were open to prostitution; and even if they were, they were selective as to type of customer.[52]

Prostitution may also enjoy social esteem by association with religion, as it did throughout much of the ancient world, including Greece (apart from Athens) and India.[53] Similar considerations apply to the type of prostitution practiced in some societies whereby the girl obtains a dowry for her subsequent marriage.[54]

In modern society about all that is left of the types of prostitution is the commercial form in which one party uses sex for pleasure, the other for money. To tie intercourse to sheer pleasure is to divorce it both from reproduction and from any sentimental social relationship. To tie it simply to money does the same. Purely commercial prostitution and the women who practice it are denigrated in all societies. This does not mean that people feel as strongly about prostitution as they do about thievery or arson. A survey conducted by *McCalls Magazine* found that only 7 percent of respondents said they would clear the streets of prostitutes if they had a chance. The disesteem for prostitution is manifest mainly by a reluctance to have a bordello in the neighborhood or to be identified with the business or its personnel.[55]

The "Causes" of Prostitution

If prostitution offends moral imperatives, why does it persist? And if denigrated, how does it recruit? To explain prostitution in economic terms is begging the question. Since prostitution is defined as selling sexual favors, one

[51] Hans Licht, *Sexual Life in Ancient Greece* (London: Routledge, 1932), pp. 332–363, 395–410. See also Alfred Zimmern, *The Greek Commonwealth* (Oxford: Clarendon, 1931), pp. 341–344.

[52] Alice Bacon, *Japanese Girls and Women*, rev. ed. (Boston: Houghton Mifflin, 1919), pp. 286–287, 288–289.

[53] Abbe J. A. Dubois, *Hindu Manners, Customs and Ceremonies*, 3rd ed. (Oxford: Clarendon, 1906), pp. 584–586; Edward Westermarck, *Origin and Development of Moral Ideas*, Vol. 1 (London: Macmillan, 1908), p. 224. "In Morocco supernatural benefits are to this day expected not only from heterosexual but also from homosexual intercourse with a holy person."

[54] Havelock Ellis, *Studies in the Psychology of Sex*, Vol. 6 (Philadelphia: Davis, 1913), p. 233.

[55] *McCalls Magazine*, February 1965.

might as well say, with equal perspicacity, that retail merchandising has economic causes. The assumption is often made that the sole question concerns the factors leading women to enter the business. Actually, there are at least five separable questions: (1) Why does prostitution exist? (2) Why are there different types of prostitution? (3) What factors influence the rate or amount of prostitution? (4) What leads women to enter or not enter the profession? and (5) What leads men to patronize or not patronize prostitutes? Let us keep these separate questions in mind.

On the physical side, human females are sexually receptive year round. This introduces sex as a permanent element in social life and favors constant association of the two sexes. Further, the sexual response may be used not only (or not at all) for the individual's own erotic gratification, but as a means to some ulterior purpose. This being true, the next question is why it should be used for money or other valuable favors and why it is usually the male rather than the female who buys. (It is significant that when men are prostitutes they are usually homosexual prostitutes—that is, for other men.) Here the roles of the family and social stratification are relevant. The demand for the prostitute's services arises out of the regulation of sex itself and the limited liability of the commercial relationship. If the customer has the money, he can obtain satisfaction with no further obligations. He does not become enmeshed in "courtship," "friendship," or "marriage." Every male finds himself sometimes, and some males most of the time, in circumstances where release through more reputable channels is impossible. Furthermore, the division of labor by sex, derived from the female's greater association with reproduction and hence the family, makes women dependent to some extent on their sexual attractiveness and gives men more control of economic means. Since the economic means are distributed unequally between classes but female attractiveness is not, some women of lower economic means can exploit their attractiveness for economic gain. For these reasons, demand and supply are broadly based and inextinguishable. This is why, when prostitution is outlawed, it falls into a category of crime that is notoriously hard to control—the type in which one of the guilty parties is the ordinary law-abiding citizen, who is receiving an illicit service. It is economically and politically foolish to punish a large number of a society's productive and otherwise orderly members for a vice that injures no one.

> The professional prostitute being a social outcast may be periodically punished without disturbing the usual course of society; no one misses her while she is serving out her turn—no one, at least, about whom society has any concern. The man, however, is something more than partner in an immoral act: he discharges important social and business relations, is as father or brother responsible for the maintenance of others, has commercial or industrial duties to meet. He cannot be imprisoned without deranging society.[56]

Of course, not all males visit prostitutes, nor do most of those who do

[56] Abraham Flexner, *Prostitution in Europe* (New York: Century, 1920), p. 108.

depend on them for a major share of their sexual outlet. In Kinsey's sample, about 30 percent never have contact with prostitutes. Of the rest, many "never have more than a single experience or two, and not more than 15 or 20 percent of them ever have such relations more often than a few times a year, over as much as a five-year period in their lives."[57] This still leaves a substantial portion of the adult male population. For them, what does prostitution provide that other outlets do not provide?

The advantage of prostitution is its impartiality, impersonality, and economy. Attracting and seducing a woman can be costly. Kinsey states that before World War II the average cost of intercourse with a prostitute "was less than the cost of a single supper date with a girl who was not a prostitute."[58] By its very effort to place the sex drive in a meaningful and enduring social relationship, society creates advantages for prostitution. For instance, the impersonality

[57] Kinsey et al., *Sexual Behavior in the Human Male,* p. 597.
[58] *Ibid.,* p. 607.

of prostitution makes it particularly suited to strangers. The man away from his wife or his circle of girlfriends cannot in a short time count on seducing a respectable woman in the place he happens to be. Also, by defining certain coital techniques as immoral and hence out of bounds for wives and sweethearts, the moral order gives an advantage to the prostitute. Further, the man who is in a stable relationship with a woman may nevertheless find his sex life with her thwarted by the vicissitudes of interpersonal relations or the staleness of age or familiarity.[59] Seen in this light, the demand for prostitution will not be eliminated or seriously altered by a change in the economic system. The underlying basis for the demand is inherent in human society.

On the supply side, it used to be said that prostitution could be abolished by raising women's wages or by abolishing capitalism. Such a view rests on the assumption that girls enter the profession because of economic necessity, but the earnings may well exceed what they could earn otherwise. Their wages are not primarily a reward for labor, skill, or capital, but a reward for loss of social standing. "No practicable rise in the rate of wages paid to women in ordinary industries can possibly compete with the wages which fairly attractive women of quite ordinary ability can earn by prostitution."[60] Also, if prostitutes are on their own, they can set their own hours, determine their own vacations, as well as escape income taxes.

It was widely believed in the 1930s that the Soviet Union had abolished prostitution. But in 1959, a reporter who had just completed a long stay in Russia had this to say:

A stroller in the central Moscow streets of an early evening is apt to be approached near big hotels. The women are strange sights—heavily rouged, gaunt-faced and costumed as in sketches by Hogarth.

Around the Hotel Astoria in Leningrad prostitutes may also be seen. Typically, the Leningrad women are smartly attired, affect high heels and pony-tail hairdos.[61]

It will take more than communism to eliminate the world's oldest profession.

Prostitution has an uncanny ability to adapt itself to any institutional system. Whether tolerated as an established evil, as in medieval Europe, or outlawed, it always manages to thrive. During the Prohibition era in the United States, the vice syndicates were linked to bootlegging and did a fabulous business running into millions of dollars. After Prohibition, the link with bootlegging was replaced by linkage with labor unions, coin-machine operations, record pirating, and pornographic activity. In 1954, two underworld figures worked out a scheme to take over vice operations in Portland, Oregon. With top officials of the Teamsters Union, they elected a district attorney who then

[59] Most patrons of prostitutes are married. Kinsey et al., *Sexual Behavior in the Human Male*, p. 288.

[60] Havelock Ellis, *Studies in the Psychology of Sex*, Vol. 6, p. 263. "There are call-girls who earn between fifty and a hundred thousand dollars a year." John M. Murtagh and Sara Harris, *Cast the First Stone* (New York: McGraw-Hill, 1957).

[61] Harrison Salisbury, *The New York Times*, September 10, 1959, p. 10.

worked with them to set up facilities for pinball, punchboard, and card-room operations, off-track betting, and prostitution. The Teamsters Union threatened to stop deliveries to restaurants, cafeterias, and bars that refused to use the syndicate's equipment.[62] By 1970 the expansion of drug abuse and the consequent demand for narcotics brought a new phase to organized prostitution.

> Mary is only 15. Until a couple of weeks ago, she worked as a prostitute . . . to support her "old man," an 18-year-old heroin addict.
> . . . prostitution and heroin addiction [among residents of Potrero Hill, a section of San Francisco] are spreading to the very young at a startling rate. . . .
> A girl hustling on the streets can make up to $400 or more a night, depending on where she works. Territories are strictly enforced. . . .
> At Everett Junior High it was said that groups of ninth grade boys often deal in narcotics and prostitution, with seventh and eighth grade girls "turning tricks." . . .[63]

The Debate over Legal Regulation

Because of its chameleon-like quality, prostitution has always outwitted all systems of legal control. Attempts to abolish it by declaring it a crime have merely driven it underground and into the hands of criminal syndicates and corrupt officials. Efforts to regulate only its public manifestations or its consequences have also had little success, because prostitution must and will advertise, if not on the streets then in massage parlors, bars, dance-halls, and hotels. The Wolfenden Committee, appointed in Great Britain in 1954, favored removing legal bans on prostitution per se but wanted stiff penalties for repeated street solicitation, rental of premises for purposes of prostitution, and living off the earnings of prostitutes. However, when its recommendations were enacted into law in the Street Offenses Act of 1959, the effects were other than those intended. Since the law merely cautioned for the first two street offenses, it increased the mobility of prostitutes, who left each district after they had accumulated two offenses. Also, both the law's rental clause and its refusal to penalize customers encouraged the use of automobiles for cruising and intercourse.[64]

Alternatively, a return to licensed brothels, inspected for purposes of health and crime prevention, is often recommended. It was this system that Abraham Flexner described and condemned in his famous report, *Prostitution in Europe*, in 1920. Flexner's criticism was that licensed brothels encourage prostitution and all its evils, including the spread of venereal infection. Actually, they were already a dying institution. Although they are occasionally revived—for exam-

---

[62] Robert F. Kennedy, *The Enemy Within* (New York: Popular Library, 1960), pp. 245–250.

[63] *San Francisco Chronicle*, March 10, 1970, p. 4.

[64] Nicholas Swingler, "The Streetwalker Returns," *New Society* (January 16, 1969), summarized in Gilbert Geis, *Not the Law's Business* (Washington, D.C.: Government Printing Office, 1972), pp. 187–189.

ple, under local option in certain Nevada counties—the publicity attending these arrangements show their rarity. In societies where nearly everyone gets a high-school education and where the level of living frees everyone from absolute servitude, the idea of licensing entrepreneurs to sell women's bodies is repugnant. If it means permitting prostitution *only* in official brothels, it represents distasteful and unenforceable compulsion. Many women who wish to sell themselves do not wish to work in brothels, and many customers do not prefer brothel inmates. In fact, any licensing of prostitutes encounters the obstacle that the occupation not only has pariah status (leading women to resist being identified with it) but also is highly mobile in a mobile society. It is unskilled, requires no equipment or fixed premises, and is often part-time and transitory as well.[65]

Legal regulation of prostitution will therefore probably remain an effort to keep it out of sight and out of contact with respectable women. People do not want prostitution in their neighborhoods or on public display, nor do they want girls recruited by guile or duress. Officials try to satisfy these desires by limiting the locations and evidences of the trade. Beyond that, the main control is not legal but pejorative; it lies in the low status given the occupation.

Prostitution and Sexual Freedom

The main competitor of prostitution is sexual freedom. Kinsey found that the reported frequencies of paid intercourse were two-thirds to one-half less for males of recent vintage than for those of the older generation. "The frequencies of coitus with females who were not prostitutes had increased to an extent which largely compensated for the decreased frequencies with prostitutes."[66] Paul H. Gebhard found a drop from 25 to 7 percent between the fifties and sixties in the proportion of male students experiencing their first coitus with prostitutes.[67]

If we reverse the proposition that increased sex freedom reduces the role of prostitution, we must admit that increased prostitution can reduce the sex activities of respectable women. This was, in fact, the ancient justification for tolerated prostitution—that it "protected" the family and kept the wives and daughters of the respectable citizenry pure.[68] In modern society, however, fewer people consider such protection necessary. This change has occurred mainly because of the mobility and anonymity associated with an urban-industrial system. Friendly sexual relations are now impossible to control. At the same time, being a prostitute is less of a fixed status. In a small city like ancient Athens, the difference between an educated alien who was a prostitute

[65] Anne Van Haecht, *La Prostituée: statut et image* (Bruxelles: Universite de Bruxelles, 1973), p. 47.

[66] Kinsey et al., *Sexual Behavior in the Human Male*, p. 411.

[67] Cited in Lester Graham, *No More Morals: The Sexual Revolution* (New York: Pyramid, 1971), p. 141.

[68] W. E. H. Lecky, *History of European Morals*, Vol. 2, 3rd ed. (London: Longmans, 1877), pp. 282–283.

and an uneducated citizen who was a wife was known to everyone. Today, in Paris, New York, or Moscow, prostitutes often marry or enter another occupation. Movement in and out of prostitution is relatively easy. For most women the occupation is pursued at the age when it is most lucrative, and then abandoned.

HOMOSEXUAL BEHAVIOR

To understand attitudes toward homosexuality, let us recall that the strongest sex norms are those concerning prohibited partners. Masturbation involves no partner at all; incest, a kinsman within the nuclear family; adultery, a partner other than one's spouse; homosexuality, a partner of the same sex. Although these norms are modified by other rules (such as those concerning the proper erotic techniques or the degree of impersonality), they are nonetheless basic, including the rule against same-sex intercourse.

How Widely Is Homosexuality Disapproved?

Historically, in all complex societies, there were people who engaged in homosexual practices. The works of some contemporary writers can always be cited as evidence of approval, but the attitude of the general public, though more poorly documented, appears to have been unfavorable. Hans Licht, for example, citing art and literature, has painted a picture of idealized homosexuality and of homosexual prostitution in ancient Greece.[69] Athens, however, was a small city and its people were suspicious of the intellectuals. Anaxagoras was condemned and exiled for impiety; Protagoras was expelled from the city and his books burned; Socrates was condemned to death. These men were charged with "corruption of youth," which probably meant disrespect for Athenian institutions. In reaction, Greek parents of the citizen class put great care into the education of their sons.

> Far from casting out their sons into public schools, with the full knowledge that they will there lose all their simplicity and innocence, Greek parents of the better sort kept their sons constantly under the eye of a slave tutor or pedagogue, . . . who never let them out of their sight.[70]

The Romans, after losing their early rustic morality, evidently tolerated a considerable amount of homosexuality, and the poets of the empire adopted a matter-of-fact attitude toward it.[71] However, ascetic and stoic philosophies were also strong in Rome, and again it seems difficult to document actual public

---

[69] Licht, *op. cit.*

[70] J. P. Mahaffy, *Social Life in Greece*, 5th ed. (London: Macmillan, 1883), p. 331. See also H. D. Kitto, *The Greeks* (Baltimore, Md.: Penguin, 1951), pp. 219–236.

[71] Otto Kiefer, *Sexual Life in Rome* (New York: Dutton, 1935), Ch. 5.

opinion. The Hebrew moral code strongly condemned homosexuality, as did that of classical Hinduism, but without preventing homosexual behavior or homosexual prostitution.[72] In sum, complex societies seem to tolerate a certain amount of homosexual behavior (and literary praise of it) without giving it respect.

Primitive societies furnish some examples of accepted but not esteemed homosexuality under restricted circumstances. "Nearly all societies," says George P. Murdock, "seek to confine marriage and sex relations to persons of complementary sex. Some permit homosexuality in specifically delimited contexts, and a very few manifest wide latitude in this respect."[73] Clellan S. Ford and Frank A. Beach list, in a total of 77 societies, 49 (all primitive) in which "homosexual activities of one sort or another are considered normal and socially acceptable for certain members of the community." Most of these cases represent acceptance of the berdache, "a male who dresses like a woman, performs woman's tasks, and adopts some aspects of the feminine role in sexual behavior with male partners." But the reversal of roles is rare and is not approved for men generally. The Chukchee berdache was "believed to have been involuntarily transformed by supernatural power and some men fear being thus changed. . . ." Among the Lango of Uganda, the men taking the feminine role were "believed to be impotent and to have been afflicted by some supernatural agency."[74] In other words, the existence of institutionalized homosexuality does not necessarily mean that it has high standing or that it is widely practiced.

The law in modern societies may be permissive even when public attitudes are negative. The British commission's report in 1957 recommended "that homosexual behavior between consenting adults in private be no longer a criminal offense."[75] Eventually enacted into law, this did not mean that the British public favored homosexuality. A Gallup Poll taken shortly after the report was issued showed 38 percent favoring legalization, 47 percent against, and 15 percent uncertain.[76]

Why the Disapproval?

Homosexual intercourse is disapproved because it is incompatible with the family and the sexual bargaining system. It affronts the norms and attitudes required to get reproduction and sexual allocation accomplished. The threat to the main system is least when homosexuality is purely instrumental—that is, when it is simply a means of sexual release—but this conflicts with the principle of harnessing the sex drive. When it is the preferred sexual mode, homo-

---

[72] Robert Wood, "Sex Life in Ancient Civilizations," *Encyclopedia of Sexual Behavior*, pp. 130–131; and Shah, *op. cit.*, pp. 533–544.

[73] Murdock, *op. cit.*, p. 317.

[74] Clellan S. Ford and Frank A. Beach, *Patterns of Sexual Behavior* (New York: Harper & Row, 1951).

[75] *Report of the Committee on Homosexual Offences and Prostitution* (1957), p. 115.

[76] J. E. Hall Williams, "Sex Offenses: The British Experience," *Law and Contemporary Problems*, Vol. 25 (Spring 1960), pp. 354–355.

sexuality is strongly condemned. Thus when boys indulge in mutual sex play as a passing sport in the absence of girls, or when prisoners are forced into it by isolation, the activity carries little or no implication of a "homosexual way of life" and is only mildly censured, but voluntarily seeking transitory encounters, such as those that take place in public lavatories,[77] is considered degrading. On the other hand, when durable homosexual relations involving affection are entered into, this at least brings sexual gratification into a social relationship. Such devotion is held as the ideal by most homosexuals, despite the fact that "complex personality and social variables" prevent most from realizing it.[78] One study found lesbians "almost without exception" to desire "an enduring love relationship," exhibiting "an almost nineteenth-century commitment to romantic ideals."[79] Such relations often mimic heterosexual love, as when the pair are "married," set up "housekeeping" together, demand mutual fidelity, and distinguish between the "masculine" and "feminine" roles. Such attachment plainly competes with male–female relationships and is thus felt as a strong threat by the general public.

Strengthening this interpretation is the fact that the public in general and homosexuals themselves hold in low esteem the one who takes a physiologically inappropriate role. This is evidently due not only to the anatomical inappropriateness but also to the greater difficulty of resuming the normal heterosexual role. In prison populations it is most often the partner who has kept his regular role (the "femme" in lesbian and the "wolf" in homosexual relations) who returns to normal sexuality after release.[80]

One may object that this theory ignores new conditions. Why do people still disapprove of homosexuality, even if they do not actually condemn it or favor legal controls, since a high birth rate is not needed? Why do they feel this way about *homo*sexual behavior when *hetero*sexual behavior has been "liberated"? The answer is that the questions are wrongly phrased. A high birth rate is not desired, but children are. And heterosexual relations have by no means been decontrolled. Whatever the future may bring, the nuclear family is still cherished; in industrial societies, it is virtually the only kinship unit left. Although the age at marriage has risen in recent years, the proportion who ever marry is higher than it was a century ago. Despite numerous divorces, about two-thirds of the couples who get married stay married. In contrast, even in special groups where opinion is pro-homosexual, homosexual relations are notoriously instable. Without doubt, as we shall see, the social handling of homosexuality is changing, but not toward giving it high standing.

[77] These are described in graphic detail in Laud Humphreys, *Tearoom Trade: Impersonal Sex in Public Places* (Chicago: Aldine, 1970).
[78] Evelyn Hooker, "An Empirical Study of Some Relations Between Sexual Partners and Gender Identity in Male Homosexuals," in John Money (ed.), *Sex Research: New Developments* (New York: Holt, 1965), p. 46.
[79] William Simon and John Gagnon, "The Lesbians: A Preliminary Overview," in John N. Edwards (ed.), *Sex and Society* (Chicago: Markham, 1972), p. 104.
[80] David A. Ward and Gene G. Kassebaum, *Women's Prison: Sex and Social Structure* (Chicago: Aldine, 1965), pp. 179, 194.

Becoming a Homosexual

The two approaches to explaining homosexual preference—an inherited or physiological aberration versus a psychosocial mechanism in childhood or adolescence—are commonly regarded as being mutually exclusive, but they are not logically so. Biological and environmental factors often work together, and may well do so in this case. Moreover, since homosexuals differ greatly among themselves, it is extremely unlikely that there is a single cause common to all cases. Favoring a hereditary hypothesis is a famous study of 85 male homosexuals and their twin brothers, by F. J. Kallman.[81] Forty of the 85 were *identical* twins, and for 37 of these Kallman managed to trace the brother. He found that in *every* instance the brother was homosexually inclined, 28 being exclusively homosexual. In contrast, among the brothers of the *nonidentical* twins (of whom he traced 26), only 3 were homosexual. However, other investigators have found identical twin pairs in which one was homosexual and the other heterosexual.[82]

If heredity plays a role, it may do so by affecting temperament, predisposing an individual to accept homosexual stimuli if presented. Since homosexuals have a low rate of reproduction, any specifically homosexual trait would be rapidly bred out of the population; only a frequently recurring homosexual mutation of some sort (say, a hormone abnormality) could maintain the trait. As indicated earlier, however, the human sex drive is capable of a great deal of conditioning. Hence any individual can, through early experience, develop a preference for same-sex gratification.

In view of sexual malleability, the question is not why so many people deviate from heterosexual norms, but why so few do. Only 4 percent of Kinsey's male respondents and 1 percent of his female respondents were exclusively homosexual. If accurate, these figures demonstrate the power of social censure over opportunity, because each society, in regulating male-female relations, inadvertently facilitates homosexual contacts. Boys are encouraged to be with boys, girls with girls—in dormitories, camps, and jails. Under such arrangements virtually every adolescent has opportunities for same-sex stimulation of the *faute de mieux* sort. Such incidents are not "homosexual" in an emotional or exclusive sense, and are generally not taken seriously. What deters young people from becoming emotionally committed to this form of release is doubtless its negative evaluation by peers and social rewards that are contingent on normal heterosexual relations. The few who turn into "true" homosexuals are presumably like the few drinkers who turn into confirmed alcoholics: they do so both because they drink too much and because they cannot make the normal

[81] F. J. Kallman, "Twin Sibships and the Study of Male Homosexuality," *American Journal of Human Genetics,* Vol. 4 (1952), pp. 136–146 and "Comparative Twin Study of the Genetic Aspects of Male Homosexuality," *Journal of Nervous and Mental Diseases,* Vol. 115 (1952), pp. 283–298. The study is described by D. J. West, *Homosexuality* (Baltimore: Penguin, 1960), pp. 107–109.

[82] West, *op. cit.,* pp. 109–110.

adjustments in life. Once the homosexual habit is fixed by the reinforcement of frequent gratification, it becomes extraordinarily difficult to break.

That most homosexuals seek sentimental and emotional satisfaction as well as organic release is comprehensible. Sex is woven into social relations. One's self-image, one's motives and emotions, depend not on sheer physical gratification, but on sexual activity as an expression of companionship and affection. It happens that in most aspects of life, one shares one's emotions with others of the same as well as different sex. It is a complex process for the growing individual to learn to discriminate between who is suitable for erotic feelings and who is not, especially since erotic motivation is often subtle and unrecognized as such. A relatively slight upset in the mechanics of personal-social development—caused either by prolonged homosexual practice itself or by neurotic problems—may cause a failure in this discrimination.

That same-sex segregation is conducive to homosexual behavior is well known. Donald Clemmer estimated that of 2,300 adult male prisoners he studied, 30 percent were partly homosexual and 10 percent "true homosexuals."[83] David A. Ward and Gene Kassebaum, two sociologists, began their study of a women's prison in California with the idea of analyzing personality types. They found lesbianism so prevalent (with at least 50 percent of the inmates participating) and so important in inmate social organization that they concentrated on that subject instead and entitled their book *Women's Prison: Sex and Social Structure.*

One might expect homosexual behavior, like prostitution, to diminish as heterosexual coitus becomes easier. In fact, however, the opposite seems true. The reason may be that the rise of heterosexual freedom is in part a function of social disorganization rather than reorganization, giving rise to personal anomie encouraging homosexual relations. Also, to the extent that heterosexual relations become commonplace they become boring, whereas homosexual relations retain something of the risqué and are therefore erotically stimulating.

Problems of Homosexual Behavior

Whatever its causes, homosexual behavior gives rise to serious problems, the most important being homosexual prostitution, venereal disease, crime, fraud, and youth corruption.

Homosexual prostitution by males in their teens and early twenties is widespread in many countries. It is "probably much more prevalent in the United States than ever before. . . ."[84] Young boys are often inducted or forced into "hustling" by older gang members. They do not consider themselves homosexuals but are out to make easy money and satisfy gang leaders. For some gangs, "the practice becomes one of 'queer-baiting,' to role the 'queer' for his

---

[83] Donald Clemmer, *The Prison Community* (New York: Rinehart, 1958), pp. 257–264.
[84] Benjamin and Masters, *op. cit.*, p. 290.

money, since he fears legal recourse. . . ."[85] Since the service involves orgasm by the boy, the end of prostitution is frequently that he himself, despite his intentions, becomes a confirmed homosexual. The customers' eagerness for youthful partners is such that the career of the homosexual prostitute is usually ended by age 25; a premium is placed on youths from 12 to 20.[86]

In the 1920s homosexual behavior was a minor source of venereal infection, but by the late 1960s it had become a major factor, with countries reporting anywhere from 10 to 90 percent of venereal cases as homosexual in origin.[87] In surveys in Los Angeles from 1959 to 1961, from 50 to 77 percent of infected males named purely homosexual contacts; in some districts the percentage was as high as 86 percent.[88] Not surprisingly, over the same period, the young age groups showed greater rises in VD rates than older groups. The reason homosexuals are so vulnerable to VD is their tendency to promiscuity (50 different contacts a month in some cases) and their furtiveness (which overcomes caution). Also, gonococcal infection of the rectum, like infection of the female vagina, is usually not recognized until it has spread to other parts of the body.[89]

Apart from robbery and violence, both frequent in male as in female prostitution, the main crises arising in homosexual relationships are blackmail and homicide. Any prominent homosexual runs the risk of blackmail, not only because of the threat of arrest or loss of job, but also because of fear of public exposure. No one knows how many stabbings and murders occur in homosexual quarrels, but the circumstances in newspaper accounts suggest they are frequent.

There are other injuries, however, in which the homosexual is not the victim but the perpetrator. One of these is marriage to a normal person without revealing one's homosexuality.[90] Curiously, in the literature on sexual deviance, this tragic situation is discussed exclusively from the standpoint of its effects on the homosexual, not its damage to the innocent spouse and children. Another crime is inducting children into a homosexual way of life. New laws permitting all sexual acts between consenting adults still usually define such acts with a minor as a felony. Similarly, there is resistance to permitting employment of known homosexuals in situations that give them authority over children. Police records do show arrests for seduction of youths by adult homosexuals. In a 1970 na-

---

[85] Albert J. Reiss, "Sex Offenses: The Marginal Status of the Adolescent," *Law and Contemporary Problems,* Vol. 25 (Spring 1960), p. 323.

[86] Benjamin and Masters, *op. cit.,* pp. 294–295, 299–302. See also Charles Winick and Paul M. Kinsie, *The Lively Commerce* (Chicago: Quadrangle, 1971), pp. 89–96.

[87] World Health Organization, "V.D. Around the World," *Today's V.D. Control Problems,* 1968.

[88] Evelyn Hooker, "Male Homosexual Life Styles and Venereal Disease," in *Proceedings of the World Forum on Syphilis* (U.S. Public Health Service, 1964).

[89] Richard Stiller, *The Love Bugs: A Natural History of the VDs* (Nashville: Thomas Nelson, 1974), pp. 106–107.

[90] Martin S. Weinberg and Colin J. Williams [*Male Homosexuals: Their Problems and Adaptations* (New York: Oxford, 1974), pp. 241–243] found that about 7 percent of their sample of homosexuals in the United States were living with a wife.

tional sample of children aged 13 to 19, among those who had had homosexual experience, 12 percent of the boys but virtually none of the girls had their first experience with an adult.[91]

Will the "Homosexual Community" Be Recognized?

In recent years, homosexuals have begun to demand that they be allowed to practice their own beliefs just like any other minority. Numerous homosexual associations have sprung up—to parade, picket agencies that refuse to hire homosexuals, demand legislative changes, furnish speakers to churches, schools, and television, and encourage homosexuals to admit and be proud of their "sexual orientation." The Mattachine Society of New York, for example, successfully challenged the constitutionality of New York's "anti-drag" law, which prohibited males from dressing as women, and in collaboration with the New York Civil Liberties Union and the Episcopal Diocese, it helped to end police entrapment of homosexuals in New York City. Indeed, the battle to end discrimination against homosexuals in employment is quickly being won. In September, 1975, for example, over the strong objections of the Chief of Police, the Los Angeles City Civil Service Commission voted unanimously to allow homosexuals on the police force.[92]

In removing legal restrictions on the employment, adult sexual behavior, and public display of homosexuality, the movement is proving more successful than most observers expected.

Evidence from contemporary industrial societies, however, indicates that the general public is not as tolerant of homosexuality as legisators are. In Denmark and Holland, two countries commonly praised for legal permissiveness, the attitude is at best one of grudging tolerance.

> Even in Amsterdam, to be a homosexual is to be in a disvalued minority . . . In referring to heterosexuals and homosexuals, the Dutch use words which mean "normals" and "homos." Even Dutch homosexuals refer to heterosexuals as "normals." . . . In summary . . . despite tolerance . . a lack of genuine social social acceptance does cause problems even for the Dutch homosexuals.[93]

In the United States, 81 percent of boys and 77 percent of girls in Sorensen's national sample[94] expressed the opinion that two boys (or girls) having sex is "abnormal" or "unnatural." An Australian poll showed that "a much larger percentage of the population oppose the liberalization of the laws relating to homosexuality than those relating to abortion and prostitution."[95] Clearly, the liberalization of laws is one thing, public approval another.

[91] Robert C. Sorensen, *Adolescent Sexuality in Contemporary America* (New York: World Publishing, 1973), pp. 286, 290, 432.
[92] *San Francisco Chronicle*, September 29, 1975.
[93] Weinberg and Williams, *op. cit.*, p. 86; see also Chaps. 2–7.
[94] Sorensen, *op. cit.*, p. 289.
[95] Paul R. Wilson and Duncan Chappell, "Australian Attitudes Toward Abortion, Prostitution and Homosexuality" *Australian Quarterly*, Vol. 40 (June 1968), pp. 7–17; cited in Geis, *op. cit.*, p. 39.

In the haste to make homosexuality respectable, the possibility of prevention has been largely overlooked. If homosexuality is mainly a conditioned rather than an inherited response, an effort to remove its causes and thus greatly lower its incidence would appear reasonable, but this possibility is almost never considered. Instead, great efforts are made to help homosexuals through psychiatric treatment and counseling, but *after* they have become homosexual. Many homosexuals regret their abnormality and would not like their children to become homosexual. For example, in a poll of 300 male homosexuals, 83 percent said they would not want a son to be homosexual, only 2 percent said they would want him to be, and the rest said they would leave it up to the son.[96] Merle Miller, a prominent author who has acknowledged his homosexuality, said in an interview that he could think of no advantages to homosexuality.[97] Given this attitude, the absence of preventive effort is puzzling.

A successful effort to make homosexuality respectable would require more than the abrogation of old rules. It would require new rules, because respectable behavior always involves defined rights and obligations. If given the same status as heterosexual behavior, homosexuality would entail an orderly distribution of that scarce resource—youthful homosexual attractiveness. Sexual bargaining would be linked to economic and social obligations and interpersonal equity in much the same way as heterosexual bargaining. Under such a regime, the role of homosexual intercourse in personal life would be altered as well. It would no longer have the stimulus of being illicit. Such a regime hardly seems likely, however, for it would compete too directly with that other institutionalized system—marriage and the family.

SUMMARY

1 The theory of why sex is regulated in all societies is a part of the theory of norms in general, but as applied to sexual behavior there are certain propositions that are helpful.

2 Since the sexual impulse is both powerful and capable of intricate conditioning, it can serve as an important source of motivation for inducing people to behave in ways contributing to group existence.

3 The major way in which the sex impulse is harnessed is by linking it with marriage and the family—for instance, by making marriage normatively superior to other kinds of sexual union.

4 However, since sexual attractiveness is found about equally in all social classes, a trade-off between economic status and sexual access is inevitable. All systems of sex regulation can therefore be understood as functions of the family and social stratification.

5 The variety of sex norms is so great that it is difficult to categorize societies in terms of any single facet, but underneath the variations in detail from one society to another, it is possible to detect certain uniformities.

[96] Geis, *op. cit.*, pp. 26–27.
[97] *The Washington Star*, October 24, 1971, p. B–2.

6 For one thing, premarital sex behavior offers the least threat to marriage, and it is here that one finds the widest range of regulations.

7 With respect to extramarital behavior, there is much less variation, especially for the wife. Communal sex and group marriage arrangements are rare and disapproved.

8 Prostitution is also disapproved insofar as it is purely commercial and removes sex from a durable social context. Yet it provides a sexual outlet free of the obligations surrounding marriage and the family, and thrives where marriage is an unbreakable union and respectable women are strictly controlled.

9 Homosexuality suffers even more scorn because it not only takes place outside the family system, as does prostitution, but also with the wrong sex. Like prostitution, however, it tends to be tolerated as an inescapable phenomenon in all industrial and some primitive societies.

10 In contemporary societies, where sex rules are being relaxed, there is much dispute as to whether this means a substitution of *new* standards (as yet unclear) or a *breakdown* of standards. Some profess to see a new order emerging, but others feel that the few remaining democracies have become too indecisive to enforce standards and will therefore be replaced. If sexual regulation is rooted in the nature of human society, as is maintained in this chapter, a breakdown indicates competitive weakness.

RECOMMENDED READING

For a discussion of the theory of norms, see Judith Blake and Kingsley Davis, "Norms, Values, and Sanctions," in Robert E. L. Faris (ed.), *Handbook of Modern Sociology* (1964). The classic account of sex practices in various cultures (mostly primitive) is still Clellan S. Ford and Frank A. Beach, *Patterns of Sexual Behavior* (1951), which consists of ethnographic reports of varying reliability. An attempt to develop a systematic theory of sexual regulation based on cross-cultural materials is found in Chapters 9 and 10 of George P. Murdock, *Social Structure* (1949).

Of necessity, the accounts of sexual practices in ancient civilizations are based primarily on literature and works of art. A scholarly analysis of Greek sexual regulation in relation to the family and social classes is found in W. K. Lacey, *The Family in Classical Greece* (1968). When future historians write on sexual behavior in present-day industrial societies, they will not have to rely on indirect sources or ethnographic impressions but will have the advantage of numerous surveys. Among these the most comprehensive is the prolonged survey made by Alfred C. Kinsey and his associates, resulting in *The Sexual Behavior of the Human Male* (1948) and *The Sexual Behavior of the Human Female* (1953). Other studies from the Institute of Sex Research at the University of Indiana include *Sex Offenders: An Analysis of Types* (1965) and *Pregnancy, Birth and Abortion* (1958).

Most surveys have been more limited in scope and more focused on particular sexual topics than Kinsey's study. For instance, numerous surveys of adolescent and student sexual behavior and attitudes are referred to in the present chapter. A pioneering study of this type was Ira L. Reiss, *The Social Context of Premarital Sexual Permissiveness* (1967). A survey of a different sort is that by Martin S.

Weinberg and Colin J. Williams, *Male Homosexuals Their Problems and Adaptations* (1974), where interviews with homosexuals in three countries—United States, Holland, and Denmark—are reported. Numerous surveys of public attitudes toward abortion, distribution of contraceptives to unmarried teenagers, and illegitimacy are described or cited in various articles by Judith Blake, Charles C. Westoff, and other authors. The most comprehensive symposium on abortion is that of Howard J. and Joy D. Osofsky (eds.), *The Abortion Experience* (1973). There have been polls of attitudes toward prostitution, but few surveys of prostitutes themselves, partly because of the difficulty of getting a representative sample. Some interview data are reported in Gilbert Geis, *Not the Law's Business* (1972) and Anne Van Haecht, *La prostituée* (1973). More general works on prostitution are Harry Benjamin and R. E. L. Masters, *Prostitution and Morality* (1964) and Fernando Henriques, *Prostitution and Society* (1968).

Because homosexuality is one of the most covert forms of sexual behavior, much of the information about it is based on a few interviews or autobiographical accounts. Evelyn Hooker has written numerous articles based on her interviews with male homosexuals with whom she could establish contact. Autobiographical is Peter Fisher's *The Gay Mystique* (1972). An account of the beginning of the gay militant movement is found in Donn Teal's *The Gay Militants* (1971) and Laud Humphreys' *Out of the Closets: The Sociology of Homosexual Liberation* (1972). Discoveries with respect to venereal disease are being made so rapidly that the best sources are the technical journals on medicine and public health. However, a quick survey is available in Kenneth L. Jones, Louis W. Shainberg, and Curtis O. Byer, *VD* (1974) and Richard Stiller, *The Love Bugs* (1974).

There are many symposia and collections of readings on sexual behavior. Among these the following may be mentioned: John N. Edwards (ed.), *Sex and Society* (1972), John Money (ed.) *Sex Research* (1965), Ralph W. Weltge (ed.), *The Same Sex* (1969), Jack and Joan De Lora (eds.), *Intimate Life Styles: Marriage and Its Alternates* (1972), and Lester A. Kirkendall and Robert N. Whitehurst (eds.), *The New Sexual Revolution* (1971). Up-to-date articles on various aspects of sex relations will be found in journals such as *Social Problems, Journal of Marriage and the Family, Sexual Behavior,* and *Journal of Sex Research.*

Part Two

Social Disorganization

6

The World's Population Crisis

KINGSLEY DAVIS

carcely any other subject reveals the human paradox as clearly as the question of human population growth. The population problem arises from the unique success of the human race in coping with the environment. Made invincible by our accumulated technology, we have multiplied until we are getting in our own way. With other animals driven to the wall and the earth despoiled, we are now engaged in a new enterprise—a search for a way to curb our own expansion deliberately before it is curbed for us by some catastrophe.

Understanding the situation requires a grasp not only of the astonishing facts of population growth but also of its causes and consequences. In this chapter we shall look first at the world as a whole and then at the developed and less developed regions. Later we shall consider prospects for the future and examine the policies that have been proposed to limit population growth.

THE POPULATION JUGGERNAUT

The basic facts are crystal clear. In 1975 the human population stood at 4 billion, twice the number in 1930. As Table 6-1 shows, the rate of increase has also shot upward. The average rate between 1950 and 1975 was 2.3 times the rate between 1900 and 1950; it was enough to double the population every 37 years. If the recent rate were to continue, the world's population would be 26 billion within a century and 167 billion within two centuries. Of course, nobody expects the rate to continue indefinitely. If we are having difficulty caring for 4 billion now, how will 26 billion be accommodated a century from now? The question is therefore *how* the growth can or will be stopped, and its possible consequences in the meantime.

Table 6-1   Growth of the Human Population

	Estimated population (millions)	Percent average yearly growth in prior period	Number of years to double population at given growth rate
400,000 BC	0.5		
8000 BC	5	.001	59,007
AD 1	300	.05	1,354
1750	791	.06	1,250
1800	978	.43	163
1850	1,262	.51	136
1900	1,650	.54	129
1950	2,486	.82	85
1975	3,967	1.89	37

Source: The first figure is conjectural but conservative; Homo sapiens may have originated millions of years earlier. The estimates for the period 8000 BC to 1900 AD are from John D. Durand, "The Modern Expansion of World Population," *Proceedings of the American Philosophical Society,* Vol. 3 (June 1967), p. 137; the 1950 estimate is from the United Nations *Demographic Yearbook, 1973;* the final estimate is from *World Population Prospects, 1970–2000, as Assessed in 1973* (New York: United Nations, March 10, 1975), p. 12.

Accelerated Growth

The modern speed of human multiplication contrasts sharply with the distant past. During at least 98 percent of human existence, the species dawdled, in an evolutionary sense. It multiplied temporarily in some areas, declined in others, but remained sparse everywhere. If the first period shown in Table 6-1 is even remotely correct, the population doubled itself only about every 60,000 years on the average. But around 8000 BC, something happened. The invention and spread of agriculture, animal husbandry, pottery, and eventually metallurgy speeded up the rate of population growth immensely. After that there was little change until 1750, when the Industrial Revolution got under way. After World War II, when the diffusion of advanced technology became worldwide, the rate reached an even higher level. Thus there were at least three escalations in human increase: one around 8000 BC, another around 1750, and a third around 1945. The following figures, derived from Table 6-1, show the approximate magnitude of the shifts:

	Percent average yearly increase*	Ratio to prior rate
400,000–8000 BC	.001	
8000 BC–1750 AD	.058	58:1
1750–1950	.580	10:1
1950–1975	1.869	3:1

* The use of averages over long periods tends to exaggerate the shifts, but the jumps are nevertheless so large as to be impressive.

Impressive as the rise in the rates is, the absolute increments are even more dramatic. For example, during 1950–1975, when the average growth rate was 1.89 percent per year, the number of people added was 1,481 million. A century earlier, the same rate for the same length of time would have produced a gain only half as great. With the huge size of the world's present population, even a small rate of growth yields a large addition. Since the actual rate is unprecedentedly high, the additions are staggering. By the end of the century, according to projections by the United Nations, the human population will be 6.64 billion (high), 6.25 billion (medium), or 5.84 billion (low).[1] The high projection means an addition of 2.3 billion, or 1.2 billion more than were added during the preceding 25 years. Even the low projection would mean an additional 1.9 billion, far more than were added previously.

Technological Backwardness and Population Growth

In the past, as Table 6-1 suggests, man's accelerating increase was associated with technological progress. For the most part, however, we lack information about the exact relationship. Only in the modern period are the facts adequate

[1] *World Population Prospects, 1970–2000, as Assessed in 1973* (New York: United Nations, March 10, 1975).

to pursue the relationship on a regional basis. They indicate that during most of modern history population growth did rest on technological advancement, but that in the twentieth century there was a curious shift. Before World War I the most rapid increase occurred in the technologically advanced nations. As a consequence, the northwest Europeans, who spearheaded the Industrial Revolution, multiplied more rapidly than the rest of the world's people. In some two and a half centuries their proportion in the world (in Europe and elsewhere) nearly doubled, rising from about 18 percent in 1650 to approximately 35 percent in 1920. Since 1920, however, the underdeveloped countries (overwhelmingly non-European in race and culture) have exhibited the more rapid growth, their advantage widening with time. Since 1940, as Table 6-2 shows, their growth rate has been, on average, about twice that of the industrial countries; according to the United Nations medium projections, the ratio of population between less developed and developed nations will reach 3½ to 1 between 1975 and 2000.

Table 6-2   Population Increase in Developed and Less Developed Countries in Each Decade from 1900 to 1970

| | Population (millions) | | Percent increase | |
	Developed	Less developed	Developed	Less developed
1900	251	1,399		
1920	309	1,551	11.0	5.3
1920	317	1,543		
1930	349	1,721	10.1	11.5
1930	528	1,542		
1940	565	1,730	7.0	12.2
1940	649	1,646		
1950	674	1,843	3.9	11.8
1950	741	1,776		
1960	845	2,160	14.0	21.6
1960	965	2,017		
1970	1,082	2,550	12.1	26.4
1970	1,117	2,515		
1975	1,167	2,800	9.2	23.9

Source: For each period, the countries in each category are the same, but between one period and the next certain countries are switched from "less developed" to "developed" as their progress justifies. Percent increase is per decade. Data chiefly from Durand, *op. cit.,* p. 137; United Nations, *Demographic Yearbook* (1970 and 1973); and United Nations, *World Population Prospects, 1970–2000, as Assessed in 1973.*

The shift did not occur because of a population slowdown in the industrial countries, for these continued to experience a substantial population increase, particularly between 1950 and 1970. Instead, there was a spectacular increase in population growth in the less developed regions. Since the less developed regions make up some two-thirds of the entire world, it is their spectacular increase that explains the acceleration of the world's population growth during the present century.

This "demographic success" of the poorer countries is one of the most tragic circumstances of the modern demographic situation, because these nations are precisely the ones that have least need for, and that can least afford, inflated numbers of human beings. Many of them are already extremely overcrowded. On the average, they are more densely settled than the industrial nations, and the discrepancy is widening:

Status of countries in 1950	Population per square mile	
	1950	1975
More developed	34.2	45.5
Less developed	57.9	100.0
Ratio	1.7	2.2

WHY THE POPULATION EXPLOSION?

In explaining modern population growth we are faced with two questions: Why did the world's population as a whole increase at an accelerating pace? Why has the fastest growth shifted from the more advanced to the less advanced nations?

In strictly demographic terms, the explanation of the great wave of population growth in the last two centuries is the decline in the death rate, not a rise in the birth rate. The long-run trend of the birth rate, taking the world as a whole, has been generally downward, but it has not fallen as fast, or as consistently and widely, as the death rate.

The Theory of the Death-Rate Decline

The standard explanation of why the death rate declined has been economic. At first the decline was limited to those countries experiencing real economic progress. It began gradually but gained momentum as the Industrial Revolution proceeded. The Western gains in agriculture, transportation, and commerce during the eighteenth and nineteenth centuries made better diets possible; the gains in industrial manufacturing made clothing, housing, and other amenities more widely available; the rise in real income facilitated the growth of public sanitation, medical science, and popular education. "It is no disparagement of medical science and practice," said Warren Thompson in 1953, "to recognize that the great decline in the death rate that has taken place during the last two centuries in the West is due, basically, to improvement in production and economic conditions."[2]

This view fails to explain why, in the industrial nations, the fastest drop in

[2] Warren S. Thompson, *Population Problems,* 4th ed. (New York: McGraw-Hill, 1953), p. 77.

mortality occurred not during the great burst of industrialization in the nineteenth century but rather in the twentieth century.[3] It also fails to explain why in less developed countries death rates have recently fallen three to five times as fast as they did earlier in the industrial nations and have reached an "industrial" level prematurely—that is, at an earlier stage of development.

To account for these facts one must recognize that modern technology has two parts that reduce mortality by different means and with different timing. The first part, the one that traditional theory has in mind, is *productive* technology. In some ways, by enlarging cities and intensifying travel and contact, early industrialism tended to increase mortality, but on the whole it decreased it by improving diets, clothing, and shelter and thus giving people greater resistance to disease. Economic development, however, did not attack the specific agents of disease, such as bacteria, viruses, parasites, vectors, and organ failure. To deal with these directly, a special technology, medicine, arose. At first, despite thousands of years of effort, this technology was ineffective; the ill effects of medical effort just about canceled the good effects. In the latter half of the nineteenth century, however, a rising tide of medical inventions greatly helped to lower death rates. Their influence was *added to* productive technology, which explains why mortality lessened more in the late than in the early stages of industrialization.

The Linkage of Poverty with Rapid Mortality Decline

What about the underdeveloped countries? Dominated politically and economically by Europe and exposed to new diseases, their populations generally showed only slow declines in mortality until around 1920. After that, however, an amazing decline in death rates began, because the medical discoveries that had been made slowly and painfully in the industrial nations could be transferred far more easily than productive technology to backward nations. The transfer began after World War I but speeded up after World War II as new inventions came to be diffused overnight. As a consequence, the underdeveloped areas, regardless of whether they were prospering or not, experienced a faster drop in death rates than the northwest European peoples had ever known.

The main triumph of medical technology was the conquest of infectious diseases, and it was the extension of this conquest to less developed areas that brought down their death rates. Under the auspices of philanthropic foundations and international agencies, widespread diseases such as malaria, yellow fever, yaws, trachoma, cholera, plague, typhoid, diphtheria, smallpox, tuberculosis, and dysentery were controlled on a mass basis at low cost. Most of the

---

[3] In Sweden life expectancy at birth *declined* between 1843 and 1858. The period of rapid improvement was from 1860 to 1950, with the years from 1918 to 1928 showing the greatest gain. Suitable life tables for the United States go back only to 1900, but after that the greatest gain in life expectancy was around 1910 to 1928 and 1940 to 1950. Derived from Statistiska Centralbyrån, *Historisk Statistik för Sverige*, Part 1 (Stockholm: 1969), p. 118, and U.S. National Center for Health Statistics, *Vital Statistics of the United States*, *1973*, Vol. 2, Section 5, p. 5–14.

discoveries making this possible, including DDT, sulfa drugs, penicillin, and BCG, were made during World War I or later. Armed with these weapons, preventive public health programs employing only a handful of specialists could save millions of lives at costs ranging from a few cents to a few dollars per person per year.

An example is Sri Lanka (Ceylon). Afflicted with chronic malaria, its crude death rate (deaths per thousand people) averaged 26.9 during 1920–1929. In 1945 the rate was still 21.5, but in 1948 it was 12.9, a 40-percent decline in three years. By 1954 it was down to 10.4, and in 1972 it was 7.7. The main factor in the decline was the use of DDT as a residual spray, which controlled malaria and also lowered mortality from other causes. The costs were negligible (less than $2 annually per head for all medical services), but even these were partly met from World Health Organization funds. The DDT, first invented in Switzerland, was imported; the experts involved either originated or were trained outside the country. Nothing was required of the Ceylonese themselves. Their houses were sprayed for them. They were not required to change their habits or institutions, to acquire a knowledge of malaria, or to take any initiative. The spectacular decline in the death rate came about through no basic economic development or change in the institutional structure.

Similar attacks on malaria occurred wherever the disease was endemic. In 1970 the world's population living in malarial areas (excluding China, North Vietnam, and North Korea) was approximately 1.8 billion. For some 1.34 billion of these, malaria was either under control or currently being controlled.[4] Numerous other causes of death were also eliminated or greatly reduced. Worldwide programs to eradicate smallpox were started in 1967. In Cuba, where a campaign was launched in 1963 to reduce diarrheal diseases (which mainly kill children), the mortality rate from these diseases fell 63 percent in four years. Miraculous declines in death rates occurred in nearly all less developed regions. From 1940 to 1965 the drop was 59 percent in Mexico, 63 percent in Puerto Rico, 72 percent in Taiwan, 65 percent in Mauritius, 44 percent in Egypt. In the same number of years from a similar starting level in 1856, Sweden's rate fell only 22 percent.

Poverty, Fertility, and Population Growth

Since disease control in less developed countries has come mainly from outside aid rather than internal change, birth rates have remained high. They were higher to begin with in most of these regions than they ever were in northwestern Europe, and they have remained much higher relative to the death rate. Whereas the presently industrial countries began lowering their birth rates *before* their sharpest decline in mortality, the backward areas of today are doing so, if at all, long *after* their mortality has reached a low level. It is this dual fact—the unprecedented conquest of mortality and the postponement

[4] R. G. Sholtens, R. L. Kaiser, and A. D. Langmuir, "An Epidemiologic Examination of the Strategy of Malaria Eradication," *International Journal of Epidemiology* (Spring 1972).

of the birth-rate decline—that explains the extraordinarily fast population growth in the two-thirds of the world that still remains underdeveloped.

CONSEQUENCES OF POPULATION GROWTH: UNDERDEVELOPED COUNTRIES

With this explanation of how the modern upsurge in population has come about, we can more clearly understand the consequences. If, for example, the most rapid multiplication is occurring in the underdeveloped countries, and if this is attributable to causes other than economic development, we can see at once that human increase may be retarding the rise in level of living or thwarting it altogether. For this to happen, the country does not have to be densely settled already. An area such as Brazil may be sparsely settled and still have too fast a population growth from an economic point of view. Furthermore, a country may be prosperous, even heavily industrialized, and still have too fast an increase. Let us consider the agrarian nations.

Rising Numbers, Poverty, and "Development"

Strictly speaking, economic development does not mean a gain in total national income, but a gain in *per capita* income. This requires that capital be added to production faster than labor. With a constant population, a rate of investment of 3 to 5 percent of national income is required to produce a 1-percent increase in per capita income; with a population growing at 3 percent per year, investment of between 12 and 20 percent of national income is required. A poor country finds it difficult to invest even 10 percent of its national income in economic development. Since most underdeveloped countries now have a rate of population growth of 2 to 3.5 percent, they have come dangerously close to making genuine economic development impossible for themselves. Even if they achieve such development, it will be at a slower rate than would be the case with a less climactic population growth. For instance, in 1960–1973 Africa's gross investment was 16.5 percent of its total product. Had there been no population growth, this high investment coefficient would have increased per capita income by 4 to 5 percent per year, but since the population grew at an annual rate of 2.6 percent, the yearly rise in per capita income was only 2.2 percent. In short, more than half of Africa's economic expansion was used simply to accommodate more people.[5]

An idea of the effect of surplus population can be obtained by looking at particular countries. Let us take Egypt.

[5] Computed from United Nations, *World Economic Survey, 1974*, pp. 45, 77, and *Demographic Yearbooks*. The literature on population and economic development is large. Useful books are J. D. Pitchford, *The Economics of Population: An Introduction* (Canberra: Australian National University Press, 1974); Alfred Sauvy, *General Theory of Population* (New York: Basic Books, 1969); and United Nations, *The Determinants and Consequences of Population Trends*, Vol. 1 (New York: United Nations, 1973). A journal that has many articles on the subject is *Economic Development and Cultural Change*.

Since Egypt is mostly desert, its population is squeezed into a zone along the Nile comprising only 3.6 percent of the national territory—a strip legendary for its density and poverty. In 1949, shortly before King Farouk left and social reforms began, there were 2,114 Egyptians per square mile of arable land, 404 of them males trying to make a living by farming. To alleviate the extreme poverty, a high dam at Aswan was proposed. It would create a lake 300 miles long, furnish needed electrical power, and irrigate over a million acres of desert. The dam was built; combined with lesser projects, it had by 1971 expanded Egypt's arable land by 12.2 percent. However, the nation's population had also expanded by more than 14 million, or 71.3 percent. The death rate, about 26.8 per 1,000 population in 1940–1944, dropped to 13.1 in 1971, while the birth rate (admittedly underregistered) did not budge until after 1965. In 1960–1964, the natural increase was the highest in Egypt's history (26.1 per 1,000 population), and in 1973 it was still 22.5. Thus, while the Aswan dam and the new canals were under construction, population growth outstripped the gain. By 1971 there were 3,226 people, including 442 male farmers, per square mile of arable land. To satisfy the rising need for food, the government curtailed the acreage of the most profitable crop, cotton. Although reforms had long since banished the absentee landlords by limiting holdings to 50 acres, land scarcity continued. Productivity per worker in agriculture diminished. Massive migration of destitute rural people to the cities created huge squatter areas. The annual addition to the manpower pool was said to be 27 times the number of industrial jobs available. To provide employment, the government instituted elaborate make-work schemes, and to keep everyone alive, it expropriated all income above a modest level. Make-work and equality do not, however, guarantee production. Per capita income in 1970 was only $202. The nation's economic expansion during the 1950s and 1960s had been used to support more people poorly rather than fewer people better. Small wonder that Egypt lost three wars to Israel, although it had eleven times Israel's population. Small wonder that the Egyptian authorities in the 1960s began a national antinatalist policy.[6]

In many other agrarian countries—India, Indonesia, Haiti, Mauritius, Ghana, Pakistan, and Sri Lanka, to mention only a few—per capita income has risen little if at all, despite a rise in national income. Even an apparent rise in income is often deceptive, because some of it is due simply to greater monetization of the economy.

Youthful Populations and Political Instability

Further problems in these countries arise from their young age structure. When mortality is reduced rapidly with little or no change in fertility, the result is an extremely youthful population, because the greatest saving of lives

[6] See H. T. Croley, "United Arab Republic," in Population Council, *Country Profiles* (August 1969); Abdel R. Omran (ed.), *Egypt: Population Problems and Prospects* (Chapel Hill: Carolina Population Center, 1973); The Economist Intelligence Unit, *Quarterly Economic Review,* annual issues on Egypt and Sudan.

is made in infancy and early childhood and the mortality decline thus acts like a rise in the birth rate. Accordingly, when fertility begins to fall, many of these countries have the youngest populations ever known. The contrast with industrial countries is shown in Figure 6-1 and Table 6-3. El Salvador, whose death rate dropped 60 percent in 30 years but whose birth rate remained high (4.7 times the death rate in 1970–1972), has 120 children under age 15 for each 100 adults aged 20 to 59. Denmark, on the other hand, has only 39 children per 100 adults in their prime. With such a burdensome child-dependency

Table 6-3 Persons in Selected Age Groups per 100 Adults Aged 20 to 59

	Children under 15	Youths 15–19	Elderly 60+
Less developed countries			
Nicaragua, 1971	133	30	13
Iran, 1971	124	26	13
Mexico, 1970	123	28	15
Ghana, 1970	121	24	14
El Salvador, 1971	120	26	14
More developed countries			
Taiwan, 1971	89	27	12
Canada, 1971	60	20	24
United States, 1974	52	20	29
France, 1971	48	16	38
Japan, 1970	42	15	19
Denmark, 1970	39	13	30
Stationary ZPG			
Life expectancy 75 years	39	13	47
Life expectancy 83 years	38	13	60
Life expectancy 100 years	38	13	98

Sources: For first two panels, United Nations, *Demographic Yearbook, 1973* or *America en Cifras, 1974, Situacion Demografica*. ZPG with life expectancy of 75 years is female life-table population of the United States for 1967; the one with an 83-year expectancy is made by the author, and the one with 100-year expectancy is made by Judith Kunofsky (unpublished, International Population and Urban Research, University of California, Berkeley, 1975).

ratio, women in underdeveloped countries are too occupied with pregnancy and child care to participate in production beyond the traditional tasks of home and garden. Their children are put to work at an early age, but child labor, by depriving children of schooling, limits the acquisition of ideas and skills suited to a modern technology. Any effort to provide adequate schooling uses a huge portion of the national budget and yet is defeated by the ever-larger waves of new pupils each year.

Educated or not, the expanding contingents of youth entering the labor market each year create an employment problem. Table 6-3 shows that Mexico,

Figure 6-1 Age Pyramids for El Salvador and Denmark

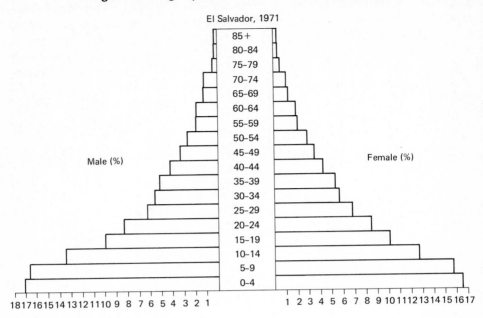

El Salvador, 1971

Male (%)　　　　　　　　　　　　Female (%)

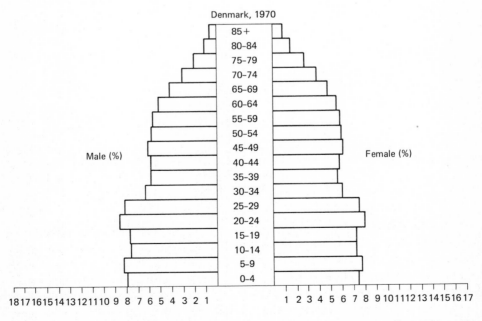

Denmark, 1970

Male (%)　　　　　　　　　　　　Female (%)

Source: Organization of American States, *America en Cifras, Situacion Demografica, 1974*, p. **29**; United Nations, *Demographic Yearbook, 1973*, pp. 168–169.

for example, has 28 young people aged 15 to 19 for each 100 adults aged 20 to 59, whereas Denmark has only 13 and Japan 15. To absorb so many youths, an economy must expand rapidly. If it falters, large numbers become unemployed. If they attend school, they become a class of "educated unemployed." With youthful energy and idealism but no stake in the existing society, they are politically explosive, ready to follow any leader who promises a quick and violent solution. Their impatience threatens a ruler who pursues a policy of basic economic development, for that is too slow. They are more impressed by threats of war, confiscation of foreign assets, liquidation of the wealthy, and nationalistic zeal.

Functionless Fertility and the Family

The dilemmas of rapid population growth can also be seen in families. The head of the household in an agrarian country often sees the problem as how to get enough land. Hence, a scheme of land distribution generally receives popular support regardless of how uneconomic it may be. But, as the case of Egypt shows, distributed land quickly becomes overcrowded. Short of land, the peasant finds it hard to maintain his children, much less educate them. His aspirations for them may be high, because he sees the futility of the village compared to urban employment and schools, but he cannot meet these aspirations. His wife is burdened with the same round of childbearing that her ancestors experienced, but with one difference—a far greater proportion of the offspring remain alive. It is this larger living family that makes child care more burdensome, land more scarce, and security more remote.

Environmental Degradation

At the United Nations Conference on the Human Environment in Stockholm in 1972, to the surprise of many idealists, the less developed nations showed more interest in "economic development" than in environmental protection. One reason for their attitude was population pressure. To officials of countries faced every year by millions of new mouths to feed, environmental degradation is of no concern unless it curtails production. Changes that are merely irritating, inconvenient, unhealthful, unaesthetic, or potentially dangerous must be ignored. If wild animal species become extinct, so be it; the important animals are those people use and eat. If smoke stains the atmosphere, if slag heaps ruin the landscape and lumbering denudes the mountains, it is regrettable, to be sure; but it does not immediately impede economic growth.

In longer perspective, of course, this concentration on immediate growth at any cost eventually does endanger development. It thus repeats the earlier mistakes of the industrial countries, but it does so in lands that are more crowded and hence more damaged already. In Pakistan, Afghanistan, and the Near East, for example, dams have been built and irrigation schemes developed that greatly increased agricultural production for awhile but eventually, due to waterlogging and salination of the irrigated lands and deforestation of the hills, created wastelands. Rectifying these conditions calls for huge investments in energy and machinery, which have their own environmental effects.[7] In Africa, where disease control and increased watering places keep more animals alive, millions of acres of grassland have been overgrazed, "leaving large areas of bare soil having a compacted surface" that will absorb little rainfall.[8] In Nepal and mountainous parts of Northern India, deforestation to obtain fuel and timber, and terracing to create rice paddies, have caused frightful erosion. Contamination by modern commercial fertilizers and pesticides is being added. Such destruction of the environment is difficult to stop when the population is desperate for sustenance and land is extremely scarce. Now this agrarian destruction is to be joined by unimpeded industrialization, whose environmental effects are notorious.

The Geographical Shift of People

In the process of development, agrarian countries face a movement of something like 60 percent of their people from the country to the cities. This movement is so greatly complicated by rapid population growth that few governments seem ready to face it realistically. Yet it is inevitable because, for industrial purposes, the present population is located in the wrong places. Since in agriculture the chief instrument of production is land, farmers are always dispersed in small villages or isolated farmsteads. In most other industries, however, land is used as a site, which means that enterprises are concentrated together in cities to minimize the "friction of space." Accordingly, whereas agrarian countries are predominantly rural, industrial countries are predominantly urban. As new industries arise in urban centers, the old industry, agriculture, is transformed by the substitution of energy for labor. Surplus farm workers go to the cities, where new occupations can pay higher wages; urban growth in turn stimulates further technological improvement on farms by increasing the demand for agricultural products. As a consequence, the loss of labor to the cities does not lower farm production but raises it; the few farmers who remain make a better living.

The magnitude of the transformation can be seen from the history of the United States:

---

[7] See Aloys A. Michel, "The Impact of Modern Irrigation Technology in the Indus and Helmand Basins of Southwest Asia," in M. Taghi Farvar and John P. Milton (eds.), *The Careless Technology* (Garden City, N.Y.: Natural History Press, 1972), pp. 257–275.

[8] E. W. Russell, "The Impact of Technological Developments on Soils in East Africa," in Farvar and Milton, *op. cit.*, p. 574.

| | Percentage of population | |
	On farms	Not on farms
1820	72*	28
1972	4.6†	95.4

* U.S. Bureau of the Census, *Historical Statistics of the United States* (Washington, D.C.: Government Printing Office, 1960), p. 74. Refers to *gainful workers* in agriculture. No data exist on the *farm population* in 1820, but its proportion of the total population should differ little from the proportion of farmers among gainful workers.

† U.S. Departments of Commerce and Agriculture, "Farm Population of the United States: 1972," *Current Population Reports*, Series Census-ERS P-27, No. 44, June 1973.

During the half-century from 1920 to 1973, the average net migration from American farms was 3.36 percent of the farm population each year. Since the average natural increase on farms was 1.23 percent, the net migration was large enough not only to cancel that natural increase but also to reduce the farm population by 2.13 percent per year. After its peak in 1917, the farm population declined as follows:

	Farm population	Percent of total population
1917	32,236,000	31.2
1940	30,545,000	23.1
1960	15,635,000	8.7
1973	9,472,000	4.5

On the average, present-day underdeveloped countries are about 25 percent urban, a level reached by the United States in 1868. They are thus more than a century behind, but because their demographic conditions are fundamentally different, they should not be thought of as repeating the history of the industrial nations. Their populations are more crowded and growing faster, the contrast in rate of growth being greater for rural than for urban areas. Their cities are growing just as fast (4.6 percent per year between 1950 and 1970) as those of the past, but their rural populations are growing three or four times as fast as the rural populations did. Why? Urban populations of the past usually failed to replace themselves because, cities being deadly places, their deaths far exceeded their births. Their growth depended entirely on migration from the countryside. Today, however, the cities of the Third World—thanks to modern public health—are growing rapidly by their own excess of births over deaths. This means that they cannot absorb migrants as fast as the industrializing cities of the past could. As a consequence, the rural population, which also has a higher natural increase than in the past due to decreased mortality, cannot get rid of as large a portion of its natural increase. Although millions of destitute migrants do go to the cities, rural inhabitants accumulate on the land. They squat on marginal lands, subdivide holdings, and impede agricultural modernization.

Simultaneously in the cities, rapid growth and poverty are creating the greatest housing shortage in human history. There are millions of urban squatters living at high density on land that does not belong to them in shacks they built themselves with waste materials. Called *paracaidistas* (parachutists) in some Latin American countries, they settle overnight in parks, school grounds, and vacant lots, or on steep hillsides or sidewalks. In some cases they compose a third to a half of the total city population. Even outside the squatter areas, housing is crowded. In Hong Kong, where "bed space" is a distinct housing category, the average per capita house size (assuming a square shape) is less than six feet per side.[9] In Delhi, India,

> a lower middle class person has to pay around 70 percent of his monthly income as house rent for his minimum housing needs and if we add another 70 percent (for the food bill) one arrives at a figure of 140 percent necessary for food and housing alone! So the choice is often between food and shelter and obviously the former gets preference. This explains to a substantial extent the [squatter] colonies in urban Delhi . . . which house over 500,000 people.[10]

In Bangkok, to meet only the low-income housing needs during the next 10 years, construction costs "would amount to 35 times the present yearly government expenditure."[11]

Governments in underdeveloped countries are justly suspicious of growing urban masses, because these bring insuperable problems of housing, sanitation, education, and public order. Violent agitation is a constant danger, heightened by the predominance of youths in the population. The officials, however, generally misconceive the cause of city growth. They think of rural–urban migration as the chief culprit and sometimes try to forbid such movement. But since the cities are growing rapidly from their own natural increase, to stop migration would both fail to prevent their expansion and enormously worsen the plight of the rural masses.

CONSEQUENCES OF POPULATION GROWTH: INDUSTRIAL COUNTRIES

With less than half the rate of population increase of poorer countries, the advanced nations nevertheless expanded their population 17 percent between 1960 and 1970. This growth came not only from the postwar baby boom that lasted into the sixties but also from massive immigration from less developed areas. The United States, during 1960–1975, for example, added 32.8 million people—27.6 million from excess births over deaths, 5.2 million from net immi-

[9] D. J. Dwyer (ed.), *Asian Urbanization: A Hong Kong Casebook* (Hong Kong: Hong Kong University Press, 1971), p. 35.

[10] Ashish Bose, *Studies in India's Urbanization, 1901–1971* (Bombay-New Delhi: Tata McGraw-Hill, 1973), p. 13.

[11] Sidney Goldstein, *The Demography of Bangkok* (Bangkok: Institute of Population Studies, Chulalongkorn University, 1972), p. 37.

gration.[12] The reduced birth rate in industrial countries in the late 1960s and early 1970s has been widely interpreted as implying permanent low fertility, but it is more probably merely a cyclical lull. The 1930s, a period of low fertility, were followed by a peak in 1947, then a lull, then a second peak in 1957, and finally a lull again. A low birth rate is itself evidence that a reversal will come, and the waves of migrants entering industrial countries bring with them the high fertility of their home countries.

The Strain on Resources

While for poorer countries population growth brings problems because of poverty, for richer ones it brings troubles because of affluence. As individual consumption mounts and population multiplies, two exponentials are added to produce an extremely high rate of total consumption. Between 1960 and 1975 in the United States, for example, the population increased 1.1 percent per year, and per capita consumption of energy increased 2.8 percent per year. Accordingly, total consumption of energy increased as the sum (3.9 percent) of these two rates, doubling in 15 years and adding the equivalent of 1.2 billion tons of coal to the nation's annual energy consumption.

The congestion of people and possessions tends to be self-defeating. An ever-higher proportion of effort and energy is expended simply to mitigate the effects of a high level of effort and energy. As the giant urban aggregates grow larger, for example, the congestion becomes more costly and frustrating. Automobiles, radios, television antennae, boats, houses, freezers, and myriad other possessions multiply relentlessly. To enjoy and store their goods and to escape the noise and pollution of the central city, families move to the suburbs, but the costs are enormous. Freeways and mass transit systems, shopping centers, schools, water systems, and sewage plants must be built, and land is removed from agriculture. Yet the problem of urban crowding is not solved. The escape from congestion simply creates more congestion. As the urban population grows, the quest for space moves the suburbs farther out and multiplies the connecting links. The home that was once "in the country" or "in a pleasant little suburb" becomes a dot in a continuous sea of housing developments and shopping centers. The freeway that was so spacious and convenient when finished soon becomes an exasperating trap at rush hours. The industries that supply the material wealth, the automobiles and buses that travel greater distances between home and work, the dumps where growing mountains of refuse are burned—all combine to create an environmental blight, smog. The air pollution extends far beyond the cities themselves, injuring crops and forests. In their unquenchable thirst for water, the cities go hundreds of miles, altering the topography and damaging the economy of rural areas. Many

---

[12] U.S. Bureau of the Census, *Current Population Reports*, Series P-25, No. 545 (April 1975). Births to immigrants are not counted as immigration. For an account of migration into the industrial countries, see K. Davis, "The Migrations of Human Populations," *Scientific American*, Vol. 231 (September 1974), pp. 92–107.

metropolitan areas expand spatially until they collide, thus creating what have been called megalopolises and making escape all the more difficult.

As is well known, cities generate heat. When summer comes, millions of air conditioners are switched on, not simply to modify natural heat but also to cancel the extra heat of the city. Air conditioners, however, use energy at a prodigious rate. The power plants required to run them pollute the air further and generate still more heat, in turn requiring the air conditioners to work harder.

An example of a natural paradise despoiled by population growth and a high level of living is California. It added 5 million people to its population between 1960 and 1975, making it the twelfth most densely settled state in the union. Most of its population is concentrated in a semi-desert running from Santa Barbara to San Diego, which contained more than 12 million people in 1975. Air pollution from this urban belt is damaging forests in the coastal range and the Sierra and injuring crops in the Central Valley, the world's richest agricultural region. The largest city, Los Angeles, has more than 30 times the population that could be supplied with the scant local rainfall. Long ago (in 1913) Los Angeles took all the water from the Owens Valley, 250 miles away, making a wasteland of the valley. Later it took water from the Mono Basin and next from the Colorado River, depriving Nevada, Arizona, and Mexico of their rightful supply. Finally it used its overwhelming concentration of votes to pass in the state legislature the "California Water Plan," a scheme to dam the rivers of the northern part of the state and transport their water several hundred miles to Los Angeles. The canals, pipes, and tunnels required are 6,265 miles long; when the system is fully operative, the total energy required to pump the water, which must go over high mountains, is scheduled to use 10.6 percent of the state's production of electricity. The northern part of the state considers the damage to its agriculture and environment incalculable. Nevertheless, in the Los Angeles area the herculean effort is justified in the name of growth. As one progress report said, it "will stimulate the development of industry, population growth, and in-migration."

The Lowered Quality of Life

As an index of the level of living, per capita income is simply a summation of all economic transactions divided by the population. It is not an index of human welfare. Many transactions injure the community at large or even persons directly involved, and many merely remedy the ill effects of other transactions. For example, when billions are spent to reduce the noxious emissions of automobiles, this "investment" is included in the national income, yet its sole purpose is to mitigate an evil that affluence and population growth have created. If a high level of consumption is the ideal, then to minimize congestion and resource depletion the demographic goal should be a reduction, not an increase, in human numbers. If Japan's per capita income is barely more than half of Sweden's while its environmental problems are worse, this is because its population density is more than 16 times that of Sweden.

Thus the advanced countries demonstrate that the dream of the less developed countries, industrialization, is likely to turn into a nightmare caused by rapid population growth. What are the future prospects?

POPULATION, RESOURCES, AND THE FUTURE

Unfortunately, nobody can predict the future for certain. All that we can do is use our knowledge of the past to say what will happen if certain assumptions hold true. Whether or not they will actually hold true cannot be predicted. For instance, it can be calculated that *if* world mortality drops to the lowest levels now found in advanced countries, and *if* world fertility (rate of births) falls by 44 percent, the human population in the year 2000 will be 5.1 billion.[13] These are big "ifs." Any prediction that they will come true must rest on other assumptions, and these in turn, if predicted, must rest on still others, and so on.

Given the uncertainty, we can understand why the main controversies over population turn on differing views of the future. Almost nobody maintains that population can continue growing forever, but there are contrasting schools of thought concerning the rate in the next decades, its consequences, the factors affecting it, and the policies (if any) that should be adopted to deal with it.

Fundamentally, there are two questions at issue: First, will population growth have consequences that will automatically cause the growth to cease? If so, what kind of consequences and when? Second, will the growth be stopped deliberately before it reaches the point of automatic shut-off? If so, when and how? The first question is usually discussed in terms of the capacity of the earth's resources to support people, and we shall now turn to that subject. The second question refers to policy, and we shall consider that later.

The Limits to Growth

Although the notion of an automatic limit to human increase is old, attempts to be specific about time and circumstances are relatively new. The most recent and most ambitious is that of a group at the Massachusetts Institute of Technology under the sponsorship of an association called the Club of Rome.

Inspired by the concepts and preliminary work of an industrial engineer, Jay W. Forrester, the MIT group produced models of possible world developments during the next 130 years. The results were described in a book called

---

[13] Tomas Frejka, "The Prospects for a Stationary World Population," *Scientific American*, Vol. 228 (March 1973), p. 21. See also Thomas Frejka, *The Future of Population Growth* (New York: Wiley, 1973).

The Limits to Growth.[14] The researchers recognized that there is not simply one restraint on population growth but several, and that the task of assessing future possibilities requires not only an assessment of the earth's potential but also a knowledge of how processes of change affect one another. To determine the limits, the group studied land and natural resources. To establish causal relationships, they studied trends from 1900 to 1970. The researchers then used a computer to trace out the complex consequences of hypothetical trends in one or more of five variables: population growth, industrialization, food production, nonrenewable resources, and pollution. Other variables were added as parts of feedback loops or linkages between the five main variables.

In the "standard run" the authors assumed that the 1900 to 1970 trends would continue as long as possible. The result, shown in Figure 6-2, is "overshoot and collapse," triggered by the depletion of nonrenewable resources. With population and industrialization both growing, the drain on resources quickly (within a century) becomes so large that reserves are exhausted.

> As resource prices rise and mines are depleted, more and more capital must be used for obtaining resources, leaving less to be invested for future growth. Finally investment cannot keep up with depreciation, and the industrial base collapses, taking with it the service and agricultural systems, which have become dependent on industrial inputs. . . . Population finally decreases when the death rate is driven upward by lack of food and health services.[15]

The standard run assumes that the supply of nonrenewable resources is equal to 250 years at 1970 rates of usage. In another run the researchers asked what would happen if, through technological advance, the recoverable resources were doubled and energy became limitless. The result, as far as population is concerned, is largely the same as in Figure 6-2. In fact, population decline sets in about 10 years earlier.[16] The collapse in this case, however, is due not to depletion of resources but to pollution. Temporarily released from the resource restraint, the growth of population and industrialization poisons the environment and drives up the death rate precipitously.

But suppose that technological advances reduce the pollution per unit of industrial expansion by a factor of four. What then? There is no pollution crisis

---

[14] Donella H. Meadows et al., *The Limits to Growth* (New York: Universe Books, 1972). A preliminary work was Forrester's *World Dynamics* (Cambridge, Mass.: Wright-Allen Press, 1971). See also his article, "Counter-intuitive Nature of Social Systems," *Technology Review*, Vol. 73 (1971). Subsequently, the models were made more complex and based on more historical data under the direction of Dennis L. Meadows, then an economist at MIT, and published in *The Limits to Growth*. Still another study under Club of Rome auspices was Mihajlo Mesarovic and Eduard Pestel, *Mankind at the Turning Point* (New York: Dutton and Reader's Digest, 1974), which attempted to deal with regions, whereas the Meadows report considered only the world as a whole. A thorough critique of the Meadows study is by a group at the University of Sussex in England—S. D. Cole, Christopher Freeman, Marie Jahoda, and K. L. R. Pavitt (eds.), *Models of Doom* (New York: Universe Books, 1973). The present exposition draws on this critique and *The Limits to Growth*.

[15] Meadows et al., *op. cit.*, p. 125.

[16] Compare the charts in Meadows et al., *op. cit.*, pp. 124, 127, and 132.

Figure 6-2 The Future World Model Produced by the "Standard Run" (extrapolation of 1900–1970 trends except as they interfere with one another)

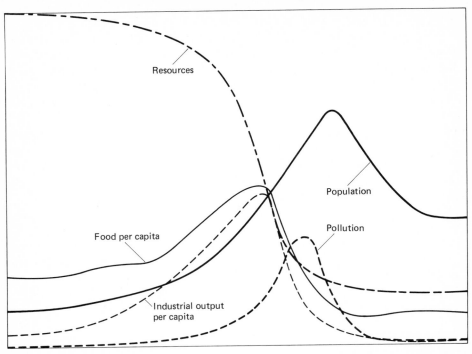

Source: The Limits of Growth: A Report for the Club of Rome's Project on the Predicament of Mankind, by Donnella H. Meadows, Dennis L. Meadows, Jorgen Randers, William W. Behrens III. A Potomac Associates book published by Universe Books, New York, 1972.

before 2100, but there is still a reduction in population, this time because of a shortage of food. Loss of arable land through erosion and conversion to industrial use eventually overcomes the gains in yields. As per capita food consumption drops, the death rate rises.

Now suppose both that agricultural yields for the entire world are doubled and that pollution per unit of industrialization is reduced by a factor of four. The population still reaches a limit and declines, paradoxically because of pollution. Even though the pollution ratio is reduced by a factor of four, industrialization is so enormous that it overcomes this reduction and overloads the environment, raising the death rate.

In sum, all the MIT models show that if population and industrialization continue to expand, population will rise temporarily above some limit and then collapse, probably in less than 130 years. The only way to avoid such a catastrophe is to limit growth by deliberate policy *before* it reaches a natural limit. If, for instance, population were stabilized by 1975 and industrialization by 1985, resource depletion and pollution would be sufficiently reduced to avoid collapse before 2100.

The Limits to Growth caught the world's imagination overnight. It confirmed scientifically a long-held fear, that mindless population increase and "development" are leading to world calamity. Yet it also showed how this calamity could be avoided by deliberate intervention to stop growth.

Despite its new computerized trappings, however, the basic message was not new nor the uncertainty overcome. By definition, in any closed system of mutually dependent variables, exponential increase must lead to feedback effects that will stop the increase. The MIT group made assumptions concerning the fixed character of the earth and then selected five variables. Investigating the behavior of these variables historically, they developed equations embodying their mutual effects. Feeding these to the computer, they obtained the results of different assumed changes in the variables. Through time lags in feedback, they added the refinements of "overshoot" and "collapse." The key question is not whether their basic logic is correct but whether the assumed limits and the assumed causal relationships are true. One of their most startling conclusions is the speed with which collapse arrives. This would not happen, however, if their assumptions about the earth's resources were drastically altered. The authors mention three limits—fresh water, land, and nonrenewable materials. Fresh water is not discussed, except to admit that desalination would expand it. As for land, 7.86 billion acres is taken as the potentially arable limit. Even if this is all utilized, the authors say, there will be "a desperate land shortage before the year 2000 if per capita land requirements and population growth rates remain as they are today."[17] Quadrupling soil productivity would merely postpone the shortage about 50 years. Notice, however, that an admission of possible soil improvement removes the fixed limit (land) as a determinant of the food supply. There is no way of proving that soil productivity could not be raised 20 times, or for that matter that food could not be manufactured rather than grown. Such possibilities do not prove that exponential population growth can go on forever, but simply that any time scale for its stoppage is dubious.

As for the other fixed limit, nonrenewable resources, the assumption that the total amount available is either a 250-year supply at 1970 consumption rates or twice that amount, is questionable. No one can predict for sure which materials in the earth will prove useful under future technology.

Apart from assumptions concerning limits, those concerning relationships among the variables are also debatable. Although some are guesses, most are supported by data for the period 1900 to 1970. This period, however, represents a particular moment in history. Relationships prevailing then will not necessarily prevail in the future. For example, in several of the models pollution turns out to be the triggering limit. As evidence that pollution follows industrialization, the MIT authors cite the historical fact that various pollutants increased in industrializing countries. They do admit, however, that "man's

[17] Meadows et al., *op. cit.*, p. 51.

concern for the effect of his activities on the natural environment is only very recent."[18] Who can say, then, what future pollution controls will do? As for the effect of pollution on the death rate, the authors have no evidence at all. They imply that it is the total quantity of pollution that affects mortality, but this need not be true. A small amount of plutonium, or use of nuclear weapons, could wipe out the human race.

In the real world, human increase is partly a function of technology, but in the MIT study technology is not one of the variables. Presumably it figures indirectly when resources are assumed to double or when agricultural productivity is assumed to quadruple, but it does not figure as a continuous force in its own right. Perhaps the reason for this omission is that the effects of technology are contradictory. Nuclear technology represents a new source of energy, but it can destroy the world. Bacteriology can save lives, but can also facilitate germ warfare. By definition, technology is purely instrumental. Its use, and hence its effects, are determined by human motives and relationships. The task of building realistic models of what might happen thus requires more social information than the MIT group has used.

If social and political possibilities are taken into account, the assumption that processes of change will move in an orderly fashion until physical limitations overcome them is unconvincing. The world's population growth could stop in a few months as a consequence of World War III or as a result of a decree by a world dictator. At each step in the process of change, people assess the change and try to influence its direction. With modern technology it is usually their own conflicts rather than physical scarcity or environmental pollution that causes disaster. This view is confirmed by a historical review of population and resources.

The Waning Age of the Fossil Fuels

During the last two centuries the use of fossil energy stored in the earth's crust had two effects of world-shaking importance. First, it made possible the population explosion. Second, despite this population explosion, it enabled consumption for the majority to rise far above the subsistence level. As long as production and transport depended on human muscle supplemented only by animals, wind, and sail, neither of these things could happen; the sudden release of energy accumulated during billions of years not only made the two developments possible but led to such close association between them that they both came to be regarded as "normal" and mutually dependent. As new uses of energy were elaborated, as petroleum and gas were added to coal, the idea of an ever-expanding economy, of perpetual conomic growth, gained sway. Any worry about population growth was dismissed as "pessimism."

Although an occasional voice earlier in the century disputed the idea of

---

[18] *Ibid.,* p. 69.

constant growth,[19] it was not until after World War II that worries about either world population growth or the supply of energy became common. Neither the *Encyclopedia of the Social Sciences* (published in the 1930s) nor its successor, the *International Encyclopedia of the Social Sciences* (published in 1968) had an article on resources or energy. As late as the 1950s books on population were published in which energy resources were never mentioned. In the late 1940s, however, scientists began to make systematic assessments of the world's fossil-fuel resources. M. K. Hubbert, a prominent geophysicist, wrote in 1949:

> The consumption of energy from fossil fuels is . . . a "pip," rising sharply from zero to maximum, and almost as sharply declining, representing but a moment in the total of human history. . . . The release of this energy is a unidirectional and irreversible process. It can only happen once, and the historical events associated with this release are necessarily without precedent, and are incapable of repetition.[20]

Public recognition of an "energy crisis" did not come until 24 years after Hubbert's warning. From 1950 to 1973 the consumption of petroleum in the world rose at a rate of approximately 7.1 percent per year.[21] Although such a rise in the use of a nonrenewable resource could obviously not be sustained for long, nobody paid much attention until the precipitous rise in oil prices in 1973. Until then all warnings could be dismissed as pessimism or distortion. People could claim vaguely that "other sources of energy" would become available in the future, by harnessing the sun or achieving nuclear fusion. When the crisis came, these dreams delivered no energy. The only immediate alternative was the installation of conventional nuclear power plants, and these burned a fossil fuel (uranium) that is not abundant, and they furnished only electrical energy, which is difficult to store and to use in vehicles. With notorious hazards and insoluble waste-disposal problems as well, and with the necessity of enriching the uranium before it could be used as fuel—a process requiring enormous quantities of conventional fossil fuels—nuclear energy was found to be no salvation. The development of a feasible breeder reactor would require at least a decade, and meanwhile nuclear power represented a frightful waste of both uranium and other fossil fuels. For the first time in two centuries the world, with its population now swollen, faced the prospect of *reducing* its level of consumption.

---

[19] See, for example, George H. Knibbs, *The Shadow of the World's Future* (London: Ernest Benn, 1928), p. 103: "It is obvious that the rate of population increase witnessed on earth during the last century and a quarter cannot continue under any circumstances whatever: it *must* diminish. What will bring this about? Will human intelligence cooperate, or will man be the victim of disaster, and what kind of disaster?"

[20] M. K. Hubbert, "Energy from Fossil Fuels," *Science*, Vol. 109 (February 4, 1949), pp. 103–109. Thirteen years later Eugene Ayres and Charles A. Scarlott wrote: "The problem of energy for the United States is not one of the dim future. It is upon us now." *Energy Sources—The Wealth of the World* (New York: McGraw-Hill, 1952).

[21] In the United States it rose at 4.3 percent per year, with imports furnishing 13.1 percent of consumption in 1950 and 35.7 percent in 1973.

Figure 6-3   Energy Subsidy to the Food System in the United States. (Hatched zone represents uncertainty as to exact values.)

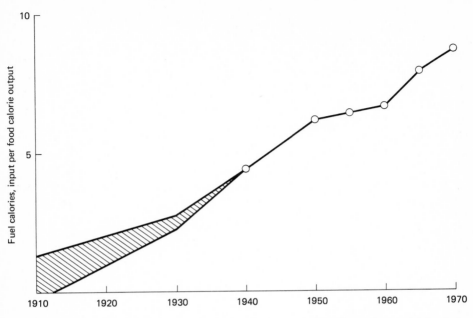

From *The Fires of Culture: Energy Yesterday and Tomorrow*, by Carol Steinhart and John Steinhart. © 1974 by Wadsworth Publishing Company, Inc., Belmont, California 94002. Reprinted by permission of the publisher, Duxbury Press.

Energy, Food, and Agriculture

The world's food supply, the resource most often discussed in connection with population, is customarily viewed as dependent on arable land. Actually, it is fundamentally dependent on energy, and the notion that this energy comes almost entirely from current sunshine is out of date. The truth is that the dependence of agriculture on fossil energy is already great and is growing rapidly. In 1910, in the world's greatest food-exporting nation, the United States, the fossil energy used in the production of human food was already tending to be more than the energy value of the food consumed (Figure 6-3). By 1970, about 8.7 calories of energy were required to produce one calorie of food for eating.[22] The world's population is currently fed at the cost of enormous infusions of mechanical energy, not only in actual cultivation but in the manufacture of fertilizers, pesticides, and machinery, and in transport and processing. If the

[22] John S. Steinhart and Carol E. Steinhart, "Energy Use in the U.S. Food System," *Science*, Vol. 184 (April 19, 1974), pp. 310–311. See also David Pimentel et al., "Food Production and the Energy Crisis," *Science*, Vol. 182 (November 2, 1973), p. 445, as well as the book by the Steinharts, *The Fires of Culture: Energy Yesterday and Tomorrow* (North Scituate, Mass., Duxbury Press, 1974), Ch. 4.

food supply were limited to what human and animal muscle could produce, a large share of humanity would starve. If the huge human population projected for the future is to be fed, the energy used in agriculture will have to increase too. It will, in fact, have to increase faster than the population, because the marginal output per unit of energy input is diminishing. This decline can be seen in decreasing yields per unit of commercial fertilizer,[23] per unit of land added to cultivation, and per unit of total energy input.[24] The so-called "green revolution," created mainly by new grain varieties, is at bottom a diffusion of high-energy agriculture. Yields per acre are increased, but not yields per unit of energy expended. The new varieties require hybrid seeds and more pesticides, fertilizer, and irrigation. It has been calculated that to feed the world's 4 billion people on an American diet would require energy equivalent to 488 billion gallons of gasoline per year, and that if the energy all came from petroleum, this use alone would exhaust the world's known oil reserves in 29 years.[25] Regardless of specific numbers, the inability of coal, oil, and gas to feed a doubled or tripled world population is clear.

Occasional famines and continuing undernutrition in major regions remind us that the human race has never been fed adequately. Lack of food has always been a factor in mortality and a restraint on population growth. It will doubtless be so in the future. Be that as it may, the growth of population in the less developed areas has given rise to the curious idea that a desirable policy is that of "labor-intensive" production (in manufacturing as well as in agriculture). The reasoning is that people need "jobs" and if many of them are employed to do what a few could do, there will be fuller employment. This idea represents a confusion of jobs with production. The genius of technology is to save human effort, not to expend it; and the genius of social organization is a division, not a uniformity, of labor. Therefore, if a task can be accomplished by three men instead of six, the use of six is a waste because the other three could be doing something else that would be productive. A "labor-intensive" policy is therefore a policy of lethargy or defeat.

In less developed regions, labor-intensive philosophy is reinforced by the prejudice against urbanization. The idea is to keep farmers on the land, simply because they are multiplying rapidly and no one knows what else to do with them. With land scarce, however, there is no need for extra labor to grow the

---

[23] In Taiwan, for example, the consumption of commercial fertilizers in ratio to crop area rose 18 times between 1903 and 1958, but the yield rose only 1.7 times. The improvement in yield was greater in the first half of the 55-year period than during the second half. Computed from data in Yhi-Min Ho, *Agricultural Development of Taiwan, 1903–1960* (Nashville, Tenn.: Vanderbilt University Press, 1966), pp. 84, 89.

[24] In American corn production, the yield in calories per calorie of energy input was 3.70 in 1945 and 2.82 in 1970. Pimentel et al., *op. cit.*, p. 445. Most American corn is fed to livestock; the energy actually consumed by human beings from corn is therefore several times less than that produced in the field. This is why, in terms of human consumption, there is a large energy deficit in American corn production.

[25] David Pimentel et al., *op. cit.*, pp. 447–448.

crops; the extra workers merely consume part of the produce that could go to the urban population, which is also growing. As noted above, the main factor responsible for modern agricultural production is not labor but inanimate energy. That is why countries such as India and Egypt, where the overwhelming proportion of the labor force is engaged in agriculture, cannot produce enough food for their population; while in industrial countries, where only 5 to 15 percent of the labor force tills the land, a surplus of food is often available for export.

The resource outlook thus gives little indication that the world's population will long continue to grow at a rate that will double it every 35 or 40 years. Such increase is particularly unlikely if all peoples insist on raising their levels of living, because this will exhaust available resources sooner. No one can forecast for sure when a cessation of increase will come, or how, or from what specific cause. No one can foretell whether it will be by a rise in mortality (either slow and grinding or sudden and catastrophic), by a policy of deliberately limiting births, or by a combination of these. But come it will, and soon.

POPULATION POLICIES

For more than a century reformers urged the repeal of laws against birth control, but the idea of curbing population growth by deliberate government intervention received no attention until the 1950s and 1960s. Cautiously at first, later more vigorously, private foundations and organizations tried to help less developed countries lower their birth rates and encouraged the United Nations and the industrial countries to assist them officially. In 1959 the Draper Committee, appointed by President Eisenhower to study military assistance abroad, recommended that the United States help countries "to deal with the problem of rapid population growth." In 1962 Sweden, with American support, finally induced the United Nations to promise U.N. technical assistance for population policies. In 1965 President Johnson declared that "less than five dollars invested in population control is worth a hundred dollars invested in economic growth." By 1968 Congress, in budgeting for the Agency for International Development, was earmarking money for population programs; in the next four years AID spent $251 million for this purpose. In 1969, in his epoch-making Message on Population, President Nixon called for a Commission on Population Growth and the American Future and for intensified population activities in AID and the United Nations. In the United Nations itself, Secretary-General U Thant in 1966 endorsed a statement, signed by 12 heads of state, declaring that population growth menaces progress and should be curbed. The next year, in order to free population activities from internal competition for funds, the United Nations established a Trust Fund for Population Activities, supported by special contributions; by 1971 the annual pledges for this fund from

46 countries amounted to nearly $30 million.[26] By 1974, 33 countries, with over 2 billion inhabitants, had official policies to reduce their birth rates.[27]

All this activity might suggest that world population growth will soon be controlled and catastrophe avoided. The mere existence of a policy, however, does not guarantee its success.

Family Planning versus Population Control

Virtually all national population policies have automatically assumed that "family planning" (furnishing couples with contraceptives) is the way to solve the population problem. With this idea, they have opened clinics, promoted research on improved contraceptives, and "educated" people on the desirability of planned births. India in 1952 was the first country to inaugurate such a program, experimenting cautiously with the "rhythm" method. Others followed, gradually using more publicity and money.

A typical example was Singapore's policy at its start in 1965, when the government reasoned as follows:

> Singapore's present population is over 1.8 million. . . . Our annual crude birth rate of over 30 per thousand is too high. . . . There is too much unnecessary human misery. . . . this can be effectively stopped through a determined effort on the part of Government to provide Family Planning on a mass basis. This we propose to do. . . .
>
> It is the intention of the Singapore Government, under its Second 5-Year Development Plan (1966–70), to bring the message to every married woman . . . that Family Planning brings her immeasurable benefits. And, at her request, to advise her on the best available methods of Family Planning which will be simple, inexpensive, and safe. . . .
>
> Each FP [Family Planning] clinic is expected to deal up to 12,500 IUCD [Intra-Uterine Contraceptive Device] insertions per annum.[28]

To lower the birth rate, a *program* devoted to family planning was assumed to be sufficient. Family planning itself was viewed as a *medical* matter, requiring *clinics* and a *near-perfect, medically supervised method*. Further, it was only for *married women* and was *entirely voluntary*. These features were, and still are, typical of virtually all national efforts purporting to lower fertility.

The basic difficulty with exclusive reliance on family planning is that it

[26] For fuller accounts of the rise of official birth-limitation policies, see Phyllis Tilson Piotrow, *World Population Crisis: The United States Response* (New York: Praeger, 1973), and Richard Symonds and Michael Carder, *The United Nations and the Population Question* (New York: McGraw-Hill, 1973).

[27] Dorothy Nortman and Ellen Hofstatter, "Population and Family Planning Programs: A Factbook," *Reports on Population/Family Planning* (December 1974), p. 24.

[28] Singapore, *White Paper on Family Planning*, Cmd. 22 (1965), pp. 1, 12, 13. Reprinted in "Government Policy Statements on Population: An Inventory," *Reports on Population/Family Planning* (February 1970), p. 10.

"Unwanted babies" from the standpoint of the nation or the world is not the same as "unwanted babies" from the standpoint of a couple. If people do not wish to have few children, offering them contraceptives will have little effect.

misconstrues the population problem.[29] Overpopulation or too-rapid growth is a condition of the society as a whole, not of the individual. The family-planning motto is that every couple should have the number of children they want, but the number of children couples want is not necessarily the number that the society should have. The "planning" is only *family* planning, whereas "population control" involves *national* planning. We do not construe planning by individual businessmen as national economic planning, nor do we regard freedom to use drugs as drug control.

[29] An early criticism of family planning as the exclusive approach to population limitation was Kingsley Davis, "Population Policy: Will Current Programs Succeed?" *Science*, Vol. 158 (November 10, 1967), pp. 730–739. (This article has been widely reprinted in books of readings.)

Implicitly, the family-planning approach assumes that the sole cause of the population problem is *unwanted* babies. It says, in effect, that if couples plan all their offspring there will be no unwanted babies and hence no population problem. But "unwanted babies" from the standpoint of the nation or the world is not the same as "unwanted babies" from the standpoint of a couple. As surveys indicate, people can want many children as well as few. In the advanced countries the desired number usually exceeds the actual number. In the underdeveloped countries, both rural and urban couples want sizable families. In South Korea, where a national family-planning program began in 1964, a survey in 1967 found no change in ideal family size. "Almost every respondent says she wants two or three sons with one or two daughters."[30]

It is conditions, not contraceptives, that determine the number of children desired. Given the right conditions, women will lower their fertility with or without a government program. The long decline of the birth rate in advanced countries from 1870 to 1932 took place in the teeth of governmental, religious, and medical opposition to birth control.

It follows that a national policy that confines itself to furnishing contraceptives cannot provide adequate population control. The only contribution it can make is perhaps, in the transition from a peasant-agrarian to an urban-industrial type of society, to facilitate the adjustment of reproductive behavior to the new conditions. In this transition, the individual's ability to adjust to new conditions is not perfect, and furnishing the means may speed the adjustment.

As part of a population-limitation program, then, furnishing contraceptives makes sense, but to assume that it alone is adequate is to deflect attention from the social changes that are also required. These changes would necessarily be unorthodox, because they go against the pronatalist institutions and values built into the structures of all preindustrial societies. An exclusive emphasis on family planning enables people to ignore these inconvenient changes and delude themselves into believing that the population problem is being solved painlessly. Until the abortion movement became popular, the family planners opposed legalizing abortion—in fact, they justified contraception as a way of combatting "the abortion problem." By concerning itself with *married* women and *family* planning, and by linking its services with *maternal* health, the family-planning approach reinforced familistic ideology. It viewed women's sole concern as childbearing. By declaring family planning to be a "health" service, and by promoting contraceptive techniques that require medical attention, the movement subordinated contraceptive programs to scarce and expensive medi-

[30] "Korea: Trends in Four National KAP Surveys, 1964–67," *Studies in Family Planning*, No. 43 (June 1969), p. 7. In Ghana 94 percent of women in an urban sample and 98 percent in a rural sample wanted four or more children. D. I. Pool, "Ghana: A Survey on Fertility and Attitudes Toward Family Limitation," *Ibid.*, No. 25 (December 1967), p. 11. In Ethiopia in 1970–71, 76 percent of rural inhabitants refused to answer the question on ideal number of children or said it was up to God, and only 7 percent said the ideal was fewer than four. In the capital city, Addis Ababa, 47 percent gave the up-to-God or don't know answer and only 15 percent the fewer-than-four answer. Wen Pin Chang, "Knowledge, Attitudes, and Practice of Family Planning in Ethiopia," *Ibid.*, No. 11 (November 1974).

cal personnel. Women seeking contraception were "patients," although they were not "sick." The population problem, an economic and social matter, was given to physicians to solve, although they are not trained in economics and demography—in fact, their accustomed concern and skills of necessity lean the other way, toward saving lives and bringing babies into the world.

Social Change and Population Control

Family planners reply that their approach is a "first step," that it has the advantage of being "acceptable," and that its program is "voluntary" whereas other measures are "compulsory."[31] To this the critics respond that if various steps are needed, taking one and not the others will delay the possibility of controlling population. This defense, they say, proves the family-planning approach to be a way of avoiding effective measures. As for acceptability, since the older mores are pronatalist, effective measures will of course be unacceptable until the institutional patterns are altered. Finally, the "compulsory" accusation is turned against the family-planning proponents themselves. In accepting the older mores in every regard except contraception, they are perpetuating the sanctions and role definitions that induce people to reproduce in abundance. They are accepting the involuntary early marriage of children in India, Nepal, and many other agrarian countries, the seclusion of women in the home and their exclusion from economic and professional opportunities, and the sexual taboos whose function was to maximize reproduction.[32] Family planners, the critics say, are not only tolerating compulsions in the old social system but also ignoring incentive measures that might motivate lower fertility. Giving people positive incentives will do more to reduce fertility than simply displacing private enterprise in the supply of contraceptives.

Zero Population Growth

Several developments have borne out the critics. One is the sudden rise of Zero Population Growth in the United States. This organization, started in 1968, had thousands of members by 1971. Its goal is hardly to be reached by merely dispensing contraceptives and encouraging people to have all the babies they want; yet public opinion has strongly favored the ZPG goal, and the Commission on Population Growth and the American Future embraced it.[33]

[31] See the debate between Kingsley Davis and William McElroy, "Will Family Planning Solve the Population Problem?" *Victor-Bostram Fund*, Report No. 10 (Fall 1968), pp. 16–17, 30–31. The most systematic attempt to answer the critics is that by Bernard Berelson, "Beyond Family Planning," *Science*, Vol. 163 (February 7, 1969), pp. 533–543.

[32] See Judith Blake, "Coercive Pronatalism and American Population Policy," Commission on Population Growth and the American Future, *Research Reports*, Vol. 6 (1972), pp. 85–109.

[33] See the Commission's *Report* (Washington: Government Printing Office, 1972), p. 110. For a fuller account of the debate over ZPG, see Kingsley Davis, "Zero Population Growth: The Goal and the Means," *Daedalus* (Fall 1973), pp. 15–30.

The Evidence of the Birth Rate

Another development that raised doubts about an exclusive family-planning policy was the bottoming-out of the fertility decline in industrial countries. This decline had begun in the late 1950s and continued all the way through the 1960s. The family-planning movement boasted that by enabling couples to prevent "unwanted births," it had achieved this decline, which in several countries had brought populations below the stable "replacement rate." By 1975, however, it was clear that birth rates in these countries had reached their low point and, unless severe recession or war intervened, would rise again.[34]

The more advanced of the developing countries also showed rapid declines in fertility. Again the family planners took credit, but the declines occurred whether the countries had official family-planning programs or not, and in countries that did have programs the drop began well before the program. In Taiwan, where great success for family planning was claimed, fertility started falling in 1952, 12 years before the family planning program was started. True, the decline was faster after 1964—4.92 percent per year as opposed to 3.65 before that—but with modernization the drop in fertility tends to accelerate anyway. In Japan there was no official family-planning program but rather legalization of abortion; yet after 1947, when fertility equaled Taiwan's 1964 level, the drop was 7.78 percent per year, much faster than in Taiwan. In Costa Rica the decline in fertility was 4.1 percent per year during four years before the government policy was started in 1967 and 5.8 percent during the four years afterwards, but the decline was due to fewer marriages, increased sterilization and abortion, and increased use of traditional contraceptives and the pill, none of which involved the official program except provision of an estimated 26 percent of the pills. The Costa Rican program mainly inserted IUDs at clinics,[35] but in nearly three and a half years, from January 1968 to May 1972, a total of 7,456 women visited the clinics—one-half of one percent of the women aged 15 to 49.[36]

If people wish to reduce their fertility and convenient means are furnished by the government at little or no cost, they will take advantage of this service, just as they would if the government offered groceries at little or no cost. Their response, however, does not mean that the government's action is the "cause" of the decline in fertility, any more than supplying groceries would be a cause of eating. Without government action, the means would be supplied by private enterprise, just as groceries are.

If people do not wish to have few children, offering them contraceptives will have little effect, as can be seen in the failure to reduce fertility when old

---

[34] See June Sklar and Beth Berkov, "The American Birth Rate: Evidence of a Coming Rise," *Science*, Vol. 189 (August 29, 1975), pp. 693–700. In 14 industrial countries, the average birth rate rose between 1973 and 1974.

[35] Jack Reynolds, "Costa Rica: Measuring the Demographic Impact of Family-Planning Programs," *Studies in Family Planning*, Vol. 4 (November 1973), pp. 310–316.

[36] Costa Rica, Servicio en Planification Familiar, *Boletin Informativo*, No. 5 (April 1973), p. 3.

conditions persist. For example, although India was first to adopt a national policy to restrain population growth, it had almost no success. There may have been a slight reduction in fertility between 1951 and 1961, but if so it was less than between 1931 and 1941 when there was an economic depression.[37]

Population Control versus Development

At the first intergovernmental World Population Conference in Bucharest in 1974 (World Population Year), delegates from the United States and other industrial countries expected the conference to stress fertility reduction through family planning. To their surprise, the less developed countries, a huge majority of the governments represented, rejected population growth as a cause of their poverty and blamed instead "neo-colonialism," "imperialism," "overconsumption," and other sins of the industrial nations. The Chinese declared:

> The superpowers raise the false alarm of a "population explosion" and paint a depressing picture of the future of mankind. This reminds us of the notorious Malthus, who, more than 170 years ago, when the population of the world was less than one billion, raised a hue and cry about "over-population" and the impossibility for the growth of production ever to catch up with that of the population. . . . Today the world population has more than trebled . . . , but there has been much greater increase in the material wealth of society. . . The creative power of the people is boundless, and so is man's ability to exploit and utilize natural resources. The pessimistic views spread by the superpowers are utterly groundless and are being propagated with ulterior motives.

The Maoist delegates, joined by the Holy See, Argentina, Brazil, and many African nations, did not deny that unemployment, poverty, and environmental degradation exist in less developed countries; they simply claimed that the causation of these evils does not lie in population growth but in international injustice. This being true, the remedy is not birth control but international reform.

> Is it owing to over-population [asked the Chinese] that unemployment and poverty exist in many countries of the world today? No, absolutely not. It is mainly due to aggression, plunder and exploitation by the imperialists, particularly the superpowers.

This old device of finding the cause of misfortune in one's enemies allowed the advanced nations to be flayed for their high level of consumption (indirect cannibalism—eating little children in Bangladesh and the Sahel) and their "plundering" of world resources. It was convincing, however, mainly because the less developed majority of countries were apprehensive of any distraction

---

[37] Prithwis Das Gupta, "Estimation of Demographic Measures for India 1881–1961," *Population Studies*, Vol. 25 (November 1971), p. 409.

from the overriding goal of development. Their anxiety was fanned by the Marxian characterization of the population question as a red herring designed to forestall social reforms, and hence development. To allay their fear, the exclusively family-planning approach to population limitation had little to offer, because in truth it does ignore social reform. Merely furnishing couples with contraceptives has little to do with economic development, but when population policy is viewed as requiring a reorganization of institutional arrangements governing reproductive motivation—that is, as requiring pro-found social reform—it is conducive to development, first by lessening the demographic burden, and, second, by speeding social changes that simultane-ously improve production. Because of their limited view of population policy, the delegates from free-world industrial countries lost the initiative at Bucharest.

Policies that Might Succeed

What are the social reforms that would reduce fertility? A clue comes from asking why fertility always falls during industrialization. Evidently it falls because low fertility is rewarded and high fertility is penalized. Urban conges-tion and formal education make children less profitable and more costly and troublesome; outside employment makes women less dependent on marriage and a husband; skilled occupations make social advancement more dependent on individual accomplishment and less dependent on kinship. Accordingly, a population policy designed to reduce fertility would systematically speed up those particular changes that not only depress fertility but also aid economic production. It would reduce unproductive housing costs by subsidizing only small family units; increase outside employment of women by educating them and giving them equal opportunities and pay; advance the average age at marriage by requiring proof of economic viability before a license is issued; foster education but require parents to pay for it; and give advantages in housing, taxes, scholarships, and recreation to single as compared to married people. These measures would probably be sufficient. If they were not, the policy could also discontinue the custom of family names and release all adult children from responsibility for their parents, thus reducing the ego-identity that plays a strong role in parental motivation; it could structure recreational life around the place of work rather than the home. It is assumed that young people would be given a realistic as opposed to a moralistic knowledge of sexual relations, family life, population problems, and individual achievement, and that means of birth control, including abortion, sterilization, and non-medical methods would be available.

Since most of these changes would either cost little or be economically advantageous, they would not compete heavily with expenditures for capital improvement such as dams, roads, bridges, and factories. Nor, of course, would all the changes listed be required; the aim would be ZPG or NPG, not a com-plete ban on babies. For this reason, a successful policy would not demand a revolutionary Utopia. There are existing societies, both free and communist, where the birth rate has long been at or near replacement level. To be sure, some of these, like Hungary, have involved hardships as depressants on fertility, but others, like Sweden, have mainly involved social changes of the kind mentioned.

The necessity of socioeconomic measures for ZPG is illustrated by Singapore. As described earlier, that country began with a conventional family-planning program. Fertility fell rapidly until 1969, but then the drop almost stopped. The government then instituted measures designed "to establish the two-child family as a social norm and to promote sterilization as a method of family limitation."[38] Among these measures were the following:

> [In 1972] higher government hospital delivery fees with each additional child; abolition of paid maternity leave after three children; and abolition of priority for large families in the allocation of subsidized Housing and Development Board flats. [In 1973] further increases in government hospital delivery fees for higher order children; lower priority in primary school admission for the fourth or higher birth order children; and permission under certain conditions for families living in Housing and Development Board flats with three or fewer children to sublet rooms. [Also] a new regulation . . . whereby immigrant workers earning less than Singapore $750 per month must seek the permission of the Work Permits Office to marry Singapore citizens.[39]

Not surprisingly, Singapore's fertility resumed its downward course, falling by 8.1 percent between 1972 and 1973, and by approximately 8.4 percent between 1973 and 1974.

THE PROBABLE FUTURE OF WORLD POPULATION

What Singapore has done the world may not choose to do. Deliberate world population control within the next half-century seems unlikely, not because contraception will be lacking (it will not be) but because the rewards for reproduction will remain strong.

Population policy, it must be remembered, is *collective* policy. The collectivities with ultimate authority are nations, of which there are some 145, but each nation harbors other cohesive groups. As is well known, rivalry between nations and between groups within nations frequently involves claims based on the relative number of people. One reads that China deserves special attention because it has 800 million people. One remembers that before World War II, Germany, Italy, and Japan justified armed conquest in the name of *Lebensraum* (living space). One knows that groups within nations frequently justify

---

[38] Wan Fook Kee and Margaret Loh, "Singapore," *Studies in Family Planning*, Vol. 5 (May 1974), p. 163. See also Saw Swee-Hock, "Singapore: Resumption of Rapid Fertility Decline in 1973," *Studies in Family Planning*, Vol. 6 (June 1975), pp. 166–169.

[39] Swee-Hock, *op. cit.*, p. 168.

political and economic claims in terms of size. How many times has one read that the *majority* in South Africa are black and that "therefore" they should rule the country? How many times has one read that the proportion of a given racial group in the American population is such and such, and that "therefore" it should have the same proportion in a high occupation? As these claims and "reapportionment" testify, democratic representation is based on the number of people.

With demographic competition thus built into the world's social organization, officials (whose careers depend on collective strength) resist "weakening" their nation or group by anti-natalist policies. While they may disavow rapid population growth because group success depends on skills as well as bodies, they seldom reject what they call "normal" growth. If they discourage immigration, it is less to restrain population growth than to protect citizens against competition and cultural invasion.

It is neighborhoods and towns that are most likely to oppose population growth. These, being "groups" only in the sense of sharing a locale and a set of amenities, have little mystical identity, yet feel the effects of population growth directly and concretely. Their power, however, is slight. When American towns and counties undertook to restrict population growth in the 1960s, they did so by restricting new housing and services, which mainly reduced migration rather than births. Even so, they encountered a storm of criticism and litigation.[40] Political power resides in nations and religio-ethnic communities rather than in local groups. For these groups, demographic weakness threatens loss of power or displacement. The Europeans did not conquer the New World by having a lesser population than the aborigines, nor are the Mexicans reconquering south Texas by having a low fertility.

Given such rivalries, national anti-natalist policies will probably not even aim at ZPG, much less achieve it. To achieve ZPG and at the same time avoid invidious differentials, all nations would have to act in unison, a highly improbable prospect. Nor does the United Nations show any sign of leading the world toward ZPG. It has become the mouthpiece of the less developed nations because they are in the majority. It has rewarded population growth by favoring emigration and special economic aid for crowded nations and by hiring people in proportion to the size of their nation. Although it has gone on record that rapid population growth endangers economic development, it has dragged its feet with respect to institutional changes that would affect reproduction.

Nor does the world seem likely, in the absence of policy, to stumble accidentally onto ZPG through individual fertility control. Some observers say that as the world becomes fully industrialized and crowded, the birth rate will "naturally" fall to a low level. If so, it will require a long time, because the world as a whole is about a century behind the advanced countries in economic development, and the very growth of population itself is the chief obstacle to

---

[40] See Rockefeller Brothers Fund, *The Use of Land* (New York: Crowell, 1973), especially Ch. 1; and Earl Finkler, *Nongrowth as a Planning Alternative* (Chicago: American Society of Planning Officials, 1972).

catching up. In the meantime, peoples with high birth rates tend to replace those with low birth rates, and the family remains a strong institution.

A rise in mortality is more likely, either a slow rise as envisaged in *The Limits to Growth* or a sudden one brought on by human conflict. In international relations population growth is an underlying and long-run irritant. As more billions with more technology struggle for the earth's resources, all-out warfare could cause not only direct casualties of unprecedented magnitude but also indirect ones from starvation, disease, and irradiation.

Out of such a conflagration might come a world-population policy hardly dreamed of today. The genetic damage among the survivors could be so great that a licensing system for parenthood would be adopted, only those persons least likely to transmit defects being allowed to reproduce. In that case, the social control of reproduction would be a reality.[41] Also a reality, in all probability, would be a world dictatorship. These eventualities would not be a solution to today's population problem, but rather the result of our failure to adopt a solution.

SUMMARY

1   As an unintended consequence of its technological success, the human species has multiplied egregiously. Until the last century the growth arose mainly from advances in productive technology, but increasingly after 1800, in the industrializing countries, it arose from medical advances as well.

2   These technological advances were readily diffused to the less developed countries. As a consequence, around 1920, the more rapid population increase shifted to the poorer countries and became a major obstacle to economic development.

3   The world's present peak growth rate will probably not continue long, because it depends on fossil fuels and other resources that are growing scarce. Even food production has come to depend overwhelmingly on mechanical energy, as the use of fertilizers, pesticides, machinery, and irrigation indicates. Worse yet, the yield of food calories per unit of energy input is declining.

4   Precisely how the world's population growth will be stopped is unpredictable, but the chance of its being stopped by deliberate anti-natalist policy appears slim. Virtually all of the existing anti-natalist policies are limited to providing family-planning services, on the theory that population growth is due to unwanted births. The evidence indicates that people *want* more children than are necessary to balance present low mortality and that the family-planning emphasis is an evasion of social reforms necessary to lower reproductive desires.

5   Individual fertility reduction seems more likely to come from changes in societies than from official family-planning policies, but it seems unlikely to fall to the present low level of mortality. People who lower their fertility that far tend to be replaced by the descendants of those who do not.

6   It seems more probable that runaway population growth will be stopped primarily by a rise in mortality. The same technology that gave the modern age an

[41] See Kingsley Davis, "Sociological Aspects of Genetic Control." In John D. Roslansky (ed.), *Genetics and the Future of Man* (New York: Appleton, 1965), pp. 173–204.

unprecedented decline in mortality, especially recently in the less developed areas, can also give it an unprecedented increase. If this happens, it will probably not be by slow attrition but by a major human conflict genereated by human crowding in a world of diminishing resources.

RECOMMENDED READING

In demography, as in other sciences, the cutting edge of development is found in journals rather than books. The chief journals in the United States are *Demography, Social Biology,* and a bibliographic journal, *Population Index,* covering the entire field in all languages. In England, *Population Studies* is the leading journal, and in France, *Population.* With respect to resources there is no one journal that covers the entire range, but an avenue to locating the most recent developments is *Science* (published weekly) and such magazines as *Natural History, Scientific American, Nature,* and *American Scientist.*

The best compilation of demographic data on countries around the world is the United Nations *Demographic Yearbook,* which has been issued every year since 1948 and generally gives emphasis to different topics in different years. Data on resources around the world are available in the United Nations *Statistical Yearbook* and *World Energy Supplies.* In addition, *America en Cifras* covers all aspects of comparative demographic and economic statistics for countries of the Western Hemisphere.

The student will find references in the footnotes to this chapter useful. In addition, the following books are recommended: The National Academy of Sciences, *Rapid Population Growth: Consequences and Policy Implications* (1971) is a comprehensive symposium on various aspects of contemporary population changes and their significance. John P. Holdren and Paul R. Ehrlich (eds.), *Global Ecology: Readings Toward a National Strategy for Man* (1971) is a good collection of readings. Eugene N. Cameron (ed.), *The Mineral Position of the United States, 1975–2000* (1973) includes graphic and expert analyses of minerals in the United States from the standpoint of supply and demand. Kingsley Davis (ed.), *Cities: Their Origin, Growth and Human Impact* (1973) is a collection of readings from *Scientific American,* including sections on city environments, cities in less developed regions, and city effects on health. Scientific American, *The Human Population* (1974) is the September 1974 issue of *Scientific American,* entirely devoted to population, in book form. Ester Boserup, *The Conditions of Agricultural Growth: The Economics of Agrarian Change under Population Pressure* (1965) ably expounds the thesis that increasing population has been the cause of technological change in agriculture, not vice versa. In Bernard Berelson (ed.), *Population Policy in Developed Countries* (1974), each author describes population policy in his country. World Bank, *Population Policies and Economic Development* (1974) is an excellent discussion of population problems in developing countries and the family planning programs supposed to solve them. William Petersen (ed.), *Readings in Population* (1972) is a collection of demographic articles. Mancur Olson and Hans H. Landsberg (eds.), *The No-Growth Society* (1973) is a reprinting of the Fall 1973 issue of *Daedalus.* Thomas T. Poleman and Donald K. Freebairn (eds.), *Food, Population, and Employment* (1973) contains original analyses of the economic, political, and demographic effects of the "Green Revolution."

7

Equality and Inequality

SEYMOUR MARTIN LIPSET

nequality and social stratification have been a source of controversy, social conflict, and, on occasion, revolution for thousands of years. They have constituted a social problem insofar as large numbers have denied the propriety of almost every effort to justify some persons' having much more income, power, and status than others. People in every epoch, from the ancient world to our own day, have sought ways of distributing the valued positions and possessions in ways that are accepted as equitable, as fair, or as divinely mandated. The question has repeatedly been raised whether people who are eminent, wealthy, or powerful are also virtuous. Moral justification for inequality has been a subject for philosophers and theologians. Until relatively recently, defenders of existing systems idealized the image of a society in which every individual was born into a specific class and inherited the rights and duties that belonged to it. The revolutions that introduced modern society, however, broke with this image. They imposed on every person the burden of his or her own freedom, with obligations enforceable only by legal sanctions, not by the morality of sacred tradition. The relationship between master and servant, for example, became a contractual one. Each was bound to the other by a cash-nexus, which destroyed all ethical meaning of the bond. Hence, the classes of industrial society are simply aggregates of persons similarly situated, and held together only by their economic interests.

The conservative and radical intellectual traditions are divided on how they perceive the basic dilemma of industrial civilization. To the conservative, the moral problem of this civilization consists in the weakening of the ties between individuals and the groups of which they are members, caused by the rapid decline of the moral standards by which individuals can orient their conduct. To the radical, the moral dilemma is oppression, the deprivation of opportunities for individual development. Oppression violates the essential human dignity, which consists of the freedom to exercise one's rational and emotional capacities to their fullest extent. Each of these traditions conceives the reform of modern society in accordance with its conception of the evil that has grown with industrialization. To the conservative reform is a matter of re-integrating the individual with the group; to the radical it is a question of creating social conditions to buttress human dignity and satisfy people's needs for self-realization.

This chapter first examines the intellectual ideas that have shaped empirical studies of social stratification in the United States and elsewhere, and second reports the findings bearing on changes in the distribution of rewards in the United States. It also deals briefly with comparable issues in the communist world, which, like the United States, emphasizes egalitarianism in its dominant political and social credo. The chapter concludes with a discussion of some of the problems raised by an emphasis on equal opportunity.

HISTORICAL VIEWS OF STRATIFICATION

Inequality of reward, power, and status and hereditary transmission of privilege have existed for as long as people have lived in complex societies characterized by a systematic division of labor. Given this fact, many analysts of stratification, of hierarchical inequality, have concluded that it is necessary for the very existence of human society. Yet the evidence also indicates that for thousands of years many have dreamed of an egalitarian society and some have attempted to reduce or eliminate inequality, seeing it as an immoral way of organizing human relationships.

Plato, in his effort to describe the ideal state, noted that people in society engage in reciprocal services, that labor is divided among them. Ideally, the individual and community would profit most if each person did exclusively what he was best fitted to do. Hence Plato envisaged an open society, with an educational system that brought out the best in each. Yet he was pessimistic about the prospects for such a society as long as the family, which he regarded as the key support of institutionalized inequality, exists. His argument, which is still followed by many contemporary sociologists, was that individuals are motivated to secure for other family members, for whom they feel affection, any privileges which they themselves attain. Hence in every society there is a built-in pressure to institutionalize inequality by making it hereditary. Plato argued that the only way to create an egalitarian society was to take children away from their parents and to have the state raise them, to eliminate the tendency toward inherited social privilege. As he put it: "Children are to be common, and no parent is to know his own child, nor any child his parent." Once "the community of property and the community of families" have been established, men

> will not tear the city in pieces in differing about "mine" and "not mine," each man dragging any acquisition which he has made into a separate house of his own, where he has a separate wife and children and private pleasures and pains. . . . They will be delivered from all those quarrels of which money or children or relatives are the occasion.[1]

Aristotle, though much less radical than Plato in his conceptions of the desirable society, also contended that the more equality, the better the state. A "city ought to be composed, as far as possible, of equals and similars. . . . Great then is the good fortune of a state in which the citizens have a moderate

---

[1] Plato, "The Republic," in *The Best Known Works of Plato*, trans. by Benjamin Jowett (Garden City, N.Y.: Blue Ribbon Books, 1942), pp. 115–122. Plato's conception was revived in the nineteenth century by the socialist thinker Robert Owen. It was even partially advocated as a policy proposal by the New York Workingmen's party, a group which ran candidates for office in the late 1820s and early 1830s and secured between 10 and 15 percent of the vote. The New York Workingmen suggested that all children, regardless of family status, be required to attend state-supported boarding schools from the age of six on, so as to equalize their social environment. See Walter Hugins, *Jacksonian Democracy and the Working Class* (Stanford, Cal.: Stanford University Press, 1960), pp. 12–13, 19; and New York Workingmen's Party, "A System of Republican Education," in Walter Hugins (ed.), *The Reform Impulse, 1825–1850* (New York: Harper and Row, 1972), pp. 135–139.

and sufficient property, for where some possess much and others nothing, there may arise 'extreme' " politics, factions, and revolutions.[2]

Plato accounted for the existence and persistence of stratification by the assumption that people vary in terms of inherent capacities; that each person does certain types of work better than others. And given the need for differentiation, the population is divided among those who labor, those who perform administrative and military duties, and those who rule.[3]

A question obviously arises as to why people accept an allocation of positions that places many, if not most, of them in inferior positions. Part of the answer lies in power relations, for the lower orders have not been in a position for much of history to challenge the authority of the privileged, who usually control access to weapons. At the same time, an ongoing system can only survive if there is a general set of ideological (or theological) justifications. There must be various mechanisms which explain, justify, and propagate given systems of inequality and which cause people to accept as legitimate the fact of their own inequality. It is extremely doubtful, however, whether any such system of beliefs could lead the underprivileged to completely accept the propriety of their inferior status. Inherent in Aristotle's maxim that "man is a social animal" is the assumption that individuals seek to maximize the esteem, the respect, they receive from others. As Thorstein Veblen argues:

> Those members of the community who fall short of [a] somewhat indefinite normal degree of prowess or of property suffer in the esteem of their fellowmen; and consequently they suffer also in their own esteem. . . . Only individuals with an aberrant temperament can in the long run retain their self-esteem in the face of the disesteem of their fellows.[4]

If people seek to maximize their sense of personal respect, it follows that those who are in low-valued positions experience low status as punishment. To be in a negatively valued position means that one is no good, that one is bad. Consequently, it may be argued that there is an inherent tension between the need to maximize esteem and the requirements of a stable stratification system, which does not rest primarily on force.

Inherent Tensions

In actual stratification systems this tension may be alleviated by various transvaluational mechanisms. In many societies there seems to be a reverse stratification system, the most enduring form of which is usually found in religion. Inherent in many religions is the belief that wealth and power are identified with sin and evil, while virtue is associated with poverty. Christianity and

[2] Aristotle, *Politics*, trans. by Benjamin Jowett (New York: Modern Library, 1943), p. 30.
[3] Plato, *op. cit.*, pp. 108–123.
[4] Thorstein Veblen, *The Theory of the Leisure Class* (New York: Modern Library, 1934), p. 30.

Hinduism, for example, both posit that the righteous poor will ultimately be able to look down upon the wicked rich. This set of beliefs, which holds out the hope of subsequent reward for adhering to the morality of the present, does not of course challenge the earthly distribution of privilege. It does, however, reflect the inherent tension within stratified society: that there is both acceptance and rejection of the value system by the underprivileged.

Yet history also suggests that in all societies some people have challenged the secular order, have rejected their inferiority, and have dreamed of a more egalitarian social order. We have little knowledge concerning the reactions of the underprivileged laborers, peasants, and slaves to their position in antiquity, although there is a record of slave revolts and of political conflicts linked to class position. Some have argued that the persistence over many centuries of the caste system in India and the feudal system in Europe, both of which emphasized hereditary inequality and denied individual mobility, demonstrates that a social order based on sharp inequalities may be accepted by the deprived within it. The fact, however, that these systems persisted does not prove that the inferior strata were adjusted to their position. In India, Islam and Christianity won millions of converts precisely in those sections heavily populated by untouchables and lower castes. In feudal Europe, many peasants ran away to join so-called robber bands and revolted against the local manorial lords. The Robin Hood story, which has been repeated in many peasant societies, describes its hero as a "bringer of justice and social equity" who "takes from the rich and gives to the poor."[5] The French historian of the Middle Ages, Marc Bloch, asserts that "revolts were inseparable from a feudal regime." Egalitarian ideologies arose in different parts of Europe in the late Middle Ages. A Czech poem of the fourteenth century likened the lords to drones and threatened them with destruction.[6] Sir John Froissart's contemporary account of the Great English Peasant Revolt of 1381 points up the diffusion of egalitarian beliefs among the oppressed of that era:

> The lower . . . orders began to murmur, saying that in the beginning of the world there were no slaves, and that no one ought to be treated as such. . . . [They were] men formed after the same likeness as these lords who treated them as beasts. This they would bear no longer; they were determined to be free.[7]

Biblical references were often used to justify such beliefs. Thus a version of the poem "When Adam delf and Eve span/ Whare was then the pride of man?" or "Wo was thanne a gentilman?" was "commonplace in this or similar

---

[5] Eric Hobsbawm, *Bandits* (New York: Dell, 1971), pp. 34–37.

[6] Leopold Genicut, "Crisis from the Middle Ages to Modern Times," in M. M. Postan (ed.), *The Agrarian Life of the Middle Ages*, Vol. 1 of *The Cambridge Economic History of Europe* (Cambridge: The University Press, 1966), pp. 735–739.

[7] Sir John Froissart, *The Chronicles of England, France, and Spain* (New York: Dutton, 1961), p. 207.

forms" in different parts of Europe, from England to East Prussia.[8] Educated lower clergy helped supply the ideological justification. John Ball, a priest who played a leading role in the English peasant uprising in 1381, regularly preached in the marketplace in these terms:

> Matters cannot go well in England until all things shall be in common; when there shall be neither vassals nor lords. . . . Are we not all descended from the same parents, Adam and Eve? And what can they [the lords] show, or what reason can they give, why they should be more masters than ourselves? . . . It is by our labour they have wherewith to support their pomp.[9]

The prolonged existence of feudalism, therefore, may have been due not primarily to the stability of its social structure, as a system of accepted values and tradeoffs among different groups involved in a division of labor, but rather to the fact that isolated peasant rebels had no means of organizing a revolt over an extended territory.

Equality and Revolution

The two classic revolutions of the eighteenth century in America and France were both made in the name of equality. Although the revolutionists came largely from fairly privileged positions, and although by equality they initially meant recognition of their social, economic and political rights by the monarchical governments, they made possible the expansion of the goal to mean greater equality for all. Alexis de Tocqueville, the great student of the consequences of these revolutions, argued effectively that once the idea of equality came into the world it was irresistible, and that it would encourage people to seek to extend it. On an individual level, it led to a greater emphasis on equality of opportunity. Once the privileges of hereditary aristocracy have been defeated, "having shattered the bonds that once held them fixed, the notion of advancement suggests itself to every mind, the desire to rise swells in every heart and all men want to mount above their station." On the biological level, Tocqueville predicted, emphasis on "equality of condition" would in time sweep away "all the imaginary or the real barriers that have separated man from woman."[10]

Most important of all to Tocqueville, however, was the fact that people have a much greater passion for equality than for freedom and liberty. Relatively few can identify personal gains with a free society, but many see equality as giving them more. As he noted, there is a "passion for equality that incites men to wish all to be powerful and honored" and that "impels the weak to attempt to lower the powerful to their own level. . . ." Hence

[8] Rodney Hilton, *Bondmen Made Free* (New York: Viking Press, 1973), pp. 211–212.

[9] Froissart, *op. cit.,* pp. 207–208.

[10] Alexis de Tocqueville, *Democracy in America,* vol. 2 (New York: Vintage Books, 1960), pp. 216, 258.

for equality their passion is ardent, insatiable, incessant, invincible; they call for equality in freedom, and if they cannot obtain that, they still call for equality in slavery [under a dictatorship]. . . . All men and all powers seeking to cope with this irresistible passion will be overthrown and destroyed by it. In our age freedom cannot be established without it, and despotism itself cannot reign without its support.

Tocqueville went on to emphasize: "Remove the secondary causes that have produced the great convulsions of the world and you will almost always find the principle of inequality at the bottom."[11]

These prescient words, written well over a century ago, seem to speak to the political and social developments of the twentieth century, particularly in poorer nations. The banner of equality has been seized by extremist political movements in less developed countries with small middle classes, and the process has overwhelmed efforts to reform them in gradual, nondictatorial ways. The triumph of communism in Russia and China and the dedication of the ruling forces in most noncommunist third-world countries to some form of socialism testify to the validity of Tocqueville's anticipation. Even in the countries of the industrialized West, with large middle classes, the goal of equality tends to inform the politics of most political parties.

If inequality is difficult to defend on moral grounds, if the passion for equality is so strong, why are systems of stratification, of institutionalized hierarchies of power and reward, so prevalent? As we have seen, explanations, often linked to justifications, of inequality are at least as old as recorded efforts to explain social behavior. Thus Plato related inequality to the supposedly inherent aspects of the division of labor.

MODERN VIEWS OF STRATIFICATION

Functionalist Theory

The modern version of Plato's way of thinking is the so-called functionalist approach in modern sociology, which is associated with such theorists as Emile Durkheim, Kingsley Davis, Robert K. Merton, and Talcott Parsons. The functionalists assume that since modern society has a complex and highly differentiated system of roles that must be performed, different people must be motivated to perform different roles. They see people as social animals whose needs are not primarily physical and satiable but, rather, culturally determined and potentially unlimited. However, if all individuals had the same set of unlimited desires, no complex social structure would be possible. Consequently,

---

[11] *Ibid.*, Vol. 1, p. 56; Vol. 2, pp. 102–103. See also Irving Zeitlin, *Liberty, Equality, and Revolution in Alexis de Tocqueville* (Boston: Little, Brown, 1971), pp. 40–42.

some social or moral force must shape and limit these potentially unlimited desires. Society prescribes different goals for different individuals and groups, sets limits on these goals, and prescribes the means that may legitimately be used to attain them.

Functionalists see stratification as the mechanism through which society encourages individuals to seek to achieve the diverse positions necessary in a complex social system. The vast variety of positions that must be filled differ in their requirements for skill, education, intelligence, commitment to work, willingness to exercise power resources against others, and the like. Functionalist theory posits that in an unstratified society—that is, one in which rewards are relatively equal for all tasks—those positions which require more work, postponement of gratification, greater anxiety, and the like will not be filled by the most able people. The stratification system is perceived, therefore, as a motivational system; it is society's mechanism for encouraging the most able people to perform the most demanding roles in order to have the society operate efficiently.

The theory also suggests that status—honorific prestige—is the most general and persistent form of stratification, because what human beings as social animals require most to satisfy their ego needs is recognition from others. Beyond a certain point, economic rewards and power are valued not for themselves, but because they are symbolic indicators of high status. Hence the functionalist school assumes that stratification, or differential hierarchical reward, is an inherent aspect of complex society and that status as a source of motivation is an inherently scarce resource.

The emphasis in functional analysis on the need for hierarchical differentiation does not, of course, explain how different individuals are evaluated in the stratification system. Talcott Parsons has pointed to three sets of characteristics which are used as a basis of ranking. These are *possessions*, or those attributes which people own; *qualities*, which belong to individuals and include traits that are ascribed, such as race, lineage, and sex, as well as traits that are attributed as permanent characteristics, such as specific ability; and *performances*, or evaluations of the ways in which individuals have fulfilled their roles —in short, judgments about achievements. Societies, according to Parsons, vary considerably in the degree to which they emphasize possessions, qualities, or performances in locating people on the social hierarchy. Thus, ideally, a feudal social system would stress ascribed qualities, a captalist society would emphasize possessions, and a pure communist system would assign prestige according to performance. Parsons has stated that no actual society has ever come close to any of these three "ideal" models; each society has included elements of all three. However, the core ideal value in each society does influence the nature of the stratification system, patterns of mobility, and the like.[12]

[12] Talcott Parsons, "A Revised Analytical Approach to the Theory of Social Stratification," in his *Essays in Sociological Theory* (New York: Free Press, 1964), pp. 386–439.

Marxist Sociology

The principal alternative interpretation of stratification stems from the writings of the father of modern social-class analysis, Karl Marx, who was concerned with elaborating the conditions under which a genuine egalitarian society, communism, could occur. Marxian analysis differs from much contemporary sociology in that it does not stress esteem as the key motivating element; rather, it begins with the premise that the primary function of a social organization is the satisfaction of basic human needs—food, clothing, and shelter. Stratification is the inevitable outcome of systems of production which cannot eliminate the problem of scarcity, which cannot produce enough to satisfy the basic needs of all. In such scarcity systems an equal distribution would leave all feeling somewhat deprived; it is inevitable that those in more commanding positions insist on receiving a disproportionate share of the goods of the society, and that the various elements of society are organized to sustain inequality. Further, once the society has gone beyond the stage of primitive subsistence economy, it requires a division of labor, which implies a sharp differentiation in levels of skill and knowledge and produces even sharper stratification.

From the Marxist perspective, the key prerequisite of a successful egalitarian society is an extremely high level of material abundance, one which permits a social system to eliminate the hierarchically organized division of labor and to give to all, regardless of variation in abilities, an equal share of material goods. Although Marx himself refrained from prescribing the way in which a communist society would operate, it seems clear from reading one of his few descriptions of such a system that it would be one in which physical work would no longer be required. In such an advanced technological society machines would do almost all the physical work, and people would be free to engage in creative intellectual and leisure tasks as they saw fit. In his book *The German Ideology*, Marx stated:

> . . . In a communist society, where nobody has one exclusive sphere of activity but each can become accomplished in any branch he wishes, society regulates the general production and thus makes it possible for me to do one thing today and another tomorrow, to hunt in the morning, fish in the afternoon, rear cattle in the evening, criticize after dinner, just as I have a mind.[13]

Clearly, Marx envisaged the complete end of the division of labor as a prerequisite for equality. As he noted in the third volume of *Capital:* "The realm of freedom only begins in fact, where that labor which is determined by need and external purposes ceases; it is therefore, by its very nature, outside the sphere of material production proper."[14]

Any effort to move toward socialism or communism, therefore, can occur

[13] Karl Marx and Friedrich Engels, *The German Ideology* (New York: International Publishers, 1947), p. 22.

[14] Cited in Joachim Israel, *Alienation from Marx to Modern Sociology* (Boston: Allyn and Bacon, 1971), p. 25.

only in a very highly developed technological society. Marx saw capitalism as preparing the way for such developments by raising levels of productivity to previously unimagined heights. But until the division of labor is eliminated, any society, whether it is based on private or public ownership of property, requires inequality in reward and in authority or power relations.

In discussing authority relationships, Friedrich Engels, Marx's closest collaborator, insisted on the need for hierarchical authority even after an anticapitalist social revolution had made "the land and the instruments of labor . . . the collective property of the workers who use them." As he noted, even under socialism the need for the division of labor meant that over the doors of all factories should be written *"Lasciate ogni autonomia voi che entrate"* (Leave, you that enter here, all autonomy behind):

> The automatic machinery of a big factory is much more despotic than the small capitalists who employ workers ever have been. . . . If man, by dint of his knowledge and inventive genius, has subdued the forces of nature, the latter avenge themselves upon him by subjecting him, in so far as he employs them, to a veritable despotism, independent of all social organization. Wanting to abolish authority in large-scale industry is tantamount to wanting to abolish industry itself, to destroy the power loom in order to return to the spinning wheel. . . .
>
> We have seen that, on the one hand, a certain authority, no matter how delegated, and on the other hand, a certain subordination are things which, independent of all social organization, are imposed upon us together with the material conditions under which we produce and make products circulate.
>
> We have seen, besides, that the material conditions of production and circulation inevitably develop with large-scale industry and large-scale agriculture, and increasingly tend to enlarge the scope of this authority.[15]

In seeking to explain the reemergence of a sharply stratified society in the Soviet Union, Leon Trotsky pointed out that Marx had anticipated the failure of efforts to create socialism, except under conditions of extremely high levels of productivity. He quoted Marx to the effect that "a development of the productive forces is the absolutely necessary premise [of socialism], because without it want is generalized, and with want the struggle for necessities begins again, and that means that all the old crap must revive."[16]

Thus, although functionalist sociologists and Marxists disagree as to the source of inequality, both agree that inequality is linked to the necessity for a division of labor in society. The Marxists are more optimistic than the functionalists as to the prospects for sharply reducing or eliminating hierarchical differentiation. While Marx stressed that stratification is ultimately the result of economic scarcity, functionalists emphasize that honor and prestige are inherently permanently scarce: Economic goods may increase, and everyone can

[15] Friedrich Engels, "On Authority," in Karl Marx and Friedrich Engels, *Basic Writings in Politics and Philosophy,* ed. by Lewis S. Feuer (Garden City, N.Y.: Doubleday-Anchor Books, 1959), pp. 482–484.

[16] Leon Trotsky, *The Revolution Betrayed* (Garden City, N.Y.: Doubleday, 1937), p. 56.

gain in an absolute sense; but since prestige is determined by *relative* ranking, if an individual or group goes up another must go down. Thus an open society with equal opportunity, unrestricted social mobility, will occasion great frustration and consequent social tensions.

Marxist critics of functionalism have argued that the great spread in income and status in modern industrial society reflects the greater power of the privileged strata rather than the need to motivate people to seek those positions which require greater ability and skill. A Polish Marxist sociologist, Wlodimierz Wesolowski, following the lead of Engels, agrees with the functionalists that complex social systems will continue to be organized on hierarchical lines, because systems of authority and command are necessary. He notes that "it would be impossible to think of any modern industrial enterprise or of the organization of the future communist society without authority- or superiority-subordination relationships."[17]

In arguing that the universality of stratification is linked to the requirements for a power hierarchy in complex society, Wesolowski has built a bridge between Marxist and functionalist sociology. For his and Engels' line of reasoning ultimately is not greatly different from that presented by the major contemporary figure in functionalist sociology, Talcott Parsons. The latter has suggested that power is inherent in the need for a division of labor and in the existence of authority roles. Holders of these authority roles are obligated to initiate acts that are socially necessary. The more complex the system, the more dependent individuals are on others for the attainment of their goals—that is, the less free or powerful they are. And power is basically control over the allocation of resources and roles which make a given system operative. Power, under any system of values, resides in having what people desire, because they will obey for the sake of getting what they want. It follows that those who possess the qualities which place them at the upper levels of the economic and status hierarchies also have the most power in modern industrial society. Money and influence, as Parsons has noted, are exchangeable for power, since power is the ability to mobilize resources through controlling the actions of others.[18]

Ideological Bases of Equality

Modern sociological analysis of social stratification in Western and communist societies has been primarily concerned with evaluating the extent to which these societies tend to reduce the inherent pressures for inequality. As noted earlier, the passion for equality, emphasized by Tocqueville and others, has led

[17] Wlodimierz Wesolowski, "Some Notes on the Functional Theory of Stratification," in Reinhard Bendix and S. M. Lipset (eds.), *Class, Status, and Power* (New York: Free Press, 1966), p. 68.
[18] Talcott Parsons, "On the Concept of Political Power," in Bendix and Lipset, *op. cit.*, pp. 92–128.

to a widespread acceptance of the objective of greater equality of reward and status. No political party today defends the propriety of aristocratic claims to the right to govern or receive respect because of ancestry. In all industrial societies access to education on all levels has been steadily widened to permit increasing numbers of those from lowly origins to gain the skills and the credentials necessary to compete for high positions. Although economic rewards remain highly differentiated, the commitment to greater equality is reflected in so-called progressive or graduated income and inheritance taxes, which are supposed to reduce differences in income and wealth. The growth of the welfare state, involving measures such as health insurance, old-age pensions, unemployment insurance, and public housing, is designed to lift the bottom, to "transfer" income from the more affluent segments of society to the poorer ones. To what extent have such commitments and the development of increased levels of production led to greater equality? This is a general question that social scientists have attempted to answer empirically. To deal with this issue, we will examine some of the evidence, primarily with respect to the two most powerful nations, the United States and the Soviet Union.

Both societies are committed to an egalitarian social order through their predominant political ideology, the American creed—the basic values of American society laid down in the Declaration of Independence—and Marxism. Some have even argued that, property relations apart, both idealize the same social objectives—that is, they define the good society in similar terms. A socialist writer, Leon Samson, has argued:

> Every concept in socialism has its substitutive conterconcept in Americanism, and that is why the socialist argument falls so fruitlessly on the American ear. . . . It is this socialist fantasy [of an egalitarian society] in the mind of the American that acts as an anticlimax to the socialist agitation. The American does not want to listen to socialism, since he thinks he already has what it purports to offer.[19]

Ideological egalitarianism has taken on a similar meaning in both the United States and the Soviet Union, and this similarity is not any less important because it has been contradicted by the existence of economic and status differences in both. The doctrine of egalitarianism insists that these are the accidental, not the essential, attributes of people. It enables people of humble birth to regard upward mobility as attainable for themselves, or for their children. It facilitates their acceptance as social equals if they succeed in rising economically. It mitigates the emotional distance between persons of different rank. And it fosters in elites the persuasion (however mistaken this may be) that their eminence is the result of individual effort, and hence temporary. As David Potter has stressed: "The American ideal and practice of

[19] See Leon Samson, "Americanism as Surrogate Socialism," in John Laslett and S. M. Lipset (eds.), *Failure of a Dream? Essays in the History of American Socialism* (Garden City, N.Y.: Doubleday-Anchor Books, 1974), pp. 426–442.

equality . . . has implied for the individual . . . opportunity to make his own place in society . . . [and] emancipation from a system of fixed status."[20]

A leading Polish sociologist, Stanislaw Ossowski, has noted that the "American conception combining classlessness with the maintenance of great differences in . . . income, which is contained in a certain version of the American Creed, is by no means alien to the Soviet Union and the People's Democracies in relation to their own societies." He goes on to note:

> The Socialist principle "to each according to his merits" is in harmony with the tenets of the American Creed, which holds that each man is the master of his fate, and that a man's status is fixed by an order of merit. The Socialist principle allows of the conclusion that there are unlimited opportunities for social advancement and social demotion; this is similar to the American concept of "vertical social mobility." The arguments directed against *uravnilovka* [equalization or leveling of wages] coincide with the arguments put forward on the other side of the Atlantic by those who justify the necessity of economic inequalities in a democratic society. "The maximisation of effort in an achievement-oriented society calls for considerable inequality"—wrote [the American sociologist J. J.] Spenger in 1953. This sentence could equally well have been uttered by a statesman in the Soviet Union or the People's Democracies.[21]

To what extent do these two societies live up to their commitment to equality of opportunity?

EQUALITY AND INEQUALITY IN THE UNITED STATES

Social Mobility

Many European commentators seeking to explain the relative absence of radical class-consciousness among the lower strata in the United States have suggested that America, as a new-frontier society without an aristocratic past, was much more "open" than European societies and hence had much higher rates of social mobility. Writing in the 1850s about the United States, Karl Marx asserted: "Though classes, indeed, already exist, they have not become fixed, but continually change and interchange their elements in a constant state of flux."[22] Fifty years later, in trying to answer the question "Why is there no socialism in the United States?", a German sociologist, Werner Sombart, stressed "the chances of the worker rising out of his class," contending that the American system "not infrequently operated to allow the ordinary worker to climb up the ladder of capitalism to the top, or almost to the top. The much

[20] David M. Potter, *People of Plenty* (Chicago: University of Chicago Press, 1954), p. 91.
[21] Stanislaw Ossowski, *Class Structure in the Social Consciousness* (New York: Free Press 1963), p. 114.
[22] Karl Marx, *The Eighteenth Brumaire of Louis Bonaparte* (New York: International Publishers, 1963), p. 25.

greater extent of their savings . . . enabled still other workers to become inde-pendent as *petits bourgeois*, i.e., shopkeepers, saloonkeepers, etc."[23]

Mobility patterns   If socialism was weak in nineteenth-century America because of the opportunity system of the society, many assumed that increasing "rigidification" would occur with the increase in large-scale factories and the need for more factory workers. The growth of monopoly capitalism and power-ful corporations and the decline in the importance of small independently owned businesses would also sharply reduce chances for upward mobility. But a number of analyses of the pattern of opportunity in American society clearly indicate that there has been no decline in social mobility; in fact, in some re-spects American society today is less rigid in terms of social advancement than it was in the past. A *Scientific American* survey of the backgrounds of big-business executives (presidents, chairmen, and principal vice-presidents of the 600 largest U.S. nonfinancial corporations) found that as of 1964 the business elite had been opened to entry from below in a way that had never been true before in American history. Since this study has never been widely dissemi-nated, it may be worthwhile to reproduce some of its findings here:

> Only 10.5 percent of the current generation of big business executives . . . are sons of wealthy families; as recently as 1950 the corresponding figure was 36.1 percent, and at the turn of the century, 45.6 percent. . . . Two-thirds of the 1900 genera-tion had fathers who were heads of the same corporation or who were independ-ent businessmen; less than half of the current generation had fathers so placed in American society. On the other hand, less than 10 percent of the 1900 genera-tion had fathers who were employees; by 1964 this percentage had increased to nearly 30 percent.[24]

Surprisingly both to scholars in the field and to those radicals convinced that a mature capitalism would become increasingly immobile, particularly with respect to sharp jumps into the elite, the evidence indicates that the post-World War II period brought the greatest increase in the percentage of those from economically "poor" backgrounds who entered the top echelons of American business (the proportion rose from 12.1 percent in 1950 to 23.3 per-cent in 1964). There was a correspondingly great decline in the percentage from wealthy families (from 36.1 percent in 1950 to 10.5 percent in 1964). A number of the underlying structural trends that were expected to limit mobility appear to be responsible for this development: the replacement of the family-owned

[23] Werner Sombart, "American Capitalism's Economic Rewards," in Laslett and Lipset, *op. cit.*, p. 605.
[24] See *The Big Business Executive 1964: A Study of His Social and Educational Back-ground*, a study sponsored by *Scientific American*, conducted by Market Statistics, Inc., of New York City, in collaboration with Dr. Mabel Newcomer. The study was designed to up-date Mabel Newcomer, *The Big Business Executive—The Factors That Made Him: 1900–1950* (New York: Columbia University Press, 1950). All comparisons in it are with ma-terials in Dr. Newcomer's published work.

enterprise by the public corporation; the bureaucratization of American corporate life; the recruitment of management personnel from the ranks of college
graduates; and the awarding of higher posts on the basis of a competitive-
promotion process similar to that which operates in government bureaucracy.
Because of the spread of higher education to the children of the working
classes (almost one-third of whom now attend college), the ladder of bureaucratic success is increasingly open to those from poorer circumstances. Privileged family and class backgrounds continue to be enormous advantages in the
quest for corporate success, but training and talent can make up for them in an
increasing number of cases. These findings, drawn from observations of the
backgrounds of the big-business elite, are reinforced by national surveys which
indicate that opportunities "to enter high-status occupations appear to have
improved in successive cohorts of U.S. men for at least the last 40 years, irrespective of those men's occupational origins."[25]

Other, more broadly focused studies provide further evidence that there
has been no hardening of class lines in American society. According to Stephan
Thernstrom (who has played the leading role among historians both in doing
research and in stimulating work on the part of others), there has been a
continuation of a high rate of social mobility over a 90-year period. In Boston,
which Thernstrom studied in detail, there was "impressive consistency" in
career patterns between 1880 and 1968: "About a quarter of all the men who
first entered the labor market as manual workers ended their careers in a middle-class calling; approximately one in six of those who first worked in a white-
collar job later skidded to a blue-collar post." Patterns almost identical to
Boston's have been reported in a "dozen samples [from various cities] for the
period from 1850 to World War I"; about 30 to 35 percent of those from working-class backgrounds moved into middle-class positions in various surveys.
Rates of downward mobility also did not vary a great deal; the large majority
of those from middle-class backgrounds (between 70 and 80 percent) maintained middle-class status.[26]

Thernstrom notes that these findings challenge the often voiced belief that
changes in American capitalism have created a permanent and growing class
of the poor. In fact, all the available evidence points in the opposite direction.
Statistical data from Poughkeepsie, New York in the 1840s, Boston in five different samples from the 1880s to recent years, and Indianapolis in 1910, as
well as from various surveys local and national after World War II, indicate
that most of the sons of unskilled workers either moved up into the ranks of
the skilled or found middle-class jobs of various kinds.

Family occupational status and mobility   These conclusions are reinforced
by the most comprehensive and methodologically sophisticated national sample

---

[25] Robert M. Hauser et al., "Temporal Change in Occupational Mobility: Evidence for
Men in the United States," *American Sociological Review*, Vol. 40 (June 1975), p. 280. The
authors cite a number of studies to this effect.

[26] Stephan Thernstrom, *The Other Bostonians: Poverty and Progress in the American Metropolis, 1880–1970* (Cambridge, Mass.: Harvard University Press, 1973).

survey of the American population, that of Blau and Duncan in 1962. Analyzing the mobility patterns of American families over several generations by relating family occupational background to first job (thus permitting a comparison of the very young still on their first job with the experience of the very old when they were young), they found that "the influence of social origins has remained constant since World War I. There is absolutely no evidence of 'rigidification.' "[27]

A recent effort by a group of sociologists at the University of Wisconsin to update the Blau-Duncan research reports similar findings. And an examination of the results of a number of surveys taken up to 1972 suggests that "the dependence of sons on father's occupation has been remarkably stable for more than half a century."[28] In evaluating the social implications of these findings, it should be noted that they were obtained by holding changes over time in the occupational structure constant. Since the proportion of higher-status, higher-paying positions requiring more education and skill has been increasing steadily, there has in fact been an increase in the proportions of those securing a more rewarded position than their fathers. Hence, though relative opportunity has not increased, the absolute levels have, and this may affect the popular feeling about opportunity.

Speaking more generally to the issue of equality of opportunity, another set of studies by a group of Harvard sociologists and economists, led by Christopher Jencks, reanalyzed the data from a number of sources, seeking to specify the factors involved in occupational choice and earning capacity. These scholars, many of whom happen to be socialists politically, found that the results contradicted their anticipations:

> Poverty is not primarily hereditary. While children born into poverty have a higher-than-average chance of ending up poor, there is still an enormous amount of economic mobility from one generation to the next. Indeed, there is nearly as much economic inequality among brothers raised in the same homes as in the general population. This means that inequality is recreated anew in each generation, even among people who start life in essentially identical circumstances.

These researchers came to these conclusions by comparing the occupational status scores on the "Duncan scale" (which ranks occupations from 96 points to 0) of fathers and sons and of brothers with a random sample of unrelated individuals. They found that randomly selected individuals differed in occupational status by an average of 28 points, while brothers differed from each other by 23 points, and fathers from sons by 20 points. As they note, "there is nearly as much variation in status between brothers as in the larger population. Family background is not, then, the primary determinant of status." These findings imply that

[27] Peter Blau and Otis Dudley Duncan, *The American Occupational Structure* (New York: Wiley, 1967), p. 107.
[28] Hauser et al., *op cit.*, p. 280.

brothers raised in the same home end up with very different standards of living. In 1968, for example, if we had compared random pairs of individuals, we would have found that their earnings differed by an average of about $6,200. If we had had data on brothers, our best guess is that they would have differed by at least $5,600. . . . When people have had relatively equal opportunity, as brothers usually have, they still end up with very unequal incomes.[29]

These results, of course, do not mean that a father's status has no effect on the occupational achievements of his offspring. Rather, as Jencks and his collaborators note:

[The] role of a father's family background in determining his sons' status is surprisingly small, at least compared to most people's preconception. The correlation [indicator of association] between a father's occupational status and his sons' is less than 0.50. If two fathers' statuses differ by, say 20 points [on the Duncan scale], their sons' statuses will differ by an average of 10 points.

But if fathers do have "some" effect on the occupations of their sons, a more recent analysis by Jencks of relationships over three generations indicates that

paternal grandfathers have little or no direct effect on their grandsons' life chances. Whether the father inherited his status, climbed up to it, or slid down to it seems to make little difference to the son's life chances. . . . The longer we make our time horizon, the more equal opportunity looks.[30]

Ethnicity and Race

The analysis of rates of opportunity is far from the whole story with respect to the underlying pattern of opportunity over time. It is important to recognize that in America occupational position has been differentially distributed among sex, ethnic, and racial groups. For much of its history the United States has been divided between "majority" and "minority" ethnic groups. The latter have, in effect, repeatedly provided new sets of recruits for the low-paid, low-status positions, thus enabling others of less recent settlement to rise. An analysis of census data by E. P. Hutchinson shows that in 1870 and in 1880 "the foreign-born were most typically employed in the factories, in heavy industry, as manual laborers and domestic servants. Clerical, managerial, and official positions remained largely inaccessible to them." The 1890 Census gathered information for the first time on the occupations of the native-born children of immigrants, thus permitting a comparison of the two generations. As Hutchinson shows, occupational status varied considerably:

[29] Christopher Jencks et al., *Inequality: A Reassessment of the Effect of Family and Schooling in America* (New York: Basic Books, 1972), pp. 7–8, 179, 219–220.

[30] Christopher Jencks, "The Effects of Grandparents on Their Grandchildren" (Unpublished Paper, Cambridge, Mass., Department of Sociology, Harvard University, January 30, 1975), pp. 15, 17.

Unlike the immigrant males who were in highest proportion among domestic and personal service workers, the second generation males were most numerous relatively among workers in trade and in transportation and manufacturing. It is also notable that those in the second generation were more successful in entering the professions, even though not as successful as members of the native stock (the native-born of native parents). . . . Altogether, the second generation conformed more closely to the occupational distribution of the entire white labor force than did the foreign-born.[31]

This pattern, in which the second generation was, as a group, in a much better position than the immigrant generation, continued for the duration of mass immigration. Thus Hutchinson reports that in 1900 "the foreign-born were no more widely distributed by occupation . . . than in 1890, but that the second generation became more widely distributed and moved closer to the occupational distribution of the entire labor force in 1900." After 1910 the census was not as comprehensive in gathering comparable occupational data, but the evidence clearly indicates patterns comparable to those summarized above for the remaining period of mass immigration through 1924.

The most recent study of the relative position of different ethnic groups in the United States, one based on the analysis of 12 national opinion surveys conducted by the National Opinion Research Center of the University of Chicago between 1963 and 1974, indicates that among the non-Spanish heritage white population, those of non-Anglo-Saxon non-Protestant background have overcome and surpassed scions of those ethno-religious stocks who were here before them. Andrew Greeley summarizes his findings as follows:

> The most wealthy Americans are Jews, with an annual income of $13,340. Irish Catholics are in second place, some $900 behind the Jews, and Italian Catholics are third, a little less than $700 behind the Irish Catholics. German Catholics, Polish Catholics take fourth and fifth place, and Episcopalians and Presbyterians only then find sixth and seventh place on the income ladder. . . . At the bottom of the economic heap are the Scandinavian Protestants ($9,597), the American Protestants ($9,274), Irish Protestants ($9,147), and Baptists ($8,693). . . . In the American economic game, then, whether nationally or in northern cities, Jews, the Irish, German and Italian Catholics are the big winners, and the Baptists, the Irish and "American" Protestants seem to be the big losers.

In seeking to explain why the members of the more recent immigrant groups have done better economically than the descendants of old-stock Protestants, Greeley suggests that a phenomenon of "overthrust" or "overcompensation" is at work. The members of a less privileged, lower status group "that 'makes it' in American society does so with such tremendous energy and such tremendous 'need for achievement,' that they not only do as well as everyone else, but better because of the sheer, raw power of their elemental drive for respectability and success." Greeley goes on to ask, "May it be that in another

[31] E. P. Hutchinson, *Immigrants and Their Children* (New York: Wiley, 1965), pp. 114, 138–139, 171.

generation or two, the effect may wear off, and the Catholic and Protestant and Jewish ethnic groups will have relatively similar levels of achievement—while the blacks and the Spanish-speaking profit from the 'overthrust' phenomenon."[32]

It must be noted, however, that these still underprivileged groups—blacks, Puerto Ricans, Mexicans, and to a small extent French Canadians—have furnished the bulk of the less skilled labor force in post–World War II America. As an analysis of mobility processes in the late 1950s put it:

> Now, as before, there is a close relationship between low income and membership in segregated groups. A large proportion of seasonal farm laborers and sharecroppers in the South and Southwest come from them. In the cities, Negroes, Mexicans, and Puerto Ricans predominate in the unskilled, dirty, and badly paid occupations. These twenty million people earn a disproportionately low share of the national income; they have little political power and no social prestige; they live in ethnic ghettoes, in rural and urban areas alike, and they have little social contact with white Americans. Indeed, today there are two working classes in America, a white one and a Negro, Mexican, and Puerto Rican one. A real social and economic cleavage is created by widespread discrimination against these minority groups, and this diminishes the chances for the development of solidarity along class lines. In effect, the overwhelming majority of whites, both in the working class and in the middle and upper classes, benefit economically and socially from the existence of these "lower classes" within their midst. This continued splintering of the working class is a major element in the preservation of the stability of the class structure.[33]

The assumptions made in that analysis about the differences between the situations of initially underprivileged whites and blacks were given a more elaborate statistical confirmation in the largest study of American social mobility, that of Blau and Duncan in 1962. These authors found that low social origin *had little negative effect on the chances of whites—including the children of white immigrants—to advance economically.* The mobility picture for whites is such that Blau and Duncan reject the notion that a "vicious cycle" perpetuates inequality "for the population at large."

The black minority But if whites, including working-class whites, experienced a fluid occupational class system in which the able and ambitious could rise, the reverse was true for blacks. As Blau and Duncan's 1962 data indicate:

> Negroes are handicapped at every step in their attempts to achieve economic success, and these cumulative disadvantages are what produces the great inequalities

---

[32] Andrew M. Greeley, "Ethnicity, Denomination and Inequality," (unpublished paper, Center for the Study of American Pluralism National Opinion Research Center, Chicago, Illinois, 1975), pp. 44–45, 51–52. Similar empirical findings from other surveys are reported in F. Thomas Juster (ed.), *Education, Income, and Human Behavior* (New York: McGraw-Hill, 1974).

[33] S. M. Lipset and Reinhard Bendix, *Social Mobility in Industrial Society* (Berkeley: University of California Press, 1959), pp. 105–106.

of opportunities under which the Negro American suffers. . . . The multiple handicaps associated with being an American Negro are cumulative in their deleterious consequences for a man's career.

Education, which we have seen opens all sorts of doors for whites, even many of quite low social origin, has not worked in the same way for blacks:

> The difference in occupational status between Negroes and whites is twice as great for men who have graduated from high school or gone to college as for those who have completed no more than eight years of schooling. In short, the careers of well-educated Negroes lag even further behind those of comparable whites than do the careers of poorly educated Negroes. . . . Negroes, as an underprivileged group, must make greater sacrifices to remain in school, but they have less incentive than whites to make these sacrifices, which may well be a major reason why Negroes often exhibit little motivation to continue in school and advance their education.[34]

The Blau-Duncan conclusions were sustained by a reanalysis of the same data by Jencks and his associates, following a different methodological approach. Comparing blacks and whites whose fathers had the same occupations, who had attained the same level of education, and who came from similar sized families, Jencks found that blacks ended up on the average in occupations 19 points below the comparable white average (on the Duncan scale). The racial differences persisted with respect to income even among "blacks who not only had the same amount of education as the average white, but also entered an occupation of the same status as the average white," since they received "incomes 63 percent of the white mean."[35]

But during the late 1960s the situation seemingly changed sharply for the better, particularly for younger and better educated blacks. An important factor in the improvement was the passage and subsequent enforcement of the 1964 Civil Rights Act as a result of mass pressure from blacks and others. In this new political context the impressive gains which blacks had been making in education enabled many of them to press on the higher levels of the occupational system. If median school years are used as an indicator of formal educational attainment, by 1970 young blacks had come very close to parity with whites. By 1974, according to a U.S. Census Bureau report, the percentage of blacks entering college, 12.3, was *higher* than their proportion in the total population, 11.4. Black men in the professions formed 6.6 percent of all males, increased from 3.6 in 1962. Black women were 10 percent of the female professionals, up from 7 in 1962.[36] A summary by Richard Freeman for the Brookings Institution points up the substantial changes in the labor market position of blacks in the past decade:

[34] Blau and Duncan, *op. cit.*, pp. 199–205, 404–406.
[35] Jencks et al., *op. cit.*, pp. 190–191, 217–218.
[36] Stuart H. Garfinkle, "Occupation of Women and Black Workers, 1962–74," *Monthly Labor Review*, Vol. 98 (November 1975), p. 29.

The evidence that the labor market position of blacks underwent an unprecedented improvement in the 1960's is substantial and growing. . . . In some markets, such as that for female workers or young college graduates, discriminating differentials have effectively disappeared. In others, positions that were rarely filled by blacks, ranging from professional and managerial jobs in corporations to construction crafts to police and public employment beyond the laborer's level in the South, were effectively opened for the first time in history. On the other hand, certain important segments of the black labor force, notably older men who had missed out on the training, experience, and position on the seniority

ladders as a result of past discrimination, experienced much more modest rates
of relative economic advance. . . . In contrast to previous studies of the importance of education on income by race, the evidence for the late 1960's revealed
a marked convergence in the returns to black and white male investments in schooling or in the impact of education on earnings, especially among the young.[37]

[37] Richard B. Freeman, "Changes in Job Market Discrimination and Black Economic
Well-Being" (Paper delivered at Notre Dame Civil Rights Conference, South Bend, Ind., on
April 15–17, 1975), pp. 7–8.

Similar conclusions were reached by University of Wisconsin economist Stanley Masters, who independently analyzed the relative income positions of blacks and whites for the years 1948 to 1971. His results indicate that

> the trend [of reduced differentials] has significantly increased since 1964, thus supporting the liberal view that there should be a continuous improvement in the relative position of blacks once some precipitous event like the Civil Rights Act and the pressures that led to it have occurred. . . . The figures by years of school indicate that blacks have improved their relative position at all schooling levels, although blacks with the most schooling have made the greatest gains.[38]

These changes, which resulted from a combination of improvements in the education of young blacks and a variety of political and judicial actions, have not of course made up for the deficiencies imposed by past discrimination, particularly among older people. Because of the relatively recent entrance of blacks into many companies which follow a "last-in/first-out layoff policy, the position of black workers was far more sensitive to the business cycle than that of white workers."[39] Further, a much larger proportion of blacks than whites enter the labor market with major handicaps, derived from having been reared in poverty-stricken and/or broken homes.

The persistently inferior economic position of the black community as a whole shows up particularly with respect to family incomes. As of 1973 the ratio of black to white median family income was still only .58. A major reason for this discrepancy according to a 1975 U.S. Census Bureau report is that 35 percent of all black families are headed by women, as contrasted with 9.9 percent among whites. In both racial groups female-headed families have much lower incomes than those with an adult male present. Thus the ratio of median income difference between the two races among male-headed families in 1973 was .72. Further, major improvements in the ratio of black to white income have been recorded primarily for men under 35, not for older persons:

> The common thread running through each of the problem areas—family income and composition, the burden of poor backgrounds, and the lack of sharp progress among older black male workers—is that simply ending job market discrimination and guaranteeing equal employment opportunity will not achieve black/white parity in the foreseeable future.

Despite the considerable progress of certain segments of the black community, whites are still enormously advantaged by the presence of a racial minority which (together with other minority groups) handles a heavily disproportionate share of the less rewarded jobs and status positions.

It is important to recognize that the considerable progress made by

---

[38] Stanley H. Masters, *Black-White Income Differentials* (New York: Academic Press, 1975), pp. 143–145.

[39] Freeman, *op. cit.*, p. 13.

younger and better-educated blacks in the last decade did not happen as a result of the "natural" operation of sociological and economic factors, as had occurred earlier with various white ethnic groups. In the case of blacks, discrimination had to be countered by political forces. Economic analysis has demonstrated a close relationship between black progress and

> an index of anti-bias activity, E.E.O.C. [Equal Employment Opportunity Commission] spending per non-white worker. . . . Data on individual companies also suggest that governmental activities were effective, with companies facing, all else the same, greater federal pressure, increasing their employment of blacks. Qualitative evidence on company personnel practices also ties the changes to governmental action.[40]

Spanish-speaking minorities   The 10 million Americans of Spanish-speaking origin, the majority of whom were born in Mexico or Puerto Rico or had parents born in these societies, also tend to be lowly placed in the economic structure and to face discrimination. Thus 20 percent of all families of Spanish origin "had incomes below the low-income threshold of the Federal government in 1969, compared to 10 percent of white families and 30 percent of black families." The median income of the Spanish-speaking families in 1971 was $7,500, "about $3,100 below that of all white families."[41] As in the case of blacks, low income was disproportionately concentrated among female-headed families, which constituted over 17 percent of all Spanish-speaking families, almost twice the proportion among the dominant population. About half of the Spanish-origin families with low incomes in 1974 were headed by women. The educational level of Americans of Spanish origin is also significantly below that of the dominant population: As of March, 1974 only 54 percent had completed high school, as compared to 80 percent among the dominant group. Not surprisingly, the Spanish-origin population

> lagged behind the total population in the proportion holding relatively high-paying jobs. For example, about 15 percent of all persons in the United States were working in professional or kindred occupations; but only about half of that proportion, 7 percent of employed persons of Spanish origin, were in those occupations.[42]

It is difficult to estimate how much of the low economic position of persons of Spanish origin results from discrimination and how much results from a lack of qualifications flowing from the recency of their settlement in the continental United States. Some evidence that discrimination is important may be reflected in the "finding that the presence in a city of substantial employment in Federal

[40] *Ibid.*, pp. 14, 28.
[41] Paul M. Ryscavage and Earl F. Mellor, "The Economic Situation of Spanish Americans," *Monthly Labor Review*, Vol. 96 (April 1973), p. 4.
[42] U.S. Bureau of the Census, "Persons of Spanish Origin in the United States: March 1974," *Current Population Reports: Population Characteristics*, Series P-20, No. 280 (Washington, D.C.: Government Printing Office, 1975), pp. 3–8.

agencies generated a constructive spin-off in terms of better jobs for Hispanic workers." And if we compare the incomes of white male Americans 25 years or older who completed four or more years of college with those of comparably educated Spanish-origin persons and blacks, there is a clear advantage for the dominant population. The latter had a median annual income in 1973 of $14,908, as contrasted to $11,939 for those of Spanish origin and $11,294 for blacks. It seems clear therefore that, as in the case of blacks, government action "designed to generate changes in corporate policies" is needed to eliminate discriminatory processes.[43]

Sex Stratification

The contribution of minorities to the higher occupational status of those belonging to "dominant" social groups is not limited to racial and ethnic factors. Women have disproportionately filled the lower-paid, lower-status, and less interesting jobs in American and other societies. And over the years, as the nonmanual white-collar and service sectors of the occupational structure have expanded, women have filled the bulk of the low-status positions (e.g., clerical workers, telephone operators, and secretaries). By so doing, women have enabled men, often their fathers, husbands, and sons, to secure better positions.

This contribution is not a minor one. In 1974 almost 50 percent of all American women between 16 and 65 years old were in the labor force, as contrasted to 18 percent in 1890 and 25 percent in 1940. Among industrially developed countries only Finland and the Soviet Union had a higher rate. Women's participation has been growing steadily, but they are still disproportionately in the rapidly growing white-collar proletariat sector. "In 1940 women made up 40.1 percent of service workers; in 1968, 57 percent; in 1940 women were 52.6 percent of clerical workers and 27.9 percent of sales workers; in 1968 the percentages of women in the same categories were 72.6 percent and 39.7 percent respectively." In the latter year 56 percent of all working women held jobs as clerical and sales, service and household workers, as contrasted to 21 percent of employed males.[44]

Within higher-level professions, even those like elementary school teaching and librarianships, which have been primarily women's occupations, men have tended to hold the higher, better-paid positions. Thus in 1968 only 22 percent of all elementary school principals were women, though they constituted 88

[43] Jerolyn R. Lyle, "Factors Affecting the Job Status of Workers with Spanish Surnames," *Monthly Labor Review*, Vol. 96 (April 1973), p. 14; U.S. Bureau of the Census, "Money Income in 1973 of Families and Persons in the United States," *Current Population Reports: Consumer Income*, Series P-60, No. 97 (Washington, D.C.: Government Printing Office, 1975), p. 125, and "Persons of Spanish Origin," *op. cit.*, p. 40; Lyle, *op. cit.*, p. 14.

[44] Marjorie Galenson, *Women and Work: An International Comparison* (Ithaca, N.Y:. School of Industrial and Labor Relations, Cornell University, 1973), pp. 15–19; Kirsten Amundsen, *The Silenced Majority* (Englewood Cliffs, N.J.: Prentice-Hall, 1971), p. 54; Marijean Suelzle, "Women in Labor," in M. E. Adelstein and J. G. Pival (eds.), *Women's Liberation* (New York: St. Martin's Press, 1972), p. 115.

percent of the teaching force. Similar patterns of male dominance existed among librarians, an occupation which is 90 percent female.[45]

Data from various government reports and special studies clearly indicate that on the average women, like blacks, have been employed in lower positions than men of similar educational attainments, and that within the same occupational classifications they have been paid less. Thus, according to the U.S. Census Bureau, salaried professionals who were males earned 146 percent of the average national income for all full-time year-round workers in 1970, while the corresponding percentage for females was 91.8 percent. Among clerical workers, men received 102.3 percent, as compared to 66.5 percent for women. Males in service occupations secured 84.4 percent of the average national income, while females in the same category were paid only 46.8 percent. Considering all occupations, the median earnings for women employed in full-time jobs in 1972 were $8,925 for college graduates, $5,577 for high school graduates, and $4,305 for those who did not finish elementary school. The corresponding figures for comparable educational groups of men were much higher—$14,660, $10,075, and $7,575.[46]

Perhaps reflecting awareness of the fact that the job market discriminated against them, women, again like blacks, have been much more prone to enter government employment, where hiring and promotion are more likely to be based on competitive examination, than members of the dominant group. Thus in 1960, 27 percent of all female lawyers worked for a government agency, as compared to 14 percent for males; the corresponding figures among doctors were 30 percent for females and 14 percent for males, and among engineers, 32 percent for females and 17 percent for males.[47]

It can be reported, however, that the occupational and economic status of women improved considerably during the civil rights decade of the 1960s and early 70s. Between 1960 and 1970 the number of women in the labor force increased by 38 percent. The increase in the number working in skilled blue-collar jobs was most dramatic, jumping almost 80 percent, or "eight times the rate of increase for men in the skilled trades." Passage of the Equal Pay Act of 1963 and the Civil Rights Act of 1964 clearly played a role in these developments. As Hedges and Bemis note: "With their legal rights to equal employment opportunity established, women were drawn to work that paid well. For those with a high school education, such jobs were most likely to be found in the skilled trades."[48]

Changes in the upper levels of the occupational structure, particularly in professional jobs, have been almost as striking. Between 1960 and 1970 the

[45] Amundsen, *op. cit.*, pp. 39–40.

[46] Jencks et al., *op. cit.*, p. 225; Elizabeth Waldman and Beverly J. McEaddy, "Where Women Work—An Analysis by Industry and Occupation," *Monthly Labor Review* 97 (May 1974), p. 12.

[47] Cynthia Fuchs Epstein, *Woman's Place* (Berkeley: University of California Press, 1971), p. 171.

[48] Janice N. Hedges and Stephen E. Bemis, "Sex Stereotyping: Its Decline in Skilled Trades," *Monthly Labor Review* 97 (May 1974), p. 18.

proportion of women entering the higher professions increased by 61 percent, much more than for men.

> In the broad category of professional occupations, women constituted 40 percent of all employees in 1974, up from 36 percent in 1962. Rapid progress occurred in a number of the higher paying professions, among physicians and surgeons (6 to 10 percent), and lawyers and judges (3 to 7 percent). . . . Women have also made slow but steady gains in accounting, from 19 to 24 percent; in personnel and labor relations work, from 27 to 35 percent; in college and university teaching, from 19 to 31 percent; and in drafting from 4 to 8 percent.[49]

The improvement has been particularly striking in higher education. A detailed statistical study of first-job placements among new holders of Ph.D. degrees indicates that "earlier discrimination in teaching appointments disappeared by 1973."[50] An independent analysis concluded that sex-related salary differentials, widely prevalent in academia, had been eliminated for new appointees by 1972. Among older established faculty, salary differentials between men and women still persist, but they have declined considerably. "In 1968–69, an average raise for women of more than $1000 across all ranks would have been required for equity in accordance with the predictors of men's salaries. The comparable figure in 1972–73 was $600."[51]

The improvement in the position of women in the higher professions is likely to continue, both because of government-enforced policies and because of a steady increase in the enrollment of women in professional training programs. Thus the proportion of women among recipients of the Ph.D. degree rose from 12 percent in 1967 to 18 percent in 1973.[52] The proportion of women enrolled in law schools rose from 5 percent in 1966 to 12 percent in 1972. In medicine it grew from 8 to 13 percent; in pharmacy, from 15 to 25 percent.

> First-year enrollment figures suggest the rise in the proportion of women in proportion of women in professional training is likely to continue. . . . In dentistry, there were as many women enrolled in the first year of study in 1972 as were enrolled in all class years in 1970, and in law as many women were in first-year study in 1972 as in all years in 1969.[53]

The evidence regarding the change in the occupational position of women generally has been summed up by Bayer and Astin: "It is fair to say that substantial progress has been made since the anti-bias regulations have been in effect. It is equally clear, on the other hand, that neither the spirit nor the

[49] Garfinkle, *op. cit.*, p. 27.

[50] Allan M. Cartter and Wayne E. Ruhter, *The Disappearance of Sex Discrimination in First Job Placement of New Ph.D.'s* (Los Angeles: Higher Education Research Institute, 1975), p. 25.

[51] Alan E. Bayer and Helen S. Astin, "Sex Differentials in the Academic Reward System," *Science*, May 23, 1975, pp. 799, 800.

[52] Cartter and Ruhter, *op. cit.*, p. 8.

[53] Parrish, *op. cit.*, pp. 41–42.

objectives inherent in the anti-bias regulations and laws have yet been fully achieved."[54]

Differences in Income

The concern for greater equality does not mean only equal opportunity; it also means equal reward, summed up in the description of a communist society as "from each according to his ability, to each according to his needs." No complex society, other than perhaps the kibbutzim (collective settlements) in Israel, which encompass over 100,000 people, has ever come close to approximating this objective. And though the mobility data reported by Blau and Duncan, and by Jencks and his associates, suggest the United States is beginning to approximate equal opportunity for white males, it is clear that such a situation occurs together with sharp inequalities in income and wealth. As Jencks notes:

> This implies that even if America could reduce inequalities in income to the point where they were no greater than those that now arise between one brother and another, the best paid fifth of all male workers would still be making 500 percent more than the worst-paid fifth. We cannot, then, hope to eliminate, or even substantially reduce income inequality in America simply by providing children from all walks of life with equal opportunity. When people have had relatively equal opportunity, as brothers usually have, they still end up with very unequal incomes.[55]

The only solution Jencks sees to the problem of gaining greater income equality is government policies which "establish floors beneath which nobody's income is allowed to fall and ceilings above which it is not allowed to rise." Although this proposal may appear quite radical, it is interesting to note that leading Republicans now assert that "there is much in the new doctrine of equality of results that is solid"—to use the words of Paul McCracken, a member of President Eisenhower's Council of Economic Advisers from 1956 to 1959 and chairman of the same body for President Nixon from 1969 to 1972. McCracken, speaking to the American Business Council, noted that American society is concerned with finding an optimum balance between its traditional ideal of equality of opportunity and its growing commitment to greater equality of result:

> For economic policy we need to have a more explicit and coherent income maintenance policy. Powerful intellectual impetus for this, as for so much of the current economic policy landscape, came from Milton Friedman in his writings on the negative income tax. It was given programmatic expression four years ago in the President's Family Assistance Plan. Ours is now a rich economy, and we can

---

[54] Bayer and Astin, *op. cit.*, p. 801.
[55] Jencks et al., *op. cit.*, p. 220.

well afford it. And all of us here would have to admit that there is a substantial element of random luck in success. . . . Moreover, we need a more explicit and coherent income-sharing plan to win more leeway for using the pricing system. . . .

The optimum toward which society is trying to feel its way here will be neither pure "equality of results" nor just "equality of opportunity." A society organized solely on the principle of equality of opportunity is not acceptable, and one organized solely around the principle of equality of results would not be operational.[56]

The gradual acceptance of the community's responsibility for upgrading the lives of the underprivileged in America constitutes an important shift in our values away from the primary, almost sole, focus on opportunity implied in the original achievement and Protestant orientations of the early republic. Yet it may be argued that the initial emphasis on equality derived from the Declaration of Independence, which has led many Americans to speak of their country as a "classless society," strengthens the new trend toward using government power to eliminate "poverty."

In spite of McCracken's acceptance of much in the doctrine of "equality of results," it is also true that the great majority of Americans believe in the present pattern of income differentiation. In 1970 a public opinion survey asked Americans to suggest "a fair yearly salary" for various occupations ranging from "top management" to "lower skill"; the large majority of those interviewed suggested differentials nearly identical with existing patterns. Lee Rainwater reports the "respondents see equity in a system in which there is quite marked dispersion of income . . . [and] seem to have little complaint about the relative shares of different groups in the occupational hierarchy."[57]

Government policy has seemingly been committed to equalizing incomes somewhat beyond what would occur through the natural workings of the economy. Various policies have been used, ranging from the graduated income tax, which increases the tax percentage on higher income, to assorted income-transfer welfare programs, which give income directly to the less privileged. Such welfare policies, stimulated by the New Deal programs initiated in the 1930s, should have the effect of reducing the pattern of gross inequalities. While these policies attest to the continued significance of equality as a national value, more important in the long run in affecting income distribution are changes in the occupational structure which serve to reduce the proportion of unskilled and low-paid jobs and to increase the proportion of jobs requiring higher education in the upper ranges of the income distribution. The spread of higher education to the point where close to half of all Americans of college age continue their education beyond high school attests to the extensiveness of this process.

Recent historical research has not only challenged the conventional wisdom about mobility rates, which assumed that the growth of large corporations would mean movement from greater to lesser equality of opportunity; it has

---

[56] Paul W. McCracken, "The New Equality," *Michigan Business Review,* Vol. 26, No. 2 (March 1974), pp. 2–7.

[57] Lee Rainwater, *What Money Buys: Inequality and the Social Meanings of Income* (New York: Basic Books, 1974), pp. 163–167.

also upset long-cherished notions about the direction of change in the distribution of income from the early nineteenth century on. The tentative conclusion which may be reached from a number of studies is that Jacksonian America—described by Tocqueville and others as an egalitarian social system (which, compared to Europe, it undoubtedly was)—was characterized by much more severe forms of social and economic inequality than the society of the 1970s. As historian Edward Pessen points out:

> The explanation, popular since Karl Marx's time, that it was industrialization that pauperized the masses, in the process transforming a relatively egalitarian social order, appears wanting. Vast disparities between urban rich and poor antedated industrialization [in America]. . . . Even Michael Harrington and Gabriel Kolko, whose estimates reveal the greatest amounts of [present-day] inequality, attribute percentages of income to the upper brackets that are far smaller than the upper one percent of New York City controlled in income in 1863 or in wealth in 1845.[58]

Most other pre-Civil War American cities resembled New York in these respects, and even in rural areas the pattern of property distribution was extremely unequal.[59]

Patterns of income distribution Detailed analysis of the distribution of total personal income since 1929 by the foremost authority on the subject, Simon Kuznets, indicates that the proportion of the income going to the bottom sections of the population (the lowest fifth and lowest 5 percent) increased during the 1930s and 1940s, while the portion going to upper groups (the top fifth and top 5 percent) dropped considerably. Thus the proportions of the total family income received by the upper fifth fell from 54 percent in 1929 to 42.7 percent in 1951; the corresponding change for the top 5 percent was from 29.5 percent to 18.4 percent.[60] Since that time, however, some family income distribution studies suggest that the process has slowed down considerably, although a recent review of a number of American studies of the subject by the Organization for Economic Cooperation and Development (OECD) concludes that there

[58] Edward Pessen, "The Egalitarian Myth and the American Social Reality: Wealth, Mobility, Morality in the 'Era of the Common Man,'" *The American Historical Review*, Vol. 76 (October 1971), pp. 989–1034; and *Riches, Class, and Power Before the Civil War* (Lexington, Mass.: Heath, 1973). Pessen cites many relevant recent historical works bearing on the intense forms of inequality in this period.

[59] Merle Curti et al., *The Making of an American Community: A Case Study of Democracy in a Frontier County* (Stanford, Cal.: Stanford University Press, 1959).

[60] Simon Kuznets, "Income Distribution and Changes in Consumption," in H. S. Simpson (ed.), *The Changing American Population* (New York: Institute for Life Insurance, 1962), p. 30. See also Selma F. Goldsmith et al., "Size Distribution of Income Since the Mid-Thirties," *Review of Economics and Statistics*, Vol. 36 (February 1954), p. 20. For a contradictory interpretation which concludes that there has been little change in income distribution since 1910, see Gabriel Kolko, *Wealth and Power in America* (New York: Praeger, 1962), p. 13. Kolko's analysis, however, is based on data prepared by a private research group that have been rejected as too unreliable to be included in the *Historical Statistics of the United States* by a panel of the leading authorities on the subject in economics.

"has been a slight but perceptible tendency, over 1950–1970 period, towards greater equality in family income distribution." Thus by 1970 the proportion received by the top 5 percent had fallen to 14.4 percent.[61]

It is far from certain, however, that the egalitarian trend with respect to income is slowing down. Government welfare policies, combined with the American emphasis on individualism and the nuclear family, have led to a continuing increase in the number of separate households headed by those under 25, those 65 and older, and married women—people who in many other societies would not be living apart from relatives and would not be counted as independent family units in the income statistics. These three groups form a very large proportion of the lowest 20 percent of the income distribution. As Kuznets pointed out in 1962:

> Splitting up [family units] would, all other conditions being equal, widen the inequality in the distribution among consumer units—as measured, for it would create an increasingly large group of units at the lower end of the distribution. . . . The point to be stressed is that in so far as splitting up began in the 1930's [as a result of old-age pensions and other welfare policies] and continued thereafter, inequality in the distribution of income among consumer units declined until 1947 and was constant thereafter *despite* the underlying trend in the structure of consuming units."[62]

More recently, Kuznets has analyzed the impact of these changes on income distribution for the period 1947–1968. He finds that family units headed by women, persons over 65, or persons under 25 increased by 17.4 percent during this period. Since old people constituted half of this group, a large proportion of them were not in the labor force.

Families with young, old, and female heads make up an increasing proportion of low-income units, fully two-thirds of the lowest fifth by 1968. When these three groups are excluded from the income distribution, "the general level of the shares of the lowest fifth, and to a lesser extent of the second fifth, are raised perceptibly, while those of the [upper] 80–95 percent, and particularly of the top 5 percent group, are lowered—thus narrowing inequality significantly." Thus the share received by the bottom fifth rose from 5.8 percent after the war to 7.3 percent in 1968, while that of the upper 5 percent fell from 16 percent to 12.8 percent. In short, while the total income distribution among all families has been relatively stable, the distribution "among families with male heads aged 25–64 (what might be called 'standard' family units), showed a sustained movement of some magnitude through almost the whole period." Further, since "the young and old family head units are characterized by much smaller families than the average . . . an adjustment for these differences in

[61] OECD Secretariat, "Inequality in the Distribution of Personal Income" (Paper prepared for Seminar on Education, Inequality, and Life Chances, Paris, January 6–9, 1975), pp. 18, 20. Herman P. Miller, *Income Distribution in the United States* (Washington, D.C.: U.S. Department of Commerce, 1966).

[62] Kuznets, *op. cit.*, pp. 36–37.

average size of family would also yield an income distribution with a more sustained and larger movement toward equality over the period."

It may, of course, be argued that from the point of view of equity there is no basis for excluding these units from a general analysis of trends toward greater or lesser equality. Kuznets answers such contentions by saying:

> One could argue that from the standpoints of productivity, equity, and welfare, the incomes of these units, on a per-person basis, should be lower than those in the "standard" family units. After all, young family heads are in their training period, may look forward to much higher returns that would compensate them later, and no equity or welfare considerations warrant claiming for them a per-person return as high as that which they themselves will secure later—so long as the current returns are minimally adequate otherwise. Old family heads, largely in their retirement period, do not contribute sufficiently to earn an income equal to that of prime members of the labor force; nor do they need such income for the purposes of further investment . . . or for utilizing the variety of new products. . . . It is thus permissible to argue that the income inequality contributed by the lower incomes of the young and old units represents no contribution to unwarranted earnings differentials.[63]

Consumer goods: symbols of equality   With respect to the way in which people *perceive* the distribution of income, it may be argued that the distribution of different kinds of *consumer goods*, those people use for immediate gratification, is more important in affecting their feelings about equity than the actual distribution of income as such. In this connection, it would appear that the distribution of consumer goods has tended to become more equitable as the size of national income has increased. This relationship between wealth and the distribution of consumer goods has been commented on by the Swedish socialist economist Gunnar Myrdal: "It is, indeed, a regular occurrence that the poorer the country, the greater the difference between poor and rich."[64]

---

[63] Simon Kuznets, "Demographic Aspects of the Distribution of Income Among Families: Recent Trends in the United States," in Willy Selle Kzerts (ed.), *Essays in Honour of Jan Tinbergen,* Vol. 3, *Econometrics and Economic Theory* (London: Macmillan, 1974), pp. 223–246. Controlling for the age factor, economist Morton Paglin also finds a significant steady decline in income inequality from 1947–1972 of 23 percent. In addition, Paglin calculated the impact of transfer payments such as "public housing, rent supplements, food stamps and food assistance, Medicaid, and social services . . ." on the income distribution. Including these as income and controlling for age, he estimates that the poorest 20 percent of the population in fact received about 54 percent of what they would get if there were complete equality, as contrasted with an estimate of 27 percent, using traditional methods which do not control for age and do not include transfer payments as income.

Paglin also finds that some of the same considerations apply to the distribution of wealth. Part of "wealth inequality" reflects the age structure and the social savings function rather than fundamental (lifetime) inequality in the economics system. When controlling for age, he finds that past uncontrolled measures had "overstated the degree of interfamily inequality of wealth by about 52 percent." See Morton Paglin, "The Measurement and Trend of Inequality: A Basic Revision," *American Economic Review,* Vol. 65 (September 1975), pp. 598–609.

[64] Gunnar Myrdal, *An International Economy* (New York: Harper and Row, 1956), p. 133.

In the United States the average per capita income has increased almost sixfold during the course of this century, and this dramatic growth has brought about a wide distribution of various social and economic benefits, greater than that in almost all other countries. Thus in America a much larger proportion of the population graduates from high school (over 80 percent) or enters college (close to 50 percent) than in any other nation. The greater wealth of the United States also means that consumer goods such as automobiles and telephones are more evenly distributed than elsewhere. A recent evaluation by *The* (London) *Economist*, using 12 social indicators to assess the relative advantages of different countries as places to live, placed the United States far in the lead over eight other noncommunist industrialized states.[65]

Sociologist Gideon Sjoberg has traced the implications of such developments historically in America. He suggests that the emergence of mass production during the twentieth century has caused such a redistribution of highly valued prestige symbols that the distinctions between social classes are much less immediately visible than they were in nineteenth-century America, or in most other less affluent countries. Sjoberg argues that the status differences between many blue-collar workers and middle-class professionals have become less well-defined, since working-class families, like middle-class ones, have been able to buy goods that confer prestige on the purchaser—clothing, cars, television sets, and so on.[66] Such improvements in style of life help to preserve the belief in the reality of the promise of equality. A person who can buy his own house, or a new car, may feel that he has moved up in the world even if he has not changed his occupational or relative income position.

The discussion of rates of mobility, of income trends, and of the distribution of status-enhancing consumer goods is pertinent to the oft repeated suggestion that such attributes affect the extent to which a country is likely to experience intense class conflict, or polarized politics. Aspects of this thesis have been enunciated by a variety of contemporary sociological observers, as well as by Karl Marx and other nineteenth-century commentators.[67] A detailed effort to test some of the implications of these assumptions, particularly in the context of evaluating the political effects of social mobility, indicates that mobile individuals (up or down) are less likely to take strong class positions than the nonmobile. The political scientist James Barber concludes his study with the assertion: "The influence of mobility on the political system would seem . . . to be a moderating one: lending flexibility to the electoral process, reducing the stakes involved in elections, and diluting the class content of politics."[68]

---

[65] "Where the Grass Is Greener," *The Economist*, December 25, 1971, p. 15.

[66] Gideon Sjoberg, "Are Social Classes in America Becoming More Rigid?" *American Sociological Review*, Vol. 16 (December 1951), pp. 775–783.

[67] For a review of some of the literature on the subject, see James Alden Barber, Jr., *Social Mobility and Voting Behavior* (Chicago: Rand McNally, 1970), pp. 9–12, 264–266. See also Sombart, *op. cit.*, pp. 593–608.

[68] Barber, *op. cit.*, p. 267.

Persistence of income differentials The stress in this discussion on data supporting the continued vitality of egalitarian trends in American society does not imply that the United States even remotely approaches a state which can be described as egalitarian from any absolute point of view. This country, like all other nations maintaining some form of capitalism, has an enormous concentration of personal wealth in the hands of relatively few individuals. The top 1 percent owns over 25 percent of all personal assets. Even among white male Americans, equal opportunity does not exist, particularly with respect to the best paid positions. And as we have seen, in spite of considerable improvement in the last decade, the promise of equality remains a mockery for most mature blacks and women, as well as for some ethnic minorities, particularly American Indians and persons of Spanish origin. But as Gunnar Myrdal has convincingly demonstrated in *An American Dilemma,* the American creed is on the side of these groups, and even people who have strong prejudices against them must assent publicly to their rights and their claim to equal treatment and equal opportunity.[69]

Poverty, though concentrated among the minority groups, also affects a significant number of whites. It is particularly found among the aged, the uneducated and unskilled, migrant farm laborers, small farm operators (especially in the South), families that have lost their male heads, and that large group with individual handicaps (those with low IQ's, physical deformities, mental illness, or other chronic ailments).

Government efforts, in tandem with the emphasis on equality, are formally committed to ending discrimination and eliminating poverty. As yet such policies have had a limited effect, in part because it is impossible to remedy existing handicaps of low education, limited skill, broken families, and inadequate motivation, and in part because the nation is still not fully committed to raising the bottom levels of society. To a considerable degree also, the efforts to improve the lot of the underprivileged are limited or negated by economic declines that reduce opportunities and that press those who have advantages to resist opening more rewarded positions to new claimants. Thus the economic downturn of the mid-seventies has disproportionately disadvantaged the traditional "outsiders"—blacks, women, those of Spanish origin, the less educated, and the less skilled. Any renewed effort to enhance the promise of equality requires both a high level of employment and economic growth.

EQUALITY AND INEQUALITY IN THE COMMUNIST WORLD

The communist world, like the United States, is ideologically committed to reducing inequality and to moving toward an egalitarian society. The Communist party has governed the Soviet Union for close to six decades. In recent years the re-emergence of sociological investigations, prevented as long as Stalin

[69] Gunnar Myrdal, *An American Dilemma* (New York: Harper & Row, 1944).

ruled, has given us considerable insight into the situation in that immense country.

The evidence is clear that European communist societies are steeply stratified along almost all the dimensions normally discussed by sociologists in non-communist systems. A hierarchy is evident in the distribution of goods and services in society, the existence of considerable consensus on positions of higher and lower prestige, the differentiation of distinctive life styles, the patterning of social contacts, the structuring of satisfactions and aspirations, and so on. Particularly important is the continued existence of great inequalities in the cultural sphere in spite of measures to narrow the differentials between top and bottom in material conditions (e.g., wages and housing).[70] Yet it should also be noted that many of the structural trends reported earlier for the United States derivative from the emergence of a more highly industrialized society linked to a mass higher education system have occurred under communism as well. As the Polish sociologist Stanislaw Ossowski has pointed out,

> industrialization, urbanization, development of communications, and mass education . . . imply an increase in social mobility in socialist countries as well as elsewhere. . . . It is the "social-economic expansion" and not the revolutionary introduction of a socialist order which can be considered a necessary condition of this increase [in rates of social mobility in Eastern Europe]. Increased mobility of this type could have been accomplished also if the capitalist system had persisted. . . .[71]

The commitment in Communist ideology to a more egalitarian society has resulted in criticism of existing forms of inequality, sometimes coming from the highest circles. In Yugoslavia, where critics have raised the issue of the emergence of a "new class," the head of the Communist party and the state, Marshal Tito, continues to stress the need for a continuing struggle with the "technocracy, bureaucracy, the class enemy . . . who oppose the interests of the working class in our society." He describes the way in which some of the managers even "have amassed wealth through different machinations. . . . You have no idea how distressed I feel when I see the things we have been talking about, this rush to get rich, this scramble for the dinar. Yet I know extremely well how families with the lowest earning live."

Frankly acknowledging the problem of "authority in the hands of a few people," Tito asserts that those fostering the power of the bureaucracy are "in key positions, that is to say, in the positions where material and financial resources are being handled and where decisions can be taken concerning the

[70] For a detailed discussion of stratification in the Soviet Union, see S. M. Lipset and Richard Dobson, "Social Stratification and Sociology in the Soviet Union," *Survey*, Vol. 88, No. 3 (Summer 1973), pp. 114–185. See also Mervyn Matthews, *Class and Society in Soviet Russia* (New York: Walker, 1972).
[71] Stanislaw Ossowski, "Social Mobility Brought About by Social Revolution" (Paper presented at the Fourth Working Conference on Social Stratification and Social Mobility, International Sociological Association, Geneva, December 1957).

utilization of the fruits of other people's labor. This is where those forces may be found." And though he is the head of a communist system, Tito argues that "there are people in the Party who make it impossible to square accounts with them." Among other consequences of the growth of power and privilege is the fact that there "are fewer and fewer worker and peasant youths at the universities, because there is a fairly large number of those who are well off and who can afford to study."[72]

The second most important Yugoslav leader, Edward Kardelj, also notes the significance of "social stratification" in the country, of "non-socialist, Stalinistic, capitalist, statist, group-property, class and other elements. . . . It is not difficult to discover such phenomena, for something of all this can be found, to a greater or lesser extent, in all contemporary socialist societies. . . ."[73]

In seeking to explain sharp differences in occupational prestige and income under communism, Soviet sociologists have developed their own version of the functionalist theory of stratified differentiation, in terms quite similar to those presented by Western sociologists. L. F. Liss notes that "the prestige of an occupation is formed on the basis of societal needs." Because of variations in occupational prestige, many will compete for high-status positions—particularly through efforts to secure higher education—but relatively few will succeed. "The resultant contradiction between societal and individual interests is resolved by means of competitive selection of the most deserving, prepared and capable individuals. . . ."[74]

The philosophy underlying inequality in Soviet society has been explicated by G. V. Maltzev:

> The personal participation of every able-bodied person in the creation of social wealth is the leading social prerequisite for the holding of rights in a socialist society. . . . Labor, its quality and quantity, is the only really just measure of economic or any other kind of distribution. . . .
>
> In a socialist society . . . the idea of equality has never meant an endeavor to make everyone alike. The artificial equalization of incomes and other measures aimed at leveling the social and legal status of individuals have nothing in common with such a society. The founders of Marxism-Leninism foresaw that under the socialist organization of labor persons with very different abilities or talents could receive more from society and become wealthier than others. . . .
>
> Despite the assertion of present-day anti-communists that socialism negates all personal initiative, thereby depriving man of the right to become rich, the distributive practice of socialism is based on the continuous growth of personal in-

---

[72] An interview with President Tito, "We Must Have a Vanguard and United Party," *Vjesnik* (Zagreb), October 8, 1972, as translated in the Yugoslav magazine *Socialist Thought and Practice*, No. 49 (August–December 1972), pp. 8–9, 11, 12–13, 21.

[73] Edward Kardelj, "Contradictions of Social Property in Contemporary Socialist Practice," *Socialist Thought and Practice*, No. 49 (August–December 1972), p. 35.

[74] L. F. Liss, "The Social Conditioning of Occupational Choice," in Murray Yanowitch and Wesley A. Fisher (trans. and eds.), *Social Stratification and Mobility in the U.S.S.R.* (White Plains, N.Y.: International Arts and Sciences Press, 1973), p. 284.

come and social wealth. Socialism encourages high incomes and does not deny the right to show personal initiative.[75]

The Soviet sociologist O. I. Shkaratan has argued that one of the distinctive features of the development of socialism is "the shift of previously secondary criteria to the foreground, as it were, and their transformation into the most characteristic marks of differentiation."

> When socialism eliminates private ownership, it eliminates its consequences, the antagonistic classes; but it does not yet do away with the division of labor into socially heterogeneous kinds. . . . With the elimination of the class hierarchy, the remaining socioeconomic division of labor acquires direct and immediate (not intermediary) influence on the mechanism of interclass structure. . . . The basic social differences within the Soviet working class are therefore essentially differences in complexity of work. . . . The fact that members of one and the same class belong to groups of workers with different skills, holding unequal positions in the system of social production, is decisive today in determining the social importance of the individual.[76]

Shkaratan goes on to describe how socialist societies have a salient division "between executive-type and executor-type labor, and in the case of the latter, between mental and primarily manual labor, and between skilled and unskilled labor." The "significance of differences associated with one's role in the social organization of labor is heightened under socialism," particularly among the higher occupations which tend to get quite differentiated in status, skill, and reward.[77]

Thus we have come a full circle. The thrust of this argument is that stratification—inequality of position—is even more applicable to socialist societies than to capitalist ones.

Space limitations do not permit a detailed report of sociological research on patterns of stratification within the communist world comparable to that presented above for the United States. Those interested are referred to published materials listed in the Recommended Reading at the end of this chapter.

---

[75] G. V. Maltzev, "Social Justice and Human Rights in Socialist Society," *Sovetskoye Gosudarstvo i Pravo*, No. 11 (November 1974), pp. 10–18, as abstracted in *The Current Digest of the Soviet Press*, June 4, 1975, pp. 13–14.

[76] O. I. Shkaratan, "The Social Structure of the Soviet Working Class," *Voprosy Filosofii*, No. 1 (1967), as translated in *The Current Digest of the Soviet Press*, April 12, 1967, pp. 3–5. Likewise the Hungarian sociologist Zsuzsa Ferge affirms that "theoretical reflections, as well as empirical data, indicate that to the extent that property relations lost their importance, other social relations gain in importance, and become factors of differentiation, notably those which are linked *to place occupied in the social division of labor*." Zsuzsa Ferge, "La stratification sociale en Hongrie," in Andreas Hegedus (ed.), *Sociologues hongrois: études, recherches* (Paris: Editions Anthropos, 1969), p. 166.

[77] O. I. Shkaratan, "Sources of Social Differentiation of the Working Class in Soviet Society," in Yanowitch and Fisher, *op. cit.*, p. 19.

CONSEQUENCES OF STRATIFICATION

Sociological investigations in the United States and the Soviet Union, two societies dedicated by their public ideology to foster greater equality, reveal that in both countries considerable progress has been made toward improving the relative position of the underprivileged. The "political religion," to use Lincoln's phrase, has been used effectively by advocates of greater equality in both nations to criticize existing patterns of inequality and to demand further reforms. Yet in both societies considerable inequality continues to exist: in the United States in terms of wealth and income, in the Soviet Union in terms of economic and political power. In both societies expanding economies and educational systems have permitted considerable upward mobility, while the norms of the predominant economic and government organizations emphasizing educational attainments and personal achievements have deemphasized the relevance of direct inheritance of position and thus facilitated downward movement as well. Each society too, in violation of its fundamental credo, is characterized by lesser opportunity, status, and income for members of "minority" ethnic groups and women, although in each progress has been made.

It has been argued that the American stress on equality of opportunity serves to legitimate the claim to unequal privilege of the affluent. Similarly, some critics of existing communist society have argued that Marxism, as a political doctrine, serves the "class interests" of the "educational and scientific estate"—the new elite of advanced or postindustrial society. The Polish sociologist Jan Machajski, a former Marxist, writing at the turn of the century, paralleled the interpretation that Marxists presented of the role of populist and egalitarian slogans during the American and French revolutions as serving to conceal and to legitimate bourgeois class rule in his anticipation of the consequences of successful socialist revolution. Like the anarchist theoretician Michael Bakunin, Machajski argued that such a revolution would result in a society controlled by the mandarins, those in elite positions requiring higher education.[78]

Views similar to Machajski's have been enunciated more recently by the senior Marxist in British sociology, T. B. Bottomore, who argued that in the Soviet Union

the sentiment of equality is exploited by asserting the moral superiority of a "classless" society in which privilege is no longer privilege but only a beneficient ne-

[78] Unfortunately, little of Jan Machajski has been translated into English. For a brief sample from his book *The Intellectual Worker*, see V. F. Calverton (ed.), *The Making of Society* (New York: Random House, 1937), pp. 427–436. Max Nomad has been Machajski's main disciple and has summarized and applied his teachings in *Aspects of Revolt* (New York: Noonday Press, 1961), pp. 96–117; *Dreamers, Dynamiters, and Demagogues* (New York: Waldon Press, 1964), pp. 103–108, 201–206; and *Political Heretics* (Ann Arbor: University of Michigan Press, 1963), pp. 238–241. See also Paul Avrich, "What Is 'Machaevism'?," *Soviet Studies*, Vol. 17 (July 1965), pp. 66–75; and Marshall Shatz, "Jan Waclaw Machajski: The 'Conspiracy' of the Intellectuals," *Survey*, Vol. 62 (January 1967), pp. 45–57.

cessity on the road to perfect justice. This doctrine, which justifies the rule of an elite over the masses, is only the most recent version of an ancient, almost venerable hypocrisy.[79]

Much of American political history, as Tocqueville pointed out 140 years ago, can be interpreted as a struggle between proponents of greater equality and would-be aristocracies of birth and wealth. In communist societies, where direct transmission of private wealth plays a less important role than in the West, the struggle for equality revolves largely around access to higher education, which is a determining factor in occupational status placement in an economy without private business. The absence of political and economic rights for the less privileged in Soviet society, their inability to strike or to vote for parties seeking their support, means that the privileged strata in their country have fewer constraints on their efforts to maintain and transmit their position. Such efforts may be seen particularly in the ways in which well-to-do Soviet parents use their money to increase the chances for their offspring to gain admittance to higher education, a resource that the Soviet government does not allow to expand to meet the demand coming from less privileged youth, with the consequent effect that the proportion of university youth from privileged backgrounds steadily increases.

Efforts to Redefine Equality

Efforts to redefine the concept of equality to mean "equality of results" have had little success in both societies, although in the United States minority groups and women have made some headway in their demand for specific group quotas to increase their numbers in universities, various occupations, and trade unions (which control access to some jobs) in line with their proportion in the population. Similar proposals, with respect to securing access to higher education for the offspring of workers and peasants, were made by Prime Minister Khrushchev in the Soviet Union in the late 1950s. They were, however, dropped after his elimination as national leader in 1964. In effect, those who propose quotas have sought to break down the traditional American and Soviet emphases on equality of opportunity for the best-qualified individuals, by demanding a shift to *group* rather than *individual* rights, thus fostering group mobility.

Compliance with demands for special quotas means denial to others of positions for which they are qualified, or which they now have. If the principle of *positive* group discrimination to attain a form of equality of results is accepted, America and the Soviet Union will have adopted a version of the principle of *ascription*, of hereditary placement, to advance equal opportunity. It has been argued that "a principle of ascribed equality—a kind of perverse

[79] T. B. Bottomore, *Classes in Modern Society* (London: Ampersand, 1955), pp. 48–49.

hereditary theory—would be as insidiously destructive of individual freedom as a principle of ascribed inequality."[80]

It may appear that the argument against special prescriptive quotas for minority groups is a form of special pleading by spokesmen of the privileged elements in society. That this is so, when viewed from a pure interest-group standpoint, cannot be denied. Yet persuasive voices against quotas have been heard even from within the American black community. Orlando Patterson, a black sociologist, argues that the black American has a stake in a "conception of human dignity in which every individual is, and ought to be, responsible for himself and his action." In his opinion, for blacks to insist that they, unlike other groups, lack the ability to change their circumstances because of their social environment is to accept a demoralizing view of their situation, one that serves to discourage efforts to change it. He notes that the emphasis on the socially determined sources of black social inferiority is so strong that the issue for many is not "why the group fails, but why the miracle of occasional individual successes persists among them." For Patterson, the great need is for blacks to find ways of emphasizing personal autonomy. And in trying to do this they should lay stress upon, and find hope and pride in, "the not inconsiderable number of successful Blacks." He calls attention to the

> numerous cases of black men and women on the average no better endowed genetically than fellow Blacks they have left behind in the ghettoes, and coming from environments with the same sorry list of broken homes, crime-plagued neighborhoods, drug-infested streets, inadequate schools, and racist white authority figures, who nonetheless succeed. How are we to explain them? We cannot. They defy explanation precisely because they alone account for their success; they made their success, and they made it, first, through a rebellion against their deterministic moral environment, and then, having gained their humanity, through the much easier rebellion against their social and economic environment.

Patterson concludes that such behavior can come about only "when one accepts one's total responsibility for oneself and one's future."[81]

---

[80] See Earl Raab, "Quotas by Any Other Name," *Commentary*, Vol. 53 (January 1972), pp. 41–42; and Daniel Bell, *The Coming of Post-Industrial Society* (New York: Basic Books, 1973), pp. 416–419.

[81] Orlando Patterson, "The Moral Crisis of the Black American," *The Public Interest*, Vol. 32 (Summer 1973), pp. 43–69, esp. pp. 64–65. A similar argument has been made by Thomas Sowell, a black economist, who notes: "Perhaps the greatest dilemma in attempts to raise ethnic minority income is that those methods which have historically proved successful —self-reliance, work skills, education, business experience—are all slow developing, while those methods which are more direct and immediate—job quotas, charities, subsidies, preferential treatment—tend to undermine self-reliance and pride of achievement in the long-run. If the history of American ethnic groups shows anything, it is how large a role has been played by attitudes—and particularly attitudes of self-reliance. The success of the antebellum 'free persons of color' compared to the later black migrants to the North, the advancement of the Italian-Americans . . . , the resilience of the Japanese-American despite numerous campaigns of persecution, all emphasize the importance of this factor, however mundane and unfashionable it may be." Thomas Sowell, *Race and Economics* (New York: David McKay, 1975), p. 238.

Regardless of what happens in the current national debate about quotas, there is, however, little likelihood that the principle of "equality of results" in America will be extended much beyond efforts to enhance the income level of those now living in poverty. Lee Rainwater's survey of attitudes toward different concepts of equality indicates that "few respondents" were willing to define it to mean "very similar incomes, wealth, education and the like." Rather, the "most broadly based model of equality among our respondents is one in which equality means equal treatment despite resource inequality. . . . Everybody has the right to pursue his own life style and to be treated as a person of equal merit and value by those around him." This concept has been basic to American values for much of the nation's history. It is closely linked to the emphasis on "equal opportunity to gain unequal rewards,"[82] which is also accepted in the Soviet Union.

Heightened Awareness of Status

There is a complex relationship between the concept of equality—the belief that all persons must be given their due simply because they are human beings —and that of opportunity or achievement—the belief that everyone, regardless of background, should be given equal access to the more advantaged or interesting positions. One of the consequences of the stress on equality of opportunity in America is that it maximizes competition among the members of a society. As early as 1835 Tocqueville noted that abolition of hereditary privilege opens "the door to universal competition." A detailed analysis of late-nineteenth-century descriptions of American society by foreign travelers shows that these commentators generally agreed that "social and economic democracy in America, far from mitigating competition for social status, intensified it."[83] Some European socialists who were surprised to find American workers so concerned with conspicuous consumption—that is, with imitating the middle-class style of life—reported that the very feeling of equality pressed American workers to "make a show," since in America a worker could hope to demonstrate his achievements to others.

But if egalitarianism has encouraged competition for advancement, it has also made individuals extremely uncertain about their social position—that is, uncertain about just how much they *have* achieved. In fact, many of the foreign travelers who have been so impressed with the egalitarian social relations in America have also suggested that it is precisely because of the emphasis on equality of opportunity that Americans have been more status-conscious than those who live in the more aristocratic societies of Europe. Many have reported that it has been easier for the *nouveaux riches* to be accepted in English high

---

[82] Rainwater, *op. cit.*, pp. 168, 170–171.
[83] Robert W. Smuts, *European Impressions of the American Worker* (New York: King's Crown Press, 1953), p. 13.

society than in American. English observers from Harriet Martineau and Frances Trollope in the 1830s to James Bryce in the 1870s and Dennis Brogan in recent years, have described the way in which the absence of a legitimate aristocratic tradition, in which social rankings are unquestioned, forces Americans to emphasize status. In a more class-conscious society, everyone is aware of class distinctions and can therefore ignore them in many activities; but in a social system in which such distinctions conflict with the basic norms, those with a claim to higher status must assert that claim in a variety of ways or lose their right to it.[84]

Evidence that the similar value emphases in the Soviet Union have had comparable consequences may be found in the concern expressed in Soviet writings that few young people are willing to take manual jobs. Many recent articles note the serious problem created for the economy by such discontent with low-level employment. Concerns of this type have been repeatedly voiced by Soviet scholars and policy makers since research on these topics was revived in recent years. V. Kantorovich notes with dismay that the distaste exhibited by Russian youth for farm and manual work "is not as exceptional as it might seem."

Sociologists have noted a highly critical attitude toward physical labor, bordering on squeamishness, exists among some upper-grade secondary school students in Leningrad. It was this, actually, that the Resolution of the Central Committee of the Party on the School Reform (1958) dealt with: "Some of those who graduate from school regard it as demeaning for them to engage in physical labor."

. . . In our country (and this is by no means limited to the ranks of the salaried professionals) people are prepared to condemn a juvenile—and, even more, the parents of one—who will work *for pay*. . . . Abroad, children from diverse strata of society (except the elite, of course) regularly earn money by working as baggage-handlers, salesmen, dishwashers, maintenance workers, and so forth. Should one be surpised that having been trained from childhood only for mental work, for study, the Leningrad secondary students . . . had decided that they were born only for the professions and not for any other kind of work? When life compels them to "become a worker," this is taken as demeaning and even as a catastrophe.

. . . It is dinned into the ears of the young person that he has free access to all occupations which enjoy standing in his eyes, and that he can advance to the highest status in our society. . . . In effect, this aphorism strips all but the thoroughly intellectual occupations of all attractiveness, and thus misleads young people by picturing as excessively easy the difficult choice of a "place in life."[85]

---

[84] For an elaboration of this analysis and references to the relevant literature, see S. M. Lipset, *The First New Nation: The United States in Historical and Comparative Perspective* (Garden City, N.Y.: Doubleday-Anchor, 1967), pp. 125–134.

[85] V. Kantorovich, "Sociology and Literature," *Soviet Sociology*, Vol. 7 (Summer 1968), pp. 32, 33.

Pressures Toward Deviation

Kantorovich's suggestion that the Soviet ideological emphasis on equality of opportunity has the effect of demeaning occupations which require less training is comparable to the analyses of the dysfunctional consequences for American society of the notion that "all should strive for the same lofty goals, since these are open to all." In specifying the consequences of the emphasis on opportunity for all, Robert Merton has suggested that failure to achieve success is felt more severely in "classless" societies than in those which place more overt emphasis on hereditary position, or in which the leftist ideology dominant in the less affluent strata persuasively rationalizes their inferior position by attributing it to structural factors, such as discrimination or social barriers. This leads Merton to infer that in societies stressing equality

> the greatest pressures toward deviation are exerted upon the lower strata. . . . Several [American] researchers have shown that specialized areas of vice and crime constitute a "normal" response to a situation where the cultural emphasis upon pecuniary success has been absorbed, but where there is little access to conventional and legitimate means for becoming successful. The occupational opportunities of people in these areas are largely confined to manual labor and the lesser white-collar jobs. Given the American stigmatization of manual labor, *which has been found to hold rather uniformly in all social classes,* and the absence of realistic opportunities for advancement beyond this level, the result is a marked tendency toward deviant behavior.

In short, Merton observes, it is the *combination* of the cultural emphasis on opportunity and the limitations in the social structure which produces intense pressure for deviation. . . . Despite our persisting open-class ideology, advance toward the success goal is relatively rare and notably difficult for those armed with little formal education and few economic resources." And in a note Merton goes on to emphasize that "numerous [American] studies have found that the educational pyramid operates to keep a large proportion of unquestionably able but economically disadvantaged youth from obtaining higher formal education."[86]

Thus, in both the United States and the Soviet Union, evidence indicates that an emphasis on equality intensifies competition for high position, makes people sensitive to differences in status, and presses those who lack the accepted means of access to advantaged positions to use "innovative" or illegitimate means. In other words, the greater the stress on equality, the more people seek to avoid low status for themselves and their children.

The issues of equality discussed by Aristotle and Plato, and revived for modern times by Marx and Tocqueville, are clearly not resolved. But they form an increasingly important part of the domestic political agenda in many countries. People everywhere face the dilemma that it is difficult, if not im-

---

[86] Robert K. Merton, *Social Theory and Social Structure* (New York: Free Press, 1968), pp. 193, 198–199. See Merton's discussion on pp. 185–248.

possible, to defend on moral grounds the right of a person to higher status and the privileges higher income will purchase simply because of the advantages conferred by accident of birth—not just being born into a higher social position but also being born with more innate abilities, greater beauty, strength, and so on. Why should a person be exposed to lifelong punishment because of luck? But if such differences cannot be defended morally, no society has yet been able to operate a complex economy and polity without using the bait of differential reward as a source of motivation for hard, dedicated, and intelligent performance. As we have seen, differentiated privilege brings in its vain efforts to legitimate, institutionalize, and transmit it. It is likely, therefore, that people in different types of societies will continue to debate, research, and fight over issues such as these for generations to come.

SUMMARY

1   Stratification—inequality of reward, power, and status—has been a source of controversy and conflict for thousands of years. Plato accounted for the existence of stratification by noting that people vary in their inherent capacities: Each person does certain types of work better than others. Given the need for differentiation in complex societies, social systems are inevitably divided among those who labor and those who rule. Such stratified systems are based on the assumption that people seek to maximize the esteem and respect they receive from others. Those who are in high-valued positions experience high status as reward.

2   Throughout history, in all societies, those in low-valued positions have attempted to reject their inferior status and to seek a more egalitarian social order. The appeal of religion in India and feudal Europe—with its promise of reward in a future life—and the frequent revolts in peasant societies demonstrate the dissatisfaction of the underprivileged with their position. The two classic revolutions that introduced modern society—in France and America—led to the defeat of the notion of hereditary privilege and to greater emphasis on equality of opportunity for all. Hence there is an inherent tension between the need to maximize esteem and the need to maintain a stable social order.

3   The modern interpretation of stratification is the functionalist approach in sociology. Functionalists argue that since society has a complex set of roles that must be performed, people must be motivated to perform these different tasks. All societies prescribe various goals for individuals and groups, set limits on them, and define legitimate means for attaining them. Stratification—differential hierarchical reward—is the mechanism through which society motivates people to perform the diverse roles that it requires.

4   Talcott Parsons points out that stratification systems evaluate people according to three sets of characteristics: *possessions*—attributes that people own; *qualities* —traits ascribed to people or attributed to them as permanent characteristics; and *performances*—judgments of how well people perform their roles. The dominant evaluating mechanism in each society determines the nature of its stratification system. In a capitalist society, possessions are stressed; in a pure communist society, performance is dominant.

5   The principal alternative interpretation of stratification is Marxist social theory. Marxists stress the primary function of society, not as motivating its members through differential reward, but as providing the means to satisfy their basic needs. Stratification, or inequality, occurs in all social systems that cannot produce enough to satisfy the needs of all. In the Marxist view, the key prerequisite of an egalitarian society is material abundance, which would eliminate hierarchically organized divisions and give equal shares to everyone, regardless of ability. But until such abundance is achieved, every society will be characterized by a division of labor and inequality of reward and status.

6   Many sociologists have assumed that industrialization—the growth of monopoly capitalism and the decline of small business—would increase social rigidification in America. Yet a number of recent analyses suggest that there is more social mobility today than in the past. Since World War II the proportion of people from economically poor backgrounds who enter the top echelons of American business has increased. Because of improvements in education, most sons of unskilled workers have moved up into the ranks of skilled jobs or entered middle-class professions of various kinds.

7   Increased opportunities for economic advancement have not held true for America's racial and ethnic minorities. In the early 1960s the median annual income of black families was 63 percent of that of whites. Greater educational opportunities combined with legislative and judicial actions throughout the 1960s have improved the situation. Nonetheless, blacks, those of Spanish origin, and other ethnic groups continue to enter the labor market with major handicaps, and improvement has occurred primarily for younger people (those under 35), rather than the older population.

8   Women, like other minority groups, have disproportionately filled the low-status, low-paying positions in American society. Since 1900 women's participation in the labor force has grown steadily, but women continue to be represented disproportionately in the unskilled and white-collar-proletariat sectors. With the passage of equal rights legislation in the 1960s, the economic status of women improved considerably. Women have gained greater access to higher education and are increasingly entering the higher professions. As with blacks and other minorities, however, the spirit and objectives of antidiscrimination measures remain to be fully achieved.

9   Recent studies have also upset long-cherished notions about trends in income distribution in the United States. Simon Kuznets found that the proportion of income going to the bottom sectors of the population increased significantly in the 1930s and 1940s. Since that time there has been a slow but steady tendency toward greater equality in family income distribution. The improvement is much greater for families headed by males between 25 and 64 years of age. This egalitarian trend will probably continue, since the U.S. government is committed— through graduated income taxes, welfare programs, and other measures—to equalizing incomes beyond the natural workings of the economy.

10   Some sociologists argue that the distribution of *consumer goods*—clothing, cars, and other items purchased for immediate gratification—is a far better indicator of people's feelings about equality than income distribution as such. The distribution of most consumer goods has tended to become more equitable as the national income has increased. Gideon Sjoberg suggests that the ability of lower sectors to buy goods that confer prestige on the purchaser has made status dif-

ferences among blue collar and middle-class families less pronounced. Such improvements in life style help to preserve the belief in the promise of equality for all.

11   Despite the greater economic opportunities available in America today, sharp differences in income and wealth remain. Poverty, though concentrated among minorities, also affects whites. It is predominant among the aged, the unskilled and uneducated, families without male heads, farm laborers, and the handicapped. Government efforts to end discrimination and poverty are hampered by the difficulty of remedying the problems of poor education, broken families, and limited skills, and by economic declines that reduce occupational opportunities. Any renewed effort to achieve greater equality will require both a high level of employment and economic growth.

12   The communist world, like the United States, is formally committed to reducing inequality and to moving toward an egalitarian social order. Nonetheless, European communist societies are stratified along almost the same lines as noncommunist societies. Studies by sociologists of communist countries show a concentration of power among the political elite, intensified competition for higher education, consensus on high-prestige and low-prestige occupations, and increasing differentiation in life styles. As in the United States, lesser opportunities are available for minority groups, although considerable progress has been made.

13   The persistence of stratification in our society has led many spokesmen for minority groups to suggest redefining equality of opportunity to mean equality of results. These spokesmen have sought special prescriptive quotas for minority groups—a form of *positive* group discrimination—to foster group mobility. Critics of this view argue that such a principle of "ascribed equality" is as destructive of individual freedom as the notion of "ascribed inequality." Moreover, surveys show that most Americans oppose a definition of equality as "equality of income, wealth, and education." The dominant view continues to be "equal opportunity to gain unequal reward."

14   Among the chief consequences of stratification in both communist and noncommunist societies are intensified competition for higher position, increased awareness of differences in social status, and greater pressure toward deviation—attempts by those in the lower strata who lack the accepted means of access to higher positions to secure them by unconventional or illegitimate means. In short, the greater the stress on equality, the more people seek to avoid low status.

15   The debate over equality begun by Plato, and carried down to this century by functionalist and Marxist theorists, will continue. Many argue that while stratification is a characteristic of every industrialized society, it cannot be defended on moral grounds. Yet no society has been able to create a complex social system without using differential reward as a motivating force for competent and dedicated performance.

RECOMMENDED READING

Articles presenting divergent approaches to stratification as well as empirical findings may be found in a number of sociological readers or anthologies. The theoretical sections generally include a number of articles presenting the functionalist approaches, as well as Marxist and power-oriented theories. Among these readers are R. Bendix and S. M. Lipset, eds., *Class, Status and Power* (1966); Celia Heller, ed., *Structured Social Inequality* (1969); Melvin Tumin, ed., *Readings on Social Stratification* (1970); Edward Lauman et al., eds., *The Logic of Social Hierarchies* (1970); Gerald Thielbar and Saul Feldman, eds., *Issues in Social Inequality* (1972); Lee Rainwater, ed., *Social Problems and Public Policy: Inequality and Justice* (1974); Marvin Olson, ed., *Power in Societies* (1970); Joseph Lopreato and Lionel S. Lewis, eds., *Social Stratification* (1974); André Béteille, *Social Inequality* (1969); Edward Laumann, ed., *Social Stratification* (1970).

The intellectual history of concern by American sociologists with inequality is contained in Charles Page's *Class and American Sociology* (1940). The most detailed treatment of the subject by an American sociologist is by Gerhard Lenski, *Power and Privilege* (1966). A more recent good short paperback work is Leonard Riessman, *Inequality in American Society* (1973).

Discussions of power may be found in C. Wright Mills, *The Power Elite* (1956); John R. Champlin, ed., *Power* (1971); James S. Coleman, *Power and the Structure of Society* (1974); W. D. Hawley and F. M. Wirt, eds., *The Search for Community Power* (1968).

Social mobility has been analyzed generally in S. M. Lipset and Reinhard Bendix, *Social Mobility in Industrial Society* (1959). Sophisticated empirical treatments are Peter Blau and O. Dudley Duncan, *The American Occupational Structure* (1967); James S. Coleman et al., *Equality of Educational Opportunity* (1966); Frederick Mosteller and Daniel P. Moynihan, eds., *On Equality of Educational Opportunity* (1972); and Christopher Jencks et al., *Inequality* (1972). A historical anthology that brings together studies of social mobility in the United States from colonial times to the present is Edward Pessen, ed., *Three Centuries of Social Mobility in America* (1974). The role of immigration in mobility has been dealt with comprehensively in E. P. Hutchinson, *Immigrants and Their Children* (1965) and Thomas Sowell, *Race and Economics* (1975).

The best discussions of income distribution in the United States are by Simon Kuznets. See particularly his article, "Demographic Aspects of the Distribution of Income Among Families: Recent Trends in the U.S.," in W. S. Kzerts, ed., *Essays in Honour of Jan Tinbergen*, Vol. III, *Econometrics and Economic Theory* (1974), pp. 223–246. A particularly important recent study is Morton Paglin, "The Measurement and Trend of Inequality: A Basic Revision," *American Economic Review*, Vol. 65 (September 1975). On trends in income differences by race see Stanley Masters, *Black-White Income Differentials* (1975). For studies of popular attitudes to income inequality see Lee Rainwater, *What Money Buys* (1974) and Joan Huber and William Form, *Income and Ideology* (1973).

For analyses of sex stratification in the United States see William H. Chafee, *The American Woman. Her Changing Social, Economic and Political Roles, 1920–1970* (1970), Cynthia Fuchs Epstein, *Woman's Place* (1971), and Kirsten Amundsen, *The Silenced Majority* (1971). A sophisticated comparative analysis is Judith Blake Davis, "The Changing Status of Women in Developed Countries," *Scientific American*, Vol. 234 (September 1974).

The literature on the situation of racial and ethnic groups in America is enormous. For material on blacks and Chicanos see the Recommended Reading at the end of Chapter 10. A good short general overview is Peter Rose, *They and We: Racial and Ethnic Relations in the United States* (1974). For a comparative analysis with chapter on U.S. groups, see Nathan Glazer and Daniel Patrick Moynihan, eds., *Ethnicity* (1975). On Mexican Americans, see Leo Grebler et al., *The Mexican-American People* (1970). For material on Asian Americans, see "Asian Americans: A Success Story?" a special issue of *The Journal of Social Issues*, Vol. 29, No. 2 (1973).

There is a growing literature on stratification and inequality under communism. For an excellent general analysis by a Polish sociologist, see Stanislaw Ossowski, *Class Structure in the Social Consciousness* (1963). Two very good collections of studies by Soviet sociologists may be found in Murray Yanowitch and Wesley A. Fisher, eds., *Social Stratification and Mobility in the U.S.S.R.* (1973), and M. N. Rutkevich, ed., *The Career Plans of Youth* (1969). For analyses by Western scholars see Mervyn Matthews, *Class and Society in Soviet Russia* (1972) and Frank Parkin, *Class Inequality and Political Order. Social Stratification in Capitalist and Communist Societies* (1971). An overview of Soviet sociological research on stratification is contained in S. M. Lipset and Richard Dobson, "Social Stratification and Sociology in the Soviet Union," *Survey* No. 88 (Summer 1973). Comprehensive analyses of the situations of ethnic groups may be found in Zev Katz et al., eds., *Handbook of Major Soviet Nationalities* (1975).

There are few comprehensive comparative analyses of American and Soviet society. The most recent one, which includes an analysis of stratification, sex roles, and ethnicity is Paul Hollander's *Soviet and American Society* (1973).

8

Age
and
Aging

MATILDA WHITE RILEY
JOAN WARING

Age and aging are social as well as biological phenomena. Murderers are not confined or punished as criminals *if* they are young children. College students are exempted from tuition payment *if* they are senior citizens. Hippies are especially scorned *if* they are middle-aged. Nude bathers are often subject to fine or imprisonment *if* they are over age 10. Thus age is a basic component in the ever-changing social structure. And this structure, in turn, influences age-related phenomena for every person in the society from birth to death. At what age a baby is weaned or trained to use the toilet is in large part socially determined. Social factors stipulate the boundaries and the activities of childhood, adulthood, and old age. Even the typical ages for onset of menstruation and for dying are affected by social conditions. Thus the lifelong process of aging, or growing older, is a social process. Both age and aging are imperious forces in social life. No man, woman, or child, nor society as a whole, is immune to their effects or to the problems they create.

Only recently, however, have the problems of age and aging been fully recognized as social phenomena: molded by human beings, rooted in human history, and susceptible to social intervention and change. These problems have been taken for granted as immutable, or wholly attributable to biology or "natural law." Yet, to understand their social character is to open all the possibilities of directing social change to improve the quality of life for people at every age. With the assurance that age and aging are mutable, the sociologist now faces a dual challenge: To explore how and to what degree social factors are responsible for personal troubles and social problems related to age;[1] and to find social means for ameliorating or correcting these problems. This chapter picks up the challenge.

Of the four parts of the chapter, the first offers a conceptual model to help define the major sets of social factors at work. Age, as a crucial element in the organization of individual and social affairs, is almost universally a criterion for allocating roles. Age determines eligibility for seeking a driver's license, signing a contract, running for political office, applying for retirement, or collecting social security benefits. Age also determines whether a person is obliged to attend school or to register for military service. Which roles are assigned at each age is fixed sometimes by custom, sometimes by law, sometimes by discriminatory practices, sometimes by social crises (like war or economic depression). Throughout their lives, people move through a sequence of age-ascribed roles—some congenial, some less so—that regulate and shape the course

This chapter was prepared as part of the Russell Sage Foundation Program on Age. The authors are indebted for many of the major ideas to their longtime collaborators, Marilyn Johnson and Anne Foner; for important contributions to Robert K. Merton; and for suggestions and criticism on earlier versions to Beth Hess, John W. Riley, Jr., and Elin Waring. Ideas and improvements were also suggested by Susan Kertzer and by several undergraduate majors in sociology including Robert Allen, David Austin, and Shaun Gilmore.

[1] For the distinction between personal troubles and social problems, see C. Wright Mills, "The Big City: Private Troubles and Public Issues," in Irving L. Horowitz (ed.), *Power, Politics and People* (New York: Oxford, 1963).

of their lives and are in turn reshaped by the people who pass through them.

Against this background of the social character of age and aging, the second section of the chapter considers some of the social problems arising from the division of society into age strata. This division creates inequalities among old, middle-aged, and young in the roles available and the associated rewards or punishments. Division into age strata also causes problems of age segregation and conflict between generations. The third section deals with problems that arise from the fact that people, as they age, continually move from one set of roles to another. It explores the strains and hidden sufferings that may accompany transitions at every phase of life—from entering a nursery school, beginning an active sex life, finding the first job, becoming a parent, to retiring or losing one's spouse. The last section addresses some of the possibilities and difficulties of social interventions aimed at correcting such problems. Interventions can be understood as attempts to modify the complex relationship between age and social change (described in the first section), as wars, economic fluctuations, or the changing state of science and the arts can transform both the force of age within the social structure and the ways in which people age. Age-graded roles, institutions, and aging individuals are involved in a complex feedback system that itself causes social problems yet gives room and opportunities for correction and for influencing the course of change.

A SOCIOLOGICAL PERSPECTIVE

In order to understand the problems of age and aging, it is useful to think of a society as consisting of two fluid, shifting structures: an age structure of people and an age structure of roles.[2] At any moment, age locates all persons in both these structures and forges the link between them. These structures derive from two universal sets of processes: *age dynamics,* which determine where, when, and how many *people* are located in the age structure, and *societal dynamics,* which determine and continually change the age structure of the *roles* to which people are allocated. These complex processes are in continuing interplay with one another, and their frequent disjunctures give rise to many social problems associated with age.

Age Dynamics

Aging and cohort flow—the processes that constitute age dynamics—involve *people.* Aging does not mean growing old—only growing older. In this straightforward sense, people age from birth to death; they grow up and grow old. In the course of aging, each person develops and changes his or her actions, attitudes, feelings, and aspirations. Moreover, while individuals in existing cohorts are aging and dying, new cohorts of people are continually being born and

[2] Matilda White Riley, "Age Strata in Social Systems," in James E. Birren (ed.), *Handbook of Aging and the Social Sciences* (New York: Van Nostrand Reinhold, 1976).

Figure 8-1. An Age Stratification System

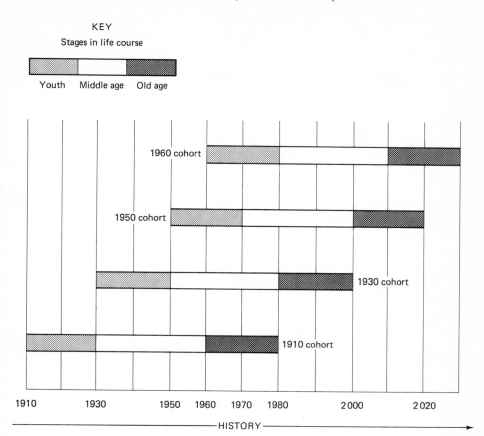

absorbed into the system. The twin processes of aging and cohort flow are indicated in Figure 8-1 by the horizontal bars, which depict the life-span of four
selected cohorts. Each of the cohorts consists of people born in the same interval of time, who age together. At each historical period (such as 1970 or 1980
in the diagram), the successive cohorts fit together to form the age structure of
the population.

Although aging and cohort flow are, at base, biological processes, the manner of their operation and their impact are primarily social. Social, not biological, explanations are needed, for example, to account for the fact that only some
40 percent of the cohort born at the turn of the last century were still in school
at the ages of 16 or 17, compared with nearly 90 percent for the cohort born in
the early 1950s.[3] Similarly, social, not biological, factors explain why recent

[3] U.S. Bureau of the Census, *1970 Census of the Population*, Vol. 1, Part 1 (Washington,
D.C.: U.S. Government Printing Office, 1973), p. 347.

cohorts have more effective means than their predecessors of controlling birth, of surviving after surgery, or of collective self-destruction. It is because of social change in such matters as health care, job opportunities, or educational norms that people in different cohorts tend to age in very different ways. And it is because of social factors—such as socially patterned decisions to have large families, to permit immigration, to use abortion, or to make military sacrifices—that cohorts differ markedly from one another in size and composition throughout their life course.

Societal Dynamics

Societal dynamics operate continually to affect aging and cohort flow. While people are being born, aging, and dying, they are being constrained and shaped by the changing age structure of *roles*. Age is not only a criterion for entering and leaving certain roles, but it also influences the nature of role prescriptions (norms as to what is expected), and the rewards or punishments allotted for role performance. For example, people are indulgent toward the cooking failures of young brides, but older wives are not similarly excused. Very different roles are open (or closed) to those at different locations in the age structure of people, and performance in roles is differently evaluated for those at different locations.

At given times (suggested by the vertical lines in Figure 8-1), we can think of the age structure of roles as a kind of screen through which different cohorts are simultaneously passing. In an educational system, for example, different cohorts are performing in the respective roles of students in elementary school, in high school, and in college. Furthermore, the role structure itself (for example, the educational system), far from being fixed, is subjected to continual modification and change as it moves through time (for example, from 1960 to 1970 to 1980). Consider the vulnerability of many structures we often accept as fixed. The usual grade sequences in schools and colleges, for example, have been challenged recently by demands for ungraded classrooms. In the future, preprimary school may become compulsory or dual enrollments in high school and college widespread. Such changes affect the *kinds* of roles available: the age criteria for entering or leaving, the normative expectations, or the sanctions (rewards and punishments). Other changes affect the *numbers* of roles available at different ages. Thus, if retirement age drops precipitously in response to economic conditions, there will be fewer roles for workers, more for retirees.

Let us look again at the "age dynamics" in relation to such changing role structures. We can now understand how *aging* means that people, over their life course, do not simply experience biological and psychological development and change; they also move through socially structured *sequences of roles* from birth to death (such as dependent child, student, worker, spouse, retiree), learning to adapt to new roles and relinquish old ones, accumulating knowledge and attitudes and social experiences. And we can understand how *cohort flow* means that, because each new cohort is born at a particular time, it con-

Figure 8-2. Educational Attainment in the United States by Age and Race, 1973–1974

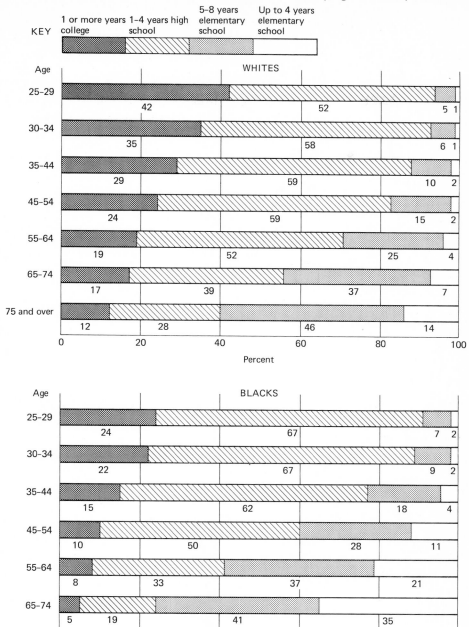

Source: U.S. Bureau of the Census, "Educational Attainment in the United States: March 1973 and 1974," *Current Population Reports,* Series P-20, No. 274 (Washington, D.C.: Government Printing Office, 1974).

fronts a unique sequence of roles and environmental events—defined as "history" (as designated in Figure 8-1). For example, the cohort born in 1930 started life during the Great Depression, experienced World War II, and entered young adulthood during a period of relative prosperity. By contrast, the cohort born in 1950 spent its early years in an increasingly affluent society and reached its majority during a period of decreased economic expansion. Each of these cohorts experienced different opportunities and disadvantages. Thus we can expect the problems of young people today to be quite different from those of young people in the past.

Age Stratification

The age strata, and many of the age inequalities we shall discuss, can be understood, then, as a cross-section of these two sets of concurrent and interacting processes: (1) the alteration of age-related roles in society as historical events occur and institutional structures change (societal dynamics) and (2) the aging of people who move through these roles, and the continual dying out and replacement of one cohort by another (age dynamics).

A few examples will begin to suggest how the interplay between societal dynamics and age dynamics result in age inequalities. Figure 8-2 shows striking age inequalities in educational attainment. Among whites, only 6 percent of the youngest stratum (aged 25–29 years) had not gone beyond elementary school, in comparison with 60 percent of the oldest stratum (aged 75 years and over). Among blacks, the age difference (9 percent for the youngest, 81 percent for the oldest) is even more striking. These dramatic differences in age strata are in large part the result of differences *among cohorts* in life-course patterns. They reflect the long-term historical rise in schooling that set its stamp on the lives of individuals in successive cohorts. And such age-strata differences in educational attainment suggest that the more recent, better-educated cohorts probably claim a greater share of social rewards (such as better jobs and higher income) than the older, less-educated ones.

Other cross-sectional differences among strata are more likely to derive from the ways in which people age *over the life course*. For example, while in our society the young are largely exempt from serious disease and disability, certain deficits in health and physical functioning tend to accumulate as people grow older, yielding such strata differences in long-term disability as appear in Figure 8-3. (Many of these may become preventable, just as acute diseases of childhood, such as polio, have.) Figure 8-3 also shows increases by age in the proportions of people whose disabilities lead to confinement in hospitals, nursing homes, and other resident institutions for health care.

Most age strata differences are more complex than those found in these examples of education or disability, since they derive from intricate combinations of life-course patterns *and* cohort differences. Whatever their derivations, such strata differences constitute a major source of social problems, as will be

Figure 8-3. Long-Term Disability by Type of Disability and Age, 1969

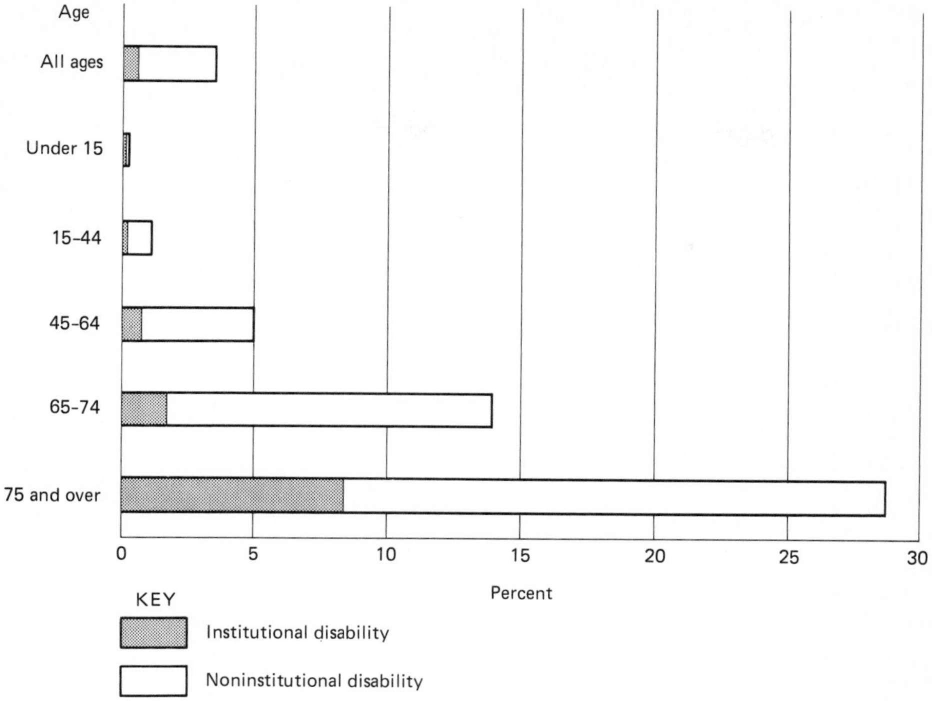

Source: Executive Office of the President, Office of Management and Budget, *Social Indicators, 1973* (Washington, D.C.: Government Printing Office, 1973), p. 11

seen in the second part of this chapter. *Within* any given stratum, people who are similar in age have much in common. They share many ideas and experiences because they are at similar points in the life course, they belong to the same cohort and so have aged together in the same historical context, and they are likely to play many similar roles. But *across* all the strata, people who differ in age differ both in the stage of their life course and in cohort membership, and have access to differing roles with differing sets of expectations and rewards. The age structure, as Merton puts it, "constrains individuals variously situated within it to develop cultural emphases, social behavior patterns, and psychological bents."[4] Many of these age-related differences in access to the good things in life are violations of societal ideals of equity or harmony. They inhibit communication and understanding between generations. They can create a sense of relative deprivation or inadequacy and feelings of hostility with reference to other age strata.

[4] Robert K. Merton, *Social Theory and Social Structure*, rev. ed. (New York: Free Press, 1968), p. 177.

Moreover, age differences often transcend other ways in which people differ. Within each age stratum, to be sure, individuals differ greatly from one another. In the United States, for example, the "typical" middle-aged male is in the labor force, while the "typical" elderly male is not, and the former has the higher "average" income. Nevertheless, some middle-aged individuals do not work and some have very low incomes, while some very old men are fully employed and some have the highest incomes in the country. Furthermore, there are marked differences among age mates that depend on their sex, race, or social-class background: Black babies are less likely to survive than white babies; college students are often treated as more juvenile than graduates from the same high school class who are working; boys in their early teens often resent the greater physical growth and emotional maturity of girls their own age; lower-class youth may feel denied the "age rights" to higher education accorded their more privileged peers. At the same time, however, age tends to unite people who differ in other respects. Figure 8-2 gives just one of many instances in which age differences are at least as great as race differences. At each age level, whites have benefited far more than blacks from educational opportunities; but for both races, the educational inequalities between the oldest and the youngest age strata are even more pronounced than racial inequalities.

Intrinsic Strains and Imbalances

Another source of social problems involving age is a built-in tension between the two sets of processes in the system—age dynamics (affecting people) and societal dynamics (affecting roles). A major insight of the sociology of age is the recognition of this inherent strain between the continuing flow of new cohorts of people and the societal changes in the roles through which the cohorts flow. Let us see what this means.

Roles change with history. Industrialization has meant drastic qualitative and quantitative changes in the overall structure of occupational roles in the United States; for example, the proportion of all workers engaged in agriculture has dropped from 40 percent in 1900 to 3 or 4 percent today. Particular roles have also altered, as the requirements for entering and performing the role of farmer have been adapted to the rise of large-scale, mechanized agriculture. Meantime, *people* change. It is widely assumed that the life course has a fixed trajectory, that aging follows a predetermined pattern. But it is now absolutely clear that *people in different cohorts age in different ways*. It is inconceivable that each new cohort should simply follow in the footsteps of its predecessors. It is inconceivable, for example, that young people today, like young people of the past, should finish school with the fourth grade. It is also inconceivable that the attitudes toward sex roles now entrenched among middle-aged men and women will be replicated by today's young cohorts (whose "liberated" women have now even broken the barrier into the military academies) as they become middle-aged in the next decades. Roles and people are

continually pressing upon one another for change. The differing life-course patterns in successive cohorts are not only changed by, but in turn change, the role structure of the society.

Given such socially structured complexity, one wonders how the system could be expected to run smoothly. People and roles often fail to mesh. People at the requisite ages may be too many or too few, or they may be overprepared or underprepared for the role openings available. So, too, there are many shifting discrepancies between the values and aspirations in the society and the actualities of age-related social roles and human behavior. As we now begin to look into the complexities of the age-stratification system, we have reason to expect it to be the source of abundant social problems—many, no doubt, latent problems yet to be recognized and studied.[5]

[5] With respect to latent problems, see the Introduction to this book.

PROBLEMS OF AGE STRATIFICATION

One set of problems derives from the pronounced differences that age creates among people in the coexisting age strata. Like social class, race, and sex, age is a basis for stratification within societies[6]—indeed, the *first* basis:

> The first class system that every individual encounters is the division between adult and child, and the complex distribution of prerogatives, compensations, dependencies, and freedom that goes with it.[7]

Age can segregate cohorts and generations. It can foment conflict between them. Most critically, it can and often does create inequalities.

Age Inequalities

Age strata are marked by differential access to the roles that provide economic rewards, prestige, and power. Some age strata have open access to prestigious roles, some have restricted access, some have virtually none—as in the case of formal age requirements for election to political office or informal ones for corporate presidencies. Age is also implicated in the uneven distribution of such other social desiderata as family affiliations, leisure and extended vacations, and health. Even such matters as opportunities for marriage after being widowed also vary widely by age, with the pool of possible mates far larger for young widowed people than for older. Not least, the sheer probability of living from one birthday to the next is age-related.

Certain of these age-derived inequalities can be biologically legitimized. The little child is not due the same income or the same power as its parents. Nonagenarians are physically unfit for active participation in professional sports. But many of the socially structured differences between strata have no necessary counterpart in the age-related, biologically grounded competencies and motivations of the people who are allotted or denied roles. Indeed, these inequalities run counter to some deep-rooted values: equality of opportunity, fair evaluation of achievement, individualism, self-reliance. The discrepancies between the ideal and the actual implied by age inequalities constitute another social problem that challenges glib acceptance of the established social order as necessarily just. For individuals, inequitable role allocations based on age can produce strain, dissatisfaction, and deviance. For society, these inequalities involve waste of human resources, unnecessary burdens of dependency, and conflicts arising from attempts to equalize rewards.

Opportunities for "success" The allocation of work roles in the United States provides one of the clearest examples of the operation and consequences

---

[6] Anne Foner, "Age in Society: Structure and Change," *American Behavioral Scientist,* Vol. 19 (November-December 1975), pp. 144–165.

[7] Philip E. Slater, *Pursuit of Loneliness: American Culture at the Breaking Point* (Boston: Beacon Press, 1971), p. 89.

of age stratification. Work roles in this society are the means for achieving not only economic reward and power, but also social esteem. They are crucial to "success," with its associated symbolic meaning of being wanted. But these valued roles and the rewards they bring (sometimes, to be sure, balanced by the burdens of responsibility) are not equally available to all age strata. Indeed, both formal and informal norms—as well as actual prejudice in hiring and firing —conspire to keep full participation from both the young and the old.

Table 8-1 U.S. Labor Participation Rates Force According to Age, 1900–1970, with Projection to 1985 (percent in labor force)

Age	1900	1920	1940	1944	1950	1960	1970	1985
Males								
14–19	63.6	52.6	44.2	70.0	53.2	—	—	—
16–17	—	—	—	—	—	45.9	46.7	45.6
18–19	—	—	—	—	—	73.1	68.8	65.1
20–24	91.7	91.0	96.1	98.5	89.0	88.9	85.1	82.4
25–34	—	—	98.1	99.0	96.2	96.4	95.0	94.4
25–44	96.3	97.2	—	—	—	—	—	—
35–44	—	—	98.5	99.0	97.6	96.4	95.7	94.9
45–55	—	—	95.5	97.1	95.8	94.3	92.9	91.7
45–64	93.3	93.8	—	—	—	—	—	—
55–64	—	—	87.2	92.1	87.0	85.2	81.5	78.1
65+	68.3	60.1	45.0	52.2	45.8	32.2	25.8	20.0
Females								
14–19	26.8	28.4	23.3	42.0	31.5	—	—	—
16–17	—	—	—	—	—	28.6	34.6	36.7
18–19	—	—	—	—	—	51.0	53.4	55.7
20–24	32.1	38.1	49.5	55.0	46.1	46.1	57.5	64.9
25–34	—	—	35.2	39.0	34.0	35.8	44.8	50.9
25–44	18.1	22.4	—	—	—	—	—	—
35–44	—	—	28.8	40.5	39.1	43.1	50.9	54.4
45–54	—	—	24.3	35.8	38.0	49.3	54.0	57.4
45–64	14.1	17.1	—	—	—	—	—	—
55–64	—	—	18.7	25.4	37.0	36.7	42.5	45.4
65+	9.1	8.0	7.4	9.8	9.7	10.5	9.2	8.5

Source: Data for 1900–1950 from Donald J. Bogue, *The Population of the United States* (Glencoe, Ill.: Free Press, 1969), p. 426. Data for 1960, 1970, 1985 from U.S. Bureau of the Census, *Statistical Abstract of the United States, 1974* (Washington, D.C.: Government Printing Office, 1974), Table 543.

Table 8-1 shows male participation in the work force by age.[8] In 1970, rates of labor force participation are low among youths, highest among men 25 to 55 years old, and then fall off sharply in the older age strata. Middle-aged

[8] Work roles of women, still in a formative stage, have shown very different age patterns, with one peak in early adulthood and another in the middle years. For a fuller discussion see: Matilda White Riley, Marilyn Johnson, and Anne Foner, *Aging and Society, Vol. III, A Sociology of Age Stratification* (New York: Russell Sage Foundation, 1972), pp. 54–57.

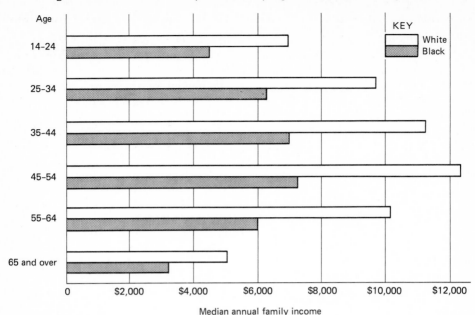

Figure 8-4. Median Family Income* by Age and Race of Family Head

Median annual family income

* Average, 1968–1971.
Source: Executive Office of the President, Office of Management and Budget, *Social Indicators, 1973* (Washington, D.C.: Government Printing Office, 1973), p. 155.

people are not only in the most favored age stratum in terms of claims to occupational roles, but are also most favored in terms of income for the roles they do perform. Median incomes for families in the several age strata in the United States (Figure 8-4) tend to form a bell-shaped curve in which younger people (heads of families) in their 20s, and older people 50 and over, have incomes sharply lower than people in their middle years.[9]

A glance at history shows how chronological age does not itself provide a fixed or compelling basis for determining labor-force participation. At the turn of the century, one-quarter of boys 10 to 15 years old were gainfully employed[10] and most men did not retire at 65 but continued their participation in the work force. Since 1900, the general trend (Table 8-1) has been toward increasing concentration of economic activity in the middle years. In general (with spot

[9] These strata differences cannot be explained by aging alone, since the earnings of most people start to decline, not in the middle years, but closer to the age of retirement. A further explanation lies in economic growth: the younger cohort benefited more than the older from the continuing overall rise in income. By starting later in history, they started at a higher level.

[10] These data are not shown in Table 8-1 since, after 1930, the Census stopped counting children under 14 in compiling labor force statistics and in 1967 stopped counting children under 16—facts further documenting the changing age criteria for role entry.

exceptions, as in 1944 because of World War II), the average age of entry into the labor force has tended to rise, and the average age of exit has fallen precipitously: In 1900, two-thirds of men 65 and over were still in the labor force, a fraction that had declined to one-fourth in 1970 and is predicted to reach one-fifth by 1985.

These drastic changes in the age structure of economic roles for men (changes paralleled in most industrial countries) give dramatic evidence that current inequalities of opportunity are not immutable. Although there are no definitive explanations, the long-term trends in age of employment have been associated with a complex of interacting factors including massive declines in both agricultural and self-employment, the extension of formal education, the establishment of rules governing age at starting or discontinuing a job, and the extension of public and private pension plans that afford alternative (though modest) sources of income and often specify mandatory ages of retirement. This is only one of many instances in which social roles allocated to age strata at any given time are by no means biologically determined, but result from historical changes in the organization of society.

Marital roles   The middle-aged also have the greatest access to marital roles which, despite the accompanying responsibilities and frequent disillusionment, constitute a major source of happiness and satisfaction.[11] Age patterns of marriage differ somewhat by sex. Young men tend to marry slightly later than young women. Old men, in contrast, tend to remain married (or remarried) up to extreme old age, whereas substantial proportions of women are already widowed by age 55. Because mortality rates for men are higher than for women, over two-thirds of women aged 75 and over are widowed, while two-thirds of men at that age are married. Thus in our society many more elderly women than elderly men lead solitary lives (many of them live entirely alone)—although they usually remain in frequent contact with at least one of their adult children.

Matching of people and roles   Such inequalities arise partly because of the age norms built into the changing role structure, and partly because of historical changes in the numbers and kinds of people in the strata. The solitary lives of elderly women today derive partly from the pronounced excess of females over males at the later ages. And, regardless of sex, there may be too many or too few people in a stratum to be readily accommodated in the available roles. The differing shapes of the age pyramids in Figure 8-5 illustrate striking changes in the relative sizes of strata in the United States since

[11] Angus Campbell et al., *The Quality of American Life: Perceptions, Evaluations, and Satisfactions* (New York: Russell Sage Foundation, 1976); Norval D. Glenn, "The Contribution of Marriage to the Psychological Well-Being of Males and Females," *Journal of Marriage and the Family* (1976, forthcoming).

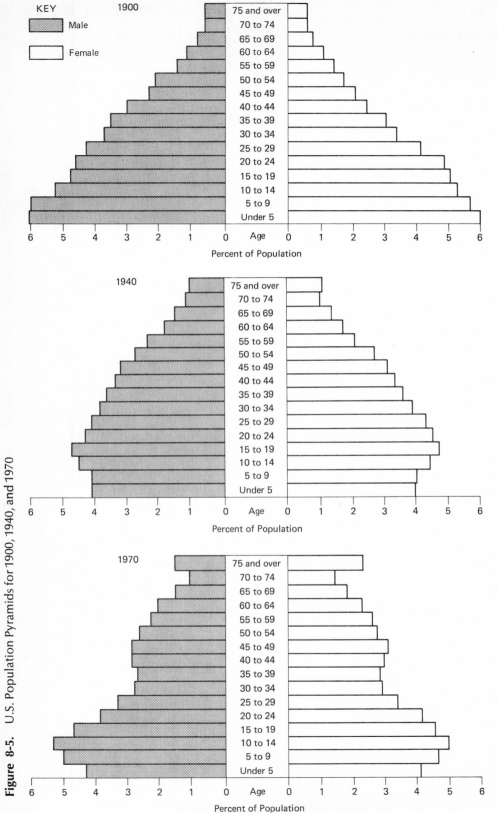

Figure 8-5. U.S. Population Pyramids for 1900, 1940, and 1970

Source: Executive Office of the President, Office of Management and Budget, *Social Indicators, 1973* (Washington, D.C.: Government Printing Office, 1973), p. 238.

1900. For example, the proportion of the total population aged 65 and over has risen sharply (from 3 percent in 1900 to nearly 10 percent in 1970) as has the proportion aged 45 to 64 (from about 10 percent in 1900 to 20 percent in 1970).

Such changes in age composition reflect changes in fertility levels over time. For example, by 1970 (as can be easily seen in Figure 8-5), there are large numbers of males and females aged 10 to 14, resulting from the peak of the "baby boom" in the mid-1950s. But there are far fewer children in the younger cohorts coming along to fill their places in the schools. To carry the responsibilities of middle life, there are also comparatively few persons aged 30 to 39 (the Great Depression cohorts).

Besides fertility, another important factor affecting the population and the mesh between people and roles is the spectacular increase in longevity. In the United States the average length of life has risen from about 40 years among cohorts born in the mid-nineteenth century to an estimated 70 years among those born in the 1970s—for the first time in history, most people can expect to grow old. As increasing proportions of people live into their later years, these changes act in turn upon the age structure of roles. Witness the virtual revolution in the number of family relationships. Just a century ago, all the living members of a family typically constituted only two generations (parents and their children living together in a nuclear household). Occasionally a grandparent was still alive. Today several generations of a family are often alive at one time (and each typically lives in a separate nuclear household): the young couple with their dependent children, two sets of middle-aged grandparents of these children, and not infrequently a few surviving great-grandparents. Many problems of the American family, and many of its strengths, arise from the long life of family members, combined with the norm and the resources for separate residence. Postparental couples, who now spend an average of a decade and a half together during the "empty-nest" stage, must readjust their whole way of life and their relationship to each other after the children leave home. With only two members, the family group is vulnerable to dissolution from the loss of either one; concern over death is focused not on which one will die but on the difficulties of the survivor.[12] With death usually striking late in life, widows today are far older than in the past; but they are also far more likely to live alone, only occasionally residing with an offspring (who may herself be over 65!) and, in rarer instances, in a nursing home (Figure 8-3). Yet the same increased longevity that causes problems for the elderly has now largely dispelled the major social problem of orphanhood that once afflicted children.

Thus, as more and more people survive into the middle and later years, they outstrip the numbers and kinds of roles traditionally available. They may also reject these roles. The social "excess" of people at the later ages, and their evolving behaviors and needs (as "empty-nest" parents, ancient widows, re-

[12] John W. Riley, Jr., "What People Think About Death," in Orville G. Brim, Jr. et al. (eds.), *The Dying Patient* (New York: Russell Sage Foundation, 1970), Ch. 2.

tirees) not only cause current problems but also gradually press to reshape some existing social roles and institutions.

Age Inequality and Deviance

An important agenda for sociological investigation is tracing the connections between age inequalities and the various forms of deviance examined in this book. Age inequalities arise, as we have seen, when people of particular ages are denied access to role opportunities that are socially valued. Still another type of social problem stems from age-patterned discrepancies between actual role opportunities and individual aspirations for roles and rewards. These socially patterned discrepancies often lead to deviant behavior and attitudes. Thus we might ask what the connections are between denying major economic roles and rewards to adolescents and the fact that crime rates in the United States typically peak in adolescence or early adulthood, and then tend to decline over the middle and later years (see Chapter 1). What are the connections between rising crime rates and decreasing access to first jobs during periods of economic recession? We should expect such connections, once identified, to open new avenues for understanding criminal behavior from the perspective of age stratification. (Conversely, understanding of the age patterns of deviance can point to strains resulting from particular types of age inequalities.)

The concept is noted throughout this book that behavior is deviant only *relative* to a set of norms defined by particular groups as appropriate or binding. The term is not disparaging; what is deviant in one context may be conforming in another. "Childishness" is deviant for an adult, but not for a child.

Disengagement and retreatism   As one example of how age-related behaviors may be better understood as forms of deviance, consider how older people—shut off from major economic roles—respond to the role of retirement.[13] Some welcome the new role and increase their interest in various unpaid activities, but others develop low morale or find it difficult to keep occupied, spending much of their time passively—sitting, standing, looking out a window, or napping. This raises the questions: Are such responses peculiar to the state of being old, or can they be defined as "deviant" responses induced not by age but by the particular circumstances of older people in today's society? If jobs were widely unavailable to people of all ages, would the responses of the young and the middle-aged be similar to those of many retired older people?

Some answers are available from studies that probed into just such a situation—the widespread unemployment in several countries during the Great Depression.[14] A few of the unemployed found compensating activities (such

[13] Matilda White Riley and Anne Foner, *Aging and Society, Vol. I, An Inventory of Research Findings* (New York: Russell Sage Foundation, 1968), pp. 453–458, 513–517.

[14] Matilda White Riley et al., "Socialization for the Middle and Later Years," in David A. Goslin (ed.), *Handbook of Socialization Theory and Research* (Chicago: Rand McNally, 1969), pp. 951–982.

as home repair or gardening) for their lost jobs. Others became resigned to unemployment, renouncing their earlier expectations of success and making virtues of their substitute roles as homemakers or parents. And still others were defensive or deviant in their reactions, finding scapegoats for their misfortunes, losing their self-esteem, or resorting to excessive drinking or to criminality. Such reactions fit precisely into the paradigm devised by Merton for analyzing basic forms of deviance.[15] Of all the responses to unemployment, Merton's "retreatism" (or "disengagement," as it has also been called[16]) was by far the most common, often giving way to complete apathy and indolence, and sometimes deteriorating into physical or mental illness. For many, impairment of skills and gradual acceptance of the unemployed status tended to result in complete unemployability. In short, when circumstances are similar, the responses of younger adult workers are strikingly parallel to those of older workers. Both older retirees and young unemployed people often resort to deviance when loss of work roles is involuntary or of long duration. For all age strata, barriers in the social structure can destroy the motivation to perform in accustomed roles. And once motivation is lost, a vicious circle sets in: Skills and capacities deteriorate through disuse, and the disuse fosters actual physical and mental incompetence. As incompetence becomes apparent, social stereotyping (or labeling) follows, and this stereotyping in turn further undermines motivation to perform.[17] Ultimately, many people come to believe in the desirability of losing the role—a phenomenon that might help account for frequent positive attitudes toward retirement today.

This example underscores a central point: it is not age alone that elicits particular responses. Many of the attitudes, satisfactions, and performances—and the accompanying stereotypes—that characterize particular age strata are evoked by socially structured inequalities, not by age as such. Various types of illness, even death, may also be traceable to such socially structured inequalities. Brim has summarized much evidence showing that people who have lost a sense of control over their lives become vulnerable to mental depression, physical ailments, and "submissive death."[18] And it is old people, of course, the special target population for disability and chronic illness, who are often deprived of social incentives to get well. Again there is the risk of a self-fulfilling prophecy. If stereotyped as "too old" to recover, the old may indeed retreat permanently into inactivity and invalidism. The sick role becomes a deviant role—often a terminal role—when the old who might get better are no longer expected to do so. (On the mechanism of the self-fulfilling prophecy, see the Introduction to this book.) Not unrelated is the fact that suicide rates

---

[15] Robert K. Merton, *op cit.*, Chs. 6, 7.

[16] Elaine Cumming and William E. Henry, *Growing Old: The Process of Disengagement* (New York: Basic Books, 1961).

[17] *Cf.* Lissy Jarvik, "Thoughts on the Psychobiology of Aging," *American Psychologist* (May 1975), pp. 576–583.

[18] Orville G. Brim, Jr., "The Sense of Personal Control Over One's Life," address to the Annual Convention of the American Psychological Association, September 1974 (mimeographed).

for men in our society characteristically show a clear age pattern, rising steadily with age to a peak at age 80 and over.[19] All this raises a question, still insufficiently studied, of a relationship between these forms of deviant behavior and age inequalities.

Societal repercussions Deviance within an age stratum can affect other segments of society as well. For example, it is not unthinkable that, as younger and more affluent people retire,[20] some retirees might develop retreatist, hedonistic, or nihilistic adaptations that spread from such deviant groups through the larger society, reinforcing in younger cohorts such manifestations as repudiation of deep-rooted values, self-indulgence, or drug addiction. Or the old themselves may become active agents of change (Merton's "rebellion"), demanding fuller social citizenship through either conflict or cooperation with those in other strata.

Age Inequality and The Quality of Life

We have been discussing connections between age inequality and forms of deviance that may arise from the age-patterned discrepancies between people's aspirations and their actual role opportunities. But how are these inequalities and discrepancies experienced? Some inequalities have subtle effects that operate below the level of awareness of the individuals involved. Other inequalities, of which each individual is acutely aware, are often suffered in secret. We know little about such hidden sufferings. Yet many people in disadvantaged age strata undoubtedly confront their own strains, anxieties, and dissatisfactions, believing that these troubles are unique to them, a result of some personal flaw. Such negative feelings may take the form of vague discontent. Or they may be recognized as inequities and regarded as unfair and illegitimate. When shared with others, such perceptions of inequity become aggregate dissatisfactions that provide soil for conflict and social movements or for mutual aid and support.

A striking set of findings on the feelings and reactions of people in the several age strata is provided in a study of "the perceived quality of life."[21] The survey uses two indicants of quality of life: "happiness," which assesses a person's current emotional state and feelings, and "life satisfaction," which assesses a person's current definitions of the situation. The findings show

[19] Recent increases in suicide rates among adolescents may reflect declines in the demand for younger workers—perhaps even marking the start of a decline in the high premium placed on youth (U.S. Bureau of the Census, *Statistical Abstract of the United States, 1974* [Washington, D.C.: Government Printing Office, 1975], Table 90).

[20] Bernice L. Neugarten, "The Future and the Young-Old," *The Gerontologist*, Vol. 15, No. 1 (February 1975), Part 2, pp. 4–9.

[21] Campbell et al., *op. cit.*

(Figure 8-6) that "happiness" is highest among young people (25–34 years old) and lowest among the very old (75 and older), whereas "life satisfaction" is conversely patterned—lowest in young adulthood and highest among the old. Only among the middle-aged (45–54), caught between heavy responsibilities and diminishing opportunities for success, are both measures simultaneously low. In interpreting these opposing tendencies, the authors suggest that the young, though dissatisfied with most aspects of their lives, can be happy because they look to the future; whereas the old, without hope or joy, have nevertheless become resigned to their life circumstances. In investigating how resignation could coexist with high "life satisfaction," the researchers requestioned the respondents and discovered two further age-patterns, both highly relevant for our understanding of social problems. First, aspirations decline with age: the older people are, the less they expect of life. Second, the gap between aspirations and perceived actuality also decreases with age.[22] It is precisely this gap between aspirations and perceived actuality that constitutes a social problem. (This definition is in the Introduction.) In other words, this study indicates that the older people are, the less they experience the quality of their lives as posing major problems for them.

Of course, the findings do not answer all the questions. Cross-section data from a single time period cannot rigorously describe how individuals change with aging over the life course. Pending further investigation that will trace these same cohorts into the future, the data do make us think about two complementary life-course processes that, to an unknown extent, are simultaneously at work. One possibility is that actual conditions may tend to improve for most people as they grow older. The lifelong search for a better mesh between person and role may have produced a gradual shedding of unsatisfactory roles (such as unhappy marriages or uncongenial jobs) and increasing commitments (for example, to home or neighborhood) in the meaningful roles remaining. This life-course pattern would indeed improve the quality of life, helping to account for increasing satisfaction as one ages. A contrasting possibility is that aspirations generally shrink over the life course because people learn to accommodate to bleak realities. Shrinking aspirations can help bridge the gap to actuality. This second process also can account for the comparatively high satisfaction—in the special form of resignation—expressed by old people. If old people are closing their eyes to the difficulties confronting them, a whole new set of social problems—latent problems—require attention. That latent problems may in fact exist is supported by the original finding (Figure 8-6) that the very old combine the highest degree of satisfaction with the lowest degree of happiness.

Whatever the ultimate explanations, this study makes clear that many people in the older age strata have come more nearly to terms with their lives than people in the younger strata. As we shall see in the third part of this chap-

---

[22] These findings are primarily suggestive, since the researchers reinterviewed only a small, though carefully selected, sample (less than 300) of their respondents.

Figure 8-6. Average Levels of Happiness and Life Satisfaction, United States, 1971 (Standardized Scores)

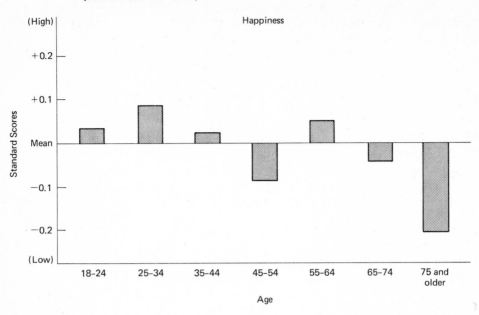

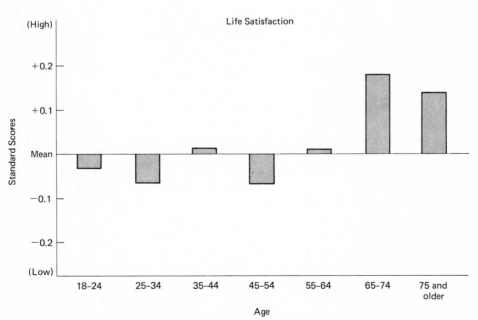

Source: Angus Campbell et al., *The Quality of American Life: Perceptions, Evaluations, and Satisfactions* (New York: Russell Sage Foundation, 1976).

ter, no matter what the objective hardships and inequalities, the old seem better able to explain the actuality away,[23] while many of the young seem both happy and expectant that their current dissatisfaction will be resolved.

Unlike the old and young, with their complex and ambivalent feelings, the middle-aged, especially those aged 45 to 54 (Figure 8-6), rank low on both measures: compared to the others, they are both unhappy and dissatisfied. Evidently, in spite of the many roles and rewards available to them, they feel themselves overburdened with responsibilities and, perhaps, are fearful as they perceive the decline of opportunities ahead.[24]

Integration versus Segregation of Age Strata

Not only does the stratification of society by age create inequalities and induce deviance, but it also contributes to other types of societal strain. Because age often channels human relationships and activities, it can serve to divide people or bring them together. It can become an agency of social segregation or of integration—and thus of social conflict or of cohesion. What, then, do age segregation and age integration mean for society? How do they operate as sources of individual and social problems? And can these problems be remedied?

Within strata, similarity of age often serves as an integrative mechanism. We have seen how similarities in cohort membership and stage in the life course provide roughly similar experiences for individuals. Age-peers may often be fiercely competitive, but their common positions and commonality of experience can nevertheless foster shared orientations, cooperation toward common goals, and the development of organized groups. Feelings of solidarity are promoted where age-peers are in a position to communicate about their similar tasks, needs, and problems, and about the intensification of these problems at points of major transitions in life. The sociological literature on friendship shows that in the United States people of all ages (but in particular adolescents and old people) tend to have friends of their own age—a status characteristic that signals mutuality of experiences, tastes, or values.[25] And, of course, age-based friendships often provide important social support in times of trouble.

But in the process of "solving" certain problems, age-based solidarity can cause new problems. Age solidarity can provide emotional support and opportunity for interaction and communication for individuals within a stratum, but

[23] See Riley and Foner, *op. cit.*, Chs. 14, 15.
[24] Orville G. Brim, Jr., "Selected Theories of the Male Mid-Life Crisis: A Comparative Analysis," address to the Annual Convention of the American Psychological Association, September 1974 (mimeographed).
[25] Such age "homophily" is a special case of widespread homophily—similarity of specific attributes among friends—in a variety of statuses and values (Paul F. Lazarsfeld and Robert K. Merton, "Friendship as Social Process: A Substantive and Methodological Analysis," in M. Berger et al. [eds.], *Freedom and Control in Modern Society* [Princeton, N.J.: Van Nostrand, 1954]).

as Blau points out, in the process it frequently fosters cleavage between the strata.[26]

Between strata, age operates differently, often segregating sets of people from one another and differentiating many of the roles they play. We have seen how people in different age strata tend to have disparate rather than similar experiences and interests because they differ in life-stage, in cohort-membership, and in the roles they occupy. Several historical trends in this country have encouraged the increasing segregation of age strata: the spread of education, which is usually age-graded; the development of age-homogeneous housing arrangements (young people in college dormitories or military quarters, old people in retirement communities, middle-aged people in suburbs where they settled as young couples). Even the nuclear family has become more polarized by age. The smaller number and closer spacing of children in the family has meant that parents and their children now form two distinct generations in contrast, for example, to the wide range of ages created by the large number of children in colonial families.

Age segregation has disadvantages. It can interfere with reciprocal socialization by preventing young people and their grandparents, for example, from teaching each other. It can reinforce age barriers, reducing the communication and ties, for example, between students currently in college and earlier cohorts of students now established in adult roles. It can create damaging and unfair stereotypes, highly competitive political constituencies, or destructive social movements. When age-based inequalities are widely viewed as inequities, strong cleavages or open conflict may develop, as young people or the elderly attempt to claim their rights.[27] Youth groups are likely to revolt against their elders in nonliterate as in modern societies;[28] and, even when not overt, there is undoubtedly a continuing struggle for position between young and old.[29] Sometimes, to be sure, age segregation allows hostile feelings to dissipate, as when avoidance of mothers-in-law is facilitated.

These problems of age cleavage are mitigated by opportunities for interaction among people of diverse age. A major source of cohesion between age strata is the family network of interdependence and exchange between parents and offspring. Among old people, ties to friends, who are generally age peers, are far less significant than ties to children and grandchildren. Some three-fourths of people over 65 in the United States have living adult children, and

---

[26] Peter M. Blau, "Perimeters of Social Structure," *American Sociological Review,* Vol. 39 (1974), pp. 615–635.

[27] For mechanisms tending to encourage age-based conflict or to reduce it, see Anne Foner, "Age Stratification and Age Conflict in Political Life," *American Sociological Review,* Vol. 39 (April 1974), pp. 187–196; Anne Foner (ed.), "Age and Society," *American Behavioral Scientist,* special issue (November–December 1975), and in particular in this issue, Anne Foner, "Age in Society: Structure and Change."

[28] S. N. Eisenstadt, *From Generation to Generation: Age Groups and Social Structure* (Glencoe, Ill.: Free Press, 1956).

[29] Pitirim A. Sorokin, *Society, Culture and Personality* (New York: Harper, 1947); Gerhard E. Lenski, *Power and Privilege: A Theory of Social Stratification* (New York: McGraw-Hill, 1966).

most, though living separately, maintain regular contact with at least one child and with their grandchildren.[30] Although some commentators postulate the complete immersion of recent generations in a "youth culture,"[31] adolescents show marked tendencies toward continuing filial bonds and continuing parental influence in preparation for adult life.[32] A recent United States survey shows that, both in the population at large and among people 65 and over, three out of four people say they would prefer to spend most of their time with people of different ages, rather than only with people their own age.[33]

Such linkages, fostering interaction and communication across age lines, reduce some of the strains on group solidarities and loyalties, and can help to alleviate some of the problems of age inequality. The policy proposals to be discussed in the closing section of this chapter include possible ways of intensifying cross-age linkages and of integrating the young and the old into the society.

PROBLEMS OF AGING

Just as age as a basis for social stratification creates inequalities and conditions for conflict, so the process of aging creates problems—though of a different order. The inevitability of aging makes moving from one age stratum to the next equally inevitable. From birth to death, as people move from one life stage to the next, they must pass through the socially structured sequence of roles, thus continually assuming and relinquishing roles. Such role transitions are seldom easy to negotiate, since they require that a person learn how to perform in the roles ascribed to the new life stage and surrender the gratifications of earlier, now inappropriate, roles.[34] In this section we examine the problems that attend the process of aging and the accompanying role transitions, touching upon the nature of transitions, how problems arise, and conditions that ease or intensify the strains generated by these role transfers.

The Nature of Role Transitions

Role transitions punctuate the life course. Although each transition has unique characteristics and poses distinctive problems, and each is met with varying degrees of trauma or resiliency, most transitions have features in common.

---

[30] Riley and Foner, *op. cit.,* pp. 541–549; Ethel Shanas, *Old People in Three Industrial Societies* (New York: Atherton Press, 1968).

[31] James S. Coleman, *The Adolescent Society* (New York: Free Press, 1961).

[32] Denise B. Kandel and Gerald S. Lesser, *Youth in Two Worlds: United States and Denmark* (San Francisco: Jossey-Bass, 1972); Matilda White Riley et al., "Adolescent Values and the Riesman Typology: An Empirical Analysis," in S. M. Lipset and Leo Lowenthal (eds.), *Culture and Social Character* (New York: Free Press, 1961).

[33] National Council on the Aging, "The Myth and Reality of Aging in America" (Washton, D.C., 1975, mimeographed), p. 71.

[34] Riley et al., "Socialization for the Middle and Later Years"; Barney Glaser and Anselm Strauss, *Status Passage* (Chicago: Aldine, 1971).

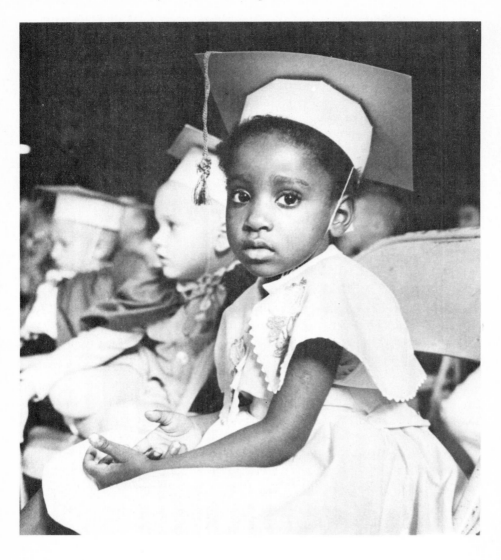

By specifying these features we can begin to understand the problems they generate.

Types of problems Two types of difficulties are common to nearly all transitions. One is the strain of learning: orienting to new roles, making myriad adjustments, resolving conflicts with the competing demands of the other roles the person plays. In making life's first great transition, the fetus becomes a baby and must learn to breathe and eat, to behave as a baby is expected to. The young child, making the transition to school, must conform to new authorities and new schedules and must handle new influences that often run counter to the influences of the family. The youth, in making the transition to the roles of adulthood, must often cope, within a short time, with many new demands at work, in the family, and in the community. Mature adults, making the transition to the roles of old age, must find ways to structure the free time imposed by retirement, widowhood, or invalidism.

The second type of difficulty pervading most role transitions inheres in the dual nature of the process: each time, a new role must be taken on and an old one given up—and giving up a role involves considerable additional learning and adjustment. It also means relinquishing the former rewards and abandoning that portion of one's self that had become invested in the previous role. Learning the role of first-grader involves renouncing full-time play; learning the role of husband or wife involves renouncing the unmarried state; learning the role of retiree involves renouncing the role of worker. In the long chain of transitions over the life course, each new change creates discontinuity with the past. It also requires fresh commitment to a new role which must, in turn, eventually be abandoned.

Both types of difficulties are often endured privately, thus constituting a latent social problem of unknown magnitude. Transitions in the life course are often taken for granted, and each person may be unaware that others also experience them as stressful. People at each stage, however brave their front to the world, confront role changes with unknown risks of emotional punishment, and untold threats to the sense of their own identity and to feelings of competence and mastery over life.

Role transitions vary widely, of course, in the extent and severity of the problems they cause. Often they are a rich source of new opportunities, challenges, and alluring rewards. They can hold promise of heightened self-esteem. But even under the most auspicious circumstances, the potential difficulties are there beneath the surface. Under less than auspicious circumstances, transitions lead to a sense of failure and to hurt, defensiveness, and withdrawal. Let us consider how problem-laden transitions differ from easier ones.

We can hypothesize a process in which the transition is accomplished—the new role learned and the former role relinquished—with no difficulty or trauma. By studying departures from such a model as a standard for comparison, we can see the nature and sources of the strains of continual learning and adjusting and the pain associated with loss of role.

Learning a new role   In a problem-free model of learning, or becoming *socialized* to, a new role, the individual acquires competency, commitment, and satisfaction in the role. In this imaginary process, a perfect fit between person and role is hypothetically achieved: the child learns to become autonomous in school, for example, or the young person independent in the workplace. Such learning involves a complex transaction between the individual and society, a careful dovetailing of individual and societal contributions to the process. The individual, because of self-ideals developed in earlier roles, *wants* to assume the new role. There is perfect congruence between the aspirations of the individual and the social norms and expectations of the role. The individual willingly submits to the role of learner, making a serious commitment to learn the obligations and the skills required by the new role, and learning to relinquish the old role and its no longer appropriate gratifications. In the interaction between individual and society, complementary societal contributions are made. Role expectations are explicitly defined. Facilities and resources for learning (such as exemplary schools) are provided, and persons (such as well-trained teachers) are made available for teaching the role. Approval and other rewards (sanctions) are given for behavior that meets social expectations, and disapproval and other punishments for unacceptable behavior. The individual is thus guided to satisfying performance in a clearly defined role valued highly by both self and society. When aging terminates the commitment to this age-related role, the process begins all over again.

In practice, of course, such conditions do not occur in this extreme form —nor *should* they if, as we stress later, the social structure is to be flexible and the individual free to alter it. Individuals may not meet the conditions: Not everybody wants to assume the roles prescribed by society; some do not learn roles readily; and very few can learn them to perfection. And the society rarely meets the conditions of the hypothetical model: Continual social change means that socially defined role expectations are often unclear; facilities for learning the role are often inadequate; or there are no suitable persons to teach the role, to provide models for role performance, or to express approval when the individual does well. Moreover, the transactions between the individual and society may not meet the conditions: Strains develop in the relationship between socializer and the individual being socialized, or the values of the individual may conflict with those prevailing in society. As a result of these discrepancies between the actual and the hypothetical, the transition experience can create feelings of inadequacy and insecurity; it can create intolerable strains; it can create pressures for deviance.

Relinquishing a role Before summarizing the complex process of learning a new role during the life course, we must take note of the complementary process of relinquishing a former role. Here too we need a model in which, hypothetically, a new mother or a new bridegroom, for example, learns without difficulty to forsake the freedoms of an earlier, less responsible period, or a new pupil learns to give up the day-long dependency on the home, or the retiree learns to renounce the role of worker. The interaction between individual and society involved in learning to surrender a role is the mirror image of the interaction involved in learning the expectations and competencies of a new one. The individual is no longer expected to perform in the former role or rewarded for doing so. Social facilities and supports for learning that performance are replaced by other facilities and supports for discarding it. In the process, the individual is (hypothetically) satisfied to drop the former routines and to give up the former rewards (such as approval or income).

The hypothetical model again directs our attention to the problems actually involved in relinquishing a role. While some roles are easily, even eagerly, dropped, the loss of other roles is often painful. In practice, the requisite social supports are often missing. Or the individual is not satisfied to give up the accustomed rewards, or to forego the familiar enactment of performances once highly valued. People may even see social betrayal in the expectation that they abandon the commitments they were once required to undertake.[35]

Relinquishing a role can cause difficulties because, as in role acquisition, it requires adjustments and efforts to learn. Also involved is a special *sense of loss*. The feeling of loss is apparent to greater or lesser degree in all major life-course transitions. Young children making the transition to nursery school or kindergarten often respond by regressing to earlier, more familiar life stages (manifested by bedwetting, thumb sucking, crying, clinging to the mothering one). Youth pressing toward adulthood are enjoined to "put away childish things," but have difficulty doing so, as well-known conflicts of adolescence attest. Though professing to look forward to the last child's leaving home, mothers often develop symptoms of emotional disturbance and feel apprehensive about the future.[36] Even mental patients and prisoners sometimes experience distress when discharge forces them to relinquish familiar institutional roles and resume the customary roles of their life-stage.

Conditions for easing transitions   In outlining the process of learning new roles and relinquishing old ones, we have touched on several societal conditions that can ease (or hinder) role transitions. Among these, two major conditions stand out as potentially helpful for alleviating transition problems. (Others will be identified in the discussion of selected examples.) One of the major conditions is that the new role be highly valued by both individual and society; devalued roles provide little incentive for executing the transition smoothly. The second condition is that *adequate social support* be provided. Social support can be primarily instrumental—from the facilities, resources, and teachers (socializers) that aid the process of learning—or emotional—from friends, advisors, and opportunities for constructive release of frustrations and unhappiness engendered by the transition. When these conditions of role valuation and social support are met, life-course transitions are negotiated with minimum strain. In few transitions, however, are both simultaneously met.

Valued vs. devalued roles   Roles vary widely in the personal and social esteem accorded them. For the individual, they differ in the degree of compatibility with previously learned values; for the society, they differ in the degree to which they serve established social, economic, or political ends. Since a transition involves both an old role and a new, each more or less valued, it presupposes some kind of calculation of rewards and costs. The net losses (or gains) serve as a rough measure of its difficulty (or ease) of mak-

---

[35] Ruth Benedict, *Patterns of Culture* (Boston: Houghton Mifflin, 1934); Ruth Benedict, "Continuities and Discontinuities in Cultural Conditioning," *Psychiatry*, Vol. 1 (1938), pp. 161–167.

[36] M. F. Lowenthal et al., *Four Stages of Life* (San Francisco: Jossey-Bass, 1975).

ing the transition. Through much of the life course, the balance is in the individual's favor: Most role transitions are individually experienced and socially defined as a series of promotions. A person is promoted from second to third grade, from freshman to sophomore in high school, from high school senior to college freshman, from trainee to foreman or junior executive. Although normatively defined as desirable (and surely preferable to "staying back"), even such positive transitions can create distress and disorientation. People are forced to acquire new skills and to adjust to new teachers, new peers, new locales, new responsibilities, or new modes of work. Even the lure of adult rewards and esteem, for example, is seldom enough to make the adolescent transition a smooth one. But it is, of course, the transitions that are individually and socially defined as demotions—the shift from college to job aspirant (or unplanned unemployment), from work to retirement, from spouse to widow—that are far more unsettling and personally threatening. It is ironic that the prolongation of life has resulted in more people living long enough to undergo more of such role-demotions. Society has lagged in developing significant new roles for those at the distal end of the life course.

Adequacy of social support Particular roles, highly valued or not, vary in the degree and kinds of available social supports for learning them. A major source of transition problems—problems that call for attention by relatives, friends, and professionals who work with people—is that the support currently given to people in a wide variety of role transitions is insufficient or inappropriate. Even where physical facilities and resources for role learning are adequate, as in entry to high school or college, significant other persons may be insensitive to the needs for emotional support, or improperly tutored to provide it during critical phases of learning. The role of doctor, for example, is one of the most highly esteemed and highly rewarded roles in American society. The high esteem accorded it provides powerful motivation for the individual to undergo the long period of preparation. The society provides physical facilities and expert teachers, and even subsidizes the cost of medical education. Yet learning the role of doctor is often pervaded by anxieties, discontents, frustrations, withdrawal, and cynicism.[37] Ideological conflicts arise between faculty and students. Role expectations are sometimes far from clear.

For people going through transitions to less valued roles, a full complement of social supports is also ofen missing, though needed more. Many high school students destined for blue-collar jobs feel alienated from a school in which the emphasis is on going on to college. For their working-class future, these school-emphasized expectations seem pointless, the curriculum and activities meaningless, the rewards more like penalties. Rebellious behavior often occurs among students in this predicament.[38]

It will be helpful to consider some examples in detail in order to probe

---

[37] Samuel W. Bloom, *Power and Dissent in the Medical School* (New York: Free Press, 1973).

[38] Arthur L. Stinchcombe, *Rebellion in a High School* (Chicago: Quadrangle, 1964).

more deeply into the factors of role valuation and social support that intensify or reduce the problems accompanying role transitions.

Transition to a Valued Role

Few roles in American society have been as unassailable as the role of mother. For the young woman, motherhood typically confers adult status, commands social respect, and can also deepen her sense of self-fulfillment. Although some advocates of women's liberation may have tried to change this high evaluation of motherhood, most young people today, though ready to accept the norm of childlessness for others, still aspire to become parents themselves. In a recent study 96 percent of young women aged 14 to 25 said that they planned to have at least one child, and the majority were committed to having two or more children.[39] Nor is this simply a matter of what people say. In actual practice most women choose the mother role. Because motherhood has become increasingly elective, their choice testifies to the high value of the role. Though "accidents happen," of course, other options have opened up with the wider availability of contraceptives and abortion, competing educational and career opportunities, and financial support in old age from social security rather than mature offspring. Yet the high valuation put on the role by both individual and society scarcely makes the transition to motherhood free from stress.[40] As we consider the supports available for this transition, we shall see how it is often impeded by restricted opportunity for practicing and learning the role, inaccurate representations of the responsibilities involved, and limited outlet for the frustrations that go with it.

Anticipatory socialization   Despite the attractions and social importance of the role of mother, little explicit training for it is provided in American society. Most preparation is casual, based largely upon (often imperfect) observation of role models: girls watch their mothers or other women perform the role or observe (often misrepresented) mothering behavior in the mass media. Beyond this, there is only limited opportunity for *anticipatory socialization*[41]— the patterned, but often unplanned, learning of a role in advance of assuming it. Ideally, anticipatory socialization is a major way of easing role transitions. In practice, however, small families with closely spaced children afford a child limited opportunity to learn parental responsibilities by caring for younger siblings, or especially newborn infants. Occasional baby-sitting or other child-related work may afford some experience but can rarely convey the sense of onerous responsibility that motherhood can actually bring.

[39] Young wives are much less likely than older wives to prefer large families—four or more children. Institute of Life Insurance, "Women," *Data Track*, No. 1 (1974); Current Population Reports, P-20, No. 279 (1975), pp. 3, 6.

[40] Alice S. Rossi, "Transition to Parenthood," *Journal of Marriage and the Family*, Vol. 30 (1968), pp. 26–39.

[41] Robert K. Merton and Alice S. Rossi, "Contributions to the Theory of Reference Group Behavior," in Merton, *op. cit.*

Although prior practice in the role is limited, there is often anticipatory learning of attitudes. Even so, such early socialization sometimes hinders rather than helps. Especially detrimental is that anticipatory socialization that is based on representations of motherhood's joy and fulfillment and none of its difficulties and responsibilities. Such preparation simply complicates the problems entailed in what is, in fact, a many-faceted experience. Youthful dreams and adult realization end miles apart, with consequent disillusion or feelings of incompetence.

Active preparation for the role, which typically begins with the announcement of the pregnancy to others, is often brief and restricted.[42] During pregnancy, the relationship between mother and future child is largely fantasized; the imagined interaction cannot be actually tried out.[43] Visits to the hospital, purchase of baby equipment, baby showers—all serve to underscore the reality of the coming event, but afford little help in mastering the future role. Classes in child care or the reading of manuals, while informative, seldom convey a sufficient sense of the fatigue, anxieties, and around-the-clock effort of caring for a newborn child. Conflicting advice from "experts" is common. And the attention and solicitude evidenced for the pregnant woman abruptly shifts to the baby as soon as it is born.[44] Social support for the mother's transition becomes submerged in the baby's transition from intrauterine life to infancy. Yet it is the mother who, in the main, must manage both her transition and the baby's.

Problems of becoming a mother   The manifold demands of becoming a mother for the first time ensure that a woman's life will be dramatically changed. She must respond to the urgent but often unclear needs of the infant. She is held personally and often solely responsible for the physical and mental health of the child as it grows, a responsibility that is imposed without adequate guidelines for fulfilling it. Actual learning of the role begins only after she actually takes it on. In a way, it is the infant itself who provides the most important and effective socialization. It is the baby who teaches parents what is expected: food, dry clothing, touching, comforting. And it is the infant who —by sighing, sleeping, squirming, or crying all night—provides the parents with rewards when they meet its needs and punishments when they do not.[45]

Other changes in the life of the young mother add to the problems. Financial commitments begin to mount. Former social relationships are altered. The mother's relationship with her husband (and his with her) must take account of the child and the immediacy of its needs. The demands, feeding schedules, and spatial restrictions imposed by the infant reduce opportunities for interaction with friends. Thus the newly acquired role of mother—at least initially—

---

[42] Helena Z. Lopata, *Occupation: Housewife* (New York: Oxford, 1971).

[43] Alice S. Rossi, "Transition to Parenthood," *Journal of Marriage and the Family*, Vol. 30 (1968), pp. 26–39.

[44] Conspicuously absent from our current practices are the rituals widely used in preliterate societies to signal the changed status of the mother. For an example, see Jane C. Goodale, *Tiwi Wives* (Seattle: University of Washington Press, 1971).

[45] Harriet Rheingold, "The Social and Socializing Infant," in Goslin, *op. cit.*

often removes other familiar and satisfying roles from the woman's active repertoire and restricts sources of help and emotional support just when they are most needed. This is especially true if, as is typically the case today, the woman had been in the full-time labor force, so that becoming a mother was somewhat like retirement. The combination of recurrent and often unexpected assaults on physical and emotional well-being is typically endured in private by young mothers. Some are made highly anxious by their new responsibilities. Some feel embarrassed or guilty over their own fatigue and dismay. Such feelings may manifest themselves in outbursts of tears or a nagging sadness. Occasionally the responses take more serious forms, such as postpartum depression, which sometimes requires hospitalization of the mother.

Ironically, even a role so nearly sacred in the popular opinion as that of mother can lack organized social support. Many women, no doubt, accomplish the transition smoothly and achieve its rewards. But many others are disturbed, at least for a time, and without full understanding of the sociologically identifiable sources of their disturbance: that expectations are unclear, opportunities for learning the role notably inadequate, and emotional support during the transition period insufficient or inappropriate. Even in transition to what are socially defined as the happiest stages of life, there can be an abundance of problems.

Importance of timing   Another factor that affects the impact of the transition is the timing of the birth in the mother's life course. The typical or modal age of women at first pregnancy tends to become a socially acceptable age, and special problems are encountered by women making the transition ahead of schedule. A study of New York women who had recently become first-time mothers found that unplanned first births and illegitimacy were far more prevalent among the youngest women (aged 15 to 19) than in any of the older age strata. Most of the youngest mothers would have preferred to postpone the first birth, whereas older ones were typically satisfied with its timing.[46] Clearly, it is socially defined age norms, not mere biological readiness,[47] that signals the appropriate timing for motherhood and sets apart those who are "off time."[48] Other social and economic pressures attending premature entrance into motherhood can aggravate the difficulties inherent in the transition and militate against the woman's future development. Being ahead of schedule can have adverse effects on the marriage. It can prevent the young woman from developing competence in nonfamily roles because of premature termination of schooling or employment.

Early motherhood is a conspicuous instance of the special problems of ne-

[46] Harriet Presser, "Early Motherhood: Ignorance or Bliss?" *Family Planning Perspectives,* Vol. 6, No. 1 (Winter 1974), pp. 8–14.

[47] In contrast with a century ago, women today experience menarche at earlier ages and menopause at later ages, although recent cohorts now spend fewer years of their lives in child bearing.

[48] Bernice L. Neugarten et al., "Age Norms, Age Constraints, and Adult Socialization," *American Journal of Sociology,* Vol. 70 (1965), pp. 710–717.

gotiating transitions where individuals are ahead of, or behind, the usual or socially prescribed schedule. During a recession, prolonged denial of jobs can impose lifelong handicaps on those members of a cohort who are out of step with their more fortunate age-mates and with those in other cohorts who started work on time. The 1975 recession has resulted in extensive unemployment and job discouragement in the cohort under age 25 (most especially among blacks and females).[49] This involves long-term losses in job skills and seniority relative to other employees entering the labor force before (and presumably also those entering after) the recession. Wars too can upset life-course schedules by delaying the entry of many young men and some young women into adult civilian life, or promoting divorce, suicide, drug addiction, and unemployability among many veterans.

Counterpart Transitions

So far we have directed attention to the strains and problems facing the individual who, with aging, moves from one role to another. Given the nature of social bonds, it is evident that others close to each person in transition are also affected. The transition to motherhood, for example, is accompanied by the infant's own entry into the legally defined role of dependent child, by the husband's transition to fatherhood, by the transformation of the couples' parents into grandparents. The new mother's successes and failures in negotiating her transition greatly affect the complementary or *counterpart transitions* of those relating to her as a mother (her role-set). If she is distressed by the change, she communicates her distress to these others who must also cope with the recent and related changes in their respective lives. Even when she negotiates the transition successfully, the others must adjust their relationships to her to make room for her new role commitments. If her husband prepares himself for the counterpart transition—for example, by joining her while she goes through "natural childbirth" or by sharing infant care—many drastic alterations in *his* life are then required.

Consider other cases in point: When a young man makes the transition to marriage and experiences the attendant strains, complementary strains are imposed on the groups he leaves behind—his parents, his extended kin, or his bachelor friends who, at least temporarily and to a degree, must relinquish him. At the same time, new groups, such as his wife's family, must find ways of including him. Or consider the case of a male executive who retires. In the office, his assistants, ordinarily younger than he, are often cast adrift, especially his secretary who may have been devoted to "the boss" for years. And at home his wife must take account of his newly acquired "free time" as she pursues her usual (or now probably changed) activities. In another type of case, middle-aged men, forced into unemployment by the closing of the factory in which they had worked, experienced a decline in health; when the wife's counterpart

[49] Urban Institute, "Unemployment and Job Discouragement," *Search*, Vol. 5 (Spring 1975), pp. 3–7.

transition took the form of finding employment for herself, the health of her unemployed husband either failed to improve or deteriorated.[50]

At times, these complementary strains serve as tonic rather than setback. Parents, for example, often find fresh marital happiness when their children leave home. When wives work, deference from their husbands often increases.[51] In the Great Depression, the father's loss of employment often meant that children, by taking on new responsibilities for the family welfare, not only felt needed but "grew up faster."[52] Yet counterpart transitions, like all transitions, pose personal problems in the individual case and social problems in the aggregate and typically involve at least a period of learning and strain.

Transition to a Devalued Role

The role transition from wife to widow, as the counterpart transition to the husband's dying, illustrates the strains and potential problems generated by the role transition of a significant other.[53] In a later example, we shall see how the husband may approach his own death. Complementary to his reactions are those of the widow. Her transition also illustrates other basic aspects of role transitions generally, such as the process of mourning and the problems incurred when the new role, widow, is negatively valued both by society and by the widow herself.

The process of mourning Persons who lose a loved one through death typically undergo an extended, but usually limited, period of mourning. The process corresponds roughly to a role transition in which differing emotions are evoked by loss of the former role (wife), by adoption of the new role (widow), and by the hiatus—sometimes lasting several months or years—before the losses are resolved and the fresh start is made. The wife's emotional preparation for the loss may begin as she and family members share their feelings and socialize each other for the impending death, or as she takes on responsibilities formerly assigned to the dying person. This anticipatory behavior can serve to mitigate grief but does not prevent it entirely. When the death is sudden or the deceased is young, grief is typically intense. An initial sense of bewilderment is followed by a shifting composite of disbelief, anger, guilt, depression, and preoccupation with the image of the dead person. Physical illness is common.[54] In a recent book a young widow described her experience: first a protective

---

[50] Sidney Cobb and Stanislav V. Kasl, "Some Medical Aspects of Unemployment," *Report to Respondents* (Ann Arbor: University of Michigan Survey Research Center, May 1971).

[51] Robert O. Blood, Jr., and Donald M. Wolfe, *Husbands and Wives: The Dynamics of Married Living* (New York: Free Press, 1960).

[52] Glen H. Elder, Jr., *Children of the Great Depression* (Chicago: University of Chicago Press, 1974).

[53] The concept of the "significant other," introduced by George Herbert Mead (*Mind, Self and Society*, 1934), postulates that it is through day-to-day interaction with certain persons ("significant others") that one's social self is formed and maintained.

[54] E. Lindemann, "Symptomatology and Management of Acute Grief," in R. Fulton, *Death and Identity* (New York: Wiley, 1965), pp. 186–200.

numbness, then a "crazy" stage of disastrously wild decisions, followed by a garrulous period of telling her troubles indiscriminately.[55] In time, the loss begins to be accepted and the self is reinvested in a world without the loved one.

Such responses are "normal." They are normal in the triple sense of being usual, being socially defined as appropriate, and of being psychologically essential to adjustment to further stages in the transition. Like the parallel reactions of those who learn of their own terminal illness,[56] such a process of mourning is not restricted to loss through death but, to varying degrees, characterizes most transitions where a former role—a former investment of self— is lost. Performance in highly esteemed roles like spouse or worker typically provides many gratifications and becomes a basis for positive self-valuation. When tenure in such a role is of long duration, as it commonly is, commitment to the role is further intensified[57] and more of the self is invested in it. Relinquishing any socially valued and self-defining role is therefore often experienced as losing part of the self and, like other losses, commonly evokes reactions of grief. As with bereavement, if the grief is not worked through, prolonged despair will characterize the next life stage, and there will be no satisfying reinvestment of the self in new roles and activities.

Few institutional arrangements exist for acquainting people with the mourning process and its characteristic reactions. At the least, such arrangements could help people recognize that their feelings will change with time and that they are far from unique, being part of the human experience.

Relinquishing the role of wife   In terms of role relinquishment, the death of a spouse represents a double loss. Not only is there loss of a close personal relationship, to the husband, but also loss of a socially valued and self-defining role as wife. During the period of immediate crisis strong emotional supports are usually available, and expression of grief is encouraged. Much of the support takes the form of ritual, of a symbolic declaration of solidarity between the bereaved and the kin and community to which the deceased person belonged.[58] In American society, the specialists available at this point to orient and aid the socialization of the widow include doctors, ministers, social workers, lawyers, insurance agents, and funeral directors. Relatives and friends stand by, although in the case of the aged widow whose parents are dead and whose children may have grown apart, *close* kin are often absent and close friends (too infirm or no longer living) even more often absent. Significantly for the outcome, the assistance available during the initial shock is generally

[55] Lynn Caine, *Widow* (New York: Morrow, 1974).

[56] Elisabeth Kübler-Ross, *On Death and Dying* (New York: Macmillan, 1969).

[57] Howard S. Becker, "Notes on the Concept of Commitment," *The American Journal of Sociology*, Vol. 66 (1960), pp. 32–40.

[58] Emile Durkheim, *Suicide: A Study in Sociology* (Spaulding and Simpson, trans.) (Glencoe, Ill.: Free Press, 1951); Talcott Parsons and Victor Lidz, "Death in American Society," in Edwin S. Shneidman (ed.), *Essays in Self Destruction* (New York: Science House, 1967). For more general discussion of the place of ritual in life course transitions, see the classic work by Arnold Van Gennep, *The Rites of Passage* (Visedom and Caffee, trans.) (Chicago: University of Chicago Press, 1908, 1960).

withdrawn before the lengthy stages of mourning are completed. For the widow, adapting to her loss is often a solitary experience.

Learning the role of widow   The bereaved woman is expected not only to relinquish her former role as wife but also, in due course, to recover from her grief and resume her usual activities in the new role of widow. She is expected to shop, interact with friends, and continue work if not already retired. She is *not* expected to withdraw from role participation. Yet such activities often seem pallid substitutes for her foregone activities as wife. And they are less socially valued. For the elderly widow—and most widows are elderly—the major residual of her past role of spouse is in home maintenance (housekeeping or gardening), as most older people continue to inhabit and operate their own homes up to the stage of decrepitude. But this activity no longer draws meaning by focus on a significant other; rather it is only for the self.

In addition, the norm of separate residence tends to inhibit replacing the lost relationship with a new major involvement with other kinfolk. Thus the widowed old person—except under special conditions of illness or disability— typically lives, often entirely alone, near children but not with them.[59] Moreover, a widowed grandparent, if perceived as a possible usurper of parental prerogatives of authority or responsibility, may even be denied warm relationships with grandchildren and harmonious ones with adult offspring. Opportunities for other interpersonal involvements are also scarce. Although widowed males tend to remarry, the supply of second husbands for widows is limited by the higher death rates among men than women. And widows are excluded from many forms of social activity for which escorts are required or, when included, feel like a "fifth wheel."[60]

In sum, widows, especially old ones, often find little support for their attempts to overcome grief and to restructure their lives without a husband and in a devalued role. Studies attesting to the consequences of this lack of support show that the widowed, on the average, have fewer contacts with children, greater unhappiness, and higher rates of suicide and death than do married persons of similar age.[61]

Retirement: a related case in point   Retirement provides another case of a transition to a devalued role similar in many respects to widowhood, but different in one basic respect: retirement involves the loss of a valued role but *not* of a valued person. Like widowhood, retirement involves surrendering one part of the self, the part that was invested in the lost role. The process of retiring also lets us see how a prized former role, that of paid worker, is relinquished.

[59] Ethel Shanas, *The Health of Older People: A Social Survey* (Cambridge, Mass.: Harvard University Press, 1962); P. Townsend, *The Family Life of Old People: An Inquiry in East London* (London: Routledge & Kegan Paul, 1957).
[60] Lopata, *op. cit.*
[61] Riley and Foner, *op. cit.*

In many societies, including our own, performance in a work role bears witness to the traditional ethic of work, and therefore commands respect. When that role is given up, respect diminishes. There may be residual esteem for past performance, but the base for generating new esteem is largely lost. Other gratifications are also removed. Apart from pension and social-security payments, income derived from the role is gone. The comradeship and personal support of fellow-workers is left behind. A familiar, day-long routine has disappeared. Competencies of long standing no longer have a focus. Although the mourning process is predictably less intense for the retiree than for the widow, it is not surprising that a good many face retirement with dismay and disorientation rather than happy anticipation.

Current problems of retirement derive in large part from the failure of society to address the question: What should retirement be a transition *to*? People entering the role of retiree often have little comprehension of what the absence of work entails and lack direction for finding roles that could provide substitute gratifications. Unpaid volunteer work has become an alternative activity for only one in five old people.[62] Expensive leisure pursuits are generally prohibited by reduced income. Organizations for "senior citizens" entice relatively few. Perhaps rightly, retirement has been called a "roleless role." Its lack of content and its uncertain rewards exacerbate the troubles and problems of transition. For some old people, this lack of content is an advantage, permitting them to fashion new roles consonant with their energies, interests, and financial resources. Yet, should increasingly better educated cohorts continue to retire at ever-younger ages, in the course of time still-to-be-defined new roles for retirees will probably become institutionalized.

Death: The Last Transition

As a final case in point for specifying problems and troubles of transition, the dying person can be thought of as undergoing life's final transition. For people who reject the possibility of life after death, it is a truncated transition—all roles relinquished, but no new ones assumed. It represents the ultimate loss of investments of self. As with other losses, the knowledge of impending death evokes a grief response that requires expressive support.

In America today death is also a devalued transition. The prevailing assumption is that life is to be prolonged and death averted at almost any price. Medical practitioners and families often insist that life-preserving measures be instituted and maintained even when recovery is impossible and death imminent. In the efforts to sustain life, the dying person is frequently deprived of a "death with dignity" as well as the final solicitude of loved ones.

Compared to other transitions, the passage to death is especially devoid of social supports. In America, this lack of support is partly attributable to an historical change in the locus of death, from the home to the hospital. Hospitals

---

[62] National Council on the Aging, *op. cit.*

are geared to saving lives, not to presiding over death. In contrast to earlier times, the dying person today is rarely given center stage. Caretakers for the dying are now typically recruited from overdemanded health professionals rather than from close relatives and friends. The lack of support may result also from the fact that, with increasing longevity, most deaths now occur among the old. The old, sometimes viewed as repugnant, sometimes as having had their chance at life, often receive a low priority for care and attention. The relative inadequacy of professional support derives further from the frequent discomfort of the well in the presence of the dying. Unlike the clergymen who earlier ministered at the deathbed, doctors are generally reluctant to tell patients of their impending death, explaining that "miracles can happen" or confessing inability to deal with possible outbursts resulting from disclosure.[63] Although many nurses show their concern,[64] they too are sometimes reported to reduce contacts with the dying and to focus on those whose health can be restored. Not infrequently, pretense characterizes interactions between the dying person and others, as doctors, nurses, and even family members and friends pretend not to know. The dying person who correctly senses the gravity of his or her condition may also feign ignorance. Such cover-ups and brave fronts only add to the strains, in some cases diverting energies better used in support of the dying person and the significant others.

By contrast, when an "open awareness" of the impending death distinguishes the interaction between the dying person and his role-set,[65] mutual support can develop and a more satisfactory negotiation of the final phase of life becomes possible. In the case of the hospital staff, dying patients sometimes ask and are allowed exemption from bothersome routines, or may directly request someone to listen to their concerns. With family and friends, previously unspoken affirmations of appreciation and love can be expressed, financial arrangements for heirs cooperatively attended to, old enmities ended. If physical conditions permit, foregone pleasures of the past—the leisure activities or vacations crowded out by the daily round—can now be jointly pursued. The dying and the surviving together may even make decisions about the conditions under which death will take place or plan the funeral ritual. Such forthrightness in the face of death can provide much comfort and deep satisfaction both to the dying and to those close to them.

Individual Reactions

These cases are enough to demonstrate that role transitions are probably more difficult than is generally recognized—that they lead to periodic eruptions of personal troubles throughout the life course and, in the aggregate, to latent

---

[63] Barney G. Glaser, "Disclosure of Terminal Illness," *Journal of Health and Human Behavior,* Vol. 7 (1966), pp. 83–91.

[64] Jeanne Q. Benoliel, *The Nurse and the Dying Patient* (New York: Macmillan, 1973).

[65] Barney G. Glaser and Anselm Strauss, *Awareness of Dying* (Chicago: Aldine Press, 1965).

social problems. Postulating two requirements or conditions for easing transitions, we have seen how certain transitions fail to meet the first requirement of promotion to a valued role, and a great many others fail to meet the second requirement of adequate social support.

Although there is only limited evidence about individual reactions to these difficulties, it appears that each type of transition evokes a wide range of responses, from autonomous mastery to defensiveness and withdrawal. Even with those transitions that objectively fail to meet both requirements, some people seem able to cope. For example, many old people claim that they are satisfied with retirement,[66] despite the low valuation generally made of it and the lack of adequate support. This phenomenon raises important questions: By what process does a negative situation become redefined as positive? And is it beneficial to the individual for such redefinition to occur?

Finding "silver linings" may represent active efforts to cope with the challenge of a bleak situation. Or they may only represent efforts to explain away feelings of resignation and powerlessness. Some tentative empirical evidence lends credence to the latter explanation. We have seen that generally, the older people are, the lower their aspirations. People aged 65 and over exhibit the smallest gap between aspirations and self-definitions. At the same time, they are the most likely to say they are satisfied—but not happy—with their lives (Figure 8-6). We have also seen that this set of findings might mean that people gradually learn, as they become older, to expect less and less of life, to adapt, and—toward the end of life—to become resigned. (As previously noted, the cross-section data can only *suggest* the interpretation of change with aging over the life course, not demonstrate it.)

This raises the question whether these tendencies are relevant to redefining a bad situation as a positive one. Data suggest that old people often unwittingly engage in such redefinition.[67] Objectively, the health of older people is generally poorer than that of the young. Although older people have fewer acute illnesses, they are more widely subject to chronic conditions such as failing vision or hearing, rheumatism and arthritis, heart disease, and high blood pressure. Some four out of five persons 65 and over have at least one chronic condition, and there are steady increases by age in physician visits, in the number and duration of hospital stays, and in the number of days spent in restricted activity or in bed.

In assessing their own health, older people regard themselves as less healthy than younger people regard themselves. Nevertheless, relative to medical evaluations of their condition, many older individuals assess their health quite positively. Many have learned to take their aches and pains for granted, accepting them as inevitable or unimportant. And despite their widespread chronic afflictions, only a small minority of chronically ill old people report themselves

---

[66] Riley and Foner, *op. cit.*; National Council on the Aging, *op. cit.*
[67] *Ibid.*

to be so severely handicapped that they are unable to carry on their major activity, whether it be a job outside the home or housework.[68]

Not only do older people typically minimize health deficits, but they also minimize the importance of their relative lack of education. Especially as long as they maintain their health, older people tend not to regard themselves as "old." Many believe that they themselves make a "better appearance" than others their age. It may be that each old person's unfavorable image of "other old people" serves as a negative reference group by which he or she—by being different—is able to accentuate the positive and thus to reconstruct the reality.

Although such attempts at coping sometimes make life tolerable for old people, they are not necessarily useful adaptations. Resignation to a bleak situation almost always serves to maintain a negative situation when, in fact, it may not be unavoidable. When the situation *is* improvable, such resignation only masks a social problem. Since we cannot take what old people *say* as an accurate description of their situation or as an index of the sufferings to which they have become resigned, there is all the more reason to look for hidden sufferings and, as in the case of poor health, to bring the sources of these sufferings to attention as social problems.

A Societal View

We have been examining the personal troubles associated with aging and role transitions from the standpoint of individuals; we turn now to certain causes and consequences of these problems in the society.

The inevitability of the problems is directly traceable to the age stratification system itself, which, as we have seen, involves two shifting age structures, each with its own dynamism: an age structure of people who, in the aggregate, are continually being born, aging, dying, and being replaced; and an age structure of roles changing along with particular historical events and other social changes. We can now understand how individuals are continually forced through the sequence of role transitions not only by biological aging, but also by the demands of the role structure and by the pressure of new cohorts coming along behind them. And we can understand how changes in the role structure make it hard for individuals to anticipate many of their future roles. We have also considered the inherent strain between the changing biographies of people and the changing configuration of the role structure—when there are too many or too few people at the requisite ages, or when people are over-prepared or under-prepared for the role openings available. These tensions and imbalances produce intrinsic problems of role transition. Individuals are caught in the massive societal dialectic between people who are aging (growing

---

[68] Interestingly, many more old people give poor health as their reason for retiring than describe themselves as handicapped by poor health. One inference from this discrepancy is that people say they are too sick to work, not because they feel so, but because they have been told so (see National Council on the Aging, *op. cit.,* pp. 89–91).

older) and social changes in roles. Each individual must negotiate the series of transitions through these two changing structures, often without regard for personal needs or personal time schedules.

As millions of individuals within the age strata of a society like ours undergo similar role transitions simultaneously, their collective experiences have repercussions throughout the social system and its institutions. For example, when especially large cohorts of children make the transition from home to school, or when increasingly large proportions of old people make the transition from work to retirement, drastic adjustments in social supports and existing facilities are required as a consequence. Before considering such adjustments, we must stress once again that those consequences of transitions that may seem best for individuals need not be best for society, and vice versa. We have noted requisite social conditions for easing life-course transitions, based on the criterion that the path should be smoothed for individuals. But for the society, meeting such requirements often serves to preserve the status quo, to rigidify the social structure—for the socialization of individuals to fit readily into existing roles limits the chances that they will contribute to structural change. Difficulties in role transition can be a source of social change as individuals act to remedy the faulty mesh between the changing age structures of people and of roles. Policy makers are often faced with difficult choices in trying to find any optimum balance between easing the way for individuals and providing flexibility for wanted change in the social structure.

ADDRESSING PROBLEMS OF AGE AND AGING

The social character of age and aging makes possible many kinds of programs and policies to alleviate or prevent age-related problems. In this final section we examine some approaches to three general kinds of problems related to age and aging: problems that go undetected because of public ignorance or that arise from widespread misperceptions; problems created by the current configuration of the age structure of roles; and problems occurring because social change continually undermines the meshing of people and roles.

Dispelling Myths and Misperceptions

If the existing problems of age and aging are to be addressed, efforts to dispel ignorance of widespread difficulties and to correct misunderstanding must become part of the social agenda. Private troubles must become public concerns and damaging myths about age and aging must be exposed.

Pluralistic ignorance   When the discontents that accompany age and aging are kept hidden, they constitute social problems of unknown scope and gravity. Until such latent problems are identified and brought to public attention they elude any possibility of solution. Yet, as we have seen, individuals in particular age strata or those making role transitions frequently assume that they are alone in the troubles they experience. In their "pluralistic ignorance," as this has been called,[69] they are unaware that others, also in private, have similar troubles. As we have further noted, people are typically strengthened to learn that they are not unique in their feelings of inadequacy, disillusion, or grief. Even the mere recognition that a problem is common brings relief from the burdens of secrecy. Furthermore, once widely recognized, problems can often be reduced or eliminated by provision of social supports—professional aid, anticipatory socialization, or even old-fashioned day-to-day human kindness.

Myths and their consequences   In addition to people's ignorance of the fact that their age mates share their personal troubles, numerous myths pervade public thinking about age and aging. Such myths set false standards and lead people to expect either too much or too little of themselves and of others at various life stages and while undergoing transitions.

Where public images are unrealistically positive or expectations too high, they engender disillusionment, as for example when the idealized rewards of parenthood conspicuously fail to match the actual experience. Or they produce feelings of incompetence, as in the anxiety or actual impotence experienced by young males who believe that "everybody else my age" is already enjoying sexual intercourse. Or feelings of conflict result, as when the widow is expected to "cheer up" well before her "grief work" is completed.

Where public images are unrealistically negative or expectations too low, they may become self-fulfilling prophecies, making actual behavior conform to the level of popular belief (see the Introduction). If it is generally accepted that the young child is not ready to learn to read or do arithmetic, the child is not taught. Then, ipso facto, the child fails to learn and the failure is taken to confirm the original belief. Yet early nineteenth-century "infant schools" taught such skills and steps are once again being taken to institute similar programs.[70] If it is generally accepted that preparation for particular jobs requires 12 (or 16 or 20) years of schooling (high school, college, or graduate school), jobs will not be provided in the occupational system for youths with less education. Yet job skills might actually improve were some students allowed to leave school and begin work earlier. Indeed, unnecessarily prolonged schooling can actually create disabilities when high schools are experienced as "prisons" or vocational schools as "aging vats."

Stereotypes of old age   One program introduced by the National Council on Aging illustrates what can be done to uncover, and then expose, myths about the elderly (who have been especially victimized by stereotypical views). Their study compares public perceptions of old people and old age with self-

[69] Floyd H. Allport, *Social Psychology* (Boston: Houghton Mifflin, 1924).

[70] Maris Vinovskis and Dean May, "A Ray of Millennial Light: The Infant School Movement in Nineteenth Century Boston," in Tamara K. Hareven (ed.), *Family and Kin in American Urban Communities: 1700–1930* (New York: New Viewpoints, 1976).

reports from old people about themselves and their circumstances (Table 8-2). A major finding is that old people aged 65 and over typically describe themselves more positively than does the general public (aged 18 to 64). Sixty-three percent of old people, for example, see themselves as "very open-minded and adaptable," whereas only 21 percent of the public attribute this characteristic to "most people over 65." Only 31 percent of old people report that they personally spend a lot of time "sitting and thinking," whereas 62 percent of the public believe this to be a common behavior of most people over 65. Less than 10 percent of old people say "not having enough to do" is a very serious problem for them, yet nearly 40 percent of the public offered that view of the old (not shown in Table 8-2). In numerous other respects, including health, finan-

Table 8-2   Old People's Perceptions of Themselves Compared with Public Perceptions of "Most People over 65"

Characteristics of people over 65	Self perceptions of people 65 and over (percent)	Public perceptions of "most people over 65" (percent)	Net Difference
Very friendly and warm	72	74	+ 2
Very wise from experience	69	64	− 5
Very bright and alert	68	29	−39
Very open-minded and adaptable	63	21	−42
Very good at getting things done	55	35	−20
Very physically active	48	41	− 7
Very sexually active	11	5	− 6
How people over 65 spend "a lot of time"			
Socializing with friends	47	52	+ 5
Gardening or raising plants	39	45	+ 6
Reading	36	43	+ 7
Watching television	36	67	+31
Sitting and thinking	31	62	+31
Caring for younger or older members of the family	27	23	+ 4
Sleeping	16	39	+23
Just doing nothing	15	35	+20
Working part time or full time	10	5	− 5
Doing volunteer work	8	15	+ 7

Source: Adapted from National Council on the Aging, "The Myth and Reality of Aging in America," Washington, D.C. (mimeographed), 1975, pp. 53, 59. Based on 4,000 respondents in a U.S. cross-section survey conducted in 1974 by Louis Harris and Associates, Inc.

cial circumstances,[71] and activity level, old people describe their situation more positively than the general public does.

[71] Of course, the relatively small fraction (15 percent) of old people who said that "not having enough money to live on" was a very serious problem for them is large in number (some 3 million).

Although we have noted the possibility that many old people may conceal their handicaps or adapt passively to real problems in their life situation, nevertheless a negative public image of what it is like to grow old can itself create a social problem of the first order. As we know from the self-fulfilling prophecy, stereotypes that label people as incompetent, unless corrected, help make them targets for discrimination in the job market, in continuing education, and in other domains of social life. Should oncoming cohorts of old people themselves accept such negative self-definitions, they are well on their way toward submitting to the inactivity that can in fact lead to physical and psychological deterioration. Such negative stereotypes do not have to be perpetuated. Through the mass media and professional channels of communication much can be done to break down the invidious stereotypes, to provide information and role models, and to substitute positive for currently negative images.[72]

Modifications in Role Structure

Very different from interventions to correct myths and to uncover latent problems are proposals arguing for fundamental changes in roles and institutions. If many problems of age and aging derive from the social structure, then a logical target for intervention is the structure itself.

Age-based role allocation   As we have seen, a critical feature of the social structure is the use of age as a criterion for entering or leaving roles. Age criteria often seem arbitrary and capricious, yet operate as a major source of inequalities in access to desirable roles, of age segregation, of required role transitions, and of other social ills. Since age criteria are so instrumental in causing social problems might it not be useful to abandon age as a basis of role allocation? Removing the cause might well remove the problems.

Consider briefly the implications of such a proposal: No individual could be excluded from any sector of the work force for being too young or too old; members of all age strata would have equal access to roles. On what basis, then, would these roles, especially if "scarce," be distributed and held? In a universalistic society, a major alternative criterion might be ability. If ability is largely defined, however, by credentials of recent training and skills or by physical stamina, then ability as a criterion would create a new set of age inequalities. The middle-aged and old would find job opportunities preempted by a large, well-educated, and healthy cohort of the young. Moreover, they might have to surrender their current roles to the better trained and stronger young.[73] If, by some chance, length of experience were to be the chief principle for allocating roles, then the inexperienced young would continue to be excluded from the roles considered socially desirable. If financial need be-

---

[72] Beth Hess, "Stereotypes of the Aged," *Journal of Communication,* Vol. 24, No. 4 (Autumn 1974).

[73] *Cf.* Michael Young, *The Rise of the Meritocracy* (Baltimore: Penguin Books, 1961).

came the dominant allocative principle, then middle-aged household heads supporting adolescent children would have first access to work roles, since need is closely tied to family size and stage of family cycle.[74]

This mental experiment suggests that eliminating age as an allocative principle could create even greater age inequalities, failing to transcend the universal processes of aging and cohort flow that form the age strata. And substituting new allocative bases can merely intensify current problems, further narrowing age boundaries for roles that bring material rewards and social esteem. Thus it seems clear that, despite the problems they create, current age norms that forbid paid labor by children or mandate retirement at given ages cannot be abandoned without a careful evaluation of the consequences of such change. Many "obvious solutions" to age problems run the risk of enshrining a new arbitrariness with new inequalities—perhaps even worse than the old.

Redistribution of work, education, and leisure   While abolishing age-based allocation is not being considered seriously as a corrective, a variety of modifications of existing age criteria might well serve to prevent or reduce age inequalities, age segregation, or age conflict. For example, one set of proposals suggests not only the desirability but the possibility of redistributing education, work, and leisure over the life course, as a way to offset inequalities and inequities among the age strata and to help integrate the young and the old into the mainstream of social activity. Two panels of scientists,[75] one convened to focus on problems of youth, the other on problems of old people, made independent but strikingly parallel recommendations for changes in institutional structures with which the young and the old are affiliated.

The report of the panel on youth challenges the adequacy and efficacy of existing institutions, especially schools, to prepare the young for adulthood. It asks that more options be made available. As background for its specific proposals, the panel identifies three historical phases in this country's treatment of youth since its agrarian beginnings. In the historical "work phase"— from the Revolution well into the nineteenth century—young children were trained from a very early age to participate in the economic activity of the family. In the more recent "schooling phase," young people are kept as long as possible in school (or college) and thereby out of the labor force. In the proposed third phase, youth will mature in a widened environment that will include school but will neither be defined by nor limited to the current school environment (which the panel describes as individualistic, stressing cognitive achievement, and imposing dependency on those kept in the role of student).

The report of the panel on old age makes a remarkably similar analysis. This panel describes as an historical "work phase" the earlier era in which

---

[74] Valerie Kincade Oppenheimer, "The Life-Cycle Squeeze: The Interaction of Men's Occupational and Family Life Cycles," *Demography*, Vol. 11, No. 2 (1974), pp. 227–244.

[75] For details of these panels and their recommendations, see James S. Coleman et al., *Youth: Transition to Adulthood* (Chicago: University of Chicago Press, 1974) and Matilda White Riley, "The Perspective of Age Stratification," *School Review*, Vol. 82, No. 1 (November 1974).

older workers seldom retired (Table 8-1) and, as an historical "retirement phase," the subsequent era during which larger and larger proportions of older workers retire from economic activity. For old people, too, a future third phase is projected that would not be exclusively limited to or defined by mandatory retirement rules.

The two reports are linked by their several specific proposals for the development of such a third phase. The panel on youth, recommending some admixture during youth of self-development (learning) and economic productivity, examines (but is cautious about positively advocating) such changes in the dominant pattern as alternating full-time school and full-time work, job training in the school as well as on-the-job training, and continuing education for full-time workers. Though designed exclusively for youth, such changes must ultimately involve all age strata in the society—for work, education, and leisure can scarcely be spread over the life-course without affecting old as well as young. The complementary proposals made by the panel on old age suggest not only making continued work available to retired employees but also respacing education and work over the entire life-course (after suitable experimentation in selected high schools, universities, and employing firms). Both panels agree that work roles should be more widely shared among the age strata. Both suggest spreading work more evenly over the life-course, rather than continuing to crowd it into the relatively few years between leaving school and entering retirement.

The feasibility of such a massive plan remains to be tested, although many relevant developments are already underway,[76] among them the large-scale return to school by older adults. No longer is college age just the years from 18 to 22; people over 22 are the fastest growing age segment in higher education and now constitute nearly half the total enrollment in college. Among those 35 or older are many women who had started jobs or families and then gone back to school.[77] There is also the growing practice of having professionals, such as doctors and lawyers, take refresher courses. Another expression of this general trend is the recent report that nearly half of the business managers in a survey had changed or considered changing their occupation in the previous five years.[78]

Although the case for major changes in age-related role structures requires testing, the proposal has much in its favor. If some work opportunities, paid or voluntary, were provided from early adolescence through the later years, both young and old would once again be directly involved in the workings of the society. By sharing work, leisure too would be more equitably distributed. The middle-aged could then also claim periods of "rest and recreation," and thus reduce the stress from intensive involvement in both work and family roles. As

[76] Lowell Eklund, "Aging and the Field of Education," in Matilda White Riley et al. (eds.), *Aging and Society: Aging and the Professions,* Vol. 2 (New York: Russell Sage Foundation, 1969), pp. 324–351.

[77] Current Population Reports, P-20, No. 279 (1975).

[78] Institute of Life Insurance, "The Life Cycle," *Trend Report* No. 8 (New York, n.d.).

the number of productive workers at various ages increased, the dependency burden would also be more equitably distributed.

Relation to Social Change

Basic changes in the age structure of roles are by no means limited, of course, to deliberate efforts toward social improvement. Social change, whether cataclysmic events or more gradual historical trends, is endlessly at work to alter the age stratification system. Social change brings its own problems, as it continually endangers the meshing of the age structure of people and the age structure of roles. At the same time, social change gives room and flexibility for problem-solving intervention in the manner of aging and in age-related social institutions. Moreover, the processes of aging and cohort flow that effect change in the age structure can be analyzed for clues to possible future changes, so that potential problems can be identified well ahead of their actual emergence. By examining the number of children born this year, for example, the number of kindergarten classroom spaces needed five years hence can be estimated. Or, by observing the number of people currently middle-aged, the future demand on social security resources can be assessed.

Balancing people and roles   Changes in society not only promise solutions to some problems of age and aging but are also a perpetual source of new problems. Because the age structure of people and the age structure of roles undergo continual change, each according to its own dynamic, there are persistent failures to maintain a match between the two (as we saw in the second part of this chapter). Often the *numbers* are out of balance; there are too many or too few people in particular cohorts for the numbers of roles available—more students ready for high school, for example, than places available, more youths seeking first jobs than the number of entry level openings in the workforce, more old people than facilities to assist them. Or there are too few pregnant women to support the continued operation of obstetrical units, too few children to maintain the continued operation of schools, or too small a local labor force in communities that young people have left in search of opportunities elsewhere.

Sometimes the number of roles is satisfactory, but the *nature* of role openings is incompatible with people's aspirations or capabilities. Thus people may reject or be unprepared for allocation to the roles in particular age strata. The college-educated may be dissatisfied with roles that are not intellectually challenging or are "out of their field." Blacks and women may refuse the "typed" roles customarily allocated to them, wanting equal consideration for the roles historically reserved for white males. High-school drop-outs or English teachers are not prepared to take on the roles of needed physicians.

Such people–role imbalances create immediate problems for the affected age stratum and its corresponding institutions. As we have seen, people without roles often resort to deviance, and people assuming too many roles at once often suffer debilitating stress. Similarly, institutions attempting to accommodate an unusually large cohort can be strained beyond capacity, and those recruiting role players from too small a cohort may be so understaffed that their operation is impaired.[79] If the people–role balance is to be restored in such instances, social intervention of some kind is often necessary.

Although in principle the imbalance could be corrected by changes either in people or roles, the focus of intervention is generally the age structure of roles. Over the short term, changing the numbers and capacities of people to match the available roles is not ordinarily feasible. To be sure, immediate crises can sometimes be handled by encouraging people to migrate or by intensive retraining; but many other "people" solutions require time enough for new cohorts to be born or educated. For example, to change substantially the numbers seeking roles in the workforce through discouraging or encouraging fertility would require at least 15 to 20 years.

While the more promising solutions involve modifications of the age structure of roles, even these modifications are contingent upon availability of necessary resources and upon willingness to commit them. Given the resources, institutions such as schools or colleges can often be expanded to accommodate additional numbers seeking entrance. Or, when few seek entrance, roles can often be trimmed, institutions consolidated, or labor-saving devices introduced.

People–role imbalances can also be remedied by modulating the *rate of cohort flow* through age-graded institutions. This rate can be altered by a change in the age criteria for entering or leaving particular roles. Cohort flow can be *decelerated,* for example, by extending the age limits of a role. By protracting the period of education, the flow of young people into the workforce is retarded and competition for jobs is reduced. By narrowing the age boundaries for roles, cohort flow may be *accelerated,* as lowering the retirement age hastens the movement of adult workers through and out of the workforce, thus making room for younger workers. Because of its great flexibility, the proposal for interspersing periods of education, work, and leisure through the life course would make people–role imbalances not only less age-specific but also less likely.

Anticipating social change   Often such people–role imbalances can be foreseen, hence sometimes prevented, forestalled, or prepared for. To help in anticipating future problems, as well as in assessing possible consequences of social intervention, the sociology of age has a special tool: cohort analysis.[80]

Cohort analysis is a direct translation into research methodology of the model of the changing age structure of people, diagrammed in Figure 8-1. Three features of cohort analysis distinguish it from more familiar procedures of studying change through a sequence of cross-section surveys: Cohort analysis (1) traces the life-course patterns of each cohort, as the size of the cohort

---

[79] See Joan M. Waring, "Social Replenishment and Social Change: The Problem of Disordered Cohort Flow," *American Behavioral Scientist,* Vol. 19 (November-December 1975), pp. 237–256.

[80] For details, see Riley, Johnson, and Foner, *op. cit.,* Ch. 2.

changes (through death or migration of its members) or as people's characteristics change in the process of aging; (2) compares the differences and similarities among cohorts in these life-course patterns; and (3) shows how consecutive
cohorts, each lagging behind its predecessor in the process of aging, fit together
to form the changing structure of the society. The method increases confidence
in estimates of the future through its use of past history and established facts
about each cohort already born (cohort size; characteristics of cohort members
such as race, educational attainment, marital status, or occupation; and past
changes in all these characteristics).[81] And the method can give clues to how
the basic processes of aging and cohort flow contribute to particular social
changes and to the associated social problems.

One example suggests how cohort analysis is used in examining and interpreting change in the sizes of coexisting age strata—information important for
policy determination. Census data indicate that dramatic changes in size can
occur in a single decade.[82] There are, for example, 50 percent *more* 20- to 24-
year-olds in 1970 than in 1960 and 44 percent more 15- to 19-year-olds. By
contrast, there are 11 percent fewer people aged 35 to 39, and 16 percent fewer
in the youngest stratum, aged 0 to 4. Such rapid changes in the age structure of
people clearly presage changes in demands for age-graded roles and facilities.
For example, the precipitous growth in the young-adult stratum is obviously
connected with the past over-crowding and expansion of the educational establishment and with the difficulties that many young people have in finding jobs
in the 1970s.

Cohort analysis helps to understand such changing sizes of the age strata
by pointing up possible antecedents of the changes and indicating social problems, past and future, that may be involved. With the sizes and the historical
backgrounds of the particular cohorts succeeding one another in the strata
established, differences in the sizes of the cohorts at birth are determined from
Census records. (Such cohort differences are reflected in the age pyramid for
1970 in Figure 8-5.) The cohort born in 1946–1950 (the familiar post-World
War II "baby boom" cohort that reached age 20–25 in 1970) was far larger than
cohorts born in previous years. Subsequent cohorts born in the 1950s (aged
11–20 by 1970) were larger still. Cohorts born in the late 1960s (those in the
youngest age strata by 1970) were markedly smaller as fertility began to drop.
Smallest of all was the Depression cohort born in 1931–1935 (aged 35–39 by
1970). The impact of this small cohort on the changing age structure can be
seen in Figure 8-5. (Compare age 5–9 in the 1940 pyramid with age 35–39 in
the 1970 pyramid.)

For each of these unequally sized cohorts, the researchers assisting policy
makers can estimate the approximate pattern of the cohort's movement into
the future. By using current knowledge about rates of death and migration,

---

[81] Social indicators of many trends are being developed and, where appropriate data on
age are included, can be rearranged to take advantage of methods of cohort analysis.

[82] U.S. Bureau of the Census, *1970 Census of the Population*, Vol. 1 (Washington, D.C.:
Government Printing Office, 1973), p. 259.

they can project the probable size of each cohort in the year 2000, for example, or 2020 (when surviving members of the large 1950 cohort will have reached age 50 and 70, respectively). These estimates can be close to the mark for the reason we have noted: much is already known about the size, composition, and past history of each cohort already born. Predictably, the large baby boom cohorts, sandwiched between cohorts of more modest size, will continue to threaten people–role dislocations up to the end of their life course.[83] Now young and inexperienced, these cohorts are making heavy demands on entry-level jobs and housing; considerably more experienced by 1990, they will be seeking larger numbers of high-level jobs than their smaller predecessor cohorts will be vacating. Early in the new century, they will become a flood of retirees.[84] Meantime, the small size of recent cohorts implies declining school enrollments for the next decade or more, and subsequent declines on the pressure for jobs and housing. To be forewarned is to be alerted to future needs for increased absorptive capacity in the workforce or for managing the dependency burden implied by the rapid jump in the number of retirees.

Cohort analysis has still other important uses. It can help estimate future consequences of current innovations. Suppose—contrary to the recommendations of the abovementioned panels—a law were passed mandating a four-year period of higher education immediately following high school. From information about the size, characteristics, and past history of cohorts now in high school,[85] some of the effects of the legislation could be worked out. From such information can be calculated the approximate number of additional college spaces and staff needed and how much more money would have to be appropriated for higher education. The impact on the labor force could also be estimated, in terms of the immediate loss of those members of the cohort ordinarily moving directly from high school to work, and the future addition of the highly educated cohorts once they had graduated from college. In such ways the perspective of age stratification and the related method of cohort analysis can often provide a wide grasp of future ramifications of current attacks on social problems.

Cohort analysis may also suggest that certain problems will become less acute or even disappear. Even now there are hints that the current lack of structure in the retirement role will be partly self-correcting. In the future, each new cohort of old people will be better educated and (barring economic crises) more financially secure than the one before.[86] Thus future cohorts may be better prepared to press toward new definitions of the retirement role. Moreover, husbands and wives can utilize the extended middle-life period, with its

[83] Norman B. Ryder, "The Demography of Youth," in Coleman et al., *op. cit.*

[84] Since the direct focus of cohort analysis is on the changing age structure of people, other methods are needed for estimating concurrent changes in the age structure of roles—for example, whether the number of high-level jobs will have expanded by 1990, or new roles for retirees institutionalized by the turn of the century.

[85] Such information is supplemented by other information, of course, such as accounts of the effects of the earlier parallel change to compulsory high school education.

[86] Neugarten, *op. cit.*

peak incomes and freedom from child rearing, to prepare for retirement by developing new patterns of leisure time interests and of relationship to family and friends. Because of the changing character of successive cohorts, new roles for older retirees may be developed. The restructuring of patterns of work, leisure, and education may be insisted upon, and new value may be attached to close relationships both for old people and for people of all ages.

Constraints on Intervention

Before concluding we must consider some constraints on intervention as these apply specifically to age-related problems. A foremost constraint derives from the interconnectedness of the age strata as parts of the system of age stratification (described in the first part of this chapter). A significant change to alleviate the problems of one stratum typically has consequences for other strata and for society as a whole. For example, advancing the age of retirement to 75 or dropping it to 50 would change not only the role prescriptions for persons at these ages; it would also change the work roles available to other age strata, the kinds of training needed by the young and how long they stay in school before taking a job, and the weight of economic dependency carried by the middle-aged. Thus any proposed intervention affecting one age stratum must be carefully evaluated in terms of its possible ramifications through other strata.

Another constraint derives from a general reluctance to recognize that age problems are not inevitable nor biologically ordained. Little can be done about problems as long as people take for granted that, through the mere process of aging, unpleasant conditions will automatically dissipate or intensify. Still other constraints arise from ethical concerns: Should policies be implemented to benefit one stratum if they create deprivations for another? Should monies currently allocated for the support of higher education or welfare aid to dependent children be reduced in order to support increased medical services for the old or to expand day-care institutions? Is it ethically defensible for one stratum to have priority over another? Should breakfast programs for the elderly poor take precedence over those for economically disadvantaged children? Should assistance with transition problems be given to widows before young mothers? Indeed, should transition problems be eased at all if their amelioration reduces motivation for socially valued innovation or greater efforts at social reform?

Intervention is further restricted by the danger of abridging civil liberties in the pursuit of a higher social value. Should couples be required to submit to genetic counseling or be forced to abort a defective fetus in order to ensure healthier new generations? Should old people or youth be prevented from living in age-segregated communities in order to foster age integration? Should the middle-aged be held financially responsible for their elderly parents?

The ultimate constraint is a practical one. Assuming that the institutional changes are thought by many to be desirable, how are they to be accomplished?

How are necessary funds to be procured? What processes of consciousness-raising, organizing, or lobbying would persuade decision-makers to implement such proposals? Such practical questions are of course presupposed by proposals and plans for restructuring age-related roles. But basic structural changes are not outside the realm of possibility, as amply evidenced by recent changes in the structure of sex roles (see Chapter 9). The challenge is to draw attention to problems of age and aging and to help mobilize public support for correcting these problems.

In sum, the dynamics of the age stratification system create social problems and also contain an inherent potential for alleviating them. Social problems spring from the impact of social change on both the age structure and the ways in which people age. Age-graded roles, institutions, and aging individuals are all implicated in a complex system that generates age inequalities, age segregation, age conflict, and difficulties of role transition. But the dynamics of this system also give flexibility for future changes in roles, for providing social supports during role transitions, and for improvement in the conditions of life for people of all ages. Clearly, though age and aging are inevitable, the age structure of roles and the manner of aging are both socially constructed and subject to social control.

SUMMARY

1   Age and aging cause problems for individuals at all stages of life and for society as a whole. Most of these problems are social, not biological, in origin.

2   A new field, *the sociology of age,* is concerned with understanding the social causes of age-related problems and finding ways to alleviate or prevent such problems.

3   One set of social problems arises from *age stratification.* Both people and roles in society are stratified by age. As a result there are age inequalities, age segregation, and age conflict. Age differences among people intensify these problems. The young, middle-aged, and old differ from one another not only in life-course stage, but also in past experiences and in the birth cohort to which they belong. (A cohort consists of people born at the same time. Members of the same cohort age together and share the same historical context.)

4   *Age inequalities* occur when people in some strata have less access than other people to valued roles and their rewards. For example, many teen-agers and people over 65 are denied work roles and the associated income and social esteem. Age inequalities are a source of obvious deprivation, hidden but widespread suffering, and various forms of deviance.

5   *Age segregation* pervades our social institutions. For example, children in age-graded schools are discouraged from interacting with children older or younger than they. Old people in retirement communities are shut off from younger relatives and friends. Although it has certain advantages, age segregation interferes with the flow of mutual support and mutual influence (socialization) between age strata.

6   Age inequalities and age segregation breed misunderstandings, cleavages, and

potential *conflict* between age strata. For example, negative stereotypes often develop from misunderstanding of young people as "too inexperienced" or old people as "no longer able" to work, and negative stereotypes can become self-fulfilling prophesies.

7 Another set of social problems accompanies the *process of aging* from birth to death. As people grow older, they move through a socially structured sequence of roles. Age is a criterion for entering and leaving these roles and for evaluating role performance.

8 Problems of aging are intensified during *life-course transitions* (such as entering the first grade, finding the first job, retiring, or losing a spouse). A transition involves relinquishing a former role as well as assuming a new one.

9 Life-course transitions present two types of problems: (a) the strains of learning the new role and adjusting to it and (b) the pain associated with loss of the former role. Relinquishing a valued and familiar role often invokes a period of grief, especially when the self has been deeply invested in the lost role.

10 Role transitions can be positive experiences when the new role is socially valued and when people (for example, *significant others* or professional counselors) provide adequate social and emotional support during the transition. For many transitions there is *no* adequate support—as in becoming a husband or wife, starting a job, becoming a parent, dying alone in a hospital, or facing widowhood.

11 *Social change* continually affects age and aging, sometimes causing new problems but sometimes eliminating old ones. For example, the tenuous balance between age-graded roles and people of the appropriate age to fill these roles is constantly being undermined by war, economic fluctuations, changes in the state of science and the arts, etc.

12 The age structure of roles is subject to special disturbances when *successive cohorts differ markedly in size,* as the outsized "baby boom cohort" first increased the demand for schools and teachers and then left in its wake an over-supply of educational facilities.

13 Because of social change, *members of different cohorts age in different ways* and are less likely than in a comparatively stable society to share and understand one another's experiences. By creating cohort differences in life-course patterns, social change exaggerates age differences and the problems of age cleavage, misunderstanding, and potential conflict.

14 The impact of social change on the age structure of people and roles exacerbates social problems but also gives continuing *opportunity to correct problems of age and aging.*

15 Some problems can be reduced or prevented through changes in the aspirations or capacities of *people* at particular ages. For example, middle-aged doctors or lawyers can be retrained to be on a par with recent graduates, or old people can be made to realize that not all of their physical handicaps are untreatable.

16 Some problems can be alleviated by dispelling negative stereotypes and by bringing to the attention of policy makers the hidden, but widespread, difficulties of age and aging.

17 Judicious interventions are also possible in the age structure of *roles.* Unplanned changes are continually underway as some roles disappear, new ones emerge, and others are redefined. Deliberate changes can aid in solving particular problems through role redefinition, or through raising or lowering age criteria for entering or leaving a role.

18   *Cohort analysis* can be used by sociologists as an aid to understanding past problems of age and aging, anticipating future problems, and assessing possible consequences of social change.

RECOMMENDED READING

Since a sociology of age is only now developing, the works of relatively few scholars have made use of a broad sociological perspective for examining problems of age and aging. Important and highly readable forerunners are Karl Mannheim's "The Problem of Generations" (1928) in Kecskmeti (ed.), *Essays on the Sociology of Knowledge* (1952) and Talcott Parsons' "Age and Sex in the Social Structure of the United States," *American Sociological Review* (1942). Updating and extending Mannheim's work are illuminating essays by Norman B. Ryder, "The Cohort as a Concept in the Study of Social Change," *American Sociological Review* (1965) and by Leonard D. Cain, Jr., "Life Course and Social Structure," in Faris (ed.), *Handbook of Modern Sociology* (1964). A comprehensive statement is to be found in Matilda White Riley, Marilyn Johnson, and Anne Foner, *Aging and Society, Volume III: A Sociology of Age Stratification* (1972).

For the study of particular age strata, a considerable literature is available, part of it in handbooks or books of readings. On adolescence, S. N. Eisenstadt's *From Generation to Generation* (1956), a monumental analysis of youth group formation, presents extensive cross-cultural and cross-temporal data. In *Youth: Transition to Adulthood* (1974), James S. Coleman and a panel of scientists evaluate past and present adolescent experience. Useful for studying adulthood, though reflecting the paucity of work on the middle years, is the reader edited by Bernice L. Neugarten, *Middle Age and Aging* (1968). Countless books, government documents, and specialized journals deal with problems of old age. Convenient and well-organized compilations are Clark Tibbitts' *Handbook of Social Gerontology* (1960) and James E. Birren's *Handbook of Aging and the Social Sciences* (1976). A synthesis of the social-science research on the middle and later years appears in Matilda White Riley and Anne Foner, *Aging and Society, Volume I: An Inventory of Research Findings* (1968). For study of the problems of old age, the reader edited by Beth Hess, *Growing Old in America* (1976) is recommended.

On life-course transitions, Arnold van Gennep's *The Rites of Passage* (1908) is the classic work. Important contributions have since been made by Orville G. Brim, Jr., "Socialization through the Life Cycle," in Brian and Wheeler (eds.), *Socialization after Childhood* (1966) and by Barney Glaser and Anselm Strauss, *Status Passage* (1971). A provocative account of the problems of one transition is Alice Rossi, "Transition to Parenthood," in *Journal of Marriage and the Family* (1968).

Using a multidisciplinary approach to the study of age, Pierre L. van den Berghe's small paperback, *Age and Sex in Human Societies: A Biosocial Perspective* (1973) offers a lively overview. Well worth reading are several investigations of the impact of historical events and social change on the patterning of the life course: Philippe Ariès, *Centuries of Childhood: A Social History of Family Life* (1962), delightfully written, containing inferences from family portraits; Glenn H. Elder, Jr., *Children of The Great Depression* (1974), a sensitive, though somewhat complicated, re-analysis of longitudinal data; and Peter Uhlenberg, "Cohort Variations in Family Life Cycle Experience of U.S. Females," in *Journal of Marriage and the Family* (1975), an imaginative demographic analysis. Other examples of the varied studies of age-related social problems are contained in Anne Foner (ed.), *Age and Society* (1975).

9

Sex
Roles

CYNTHIA FUCHS EPSTEIN

M ost people are aware of the striking changes in the sex roles of many men and women in America during the past decade. The new work roles of women and the changing definitions of men's roles in the family are evidence both of widespread discontent with the traditional view of sex roles and of concern with the wider issues of equality and participation in the society. They also reflect changes in individuals' behavior that are making conventional attitudes obsolete. Although these changes are a partial solution to the social problems that gave rise to them, they are creating new social problems in the clash of old and new norms, old and new interests. Women especially, by their challenges of the roles traditionally assigned to them because of their sex, are forcefully questioning the division of labor and distribution of rewards in all of society's basic institutions.

All societies assign an array of roles to individuals—as family members and workers, as religious and political leaders, as children and adults—because of their sex. Under all cultural belief systems, these roles are considered correct, particularly since they are thought to be an expression of assumed physical and mental differences between the sexes. They are also believed to be "just" and best for the proper functioning of society.

Two important sets of issues are being raised in the United States and other societies today with regard to traditional sex-role assignments and the beliefs supporting them. One set questions the constraints nature imposes on how men and women can behave. The other deals with the social consequences of sex-role assignments, speculating on whether men and women are justly treated in the way they are assigned their places in the world, and whether the present existing system of assignments benefits most individuals or only privileged groups..

New research in the social sciences and physical sciences suggests that much of what once was accepted as scientific fact about sex differences based on biology may have in fact been based on cultural biases. Apart from the roles linked directly to women's bearing of children, few gender roles assigned by society can now be said to be functionally related to physiology. As we shall see, the perpetuation of differential social roles for men and women is related to social rather than physiological causes.

Although differences in social roles based on sex always affect men as well as women, the problems that result place emphasis primarily on women's sex roles. This is partly because the problems for men that result from stereotyping male behavior—such as the demand for lifelong economic activity and the emphasis on emotional control—have not yet been defined as social problems. Women's role problems, however, have been defined as social issues affecting the entire society.

In recent years, women have become increasingly conscious of their exclu-

The research assistance of Susan Ogulnick in the preparation of this chapter is gratefully acknowledged, as well as the extraordinary aid and critical assistance given by Howard M. Epstein and Robert K. Merton.

sion from positions of power and their lack of freedom to exercise personal choice in careers and in their family lives. Many men too have become aware of the inequalities women face in American society and have become partners in the struggle to end them. But the commitments of most American men and women to equality remain ambiguous, both because of traditional views about the essential nature of men and women, and of fears of the costs and consequences of equality for the family and other institutions. Men and women alike fear that in addition to the economic cost of childcare facilities, for example, women's equality would weaken the family and disrupt traditional sex-segregated ways of work, education, and government.

The inequality of men and women goes back to the beginning of recorded time, although it has appeared in differing forms. In most societies, women have been restricted more than men, have been ranked lower in the status hierarchy, and have been given less recognition for the work they do. All societies have regarded women as very different, not only biologically but emotionally and intellectually, and almost always to their disadvantage. Christian, Jewish, Hindu, and Moslem beliefs all support the notion that women should hold inferior positions in society, and, until recently, this inferiority has been written into law in nearly all societies.

Although some groups of men also suffer deprivation and restriction, women in all groups have been affected by laws denying them the right to hold property, to vote, to go to school, to travel, to borrow money, and to enter certain occupations. In many societies, men of wealth and prestige could not, except in rare cases, make their daughters chiefs, send them to institutions of higher learning, buy them seats on the stock exchange, transfer property to them, or arrange public office for them.

This is what it means to hold an ascribed, immutable status—one that, like a racial status, is acquired at birth and cannot be changed. The consequence of status immutability is that the members of the group cannot solve their problems even when as individuals they possess resources for doing so. The invidious distinctions between the role assignments society imposes on men and on women create a good many of the social problems we are concerned with in this chapter. The inflexibility of sex-role assignment also creates problems for individuals who cannot or do not wish to subscribe to the role assignments of their sex. This is variously true in all societies. But it is felt most oppressively in the modern world, where options and freedoms for all categories of people are spelled out and more individuals feel constrained by traditional and rigid definitions of who they are, what they are worth, and what they should be doing.

Since the issues stemming from these distinctions are universal and bear directly on the lives of all men and women, one wonders why they have been defined as a social problem only in the last decade.

There is no easy answer. But a number of factors have contributed to this new awareness. One very important factor is the ever-growing participation of women in the labor force, now up to 42 percent in the United States. There is also women's new ability and willingness to control fertility, particularly through use of the birth control pill, which has given them greater choice in the exercise of their motherhood role. Another is women's participation in the two world wars and in wars of national liberation. Political and ideological discussions of equality for all people—including attempts to provide equal opportunity in Western and socialist societies—have also been major elements, though no lasting "solutions" have been found anywhere.

Finally, the ideological challenge of the women's movement in the United States has brought the problems of sex-role inequality to the eyes and consciousness of millions of women and men, defining individual frustrations and dissatisfactions as socially induced and therefore appropriate targets for change on a societal basis.

MOVEMENTS TOWARD SEX EQUALITY

The Women's Movement

The women's movement that began in the 1960s is unique in the American experience. The position of American women has altered more in the late 1960s and early 1970s than in decades before, and it seems clear that the women's movement has been the driving force.

Active women's movements existed in the nineteenth and early twentieth centuries in England and in the United States. They were effective in winning the vote for women[1] but not in achieving their other goals—to obtain for women the right to own property, to seek a divorce, to work in occupations of their choice, and to control their own incomes. Elizabeth Cady Stanton, who with Susan B. Anthony organized the first women's rights conference in 1848, dismissed the winning of suffrage as "not even half a loaf . . . only a crust, a crumb." Her reservations were justified, since possession of the vote did not, as expected by some, put women into the political mainstream. Women's political activity in the 1920s was limited to pressures that led to protective work legislation. It was not until the 1970s that women's effectiveness and interest in political activity on their own behalf became significant.

Most social commentators agree that Betty Friedan's book *The Feminine Mystique,* published in 1963, provided the main ideological basis for the new women's movement. In it, Friedan sketched the problems women faced in a society that claimed to judge itself by the degree of equality it offered its citizens, while excluding women from that judgment. The problems of black people had become obvious to most concerned Americans, but whether inequality was a problem for women—and, if so, how important a problem—seemed unclear even to women themselves. Friedan wrote that women faced a

---

[1] Suffrage was won for women in 1918 in England and in 1920 in the United States.

malaise that had "no name." She gave it a name—the "feminine mystique"—which identified the aimlessness and lack of self-worth that women experienced because they were not recognized as productive members of American society. Analyzing the structural reasons for it, she contended that women's powerlessness restricted them to lives of vicarious fulfillment and that, as consumers but not producers, they were playing roles that were personally frustrating, even if functional for the American economy.

The tumultuous response to her work[2] helped to create the new movement with Friedan as its leader. She organized the National Organization for Women (NOW) in 1966, and has remained a leading feminist, working with others prominent in the movement to help found the National Women's Political Caucus and the First Women's Bank.

The women's movement has expanded into labor, academic, and professional organizations of all types and has created thousands of informal discussion groups linked by their participants' discoveries of common concerns.

Certainly the new feminist message has spread rapidly throughout the United States. Although media coverage of women's attempts to improve their situation has frequently been tinged with derision and humor, and often only the dramatic and radical activities have gained attention (picketing and those oft-cited but infrequent bra-burning demonstrations), millions of women throughout America have come to reassess their roles as housewives and mothers. They have become sensitive to the discrimination they face getting jobs and specialized education; to the condition of dependency that marriage engenders; and to the disorienting anomie that divorce may create. Consciousness-raising groups sprang up in cities and suburbs, with middle-age women following the path set by college-age women.

One indicator of the change in attitudes brought about by the movement are the findings of opinion polls, which show a sharply increased sentiment on the part of women in support of more sexual equality. A 1973 poll by the Roper Organization showed that 57 percent of the women questioned nationally favored efforts to strengthen their status, an increase over the figures reported in 1971 and 1972 by Louis Harris, in which 40 percent and 48 percent expressed such support. Almost equal percentages of men agreed with the women. A 1974 poll reported that almost half the women (46 percent) in a national sample preferred a marriage "where husband and wife share responsibilities more—both work, both share homemaking and childcare responsibilities."

Still, large questions remain about the movement's permanent impact on society. The major fear feminists have is that the great strides apparent today will turn out to be token changes, in time forgotten, as were the goals of the first women's movement. In 1975 Friedan and a group of feminists active in the National Organization for Women began efforts to reassess the direction of the movement. They called for organized efforts on behalf of housewives and

---

[2] *The Feminine Mystique* sold over three million copies and continues to be read widely.

working women and for action to combine women's liberation with more options and freedom for men. The aim of the movement, they claimed was, as before, women's truly equal partnership with men.

Men's Liberation

Although very few men have become active in the women's movement, it is clear that many men support women's equality, especially in education and work. A number of men have reacted to the changes in their wives' attitudes toward work by encouraging them and by sharing responsibility for housework, at least in principle. Middle-class men, who a decade before would have been uncomfortable wheeling a baby carriage except on Sunday outings, now carry youngsters in backpacks, dashing down the aisles of supermarkets to participate in family shopping.

The men, like the women, are not without ambivalence. Mirra Komarovsky, in a study of college men, found that many conceded the case for equality but were disturbed to think of its effect on their personal lives, and hoped that their wives would conform to a traditional pattern, staying home until the children were of school age and assuming primary responsibility for the home.[3] Even men who actively support women's equal participation in work often are constrained by the institutions in which they work. Husbands who wish to help care for children do not find it easy to get time off from work for that purpose; and the few men who are avant-garde enough to want to share one job with a wife find it harder to manage in reality than in ideological terms.

A few younger men have been so personally affected by the activity and ideology of the women's movement that they have sought to follow the path of consciousness raising and liberation, first to understand and deal with the women they know, and then to cope with their own problems stemming from stereotyped ideas about masculinity in American society. In consciousness-raising groups, for example, they have questioned their shame at displaying emotions such as tenderness and fear, and the difficulty of making intimate friends of other men and women. Some have formed male liberation groups, which sprang up on college campuses and elsewhere through the efforts of a few leaders such as Warren Farrell.[4]

The focus on male liberation is the excessive—sometimes overwhelming—demands made upon men by the marketplace. Unlike women activists, who are seeking access to the competitive arena of high-commitment work, many of these men seek freedom from the "rat race." Social scientists have begun to analyze the problems attached to male roles and the stereotyping of men's

---

[3] Mirra Komarovsky, "Some Problems in Role Analysis," *American Sociological Review*, Vol. 38 (1973), pp. 649–662.

[4] Warren Farrell, *The Liberated Man* (New York: Bantam, 1975).

personalities; the ambivalences created by the disparity between men's emotions and the constraints on the expression of these feelings; and the consequences of men's assignments in the work world.[5] Some change is already discernible on the legal level, reflecting in part a consideration of these ideas; men are beginning to win child custody in divorce cases, and some have won suits demanding paternity leave from schoolteaching, and equal rights to Social Security survivors' benefits as widowers.

Equal Rights Legislation

The upsurge of women's activities in the United States began at the same time as the passage of the Civil Rights Act of 1964, originally intended to stop discrimination against minorities but amended at the last minute to include a ban on sexual discrimination.[6] The act provided the legal foundation for women's rights activity, and the combination of law and of women's organizations proved to be powerful.

The Equal Employment Opportunities Commission (EEOC), whose major activity has been in handling cases of minority discrimination, established guidelines for compliance with Civil Rights Act provisions relating to women. It was the EEOC and a number of feminist lawyers who sued the American Telephone and Telegraph Company, the largest employer of women in the world, and won a landmark agreement forcing AT&T to provide goals and timetables for the hiring and promotion of both women and minority employees. AT&T was also forced to pay $15 million in back pay to persons who had been denied promotion because of discrimination and $23 million in immediate annual pay increases to women and minority males who were deemed underpaid in their job classifications.

The EEOC action against AT&T demonstrated that women could muster and use power, and that there was support for their position in and out of government. Some critics had labeled the women's movement an enterprise of privileged, white, middle-class women, but the AT&T case proved that women were affected by the movement's activity at all levels of the socioeconomic pyramid. It was now clear that legislation giving middle-class women an opportunity to be hired as lawyers also gave working-class women the opportunity to be promoted as supervisors in factories and businesses.

[5] See Joseph H. Pleck, "The Male Sex Role: Definitions, Problems, and Sources of Change," *Journal of Social Issues*, forthcoming.

[6] The amendment was the last-minute contribution of Representative Howard W. Smith (D.-Va.), who thought that broadening the act to bar sex discrimination would doom the legislation. Smith was bitterly opposed to equality for minorities or women and thought that including sex in the bill would make it so preposterous that other legislators could not vote for it.

SEX ROLES AND WORK

Few of us think of work as being as much a part of human existence as eating, sleeping, or sexuality. Yet all human beings—men and women, children and adults—work at feeding and clothing themselves and others, at building, at making things, and at teaching and learning. They work at different levels of talent and training and according to rules set down by society.

Societies divide labor among their members differently and reward their labor differently. All societies use age, race, ethnicity, and sex as criteria for allocating work and the rewards attached to it, but not all societies allocate work and rewards according to the same criteria. Some universal patterns emerge, however, and certain relationships between kinds of work and kinds of workers and the rewards they receive are normative in all societies.

In Western societies—especially in the United States—women increasingly are challenging the traditional criteria allocating work and rewards according to the sex of the worker.

Norms and Realities

In all societies, females are expected to attend to childcare, and do so. According to the norms of Western societies, adult men are expected to engage in market activity (paid work), and adult women are not supposed to work for pay unless forced to by economic need. Yet nearly 43 percent of American women over the age of 16 work, many of them married women with children. More than 57 percent of all wives with children between the ages of 6 and 17 worked during 1972, as did 45 percent of the women with children under 6. Among wives with children under the age of 3, 29 percent were in the labor force in March 1973, an increase of 10 percent in a decade. From 1969 to 1972 the proportion of black working wives with preschool children rose from 26 to 41 percent.

The substantial and growing participation of American women in the economy—they make up 41 percent of the labor force—is matched in other industrialized countries, yet in no Western society is paid work outside the home considered desirable for married women and mothers. Only in some of the East European countries, in China, and in some other Asian and African societies are women expected to work and contribute to the economy equally with men.[7]

It is widely assumed that American women would not work if the income of their husbands were sufficient to support a middle-class life style. For many families it is true that a middle-class standard of living requires that both partners hold jobs: in 1968, 60 percent of the families with annual incomes of $10,000 or more passed that point only because the wife worked; employed women contributed 38 percent of family income in 1972.

People of both sexes usually claim they are working because of economic need. But it is widely recognized that men work for other reasons as well. American culture has always emphasized that a man should define himself in terms not only of how much money he makes but also the kind of job he holds. Professional, businessman, salaried employee, factory worker, truck driver—which of these positions a man holds does much to determine his sense of identity and his family's social status, as well as their income level. In reality, most American men work even if they have inherited wealth or married rich women. No "self-respecting" man, it is thought, "lives off" his father or his wife.[8] A man is expected to involve himself in earning money whether he needs it or not, and to gain from his work self-definition, a sense of autonomy, and social contacts.

---

[7] Ester Boserup, *Woman's Role in Economic Development* (New York: St. Martin's Press, 1970).

[8] There are exceptions to this. For example, Jewish scholars who studied the Torah in the *stetls* (village or town) of Eastern Europe were not expected to work in the marketplace. Instead, their wives devoted themselves to income-producing activity to support the family without demeaning the husband, who still was regarded as "head of household." See Mark Zbrowski, *Life Is with People* (New York: International Universities Press, 1952).

American culture traditionally has defined money and work roles for women quite differently, however. Women could earn money, but it was preferable if they obtained it from men—husbands or fathers—for use as consumers. A woman was not encouraged to define herself or establish her identity in terms of the work she did or the money she made, but rather in terms of her husband's or father's work and in the way she spent his money. In recent years the change in this set of attitudes has been dramatic. People have begun to acknowledge that women, too, can *want* to earn money even if they do not *need* to, and that they too may properly use work as a way to acquire autonomy, status, friendships, and personal identity. Upsetting the mandate of economic necessity as the only justification for women's work (although recognizing its reality for women as well as men) is one of the main achievements of the women's movement.

Sex and the Ranking and Division of Labor

In all societies, some work is considered "good" and carries high prestige, and some work is considered onerous and has little prestige.[9] Women are not usually found in the jobs ranked high in prestige. The work considered most boring, dirty, and least rewarding has always been assigned by societies to slaves, the poor and lowest castes, the young, and women.

In the United States since World War II, women have entered the labor force in relatively low-prestige jobs as clerks, secretaries, telephone operators, and food handlers (72 percent of all waiters and waitresses, cooks, and bartenders are women). Women comprise 57 percent of all service workers and 97 percent of all domestic servants.[10] More than two-thirds of the women employed in Eastern Europe and the Soviet Union work in the service sector, especially in public health and education. Female employment in East European industry is concentrated in textiles and clothing manufacturing. A similar pattern of female concentration in low-skilled, low-paid work exists in Western Europe.[11]

In all societies the division of labor, whether on the basis of sex or other status, is legitimated and supported by the society's system of beliefs, religious or ideological, and is rationalized as "natural" and usually as necessary for the social good. Changes in belief systems and work assignments occur from time to time, but in no society is there merely a random relationship between kinds of work and the entire pool of possible workers. Work assignments are always linked to certain categories of persons; sex status is almost always one of the criteria for these assignments.

[9] Everett Cherrington Hughes, *Men and Their Work* (Glencoe, Ill.: The Free Press, 1958), pp. 49ff.

[10] Alice H. Cook, *The Working Mother: A Survey of Problems and Programs in Nine Countries* (Ithaca: New York State School of Industrial and Labor Relations, Cornell University, 1975), p. 11.

[11] *Ibid.*, p. 9.

The sex typing of jobs occurs in entire professions (medicine for men, nursing for women) and in specialties within professions (if women are doctors they tend to become pediatricians or obstetricians, while surgery is an almost exclusively "male" specialty); in whole industries (mining is male) and in job sectors within industries (clerical work is usually female; skilled production work is usually male). A few jobs may be gender-neutral, but this is often true only when they are new, perhaps as the result of developing technology.

The sex-role revolution is addressed most directly to the problems experienced by groups of individuals, male and female, who have become discontented with existing job and group classifications and the constraints they impose. Men and women experience frustration and pain when, merely because they come from a devalued group, they are limited to working in occupations that do not suit them. They are questioning occupational constraints based on either ascribed or achieved statuses that are not germane to the work performed but serve rather to restrict favored jobs to individuals and groups who now control them. There are growing objections to stereotyping in any form because of the new consciousness that when men or women are expected to choose a set of activities only because of their sex, their freedom to pursue individual interests is diminished. For example, women have become aware that a belief that they possess special traits as a group is used to *prevent* them from having a wide array of good jobs. Often the reasoning is illogical as well as incorrect. Women are believed to be more sensitive than men and are thus discouraged from becoming doctors and business managers. Yet an argument could be made that if women really are more sensitive, they are well suited to demonstrate the qualities we ask of these professionals: tactfulness, responsiveness, and an ability to know intuitively "what is going on."

Men, especially younger men, are questioning the idea that they are abnormal, lack drive, or "are not men" if they prefer undemanding careers. Many young people today feel that varied activities that make life balanced and pleasurable (such as spending time with children or engaging in crafts) have been undervalued in favor of those that produce goods and wealth. The idea that men should work to the limits of their endurance and that women should handle childcare, meals, and home maintenance is being challenged by both sexes.

Whether a job is autonomous or subordinate determines to what extent it will be sex-typed. A high proportion of female jobs are subordinate to male-labeled jobs, as in the nurse–doctor, secretary–executive cases. When male jobs are subordinate, they are rarely if ever subordinate to female-labeled jobs. For example, hospital orderlies (usually males) do not report to nurses (females who are higher in rank) but to the hospital administrator (usually a male).

Jobs that are relatively autonomous (truck driver, salesman) are typically male. Women are less often self-employed than men, even when both are performing the same work. Most male doctors, dentists, and lawyers in this country are self-employed; most females in these professions are not.

Perpetuation of Sex Typing

Social controls work to keep the sexes in their place in the division of labor— to keep male-typed occupations male, and female-typed occupations female. These controls work in overt and subtle ways, by customs and by rules. As we noted before, laws and rules kept women out of many occupations in the past. But ridicule, embarrassment, and forms of disapproval have kept low the number of men and women in occupations for which they are believed unsuited.

A man who becomes a nurse, secretary, or kindergarten teacher may be thought to lack ambition or self-reliance or to be neurotic because he wishes to spend the workday with women or children rather than with other men. A woman who becomes a taxi driver or construction worker may be considered "too tough" for a woman and at the same time "not tough enough" for the job. Female professionals and business executives are suspected of being "unfeminine": too brainy, too committed to their work (and not committed enough to their families), too aggressive.

Because the attitudes linking sex roles with particular work roles are so enmeshed with the belief that violation is both wrong and "sick," occupational "crossing over" is made very difficult for the individual man or woman who attempts to do so. The person faces opposition not only at the point of entry to the occupation but continuously through his or her work career. The longer a job tends to remain the domain of one sex or the other, the more difficult it is for the person of the "wrong sex" to be treated as an equal within it.

Sex labeling and the reward structure   Women tend to be paid less than men even when they work at essentially similar jobs. This is true throughout the world for professional work as well as factory work, even though most countries have official commitments to the doctrine of equal pay for equal work.[12] The discrepancy is often attributed to women's pattern of part-time employment and to their high job turnover, but when full-time workers are compared, women still are paid less, probably because they are less militant and fewer are organized in unions.[13]

In the United States the federal government has acted recently to redress this inequality.[14] A number of courts have interpreted the Equal Pay Act of 1963 to ensure that when workers did essentially the same work, they were to be paid the same, even though their job titles were different. During fiscal 1974, nearly 33,000 employees were found to have been underpaid by more than

[12] *Ibid.,* pp. 22–24.

[13] Isabel Sawhill, "The Economics of Discrimination Against Women: Some New Findings," *Journal of Human Resources,* Vol. 8, No. 3, pp. 383–395; Larry E. Suter and Herman P. Miller, "Components of Income Differences Between Men and Career Women," *American Journal of Sociology,* Vol. 78 (January 1973), pp. 962–974.

[14] Citizens Advisory Council on the Status of Women, *Women in 1974* (Washington, D.C.: U.S. Government Printing Office, 1975), pp. 7–8.

$20.6 million under the Equal Pay Act. The guidelines thus established provided that men and women doing substantially the same work could not be segregated in separate departments, classified as performing different jobs, or paid at different rates.

As we have noted, however, women and men generally do perform different kinds of work, and women's jobs pay less. In some cases other compensations are offered in lieu of high salary. It has been suggested that women are often directed into roles that bring vicarious fulfillment;[15] they are expected to derive satisfaction from serving men (as nurses or secretaries, for example) and to share the prestige of the men with whom they form role relationships. Just as a wife's status rises when her husband gets a better job, so a secretary's rises when her boss is promoted and he "takes her with him." Riding on a man's coattails may seem an easy way to improve one's position, but there are disadvantages to what has been called "vicarious rank."[16] The woman's career is likely to be tied to that of a particular man rather than to his position or to her own abilities. Others may wonder about the personal relationship between the woman and her boss if she is sexually attractive. Even if this is not the case, the woman's training is not defined as apprenticeship, and her skills are not easily transferable to another boss or a higher-level job for herself.

When the woman's job is evaluated in terms of the personal relationships it entails, her rewards are apt to be outside the usual occupational reward system and may not correspond to the normal rewards men on the track to success expect, such as raises and promotions.[17] But women are often compensated with rewards appropriate to a friendship or family system. Their "pay" may be in the form of lunches, flowers, affection, and attention. Yet for women who are cut off from the usual reward structure, love, friendship, and the promise of continuity of relationship become highly prized rewards, and such women may alter their expectations to conform to what they can get rather than what ought to be an appropriate reward in the work situation.

Sex labeling and the tracking system   Why do women fail to climb the ladder in the occupational hierarchy when they often have appeared to start in jobs on the road to achievement? Part of the answer lies in the fact that separate sex-differentiated job tracks exist for men and women. Although they may be parallel at some points, the male track inevitably leads higher. A higher-ranking female job may provide less of a future for a woman than a lower-level position provides for a man, because his job is one that leads to promotion and hers is not.

[15] Jean Lipman-Blumen, "The Vicarious Achievement Ethic and Non-Traditional Roles for Women." Paper presented at Annual Meetings of the Eastern Sociological Society, April 13–15, 1973.

[16] Harris Schrank and John Riley, Jr., "Women in Work Organizations," in Juanita M. Kreps (ed.), *Women and the American Economy* (Englewood Cliffs, N.J.: Prentice-Hall, 1976).

[17] Cynthia Fuchs Epstein, "Sex Role Stereotyping, Occupations and Social Exchange," *Women's Studies*, Vol. 3 (1976), pp. 185–194.

Women today are getting higher-level jobs than they have ever had before, but their jobs are still being labeled female and are not on the same track to the top as men's.[18] Women are now being made corporate assistant vice-presidents, but they are being put in charge of affirmative action plans, personnel programs, and other dead-end positions—not the production, sales, and financial posts on the track to top management posts.

It has been suggested that competent women are often unwilling to cross to a male track because of their early socialization and the possibility that they will attain higher rank and income than their husbands. This may explain some women's behavior, but it ignores the real discriminatory patterns that block women in the occupational structure. When distinctions are made between male and female jobs and the best jobs then are labeled "male," women are blocked from advancement. In occupations sex-typed male, women are often excluded by rule; even if they enter, they have almost no chance to attain top places. Yet when women predominate in an occupation, fewer formal rules exclude men, and the few men in such fields have a better chance than the women around them to rise to leadership positions.

There are also subtle dimensions to tracking. In many professional fields, competence is created largely through experience rather than preliminary training. Trial lawyers learn court procedures and acquire skill in handling cases in the courtroom. Surgeons learn advanced techniques in the operating room, from senior people who have chosen them as assistants. Many business executives are former protégés of corporate officers who have provided them with contacts and taught them the secrets of the inner circle.

Women have not usually had access to informal training of this sort, even when the jobs they hold would make it appropriate. Sexual stereotypes make senior people reluctant to invest training or affix such labels as "promising" and "brilliant" to women, just as racial stereotypes keep the same labels from blacks; neither are considered good risks for inner circles. This prevents women and blacks from receiving the stimulation and attention they need to develop, and sometimes even from entering fields they might do well in. Yet a close look at the lives of "self-made men" make it clear that such structuring and supports are usually as necessary to their growth as talent and the will to succeed.

Recruitment Patterns and Sex Typing

Occupational sex typing is perpetuated not only by labeling but also by selective recruitment practices. These practices range from sex quotas in training schools and exclusion from professional associations to the way in which job information is communicated to potential recruits.

[18] Cynthia Fuchs Epstein, "Tracking and Careers: The Case of Women in American Society," in Eleanor L. Zuckerman (ed.), *Women and Men: Roles, Attitudes and Power Relationships* (New York: The Radcliffe Club, 1975), pp. 26–34; "Institutional Barriers: What Keeps Women Out of the Executive Suite?" in Francine E. Gordon and Myra H. Strober (eds.), *Bringing Women into Management* (New York: McGraw-Hill, 1975).

Until a recent ruling by the Equal Employment Opportunities Commission that the practice was discriminatory, there were two categories of job advertisements in newspapers: "Help Wanted—Male" and "Help Wanted—Female." Thus jobs for typists and domestic workers were listed as "female," and jobs for salesmen and truck drivers were listed as "male." This seemed a reasonable matching of jobs and persons seeking employment, the newspapers claimed. But when the Civil Rights Act of 1964 was passed and the EEOC was charged with creating guidelines for its implementation, many social scientists testified that the effect of the separate-sex listings was discriminatory. The work of two social scientists, Daryl and Sandra Bem, was cited in a California Supreme Court decision banning sex-segregated classified ads.[19] Bem and Bem showed that few men in a sample responded to telephone company job ads for operators and service representatives when these were described as women's jobs. When ads for lineman or frameman described these as men's jobs, only 5 percent of a sample of women expressed interest in them. When these same jobs were described in a sex-neutral way, 25 percent of the women in the Bems' sample expressed interest, and when they were described as appropriate for women, the figure jumped to 45 percent. The EEOC submitted the results of this study as part of its overall complaint against the American Telephone and Telegraph Company, and AT&T has directed that its advertising and recruiting materials be rewritten to remove sex bias.

Apprenticeship programs Apprenticeship is an important channel of recruitment for many male-dominated occupations, in some cases the only one. Apprenticeship programs have usually been closed to women and to men of undesired minority groups. Years ago, it was possible for a person to become a doctor or lawyer by apprenticeship to a professional practicing in the field. Today a formal degree is necessary in those professions, but apprenticeship still takes place at the level of specialization, where senior professors of medicine or senior partners in law firms take on junior colleagues and teach them specialty roles. Apprenticeship is also the typical point of entry to many skilled trades and craft industries offering opportunities for high-paying, interesting work at the top of the blue-collar pyramid.

In 1970 there were 280,000 men in apprenticeship programs in 350 recognized trades and crafts. There were only 12,000 women apprentices, many of them working in hairdressing establishments. The problems women face in obtaining apprenticeship training are illustrated by a study conducted in a Wisconsin town.[20] Most employers polled said they would not give training in skilled work to women because of the harsh conditions under which they would have to work. But it was found that these employers hired women to do unskilled work under the same harsh conditions. The survey also found that many plants posted information about apprenticeships in places where women

---

[19] Daryl Bem and Sandra Bem, "Does Sex-Biased Advertising 'Aid and Abet' Sex Discrimination?" *Journal of Applied Social Psychology,* Vol. 3 (1973), pp. 6–18.

[20] Lisa Hammel, "Why Do Few Women Hold Apprenticeships?" *The New York Times,* July 2, 1974, p. 26.

would be unlikely to see them, such as the men's washroom. Finally, most of the male apprentices were between 18 and 24 years old. Although young recruits are preferred in most craft programs, many women do not wish to enter apprenticeship programs until they have married and had families.

Agencies such as the Women's Bureau of the Department of Labor have made a considerable effort to open apprenticeship programs to women. Probably the greatest barrier facing new applicants (not only women but men from some racial and ethnic groups) is the attitude of the established craftsmen, many of them with working-class backgrounds and beliefs. In many crafts, it is traditional that recruits be not only young but from a particular ethnic or racial group, and apprenticeship programs often have operated to exclude those deemed undesirable. Apprenticeship requires some rapport between teacher and trainee, and many crafts have developed close-knit comradeship groups. They view present attempts to open their ranks as violations of their rights to autonomy and selection of the people who they believe fit in best. It seems doubtful that their customary apprenticeship practices will be changed easily or quickly.

Sex status and trade union activity   Trade unions win their members higher wages, better working conditions, and more fringe benefits, and workers who are not union members or are not covered by union agreements are comparatively disadvantaged. In most countries the percentage of women workers who are union members is lower than the percentage of men; in the United States the figures are 10.4 percent for female workers and 28 percent for male workers. Women are also a disproportionate minority in union decision-making bodies, whether in communist or noncommunist countries. With only a few exceptions, labor unions have never been strong or early advocates of job equality for women. Most unions have upheld sex segregation, creating separate seniority rosters for men and women and ratifying different wage scales for the two sexes.

Very recently, union women have become more active and demanded more representation in union decision-making bodies. In 1974 a national coalition of women from the AFL–CIO and independent unions was formed in the United States. Similar groups have been started in some other countries. Although the activity of women in unions, as elsewhere, is constrained by their lack of education and training and by the demands of home and children, there is a growing feeling that women should participate more in union affairs to get a hearing for their demands at the bargaining table: equal pay, equal promotion opportunities, the elimination of sex segregation, and childcare facilities.

High-Prestige Occupations and Professions

Some of the first assaults on sex-based occupational exclusions were by feminists demanding equal access to high-ranking male-dominated occupations and professions. Law, medicine, university teaching, scientific research, and executive positions in corporations had all included only tiny percentages of women since the early 1900s. Excluding women meant that the jobs highest in remuneration and power in the society were reserved for men.

Members of the elite professions have a disproportionate amount of power in society because of their prestige, education, and wealth. Doctors are the highest-paid professional group in the United States, and lawyers rank second. Most of our political leaders are lawyers, and many business executives have training in law or engineering. Excluding women from these fields compounds the consequences of inequality because they cannot compete with men who have the credentials for important positions in politics and business.

Unlike lower-stratum occupations such as mining or construction work, it could not be argued that the professions require more physical strength than women typically have; the higher one goes in occupational rank, the more "mental" is the activity. Instead, it was claimed that women lack the stamina and temperament for top-level work; that their home obligations are too demanding; that they lack the commitment to work and the ambition necessary to succeed.

Other reasons used to justify their exclusion from the professions are similar to those used to rationalize their exclusion from apprenticeship. Many top occupations share the characteristics of communities in that they tend toward homogeneity, shared norms, and common attitudes.[21] Therefore it is difficult for those who already belong to accept persons who lack the appropriate status-set, persons who are "different." Women, it is supposed, would not understand the unstated norms and casual professional exchanges; they might "spoil" the work group or simply make everyone uncomfortable.

This problem is particularly acute for the first few women to enter a male-dominated occupation. "Tokenism" can be a first step toward equality, but it may be years before the next step is taken. In the meantime the token person—whether female, black, young, or old—stands out, and the situation is awkward for everyone.

Changes in women's representation in the professions   During the 1960s women's representation in the professions increased, but only in about the same small percentages that it had in the preceding decades. According to census figures, 2.4 percent of American lawyers in 1940 were women, 3.5 percent in 1960, and 4.9 percent in 1970. In medicine, women constituted 6.5 percent of the profession in 1960 and 9.3 percent in 1970. Considering the strength of the women's liberation movement in the late 1960s, the recent increases are not striking. The relatively small size of the increases is accounted for by the long lead time required for entry into the legal and medical professions. The 1970 census reflects decisions made by professional schools and prospective applicants during the mid-sixties.

The rise in the number of women in professional schools today is nothing short of dramatic. In the fall of 1974, first-year law school classes were 23.7

---

[21] William J. Goode, "Community Within a Community: The Professions," *American Sociological Review,* Vol. 22 (April 1957), pp. 195–200; Robert K. Merton et al. (eds.), *The Student-Physician* (Cambridge: Harvard University Press, 1957).

percent female, up from 15.7 percent in 1971. In medical schools, 22.2 percent of the 1974 entering class were women, exactly twice the percentage reported in 1970. During the early 1970s, women were also busy acquiring credentials for management jobs. To illustrate, the Columbia University Graduate School of Business' student body was only 7 percent female in 1970 but 24.2 percent in 1974. It seems likely that women more than men need the legitimation that an M.B.A. provides, but only recently have they had access to it. Harvard, for example, did not admit women to its M.B.A. program until 1963. Other leading business schools admitted women earlier, but there were quotas on their number, and few women applied. The jump in applications and admissions now that quotas have been curbed suggests that the shortage of female applicants in the past was an expression not of women's preferences but of their understanding that they were not wanted. The popular assumption that women are not interested in business may be incorrect.

Women's participation at the top levels of all high-ranking occupations has been minuscule. At present, for example, women constitute only about 10 percent of management personnel in banking, even though the term "management" is used loosely in banking to include supervisory jobs. Today's affirmative action programs mean that businesses and other institutions must consider upgrading the women on their staffs and begin programs to produce a flow of women into management jobs. The test of these programs remains whether women ultimately will be assimilated into the leadership of business, industry, and the professions in sizable numbers. Today there are just 15 women among the 2,500 presidents, key vice-presidents, and board chairpersons who direct the country's major corporations.

Professional associations and activities   Membership and participation in professional associations characterizes the active professional and reinforces professional identity. Such associations act as educational and self-monitoring bodies that uphold standards and provide important social contacts. At one time, women were almost entirely excluded from professional societies.[22] They often formed separate associations, such as the Women's Medical Association, the National Association of Women Lawyers, and the Association for Women Geographers. These groups had low prestige and little power, however; they reflected the low status of women practitioners themselves.

During the past few decades, when women have been permitted to join the male-dominated organizations, they have generally been kept off important policy-making committees[23] and assigned instead to service roles in which they chair social committees and deal with the organization's "housekeeping." More recently, they have become aware of the peripheral nature of their membership and have begun campaigning for equality; women's caucuses and groups have been formed in occupational associations as diverse as the American Bar Association, the Association of Cell Biologists, and the American Management As-

---

[22] See Cynthia Fuchs Epstein, "Encountering the Male Establishment," *American Journal of Sociology,* Vol. 75 (May 1970), pp. 965–982.
[23] *Ibid.*

sociation. These groups have worked both to increase the representation of women in the professional associations and in graduate and professional schools and to help women obtain equal access to financial aid.

Women's growing awareness of discrimination has led them to fight for a broad review of sexist attitudes in professional activities. For example, women in medicine have urged more respect for women as patients and a more serious study of diseases associated with their sex. They have accused male physicians of patronizing behavior toward female patients, and the medical profession of considering gynecological problems less important than other illnesses. Women in sociology have exposed sexism in the media and in textbooks, protesting biased and inaccurate statements about women. A study of medical school texts[24] showed them to contain grossly incorrect and stereotyped characterizations of the personality and emotional makeup of women. And women lawyers have found that in addition to the profession's often negative attitude toward women, in a number of states women defendants received a different kind of "justice" from men. Until women lawyers called attention to the matter, for example, it was more common to give indeterminate sentences to women than men. One dramatic instance of change brought about by lawyers in the women's movement concerns rape. It was common for women who had been raped to be blamed for complicity in the crime. Police and judges underestimated the psychological and physical damage suffered by the victims. There has been a complete reappraisal of both the causes and consequences of rape, as a result of the work of feminists throughout the legal system, from the new women police officers who bring greater sensitivity in dealing with victims, to women lawyers and political leaders who have effectively worked to change legislation that makes prosecution of rapists easier. By creating a climate that removes some of the shame women experienced before, they have also made it possible for more women to report attacks.[25]

Thus, women's participation in the professions and occupations previously closed to them has had an impact not only on the professions' membership, but on their practices and the content of their work as well.

SEX ROLES AND POLITICAL BEHAVIOR

Politics has been viewed traditionally in the United States as a male activity. Cigar-chewing, hard-drinking men making political deals in back rooms—such is the stereotype attached to politicians in the United States. For most citizens,

[24] Diana Scully and Pauline Bart, "A Funny Thing Happened on the Way to the Orifice: Women in Gynecology Textbooks," in Joan Huber (ed.), *Changing Women in a Changing Society* (Chicago: University of Chicago Press, 1973), pp. 283–288. Some of the examples cited from the texts: "The traits that compose the core of the female personality are feminine narciscism, masochism and passivity." "Sexual pleasure is entirely secondary [to the urge of motherhood] . . . sexual pleasure is entirely absent or secondary."

[25] One of the most forceful statements depicting rape as more than individual assault—as an extension of the general subjugation of women in society—has been written by Susan Brownmiller, in *Against Our Will: Men, Women and Rape* (New York: Simon & Schuster, 1975).

political talk is considered the province of men sitting around the cracker barrel at the country store, over brandy at dinner parties, and at meetings and business lunches. Women are thought to be uninterested in politics and eager to retreat to conversation about babies, clothes, and cooking while the men discuss who shall rule and how. Women's exclusion from business and law and their isolation from the political "old-boy" networks has in fact prevented them from playing effective political roles in the past. But as barriers have broken down in those arenas, women have begun to press for more political participation and have had some success.

Laws and informal practices have kept women from positions of political leadership and decision-making almost everywhere in the world. Yet women have been leaders in a few small societies[26] and new historical studies are uncovering evidence of forgotten political activity by women in many societies. It is worth remembering a few who stand out in history: Aspasia and Hecuba in ancient Greece, Madame de Staël and George Sand in France, the Duchess of Sagan in Austria, Jennie Churchill in England. All were women actively interested in politics in their societies, although none could hold political office nor were expected to. Their political role was exercised through others, in the manner that women have had to use through the ages. Only a few women monarchs, such as Catherine the Great, Eleanor of Aquitaine, Queen Elizabeth, and Queen Victoria, who held office by ascribed designation in the absence of male heirs, have held power in their own right and exercised it.

Most women, however, have been bound by the restraints on their political interest and participation and by the cultural definitions of political activity as inappropriate for women. Men, brought up to feel that it is demeaning to be subordinate to a woman, rarely feel comfortable with women in positions of leadership, and political leaders have sealed their exclusion by naming only tiny numbers of women to appointive office. Further, women's roles as wives and mothers conflict with political roles in the same ways they do with work roles. Meeting the demands of childcare (when fathers do not share these with mothers) often makes political activity impossible and may even depress interest in it. Local politics and elections are primarily evening activities, and the woman who defers to her family's claims rather than carefully planning her efforts will not be free to leave her responsibilities to campaign or to attend meetings. A study by Lynn and Flora of the 1968 U.S. election showed that mothers feel less politically effective than nonmothers.[27]

Women who do manage to marshal their energies and have support from their families often face hostile and condescending attitudes because they have

[26] Oral tradition and written documents suggest that for centuries women in the Mende ethnic area of Sierra Leone (West Africa) have enjoyed high office as lineage heads, heads of secret societies, and chiefs. Even in 1970, 9 percent of the Mende chiefdoms were ruled by women (Carol P. Hoffer, "Mende and Sherbro Women in High Office," *Canadian Journal of African Studies,* Vol. 6 [1972], pp. 151–164; "Madam Yoko: Ruler of the Kpa Mende Confederacy," in Michelle Zimbalist Rosaldo and Louise Lamphere, *Women, Culture and Society* [Stanford: Stanford University Press, 1974], pp. 173–188).

[27] Naomi B. Lynn and Cornelia Butler Flora, "Motherhood and Political Participation: A Changing Sense of Self," *Journal of Military and Political Sociology,* Vol. 1 (March 1973).

withdrawn from family activities (as men do) during a campaign. When a Milwaukee woman, Cynthia Kukor, ran for election as alderman, she was opposed by a group who called themselves "Concerned Mothers for the Kukor Children." Although male candidates usually try to show that they have strong family ties and the support of their wives and children, they seldom face questioning as to the quality or extent of the care they give their children or the affection they give their wives.[28] When women in the public eye campaign as vigorously as men, they are apt to be considered neglectful wives and mothers; if they claim to be attentive mothers, their ability to devote energy to public office is questioned.

Women as Voters and Political Participants

Few differences in the voting behavior of Americans can be attributed to sex. A somewhat smaller proportion of women than men have voted in national elections, but that gap narrowed in 1972.[29] Voting is also related to work activity and level of education, both of which are rising for women. Party affiliation does not vary by sex. Studies of female political activists—women in pressure groups, party workers, legislators, and bureaucrats—show marked differences in levels of participation from male activists, although there is evidence of a steady increase over the past two decades.[30] In 1974 women accounted for less than 5 percent of U.S. legislators and top-level bureaucrats.

There is some irony in the consistent finding that women do not vote very differently from men. It was believed that when women gained suffrage they would use their votes differently from men—against militarist and prowar candidates and for those promising to aid the underdog. But the views of women voters are similar to those of men voters on political issues,[31] and since 1956 women have not varied much more than 5 percent from men in their preference for presidential candidates.[32] These findings suggest that women do not constitute a group with a sense of political self-interest, that they share with men the beliefs and attitudes of their social backgrounds and groups. This is not true, however, for women active in politics, as we shall see below.

Popular attitudes toward women's family status and obligations are only part of the problem women face on entering the political realm. Backing a woman for election to even a moderately important office is usually considered a poor investment. Party leaders collect funds and acquire power by supporting

---

[28] The memoirs of prominent national political figures show that, whatever their public stance as family men, as a rule they have rarely permitted their families to interfere with their work or careers. See Myra MacPherson, *The Power Lovers: An Intimate Look at Politicians and Their Marriages* (New York: G. P. Putnam's Sons, 1975), for accounts of the personal lives of Washington's political wives today.

[29] Marjorie Lansing, "The American Woman: Voter and Activist," in Jane S. Jacquette (ed.), *Women in Politics* (New York: Wiley, 1974), p. 22.

[30] *Ibid.*

[31] Jeanne J. Kirkpatrick, *Political Woman* (New York: Basic Books, 1974), p. 139.

[32] Lansing, *op. cit.*, p. 15, Table 1.10.

winning candidates and then brokering their obligations of patronage. Since women have not been viewed as winners, few political bosses have been willing to back them.

Financing political campaigns is unusually difficult for women. Women do not ordinarily have free use of substantial wealth, even if they are from prosperous families; they rarely have the contacts to tap financial resources that men have. Since they do not make the kinds of contributions men make, women do not get political patronage in return. This will probably change; as women make money that is defined as "theirs," they will feel free to contribute to causes that will advance their interests and careers.

The NWPC and Indicators of Change

In 1971 women activists formed a new group, the National Women's Political Caucus, to seek the development of the political potential of women and political action on the issues raised by the movement. NWPC, active in nearly every part of the United States,[33] has raised campaign funds and brought about the seating of more women delegates at political conventions. It has increased its strength to the point that women candidates have sought caucus endorsement, subscribing to its positions on issues of women's equality even when they were not committed to these issues in the past.

While not a strong and pervasive organ when compared with the major party organizations, NWPC has been important as a symbol of women's growing political consciousness and frustration. Together with groups such as the National Organization for Women, the Women's Campaign Fund, and the Women's Lobby, NWPC represents a new form of political activity. Not since the first years after suffrage have women's political associations been organized to work for legislative and executive action on specific issues. The League of Women Voters is a nonpartisan organization dedicated to principles of good government and voter information, but it is not a lobby and has never organized women politically. Faced with a loss of membership to the new activism, some of the more established women's groups are adopting a more active political stance.

One of the key changes in the political life of women is what appears to be their growing success as political leaders. Over the past half-century, so few women held office in the House of Representatives, the Senate, or the State Houses that the election or defeat of one or two women might double their number or eliminate them entirely.

Most women who attained high posts either were appointed (as was Frances Perkins, Secretary of Labor under President Franklin Roosevelt) or succeeded their husbands or fathers to office. In 1974, though their numbers remained small, women were elected to several important posts in their own

[33] NWPC's first convention, held in Houston, Texas, February 9–11, 1973, was attended by delegates from 48 of the 50 states.

right. Ella Grasso was elected governor of Connecticut, the first woman to "make it on her own" to a governorship. Mary Ann Krupsak of New York won the office of lieutenant governor, the first woman to fill that post in any state. To complete the picture, however, no woman was elected to the Senate (which currently has no women) in 1974, and there were fewer women in both houses of Congress (18) than in 1962, the record year, when there were 20. Women constituted 8 percent of state legislators in January 1975 (610 out of 7,561).[34]

A recent study by Jeanne Kirkpatrick, the first of its kind, shows that women who held state political office in the past typically came from backgrounds in volunteer service and had been active in church and school affairs. They were older on the average than male legislators, usually first running for office after the age of 40, while 90 percent of a matching group of male legislators had made their first political attempts before that age. Kirkpatrick sees a change in that more women are running for public office at a younger age, and those seeking higher office are almost all lawyers. It is likely that if women continue to attend law schools in the proportions they have in recent years, they will increasingly seek political office and will come to it equipped with experience in debate and negotiation.

Many Americans believe that women are "cleaner" than men in politics, and to some extent this has been true. Women played no important roles in the recent political scandals. However, their "cleanness" may come from the fact that they have not been part of the party machines or of established political networks. In countries where women have held high executive office they have engaged in the same machinations, legal or extra-legal, as men have. This has been true of Indira Gandhi in India, Golda Meir in Israel, Sirimavo Bandaranaike in Sri Lanka, and Isabel Peron in Argentina.

It is difficult to envisage that sex status will ever become irrelevant to politics. Since politics is the arena of the highest stakes of power in a society, it is guarded closely, and the interlocking networks of economic position, political patronage, informal associations, and entrenched party machinery all act as barriers to outsiders. For women to become insiders they will have to progress in political careers by all the routes men take, or band together with other women to form powerful pressure groups.

SEX ROLES AND EDUCATION

Education has long been one of the most important channels of mobility in the United States, especially for immigrants and other disadvantaged groups. Yet the educational system at every level has always been stratified and not equally accessible to all in the society. Women were barred from higher education until the middle of the nineteenth century. Cultural attitudes that regarded women as having less need for education (it was assumed they would rarely have

[34] Citizens Advisory Council on the Status of Women, *op. cit.*, p. 22

careers) continued to discourage them from education in many areas, particularly at upper levels. Indeed, until the 1960s many women who began college dropped out to get married.

The changes in women's attitudes toward careers and their growing awareness of the need for educational credentials have, in the past few years, stimulated more young women to complete college and go on to graduate school. Furthermore, over a million women who had never gone to college or had abandoned their studies were enrolled in college in 1972. Nearly half (475,000) of them were over 35 years of age. For the young mother with small children, and for the older woman, return to school brought problems working women have had to contend with: the need for childcare assistance, for cooperation and encouragement from husbands and others, and for flexible school schedules to permit mature students to meet the demands of their other roles.

Women and Admissions Policies

Women's increased interest and presence in higher education has also been related to an easing of admissions policies. Women were excluded from many institutions of higher learning, including the professional schools, far into the 1960s.[35] Harvard University, one of the last to surrender, excluded women from its law school until 1950. Professional schools that admitted women prior to the 1970s usually imposed informal quotas on their admission, keeping women students at about 5 percent of the total. Furthermore, the higher the status of the institutions—and the more elite the law firms and hospitals their graduates entered—the more they tended to discriminate against women.

Typically the reasons offered for the exclusion of women were not very different from those of a century ago; they ranged from women's presumed delicate constitutions and lack of commitment as professionals, down to the absence of restroom facilities for them.[36]

Unlike minority-group applicants, women seeking professional education have possessed status-sets almost identical to those of the men who excluded them; they came from the same kinds of families and received similar college educations, although sometimes in separate-sex institutions. Thus even privileged women with credentials have been effectively prevented from progressing in a status-squence (college to specialized professional training to career) appropriate to their training, capacities, and interests.

In the field of education as in other fields, the discriminatory mechanisms used against women have been the same as those used against blacks and other minority-group members. The civil rights movement was crucial in striking

[35] This subject was treated more extensively in the section on professions and occupations.

[36] The restroom argument has often been seriously used against women's admission to male-dominated occupations and associations. In New York City, two bar associations avoided the equality issue by maintaining that they had no restroom facilities for women. The Princeton University graduate schools also used this excuse, as did Cambridge and Oxford universities in England. (See Cynthia Fuchs Epstein, *Woman's Place* [Berkeley: University of California Press, 1970], p. 185.)

down barriers based on race or ethnic affiliation, and in the late 1960s and 1970s the women's movement won action to prevent exclusionary quotas on the basis of sex. Institutions were also forced to adopt affirmative action programs redressing past sex discrimination by seeking recruits among minority groups and women.

As a consequence, women are moving into professional and graduate schools in greater numbers. At the same time there was a movement to desegregate the separate-sex colleges on the grounds that separate education is unequal education. Long years of tradition were altered when elite schools such as Princeton and Yale universities and Vassar College became coeducational.

New regulations have been proposed by the Department of Health, Education, and Welfare to end all forms of sex discrimination remaining in education and to broaden the participation of women in education at all levels. There is opposition to these changes from a variety of sources. Some school administrators have protested that the new regulations will be difficult to enforce and destructive in impact. For example, supporters of competitive-sports programs fear that the requirement that schools provide comparable athletic training for girls will make it impossible to have the top-quality teams that many communities demand. Yet advocates of equal athletic preparation for girls maintain that women are disadvantaged by the inferior physical education they receive and by not having the same opportunities for attaining "star" status and engaging in team work, both useful to career development in adulthood.

Sexism in Textbooks

The ways in which males and females are portrayed in books and in the media have important consequences for the ways both sexes learn to think of themselves and to develop self-images and life perspectives. Schoolbooks have tended to present children and adults playing the stereotyped roles idealized by the culture. Stereotypes not only give a narrow picture of the way people of certain categories act and behave; they are often entirely incorrect. They show girls acting demure and docile, not arguing and getting dirty at work and play; mothers smiling and baking cookies, not working as typists or in factories or as teachers. Books also stereotype males: fathers go off to work with briefcase or lunch box, to arrive home smiling and in good cheer (not tired or abusive to children); boys run and plan adventures (but do not hide behind mothers' skirts in fear of animals or the dark, or play with dolls and draw in coloring books).

In the early 1970s a number of studies documented the stereotyped images of men and women in children's picture books, primers, and textbooks,[37] and teachers and parents, in many cases led by members of feminist groups, de-

---

[37] Marjorie B. U'ren, "The Image of Women in Textbooks," in Vivian Gornick and Barbara K. Moran (eds.), *Women in Sexist Society* (New York: Basic Books, 1971); Aileen Pace Nilsen, "Women in Children's Literature," *College English,* Vol. 32 (May 1971), pp. 918–926.

manded that the stereotypes be eradicated. As a result, a number of state departments of education, as well as the American Association of School Administrators, took action to amend textbooks; many text publishers have warned their authors against depicting women and girls in demeaning ways, or ignoring the many roles that women have. A number of feminist presses that developed in the 1970s also have begun to publish books showing boys cooking and playing with dolls; girls being mischief-makers and biking on paper routes; and mothers at their jobs and fathers taking care of children.

Sexism in the Classroom

Because most elementary school teachers are female and most high school and college teachers are male, it has been suggested that, at each level, opposite-sex students may suffer disadvantages in their educational experience. Patricia Sexton suggested in *The Feminized Male* (1969) that working-class boys are discriminated against by women teachers who tend to reward boys according to a feminine model—favoring those who are compliant and effeminate. Joseph Pleck,[38] however, suggests that the traditional "masculine" attributes are probably inappropriate to the tempered and moderate behavior most men will be expected to exhibit as adults.

The lack of role models has been pointed to as a problem in college and beyond for girls who do well in grade and high school. It has been suggested that with few or no women professors as part of her experience, the young woman may well wonder whether there is a place for her in academic life or the professions. In hearings on sex discrimination at various universities in the 1970s, women have reported in detail on their offhand treatment by male professors who believed they were not worth an investment of time and effort because they would probably abandon their work to have a family or were only in school "to catch a husband." Although many of these practices have changed, women still report subtle resistance to their full participation in academic training.

Older Women in School

The return to school of women who left for family reasons earlier in their life is a phenomenon of our time and brings an entirely new range of problems into the classroom. These women fall into two categories: those who return to school in their 40s and 50s, after their children have grown up, and women in their 30s. The latter group is made up largely of those who resume their education as soon as their children are in school or who choose to go to a professional school because the jobs open to them with liberal arts degrees have proven to be dead ends.

[38] Joseph H. Pleck, "The Male Sex Role: Definitions, Problems, and Sources of Change," *Journal of Social Issues,* forthcoming.

Women who return to the classroom create demands for flexible time schedules, new and less rigid educational programs, and part-time fellowships. In fact, it is becoming necessary for both men and women to have access to a more variable educational structure than now exists, predicated as it is on the model of the unmarried, male student. Older women returning to school are also becoming an organized force and have been instrumental in initiating women's groups on campus. Some of their current activity includes pressuring for guidelines under the new Title IX of the Education Act Amendments of 1972 to bar discrimination against women who, because of family responsibilities, attend school part-time and/or at a later age.

Many women who complete school late or outside the usual track find they are a peripheral group in the labor force. Their newly acquired college degrees may be worth very little to women entering the traditional women's fields, such as social work and education, where they face severe competition for jobs. It is also true that older women are less attractive to employers, who tend to view them as uninitiated in the norms of business life, possibly resistant to authority, and not worth an investment in training. They suffer compounded discrimination because of their sex and age statuses.

It is evident that changes in educational opportunities and the new activity of older women will have consequences for the society. Women who choose nontraditional programs and older women returning to school are likely to be highly motivated and look forward to employment after their schooling. They constitute both a new resource and a new problem for business and the professions. No doubt their talents can add much in a vigorous economy. In a faltering one, they can easily form a new rank of the unemployed.

SEX ROLES AND MINORITY ROLES

Women who are members of racial and ethnic minority groups are placed in an unusually disadvantageous position in American society. Persons who possess two or more negatively valued statuses—for example, women who are black and/or old—may find they suffer cumulative disabilities.[39] (The possession of two or more negatively valued statuses may have a positive effect, but only in a few special cases.[40]) Disadvantages are further compounded when educational and other opportunities have been denied because of one or more of the unfavored statuses; for example, entry to management training is not possible without access to prerequisite levels of schooling. Disadvantage accumulates for black families because they are apt to suffer from poor education, low in-

---

[39] The idea of "accumulation of advantage" and of disadvantage has been developed in the work of Robert K. Merton and his colleagues in a series of investigations. References to these may be found in Merton, "Structural Analysis in Sociology," in Peter M. Blau (ed.), *Approaches to the Study of Social Structure* (New York: Macmillan, 1975), p. 35.

[40] Cynthia Fuchs Epstein, "Positive Effects of the Multiple Negative: Explaining the Success of Black Professional Women," *American Journal of Sociology*, Vol. 78 (January 1973), pp. 912–935.

come, and lack of work skills. But when one compares higher-income black families with white families, many of the problems associated with blacks on the basis of race tend to disappear or match those of white families.

The black woman possesses a combination of statuses that creates a unique set of difficulties. Both statuses are ascribed (they are acquired at birth) and immutable (they cannot be changed). Persons who possess these two statuses suffer severe limits on their ability to change their life situation and affect the attitudes of others toward them.

It has been extraordinarily difficult for black women to break out of the mold that American society has created for them. Contrary to current misconceptions about the existence of a black matriarchy, black women are seldom powerful or even dominant in their families, except when no adult males are present.[41]

Work and Social Condition of Black Women

Black women are slightly more apt to work than white women of the same age and education.[42] In 1973, 49 percent of all black women were workers,[43] compared with 44 percent of white women. Black women workers are more likely than white women to be wives and mothers. They generally have less education, suffer more from unemployment, and fill the least-skilled, lowest-paying occupations.[44]

It may be this set of harsh circumstances that makes black women—contrary to popular belief—vigorous in their approval of attempts to improve the status of women. In 1972, 62 percent of the black women polled in a national sample (contrasted with 45 percent of the white women polled) favored efforts to strengthen or change women's status in society. Sixty-seven percent of the black women were sympathetic to women's liberation groups, as opposed to 35 percent of the white women.[45]

Black women are less ambivalent than white women about working, partly because their expectation that they will have to work is less ambiguous and contingent. More black women are heads of families than white women. One out of five minority women is a family head, and almost three out of ten black families are headed by a woman. Even those black women who are married with husbands present in the home (nearly half of minority women workers are in this category) will more likely become workers than white women, because of their need to supplement the family income. Sixty-one percent of mi-

---

[41] See Richard B. Hill, *Strengths of Black Families* (New York: Emerson Hall, 1971).

[42] U.S. Bureau of the Census, *Current Population Reports,* P-60, No. 75, Table 50 (Washington, D.C.: Government Printing Office, 1970), p. 113.

[43] The figures for racial minorities include 3 or 4 percent Asians; they have usually been included in data for "minorities" or "blacks."

[44] Unless otherwise indicated, figures are from publications of the U.S. Department of Labor Women's Bureau.

[45] "The 1972 Virginia Slims American Women's Opinion Poll," conducted by Louis Harris and Associates, Inc., pp. 2, 4.

nority women with children 6 to 17 years of age, and 47 percent of those with children under 6, were labor-force members in 1971. Among white mothers the comparable figures were 51 percent and 29 percent, respectively.

Black women and their families are one of the most deprived groups of workers in American society. Although any child, black or white, is subject to the negative influences of the street in impoverished city areas, especially if unsupervised, delinquency is a greater problem in black families. There were about 4.4 million children of black women workers in 1974 under the age of 18. But institutional childcare facilities are insufficient and in many areas do not exist at all; small children are typically cared for by older siblings wise in street experience. The lack of adult supervision also means that children get less of the attention important to psychological well-being, formation of positive life goals, and good school habits. A capable working mother can be a positive role model for her daughters and sons, but the compounded problems of poverty make for a high incidence of family problems for black mothers who work. The earnings of minority women, like those of white women, are substantially less than the earnings of men, either minority or white. In 1972 women of minority races who worked year-round at full-time jobs had a median income of $5,320, which was 87 percent of white women's median income. This was a substantial rise from 1960, when black women earned only 70 percent of the salary of white women. However, black women made only about half as much as white men, whose median income was $10,786.

Changes in the Lives of Black Women

The identification of race and sex as a social problem to be remedied by equal rights legislation has brought about the opening of some educational and job opportunities to black women and has resulted in some improvement in their situation. Between 1960 and 1971 the proportion of black working women in private household jobs (one of the lowest-paid, least-protected occupations in America) decreased from 35 to 17 percent. Black women were moving into white-collar jobs; during the same years the proportion of minority-women workers employed in professional and technical jobs rose from 9 to 22 percent. They are rapidly becoming highly visible in such professions as nursing and social work, especially in cities where minorities form a major segment of the population.

Relative to their male colleagues, black career women have done better than their white sisters. They form a larger part of the black professional community than women in the white professional world; proportionately more women are found among black doctors (12.5%) and lawyers (11%) than among white professionals, and they are nearer to male professionals in their earnings, yet their absolute numbers are small, totaling only a little over a thousand for the two professions in the 1970 Census. Nonetheless, the relative success of black career women compared to that of white career women suggests that an investment in specialized higher education for black women produces positive results.

Against the backdrop of poverty and other deprivation in the lives of most black women, a few have made spectacular personal advances. The first black woman elected to Congress took her seat only in 1969, and a number of others have followed. Of the 18 women in the Ninety-fourth Congress (1975–76), four were black. Furthermore, the black women in Congress have been vocal and in the public eye. Affirmative action programs that encourage institutions to hire women and minority people and a new consciousness regarding the responsibility of recognizing the talents of minorities have resulted in the promotion of black women into positions never before believed possible. Of the three women who are partners in top Wall Street firms, one is a black woman; a former black woman ambassador became the first woman trustee of IBM; and several black women now appear regularly as newscasters on major television stations. Their numbers are tiny but significant, indicating that the absolute barriers to black women that existed prior to the 1970s have been breached.

More and more black women can be expected to move into industry, and, following the trend of white women workers, they probably will become increasingly active in the labor movement. Already active in organizations to promote civil rights, community control of schools, and expanded welfare benefits, black women are expressing their demands and needs in stronger and more organized ways than have white women at similar economic levels. They may well take on positions of leadership in organizations that draw mainly white women at this time.

SEX ROLES IN THE FAMILY

Family roles are created and assigned to meet the needs of the members of the family and of the larger society. The basic roles are those of parenting,[46] working to provide food and shelter, legitimate sexual gratification, and conferring of social class status on children and other family members. Family roles also include the development and maintenance of family honor and prestige. Which family members should be assigned to carry out the tasks necessary to fulfill these functions, and when and how they should carry them out, is dictated by tradition, law, and the circumstances of the individual family (such as its class position) and the larger society. Biology sets broad limits on certain of these social assignments.

The family roles that individuals play have major implications for the ways they participate in other social institutions, and it follows that few major social changes occur without affecting family structure. Families can free their members to engage in outside activities or can prevent them from doing so. Most family systems have limited women members' activity in the outside society while requiring male members to participate in external activities for the benefit of the family.

---

[46] The term "parenting" is used to define certain activities that are not necessarily specific to either mother or father—such as childcare, education, and socialization.

The way in which families and societies use sex as the basis for determining their members' roles is today still another focus of concern for advocates of equality. Traditionalists believe that using sex as the basis for division of labor in the family provides stability and continuity. Their opponents feel that stability is achieved at the cost of repressing the needs and interests of men and women. They assert that many people find it difficult to integrate traditional roles with changes in the economic and political roles they play outside the family, and insist on freedom to reject the family roles they are assigned because of their sex.

The attitudes attached to assignment of family roles are among the most resistant to change in a society, even when actual changes have taken place in people's behavior. There are strong beliefs, for example, that it is "natural" for mothers to take care of babies and for fathers to work.

Family roles are embedded in the stratification system of each society. All families are affected by their society's rules determining ownership of property, division of labor, lines of inheritance, exercise of power, and control of children. These have consequences for personal relationships within the family as well. The two systems interact.

For example, the division of labor that defines the man as breadwinner of the family is reinforced by laws that oblige men to support their families. Wives usually are not legally responsible for meeting the financial needs of the family, and husbands are not obliged to look after the children when there is a mother in the home. In some states there are also laws governing the couple's obligations to engage in conjugal (sexual) relations.

There is considerable variation in actual family practices; the law usually comes into play only where there is an extreme and visible violation, such as total nonsupport or child abuse. This is because most societies depend on the customs that make it seem natural for men and women to carry out their traditional tasks as husbands and wives, fathers and mothers. In fact, only after major breakdowns in the ability of large numbers of families to perform the functions society expects of them does a society respond with institutional solutions. It is a relatively new concept, however, to consider it appropriate—and necessary—for society to assume some of the burdens of deprived families. Defining the nutritional deficiencies of poor families as a social problem, for example, led in recent years to the food stamp program; likewise, the poverty of many single-parent families, in which the mother could not both work and take care of the children, led to the federal Aid for Dependent Children program.

The women's movement has focused attention on difficulties between husbands and wives as a social problem requiring social solution. The new awareness of women has led them to question the inequality implicit in family relations and the law, in which husbands are defined as the "head of family" and their preference determines the family's legal residence, and in which physical assault on wives by husbands has been viewed by law enforcement agencies as a "domestic squabble" without legal redress. The demands of women for equality in family relations has brought many changes both in law and in attitudes concerning permissible family behavior. On another level, the sharing of domestic responsibilities formerly considered the role of women alone has become a norm among a growing proportion of young families in which women work and refuse to bear the exclusive burden of household responsibilities.

Family Roles and Social Class

Although role assignments are generally made in the family on the basis of sex and age, the family's ranking in the social structure will largely determine how these roles are carried out. Historically, for example, women in wealthy families have often assigned child rearing to other women and then themselves assumed other roles. Veblen pointed out the symbolic function of wealthy women whose major task was to communicate how wealthy their husbands were, in part by *not* working.[47] Women of the upper classes often enhance family prestige

[47] Thorstein Veblen, *The Theory of the Leisure Class* (New York: Modern Library, 1934).

through cultural activities, either by actually engaging in the activities or by raising money for them.[48] In American society, upper-middle-class women in particular take part in voluntary organizations that serve social needs. It is estimated that about $14.2 billion's worth of activity in hospitals, cultural works, and community aid of various kinds is performed by women without pay each year. An upper-class husband also engages in such voluntary activities, but he is more apt to "contribute" his wife's time. Today women are beginning to object to doing work that is no longer considered of social value except in a very general sense. They sometimes express resentment that their status is only the reflected status of their husbands and that their contribution is not acknowledged as genuine work because they are not paid for it.

Lower-class women often take on economic activity as an adjunct to their family roles. Because it is known that they "must" work for economic reasons, they can delegate childcare to others without guilt and with the social approval of friends and relatives. Working-class women can use childcare centers when they are available, but most of their children are cared for in their own homes by family members, often by husbands working another shift. Of the children taken care of outside the home, 55 percent are cared for by women in the neighborhood, often on an informal fee basis.

But a widespread ideal among working-class families is to achieve a middle-class way of life, in which the family becomes financially solvent through the husband's earning capacity alone and the wife stays home to care for the children while they are small. The women's movement may have effected some change in these attitudes. Many working-class women claim to enjoy the social contacts they have at work, but the woman's *not* working is still a frequent indicator of the success achieved by working-class families. This set of attitudes provides a constraint on the collective ability of these women to achieve economic equality with men.

Relationship of Husbands and Wives

Elizabeth Bott has shown that sex-role relationships between husbands and wives differ in the middle and working classes.[49] Middle-class couples typically share leisure-time activities with a common set of friends, and are more apt to share household work than are working-class couples. In the middle class, sex-role assignments more often overlap or are blurred, with husband and wife doing tasks together or substituting for one another. In contrast, working-class husbands and wives tend to have same-sex friends or spend time with same-sex relatives. They rarely accept tasks associated with the opposite sex and generally consider it inappropriate for a man to do woman's work or for a woman to do man's work. In her study of blue-collar families, Komarovsky

---

[48] Gaye Tuchman, "Women and the Creation of Culture," in Marcia Millman and Rosabeth Moss Kanter (eds.), *Another Voice: Feminist Perspectives on Social Life and Social Science* (New York: Anchor Books, 1975), pp. 171–202.

[49] Elizabeth Bott, *Family and Social Network* (London: Tavistock Publications, 1957).

notes that husbands and wives who are high school graduates are more likely than non-high school graduates to share the traditional division of family tasks between them; the husbands help more frequently with childcare and shopping than do husbands with less education.[50] She also found that the better-educated among her working-class sample had fewer problems communicating with each other. Blue-collar couples with little education usually had severe problems in talking with each other, making it difficult to resolve their personal problems, including sexual ones. Contrary to stereotypes, working-class husbands and wives do not feel sexually "free"; they are invariably more repressed and more bound than middle-class couples by the sexual folkways of their communities.

Interaction Effect: Family and Society

The family roles performed by men and women usually coordinate with the roles they play outside the family. Although some family systems are more egalitarian than others, the relative power of the sexes within the family reflects the rank order of the sexes in activities outside the family, such as work and politics. To some extent, the subordination of women in the family is a result of the economic dependence they are subject to when they do not work, but it is usually present even when they do work. Women's jobs inside the home are seen as service jobs, as is their work outside the home. Yet when women are active in market activity and make independent incomes, they are often afforded more equality at home. In the United States, for example, when women contribute to the family income they tend to play a larger part in decision-making than do women who are solely housewives.[51]

Anthropological evidence shows that when women contribute substantially to food production or to the economic wealth of a society, they have considerably more power within the home. When such economies change so that occupational activity becomes sex-labeled as male, the change usually results in a loss of rank for women, in both the society and the family. On this basis, it has been argued that industrialization may have had an adverse effect on women in many African and Asian societies, as women's contributions to the market economy are supplanted by a technology largely confined to male participation.[52]

At an earlier time in Western European society, the separation of work from the home as a result of the industrial revolution led to a lowered evaluation of work in the home as nonproductive and not measurable in monetary terms. Women whose work is only in the home have no basis for acquiring prestige, power, or wealth independently. These and other tangible and intangible benefits are available only to those who "work for gain."

The women's movement has focused attention on the consequences of the

[50] Mirra Komarovsky, *Blue Collar Marriage* (New York: Random House, 1964).

[51] David M. Heer, "The Measurement and Bases of Family Power: An Overview," *Marriage and Family Living*, Vol. 25 (May 1963), pp. 133–139; R. Blood and D. Wolfe, *Husbands and Wives* (New York: The Free Press, 1960).

[52] Boserup, *op. cit.*

prevalent belief that work done in the home by women or men is nonproductive. Efforts have been made to induce governments to correct the problems that derive from this view; economists have been urged to identify the economic value of housework and also ways to extend benefits to unpaid workers in the home.[53] The economist Robert Lekachman notes that national-income accounting, from its inception in the United States in the 1920s, excluded unpaid household labor from the measure of society's product.[54] The accounts are held to promote error by misrepresenting households as noneconomic units, presumably regulated entirely by altruism and affection. But conceived as an economic unit, the household is a small business enterprise in which husbands and, frequently, wives invest cash (their earnings) and labor (mostly female) in order to generate a measurable output of meals, clothes, transportation, and other services. To conceptualize the family as an economic unit in the way Lekachman suggests would perhaps require social and legal guarantees not yet available anywhere in the world, neither in socialist nor capitalist countries, developing or developed countries.[55]

In many traditional societies it has been possible to be considered both a good family member and a good worker. But in modern industrial societies where work is frequently done at some distance from the home, men and women often live with role strain and a sense of failure that comes from conflict between duties and obligations attached to their different roles. Women consider themselves as failing to be good mothers when they become committed to work outside the family; men feel they may fail as good husbands and fathers when their work commitments are so demanding that they are rarely able to spend time with their wives or children. The problem with these obligations is that they are all considered to be legitimate. Yet men and women are supposed to be helped by society's assignment of priorities on the basis of sex status.[56] Men are supposed to give first preference to their worker role; women, to their family roles.

These cultural priorities do not take into account fluctuations in the economy and the need for both female and male family members to work; nor do they take into account individual preferences. The rationalization of the econ-

---

[53] Estelle James, "Income and Employment Effects of Women's Liberation," in Cynthia B. Lloyd (ed.), *Sex Discrimination and the Division of Labor* (New York: Columbia University Press, 1975), pp. 379–400; Shirley B. Johnson, "The Impact of Women's Liberation on Marriage, Divorce, and Family Life-Style," in *ibid.*, pp. 401–426; Barbara R. Bergmann, "The Economics of Women's Liberation," in Ruth B. Kundsin *Annals of the New York Academy of Sciences*, Vol. 208 (March 15, 1973), pp. 154–160.

[54] Just as we have seen that laws reflect prevailing ideas about sex roles in the family, so we now see that even computing the "GNP" can reflect assumptions—that work done in the home does not contribute to the U.S. Gross National Product. A group of economic researchers in the Social Security Administration has estimated the value of the housework performed by the average American housewife by calculating the market cost of each of the tasks carried out. The estimate ranges from $5,389 per year for housewives aged 15 to 29, to a peak of $6,417 for those aged 25 to 29, to $2,942 for those aged 60 to 64. (*The New York Times*, January 13, 1976).

[55] Robert Lekachman, "On Economic Equality," *Signs: Journal of Women in Culture and Society*, Vol. 1 (Autumn 1975), p. 95.

[56] Cf. Robert K. Merton, *Social Theory and Social Structure*, on articulation of roles.

omy, the rise of bureaucracy with its emphasis on universal rules, the institutionalization of complex organizations—all have created an inflexibility of structure and a dominance of economic roles over family roles for men. For women who work outside the home, however, there are next to no institutionalized mechanisms to alleviate the pressures they experience from role conflict. They are expected to make the family their first priority, but once in the labor market, bureaucracy is inflexible to their family obligations. One adaptation of society to these pressures has been to segregate many women in a part-time, nonessential labor pool, available when needed but not in continuing competition with the family's needs.

Problems of time and task coordination always result in role strain; for women they are not as severe when their jobs are done in the vicinity of the home. This is true both for simple and complex societies. For example, tribal women who are gardeners and gatherers can be with their children as they work, and supervise their activities. In some industrial societies and in certain periods in most societies, women and men have done piecework in the home (this is still typical in Japan), while childcare and other aspects of family life went on around them.

Although we usually think of the separation of work from the home as creating problems for women, it has consequences for all family members. When men moved from work near the home to work far removed from it, they ceased to have contact with their wives during the day, and in many cases their roles as fathers changed. The time they spent with children was greatly reduced, and they often became remote figures. This meant that women had to spend more time with children, precisely at a time when they had fewer family members on whom to depend for help.

The transition to modern society with its structures of role priorities and its inflexibility has everywhere created problems for individual family members, as well as for the larger society. In the Soviet Union, for example, in the years immediately after the revolution, when the law made marriages easily dissoluble, families became unstable and mothers were recruited into the labor force. Deprived of care by the traditional Russian extended family, massive numbers of children went unsupervised and often formed marauding gangs.[57] Shortly thereafter, the Soviet government not only tightened its divorce policy but also began to provide institutional care for young people. This situation is not unlike that faced by mother-headed families in the United States in low-income areas with inadequate childcare and youth programs.

Divorce

Women's growing activity in the labor force is partly an expression of changes in family life, including the high percentage of marriages ending in divorce

---

[57] H. Kent Geiger, *The Family in Soviet Russia* (Cambridge: Harvard University Press, 1968).

and changed attitudes toward divorce. No doubt women's ability to become self-supporting has led many to consider ending unhappy marriages. This is a worldwide phenomenon, although the United States has one of the highest divorce rates in the world, as Goode shows in the chapter on family disorganization. The role of a divorced person is often anomic, without clearcut rules of behavior, because in all societies the expectation is that adults will be married, and most communities and institutions function on the premise that their adult members live in intact families. Major social problems have been created by the fact that today a large proportion of American families are disrupted and there are no institutional solutions for the problems they face.

Divorce has changed the family roles of millions of women who, while married, had worked only in the home. Casting off the old role—that of wife— often means taking on not one new role but two: divorcee and worker. In divorces where this does not occur, other redefinitions of roles are introduced: husbands often must support both the old and the new families. The high rate of divorce has led men and women to changing expectations of their marital roles and parental responsibilities.

Changed expectations about the durability of marriage have in subtle and important ways affected young men's and women's decisions about many aspects of their lives. Although 85 percent of the young women questioned in a 1974 Institute of Life Insurance survey said they believed people should marry, it is clear that many young women today expect permanence in their working careers but are unsure that they will have permanence in marriage. Fourteen percent of those polled rejected marriage for a variety of reasons, including the notion that it was an "outmoded" institution. These women rejected the roles that are traditional for women in marriage. These attitudes find expression among the men and women who today live together without being married. There seems to be more sharing of roles formerly assigned to one sex among such couples. Although most eventually do marry, their informal living arrangements are open to alternatives that early marriage and early childbearing would only curtail. This is their adaptation to the still-unsolved social problems created by role assignments.

Abortion

Today's liberalized abortion laws allow unmarried women who become pregnant an option other than marriage, and assure married women greater control over family size. An issue generating intense emotional reaction, abortion is of great concern to the women's movement because of the implications it has for women's right to the control of their bodies. Women's groups have fought for abortion strongly and effectively. They have gathered considerable support, from educated, middle-class white men as well as women.

Before laws were enacted that legalized abortion in many American states, the major burden of the prohibition was experienced by poor women. Middle-class women could travel to a country where abortion was legal, or find private physicians who were willing to perform the procedure. But those who could not afford these solutions were forced to bear unwanted children or to run the risks of abortion by unlicensed quacks. As Merton points out in Chapter 1, this answer to the problem violates the beliefs of many other people. The Roman Catholic Church has continued to campaign to prevent or rescind legislation permitting abortion,[58] although a 1972 Gallup poll found 64 percent of the general population and 56 percent of the Catholic population in favor of women's right to choose abortion.[59] The minority view is grounded in conservative religious philosophy and the traditional view that a woman's main function is to bear children and stay in the home. There is still a highly charged debate as to whether abortion is a private right or whether the fetus is a human being whose right to life must be protected by the state. The liberalization of abortion laws is one of the first issues that women have collectively fought for and largely won in this country; it remains an issue of great concern, both for its practical importance to women and as a symbol of their rights.

Fertility

The United States birthrate has declined to its lowest point in history—to 1.5 percent of the population in 1973 and 1974. This decline, from levels of about 2.5 percent during the 1950s and about 2 percent in the 1960s, is both cause and consequence of the altered life style of American families, and especially of women. Not only are women having fewer children, they are deferring slightly the age at which they are having first children.

Young people are now believed to express more approval for childless marriages, but it is clear that, as in the past, only a very few want to be childless themselves. A 1974 Life Insurance Institute survey found that only 4 percent of a national youth sample planned to be childless, 10 percent said they would prefer to have one child, and 46 percent said they would prefer to have two children. The Roper Organization's 1974 poll found that 49 percent of the women surveyed felt that the ideal family included two or fewer children. A Roper poll in 1952 had found that less than 25 percent of the women surveyed favored having two children and three out of four wanted larger families, a considerable change in attitudes.

Once again, the women's movement may have contributed to a significant alteration in women's behavior and attitudes. It has been forceful in combating the popular opinion—in this case bolstered by psychoanalytic theory—that women could be feminine and psychologically healthy only by having children and personally rearing them. The increase noted in women's age at birth of first child—the age at which they attain the status of "mother"—is more than slightly significant. For women as a group it means they can fulfill the obliga-

---

[58] Mary Daly, "Abortion and Sexual Caste," *Commonweal* (February 1972), pp. 415–419, reprinted in Robert Antonio and George Ritzer (eds.), *Social Problems* (Boston: Allyn & Bacon, 1975), pp. 179–184.

[59] Roberta Brandes Gratz, "Never Again," *Ms.* (April 1973), pp. 44–48.

tions of other status commitments for a longer period—specifically, they can obtain more job training and involve themselves more fully in their careers.

Institutions and the Change in Family Needs

Changing work roles of women and changing attitudes of men in American society are creating pressures on other institutions to become more sensitive to the needs of the family. For example, if women are to have jobs that offer good salaries and work satisfaction, businesses will find it more difficult to transfer husbands from one company location to another. A requirement for executive advancement in many firms, repeated transfers were not generally thought of as a social problem. Although constant moving created disorientation for the families of executives, the situation was considered unavoidable, and individual executives could not force changes in the custom. Men have suffered from the practice as well, but they faced serious punishment for rejecting a company-requested move; those who did so were believed to lack ambition. The family was regarded as subject to the occupational needs of the husband and father. Yet if other members of the family had needs that were evaluated as highly as his, the family would be viewed as a constraint on behavior necessary for his success in the business world. When women had no power to protest, and when they made no economic contribution to the family, they had few options. But with their growing sense of self and of involvement in work, there will probably be considerable pressure to change such practices.

Organizations may increasingly have to take account of the family as a unit having two economically productive members. They may be asked to find work opportunities for the spouse of the person they hire. Businesses are already being forced to adjust to many changing patterns—for example, the striking down of nepotism curbs that prevented husbands and wives from working in the same place. Probably there will be changes in the law, but pressure will also come from individuals who need more flexibility in their work lives to meet the new demand for flexibility in their home lives. The "new family" has individual needs that will aggregate into problems for the society.

Costs of Changing Sex Roles in the Family

As traditional authority patterns in the family have been disrupted, many of those who have been in authority—the men and older family members—have experienced a sense of loss. But there is no evidence that this sense of loss has resulted in men's withdrawal from economic activity or from decision-making in other spheres.

Some men have embraced these changes, feeling relief at being able to share economic responsibilities that they formerly had to carry alone. But many men do not know how to react to wives who ask and expect to share in decision making in the home and to receive a new level of respect. Many are confused about how to treat such women or how to expect such women to treat them. They realize that older models of family life are now considered inequitable and do not have new models to emulate.

The dynamics of family life will differ when the husband is forced out of the labor force because of illness or layoff and his wife steps in to support the family. In a culture that gears a man's identity to his occupation, his failure is made worse by her relative success; it does not make him prize his wife's equality in the labor market. In the family where this occurs, psychological problems are created for both husband and wife and both may experience feelings of resentment, guilt, and failure.

There is no doubt that at work men increasingly have to adjust to women's participation as equals and their expressed ambitions and aspirations. When this same situation occurs at home, it is probably much more difficult to deal with. When both husband and wife have aspirations for work achievement and a need for relaxation and solace at home, inevitably there will be problems of priorities. People today are sorting out ways to meet women's newly articulated needs. The repercussions beyond the family will persist for many years.

Overloading the Family

It is a heavy responsibility for women and men to have to perform in all the areas of life in which they are now supposed to have competence. Today the American nuclear family is overloaded in its efforts to be all things to all members. Both spouses must be not only each others' emotional supports, but satisfying sexual partners, ideal parents, successful providers, and companions in leisure activity. No doubt the demands of these roles have contributed to the high divorce rate in the United States, but some of the tensions are created by the inability of other institutions to adjust to changes taking place within the family.

Old views of efficiency may prove inappropriate to the new life styles of the young, as well as to their changing values. Even with today's economic pressures, young people do seem to want to live by more humanitarian values, and to have a family life that—ironically—fits an older, more nostalgic image of family sharing.

SUMMARY

1   All societies assign to individuals an array of roles based on sex that are usually believed to be "just" as well as natural. Yet as a result of developments in the social and physical sciences, the civil rights movement, and changes in the economic structure, men and women are questioning traditional sex-role assignments.

2   Although there are stereotypes regarding how both men and women ought to behave and what their proper roles in life ought to be, those which focus on women have been most particularly identified as a set of social problems. This is because the roles typically assigned to women—whether in the family, work,

politics, or religion—are structured to keep women subordinate to men, and out of decision-making and prestige-awarding positions.

3   Changes in expectations regarding the roles men and women will assume because of their sex have created considerable discussion and debate in American society, culminating in the women's movement.

4   The current women's movement began in the 1960s with the founding of the National Organization for Women (NOW), which has been devoted to identifying patterns of discrimination in the occupations, in schools, within the family, and in the media. NOW has worked actively with government groups to implement the Civil Rights Act of 1964 and other legislation guaranteeing equality to women. The women's movement now comprises hundreds of women's groups and caucuses within the professions and academic disciplines as well as in labor unions, political organizations, and church groups.

5   The women's movement inspired a *men's* liberation movement, considerably smaller in size and less organized, that is concerned with the consequences of masculine stereotypes. Its members have worked to change practices and laws based on the conventional assumption that only women will take care of children and men will work outside the home. As a result, rulings have occurred permitting paternity leave after birth of a child in the family and social security payments to widowers with young children.

6   Of considerable importance to the change in attitudes toward conventional sex role attitudes in the United States has been women's growing participation in the labor force, now at 42 percent. Furthermore, there has been an increase in the proportion of women with children of all ages in the work force; more than 57 percent of all women with children between the ages of 6 and 17 years and 45 percent of women with children under 6 are currently employed. An even greater proportion of black women with children work.

7   Up until recently, women have been incorporated into the work force in virtually sex-segregated jobs that are typically low ranking and have low prestige and few advancement possibilities. The jobs most frequently sex-typed as female jobs, and which employ most working women, are as clerks, secretaries, telephone operators, and food handlers. Women constitute less than 10 percent of practitioners in the high ranking professions and occupations, such as medicine (9%), law (4.9%), engineering (1%), and business management. These low percentages are a result of quotas restricting the percentage of women in graduate and professional schools, and discrimination against them in hiring.

8   Informal and formal practices tend to perpetuate sex typing of occupations and the invidious distinctions between men's and women's jobs. These include confining women to jobs and specialties that are considered appropriate, such as those related to service, child care, and "good works." Furthermore, although formal rules excluding women have been abolished through civil rights legislation, women are "kept out" of male spheres by being excluded from professional-personal networks that provide contacts and information about jobs. These include "men only" luncheon clubs, leisure activities, and friendships. Men are pressured to forsake women's occupations by social controls in the form of derogatory comments, derisive humor, and anger directed at men taking on women's roles.

9   Women typically suffer cumulative disadvantage from the fact that their jobs are low ranking and ancillary to male jobs. Women's jobs usually are not tracked

in the direction of advancement to the top of their own fields or to those jobs considered important in the society. For example, since women have been excluded from apprenticeship programs, they cannot advance from unskilled jobs to skilled jobs. Because they have not trained as lawyers, they were not in line for higher level jobs in business or government. There are signs of improvement in the rate of women's entry into all these spheres, however, as their representation in graduate and professional schools has gone up.

10   Real barriers continue to exist for women in the economic sector because society still assigns them primary responsibility for childcare, with few alternative solutions. Some families are seeking their own answers by adopting marriage styles where husband and wife share childcare responsibilities and try a flexible approach to their occupational needs. But in a society where men, though often willing to share home responsibilities, are still subject to the demands of their own occupations, individual couples may not be able to translate egalitarian attitudes into behavior.

11   Problems have also arisen from the ambiguity created in men and women who are experiencing changing expectations attached to their own and others' roles. Men are now faced with women's rising ambitions in work and their expectations of more equal treatment in both private and public life. Women and men are also faced with sorting out intimate relationships that fit in with their other obligations.

12   The general profile of American society seems to be tending toward more sharing of privileges, opportunities, and responsibilities between men and women than ever before.

RECOMMENDED READING

A broad historical overview of the changing position of women is provided by William H. Chafe in *The American Woman: Her Changing Social, Economic and Political Roles 1920–1970* (1972). An anthology of the writings of eighteenth-century feminists in England and the United States illustrates continuities in definition of women's rights as social problems—Alice S. Rossi's *The Feminist Papers: From Adams to De Beauvoir* (1973).

The Feminine Mystique by Betty Friedan (1963) as the "opening gun" of the current women's movement challenges the underutilization of women's abilities and the consequences for society. A statement on "men's liberation" can be found in Warren Farrell, *The Liberated Man* (1974).

Issues in the biosocial aspects of sex roles can be found in John Money and Anke A. Ehrhardt, *Man and Woman, Boy and Girl* (1972) and psychological aspects in E. E. Maccoby and C. N. Jacklin, *The Psychology of Sex Differences* (1974).

A comprehensive view of studies relating sex differentiation and major institutions in Western societies is Harriet Holter, *Sex Roles and Social Structure* (1970). The changing position of women in societies in transition is analyzed in Ester Boserup's excellent book, *Woman's Role in Economic Development* (1970); the books of readings edited by Carolyn J. Matthiasson, *Many Sisters* (1974), and Michelle Rosaldo and Louise Lamphere, *Woman, Culture and Society* (1974), give one a cross-sectional analysis of women in non-Western as well as Western countries.

A discussion of sex differentiation in work roles can be found in Cynthia Fuchs Epstein, *Woman's Place* (1970) and Athena Theodore, *The Professional Woman* (1971). William J. Goode's *World Revolution and Family Patterns* (1963) is the most comprehensive analysis of changing sex roles in the family, while Jessie Bernard's *Marriage and Family Among Negroes* (1966) and Mirra Komarovsky's *Blue Collar Marriage* (1964) show how sex-role differentiation in the family occurs in particular groups and strata of society.

The effect of sex status on the ways women are treated medically is discussed in Phyllis Chesler, *Women and Madness* (1972), as legal clients, in Leo Kanowitz, *Woman and the Law* (1967), and in a number of other social contexts, in the book of readings edited by Vivian Gornick and Barbara K. Moran, *Woman in Sexist Society* (1971). A compilation of studies that attempt to "put women back" into standard sociological fields such as the occupations, stratification, and culture can be found in Marcia Millman and Rosabeth Kantor (eds.), *Another Voice: Feminist Perspectives on Social Life and Social Science* (1975).

Issues that focus on social policy implications of sex differentiation can be found in Constantina Safilios-Rothschild, *Women and Social Policy* (1974), Jessie Bernard, *Women and the Public Interest* (1971), and Phyllis Chesler and Emily Jane Goodman, *Women, Money and Power* (1976).

10

Race
and
Intergroup
Relations

THOMAS FRASER PETTIGREW

A few years ago, 12 college students conducted a revealing field experiment.[1] They set out as six couples—two black, two Mexican American, and two Anglo-white—to test the renting practices of 25 apartment houses in one area of Los Angeles. The couples were similarly educated, similarly dressed, similarly articulate in English. But they were treated differently; that is the focus of this chapter.

Each of the apartments had advertised one or more available units the day before they were visited. Yet the minority couples were far more often told there were no available apartments. Even when they were offered an apartment, the minority couples were more likely to be quoted higher rents and higher incidental fees. Only five of the 25 apartment managers did not discriminate in any way. The black couples were victimized in some fashion on 75 percent of their visits; the Mexican Americans on 50 percent of their visits; and the Anglo-whites on only 17 percent of their visits.

Unfortunately, there is nothing unique to Los Angeles about these results. Despite the American "creed" of equality, despite state and federal anti-discrimination laws, blatant discrimination remains widespread in modern America. Nor is this social problem new to our nation. It has deep roots, and it has affected many groups in our history. The United States population is, after all, extremely diverse. Americans range across the major races, religions, and nationalities of the world. Not surprisingly, this heterogeneity provides one of our society's principal bases for social organization; it is also a principal source of societal strain. Whether in the North or South, before or after the Civil War, in this or the last century, racial and intergroup conflicts have been the direct cause of far more domestic violence than any other source.[2] From slavery and racial segregation to the problems of massive immigration, racial and intergroup relations have remained a major domestic concern for American society.

We shall concentrate in this chapter on the two largest groups that have been and still are victimized: black Americans and Mexican Americans. The former highlight the role of race, the latter the role of culture. Blacks and Chicanos are not, of course, the only groups who have faced similar forms of prejudice and discrimination. Indeed, as the late President John F. Kennedy aptly phrased it, we are "a nation of immigrants"; as such we are all members of one or more racial, religious, or national groups, most of which suffered difficulties in gaining acceptance.

The author wishes to thank Professor Jaime Sena-Rivera for his comments on an earlier draft of this chapter.

[1] D. A. Johnson et al., "Racial Discrimination in Apartment Rentals," *Journal of Applied Social Psychology*, Vol. 1 (1971), pp. 364–377. Reprinted in T. F. Pettigrew (ed.), *Racial Discrimination in the United States* (New York: Harper & Row, 1975).

[2] R. C. Wade, "Violence in the Cities: An Historical View," in C. U. Daly (ed.), *Urban Violence* (Chicago: University of Chicago Press, 1969), pp. 7–26.

HISTORICAL BACKGROUND

Among the stormiest histories is that of the native Americans, who "immigrated" first and numbered 793,000 in the 1970 Census. They suffered shameful maltreatment extending back to the European "discovery" of the New World. Mainland Puerto Ricans, comprised of over one and a half million people most of whom reside in New York City, share many of the problems of both other Spanish speakers and blacks. Asian Americans have also endured racial prejudice. The mixed reception provided Vietnamese refugees in 1975 recalls Asian problems of the past. Chinese Americans, who numbered 435,000 in the 1970 Census, encountered notorious mistreatment in the West in the nineteenth century. Today they struggle to accommodate immigrants from Taiwan and Hong Kong, whose annual numbers have more than quadrupled since passage of the 1965 Immigration Act. Filipino Americans, who numbered 343,000 in the 1970 Census, have experienced employment exploitation from the pineapple fields of Hawaii to the ship galleys of the U.S. Navy. They, too, have witnessed an increase under the new immigration act by about five times the annual number of new arrivals as before 1965. Japanese Americans, who numbered 591,000 in the 1970 Census, bore the ultimate act of discrimination: massive internment in federal camps during World War II despite no evidence of alleged sabotage.

Recently, European ethnic groups and their problems in America have won special attention. An "ethnic group," following Max Weber, is a human collectivity based on an assumption of common origin, real or imagined. It has at least some values that contrast with those of the larger society, and it maintains some separate institutions and rituals. But in the American case, this definition casts the net too broadly and includes virtually all identifiable groups. It is useful, then, to confine the definition to European nationality groups who immigrated to the United States after the American Revolution.

Ethnicity, under this narrowed definition, has returned in the 1970s as an issue of public discussion. The familiar point is that American society has not proven to be the "melting pot" of complete assimilation that many had thought it was. But if the melting-pot notion is clearly a myth, so, too, is the opposite notion of "complete pluralism."[3] This counter-myth views America as almost completely split into its various ethnic and racial segments, with few important bonds across groups to tie the society together. Reality, as usual, is far more complex than these simple conceptions. There *have* been both some "melting" and some group separation. American life today witnesses mass acculturation side by side with only moderate assimilation.[4] Put differently, the vast majority

---

[3] T. F. Pettigrew, "Ethnicity in American Life: A Social Psychological Perspective," in J. H. Franklin et al., *Ethnicity in American Life* (New York: Anti-Defamation League, 1971), pp. 22–34.

[4] Milton Gordon, *Assimilation in American Life* (New York: Oxford, 1964).

of Americans share a common culture of speech and manners, much of it conveyed by the mass media. But there are also considerable differences at the intimate, primary levels of friendship and family, and there are numerous barriers denying entire groups access to important societal institutions. It is these group barriers to institutional participation that often constitute discrimination for ethnic as well as racial groups.

Much of the prejudice and discrimination against ethnic groups has been based on religion. Following World War II and Nazi Germany's campaign of Jewish genocide, anti-Semitism declined sharply.[5] It has, however, flared repeatedly in the United States over the past century. Discrimination against Jewish Americans usually takes subtle forms, but sometimes it is blatant, as in exclusion from certain college fraternities and sororities, social and country clubs, particular New York City law firms, and executive positions in the utility and automotive industries. Roman Catholics have also known prejudice and discrimination in a predominantly Protestant nation. The "Know-Nothings" of the nineteenth century and the recurrent editions of the Ku Klux Klan in the twentieth provided flagrant examples of anti-Catholicism.

The election of John F. Kennedy to the Presidency in 1960 and the appointment of Henry Kissinger as Secretary of State in 1974 symbolize the partial abatement of these religious conflicts of the past. Kennedy was the first Catholic to become President in almost two centuries of the nation's history, and he won election only after facing bigoted abuse that recalled the religiously motivated elements of the defeat of Alfred Smith in 1928. Kissinger was the first naturalized citizen as well as the first Jewish American to become Secretary of State; in fact, he holds one of the highest offices any Jewish citizen has ever held in the United States.

Many of the problems faced by ethnic groups involve issues of social class and economic inequality. This is especially true for those who were among the last to arrive during the period of major European immigration, 1880–1915. Italian Americans and Eastern Europeans, especially Polish Americans, are particularly prominent among these groups. These more recent arrivals also encounter prejudiced stereotypes and discrimination, to which the continued existence of "criminal Italian" and "dumb Pole" jokes bitterly attests.

There is, then, a vast range of intergroup relations problems found in the United States. Some of the issues raised by these problems, such as economic inequality, are treated in other chapters. Here we shall focus on the social problems faced by black and Mexican Americans. These two groups share many of the problems experienced by other minorities and by each other. Each also faces a distinctive set of problems that are different in kind as well as in extent from those of other groups.

[5] C. H. Stember (ed.), *Jews in the Mind of America* (New York: Basic Books, 1966).

Figure 10-1 Six Approaches to the Study of Race Relations

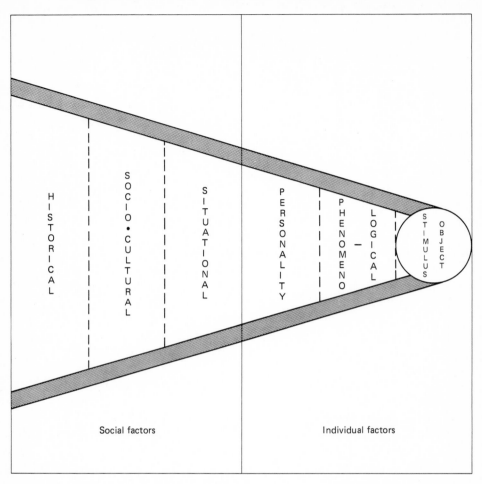

Source: Adapted from Gordon W. Allport, *The Nature of Prejudice* (Cambridge, Mass.: Addison-Wesley, 1954), p. 207.

SIX BASIC APPROACHES TO THE PROBLEM

All relations between groups are conditioned by six interrelated classes of factors: *historical, socio-cultural, situational, personality, phenomenological,* and *stimulus object.*[6] Each forms a different and necessary approach. "There is no master key," wrote Gordon Allport. "Rather, what we have at our disposal is a ring of keys, each of which opens one gate of understanding."[7] As shown in

---

[6] This scheme is adapted from one proposed for prejudice in Gordon W. Allport, *The Nature of Prejudice* (Cambridge, Mass.: Addison-Wesley, 1954), pp. 206–218.

[7] *Ibid.,* p. 208.

Figure 10-1, the six approaches form a lens model that focuses down from the broadest approach, the historical, to the principal stimulus object of the process, the minority group. This scheme helps to order our thinking, but the six sets of factors do overlap and there is interaction between such diverse factors as socio-cultural and personality.

1. The historical approach   How did black-white relations in North America begin? How was slavery unique in the American colonies and what are the consequences of these differences today? And how did the past shape the various patterns of Chicano-Anglo relations that have characterized the Southwest in this century? Only history can supply the answers.

History offers the broadest context of all of the approaches. In bold strokes, historical considerations outline the scope and direction of the process, but these considerations are incomplete in themselves. History does not spell out how particular social forces, once begun, eventually structure diverse racial patterns in similar localities. To utilize fully the general insights that history provides, it is necessary to trace them through a series of more specific approaches.

2. The socio-cultural approach   The socio-cultural category includes the many cultural and institutional factors that form the setting within which intergroup relations take place. A new set of relevant questions are now posed: How have black and Mexican Americans changed demographically, politically, and economically in this century? What is the significance for intergroup relations of the dominant social trends in American society?

3. The situational approach   The situational perspective considers the specific contexts in which groups actually meet face to face. It is here that the historical and socio-cultural factors, on the one hand, and the individual factors, on the other, come to a pointed focus and, conditioned by the particular characteristics of the situation, produce intergroup *relations* as such. We shall stress the critical importance of intergroup contact and the specific conditions under which it occurs. This is central to the design of effective remedies. We shall contend that *efforts at improving American intergroup relations are successful to the extent that they further intergroup contact under optimal conditions.* Such a contention raises situational questions like: What are the conditions for "optimal" contact? How are racial attitudes altered by new interracial experiences? Research provides interesting answers to these situational queries.

4. The personality approach   The first three approaches explain the social climate within which intergroup interaction occurs. But what about the individuals who live and act in this climate? Personality considerations make up the first of the three approaches concerned with individual factors.

Do majority Americans need, in a deep personality sense, group bigotry? This is no mere academic issue. If the answer is essentially "yes," then the modification of the country's intergroup patterns faces stern difficulties, and strategies for change should strive largely to contain prejudice while minimizing discrimination. But if the answer is "no," the reformer can set his sights higher and work for a truly democratic society with minimal prejudice and discrimination.

5. The phenomenological approach How do "Anglo-Americans" view their nation's intergroup relations and their own intergroup contacts and experiences? After all, what men and women think to be true is what actually guides their behavior. Here we discuss the prevalent intergroup stereotypes, and how these capsule images of whole groups have recently faded somewhat.

6. The stimulus-object approach Finally, we look at the focus of the issue, the minority group member himself—not just as a victim of prejudice and discrimination, but also as a reactor to oppression.

Armed with this multiple-factor model, we are now prepared to discuss America's intergroup relations problems and their causes. First, we will apply the model to black-white relations.

THE HISTORICAL APPROACH TO BLACK-WHITE RELATIONS

Slavery

Black Americans have been an integral part of the society ever since their arrival at Jamestown, Virginia from a Dutch frigate in August, 1619. It is erroneous to think of blacks as merely transplanted Africans or as a group with a culture totally divorced from the larger society. After 14 generations, black Americans truly belong in the United States. This fact poses an ironic problem: Although they constitute an integral eighth of their nation, blacks have been denied their full rights as citizens for 3½ centuries.

The roots of the problems go back to slavery. The first "twenty and odd Negroes" who landed at Jamestown were apparently not slaves. The peculiar institution was not established by law in Virginia until 1661; it placed upon blacks, alone of all American minorities, a stigma of assumed inferiority that is only now being erased. This raises an important question: Why did slavery in the United States leave such a deep and lasting scar while other areas of the world, such as Brazil, had the institution longer and yet have thrown off its effects more successfully?

One possible answer lies in the peculiar nature of slavery under English law. The historian Frank Tannenbaum points out that the Iberian countries of Spain and Portugal, unlike England, had centuries of experience with slavery prior to the founding of the New World.[8] Hence, under Iberian law there

---

[8] Frank Tannenbaum, *Slave and Citizen: The Negro in the Americas* (New York: Knopf, 1947).

evolved a special category for the slave as a human being. But English law, unfamiliar with the institution, had no such special category and treated the slave as merely dehumanized property—no different legally from a barn or an animal. Consequently, Latin America, emulating Iberian law, never developed the totally dehumanizing stigma surrounding slavery that the American colonies did, following English law. This is not to say that slavery was not also cruel in Latin America or that there are no race problems there at present; it is to say that a different legal definition of slavery left the Latin countries with less of a dehumanizing legacy of racial stigma.

Slavery expanded rapidly once it was seized upon as a solution to the labor shortage in the colonies. There were 400 times as many blacks in Virginia in 1756 (120,000) as in 1650 (300). This phenomenal growth soon led to white fears of slave revolts. Consequently, the colonial slave codes became firmly established by the early 1700s, and severely restricted the slave's movements. Slavery varied considerably among the colonies. Large slave holdings were economically feasible only in warm areas with vast, flat agricultural lands. Thus, Maryland, Virginia, and South Carolina had the most slaves and the harshest codes, while New England had the fewest slaves and the mildest codes.

Three forces combined during the late eighteenth century to spawn the first strong anti-slavery movement: the liberal philosophy of the American Revolution, the struggle for the slaves' allegiance during the Revolution, and the declining utility of slavery. This combination led to gradual abolition in all of the northern states by the early nineteenth century, and to a provision in the Northwest Ordinance that outlawed slavery in what became Ohio, Indiana, Illinois, Michigan, and Wisconsin. The movement almost succeeded in ending slavery even in the South when agriculture there fell on bad times.

Just as southern slavery was teetering, a series of history-making inventions revived and expanded it as never before. In England, new spinning and weaving machinery made possible mass production of cotton textiles, leading to a voracious demand for cotton. The South, however, could not greatly expand its modest cotton production until an efficient method for removing seeds was devised. Soon a visiting young Yankee schoolteacher, Eli Whitney, developed a satisfactory gin. Cotton became the ruling passion of the South. The amount grown in 1840 was almost four times that grown in 1820; by 1860 it had more than tripled again. Slavery now had a firm economic base and vastly increased. From less than a million slaves in the entire nation in 1800, the number rose to two million by 1830 and to almost four million by 1860.[9]

How could slaveholders treat human beings as mere property and also believe in the American ideal of human equality? Many of them never did rest easily with this glaring contradiction, though they tried to rationalize the conflict. Into the nineteenth century, believers in slavery generally employed religious rationalizations. Slavery was an effective method, some claimed, to

---

[9] U.S. Bureau of the Census, *Negro Population: 1790–1915* (Washington, D.C.: Government Printing Office, 1918), p. 53.

introduce Christianity to African heathen. God had willed that the black man serve the white man, said others. These rationalizations lost their potency as more and more blacks became Christian.

Just as the religious rationalizations were losing force, biological ideas were introduced. Almost desperately, many white Americans seized upon racist theories from Europe and accepted the divisive concepts of race and racial superiority.[10] The new feature of modern slavery—its limitation to one group—could now be explained away without religious considerations. Blacks were slaves of Caucasians because they were a lower order of human development in a Darwinian sense. Naive as it seems today in the light of subsequent advances in biology, this racist reasoning appealed to all but the thoughtful. For all one had to do was look around him. Were not slaves obviously inferior to their masters in intelligence and manners? And if such things are all biologically determined, is this not proof that whites are racially superior to blacks? So went the argument, for the sweeping importance of environment and opportunity was not yet understood.

The Ostensibly "Free Negro"

The defenders of slavery sought to strengthen their case by pointing to the lowly condition of the "free Negro." Only technically free, these blacks in the South were restricted in almost every conceivable manner. The haunting fear was that they would lead slave revolts. Most southern states kept "free Negroes" from voting, denied their right to assemble, granted them no equality in the courts, circumscribed their movements, and attempted to deny them education. Consequently, many "free Negroes" slipped below the living standards of even the slaves, who at least enjoyed a modicum of paternalistic benefits.

By 1860, there were almost ½ million "free Negroes" in the nation, about half of them in the North.[11] But those in the North fared little better prior to the Civil War.[12] Violent anti-black riots flared up in many northern cities in the 1830s and 1840s. Most northern states either denied or restricted black suffrage, five did not allow blacks to testify in court, two outlawed interracial marriage, and one, Oregon, even made it illegal for blacks to own real estate or make contracts. Many northern cities established separate black schools.

The significance of this nationwide discrimination against "free Negroes" was that it furnished a convenient and dangerous precedent for handling emancipated blacks after the Civil War. The ink was barely dry at Appomattox before North Carolina had legislatively extended to the new Freedmen the same restrictions and disabilities that had formerly applied to "free Negroes." Other states passed similar statutes. In short, the full fruits of the most dramatic action in black American history—the 1863 Emancipation Proclamation—were being denied as soon as the Civil War ended.

[10] William Stanton, *The Leopard's Spots: Scientific Attitudes Toward Race in America, 1815–1859* (Chicago: University of Chicago Press, 1960).

[11] U.S. Bureau of the Census, *op. cit.*, p. 53.

[12] Leon F. Litwack, *North of Slavery* (Chicago: University of Chicago Press, 1961).

The Roots of Modern Segregation

Then the Reconstruction era began. The victorious Union retained its military occupation of the South and set up Reconstruction state governments. This period witnessed the repeal of anti-black laws and the passage of anti-discrimination laws throughout the South. Many blacks assumed important public office. The great tragedy of this period, however, is that federal measures were not employed to strengthen the South's sagging economy and thus make permanent these sweeping improvements in race relations.

The South did not revert immediately to white supremacy when the Reconstruction era drew to a close in the 1870s. C. Vann Woodward has shown that segregation did not rush in as a system until very late in the nineteenth century.[13] Throughout the South, state government scandals and a powerful agrarian revolt movement at that time made it expedient to use the black once again as a scapegoat. White men had to stick together, argued conservative politicians who feared a class coalition between black and poor white voters. Other whites joined them out of fear that uneducated blacks would sell their votes to wealthy politicians.

By the turn of the century, southern states were disfranchising black citizens. Between 1890 and 1910 the whole complex of so-called "Jim Crow" laws were enacted—separate railroad cars, separate lunch counters, separate doorways, and separate waiting rooms. No detail was too minute: Oklahoma later required separate telephone booths, and many courts began to use separate Bibles for swearing in.

Among all the years since Abraham Lincoln's Emancipation Proclamation, this period marked the nadir of black American fortunes. It was the period of mass lynchings of blacks and the establishment of modern institutional racism. Since then, with relentless determination, black Americans have succeeded step by step in writing Jim Crow's epitaph. It is to these steps that we turn now.

THE SOCIO-CULTURAL APPROACH

Trends in six different realms provide a socio-cultural perspective on black-white relations: *legal, demographic, political, housing, economic,* and *educational.*

Legal Trends

The segregation era, 1876–1910   Reconstruction promised a sharp departure from the nation's slave past. In particular, the Thirteenth, Fourteenth, and Fifteenth Amendments to the Constitution forcefully spelled out this new direction. Witness the key passage of the Fourteenth Amendment:

[13] C. Vann Woodward, *The Strange Career of Jim Crow*, 2nd rev. ed. (New York: Oxford, 1966).

No state shall make or enforce any law which shall abridge the privileges or immunities of citizens of the United States, nor shall any state deprive any person of life, liberty, or property, without due process of law; nor deny to any person within its jurisdiction the equal protection of the laws. . . .

Yet even this straightforward guarantee was narrowed and distorted for a third of a century by the country's highest tribunal. The segregationist era of the United States Supreme Court began in 1876 with Chief Justice Morrison Waite; it repeatedly ruled both state and federal anti-discrimination laws unconstitutional.[14] Such rulings tempted the white South into establishing the first forms of legalized segregation. Under the next Chief Justice, Melville Fuller, this temptation became an open invitation. The Fuller Court from 1888 through 1910 found constitutional a series of early southern state laws requiring segregation.

The Fuller Court's most important race decision was *Plessy v. Ferguson* in 1896.[15] Homer Plessy, one-eighth black by birth, had been arrested for riding in a rail car reserved for whites under a new Louisiana law. Plessy sued and claimed that the Louisiana statute was unconstitutional. Affirming the rulings of state courts, the Supreme Court denied Plessy's plea. Only Justice John Harlan, a former slaveholder from Kentucky, dissented by maintaining that "our Constitution is color-blind." The *Plessy* ruling led to the segregationist formula of "separate but equal"—that is, separate facilities for the races may be required by state law provided that the facilities are "equal." The South was too poor to have even one set of adequate public facilities, so the precise legal formula in practice lapsed into separate but very unequal.

The preparatory era, 1911–1930 In the *Plessy* opinion, the High Court was merely accentuating the trend of the times, not manufacturing it. By 1910, however, the climate was changing, and the Supreme Court changed with it. From 1909 to 1911, four justices died and a fifth resigned. A transitional era was beginning that prepared the ground for the desegregation decisions of recent decades. This preparatory era began with a southern-born Chief Justice and ended with an ex-President as Chief Justice. Edward White was a Louisiana sugar-planter who had fought in the Confederate Army; and he was followed in 1921 by ex-President William Taft. Their leadership saw decisions that, for example: protected black voting rights by holding both the infamous "grandfather clauses" and white-only primaries unconstitutional;[16] and ruled against municipal ordinances requiring residential segregation.[17] On the legislative front, however, there was little during these years that can be described

---

[14] *U.S. v. Cruikshank,* 92 U.S. 542 (1876); *U.S. v. Reese,* 92 U.S. 214 (1876); *Hall v. DeCuir,* 95 U.S. 485 (1878); *U.S. v. Harris,* 106 U.S. 629 (1883); *Civil Rights Cases,* 190 U.S. 3 (1883).

[15] *Plessy v. Ferguson,* 163 U.S. 537 (1896).

[16] *Guinn v. United States,* 238 U.S. 347 (1915); *Myers et al. v. Anderson,* 238 U.S. 368 (1915); *U.S. v. Mosley,* 238 U.S. 383 (1915); *Nixon v. Herndon,* 273 U.S. 536 (1927).

[17] *Buchanan v. Warley,* 245 U.S. 60 (1917); *Harmon v. Tyler,* 273 U.S. 668 (1927).

as "preparatory" for desegregation. The federal government and northern states ignored racial discrimination, and southern states enacted more segregation statutes.

The desegregation era, 1930–1969   The third Supreme Court period began in 1930 when Charles Hughes became Chief Justice. The Hughes Court, and later the Stone and Vinson Courts, whittled away at the "separate but equal" doctrine by applying increasingly more rigorous definitions of "equal."

Blacks made gains early in this era in six key areas. In *due process* cases, the Court consistently ruled that the exclusion of minorities from juries is presumptive evidence of discrimination.[18] In the *employment* area, the Court agreed that states have the power under the Fourteenth Amendment to prohibit racial discrimination by labor unions.[19] In *public accommodations* cases, the Court held that interstate segregation is an unconstitutional burden on interstate commerce and that blacks cannot be denied an unoccupied Pullman seat or an unoccupied dining car seat.[20] In two cases in 1948 and 1953, the Court ruled that racially restrictive *housing* covenants could not be supported by court action.[21] The major legal breakthrough on *voting* came in 1944, when the Court reversed itself and declared that state political conventions and party memberships were state actions and hence, under the Fourteenth Amendment, could not exclude black citizens.[22]

In addition, continuous legal advances were made in *education.* The unanimous decision in *Brown v. Board of Education* in 1954 against *de jure* racial segregation in public schools finally destroyed the "separate but equal" doctrine by ruling that "separate educational facilities are inherently unequal." The Supreme Court handed down a year later a weak enforcement order with the vague standard of "with all deliberate speed." This weak standard proved to be a serious mistake. It encouraged segregationists to resist, and it necessitated an almost endless flow of implementation cases in the crowded lower courts. Only after a decade and a half of delay did the high bench call for elimination of *de jure* segregation in public schools "root and branch." The historic 1954 ruling set the course for the Earl Warren-led Court. The new "separate cannot be equal" doctrine was extended to public pools, beaches, golf courses, and theaters. Further gains were made in employment and voting; and state laws banning interracial marriage were struck down in 1967.

Belatedly, civil-rights legislation outlawing racial discrimination in public accommodations began being enacted in the late forties in such states as New York and Massachusetts. Similar state statutes in employment and then in housing followed, until today many states boast anti-discrimination legislation

---

[18] *Norris v. Alabama,* 294 U.S. 587 (1935); *Pierre v. Louisiana,* 306 U.S. 354 (1939); *Smith v. Texas,* 311 U.S. 128 (1940); *Patton v. Mississippi,* 332 U.S. 463 (1967); *Cassell v. Texas,* 239 U.S. 282 (1950); *Reece v. Georgia,* 350 U.S. 85 (1955).

[19] *Railway Mail Association v. Corsi,* 326 U.S. 88 (1945).

[20] *Mitchell v. U.S.,* 313 U.S. 80 (1941); *Henderson v. U.S.,* 339 U.S. 816 (1950).

[21] *Shelley v. Kraemer,* 334 U.S. 1 (1948); *Barrows v. Jackson,* 346 U.S. 249 (1953).

[22] *Smith v. Allwright,* 321 U.S. 649 (1944).

on their books. In 1957 and 1960 the first federal civil-rights legislation since 1875 plugged some of the gaping holes in the federal legislative armor against voting discrimination. But the important breakthrough occurred with the passage of the sweeping Civil Rights Act of 1964. It contained titles to combat discrimination in public accommodations and employment and to withdraw federal funds from institutions that practice racial discrimination. In 1965 a well-designed Voting Rights Act was enacted, and in 1968 the first federal statute against housing discrimination was passed.

To date, the practical results of this spate of civil-rights laws are not impressive. Typically the enforcement agencies are grossly understaffed and narrowly circumscribed, and enforcement is often limited to processing complaints on an inefficient, case-by-case basis. But Mayhew has shown that the typical complaints of employment discrimination are nonstrategic.[23] They are generally lodged against the firms that discriminate least, while complaints against unfair employers seldom arise. In short, racial discrimination is patterned and only patterned enforcement not dependent upon nonstrategic complaints can be effective.

The retrenchment era, 1970 on   The retirement of Chief Justice Warren in 1969 and the nomination of a series of conservatives for the Supreme Court by the ill-fated Nixon Administration signalled a new era. The Court soon surrendered its role of leadership in civil rights. The Berger Court has upheld many of the racial positions of the Warren Court, but has consistently refused to enter upon new legal ground.

Three critical cases illustrate the trend of this era. In a 1971 case involving Charlotte, North Carolina, the Berger Court supported the bussing of students throughout a large metropolitan school district in order to achieve racial desegregation. Bussing is "a normal and accepted tool of educational policy," observed the Court, and "desegregation plans cannot be limited to the walk-in school."[24] In a 1973 case from Denver, the Supreme Court made its first important school desegregation ruling for a northern district. The Justices found that intentional segregation in one area of a school system may have "reciprocal" effects throughout the system. They also noted that "Hispanos" suffer inequities similar to those experienced by blacks and must also be considered in identifying segregation.[25] A defeat was suffered by civil rights advocates in 1974 when the High Court turned down a metropolitan remedy for school desegregation in Detroit.[26] Even in the Detroit case the Berger Court upheld the basic constitutional standards enunciated by the Warren Court, but imposed stringent requirements for achieving much-needed metropolitan remedies. In 1975, the Court let stand two metropolitan cases involving Louisville, Kentucky and Indianapolis, Indiana.

[23] Leon Mayhew, *Law and Equal Opportunity: A Study of the Massachusetts Commission Against Discrimination* (Cambridge, Mass.: Harvard University Press, 1968).
[24] *Swann v. Charlotte-Mecklenburg Board of Education*, 402 U.S. 1, 29–30 (1971).
[25] *Keyes v. School District No. 1, Denver, Colorado*, 413 U.S. 189 (1973).
[26] *Milliken v. Bradley*, 418 U.S. 717 (1974).

If the Supreme Court became more cautious, the legislative and executive branches of the federal government began a full-scale retreat. In the 1970s Congress placed numerous "anti-bussing" riders on educational legislation, and even considered initiating an "anti-bussing" amendment to the nation's constitution. And the Nixon and Ford Administrations repeatedly took public positions against school desegregation. From 1969 on, the Department of Health, Education, and Welfare sharply curtailed its administrative enforcement of civil rights laws, and after 1971 the Department of Justice cut back its desegregation suits. On October 9, 1974, just as rioting over interracial schools was taking place in Boston, President Gerald Ford publicly attacked the city's desegregation court order.[27] These official actions have slowed, but have not yet reversed, the school desegregation trend. They do serve, however, to legitimate extreme segregationist resistance and make more difficult the achievement of effective integrated education.

Demographic Trends[28]

Migration to the city   In this century blacks have become urbanites. Four out of every five black Americans today reside in cities, while only one in four did so in 1910. Significant black migration to the cities began during World War I, when European hostilities provided large war orders for American industry and also stemmed the tide of immigrant labor, opening up new employment opportunities for Americans.

Not all of this human surge was stimulated by the attractive pull of new jobs; there were "push" factors as well. The high birth rate among rural southerners, the mechanization of southern agriculture, the boll weevil, government programs limiting agricultural production, and the shift of cotton cultivation to the Southwest were all factors that literally starved blacks off the southern farms. And there was always the motivation to escape from the South's oppressive racial system.

The migration increased to an enormous process in the 1920s, slowed during the depression, accelerated again with America's entry into World War II, and continued heavy during the 1950s and 1960s. Between 1940 and 1970, over 4½ million black southerners left the region permanently.[29] Natural increase, rather than migration, now provides the greater part of black growth in the North and West. Now that more blacks live outside the ex-Confederacy than in it, race relations are clearly a national concern.

They are a national concern, however, with an urban cast. Today black Americans are more urban than white Americans and are especially concen-

---

[27] T. F. Pettigrew, "Race, Schools and Riots in Boston," *New Society*, Nov. 28, 1974, pp. 538–540.

[28] For more details, see T. F. Pettigrew, *Racially Separate or Together?* (New York: McGraw-Hill, 1971), and T. F. Pettigrew (ed.), *Racial Discrimination in the United States* (New York: Harper & Row, 1975).

[29] U.S. Bureau of the Census, *The Social and Economic Status of the Black Population in the United States, 1971* (Washington, D.C.: Government Printing Office, 1972), p. 15.

trated in the central cities of the largest metropolitan areas. By 1973, 76 percent of all blacks lived in metropolitan areas and 60 percent in central cities, compared to only 67 percent and 26 percent respectively of all whites.[30] Indeed, the black populations of just eight central cities—New York, Chicago, Detroit, Philadelphia, Washington, Los Angeles, Baltimore, and Houston—account for over a fourth of all black Americans. Today more blacks live in the New York metropolitan area than in any southern state; more live in metropolitan Chicago than in Mississippi.

If the old stereotype of the black sharecropper is outdated, so is the less dated stereotype of the urban black as a raw migrant fresh from the hinterland. The typical pattern now is for blacks to come to northern cities not from the farm but from southern cities. They tend to be better-educated, though their educational level is still below that of the typical black northerner. They are also typically more militant and less religious than their parents.

Projections of the future   In 1973, black Americans numbered more than 23.7 million people and constituted 11 percent of the nation's population;[31] by 1984, they will probably number between 28 and 32 million and constitute about 12 percent of the population. Most of this expansion will be absorbed by our largest metropolitan centers in the North and West, followed by continued growth of metropolitan centers in the South. Ultimately, from 75 to 85 percent of the black population may live outside of the South.

From a national perspective, the move of blacks to the city contains many positive features. It has prevented an uneconomic piling up of near-peasant blacks in the South's depressed rural areas. In fact, the shift from farm to city is more responsible for black gains in income, education, and housing during the past generation than the reduction in racial discrimination. Urbanization has also created a more sophisticated people capable of effective protest, a people more aware of what discrimination has denied them and more eager to benefit from the full privileges of American citizenship.

These national advantages would outweigh the urban strains on public services were it not for the enforced segregation of blacks into central-city ghettos. The problems of rapid growth are multiplied both for blacks, concentrated into blighted and underserviced areas, and for the city. It is this embedded pattern of racial separation that provides the backdrop for politics, housing, economics, and education.

Political Trends

The political power of black America has increased enormously in recent decades. This new power is fueled by a vast increase in the number of blacks registered to vote, especially in the South. Black registration in the South to-

---

[30] U.S. Bureau of the Census, *The Social and Economic Status of the Black Population in the United States, 1973* (Washington, D.C.: Government Printing Office, 1974), p. 11.
[31] *Ibid.*, pp. 131–132.

Selma, Alabama

taled only 150,000 in 1940; by 1946, after the 1944 Supreme Court ruling in *Smith v. Allwright*, this figure had risen to 600,000. By 1958 about 1.4 million, or 27 percent of the black voting-age population, were registered; by 1961, about 32 percent.[32] By 1972 the number of voters had reached almost 4½ million and constituted 64 percent of the black voting-age population in the South.[33] This percentage almost equals that of black northerners (67 percent) and approaches that of whites (73 percent). The greatest gains of recent years occurred in those states covered by the Voting Rights Act of 1965. Under this act, black registration in Alabama had more than doubled by 1968, and the percentage of voting-age black citizens registered in Mississippi climbed from a low of 8 percent in 1964 to almost 60 percent in 1968.[34] This southern increase has been partly countered by a rise in white registration, but has not been cancelled out by it. The gain in black registration is the major reason for the

[32] Donald Matthews and James W. Prothro, *Negroes and the New Southern Politics* (New York: Harcourt, Brace & World, 1966), pp. 112–113.

[33] U.S. Bureau of the Census, *The Social and Economic Status of the Black Population in the United States, 1973*, p. 121.

[34] Vernon E. Jordan, Jr., "New Forces of Urban Political Power," *New South*, Vol. 23 (Spring 1968), pp. 46–51.

election, by 1975, of over 1,500 black officials throughout the South, including about 100 southern state legislators and 82 mayors.[35] Particularly significant was the victory of Maynard Jackson as mayor in Atlanta.

Less dramatic but equally important has been the increasing political organization in black communities in the North. Typically the problem in northern cities has been not in restrictions against registering, but in unifying the community and getting out the vote. Many northern black communities have only recently become organized. The results were apparent in the election of black mayors in Gary and Cleveland in 1967, Newark in 1970, Los Angeles in 1973, and Detroit in 1974.

On the federal level, in 1966 Edward Brooke, a state attorney general, became the first black U.S. Senator in this century. And black members of the House of Representatives have increased in number from only four in 1962 to 17 in 1975. Important gains, to be sure, but this still means that a people who constitute 11 percent of the population comprise only 1 percent of the Senate and 4 percent of the House.

Similarly, these total political gains pale when placed in national perspective. The number of black elected officials has risen dramatically—from only 103 in 1964 to 3,503 in 1975[36]—and yet the 1975 figure represents less than 1 percent of the country's elected officials. Moreover, black people have been virtually excluded from nonelected power circles.[37] The late 1970s and early 1980s, however, promise a continuing, if slow, trend toward correcting these inequities.

Housing Trends

The degree of housing segregation   Strict racial separation is the rule in metropolitan America. White population growth in the suburbs in recent decades has been as dramatic as black population growth in the central cities. In 1973, three out of every five whites in the nation's standard metropolitan statistical areas (SMSAs) lived in suburbs, while four out of every five blacks in SMSAs lived in central cities.[38] Even these striking contrasts understate the housing segregation by race, for within both suburbs and central cities blacks are further segregated into particular neighborhoods. To achieve racially random residential patterns, the median central city in the United States in 1970 would require 83 percent of its black households to move from black blocks

---

[35] Joint Center for Political Studies, "Black Elected Officials Triple Since 1969," *Focus*, June 1975, p. 7.

[36] *Ibid.*

[37] H. M. Baron, "Black Powerlessness in Chicago," *Trans-Action*, November 1968, pp. 27–33; K. H. Flaming et al., "Black Powerlessness in Policy-making Positions," *The Sociological Quarterly*, Vol. 13 (1972), pp. 126–133.

[38] U.S. Bureau of the Census, *The Social and Economic Status of the Black Population in the United States, 1973*, p. 11.

to predominantly white blocks.[39] From 1940 to 1950, the index of housing segregation increased throughout the nation; from 1950 to 1960, it continued to rise in the South and decreased slightly in other regions; and in the sixties, it increased again with a leveling off in the late years of the decade.[40] In addition, the relatively few blacks who reside in suburbs are also typically segregated.

The causes of housing segregation The Taeubers demonstrate that "economic factors cannot account for more than a small portion of observed levels of racial residential segregation."[41] Five other causes are more important: federal housing policies, blatant racial discrimination, the tight supply of low-income housing, suburban zoning barriers, and binding ties within the black community.

Federal housing policy has been one of the largest contributors to the present state of extreme racial separation.[42] From the first National Housing Act in 1935 until 1950, the federal government actively enforced segregation. From 1950 to 1962, federal housing policy was officially neutral but actually segregationist. Not until President Kennedy's limited anti-discrimination executive order in 1962 and the 1968 Fair Housing Act did the government turn ineffectively integrationist.

Blatant racial discrimination in the private market has achieved further separation. Public referenda against discrimination in housing have lost by two-to-one majorities in Akron, Seattle, Detroit, and California. There are essentially two separate housing markets, with the market for blacks guaranteeing overcrowding, inferior facilities, and inflated rents. True, home ownership and intact housing have been increasing among black households, but these trends have not kept pace with white advances nor have they eroded the dual markets. They result from migration to the cities and the acquisition by middle-class blacks of older homes left behind by suburban-bound whites, rather than from any relaxation of discrimination.

The problem is made worse by the unavailability of low- and medium-income housing. The supply has not been increasing fast enough to meet the needs of the expanding population, much less replace aging housing stock. In addition, suburban zoning barriers not only act to keep blacks in the central city, but also serve to force the building of low-income housing for all the poor in the tax-weak central cities. Such restrictive policies as minimum lot sizes and dwelling costs result in part from the suburbs' eagerness to attract residents who will contribute more to local taxes than they require in services.

[39] A. Sorensen et al., *Indexes for Racial Residential Segregation for 109 Cities in the United States, 1940 to 1970,* Studies in Racial Desegregation, No. 1 (Madison: University of Wisconsin Institute for Research on Poverty, 1974).

[40] *Ibid.;* K. E. Taeuber and A. F. Taeuber, *Negroes in Cities* (Chicago: Aldine, 1965).

[41] Taeuber and Taeuber, *op. cit.,* p. 2.

[42] Charles Abrams, "The Housing Problem and the Negro," and T. J. Lowi, "Apartheid U.S.A.," in Pettigrew, *Racial Discrimination in the United States,* pp. 41–53, 59–74.

Such practices nourish racial fears.[43] Both racial groups are now so adapted to dual housing markets that many whites think their security is dependent upon separation, and relatively few middle-class blacks challenge the exclusion even under favorable circumstances.[44] Equally important, residents of the black community develop binding ties of friendship that they are reluctant to give up.

Housing remedies   The goal is not to eliminate the ghetto, but to convert it from an isolated racial prison to an ethnic area of *choice*. This effort must be projected for entire metropolitan areas; it must also be systemic, closely intermeshed with such components as mass transit, education, and employment.

Economic Trends

The problem   The upgrading of black employment has not kept pace with the upgrading created by automation, nor has it substantially narrowed the gap with white employment. Yet definite gains were made during the 1960s, before the dual crises of inflation and recession gripped the nation during the 1970s. Thus, between 1963 and 1973, the percentage of employed black males in white-collar jobs rose from 15 to 23 and those in skilled blue-collar jobs from 11 to 15. But these figures still trail far behind those of employed white males, of whom 42 percent were in white-collar jobs and 22 percent were in skilled blue-collar jobs.[45] Consequently, the median black family income has remained between 50 and 61 percent of the income of the median white family since 1950.[46]

Black unemployment rates have remained roughly twice those of white unemployment since the Korean War. Even in a tight labor market with the total unemployment rate reduced to below 4 percent, as in 1968, the black adult rate of unemployment is 7 percent or more. In times of widespread unemployment, such as the mid-1970s, black adult joblessness soars up toward 20 percent and black youth joblessness toward 50 percent. Comments one economist: "What is recession for the white (say, an unemployment rate of 6 percent) is prosperity for the non-white. . . . Therefore, perhaps, it is appropriate to say that whites fluctuate between prosperity and recession but Negroes fluctuate between depression and great depression."[47] Three factors cause even these grim data to underestimate the problem. First, black jobhold-

[43] Unscrupulous real-estate dealers exacerbate these fears. For evidence challenging the widely believed notion that black neighbors lower property values, see Luigi Laurenti, *Property Values and Race* (Berkeley and Los Angeles: University of California Press, 1960).

[44] T. F. Pettigrew, "Black and White Attitudes toward Race and Housing," in Pettigrew, *Racial Discrimination in the United States*, pp. 92–126.

[45] U.S. Bureau of the Census, *The Social and Economic Status of the Black Population in the United States, 1973*, p. 54.

[46] *Ibid.*, p. 17.

[47] Rashi Fein, "An Economic and Social Profile of the Negro American," in T. Parsons and K. Clark (eds.), *The Negro American* (Boston: Houghton Mifflin, 1966), pp. 114–115.

ers are more often underemployed than white job holders, and less frequently hold jobs commensurate with their education. Second, blacks typically do not earn as much as whites in comparable jobs. Third, a disproportionately high percentage of working-age blacks withdraw from the labor force in despair and are not officially recorded as unemployed.

Economic and social data reveal an ominous trend that is masked by aggregate statistics: Some blacks have made significant gains, while many others are slipping further behind.[48] Those blacks less scarred by past deprivations have been in a position to take advantage of racial changes. There is, however, another black America that is less fortunate. Now constituting somewhat over half of all blacks, this group has not been significantly touched by racial change. Progress in improving the economic position of blacks depends upon reaching this other black America.

Blatant racial discrimination is not the sole cause of black America's economic plight. Relative to whites, blacks more often reside in the South, have received fewer years and a poorer quality of education, and form a younger segment of the labor force—all characteristics apart from race that contribute to economic marginality. Moreover, the central cities of the North and West, where blacks are concentrated, are losing manufacturing jobs. Implicit in these factors are forms of indirect economic discrimination. For instance, since most blacks cannot move to the suburbs, they cannot follow the manufacturing jobs that are shifting from central city to outer ring. Nevertheless, the major barrier is still direct and obvious job discrimination by both employers and unions. Attacks upon blatant discrimination in employment also offer more hope for short-term effects than the slower, though ultimately necessary, alterations in the indirect contributors.[49]

Economic remedies Affirmative measures in this realm can take place only within a context of vigorous economic growth for the nation. A tight labor market is essential. Following the severe recession of the 1970s, much of the anticipated expansion will come in the professional, technical, and white-collar sectors of the labor market. This will be helpful for trained blacks, but what about the poorly-educated "other black America"? There must also be substantial increases in occupations requiring less training, and these increases must be made still greater by legislation. This would not involve degrading, "makework" employment. Rather, these jobs are urgently needed now to upgrade public services in health, education, welfare and home care, protection, beautification, and sanitation. The first needed remedy, then, is for legislation at all levels of government to create public-service employment.

A second legislative direction entails effective statutes against discrimina-

[48] Andrew Brimmer, "The Negro in the National Economy," in J. Davis (ed.), *The Negro Reference Book* (Englewood Cliffs, N.J.: Prentice-Hall, 1966), pp. 261–271.

[49] O. D. Duncan, "Patterns of Occupational Mobility among Negro Men," and S. Lieberson and G. V. Fuguitt, "Negro-White Occupational Differences in the Absence of Discrimination," in Pettigrew, *Racial Discrimination in the United States*, pp. 167–206.

tion in employment. Title VII of the 1964 Civil Rights Act is directed to this problem, but it has proven only partially effective because of understaffed enforcement based largely on responding to complaints. The necessity of broad, patterned enforcement points up again the systemic nature of racial problems in America. This suggests further remedies: the creation of metropolitan job councils combining business, labor, and government interests in order "to plan, coordinate and implement local programs to increase jobs"; the federalization of public employment services, which are now ineffectively operated by states on federal funds; and the design of new mass-transit systems so that black workers have direct access to the increasingly suburban centers of metropolitan employment.

Two further directions commend themselves: retraining and guaranteed income levels. The Manpower Retraining Act needs to be revised to lower its entrance requirements (it has often rejected those who need it most) and to furnish relocation funds so that the retrained can move to where the jobs are. And private employers could be given either direct federal grants or tax credits in direct proportion to their ability to raise an impoverished worker's income.[50]

The present patchwork of welfare programs has clearly failed, and blacks are prominent among those who suffer from the failure. As an alternative, nationwide guaranteed-income plans have been proposed. The most promising is the "negative income tax plan."[51] All Americans would file an annual income tax statement, but those falling below stated poverty levels would receive graduated funds from the federal government. An equitable negative income tax system could encourage employment and keep families intact, both of which present welfare programs often discourage. The negative income tax can also be simpler to administer, avoid the indignities of many present procedures, and include all segments of the poor. The plan has been successfully tested in a number of communities. Together with local and better-designed welfare programs, the negative income tax could be an important step toward the elimination of poverty in the world's richest country.

Educational Trends

No institution is more central to the full inclusion of blacks into American society than public education. Yet problems mount faster than progress in this realm. While years of formal education for blacks as well as their percentages in school at each age level have risen, the problem of the racial segregation of schools persists.

The extent and causes of segregated education   Under federal court pressure, school desegregation gains were registered during the late 1960s. The

[50] L. C. Thurow, "An Incentive System for Upgrading Impoverished Workers," in Pettigrew, *Racial Discrimination in the United States,* pp. 360–367.

[51] James Tobin, "On Improving the Economic Status of the Negro," in Parsons and Clark, *op. cit.,* pp. 451–471.

proportion of black children in all-black public schools declined from 40 percent in 1968 to 12 percent in 1971, and the proportion of those in predominantly white schools rose during these years from 18 to 44 percent. Today, there is considerably more educational desegregation in the South than in the North. This regional shift reflects the widespread phenomenon of northern urban segregation, from big cities like Chicago to smaller ones like Des Moines.

There are four major causes for urban school segregation: (1) trends in racial demography, (2) the anti-metropolitan nature of school-district organization, (3) the effects of private schools, and (4) intentional separation of the races. The first two of these causes become apparent when we compare school-district organization with the demographic shifts already discussed. There are about 16,000 school districts in America that typically cut suburbs sharply off from central cities; yet suburbs continue to grow ever more white while central cities grow ever more black. And housing trends offer no hope for substantial relief from this pattern in the next decade. Thus, America would face an enormous problem of school segregation even if there were no intra-district separation by race.

In fact, however, there is also rigorous racial separation within school districts. Central-city segregation is heightened by the absorption of many white school children into private schools. However, much of the segregation is due to explicit and cynical efforts by politicians and school administrators.

The effects of segregated education   Most research indicates that black children tend to achieve better in predominantly white schools than in predominantly black ones, while white children tend to achieve as well in predominantly white schools as in all-white schools. The large national study of the U.S. Office of Education popularly called the Coleman Report suggests that these effects derive largely from the fact that predominantly white schools usually afford their students a more middle-class climate, one characterized by high aspirations and expectations.[52] At any rate, blacks trained in desegregated schools apparently more often finish high school, attend college, and secure white-collar jobs than other blacks.[53]

The benefits of interracial schools are not limited to academic achievement. Interracial attitudes and behavior are improved among both black and white students by positive contact. Thus, white students who attend public schools with blacks are the least likely to prefer all-white classrooms and all-white "close friends."[54] Likewise, black adults who attended desegregated schools as children themselves tend to send their children to such schools more than comparable black adults who attended only segregated schools as children. Similarly, white adults with desegregated schooling differ from comparable

---

[52] James S. Coleman et al., *Equality of Educational Opportunity* (Washington, D.C.: Government Printing Office, 1966).

[53] R. L. Crain, "School Integration and Occupational Achievement of Negroes," in Pettigrew, *Racial Discrimination in the United States*, pp. 206–224.

[54] Coleman, *op. cit.*, p. 333.

whites in their greater willingness to reside in an interracial neighborhood, to have their children attend interracial schools, and to have black friends.[55] Interracial schools appear to prepare their products for an interracial world; segregated schools, white or black, do not.

Two practical caveats must be offered concerning this research. First, these demonstrated benefits of interracial schools are strongest for the early grades, where actual desegregation occurs least. Second, a distinction must be made between merely "desegregated" and truly integrated schools. The former involve merely mixed student bodies and faculties, while the latter also involve cross-racial acceptance and optimal conditions for contact. Not surprisingly, the benefits of interracial schools are minimized in desegregated schools, maximized in integrated schools.

Educational remedies   Small and large ghetto situations must be differentiated. The small ghetto occurs in a city whose public-school population is less than one-fifth black. Its high schools, and often its junior high schools, are naturally desegregated. But its elementary schools, the most critical level for racial contact, are generally segregated. With good faith, small ghettos can be totally desegregated within their districts by applying a combination of proven techniques: (1) district-wide redrawing of school lines to maximize racial balance, (2) the pairing of white and black schools, and (3) careful placement of new schools. Two additional devices serve to desegregate the junior- and senior-high levels: (4) the alteration of "feeder" arrangements from elementary grades to higher grades in order to maximize racial balance and (5) the conversion of schools into district-wide specialized institutions.

The real problems occur in the large-ghetto situation, where small-ghetto techniques are mere bandaids at best. It is here that the four major causes of central-city school segregation must be carefully considered in order to establish criteria for effective remedies. Thus, desegregation measures in school systems with large ghettos must be metropolitan in scope; and they must encourage cooperation not only between central-city and suburban school systems but between public and private systems as well.

THE SITUATIONAL APPROACH

Mere contact between two groups does not necessarily improve relations between them. Think of the South, where the greatest amount of sheer contact between black and white Americans has occurred and there was no conspicuous development of acceptance between the races. Similar observations could be made of Chicano-Anglo contact in the Southwest. It almost appears as if the more two groups get together, the more prejudice and conflict is generated.

[55] U.S. Commission on Civil Rights, *Racial Isolation in the Public Schools*, Vol. 1 (Washington, D.C.: Government Printing Office, 1967), pp. 111–113.

Yet this conclusion, too, would be fallacious. The crucial questions are: What types of contact lead to greater tolerance and trust? And what types lead to greater prejudice and distrust?

The Conditions of Optimal Contact

Allport concluded that four situational factors are of crucial significance.[56] Prejudice is reduced and conflict minimized when two groups (1) possess equal status in the situation, (2) seek common goals, (3) are cooperatively dependent upon each other rather than in competition, and (4) interact with the positive support of authorities, law, or custom. Allport's principles are seen in operation in racially integrated situations. For example, in the late 1940s President Harry Truman ordered American merchant ships to end racial segregation and discrimination. Soon after, white seamen tended to hold racial attitudes in direct relation to how many voyages they had taken with equal-status black American seamen—the more desegregated voyages, the more positive their attitudes.[57] Interracial bonds built through optimal contact situations like this can withstand even severe crises. While black and white mobs raged in the streets during Detroit's 1943 race riot, desegregated co-workers, university students, and neighbors of long standing carried on their interracial lives side by side.[58]

Mention of neighborhood desegregation introduces the best research evidence available. Repeated investigations have found that racially desegregated living in public housing developments that meet all four of Allport's criteria sharply reduces intergroup prejudice among both black and white neighbors.[59] These same investigations demonstrate that living in segregated, even though otherwise identical, housing developments structures interracial contact so that bitterness is often enhanced.

Limitations of the Effects of Optimal Contact

Another study found that white steelworkers in the northern United States generally approved of the racial desegregation of their union to the point of sharing all union facilities and electing blacks to high office; yet they also

[56] Allport, *op. cit.*, Ch. 16.

[57] I. N. Brophy, "The Luxury of Anti-Negro Prejudice," *Public Opinion Quarterly*, Vol. 9 (Winter 1945–1946), pp. 456–466. An alternative explanation for the results of such studies is that the least prejudiced people sought out interracial contact. Many of these studies, however, rule out the operation of this self-selection factor.

[58] A. M. Lee and N. D. Humphrey, *Race Riot* (New York: Dryden, 1943), pp. 97, 130, 140.

[59] M. Deutsch and Mary Collins, *Interracial Housing: A Psychological Evaluation of a Social Experiment* (Minneapolis: University of Minnesota Press, 1951); D. M. Wilner et al., *Human Relations in Interracial Housing: A Study of the Contact Hypothesis* (Minneapolis: University of Minnesota Press, 1955); E. Works, "The Negro Minority Group," *American Journal of Sociology*, Vol. 67 (July 1961), pp. 47–52.

sternly opposed the desegregation of their all-white neighborhoods.[60] In this case, as in many others, institutional structures limited the effects of contact. Interracial attitudes and behavior had changed in the work situation, with the support of the union, but these changes had not generalized to the neighborhood situation, where a community organization resisted desegregation.

In other words, intergroup contact first affects attitudes that are specifically involved in the new situation. But such contact does not mean that a person's whole attitudinal structure will crumble unless other situations change too. Most of us are adept at "re-fencing" our prejudices and stereotypes. We meet members of a group we are prejudiced against, and we explain away the fact that we like them by insisting that they are "different." Should integration in many realms of American life finally become a reality, there could be more generalization from one situation to another.

The Power of Situational Norms

Modifying prejudiced attitudes is only a beginning, for the central problem is to eliminate discriminatory behavior. To be sure, individual prejudice often lies behind it, but the power of what others in a situation expect of us makes it common to find social circumstances where bigoted individuals do not discriminate and other circumstances where unbigoted individuals do.

There are many examples of the power of situational norms in race relations. In the coal mining county of McDowell, West Virginia, black and white miners once followed a traditional pattern of desegregation below the ground and segregation above the ground.[61] Obviously, the West Virginian miners did not change their racial attitudes each time they went into the mines or came out of them. Attitudes and behavior need not always be in agreement; particular situations can structure how most people behave in spite of the attitudes they may harbor.

Sociologists were first alerted to this by a 1934 study of verbal versus actual discrimination.[62] A traveling Chinese couple stopped at 250 sleeping and eating establishments across the United States. They were refused service only once. Later, the same places received mail inquiries as to whether they served "members of the Chinese race." About half did not reply; of those that did, over 90 percent announced they did not accommodate Chinese guests. A control sample of comparable, unvisited establishments yielded similar results.

---

[60] D. C. Reitzes, "The Role of Organizational Structures: Union vs. Neighborhood in a Tension Situation," *Journal of Social Issues*, Vol. 9, No. 1 (1953), pp. 37–44.

[61] R. D. Minard, "Race Relations in the Pocahontas Coal Field," *Journal of Social Issues*, Vol. 8, No. 1 (1952), pp. 29–44.

[62] R. T. Lapiere, "Attitudes Versus Actions," *Social Forces*, Vol. 13 (December 1934), pp. 230–237.

This phenomenon was repeated during the early fifties in 11 restaurants in a northeastern suburb.[63] Three women, two white and one black, went to the establishments and received exemplary service. Two weeks later, requests were sent to the restaurants for reservations for a similar group. Ten of the letters went unanswered, and follow-up phone calls met great resistance. Control calls for all-white parties led to 10 reservations. It is more difficult to reject another human being face to face than through impersonal letters and phone calls.

Laws Can Change the Hearts and Minds of Men

Within this perspective, a reappraisal can be made of the old saw, "Laws cannot change the hearts and minds of men." An early case in point was the 1945 anti-discrimination employment legislation enacted by New York State. This law led to the initial hiring of blacks as sales clerks in New York City department stores. Two investigators conducted separate tests of the effects of this law-induced desegregation. One study of white sales personnel revealed that those who had experienced the new equal-status job contact with blacks held more favorable attitudes toward interracial interaction in the work situation.[64] Once again, however, the initial effects of this contact did not extend beyond the immediate situation; equal-status clerks were not more accepting of blacks in eating and residential situations. The other investigation questioned customers.[65] Their responses revealed widespread acceptance of this legally-required racial change. They were concerned largely with shopping conveniently and efficiently. Many hesitated to challenge the firm *fait accompli,* and for many the new pattern was consistent with their belief in the American creed of equal opportunity.

Contrary to the old adage, then, laws *can* change the hearts and minds of men. They do so through a vital intermediate step. Laws first act to modify behavior, and this modified behavior in turn changes the participants' attitudes. Notice that this is the opposite sequence commonly believed to be the most effective method of attitude change. When people are convinced to be less prejudiced through informational and good-will campaigns, conventional reasoning asserts, then they will discriminate less. To be sure, this sequence sometimes occurs. But the preponderance of social psychological evidence indicates that behaving differently is more often the precursor to thinking differently.

[63] B. Kutner et al., "Verbal Attitudes and Overt Behavior Involving Racial Prejudice," *Journal of Abnormal and Social Psychology,* Vol. 47 (July 1952), pp. 649–652.

[64] J. Harding and R. Hogrefe, "Attitudes of White Department Store Employees Toward Negro Co-workers," *Journal of Social Issues,* Vol. 8, No. 1 (1952), pp. 18–28.

[65] G. Saenger and Emily Gilbert, "Customer Reactions to the Integration of Negro Sales Personnel," *International Journal of Opinion and Attitude Research,* Vol. 4 (Spring 1950), pp. 57–76.

THE PERSONALITY APPROACH

The Three Functions of Prejudice

Attitudes, prejudiced and otherwise, serve three vital personality functions.[66] First, there is the *object appraisal* function; attitudes aid in understanding "reality." As societies and cultures change, the social consensus as to what constitutes "reality" shifts and attitudes shift accordingly. In the second function of attitudes, *social adjustment*, attitudes aid socially by contributing to the individual's identification with various "reference groups."[67] They help people to conform to what is expected of them. Finally, attitudes can reduce anxiety by serving an *externalization* function. This occurs when an individual senses an analogy between a perceived event and some unresolved inner problem; one then adopts an attitude toward the event which is a transformed version of one's way of dealing with the inner difficulty. In short, people project their personality problems onto the external world through particular attitudes. Thus, if you have sexual problems, you may regard blacks as dangerously hypersexed. The most fashionable psychological theories of prejudice—frustration-aggression, psychoanalytic, and authoritarianism—all deal chiefly with the externalization process. The last of these, authoritarianism, has received massive research emphasis.

The Authoritarian Personality

Personality specialists intensively studied the personality dynamics of anti-Semites in the United States during the 1940s.[68] They found a syndrome of personality traits, labeled *authoritarianism,* that consistently differentiated highly anti-Semitic and ethnocentric individuals from others. Central to the syndrome is anti-intraception, the refusal to look inside oneself and a general lack of insight into one's own behavior and feelings. Authoritarians refuse to accept their own emotions and try to deny them. For instance, as children authoritarians may have been punished frequently by stern fathers and in turn felt intense hatred for them. Unable to express these aggressive feelings for fear of further punishment, authoritarians found them threatening and unacceptable, denied them, and began to project them onto others. If authoritarians feel hatred for their fathers, they see hatred not in themselves but in the dangerous outside world.

Consequently, authoritarians typically convey an idealized picture of their

---

[66] M. B. Smith, J. S. Bruner, and R. W. White, *Opinion and Personality* (New York: Wiley, 1956).

[67] A reference group supplies standards that an individual may use to guide his own behavior and with which he may compare his own position in life. Note that a reference group is not necessarily a membership group. See H. H. Hyman and Eleanor Singer, *Readings in Reference Group Theory and Research* (New York: Free Press, 1968), and Robert K. *Merton Social Theory and Social Structure* (New York: Free Press, 1968), Chs. 10 and 11.

[68] T. W. Adorno et al., *The Authoritarian Personality* (New York: Harper & Row, 1950).

parents as absolutely perfect. Generalizing this unrealistic view to include other authorities, authoritarians come to view the world in good-bad, up-and-down power terms. They are generally outwardly submissive toward those they see as authorities with power over them, and aggressive toward those they see as beneath them in status. This hierarchical view of authority naturally produces prejudice against minority groups; indeed, prejudice becomes for such individuals a *crutch* upon which to limp through life. Lacking insight into their inner feelings, they project their own unacceptable impulses on the minorities whom they regard as beneath them.[69]

The Conforming Personality

The psychoanalytically inspired theory of the authoritarian personality is a valuable contribution to an understanding of intergroup relations. But the emphasis upon the externalization function of prejudice has caused neglect of the equally important function of social adjustment. Most white Americans who hold anti-black opinions and participate in discriminatory actions do not exhibit the authoritarian personality syndrome. For many, anti-black views and behavior are not nearly so expressive as they are socially adaptive in a racist society. In contrast to the deeply rooted bigotry of authoritarianism, the bigotry of *conformity* requires prejudice as a social entrance ticket. The conforming bigot wants to be accepted by people important to him; if these people are anti-black, he reflects their attitudes.

Notice two significant differences between the crutch and conformity varieties of intolerance. Those who are anti-black for largely conformity reasons have antipathy only for those groups that it is fashionable to dislike; their prejudice does not spread to out-groups in general as does that of authoritarians. They follow the path of least social resistance, for they need to be liked rather than to hate. Moreover, conformity prejudice is not so rooted in childhood socialization. Thus, as social change proceeds and what is expected by others is altered, conforming bigots shed their prejudice with relative ease. They continue to conform, but the customs and norms that guide their beliefs and actions change. Conformity prejudice makes possible at the individual level the power of situational norms to determine racial attitudes and behavior at the social level.

The Prevalence of Prejudice Types

Do most white Americans *need,* in an authoritarian-personality sense, anti-black prejudice? Or do most white Americans who harbor anti-black attitudes do so largely in order to follow racist expectations? Of course, the two types

[69] Note that this description fits only the authoritarian of the political right. Authoritarians are also found on the political left; with equal dogmatism, they reject all authorities and evince condescending identification with minorities. The politics of the two authoritarian types may be polar opposites, but the personality style remains strikingly the same.

of prejudice as described are ideal types and seldom seen in pure form. Typically, prejudice weaves together elements of both types. Yet it is still feasible to ascertain roughly the prevalence of persons who are relatively authoritarian in their orientation against blacks as opposed to those who are relatively more conforming.

Allport estimated back in 1954 that roughly "four-fifths of the American population harbors enough antagonism toward minority groups to influence their daily conduct."[70] This crude figure includes both types of prejudice and varies widely across regional, age, and social-class groupings; it varies also according to the research question and method employed. Yet Allport's estimate continues to receive research support. Furthermore, the unprejudiced fifth noted by Allport appears to be matched by a prejudiced fifth motivated largely by authoritarian personality needs. These are the citizens whose racial beliefs are so salient that they will follow them even when they conflict with other values. They can be counted on to vote against any civil rights referendum, to favor political candidates who run on openly anti-black platforms,[71] and to answer survey questions about minority groups with prejudicial responses.[72]

Roughly speaking, then, three-fifths of white Americans may well be conforming bigots. On issues that face considerable societal disapproval, such as the bussing of children to interracial schools, most of these citizens will join the crutch-types in forming a majority resistant to change. On issues that win wide societal approval, such as the 1964 Civil Rights Act after the assassination of President John Kennedy, most of these citizens will join the unprejudiced in forming a majority favorable to change. It is they, then, who are primarily responsible for the breathtaking swings in the national mood on racial change. This analysis suggests that persons who approximate the conformity-type bigots probably outnumber those who believe and act consistently on race, including both those who approximate crutch-type bigots and those who favor racial change. Even in the South, there is evidence that conformity prejudice against blacks is considerably more common than authoritarian prejudice.[73]

Two implications flow from this personality analysis. On the one hand, it suggests that white American racial opinion is more flexible than it might at

[70] Allport, *op. cit.*, p. 78.

[71] George Wallace received as much as 22-percent survey support as a Presidential candidate in 1968 and secured 14 percent of the total vote. Pettigrew, *Racially Separate or Together?* Ch. 11.

[72] Thus, 18 percent believed in December of 1963 that "white people should have the first chance at any kind of job"—the most extreme item in Sheatsley's pro-integration scale. At the other extreme, only 27 percent *disagreed* with the statement "Negroes shouldn't push themselves where they're not wanted." P. B. Sheatsley, "White Attitudes toward the Negro," in Parsons and Clark, *op. cit.*, pp. 303–324. Similar findings emerge from other surveys: Hazel Erskine, "The Polls: Recent Opinion on Racial Problems," *Public Opinion Quarterly*, Vol. 32 (Winter 1968–1969), pp. 696–703; A. Campbell, *White Attitudes Toward Black People* (Ann Arbor, Mich.: Institute for Social Research, 1971).

[73] T. F. Pettigrew, "Social Psychology and Research on Desegregation," in Pettigrew, *Racially Separate or Together?* Ch. 7.

first appear. If major socio-cultural changes create optimal conditions for increased interracial contact, racial attitudes could continue to improve as they have since 1944.[74] Efforts toward needed structural changes should not be deterred by the initial opposition of a majority of white Americans. On the other hand, the strong possibility that the anti-black sentiments of about one-fifth of white America reflects, in varying measure, deep externalizing functions should give us pause. Over 20 million adult citizens who approximate crutch-types form a critical mass for societal conflict.

THE PHENOMENOLOGICAL APPROACH

Two Outgroup Stereotypes

In broad psychoanalytic terms,[75] two contrasting types of outgroup stereotypes emerge throughout the world. One type is rooted in superego concerns, with the outgroup stereotyped as mercenary, ambitious, sly, and clannish. The other type is rooted in id concerns, with the outgroup stereotyped as superstitious, lazy, happy-go-lucky, ignorant, dirty, and sexually uninhibited. In the United States, the prejudiced person typically projects his own superego sins of ambition and deceit on to Jewish Americans and his own id sins of the flesh on to black Americans.[76]

This psychoanalytic distinction between superego and id stereotypes is applicable to a variety of cross-cultural situations. Thus, outgroups assigned a superego stigma are usually merchants who are not native to an area—middlemen caught between the landed and the laboring classes, like the medieval European Jews. Indeed, the Chinese merchants of Malaysia and Indonesia are often called the "Jews of Asia," and the Muslim Indian merchants of East Africa the "Jews of Africa." Likewise, the id stigma is invoked around the world for groups that are found on the bottom of the social structure. In Europe, Gypsies and southern Italians are often the targets.[77] In America, both blacks and Mexican Americans inherit the id stigma.

The Slow Fading of the Id Stereotype

The id stigma branded upon blacks has begun to recede. Evidence comes from repeated surveys of the National Opinion Research Center asking: "In general, do you think Negroes are as intelligent as white people—that is, can they learn

[74] *Ibid.*, Chapter 8.

[75] Calvin S. Hall, *Primer of Freudian Psychology* (New York: New American Library, 1973).

[76] Adorno et al., *op. cit.*; Bruno Bettelheim and Morris Janowitz, *Social Change and Prejudice* (New York: Harper & Row, 1964).

[77] The superego outgroup pattern also typically involves a middle-man minority that is separatist in an expanding nationalist state that emphasizes unity. S. Stryker, "Social Structure and Prejudice," *Social Problems*, Vol. 6 (Spring 1959), pp. 340–354.

just as well if they are given the same education and training?" In 1942 only 42 percent of white respondents answered "yes." By 1946 this figure had risen to 52 percent; by 1956 it had climbed to 77 percent, where it has remained.[78]

To see how this shift is reflected in the mass media, compare contemporary materials with the magazines of four decades ago. While occasionally portraying them neutrally or as "credits to their race," *Life* in the late 1930s overwhelmingly presented blacks either as musical, primitive, amusing, or religious, or as violent and criminal; occupationally, they were usually pictured as servants, athletes, entertainers, or unemployed. Pictures included a black choir at a graveside funeral and an all-black chain gang. Dialect was common. Descriptions of blacks dancing included such terms as "barbaric," "jungle," and "native gusto."[79] Such material would not be acceptable today.

This is not to imply that the id stereotype has faded completely. A national survey in 1966 found that bedrock racist beliefs of black inferiority still persisted not only among the "authoritarian fifth" but also among many of those whose prejudice was of the conforming type. Thus, 52 percent of whites still believed that blacks "smell different" (down from 60% in 1963), and 50 percent that they "have looser morals" (down from 55% in 1963).[80]

As the stereotyped racial views slowly fade, so do white attitudes favoring the maintenance of racial discrimination. National samples have been asked repeatedly, "Do you think white students and Negro students should go to the same schools, or to separate schools?" In 1942, only 30 percent of white Americans favored "same schools." By 1956, the percentage had risen to 49; by 1963 to 63; by 1965 to 67; by 1970 to 74. In 1972, 86 percent answered that the races should go to the same schools.[81] Furthermore, white racial attitude change has been greatest in the South and has typically *followed* school and other types of desegregation in the community.[82] Social trends have simply forced a realignment in the views of blacks held by whites. The racist stereotype will continue to recede in direct relation to how dysfunctional it becomes for American society.

THE STIMULUS-OBJECT APPROACH

Within the context supplied by the previous five approaches, we now look at black Americans, first as victims of prejudice and discrimination, and next as protesting reactors to oppression.

[78] H. H. Hyman and P. B. Sheatsley, "Attitudes toward Desegregation," *Scientific American*, Vol. 211 (July 1964), pp. 16–23.

[79] The author is indebted to Dr. Patricia Pajonas for her analysis of all racial material appearing in 34 issues of *Life* sampled from November 1936 through March 1938.

[80] W. Brink and L. Harris, *Black and White: A Study of U.S. Racial Attitudes Today* (New York: Simon and Schuster, 1967), p. 136.

[81] A. M. Greeley and P. B. Sheatsley, "Attitudes Toward Racial Integration," in L. Rainwater (ed.), *Social Problems and Public Policy: Inequality and Justice* (Chicago: Aldine, 1974), pp. 241–250; Hyman and Sheatsley, *op. cit.*

[82] Hyman and Sheatsley, *op. cit.*

The "Negro" Role

Black-white contact in the United States has generally been characterized by a rigid differentiation of inferior and superior status. Such contact has reinforced racial stereotypes and been the means of imposing the oppressive racial system's effects upon individual blacks. One useful way to conceptualize such racial interaction involves role theory.[83] Discriminatory encounters between whites and blacks require that both "play the game." Whites must act out the role of the "superior." By direct action or subtle cue, they must convey the expectation that they will be treated with deference. For their part, blacks must, if traditional norms are to be obeyed, act out the role of the "inferior"; they must play the social role of "Negro." Should they refuse to play the game, they would be judged by many whites as "not knowing their place," and harsh sanctions could follow.

The socially stigmatized role of "Negro" is the critical feature of having dark skin in the United States. At the personality level, such enforced role adoption can divide an individual black both from other human beings and from himself. Of course, all social roles, necessary as they are, hinder forthright social interaction to some extent. An employer and employee may never begin to understand each other as complete human beings unless they break through the constraints of their role relationships. Likewise, whites and blacks can never communicate as equals unless they break through the role barriers. As long as racial roles are maintained, both parties find it difficult to perceive the humanity behind the facade. Many whites unthinkingly confuse the role of "Negro" with the people who must play this role. Conversely, many blacks confuse the role of "white man" with whites.

Intimately associated with this impairment of human relatedness is an impairment of the individual's acceptance and understanding of himself. Both whites and blacks can mistake their own roles for an essential part of themselves. Whites can easily flatter themselves into believing that they are in fact "superior"; after all, doesn't the deferential behavior of the role-playing black confirm it? Blacks may also accept the mythology, for doesn't the imperious behavior of the role-playing white confirm their "inferiority"?

These ideas are supported by a large body of social-psychological research. This research demonstrates that role playing has the power to change deeply held attitudes, values, and even self-concepts. Moreover, remarkable changes of this kind have been rendered experimentally by temporary role adoptions of a trivial nature. Imagine, then, the depth of the effects of having to play a lifelong role that touches most aspects of daily living. In short, racial roles have profound psychological as well as behavioral effects upon those who play them.

[83] T. F. Pettigrew, *A Profile of the Negro American* (Princeton, N.J.: Van Nostrand, 1964).

Relative Deprivation and Black Unrest

The deferential nature of the "Negro" role raises questions about assertive black protest behavior. Why did black unrest come to a boil in the 1960s? And how were the young in particular so able to break through the constraints of the accommodating "Negro" role?

Answers to these questions are suggested by the socio-cultural changes black Americans have been undergoing as a people. As noted earlier, the latest product of this dramatic transformation from southern peasant to northern urbanite is a second- and third-generation northern-born youth. This "newest new Negro" is relatively free of the principal social controls recognized by his parents and grandparents—the restraints of an extended kinship system, a conservative religion, and an acceptance of white supremacy. During his short life the young black adult has witnessed the initial dismantling of the formal structure of white supremacy. Conventional wisdom holds that such an experience should lead to a highly satisfied generation. Social psychology tells us precisely the opposite is to be anticipated.

The past three decades of black American history constitute an almost classic case of "relative deprivation."[84] Mass unrest among oppressed groups has reoccurred throughout history after long periods of improvement followed by abrupt periods of reversal. This pattern derives from three revolt-stirring conditions that are triggered by long-term improvements: (1) Living conditions of the dominant group typically advance faster than those of the subordinate group; (2) the aspirations of the subordinate group climb far more rapidly than actual changes occur; (3) there is a broadening of comparative reference groups for the subordinate group.

Each of these conditions typified the black situation in the 1960s. (1) Though the past few decades have witnessed the most rapid gains in black American history, these gains have generally not kept pace with those of white America. (2) Public-opinion surveys document the swiftly rising aspirations of black people. Finally, (3) black Americans have greatly expanded their relevant reference groups in recent years; wealthy inhabitants of the richest country on earth are now routinely adopted as the appropriate standard by which to judge one's condition. The second component of unrest—a sudden reversal—was supplied when the Vietnam War caused a reversal of black economic gains. Little wonder, then, that America's racial crisis reached the combustion point in the late sixties.

But what about the 1970s? The Nixon and Ford Administrations severely cut back federal initiatives in civil rights. The hopes and aspirations of black people diminish, understandably, as the nation turns its attention to economic and other concerns. Protests and riots have almost disappeared, as relative deprivation theory predicts that they will in such circumstances. This reduction in collective action does not mean that blacks are satisfied with their lot.

[84] T. F. Pettigrew, *Racially Separate or Together?* Ch. 7.

National survey data show growing alienation from government among black Americans. Less estranged than whites from the nation's government in 1964 and 1968, black faith sank precipitously during the first Nixon term, and in 1972 reached the lowest point recorded for any group in the 14 years of the survey.[85] Soon the United States will have to return to the search for a solution to its oldest domestic problem.

MEXICAN- AND ANGLO-AMERICAN RELATIONS

We turn now from intergroup problems based on race to those based largely on culture and national origin. Mexican Americans, comprising over 6 million people, are the second largest American minority group facing widespread discrimination. They are the largest Spanish-origin group in the nation. Despite their numbers, however, their problems have been, until recently, among the most neglected of America's intergroup concerns. This neglect is attributable in part to prejudice, in part to the group's diversity across place, generation, and social class, and in part to their concentration in five southwestern states (California, Arizona, Colorado, New Mexico, and Texas), although migrant labor pockets occur in the Midwest and Northwest, with large settlements in Chicago, Detroit, and Gary, Indiana. To understand these "forgotten Americans," we shall again utilize Allport's six approaches.

The Historical Approach

1598–1853   The diversity of the Spanish-American population and its concentration in certain areas derive from a complex history that stretches back over four centuries. Spanish colonization via Mexico in the Southwest began in 1598 just north of Santa Fe. The next two centuries witnessed almost constant warfare between the Spanish settlers and the local Indians. First the Pueblo villagers resisted the seizure of their river valleys, demands for tribute, and induction into servitude; later the nomadic Apaches, Utes, and Comanches raided Spanish settlements.[86] This long conflict helped to limit Spanish expansion.

In California Spanish colonization did not begin until 1769. During the next 52 years, under Spanish rule, the Franciscan religious order established 21 missions, spread north from San Diego about every 30 miles. The Church came to control most of the fertile land, with local Indians working it.[87]

---

[85] Institute for Social Research, "Blacks' Trust in Government Falls Sharply," in Pettigrew, *Racial Discrimination in the United States*, pp. 329–333.

[86] W. Moquin (ed.), *A Documentary History of the Mexican Americans* (New York: Praeger, 1971), pp. 43–58; D. W. Meinig, *Southwest: Three Peoples in Geographical Change 1600–1970* (New York: Oxford, 1971), pp. 14–15; E. R. Stoddard, *Mexican Americans* (New York: Random House, 1973), pp. 8–9.

[87] Moquin, *op. cit.;* Stoddard, *op. cit.*, pp. 15–16.

The dominant characteristic of these Spanish communities was isolation. Sparsely settled and weakly linked, the southwestern settlements were far from the capitals of both Mexico and the United States. Spanish development consisted largely of four south-to-north corridors that followed rivers and mountain passes: from the Rio Grande River to east Texas, from El Paso to northern New Mexico and southern Colorado, from Mexico to Tucson, and up the California coast. East-to-west travel was practically nonexistent before gold was discovered in northern California in 1848. This isolation bred diversity.[88]

The advent of Mexican independence from Spain in 1821 initiated change. The new regime made large land grants, encouraged American immigration into east Texas, and, in 1834, secularized the California missions and their vast landholdings. Anglo-Americans began to trade with Mexico, using the Santa Fe Trail or the sea route to California, and to settle in Texas.[89] Soon armed conflict burst forth, leading to the successful Texas revolution of 1836, the United States' annexation of Texas in 1845, the Mexican-American War, and the 1848 Treaty of Guadalupe Hidalgo, which also added territory to the United States. Five years later the Gadsden Purchase added more, rich in copper, but created an unnatural border.[90]

Note that many descendants of Spanish settlers in the New World became American citizens by virtue of conquest and annexation rather than by immigration. Today, especially in New Mexico, members of this group commonly call themselves "Spanish Americans" to denote the fact that their southwestern heritage extends back to before Mexican independence. Anglos were the immigrants and later the conquerors.

1853–1909   The latter half of the nineteenth century witnessed continued border conflict in Texas, rapid growth of the Anglo population in the Southwest, and declining economic prospects there for Mexican Americans of all strata.

American dominance in the Southwest was effected largely through force of arms. Understandably, there was Mexican resistance. It continued for 75 years after the 1848 Treaty, especially along the Mexico-Texas border, and is an important historical legacy for Chicano-Anglo relations today. "Bandits" to many Anglos, "*guerrilleros*" to many Chicanos, one of the best-remembered of the Mexican fighters is Juan Cortina. Beginning in 1859, Cortina led raids on

---

[88] L. Grebler et al., *The Mexican-American People: The Nation's Second Largest Minority* (New York: Free Press, 1970), p. 40; G. I. Sánchez, "History, Culture, and Education," in J. Samora (ed.), *La Raza: Forgotten Americans* (Notre Dame, Ind.: University of Notre Dame Press, 1966), pp. 5–6.

[89] "Anglo" will be used here in its broad southwestern sense: a Caucasian-American who is not of Spanish origin. "Chicano" includes all Mexican-Americans and will be discussed in detail later.

[90] J. W. Moore, *Mexican Americans* (Englewood Cliffs, N.J.: Prentice-Hall, 1970), pp. 37–38. Class as well as nationality was often involved in these changes. Though the fact is typically ignored by Texas Anglos today, prominent Spanish Americans were among the leaders of the Texas Republic and nine died defending the Alamo. Stoddard, *op. cit.*, pp. 4–5.

Texas for over a decade and urged Mexicans on both sides of the border to reclaim their lands and rout the *gringos*.[91] The American Civil War directly affected Texas and added to the conflict, and the U.S. Army, mobilized by the war, was used after 1865 for border duty and the "pacification" of Indians. Full U.S. control of Arizona did not come until the 1880s, when Indian resistance finally ended, and border "troubles" continued into the twentieth century.

The influx of Anglos into the Spanish regions of the Southwest occurred at different times in different regions. Anglos outnumbered Mexicans in east Texas as early as the 1820s and in northern California soon after the discovery of gold in 1848, but the remainder of the Southwest received Anglos in large numbers only after east-west rail connections were completed and the economy expanded. In 1887 alone the trains brought over 120,000 Anglo-Americans to California, 10 times the number of Mexicans then in southern California.[92] Mining in Arizona and New Mexico attracted many Anglos, and the spread of irrigated farming and cattle raising attracted others. By 1900, Anglos were a majority in every state except New Mexico, where Spanish Americans were a majority until 1950.

As Anglos poured in, the economic fortunes of Mexican Americans in the area suffered. Though the United States had agreed in the 1848 treaty to honor Spanish and Mexican land grants, the land began to shift to Anglo owner-ship. Trickery was a prominent factor but not an exclusive one. The old land grants were often interpreted as imprecise, and the American legal system varied sharply from Spanish practice. In California, the original landholders were obliged to sue the federal government to establish their claims. And economic stress forced southern California owners to begin selling their land even before Anglos arrived in large numbers. The invention of inexpensive barbed wire in the 1870s furthered the process. Large cattle and sheep ranchers began to enclose their vast holdings, driving out smaller ranchers. Public land use also exacerbated the problem. Large land grants were made to railroads. Over-grazing and poor farming and timber-cutting practices threatened the land. Subsequently, national forests were established from 1892 on until an eighth of all the land in New Mexico had passed into limited usage.[93] Small New Mexico villages were often cut off from their traditional grazing lands by these developments.

Irrigated farming and copper mining were both highly capitalized and labor-intensive. They left little room for small farmers and businessmen, either Chicano or Anglo. These economic forces combined to push Mexican Americans off their land and into work as unskilled laborers on the farms, in the mines, and on the railroads. They also meant that southwestern politics were generally conservative, dominated by big-business interests and, except for New Mexico, closed to Mexican-American concerns and participation.

[91] Stoddard, *op. cit.*, pp. 5–6; Moore, *op. cit.*, pp. 140–141.
[92] Moore, *op. cit.*, p. 19.
[93] Moore, *op. cit.*, p. 22; S. Steiner, *La Raza: The Mexican Americans* (New York: Harper & Row, 1970), pp. 1–26.

1909 to the present The Mexican Revolution, beginning in 1909, meant the end of near-chattel peonage for hundreds of thousands of Mexicans, now seeking employment. At the same time, rapid expansion of agriculture was occurring in the U.S. border states, and a large labor force was needed. Thus was triggered massive Mexican immigration into the Southwest. While recorded Mexican immigration for the first decade of the century was less than 25,000, it swelled to 174,000 between 1910 and 1919 and to almost half a million in the 1920s.[94] It declined sharply during the Great Depression and the 1940s, began to rise in the early 1950s, and has averaged about 40,000 a year ever since.

The immigration pattern is quite complex, given the border's accessibility and length and the different economic opportunities and wavering regulations of the two countries. There are legal and illegal entrants, permanent legal immigrants, temporary workers, even some who work in the United States and reside in Mexico. Considerable conflict has surrounded this complex pattern, for Mexican immigration into the United States is different from European immigration in important ways. It has rarely been restricted by formal quotas, but it has involved uniquely high rates of deportation and "an atmosphere of illegality." Even poor Mexicans can reach the border by rail, bus, and car, making "trial" stays and returning home relatively easy. And the economic exploitation of imported Mexican workers combined with the anti-unionization tactics of big agricultural and manufacturing interests have also given the process a controversial cast.[95]

The Great Depression of the 1930s hit Mexican Americans especially hard. Still more were driven to the cities, and efforts on their behalf by the Roosevelt Administration bound them to the Democratic party. When World War II production began in California, the incentive to go west to Los Angeles was even stronger for Mexican Americans than for others. The isolation that traced back to Spanish colonial days eroded. Concentrations in urban *barrios*, the experience of armed service throughout the world of almost a half million young Chicanos, and general contact with the wider American society all tentatively pointed to a new group consciousness. The widely publicized 1943 "zoot-suit" riot in Los Angeles between young Chicanos and sailors focused wide attention of the nation on this "new minority" for the first time.

A more aggressive, less accommodating political style emerged after World War II. New leaders, usually veterans, began to form or revitalize such organizations as the Community Service Organization and the Mexican American Political Association in California and the American G.I. Forum and the Political Association of Spanish-Speaking Organizations in Texas. Later César Chávez began his long, nonviolent attempt to unionize farm workers, and Reies Tijerina led a violent uprising to reclaim lost lands in northern New

---

[94] Grebler et al., *op. cit.*, p. 64.
[95] Moore, *op. cit.*, pp. 38–39; J. Samora, *Los Mojados: The Wetback Story* (Notre Dame, Ind.: University of Notre Dame Press, 1971).

César Chávez, leader of the United Farm Workers

Mexico.[96] More recently, the Chicano movement has introduced a militant, all-embracing ideology to which we shall return.

The Socio-Cultural Approach

Demographic trends The U.S. Census employs a range of group identifiers, and each provides a different picture of the nation's diverse Hispanic population. Thus, in 1970 5.2 million reported a Spanish-speaking country as

[96] J. L. Love, "La Raza: Mexican Americans in Rebellion," in J. H. Burma (ed.), *Mexican-Americans in the United States* (Cambridge, Mass.: Schenkman, 1970), pp. 459–472; Stoddard, *op. cit.,* pp. 195–201; R. Gardner, *Grito! Reies Tijerina and the New Mexico Land Grant War of 1967* (Indianapolis: Bobbs-Merrill, 1970); Steiner, *op. cit.,* pp. 51–96.

their or their parents' birthplace, 8 million were raised by a Spanish-speaking mother, and 9.1 million identified themselves with an Hispanic group.[97] Of greatest interest is the Southwest, where about six out of seven Mexican Americans reside. Utilizing a list of about 8,000 names, the Census calculates that in 1970 the region contained 4.7 million persons with Spanish surnames— the principal identifier we shall use.[98] This figure constitutes 12.9 percent of the Southwest, ranging from 9.6 percent of Colorado to 31.9 percent of New Mexico; it is the largest concentration of people of Latin-American ancestry outside of Latin America. It is also more than double the 2.3 million with Spanish surnames counted in 1950.

The rapid growth of the Mexican-American people in the Southwest partly reflects immigration, but even more reflects their high birth rate. They have one of the largest average family sizes (4.51 average in 1970) of all groups in the nation. Consequently, they are a young population, with a median age of only 20.2 years. But only 13 percent in 1970 were foreign-born; 30 percent were native-born with foreign parentage, while 57 percent were native-born of native parentage. The third-generation Americans are particularly young (15.8 years median); many of them are the grandchildren of the wave of Mexican immigrants in the 1920s.

Just as rapid has been the massive Mexican-American shift to large metropolitan areas and westward to California. In 1970, 85 percent of Spanish-surnamed southwesterners lived in urban areas, compared to 66 percent in 1950 and 79 percent in 1960. Almost a fourth live in the three standard metropolitan statistical areas (SMSAs) of the Los Angeles region alone, and a half live in just 10 SMSAs.[99] Californian cities have received much of this migration. Almost half of the Spanish-surnamed in the region dwelled in California in 1970 compared to only a third in 1950, and California and Texas together comprise 83 percent of the group.

Legal and political trends   As urban concentrations, the percentage of native-born, and group consciousness have all increased, Mexican-American interest in attaining full citizenship rights through legal and political means has naturally heightened. There remains an ambivalence, to be sure, for Mexican

---

[97] U.S. Bureau of the Census, *Persons of Spanish Origin*, PC(2)1C. (Washington, D.C.: Government Printing Office, 1973) (referred to below as *Origin*); U.S. Bureau of the Census, *Persons of Spanish Surname*, PC(2)-1D. (Washington, D.C.: Government Printing Office, 1973) (referred to below as *Surname*). By mid-1973, the census estimated that there were 10.6 million Americans of Spanish descent, including about 6.3 million Chicanos, 1.55 million Puerto Ricans, and 733,000 Cuban-Americans.

[98] Using the surname as identifier involves two errors that tend to counterbalance each other: Those Mexican Americans who have rare Spanish names or have Anglicized their names will be omitted, while about 87,000 rural Indians in New Mexico and Arizona and Filipinos in California with Spanish surnames are included. *Surname*, p. VII.

[99] *Ibid.* The Los Angeles region is here defined as including the three Los Angeles-Long Beach, San Bernardino-Riverside-Ontario, and Anaheim-Santa Ana-Garden Grove SMSAs. The additional SMSAs comprising the largest ten Chicano concentrations are: San Antonio, San Francisco-Oakland, El Paso, Houston, San Jose, Corpus Christi, and the border area of McAllen-Pharr-Edinburg, Texas.

Americans have had an unhappy history in American courts and politics. Yet in recent years the Mexican American Legal Defense and Education Fund has been established in San Francisco. Modeled after the NAACP Legal Defense and Education Fund, it challenges in the courts discrimination against the group.

Often legal progress is made in conjunction with the efforts of other minorities. We noted earlier that the Supreme Court included Mexican Americans as well as blacks in its Denver ruling against segregated public schools. Likewise, civil rights legislation against discrimination has benefited Mexican Americans as well as other minorities. Greater court action and pressure for legislative protections can be expected in the future, for there is much to accomplish. Basic equality in the administration of justice, for example, has yet to be established in some Texas courts.[100]

Upper-status Spanish Americans, such as U.S. Senator Joseph Montoya, have long been politically active in New Mexico. But in the remainder of the Southwest politicization awaited a native-born, urban middle class that did not emerge until the 1940s. It began with a spate of political organizations, often headed by World War II veterans. Progress, however, has been slow. Internal disagreements and a reluctance to form coalitions hurt; so did blatant Anglo resistance, such as gerrymandering, poll taxes, and English literacy tests. Yet by 1967 some gains had been made: three members of the U.S. House of Representatives (Edward Roybal of California and Henry Gonzales and Eligio De La Garza of Texas), 15 state legislators in addition to 33 in New Mexico, and numerous local elected officials in places with large Chicano populations.[101] A highly publicized political triumph came in 1963 in Crystal City, Texas, a tiny Rio Grande Valley agricultural town long dominated by the vastly outnumbered Anglos. With help from the Teamsters Union, all five city council seats were won by Chicanos. The victory was short-lived, however, for two years later intense Anglo pressure replaced the entire slate with a conservative, ethnically mixed one. Nonetheless, Crystal City had important effects on Mexican-American thinking.

Particularly revealing are the answers of 2,000 Mexican-American respondents in Los Angeles and San Antonio to surveys conducted in 1965–1966.[102] Ambivalence toward the political system is indicated by the large majority, who agreed both that "voting decides what happens" and that politics is "too complicated." Large majorities also agreed that "Mexican Americans should get together politically" but flatly rejected political coalitions with blacks. Despite this ambivalence, Mexican-American registration and voting rates in Los Angeles are beginning to approach those of the nation. The Chicano movement, beginning in the late 1960s, may hasten the process with its assertive "today not *mañana*" style. One indication of greater weight in national politics came in 1973: The National Committee of the Democratic party found it expedient to include two Mexican Americans among its new members. More recently, the

---

[100] Stoddard, *op. cit.*, pp. 233–234.
[101] Grebler et al., *op. cit.*, pp. 560–563.
[102] *Ibid.*, pp. 563–569.

election of Jerry Apodaca as Governor of New Mexico, and of Castro as the first Governor of Mexican descent of Arizona are heralded by Chicanos as indicating a new era for Mexican Americans in politics.

Housing and economic trends   Generalities about the living conditions of Mexican Americans are made hazardous by the group's diversity. Even the nature of poverty varies widely among south Texas, the vineyards of California, the tiny villages of New Mexico, and the *barrios* of East Los Angeles and San Antonio. In addition to locality, living conditions vary across generation and social class. Consider the extremes. At one end, there are growing numbers of Mexican Americans indistinguishable in general from their Anglo middle-class neighbors or fellow workers. At the other end, there are still many Mexican Americans crowded into the deteriorated housing of the *barrios* and overrepresented in low-skill, low-paying occupations. An intelligent reading, then, of social data on Mexican Americans requires a recognition of this great range.

Mexican-American housing is typically segregated.[103] For 35 southwestern cities in 1960, indices of residential dissimilarity indicate that: (1) Mexican Americans are about equally separated from Anglos and blacks; (2) this separation is about two-thirds that of Anglo-black separation; (3) it varies greatly across cities, but is greatest in Texas, in the largest cities, and where there is a high minority proportion of large families. Blatant discrimination plays a critical role in these segregation patterns, as demonstrated in the Los Angeles study described at the beginning of this chapter. But the varied origins of Mexican-American areas also play a role, from the central plazas of cities established by the Spanish (Albuquerque, for example) to the agricultural *barrios* and former labor camps swallowed up by expanding cities and the overwhelmingly Mexican-American cities like Laredo.

Old, overcrowded facilities characterize much of Mexican-American housing. In 1970 in the Southwest, the percentage of Spanish-surnamed living in units built before 1940 (30.7%) surpassed that of blacks (23.4%).[104] Overcrowding (more than one person per room) was equally bad. Almost twice as many Spanish-surnamed households (30.2%) as black households (17.6%) in the Southwest occupied overcrowded quarters.[105] In addition to direct discrimination and segregation, poverty and large families are major determinants of this situation.[106]

Family size is important in understanding the economic position of Mexican Americans. Compared to blacks, Spanish-surnamed males earned more money in 1969 with fewer years of education in all five southwestern states. Compared to Anglos, they do best in Arizona (81% as much income) and poor-

[103] *Ibid.*, Chapter 12.
[104] *Surname;* U.S. Bureau of the Census, *1970 Census of Housing. Vol. I*, Parts 4, 6, 7, 33, and 45 (Washington, D.C.: Government Printing Office, 1972), Table 41. (To be referred to as *Housing.*)
[105] *Surname; Housing*, Table 7.
[106] Grebler et al., *op. cit.*, pp. 265, 267.

est in Texas (64%).[107] The larger size of Mexican-American families, however, pushes their income *per person* in the family slightly below that of blacks in each state except Arizona, and further below that of Anglos in all five states.

These data also reflect the concentration of Mexican Americans in low-skilled, poorly paid work. Seventy-one percent of the Spanish-surnamed employed in the 1970 southwestern labor force (over 15 years old) were in blue-collar jobs, and 31 percent were either laborers or service workers. Fewer than 7 percent of the employed Spanish-surnamed were professionals and technicians in 1970; almost a third (31.6%) of all of those with white-collar occupations were female clerical workers.[108] Yet even these data represent substantial recent improvement. This improvement has been greatest for the native-born and furthered by the move from poor rural areas to prosperous California cities. Like black unemployment, however, Mexican-American unemployment remains much higher than that of Anglos. Grebler and his colleagues warn of the future possibility of a vast unskilled "ethnic proletariat" in the Southwest, comprised of poor Chicanos and blacks who have been forced permanently out of work by automation.[109]

Education   Some of the Mexican American's economic problems can be traced directly to poor and limited education. Indeed, no other form of discrimination incites the group's wrath more than the inadequate and culturally intolerant schooling many of their children receive.

First, Mexican-American adults have typically received far fewer years of education than blacks or Anglos. In 1970, Mexican Americans over 24 years of age in the Southwest had median years of education ranging between 6.7 in Texas to 9.7 in California.[110] By contrast, blacks ranged between a median of 9.4 in Arizona and 11.9 in California and Anglos between 11.9 in Texas and 12.5 in California.[111] Texas provided the most extreme case: Mexican Americans there typically had over three years less education than blacks and over five years less than Anglos. The youth in school now will close some of this gap, but it will remain for some time a major deterrent to Chicano advancement.

Second, the education that is obtained is frequently segregated and inferior. The U.S. Commission on Civil Rights, in a series of six reports, issued a stinging indictment of southwestern schools for having consistently failed to provide equal educational opportunities to Chicano children.[112] Following the segre-

[107] *Surname*, pp. 42, 50, 52, 54, 56, 58; U.S. Bureau of the Census, *1970 Census of the Population*, Vol. *I*, Parts 4, 6, 7, 33, and 45 (Washington, D.C.: Government Printing Office, 1973), Table 192. (To be referred to as *Population*.)

[108] *Surname*, pp. 60–77.

[109] Grebler et al., *op. cit.*, pp. 226–227.

[110] *Surname*, p. 21.

[111] *Population*, Table 51.

[112] U.S. Commission on Civil Rights, *Ethnic Isolation of Mexican Americans in the Southwest*, Report I (1971); *The Unfinished Education*, Report II (1971); *The Excluded Student*, Report III (1972); *Mexican American Education in Texas: A Function of Wealth*, Report IV (1972); *Teachers and Students: Differences in Teacher Interaction with Mexican American and Anglo Students*, Report V (1973); *Toward Quality Education for Mexican Americans*, Report VI (1972) (Washington: Government Printing Office).

gated housing patterns, and often with official intent, many Mexican-American schools are segregated. In both segregated and ethnically mixed schools, the Commission found many teachers openly discriminatory in their behavior and the Spanish language and Chicano culture largely ignored and "even suppressed." It recommended federal funding sanctions, mandatory bilingual programs, the recruitment of Chicano teachers, and the prohibition of at-large school board elections so as to allow Mexican-American representation.

The Situational Approach

The conditions for optimal interracial contact described earlier—equal status, common goals, cooperative dependence, and the positive support of law or custom—appear to apply equally well for Chicano-Anglo situations, although rigorous research on the point has not been conducted. And there are several differences between typical face-to-face encounters of Chicanos with Anglos and those of blacks with whites. One of these differences involves culture; another, the great diversity among Mexican Americans.

U.S. society has traditionally been intolerant of deviant cultural patterns. Immigrants are expected to speak English and "get ahead" along the typical routes for social mobility. Rural migrants from central Mexico, speaking Spanish and holding more family-centered and present-time values, would face a difficult time even if there were no additional discrimination practiced against them. Thus, linguistic and value differences between many Mexican Americans and Anglos are greater than those typically found in black-white interactions. This fact will often operate against the achievement of the condition of "common goals" for optimal contact.

The cultural clash often arises in the schools. As the Civil Rights Commission documented, Spanish has often been forbidden in the schools and Mexican culture looked down upon. Complete acculturation is seen as the educational goal, and cultural diversity as a problem rather than a resource. Yet American schools have a poor record in foreign-language instruction; and bilingual schools—with English and Spanish both utilized as media of instruction—could be exploited as an educational resource for children of all groups. Such has been the experience of the few California schools that have adopted this positive approach. And Allport's four contact conditions for reducing intergroup prejudice can be attained more easily in such schools.

The differential response of many Anglos to Mexican Americans is a result of Mexican-American diversity. If minority members have lighter skin and higher social class, Anglos typically give little recognition of their ethnic status. But for Mexican Americans of darker hue and lower social class, Anglos frequently invoke standard stereotypes and optimal contact conditions are difficult to achieve. Either way, the potentially positive effects of intergroup contact are severely limited.

Despite these problems, probably a larger proportion of Chicano-Anglo contacts than black-white contacts meet Allport's situational criteria. True,

Mexican-American tensions with police match those of blacks, and the typical interactions of Mexican agricultural workers with their Anglo employers are hardly positive. But Chicano-Anglo intermarriage rates are far higher, and residential segregation indexes far lower, than those between blacks and whites. Important, too, are the contacts provided in the armed forces. Unlike black and Japanese Americans, Mexican Americans did not fight in separate units in World War II. Thus military experience has had an enormous effect upon the Mexican-American community. Even today, Mexican-American veterans in the Southwest report higher incomes than comparable Mexican Americans there who have not served in the armed forces.[113]

The Personality and Phenomenological Approaches

Turning to the individual approaches, the same "crutch" and "conformity" personality dynamics discussed earlier apply to Anglo prejudices against Chicanos. The classic study on the authoritarian personality included two questions related to Mexican Americans, in addition to questions tapping prejudices against Jews and against blacks. One referred to "the innate dirtiness, laziness, and general backwardness of Mexicans," and the other to "zoot suiters" who "demonstrate that inferior groups . . . misuse their privileges and create disturbances."[114] These items related to the authoritarian personality syndrome as the anti-Semitic and anti-black statements did: by allowing respondents to express a rigid up-and-down power view and to project their own "unacceptable" impulses upon the minority group as a whole.

The traditional stereotypes of Mexican Americans take the "id" form discussed previously for blacks—"lazy," "dirty," "irresponsible." There are two principal images: the peasant dozing under his large *sombrero* in perpetual *siesta*, and the fiery *bandito* atop his horse, shooting pistols ineffectually in all directions. A national food company, until pressured by Mexican-American activity to do otherwise, for years used a combination of these inconsistent stereotypes as the symbol for a much-advertised product. Spanish-dialect "humor" perpetuated the simple, lovable peasant image as in the "José Jiménez" characterization of comedian Bill Dana, and western movies disseminated both images.

A further complication arises in the differentiated stereotypes of "Mexican" and "Spanish." The simple peasant and the fiery *bandito* images derive in part from the immigration of illiterate farm workers and the years of border "troubles"; they are applied explicitly to Mexican nationals and broadly to lower-status Mexican Americans. But positive stereotypes involving a distinctive culture and gracious manners are often applied by Anglos to upper-status, native-born Mexican Americans who are thought of as "Spanish" or "Hispanic." This split nationality image, while typically linked to social class, does have its

---

[113] H. L. Browning et al., "Income and Veteran Status: Variations among Mexican Americans, Blacks, and Anglos," *American Sociological Review*, Vol. 38 (1973), pp. 74–85.
[114] Adorno et al., *op. cit.*, p. 111.

pre-Mexican origins in New Mexico and southern California. It is also a continuation of the older Spanish norms that devalued Indian ancestry and valued those born in Spain.

This stereotyped differentiation between poor, ignorant Mexicans and the prosperous, cultured Spanish relates also to Anglo prejudices concerned with skin color. Consider how nationalities have been ranked consistently by Anglo-Americans over the past half-century on a measure of "social distance."[115] The English, Canadians, and northern Europeans tend to be ranked highest in acceptance; next come such southern Europeans as the Spanish and Italians; last come nonwhite groups like the Japanese, Chinese, and blacks. Significantly, Mexicans rank well below the Spanish and just ahead of the nonwhite groups.

The Stimulus-Object Approach

Like all peoples, Mexican Americans harbor their own stereotyped beliefs about themselves. One survey, conducted in 1965–1966 in Los Angeles and San Antonio, found that large majorities of Mexican Americans of varying class and locality thought their group to be "very emotional," to "have stronger family ties than most other Americans," and to be less "materialistic" and "progressive" than Anglos.[116] Beyond this limited consensus, there is considerable public debate and private confusion among Mexican Americans as to their group identity. Little wonder that answering the key question "Who am I?" is difficult for them, when one considers their marginal situation.

The marginality of many Mexican Americans is created by a host of factors: (1) the great diversity of the group across region, age, and social class; (2) the accessibility of the border, which makes it possible for new immigrants to "try out America" and easily return and keeps "the old country" vividly in view for all generations; (3) the extent and recency of the group's massive migration to the city; (4) the difficulty inherent in having to deal with Anglo authorities after a long history of bruising encounters with the Border Patrol,[117] the Texas Rangers, and local police; (5) being the largest minority in the United States with an actively maintained world language other than English (a critical point, for Spanish serves not only as a medium of communication but also as a repository for cultural values and an internal criterion of identity);[118] (6) the dilemma between "making it" in an Anglo-dominated society and retaining a distinctive culture. Exacerbating each of these marginality factors is Anglo ambivalence toward them—sometimes accepting and supporting, often rejecting and discriminatory.

---

[115] E. S. Bogardus, *Immigration and Race Attitudes* (Boston: Heath, 1928); G. E. Simpson and J. M. Yinger, *Racial and Cultural Minorities: An Analysis of Prejudice and Discrimination*, 4th ed. (New York: Harper & Row, 1972), pp. 144–145; Allport, *op. cit.*, p. 450.

[116] Grebler et al., *op. cit.*, p. 388.

[117] Samora, *Los Mojados: The Wetback Story.*

[118] Stoddard, *op. cit.*, Ch. 5.

The symptoms of this marginality and identity problem include a slow rate of naturalization and a problem over labeling. Between 1959 and 1966, for example, Grebler has shown that only about 2 to 5 percent of eligible Mexicans annually become citizens compared to rates of 23 to 33 percent for other immigrants with similar lengths of residence.[119] Labeling varies extensively. In New Mexico, "Spanish American" is highly preferred; in Los Angeles, "Mexican" or "Mexican American"; in San Antonio, "Latin American."[120] Several decades ago two political organizations, one based in California and the other in Texas, were unable to form one regional group largely because of disagreement over the label.[121]

Confronting these issues directly is the student-inspired Chicano movement.[122] *Chicano* is a widely used label today among the young and more militant. It relates to a broad ideology, resembling in important respects modern political thought among militant black youth. It rejects accommodation policies, defines politics broadly, and stresses unity in the struggle for change. *Chicanismo* in this sense includes the land protests of New Mexico, the farm-labor protests of César Chávez, the urban action of Denver's Rodolfo (Corky) González, and the high-school and college protests of Chicano youth. It aims to solve problems of marginality through cultural pride. *Chicanismo* indicates the future directions of the minority in its efforts to win acceptance in American society on new cultural terms.

A FINAL WORD

The Mexican-American problem of answering the identity question "Who am I?" is an acute example of a larger national problem. Who are we Americans? What are our national identities? What kind of nation do we want America to become? Do we want a society that emulates the melting-pot conception, boiling down group differences into a common, homogeneous culture? Do we want a culturally diverse America with "complete pluralism," where each racial, national, cultural, and religious group is largely separated from others? Or can we evolve a mixed type of society that exploits the best features of these extreme options—a diverse country with many intergroup bonds forming a common "American" identity? These are the broad questions raised by contemporary social problems involving racial and cultural relations. Whatever the ultimate answer, a broad consensus should be possible on the need to eliminate the kind of discrimination uncovered by the college students who conducted the experiment on apartment rentals in Los Angeles.

[119] L. Grebler, "The Naturalization of Mexican Immigrants in the United States," *The International Migration Review,* Vol 1 (Fall 1966), pp. 17–32.

[120] Grebler et al., *op. cit.,* pp. 385–387.

[121] Moore, *op. cit.,* p. 148.

[122] A. Cuellar, "Perspective on Politics." In Moore, *op. cit.,* Chapter 8.

SUMMARY

1 Great intergroup diversity characterizes the United States. This diversity has provided a principal base for America's social organization as well as a principal source of societal strain. Native Americans, Puerto Ricans, Asian Americans, Jewish Americans, and many other groups experience the nation's persistent intergroup problems. This chapter focuses upon black Americans and Mexican Americans.

2 There are six basic approaches to the problem. Three are social—*historical, socio-cultural,* and *situational;* three are individual—*personality, phenomenological,* and *stimulus-object.*

3 The historical roots of black-white relations can be traced back to slavery. Under English law, the slave was treated as property; this left an especially dehumanizing legacy of racial stigma. "The peculiar institution" expanded rapidly until the American Revolution, then revived again at the start of the nineteenth century with the invention of the cotton gin. Ostensibly "free Negroes," reaching a half million in number by 1860, were also mistreated in both the North and the South; and this maltreatment furnished a dangerous model for dealing with emancipated blacks after the Civil War. Modern segregation, however, was not established in the South until 1890–1910.

4 The socio-cultural approach to race relations requires an investigation of six trends: legal, demographic, political, housing, economic, and educational. Legal trends, for example, can be viewed as forming four distinct Supreme Court eras. The Segregation Era (1876–1910) featured the *Plessy v. Ferguson* case in 1896, which led to the doctrine that "separate-but-equal" facilities are constitutional. The Preparatory Era (1910–1930) saw the High Court slowly begin to interpret the Thirteenth, Fourteenth, and Fifteenth Amendments to the U.S. Constitution as defending black rights as citizens. The Desegregation Era (1930–1969) was highlighted by the 1954 ruling against the *de jure* segregation of public education. The Retrenchment Era (1970 on) is characterized by a more cautious, conservative approach.

5 Demographically, black Americans have engaged throughout this century in a massive migration out of the rural South and to the largest central cities of the nation. This shift has major political implications. Black elected officials increased from 103 in 1964 to 3,503 in 1975, including 17 members of the U.S. House of Representatives, one U.S. Senator, and the mayors of such major cities as Atlanta, Detroit, Gary, Los Angeles, and Newark.

6 There is a massive degree of housing segregation by race in the United States. It has been caused by federal housing policies, blatant racial discrimination, the tight supply of low-income housing, suburban zoning barriers, and binding ties within the black community.

7 Economic racial trends are mixed. Major upgrading of black employment took place during the 1960s. But the severe recession of the 1970s has meant disproportionately massive unemployment and economic hardship for black Americans. Effective remedies will require vigorous economic growth.

8 Educational segregation by race was significantly reduced between 1968 and 1972, especially in the South. Yet much school segregation remains, particularly in large central cities where only metropolitan remedies would be sufficient.

9 For face-to-face contact between blacks and whites to lessen prejudice and con-

flict, four situational conditions must operate: the two groups must (1) possess equal status in the situation, (2) seek common goals, (3) be cooperatively dependent upon each other, and (4) interact with the positive support of authorities, law, or custom. Yet even positive changes rendered by this optimal contact in specific settings may not readily generalize to different situations.

10   Two different personality bases for racial prejudice can be ascertained: the authoritarian and the conforming personalities. Research evidence suggests that roughly about one-fifth of white Americans are authoritarian bigots, another fifth are relatively unprejudiced, and the remaining three-fifths react to race relations in terms of their need to conform.

11   Two outgroup stereotypes characterize the phenomenology of intergroup relations throughout the world. The super-ego image portrays the outgroup as mercenary, sly, and clannish. The id image portrays it as lazy, stupid, and dirty. Black Americans have long been stereotyped in terms of the id image, though this image is slowly fading. As it fades, white American attitudes toward blacks and desegregation have sharply improved over recent decades.

12   The sixth approach to race relations concerns the stimulus object of the process— black Americans. The "Negro" role of inferiority, long expected and required of blacks in America, mediated many of the damaging effects of racism. More recently, a severe sense of relative deprivation has led to black unrest and demands for change.

13   Applying Allport's approaches to relations between Mexican Americans and Anglos, history tells us of the four centuries of diverse and often isolated Spanish development in the U.S. Southwest. Mexican independence in 1821 initiated major contact and conflict with Anglos. This conflict included the Texas Revolution in 1836, the Mexican-American War ending in 1848, and border troubles into the 1920s. The original Spanish settlers lost most of their wealth and land for a variety of factors, including trickery. The Mexican Revolution, beginning in 1909, triggered increasing immigration into the Southwest that continues today. Most of the Chicano population today derives from this twentieth-century movement across the border.

14   The demographic profile of the over 6 million Mexican-American people today reveals that they are overwhelmingly residents of the Southwest, are a young people with large families and a high birth rate, and have been rapidly shifting westward to California and to such large metropolitan areas as Los Angeles and San Antonio. These shifts have led to a growing group consciousness and political mobilization.

15   Mexican-American housing is typically segregated, old, and overcrowded. Furthermore, Mexican Americans are concentrated in low-skilled, poorly-paid work. They earn more money with less education than blacks throughout the Southwest, but because of larger families the income per person among Mexican Americans tends to be less than that of blacks. These problems are made worse by public education that is often segregated, inferior, and culturally intolerant.

16   Contact situations between Mexican Americans and Anglo-Americans are as diverse as the Chicano people. On the one hand, typical Chicano interactions with the police and with agricultural employers violate Allport's optimal conditions. On the other hand, widespread Mexican-American integration in the armed forces often meets Allport's conditions.

17   Mexican Americans have also suffered from the id stereotype of lazy, dirty, and

irresponsible. Group identity is made difficult, too, by a host of demographic, geographic, and cultural factors that enhance the marginality of many Mexican Americans. Confronting these problems directly is the recent Chicano political and cultural movement.

RECOMMENDED READING

A broad sociological overview of this field is provided in the fourth edition of George Simpson and Milton Yinger's *Racial and Cultural Minorities* (1972). The definitive psychological treatment remains the late Gordon Allport's *The Nature of Prejudice* (1954).

The field of black-white relations is blessed with a large number of readily available paperbacks that focus on particular concerns. For example, Talcott Parsons and Kenneth Clark's edited volume, *The Negro American* (1966), provides detailed analyses by a broad range of specialists; James Jones's *Prejudice and Racism* (1972) offers an original analysis using both historical and social psychological materials; Judith Porter's *Black Child, White Child* (1971) presents a vivid description of the effects of racist norms upon children; Peter Goldman's *Report from Black America* (1970) gives the results from a national survey of black American opinion. Cross-national comparisons can be made by reading about black-white relations in England and in South Africa in Nicholas Deakin's *Colour, Citizenship and British Society* (1970) and Pierre van den Berghe's *South Africa: A Study in Conflict* (1965). More detailed treatments of this chapter's themes can be found in T. F. Pettigrew's *Racially Separate or Together?* (1971) and *Racial Discrimination in the United States* (1975).

The Mexican-American bookshelf is not yet so extensive. The books cited in the footnotes constitute a good beginning. The most definitive is the tome by L. Grebler, Joan Moore, and R. C. Guzman, *The Mexican-American People* (1970). In paperback and especially informative are Joan Moore's shorter treatment from the same research project at UCLA, *Mexican Americans* (1970), and E. R. Stoddard's *Mexican Americans* (1973). More specialized but of special interest are: J. Samora's *La Raza: Forgotten Americans* (1966), S. Steiner's *La Raza: The Mexican Americans* (1970), and J. Samora's *Los Mojados: The Wetback Story* (1971). A useful general reader is *Mexican-Americans in the United States* (1970), edited by J. H. Burma.

11

Family
Disorganization

WILLIAM J. GOODE

According to eyewitnesses, the family has been in a state of constant decline for several hundred years. Commentators in generation after generation have observed that parental authority was breaking down, people were no longer observing traditional sexual taboos, husbands and wives did not trust one another, and wives were rebelling against their husbands—all in contrast to the periods of their grandfathers, when the old customs were followed and the family seemed vigorous and strong.

The family, then, presents us with a striking paradox. It seems to be constantly becoming less stable, yet it shows no signs of disappearing. Almost everyone in this and all other nations seems to get married eventually, and people who get divorced marry again, thus suggesting that the single state is not desirable. Were all those observers merely sentimentalizing the family relations in their grandparents' generation, and expressing their own dissatisfaction with contemporary family life? Or were they simply the moralists who have complained everywhere and in all times that people were not living up to the ideals of the society?

Perhaps the most fruitful interpretation would be that disorganization is *endemic* to the family, that the *normal* course of daily family life is made up of dissolving pressures, together with repeated and often stumbling reassertions of stable patterns. Under that view, to speak of family disorganization is not so much to single out peculiarities and strange deviations from some widely accepted and typical set of norms, but rather to look at expectable processes that may well be found in any family unit, or that are observable in a large minority of all families. Perhaps almost everyone experiences one or another of the various forms of family disorganization at some time.

THE LARGER SOCIAL STRUCTURE AND THE FAMILY

In the analysis of family disorganization, we must assume at times the perspective of family members who are undergoing this experience. At other times, we must stand off and consider family disorganization as part of the larger social structure. What happens in the family may affect the larger social structure—as when men's experiences in divorce motivate them to change the divorce laws in their favor—and in turn the larger social processes (e.g., war, revolution) may affect what happens in individual family units.

From the larger perspective, we shall be interested in the differing rates of various kinds of disorganization from one society to another, or over time. That perspective must, however, be corrected by data about individual experience. The contrast can be seen with reference to divorce. This is experienced

The author wishes to acknowledge the help of Nicolas Tavuchis, Joel Telles, Cynthia Fuchs Epstein, Jo Anne Costello, Lenore J. Weitzman, and Mark Johnson in various revisions of this chapter.

513

by individuals as unique, as a loss or hurt no one else has suffered in quite this form. From a larger perspective, however, we note that there were almost one million divorces in the United States in 1974, and that we can examine them to see whether (ignoring the individual differences) they exhibit various regularities—including common patterns of adjustment to divorce.

A relationship between the larger society and the family system which we are likely to assume is that when the larger social structure is changing rapidly and all the traditional social forms are being destroyed, the family system, too, will become disorganized somewhat. However, we should remember that a social system can continue relatively unchanged but contain a set of family patterns that are disorganized in many ways. That is, not all traditional family systems were highly stable; many had their own forms of disorganization. For example (we shall analyze this case later) in the "traditional" Latin American countries the rate of illegitimacy was very high. As a few of these countries have moved toward industrialization many new social problems have emerged but it also seems likely that the rate of illegitimacy will decrease. Moreover, as mortality rates drop, fewer children must face life as orphans than in the past.

Moreover, both the larger social system and the family system may continue unchanged for generations, while individual family units dissolve at a rapid rate. That is, the high rate of dissolution *is* part of the "traditional" family system. For example, very high divorce rates were normal in a number of societies, such as Arab Algeria and Japan, but that was a normal, expected part of those systems.

As a final connection between the larger social structure and the family, we note that the legal and formal structures of modern nations may reflect little concern with some of the problems of family disorganization—though they affect individual family members a good deal. For example, in the United States a husband and wife can decide to separate on their own, and no legal agency is even empowered to find out that a separation has occurred. Similarly, if a child is born an idiot or becomes severely retarded, the formal agencies of the society do not act unless asked to do so, and few social customs will help guide the family members. In short, in a number of areas, the family has considerable autonomy, and neither outsiders nor the state may have any specific right to intrude into its solution of the problem. Again, this pattern will vary from one society to another.

TYPES OF FAMILY DISORGANIZATION

Social philosophers dispute indefinitely as to what "disorganization" is. Modern analysts also object to the term because it suggests a negative evaluation. We can be satisfied here with a simple definition: Family disorganization is the breakup of a family unit when one or more members are unwilling or unable to perform their role obligations adequately, as these are viewed by other members. Using this definition, several types of disorganization can be analyzed separately: Some family units will break up as a result of *external* problems such as war, depression, death, or imprisonment, while others break up because of some failure in role obligations *within* the family unit itself.

The major forms of family disorganization may then be classified as follows:

1. *The uncompleted family unit: illegitimacy.* Although the family cannot be said to "dissolve" if it never existed, illegitimacy may nevertheless be viewed as one form of family disorganization for two reasons: (a) the potential "father-husband" conspicuously fails in his role obligations as these are defined by the society, the mother, and (later) the child; and (b) the parents of both the young mother and the young father fail in their social obligation to control the courtship behavior of the two young parents, and this is a major indirect cause of illegitimacy.

2. *Voluntary departure of one or both spouses: annulment, separation, divorce, desertion.*

3. *Changes in role definitions that result from the differential impact of cultural changes.* Social movements such as women's liberation may affect relations between husband and wife, but a major type problem in this category is parent-youth conflict.

4. *The "empty shell" family,* in which individuals live together but have minimal communication and contact with one another, failing especially in the obligation to give emotional support to one another.

5. *The family crisis caused by "external" events,* such as the temporary or permanent *involuntary* absence of one of the spouses because of death or imprisonment, or as a result of such impersonal catastrophes as flood, war, and depression.

6. *Internal catastrophes that cause involuntary major role failures; for example, mental, emotional, or physical pathologies,* such as severe mental retardation of the child, psychosis of the child or spouse, or chronic or incurable physical conditions.[1]

This rough classification emphasizes that a continuing pattern of role performance is necessary if a particular family is to continue to exist.[2] On the

---

[1] This type will not be analyzed in this chapter.

[2] Obviously, other modes of measurement or classification might also be useful. See, for example, those of L. L. Geismar, Michael A. LaSorte, and Beverly Ayres, "Measuring Family Disorganization," *Journal of Marriage and Family Living,* Vol. 25 (November 1963), pp. 479–481.

In cases of death the family is guided more definitely by customs than in cases of divorce.

other hand such a classification does not take into account a wide range of other differences in types of problems. For example, the larger society may be more sympathetic to one kind of problem than another (the family of the deserting father gets more sympathy than that of the prisoner); the society furnishes clear social rules for some participants but not others (death is more tragic than divorce, and in cases of death the family is guided more definitely by customs); or for financial reasons, the society may concern itself with only one of the participants (the deserter or the illegitimate father), not with the entire family. We shall focus on these variations as we proceed with our analysis.

We shall attempt to make comparisons of the United States with other societies and, to some extent, of the present with other time periods, simply because these may illuminate our understanding of the processes of disorganization. We shall give somewhat more consideration to divorce, because so many other types of family disorganization are likely to end in divorce sooner or later, because it is the focus of so much moral and personal concern, and because changes in the divorce rate are usually an index of changes in other elements in the family patterns of any society.

THE UNCOMPLETED FAMILY: ILLEGITIMACY

Over a generation ago, the anthropologist Bronislaw Malinowski formulated the "Rule of Legitimacy," according to which every society has a rule that each child should have a legitimate father to act as its protector, guardian, and representative in the society.[3] Like all other rules this one is violated, and those who violate it are punished in some ways. Where the rule is strongly enforced, the illegitimacy rate is low and people who violate the rule (as well as their illegitimate children) suffer more punishments. In all societies such rules move eligible young men and women toward marriage, place the new child in a specific position within a family unit that is linked within the kinship and social structure, and fix responsibility for its maintenance and socialization on that specific family unit. These regulations define "legitimacy" in the society, and therefore "illegitimacy" as well.

The social rule of legitimacy is not, therefore, caused by a simple prudishness about sex, but by the importance of giving to a specific social unit the responsibility for the next generation. In about 70 percent of the societies that we know, some degree of premarital sexual license is found, but childbirth outside marriage is not approved. That is, societies are more concerned with illegitimacy than with intercourse outside marriage.[4] We must emphasize this difference, since undoubtedly the disapproval of illegitimacy in U.S. society was partly based upon a disapproval of sexuality before marriage, but there has been a major trend toward sexual permissiveness in the United States. A great majority of the American population no longer disapproves of sexual intercourse prior to marriage, and a majority of men and women in fact engage in sexual relations prior to marriage.[5] If our analysis is correct, these changes will reduce the strong disapproval of illegitimacy and the illegitimacy rate may rise

[3] One such statement is to be found in his "Parenthood, the Basis of Social Structure," in V. F. Calverton and Samuel D. Schmalhausen (eds.), *The New Generation* (New York: McCauley, 1930), pp. 137–138.

[4] George P. Murdock, *Social Structure* (New York: Macmillan, 1949), p. 265. For different reactions to different *kinds* of illegitimacy, see the classic articles by Kingsley Davis, "The Forms of Illegitimacy," *Social Forces*, Vol. 18 (October 1939), pp. 77–89, and "Illegitimacy and the Social Structure," *American Journal of Sociology*, Vol. 45 (September 1939), pp. 221–222 and 231–233.

[5] For definitive data on these and related points, see Morton Hunt, *Sexual Behavior in the 1970s* (Chicago: Playboy Press, 1974).

somewhat in the near future, but most babies will be born to married couples in the future, as in the past.

Though societies generally disapprove of illegitimacy, they vary in how *much* disapproval is felt, in the severity of the punishments visited on child and parents, and in the position in the social structure that an illegitimate child is allowed to occupy. Some family systems control illegitimacy far more vigorously than others. In addition, toward the higher social strata of any society, where the kinship line is viewed as more important and family inheritances may be at stake, the concern about illegitimacy as well as the social pressures against it are stronger.

Rates of Illegitimacy around the World

In countries where the stigma of illegitimacy is very high, as in India, the United Arab Republic, and Japan, not only is the real illegitimacy rate very low, but the official rate is lower still, because families make every effort to hide such a shameful fact. Thus, the official rate is likely to be less than 1 percent of all live births, as in Japan. African tribes placed a generally high value on children, and a marriage would simply be arranged before childbirth in cases of a premarital pregnancy.

From the 1890s until the late 1960s, there was a slight downward trend in the illegitimacy rates of most countries, even though the sexual freedom of young adults increased greatly and in Western nations the tolerance for childbirth outside of marriage certainly increased.[6] Over the past decade, these rates rose in Sweden, Great Britain, and the United States. Whether they will continue to rise as sexual patterns change cannot as yet be predicted. In Table 11-1 some recent data are presented.

Table 11-1 Illegitimacy Rates in Selected Countries

Country	Percentage illegitimate of all live births
United States (1973)	13.0
Sweden (1973)	28.3
Italy (1972)	2.5
England and Wales (1973)	8.6
Japan (1967)	0.9
Israel (1968)	0.6

Source: Official statistical yearbooks of these countries.

[6] For a further analysis of European illegitimacy over time, see Edward Shorter, "Illegitimacy, Sexual Revolution, and Social Change in Modern Europe," *Journal of Interdisciplinary History*, Vol. 2 (August 1971), pp. 237–272, which makes reference to changes from the late seventeenth century through much of the nineteenth century.

One northwestern European rural pattern, now disappearing, throws some light on the effect of social controls on illegitimacy rates. In the Scandinavian countries and in parts of Germany, adolescent children of farmers were permitted considerable sexual freedom. This created high *official* illegitimacy rates in some rural regions. The courtships were not secret, however, and the couples were guided by both peer group and adult norms. In case of pregnancy, the father was likely to be known and by that stage in the relationship both families had at least tentatively approved of the match as well. The legal fact that the child might be born out of wedlock was important to the church and state, but was of little concern to the local community, for the marriage was a settled matter and would take place at the convenience of the couple's parents.

Low illegitimacy rates do not, then, prove that unmarried people are abstaining from sexual intercourse. As we noted earlier, social rules against illegitimacy are stricter than those against sexual behavior among the unmarried. When it is likely that a couple will marry, they are permitted more privacy and are watched less closely—but they typically get married before the child is born. Consequently, studies of past centuries as well as of the present show that some 20 to 25 percent of all marriages have occurred *after* conception.[7] That is, where illegitimacy sanctions are severe, couples are under strong pressure to marry when the woman becomes pregnant. As a consequence, at least some who might otherwise have drifted apart may feel they have to marry. However, the divorce rate among such couples is higher than among those who did not conceive before marriage. Such forced marriages should become less common now that abortion is legally permitted in the United States.

The New World (including the Caribbean and Latin America) offers an instructive contrast to illegitimacy patterns in both Europe and other great nations of the Mideast and Asia. Illegitimacy rates, ranging from 20 to 70 percent, are higher there than anywhere else on record except for urbanized slums in sub-Saharan Africa. Similarly high rates are to be found among the black population of the United States.[8]

These high rates are not a product of "Indian" or "transplanted African" cultures in which "illegitimacy in the white man's sense" has no social value.

---

[7] For data on the United States, showing that about 25 percent of all marriages are preceded by conception, see U.S. Bureau of the Census, "Fertility Histories and Fertility Expectations of American Women," *Population Characteristics*, Series P-20, No. 263, April 1974, p. 53. For a comparison with Denmark, see the older study by Harold T. Christensen, "Cultural Relativism and Premarital Sex Norms," *American Sociological Review*, Vol. 25 (February 1960), pp. 31–39, as well as the more recent study by Harold T. Christensen and Christina F. Gregg, "Changing Sex Norms in America and Scandinavia," *Journal of Marriage and the Family*, Vol. 32 (November 1970), pp. 616–627.

[8] For analyses of these patterns, see William J. Goode, "Illegitimacy in the Caribbean Social Structure," *American Sociological Review*, Vol. 25 (February 1960), pp. 21–30, and "Illegitimacy, Anomie, and Cultural Penetration," *American Sociological Review*, Vol. 26 (December 1961); pp. 910–924; and Judith Blake, *Family Structure in Jamaica* (New York: Free Press, 1961). Official data on the populations with high rates are not very precise. Rates in Latin American countries have become less available in recent years, but do not seem to have changed much in the 1970s.

Neither the older Indian nor the African family systems exhibited high illegitimacy rates. Moreover, the New World nations are Western in culture, for the most part, and every study of a specific community, whether of the black population of the United States or the native populations of Latin America, shows that people who have children prefer to have them within wedlock. On the other hand, where a high proportion of the people in a given population segment were themselves born illegitimate, no one can be singled out for much punishment or reward for not following the rule of legitimacy.

It is in the lower social strata of the New World countries that such high illegitimacy rates are found, where there are fewer family controls over the courtship behavior of the young girl or woman. Such high rates can best be understood by examining the situation of a relatively unsupervised young woman at such class levels. Since most young men take for granted that dating or going together includes sexual intercourse sooner or later, and contraceptives are little used, any young woman faces the choice of risking pregnancy and having a child out of wedlock or of not taking part in courtship behavior. If she does not, she will have little chance of marrying eventually.

Unless the young woman has outstanding personal qualities (or possibly owns a bit of land) she is in a poor bargaining position. On the other hand, the loss of esteem if she does become pregnant is not great in the social strata where rates are very high. The motivation of lower-class families, as well as their resources, for controlling the courtship behavior of young people are not as high as among families at higher socioeconomic levels. Nevertheless, most people do marry eventually even at lower class levels in New World countries, which suggests that living together outside of marriage is not preferred.

This pattern of unsupervised courtship and weak family controls resulted from cultural and social disorganization in the subordinate populations of New World countries, including of course the blacks in the United States.[9] Similar patterns have developed in sub-Saharan Africa with industrialization. It can be predicted that as these populations become more fully integrated into their national societies, and are given a more adequate economic base for existence as well as more social esteem for conformity to traditional family norms, these high illegitimacy rates will begin to drop. Although at present they remain very high among the black population in the United States, for the past 10 years

---

[9] Although succeeding data have in general supported this interpretation of New World illegitimacy, some authors have rejected it on the grounds that there is a "culture of poverty" among the black poor in many parts of the world, which supports illegitimacy and consensual unions not merely as something to be borne, but as a set of ideal principles. H. Rodman has tried to interpret the phenomenon differently, by alleging that there is some kind of "lower class value-stretch" so that the lower classes are once again seen as different, and not at all disapproving of illegitimacy. For data reviewing the Rodman thesis, and rejecting it, see C. Allen Haney, Robert Michielutte, Clark E. Vincent, and Earl M. Cochrane, "The Value Stretch Hypothesis: Family Size Preferences in a Black Population," *Social Problems*, Vol. 21 (Fall 1973), pp. 206–219. The Rodman thesis is given some support with reference to family size preferences.

the number of black *women* per thousand population who have children outside of marriage has continued to drop, except for the age group 15 to 19.[10] It should also be noted that the lowest rates of illegitimacy found among blacks in the United States occur in such states as North Dakota, Hawaii, Utah, Maine, and New Hampshire, where there are very few blacks, who are thus much more integrated into the dominant society.

Illegitimacy as a U.S. Social Problem

The public attitude   Public outcry about illegitimacy in the United States has been far more strident than the facts suggest. The striking change in the United States over the past generation is that illegitimacy has become a *social* problem, rather than a merely personal or family problem. Consequently state and private agencies, established on the conviction that the illegitimate child and mother should be helped, are far more concerned with their fate than before, and are in fact contributing to their support. This very transformation, however, has created strong sentiments against "helping mothers to have more illegitimate children," or "paying to increase the illegitimacy rate."

Indeed, the controversy on this topic is even more complex. As one family analyst has pointed out, the respectable elders of the community are affronted both by the sexual pleasure enjoyed by the women who have illegitimate children, and by the idea that their illegitimate children must be supported by the taxpayers. Many social and political leaders have opposed free abortions and the distribution of contraceptives to potential illegitimate mothers because that would make their sexual pleasure too easy, and also oppose giving welfare to unwed mothers because that rewards illegitimacy itself. On the other hand, many Black Nationalists oppose free abortion and free contraceptives because they believe such measures are a white genocidal plot against the blacks.[11]

In recent years, illegitimacy has become a larger social problem, but the apparently upward trend should be viewed with some caution. Almost certainly, compared with a century ago, black illegitimacy rates have dropped. In the post-Civil War period a large majority of black parents were not legally married.[12] In most southern states, no serious effort was made until fairly recently to collect accurate data on black births, illegitimate or legitimate. Improved

---

[10] U.S. National Office of Vital Statistics, *Summary Report, Final Natality Statistics* (Washington, D.C.: Government Printing Office, 1973), p. 4.

[11] On this controversy, see Robert F. Winch, *The Modern Family,* 3d ed. (New York: Holt, 1971), p. 196.

[12] However, as against the classic analyses of the black family in the past, such as E. Franklin Frazier, *The Negro Family in the United States* (Chicago: University of Chicago Press, 1939), Robert W. Fogel and Stanley L. Engerman assert in *Time on the Cross* (Boston: Little, Brown, 1974, pp. 126ff.) that slave family life itself was stable, and plantation owners insisted that their slaves get married. However, their work has been widely attacked for its factual weaknesses.

record keeping may make the increase in illegitimacy seem greater than it really is. In the period 1940–1960 the rates for both blacks and whites increased.

In the early 1970s, the percentage of live *births* that were illegitimate continued to increase for both blacks and whites, but the percentage of *women* who bore illegitimate children had begun to drop. This seeming paradox is a result of the way the first of these figures is calculated. It is really a ratio, a comparison of the number of children born to married couples with the number born to unmarried couples. Since fertility *within* marriage has been *dropping*, there is an apparent *rise* in that illegitimacy ratio. To understand this relationship better, consider that half or more of the children born to young women age 15 and under, either black or white, are illegitimate, because there are very few married women at such early ages, and thus the ratio of illegitimate to legitimate children born to such young people is high. If, however, the percentage of unmarried mothers continues to drop, then this ratio should eventually drop as well. It seems likely, then, that the public outcry may not be fully justified.

Since slightly more than half of the approximately 400,000 illegitimate births in the United States each year are black, it is worth commenting on the change in the situation of blacks. The contemporary conflict about racial discrimination is not an index of social disorganization, but a sign that for the first time in its history our country is actually conceding that it has oppressed the black population. Almost certainly, the steps that are being made toward integrating blacks into the mainstream of American social life will lead to a substantial decrease in the illegitimacy rate among black citizens.

Adjustment to illegitimacy   In the United States, the unwed mother has a difficult adjustment to make. In spite of increasing sexual permissiveness, the society has not yet become tolerant of the young unwed mother who wishes to keep her child as her own.[13] Some families try to deny the connection of the child with the mother and say that it belongs to a relative. If the family can afford it or if other financial assistance can be found, a preferred solution is to have the girl bear the child in a nursing home and to leave it there for adoption. The economic problems and the problem of parental control are likely to be too great to handle when there is no father available and no community support (other than economic). Perhaps only in contemporary Sweden is sufficient social assistance available to help the unwed mother care adequately for her child. Whether or not she keeps her child, the mother may suffer much emotional pain because of the social disapproval she must bear; if she allows her child to be adopted by others she may also suffer because of the strong love developed for it when it is born.

[13] Nevertheless, in recent years a greater number of unmarried mothers have decided to keep their own children, the percentage of women who are unwed mothers has been dropping, and fertility within marriage has dropped. Consequently, there has been a shortage of white children available for adoption.

No simple moral or technical solution for the problems associated with illegitimacy will arise until the society becomes willing to shoulder all of these burdens collectively, or until abortion becomes so widespread that illegitimate births do not occur. Marriage itself does not automatically create a family relationship, though it may confer the status of legitimacy on the child. Illegitimacy in the United States most often occurs precisely among couples who are not deeply involved with each other emotionally and who have shared mainly a sexual experience. Often the pregnancy occurred partly because of carelessness on both sides and partly because the father had little feeling of responsibility about the relationship, the woman, or the consequences. Marriage would give a name, but not a father, to the child. Fundamental changes in the social structure would be required to give full social rights to the illegitimate child without marriage, however, and these changes are not likely to take place in the next few generations. Moreover, the same problems apply, although somewhat less harshly, to all the communist countries in spite of the fact that there the distinction between legitimacy and illegitimacy has been "abolished by law."[14]

VOLUNTARY DEPARTURES: SEPARATION, DIVORCE, ANNULMENT, AND DESERTION

The legal differences among separation, annulment, desertion, and divorce cannot be ignored, but they should not obscure the similarity of behavior throughout this large category of marital dissolution. Focusing mainly on divorce patterns in the succeeding sections simplifies the exposition without distorting reality. However, data on the other subtypes are also used where they are relevant.

Most of us are likely to view divorce as a misfortune or a tragedy, and indeed in no country is it viewed as a cause for celebration. Our Western bias in favor of romantic love also views marriage as based on love, and divorce as failure. Thus, Americans are likely to view high divorce rates as evidence that the family system is not working well. This attitude is part of our religious heritage that made divorce a rare event until the early part of the present century, although various Protestant sects asserted the right to divorce as early as the sixteenth century, and Milton's famous plea for it was written in the seventeenth century.

All marriage systems require that at least two people live together, attempting to harmonize their individual desires, needs, and values. Thus, all systems create some tensions and unhappiness, and no system promises happy marriages

---

[14] Several Supreme Court cases over the past decade, as well as some state court decisions, have extended many of the rights of legitimacy to illegitimate children. On these, see Lenore J. Weitzman, "To Love, Honor, and Obey? Traditional Legal Marriage and Alternative Family Forms," *The Family Coordinator*, Vol. 24 (October 1975), pp. 544–546.

for all. In this basic sense, then, marriage "causes" divorce, annulment, separation, or desertion.

But though a social pattern may be able to survive even when many individuals in it are unsatisfied, it must contain various mechanisms for keeping interpersonal hostilities within some limits. Two main patterns of controlling conflict are common. One is to *lower the individual's expectations* of what to expect from marriage. For example, the pre-Revolutionary Chinese praised family life as the most important institution, but taught their children that they were not to expect either romance or happiness from it. At best, they were taught that they might achieve contentment or peace in marriage.

A second way of controlling marital conflict, widespread in pre-industrial societies (including the pre-Revolutionary Chinese), is to put less stress on the husband-wife relationship and more on the larger kin network. In such societies, elders directed the affairs of the family, arranged the marriages of the young, and intervened in quarrels between husband and wife. The success of the marriage was rated not so much by the intimate emotional harmony of husband and wife as by the contribution of the couple to the lineage or extended kin. Consequently, tensions between husband and wife were less likely to build up to an unbearable level.

In addition, all societies offer or impose some ways of *avoiding* marital tensions and thus reducing divorce. One pattern is to consider certain disagreements as trivial. For example, individuals in the United States are told that disagreement on the relative values of bowling and bridge is not important. Another pattern is to suppress some irritations. As individuals become adult, they are increasingly forced to control their anger, unless the problem is serious. Still another pattern is to mold expectations in childhood and adolescence so that spouses expect similar things in marriage.

Societies may decrease or increase the divorce rate by different definitions of what is a *bearable* level of dissension between husband and wife, as well as in socially approved *solutions* for marital difficulties. It seems likely that during the nineteenth century United States public opinion considered a degree of disharmony bearable that modern couples would not tolerate. People took for granted that spouses who no longer loved one another and who found life together distasteful should nevertheless live together in public amity for the sake of their children and their standing in the community.

Ideas as to what should be done about an unsatisfying marriage vary considerably, too, even among Western countries. Spain, Ireland, Brazil, and Peru, all Catholic countries, permit only legal separations, not divorce. Where divorce is impossible or restricted, both legal and informal separations are common. In societies where there are extended kinship networks and divorce is not permitted, husband and wife may continue their daily tasks but minimize their contacts. In a polygynous society, a man might refuse to spend any time with one of his wives if their relationship was an unhappy one. Under the family systems of Manchu China and Tokugawa Japan, a man (but not a woman) could bring a concubine into his house. In China, a dissatisfied husband might instead stay away from his home for long periods of time by working elsewhere or going on business trips—a form of separation.

These devices to avoid trouble, to divert dissension, to train individuals to put up with difficulties, or to seek alternative relationships to ease the burden of marriage show that societies generally do not value divorce highly. Very likely in no society has divorce been a valued mode of marital behavior. The reasons for this are easily seen. Divorce grows out of dissension and also creates additional conflict between the two sides of the family lines. Prior marriage agreements are broken, and prior harmonious relationships among in-laws are disrupted. There are problems of custody, child support, and remarriage, which will be analyzed in more detail later on.

In no society, however, are the mechanisms for avoiding or reducing marital conflict enough to make all couples able to tolerate their marriages. Dissolution is, then, one of the safety valves for the inevitable tensions of married life. At present we cannot say why a particular society adopts the pattern of divorce rather than that of separation, or that of living together but enlarging the household to take in additional wives, but divorce is clearly a widespread solution for the problems of marital living. In fact, the alternative solutions that various societies offer are only variations on the pattern of divorce.

Divorce differs from these variations principally in that it permits both partners to remarry. In societies without divorce, ordinarily only the man can enter a new union, even when it is not entirely a legally recognized one. For example, in the past in India a man could take an additional wife or, in China or Japan, a concubine, but no such possibility was open to the woman who was dissatisfied with her marriage. In a polygynous society a man might marry additional wives in order to have a tolerable marital life, but the woman whom he disliked was not permitted additional husbands. In those Western nations where separation is permitted but not divorce, the attitudes opposing a wife's entering into an unsanctioned public union are very strong, but the husband is usually permitted to have a mistress outside his household.

It is not correct to speak of divorce as a more extreme solution than some of the other patterns already described. For example, we do not know whether divorce creates more unhappiness than the introduction of a concubine into the household, or whether it is more extreme to divorce or to bear the misery of an unhappy marriage. In any event these choices are partly a matter of personal and societal values.

Countries with High Divorce Rates

In 1974, the number of marriages in the United States was over 2.2 million, and the number of divorces was almost 950,000. The United States has the highest divorce rate among Western nations.[15] Other countries with high rates for 1972,

---

[15] Paul C. Glick, "A Demographer Looks at American Families," *Journal of Marriage and Family Living*, Vol. 37 (February 1975), pp. 16, 22.

the latest date for which such figures are available, were Soviet Russia, Hungary, and Cuba. Other nations in the past have had higher rates than the United States, for example Israel (1935–1944), Egypt (1935–1954), and Japan (1887–1919). We shall comment on some of these countries briefly in order to understand better the relationship between divorce and the family system. In Table 11-2 various divorce rates over time are presented for comparison.

Table 11-2 Divorces per 1000 Marriages in Selected Countries, 1890–1974

Country	1890	1900	1910	1920	1930	1940	1950	1971–1974
United States	55.6	75.3	87.4	133.3	173.9	165.3	231.7	424 (1974)
Germany		17.6	29.9	40.7	72.4	125.7	145.8	186 (1971)
(1950–1971, W. Germany)								
England and Wales				8.0	11.1	16.5	86.1	279 (1972)
France	24.3	26.1	46.3	49.4	68.6	80.4	106.9	117 (1971)
Sweden		12.9	18.4	30.5	50.6	65.1	147.7	380 (1972)
Egypt					269 (1935)	273	273	204 (1971)
Japan	335	184	131	100	98	76	100	98 (1972)

Sources: All figures calculated from governmental sources and from *Demographic Yearbook* (New York: United Nations, 1974).

Note: A better measure of divorce frequency is the number of divorces per 1000 existing marriages, but the latter figure is not often available. The above rate compares marriages in a given year, with divorces occurring to marriages from *previous* years. However, changes from one year to another, or differences among countries, may be seen just as clearly by this procedure.

Traditional Japan prior to the Meiji Restoration in 1868 was a very stable society, but it had a high divorce rate. Indeed, not until the 1920s did Japan's divorce rate begin to fall below that of the United States. Nevertheless, marital instability did not undermine either the Japanese social structure or its family system.

How did the Japanese system work, with so high a divorce rate? In Japan, marriages were arranged by the elders of the two families through a marriage broker. If the family had wealth and position the couple were not expected to live separately from the groom's parents. Wealthy or not, if the groom was the eldest son it would ordinarily not set up a separate household. After marriage the matter of prime importance was whether the young bride would or could adjust well to her elder in-laws. She was under a stern obligation to pay great respect to them, to defer to their wishes, and to obey them. If she could not obtain or retain the approval of her in-laws, she would be sent back to her parents (commonly in the same village) with little regard to whether she and her husband got along well. The "divorce" in Japan, then, was a repudiation of the bride by her in-laws.

In Japan (as in most societies) the divorce rate was lower in the upper social strata than in the lower strata, in part because the nobleman could adjust to marital problems by obtaining a concubine, and a young bride had no re-sources for resisting her powerful in-laws. His wife's position was secure enough if she obtained the favor of her in-laws and bore sons for the family. And, since marriage among the nobility was often a family alliance, divorce was more undesirable because it would be more likely to cause conflict between the two families.

Changes in the Japanese family system have been extensive over the past 50 years and cannot be analyzed in detail here. For our purposes, the most important fact is the decline of the divorce rate since the 1890s, as shown in Table 11-2. One important shift has been towards an increasing proportion of marriage based either on personal choice or on personal preferences which are then approved by parents. Thus, the young wife has only to adjust to her husband's needs, not to the needs of a group of elders. Fewer young brides now live with their in-laws. Nevertheless, the culture remains family-centered to a considerable degree.

Changes in Divorce Rates as Indices of Other Social Changes

Increasing rates of divorce in various countries do not necessarily indicate that these societies are becoming disorganized, but they do show that changes are occurring within the family system as well as in the larger social structure. Clearly, the industrialization under way in most countries need not lead to an increase in their divorce rate. In Japan, the divorce rate has been dropping for well over half a century, and recorded drops in the Egyptian and Algerian rates suggest that the rates in other Arab countries may eventually decline below their highest points. By contrast, divorce rates have risen in every western European country where divorce is possible, and usually *at a faster rate* than in the United States. For example, the divorce rate in England a generation ago was about 6 percent, and is now 68 percent, of that of the United States. In the industrializing areas of sub-Saharan Africa and in the People's Republic of China, divorce rates are rising. In India the divorce rate has risen since 1955, when the Marriage Act extended the privilege of divorce to the entire population.

These two opposite developments are both results of a greater emphasis on the independent conjugal family unit in all these family systems. The new type of system has a relatively high divorce rate, but in some cases the rate may be lower than it was in the old system. Let us look at this conjugal system briefly.

Under the fully developed conjugal pattern, as in the United States, people have greater freedom of action and the right to choose their own mates. They depend less upon their older relatives, feel fewer obligations to take care of their elders, and, of course, receive less aid from them. Correlatively, the social controls on both sides are less exacting and less effective.

When husband or wife fails to find emotional satisfaction within this unit, there are few other sources of satisfaction and few other bases for common living. The specialization of service in an industrialized economy permits the man to purchase many domestic services if he has no wife, and the woman is increasingly able to support herself even if she has no property and no husband. For these reasons, the independent conjugal family is not highly stable.

On the other hand, where the union under the earlier system was fragile because of the elders, as in Japan, or dependent on the whim of the man, as in the Arab countries, the new system, with its greater independence of the young couple, more intense emotional ties of husband and wife with one another, and the increased bargaining power of the woman may mean a somewhat greater stability of the family unit.

Fluctuations and Trends in U.S. Divorce Rates

Divorce rates in the United States have fluctuated a good deal over the past century, but have shown a consistent upward trend. Table 11-3 presents this trend.

Table 11–3   Number of U.S. Divorces per 1,000
Existing Marriages, 1860–1968

Year	Divorces
1860	1.2 per 1,000 existing marriages
1880	2.2
1900	4.0
1920	7.7
1932	6.1
1940	8.7
1950	10.3
1960	9.2
1970	13.5
1974	424 per 1,000 marriage ceremonies

Source: Paul H. Jacobson, *American Marriage and Divorce* (New York: Rinehart, 1959), p. 90. The data from 1920 on contain annulments, and all these data are partly estimated since not all states are included in the divorce registration system. The earlier rates are, of course, even more open to question than the later rates. See also *Statistical Abstract of the United States* for recent data, as well as issues of *Monthly Vital Statistics Reports*. The last figure is calculated from Paul C. Glick, "A Demographer Looks at American Families," *Journal of Marriage and Family Living*, Vol. 37 (February 1975), p. 16.

Both divorce and marriage tend to follow the business cycle, increasing during periods of prosperity and decreasing during periods of depression. These data do not mean that families are happier during a depression or that people lead less contented family lives during prosperity. It is rather that the cost of the divorce itself and the still greater cost of establishing new households prevent people from embarking on such a venture during hard times. The effect can be seen dramatically in the swift change after the stock market crash in 1929. Up to that point, "the divorce rate had climbed to a new peak of 7.9 per 1,000 existing marriages. . . . In the deepening depression that ensued, the rate dropped more than one-fifth to a low of 6.1 per 1,000 in 1932 and 1933."[16] The frequency of divorce declined for marriages of long duration as well as for those of short duration. However, the return of better economic conditions soon pushed divorce rates to a new high.

The effect of war on divorce rates is somewhat less clear, but *after* the Civil War and after both world wars the rate at first rose sharply and then fell off somewhat, only to resume its upward trend after a few years. It seems clear that both wartime marriages and unions immediately upon the return of soldiers are less stable than marriages begun at other times. This is illustrated by the record total of 629,000 divorces and annulments which took place in 1946, after World War II, when in many cases the returning soldier and his wife could not adjust to one another.

In part, the higher number of divorces after a war, like the greater number of divorces during prosperity, is "caused" by the same factor: the greater number of *marriages* that occur then. The number of divorces will rise with the number of marriages, because more marriages are at risk and because the risks are greater in the first years of marriage. After the first few months of marriage the risk quickly rises, reaching a maximum during the third year. Between 20 and 25 percent of divorces occur within two years of the marriage.[17] During the past several years, short marriages have tended to break up somewhat earlier than in the past. However, there is also some evidence of an upswing in the divorce rate among people who have been married 15 years or more.

An examination of the long-term trend in United States divorce rates poses the question, "What changes in the social structure have taken place in the last 100 years that have had an effect on the family system and thus on the divorce rate?"

Perhaps the most striking changes have occurred in the general values and norms relating to divorce. Although divorce may now be viewed as an experience to be regretted, one which commands some sympathy, it is no longer considered a violation of public decency. Whether the individual is viewed as the sinner or as sinned against, divorce is generally accepted today as one possible solution for family difficulties.

Of course there are no public opinion surveys of this change of attitudes, which began during the last half of the nineteenth century. But newspaper debates, popular novelists' increasing use of divorce as a solution for bad marriages, and legislative debates in various states considering new divorce laws

---

[16] Paul H. Jacobson, *American Marriage and Divorce* (New York: Rinehart, 1959), p. 95.
[17] U.S. National Center for Health Statistics, *Vital Statistics of the United States, 1970,* Vol. 3: *Marriage and Divorce* (Washington, D.C.: Government Printing Office, 1970).

are evidence of a growing tolerance toward divorce.[18] Not even 100 years ago, however, was public opinion unanimously set against divorce. Church leaders and most public figures denounced divorce, but others attacked the idea that unhappy husbands and wives should remain together forever. The border and frontier states in particular did not have rigid views against divorce, and on the eastern seaboard Connecticut had liberal laws.

Over the past decade attitudes have changed still more, as indexed in new divorce laws. In 1969, California adopted the first no-fault divorce law in the United States. This law abolished the traditional requirement of "grounds for divorce," i.e., that husband or wife had to prove the other was at fault in order to obtain a divorce. Instead, no-fault divorce laws legitimate divorce by mutual consent, and indeed permit divorce if only one party feels the marriage is intolerable. Since 1970, 14 other states have adopted some form of no-fault divorce law, and an additional 10 states have added a no-fault provision to their existing grounds for divorce. That is, if husband and wife do not wish to be married any more, they can agree to a no-fault divorce, instead of choosing one of the traditional grounds for divorce.[19]

As disapproval of divorce waned, so did the social pressures opposing it. One hundred years ago kin and friend networks advised warring spouses to adjust, to bear the burden, and to accept their fate. A divorce would mean losing respect in one's social circle. At present, these pressures are much reduced, and it is probable that at least some people within one's network will agree that a divorce is the only sensible solution.

Much more fundamental has been a change in the *alternatives* faced by the husband or wife considering a divorce. Formerly a man found it very difficult to get along from day to day unless he had a wife, especially on the farm. Women, in turn, had almost no opportunities for employment except as domestics. Even when a woman's family had money, returning to her family was viewed as a shameful alternative. Perhaps most central is the fact that since being divorced is no longer a stigma, and there are many people who have been either widowed or divorced, another marriage is a real alternative. Generally, high divorce rates are accompanied by high *re*marriage rates in most societies.

A deeper change in values should also be noted, which affects a wide range of social behavior along with divorce—the growing belief that people have a right to make decisions on the basis of what they think will bring them happiness. This has meant that people no longer believe that the central purpose of marriage is the founding or maintenance of a family line, carrying out one's duties as spouses or parents, or contributing to the community, but instead one's

---

[18] An older compilation of this material, concentrating on the novel, may be found in James H. Barnett, *Divorce and the American Divorce Novel, 1858–1937* (Philadelphia: University of Pennsylvania, 1939, privately printed), esp. Chs. 3–5.

[19] Lenore J. Weitzman, Herma Kay, and Ruth Dixon, "No-Fault Divorce in California," paper presented at proceedings of the American Sociological Association, San Francisco, August 1974.

own self-development or growth, or at a minimum one's own satisfaction. A widespread philosophical view urges that one should seek one's own happiness when duty conflicts with one's personal wishes, even if that means the breakup of a marriage.

These pressures and patterns are not at all peculiar to the United States. The general rise in the divorce rate in Europe is not caused by the insidious influence of "bad" American customs. Rather, the United States is in the vanguard of a process which is worldwide. The European countries follow behind simply because they are going through similar phases at a later date.[20]

Where will this process end? Will the ratio of divorces to marriages rise until there are as many divorces each year as marriages? It is not easy to make adequate predictions about the future divorce rate, because we cannot be sure that we have located the major factors that have caused its rise in the past. At present, however, the alternatives that modern society presents, of different spouses as well as different marital arrangements, continue to increase. With reference to both jobs and domestic tasks, neither spouse is as dependent upon the other as in the past. There is little evidence of any greater conservatism in family values, and no prospective changes in the economic or social structure that would support an increase in marital stability are on the horizon. At present, then, it seems likely that the divorce rate will continue to rise in the future, if not at the same rate as in the past.

Divorce and Desertion in Different Segments of the U.S. Population

The similarities of people in the United States form the basis of national unity, but individuals in different positions *within* the social structure have different experiences, interpret them differently, and are subjected to different social influences. Consequently, it is to be expected that differentials in divorce, annulment, and desertion might be found among people from different socioeconomic strata, religions, races, and rural or urban backgrounds. Some of these differentials are presented and analyzed below.

Common sense has long suggested that economic factors may create marital discord, while many family analysts asserted that economic factors hide more basic conflicts, such as definitions of sex roles, personality differences, or divergent life styles. Doubtless both positions contain some truth. Neither position, however, predicts whether the divorce rate would be higher toward the lower classes. Even among the well-to-do, people experience financial problems, and other basic conflicts might be as intense in any class.

---

[20] For a more elaborate analysis of these processes, see William J. Goode, *World Revolution and Family Patterns* (New York: Free Press, 1963). For Japan, see Ezra Vogel, *Japan's New Middle Class; The Salary Man and His Family in a Tokyo Suburb*, 2d ed. (Berkeley: University of California Press, 1971), Chs. 8, 13. The same processes are also to be observed in Africa, India, and the Arab world.

Both common opinion and family analysts continued to suppose, in any event, that divorce was more usual toward the upper social strata, perhaps because it was given so much more publicity when it occurred there. The relationship between class and divorce rates was not definitely settled until the 1950s, when a full analysis disclosed that this correlation was *inverse*—that is, the divorce rate *drops* toward the *upper* socioeconomic levels, whether the index used is occupation, income, or education. It was also ascertained that the divorce rate among blacks is higher than that among whites and has been for decades.[21]

Unquestionably, the popular notion that it was the well-to-do who divorced was originally based on fact, for it was once only they who could afford it. Until about the Civil War, some states required, as in England, a special act of the legislature in order to get a divorce. Nevertheless, there was no reason to suppose that the marital *stability* of the lower strata was greater at any time in our history. The popular picture of lower-class family life as stable, warm, and inviting, with frequent exchange of kinship obligations and tightly knit against the outside world, was a literary stereotype, often used by authors who had never observed a lower-class family. Lower-class instability was probably expressed in separation and desertion when divorce was very difficult. These forms of dissolution continue to be more common among the lowest strata in our population. At just what date the lower strata began to exceed the middle and upper in turning to legal divorce cannot be determined, although the pattern was definite by the 1920s.

A more general formulation can be made, cross-culturally and historically. Where divorce is extremely difficult, and thus requires considerable resources, it is a privilege that mainly the upper social strata enjoy. As each country moves away from those conditions, and permits a more or less "free market" in divorce, the basically greater marital instability among the lower social strata exhibits itself. Where, as in Japan or the Arab countries, divorce was relatively easy to begin with, that inverse class correlation shows itself whenever it is

[21] The divorce rate among blacks, compared to the rate among whites varies according to the index used and by sex as well. The range of variation is narrower for blacks than for whites whichever index is used. (That is, the rate of marital instability is higher among blacks than whites at the higher socioeconomic levels but lower among blacks than among whites at the lower socioeconomic levels; however, the relationship is roughly inverse for both.) The relationship between income and the divorce rate is inverse for males of either race but direct, i.e. positive, for women of either race. The relationship between education and the divorce rate and between occupation and marital instability is more complex among black males, and females of either race, than among white males.

This relationship was reported in William J. Goode, "Problems in Divorce Adjustment," *American Sociological Review*, Vol. 14 (June 1959), p. 397. The first elaborate analysis of this relationship was reported in William J. Goode, *After Divorce* (New York: Free Press, 1956), Chs. 4, 5. These findings were confirmed by several later studies. As Goode notes, there were also many prior sets of data that revealed this relationship but—perhaps because it was contrary to common belief—it was glossed over or ignored as a fact to be analyzed theoretically. For data only on white women, see Larry L. Bumpus and James A. Sweet, "Differentials in Marital Instability: 1970," *American Sociological Review*, Vol. 37 (December 1972), pp. 754–766.

possible to obtain data. The relationship can be demonstrated on a worldwide basis.[22] In Table 11-4 it is shown clearly for the United States.

Table 11-4   Male Proneness to Marital Instability by Urban Occupation in the United States (1970)

Occupation	Index to proneness to marital instability*
Professional, technical	72
Managers and administrators	90
Clerical, sales	97
Craftsmen	103
Operators	112
Laborers	124
Service workers	135

Source: Calculated from U.S. Bureau of the Census, *1970 Census of the Population*, Subject Report PC (2) 4C, *Marital Status* (Washington, D.C.: Government Printing Office, 1972), p. 142, Table 5, by dividing:

$$\frac{\text{* Separated } + \text{ divorced } + \text{ married more than once as \% of total in each of those categories for each occupational group}}{\text{Number "ever married" as \% of total "ever married" for each occupational group.}} \times 100$$

What causes such a correlation? Socioeconomic factors indirectly affect many decisions within the family. Our "affluent" society tends to encourage people to want a great number of goods and services that their incomes will not afford. As a consequence, most families feel their income is insufficient. In spite of the growing egalitarianism in the society, the economic responsibility still rests primarily with the husband, and any failure is seen as his failure. In addition, every study of job satisfaction shows that men in jobs with more responsibility, prestige, and income enjoy those jobs more than men in lower-ranking jobs enjoy theirs. Thus, in terms of both job satisfaction and economic reward, there seems to be more socioeconomic dissatisfaction, and thus possibly more marital tension from that source, toward the lower social strata. These economic strains may affect noneconomic relationships, such as sexual and marital adjustment.

Other class factors also affect divorce rates. First, the network of both kin and friends is larger and more tightly knit toward the upper social strata than at lower socioeconomic levels. Thus the social consequences of divorce are likely to be greater. Second, from the husband's point of view, getting out of family obligations toward the upper social strata is harder. More prosperous

[22] For data on this point, see William J. Goode, "Marital Satisfaction and Instability: A Cross-cultural Class Analysis of Divorce Rates," *International Social Science Journal*, Vol. 14 (1962), pp. 507–526.

families are more often locked into long-range property investments which are harder to sell or dispose of wisely, if divorce requires that it be divided. More of the income is allotted to long-term expenditures such as houses, insurance, and annuities. By contrast, more of the income at the lower social strata is allocated to consumer goods such as food and clothing. Thus it is not as easy for the husband in somewhat higher socioeconomic strata to walk out on his obligations.

Third, from the wife's point of view, her potential loss through divorce is greater at higher-class levels, and thus she is more unwilling to give up the marriage. The difference between the potential earnings of the lower-class wife and her husband is smaller than between those of the middle- or upper-class wife and her husband. (Highly educated wives with high incomes would, by this reasoning, be more likely to experience divorce rates—and they *do*.)

All of these factors press in a similar direction. They make it somewhat more costly or less desirable for people toward the upper social strata to get a divorce.

Class differences also show up in desertion or separation, for lower-class husbands can more easily move and avoid being traced. Although the actual number of desertions has not dropped, a higher percentage of lower-class instability is now expressed in legal divorce than in the past. First, more working-class couples can now afford divorce. Second, husbands are now more easily traceable. Third, some states have inaugurated programs for tracking down husbands who are derelict in meeting obligations to support their children.

In general, desertion rates are higher among the poor, and higher among blacks than among whites. It is difficult to ascertain the exact number of desertions in any year, since many people separate each year and some separations become desertions or divorces. Moreover, some husbands leave their families but their whereabouts are known, so that there are no official data which distinguish between husbands who have "disappeared" and those who have simply moved elsewhere. In any event, official, legal separations are not as common as unofficial ones. In one study of approximately 3,000 families who were receiving grants for their dependent children, it was ascertained that more than four-fifths of the fathers were simply absent from home.[23] In the 1970 census, 1.5 million women said their spouses were absent, and 1.7 million said they were separated from their spouses. The percentage of both separations and absences is higher among blacks than among whites.[24]

Desertions are officially noted, although not counted, in three situations: the divorce courts, applications for compulsory support from the husband, and for Aid to Families with Dependent Children. It may well be that there has

[23] U.S. Bureau of the Census, *Statistical Abstract of the United States, 1974* (Washington, D.C.: Government Printing Office, 1974); data are from Findings of the 1973 AFDC Study, U.S. Social and Rehabilitation Service, May 1974 (Part I).

[24] U.S. Bureau of the Census, *1970 Census of the Population,* Subject Report PC (2) 4C, *Marital Status* (Washington, D.C.: Government Printing Office, 1972), Table 1.

been no real increase in the rate of desertions over the past decades. As noted, the increase in numbers may actually be due to the development of more facilities for giving help to the deserted family and for tracing absent husbands.[25]

With reference to the somewhat higher divorce and desertion rates among blacks, two broad patterns should be noted here. One is that depression and prosperity seem to have a greater effect on the black than on the white divorce rate.[26] The second is that as the black population becomes more assimilated into the dominant cultural patterns, both their marriage and divorce behavior becomes more like that of whites.

Depression has a greater effect on the black divorce rate because blacks have proportionately fewer white-collar jobs, where employment is steadier. In a comparison of black-white divorce differentials from 1890 to the present time, the only census in which the percentage of divorced blacks is lower is that of 1940, after nearly a decade of the Depression.[27] In 1973, the ratio of the black to the white percentage divorced was 1.4.[28] This is higher than in 1960, when the ratio was 1.25, but it is still lower than any of the pre-Depression decades.

The earlier figures should of course be viewed with some caution. In the period prior to World War I, most blacks were in the rural south, and the major migration to northern cities did not occur until that wartime period of job opportunities. Although the ratio of black divorces to white divorces was high in that earlier period, those census data do not prove that blacks were in fact using southern divorce *courts* to a greater extent than whites. Many blacks lived together without legally marrying, and relatively fewer attempted to obtain formal divorces. Census data simply tabulated the percentage of blacks and whites who gave the answer "divorced" to the census enumerator.

[25] Under a new federal law related to the Social Security Act, state agencies will not get federal aid for child support if they do not set up procedures for establishing parenthood, tracing parents, and applying legal pressures to force parents to contribute to the support of their children. It will thus be still harder for fathers to ignore the court provisions for child support, or to refuse support to their illegitimate children. See *Information Memorandum*, Social and Rehabilitation Service, Department of Health, Education, and Welfare, January 29, 1975. The law is Public Law 93-647. For additional data on the techniques for tracing parents, see Lenore J. Weitzman, *Social Suicide: A Study of Missing Persons*, Unpublished dissertation, Columbia University, 1970, Ch. 11.

[26] That blacks experience greater economic difficulty than whites during a depression has been documented many times and need not be reveiwed here. This point is, however, different from the assertion that unemployment affects marital instability directly, within nondepression years. One study asserts that the relationship between marital instability and unemployment is the same among whites and blacks, i.e., there is no positive association. See Greta Miao, "Marital Instability and Unemployment among Whites and Non-Whites, The Moynihan Report Revisited—Again," *Journal of Marriage and the Family*, Vol. 36 (February 1974), pp. 77–86.

[27] For an analysis of these data, see William J. Goode, *Women in Divorce* (New York: Free Press, 1965), pp. 49–51.

[28] The ratio of 1.4 between the percentage of blacks who state they are divorced, compared to the percentage of whites who give that answer, is based on a 1973 25% sample of the population 18 years and over, reported in the *Statistical Abstract of the United States, 1974.*

That meant that their spouses were no longer living with them, but it does not prove that they had obtained a legal divorce. On the other hand, such figures do show that black marital *instability* was and is greater.[29] By contrast, at the present time the figures almost certainly reflect the fact that blacks increasingly use the divorce courts, and it is now clear that at lower socio-economic levels both white and black family units are less stable.

Religious Differentials in Marital Dissolution

Ascertaining divorce differentials by religion is difficult since the U.S. census does not ask questions about religion, and all findings are based on relatively small surveys. The religious beliefs of Catholic, Protestant, and Jewish denominations are opposed to divorce, but vary in the intensity of their disapproval, the Catholic Church taking the most negative position.

Several general factors interact to produce religious differentials in marital dissolution. First, religious groups strongly opposing divorce do have lower divorce rates, but their total voluntary marital dissolution rate may be almost as high as that of other groups. For example, Catholic-Catholic marriages experience the lowest divorce rates among the major religious groups, but being reluctant to divorce does not create harmony. Catholics seek another solution: they also experience somewhat higher desertion rates.

Second, people who claim no church membership are less strongly opposed to divorce, but they may be deviant in other ways, too, so that their divorce rate is higher than that of any other group. By contrast, when both spouses are of the same religion, divorce rates will be lower, and when both spouses are affiliated with different churches their rates fall in between. Interfaith marriages are less stable, because if husband and wife come from different churches they may well come from different social backgrounds, too, and as a consequence engage in more conflict. As against that likelihood, those who marry outside their church are also less committed to its beliefs, so that purely religious conflict within the marriage may be reduced somewhat.

Third, mothers generally control the religious education of their children, but this may create some conflict in certain types of interfaith marriages. The

---

[29] It should be emphasized that the data proving the greater instability of black families cannot be called into question by the present-day, often vituperative, attacks on family sociology as having been ignorant, arrogant, or insensitive with respect to the wide differences among family types. In fact the most responsible scholars, black and white, have pointed out these differences for many decades. Some of this defensive literature has tried to emphasize the "great strength" of the black family in spite of its instability. For arguments on this point, see Andrew Billingsly, "Black Families and White Social Science," *Journal of Social Issues* (Summer 1970), pp. 127–142; as well as Leonard Lieberman, 'The Emerging Model of the Black Family," *International Journal of Sociology of the Family* (March 1973), pp. 10–22. See Robert Staples, "Public Policy and the Changing Status of Black Families," *Family Coordinator* (July 1973), pp. 335–351, who notes, however, that the family-headed household will continue to exist in large numbers among blacks in the future. The common notion of "black family matriarchy" is based on little evidence that need be taken seriously.

most likely types are those in which the husband is Catholic or Jewish and the wife is Protestant or non-Jewish. The wife then expects to control the religious affiliation of her children, but both Catholics and Jews (male or female) are likely to feel a stronger obligation than Protestants do to rear the children in their own faith. Thus if the wife is Catholic she expects as a mother to control the religious education of her children and as a Catholic feels strongly about that obligation. If her husband is Protestant, he expects her to control that education, and feels less strongly about it anyway. By contrast, if the husband is Catholic he feels a stronger obligation, but his wife expects to make the decisions about the children's religion, so that they are somewhat more likely to be in conflict. The same type of conflict is somewhat more likely to occur when the husband is Jewish and the wife is not. Thus the likelihood of conflict about religion is greater when the husband is Catholic or Jewish and the wife is not than when the wife is Catholic or Jewish and the husband is not.

Two final comments should be added here. First, more analysts of religious behavior argue that the differences among members of different churches have been declining for some decades. Second, differences in family behavior between those who attend no church at all and those who attend church regularly are often greater than the differences among people who are affiliated with different churches.[30]

Differences in Social Background

We have moved from the broad institutional factors that create or rule out the option of divorce to some of the class, race, or religious factors that lower or raise the likelihood of marital instability and divorce. Here we shall assess the effects of still more specific background traits of couples on their rates of marital dissolution. Later we shall analyze the complaints and countercharges of divorcing couples.

Some of the findings from various research studies may be summarized as follows:

BACKGROUND CHARACTERISTICS ASSOCIATED WITH GREATER

OR LESSER PRONENESS TO DIVORCE

Greater proneness	*Lesser proneness*
urban background	rural background
marriage at very young ages (15-19 years)	marriage at average ages (males, 23; females 20) or older ages
shorter acquaintanceship before marriage	acquaintanceship of two or more years prior to marriage
short engagement, or none	engagement of six months or more

---

[30] With reference to religious differences, see Thomas P. Monahan, "Some Dimensions of Interreligious Marriages in Indiana, 1962–1967," *Social Forces,* Vol. 52 (December 1973), pp. 195–203.

parents with unhappy marriages	happily married parents
couples who do not attend churches, or are of different faiths	couples who attend church regularly, are Catholic, or adhere to the same church
kin and friends' disapproval of the marriage	kin and friends' approval of the marriage
general dissimilarity in background	similarity (homogamy) of background
disagreement of husband and wife on their role obligations	agreement of husband and wife on their role obligations

The following are operating factors in these relationships: (1) individual values—whether persons from a particular religious or social background are more strongly opposed to divorce than other people are; (2) pressures from kin and friends; (3) mate-selection processes; and (4) the ease of marital adjustment, depending on the similarity of social backgrounds.

All of these considerations, of course, may play some role in any of the regularities noted above. We have already noted the influence of religious factors. Rural populations are more strongly against divorce than residents of urban areas.[31] In general, people from a "conventional background"—who are also more inclined to say that they are "contented"—are more opposed to divorce and so are less likely to resort to it.[32]

Opposition to divorce may not lessen the possibility of *conflict* by much, but it does lessen the likelihood that individuals will use divorce as a solution for their conflict. Of course, differences associated with some of these background traits have been reduced over the past several decades—for example, religious differences and rural-urban social differences. In any event, rural-urban differences play a smaller role in social life simply because the rural population is now so small a percentage of the total population.

As noted earlier, when one's social circle of kin and friends is opposed to divorce, one is less likely to seize upon that solution to marital unhappiness. This applies to religious differences, as well as to rural-urban differences. Kin and friends are also relevant in understanding the seemingly trivial impact of long- or short-term acquaintance, and long- or short-term engagements.

The approval of kin or friends is often thought of as unimportant, since many modern commentators assert that each individual should follow his or

---

[31] On the rural-urban differences, see Karen Hillman, "Marital Instability and Its Relation to Education, Income, and Occupation," in R. F. Winch et al. (eds.), *Selected Studies in Marriage and the Family* (New York: Holt, 1962), pp. 603–608.

[32] As the reader might suspect, whether people will assert that they are contented or happy in marriage is partly determined by whether they want to respond with "socially approved" answers. On this point, see Vernon H. Edmonds, Glenne Withers, and Beverly DiBatista, "Adjustment, Conservatism, and Marital Conventionalization," *Journal of Marriage and the Family*, Vol. 34 (February 1972), pp. 96–103.

her own choice of a spouse. In fact, however, much social research shows that members of a social network do have very great influence on most fellow members' attitudes and behaviors. In any event, the approval of kin and friends has a double aspect. On the one hand, it is simply a *prediction:* These people know the engaged couple and have a judgment as to whether they are fitted for one another. On the other hand, approval actually helps to bind the couple together, for it makes the interaction more pleasant between the engaged or married couple and others.

Similarly, length of acquaintance or engagement is an *index* of the couple's commitment to one another, but it also reflects a longer period of shared experience, during which the two people involved may adjust to one another or decide that they cannot tolerate one another. With reference to the length of acquaintanceship or engagement, however, we should keep in mind that this, too, is a *class* factor, as longer engagements are more common in upper-class families. A very short engagement in an upper-class or upper-middle-class social stratum is more likely to be a deviant union in some respects than it would be in the lower social strata.

With respect to age at marriage, the reader should be reminded that a very high proportion of the marriages involving females at about 15 years of age are likely to be preceded by conception, and thus are likely to be forced marriages. As a consequence, compatibility between the two spouses is likely to be lower than for people married at later ages, aside from any other factors that might be of importance. Thus, again, a short engagement is but an index of other social and cultural events.

Grounds, Complaints, and Conflicts in Divorce

From the Civil War until about the time of World War II, the *legal* grounds for divorce did not change in any fundamental fashion, but the *interpretation* of those grounds did change. Specifically, cruelty had always been a popular basis for a divorce complaint, but its meaning changed from physical cruelty, or unusual personal indignities, to mental cruelty, which has been interpreted to mean little more than a charge of "incompatibility." In the 1880s, about 40 percent of all divorces granted were for desertion, but as other grounds have become more easily available, desertion has played a lesser role in divorce complaints. Since World War II, as noted earlier, there has been a steady move toward some version of "no-fault" divorce, which has meant in most states that neither spouse has to prove the other is "guilty." In fourteen states, this means something much more specific: the possibility of obtaining a divorce even if the other spouse is *opposed* to it, without making additional complaints about drunkenness, adultery, or neglect to provide.

Thus, divorce complaints may be classified in three great time patterns since the Civil War: (1) a very long period in which extremely serious charges still had to be made in court, and one spouse was presumed legally to be "guilty," while a gradual change occurred in the direction of accepting less serious complaints as an adequate basis for divorce;[33] (2) a period beginning before World War II, and continuing after it, in which "cruelty" was increasingly viewed as including almost any behavior that the complaining spouse objected to; and (3) the last decade, in which a larger number of states have added the possibility of a "no-fault" divorce, or even made that the exclusive basis of divorce, requiring only that one spouse assert that he or she no longer wants the marriage.

From these changes, it is clear that at no time in the past or present can a tabulation of divorces according to the *legal* grounds of the divorce complaint be viewed as a description of the real *conflict* that was taking place within the marriage. At best, such a tabulation of the official grounds in the past reflected only the fact that our legal system required one party to prove that the other party was "guilty." In general, those divorce grounds were chosen that permitted the easiest possible divorce, while preserving both parties from any serious inquiry into their actual behavior. We can conclude that when very serious charges were made they are very likely to have been correct, but most divorcing parties have chosen relatively innocuous charges, if their lawyers felt that would guarantee a divorce.

We cannot, however, assume that we have obtained the "real" grounds for the divorce when we have turned away from the divorce suit itself, with its legally correct formulation, to direct *questions*. The real complaints of husbands and wives against one another are not always "real causes." A wife may complain that her husband has had an affair, but she does not ask what failure on *her* part made an outside solace attractive to her husband. A husband may complain that sexual relations with his wife were always unsatisfying, but never know that *his* ineptitude was the major cause of her frigidity. Neither may express a complaint about financial matters, but both may have lived under great tension because of their economic problems. In short, we cannot assume, even when we have asked the suffering and complaining partners the "real" causes of their divorce, that their answers state the reality.

When divorced spouses are offered a list of the serious complaints they had about their marriages, they check a large number of them. The conflicts they check are likely not to be very different from the answers given when the spouses are asked, "What was the *main* cause of your divorce?" In both cases, they are likely to mention whatever are the *main areas of social life together*. A large percentage will say that their spouses paid too much attention to someone else, or had an affair; about one-third to one-half of the wives will complain that their husbands did not support them adequately; an equally large group will say that their husbands drank or gambled. Almost as many will make some complaint that could be viewed as a conflict of "personality."

Efforts to understand the deeper meaning of these complaints—sometimes called "causes"—are not very successful. For example, very likely almost one-

---

[33] For some historical data on divorce complaints, see Jacobson, *op. cit.*, p. 124.

half of these complaints will center about some aspect of *affectional life*—poor sexual adjustment, flirting with others, unresponsiveness or hostility, or no longer being in love. The complaints are real enough, but one may assume those same husbands and wives acted differently at the beginning of the marriage. What caused them to change? That is, what are the causes underlying those complaints? "Nonsupport" is common too, and certainly causes marital dissension, but this role failure may in turn occur because the husband no longer wants to support his wife and family, often because he has become involved with someone else, or at a minimum because he has become hostile toward his wife. Thus, each such complaint, when challenged, forces us to a deeper level of probing, where we once again have to ask, "What caused *that* failure?" A generation ago, sexual maladjustment may have been caused by a repressive childhood, but now it is mainly caused by a growing coolness or animosity between the spouses. But again one seeks in vain for some underlying, basic "cause."

However, it is not necessarily true that great events have great causes. Doubtless, a few marriages end because of some large, single cause, such as the husband's violence or the wife's neurosis. But most modern divorces are the result of a multitude of smaller difficulties, which create a continuing, cumulative process of conflict in which spouses gradually come to reject both the relationship and each other; in the process both persons begin to change as well. At the end, it is really true that neither can find in the other the delightful, attractive person he or she had originally married, for that person does not exist any more[34]—at least not for his or her marital partner.

Patterns of Conflict

In newspaper accounts and novels, divorce conflict is often presented dramatically, but the final battles are the climax of a long, drawn-out series of often minor maladjustments and difficulties. Typically, the period of serious conflict extends over years (and is likely to be two years or more even from serious consideration of divorce to the final decree), and is usually punctuated by harmonious periods as well as episodes of anger. That is, a divorce conflict curve would not be a simple upward or downward line. It would be a kind of spiral in which husband and wife come back to disagreements and agreements from time to time, but gradually move further away from any possibility of real reconciliation.

In one common pattern of conflict, husband and wife are wounded in some disagreement, and one or the other withdraws some of his or her affection. On the other hand, they must work together and live together, while the with-

---

[34] For tabulations of such complaints, see Harvey J. Locks, *Predicting Adjustment in Marriage* (New York: Holt, 1951), pp. 75–76, as well as Goode, *Women in Divorce*, p. 123. See also Judson T. Landis, "Social Correlates of Divorce or Non-divorce among the Unhappily Married," *Journal of Marriage and Family Living*, Vol. 25 (May 1963), pp. 178–180.

drawal of affection makes that more difficult. Thus, at the next stage they are even less prepared to reconcile their differences, for they have been forced to cooperate when in fact they still felt hostile.

As the periods of coolness or annoyance increase in frequency or duration, there may come a time when one spouse or the other decides that he or she simply does not care much any more what the other one does or even thinks. The conflict proceeds to the point where they begin to look at each other as strangers, and thus each need not tolerate any longer the bad habits, the domineering qualities, the selfishness, or the nagging of such a stranger.

It is this *reciprocality* of the conflict, the contribution that *both* husband and wife make to the eventual divorce, that renders the old legal theory of a fault divorce so hollow. A fault-oriented legal procedure requires that the innocent party bring suit against the offender, to prove that the erring spouse has broken the rules of marriage. This legal theory also assumes there is no collusion between the spouses in getting a divorce. Both of these elements violate the facts.

Although an increasing percentage of divorces are granted to men, the majority are still granted to wives. Nevertheless it cannot be assumed that wives are the innocent parties in all of those cases. Rather, the kinds of charges that are required in most divorce courts can be brought against the husband without hurting his reputation, while the corresponding charge brought against a woman might damage hers to some degree. In general, husbands and wives use the legal grounds that are least accusatory but most effective in getting the divorce approved by the court.

One study of the divorce conflict process suggested that husbands want to break up the marriage more often than do wives, for some of these reasons: (1) the husband invests less of his total emotion in the family than does the wife; (2) the husband still has more opportunities to become involved with alternative mates outside of marriage; and (3) the adjustment to a divorce is easier for a husband than for a wife, on both social and economic grounds.

Thus, husbands want to get a divorce before their wives do, and they face the problem of leaving a marriage when the wife is somewhat less willing.[35] This analysis[36] suggests that our society permits the husband to engage in behavior that would bring about an end to the marriage. Specifically, he can engage in a wide variety of activities that cause still greater conflict and difficulty at home, but for which he will lose little respect from his friends or fellow workers. For example, he can consistently come home late to dinner, or can plead a heavy burden of work and thus neglect his family. He can spend more time in social activities outside the home, without his wife. He can refuse to take part in any other responsibilities of the home, pleading either lack of time or even his "rights as a husband" to be free of such burdens.

In short, he may eventually make himself so obnoxious, without harming

[35] The reader should remember that about half of all states now have at least a no-fault provision in their divorce laws.

[36] Goode, *Women in Divorce*, Ch. 11.

his reputation as a fine fellow, that his wife becomes as willing to break up the marriage as he is. One consequence of her then being willing to take the initiative is that he can feel somewhat freer of guilt than he otherwise might for setting in motion the process of conflict that eventually led to the divorce.

INTERNAL DISSOLUTION: THE "EMPTY SHELL" FAMILY

The state may ask many questions of the individual, but so far it has not dared to ask whether a supposedly intact family is in truth merely a physical household unit, in which the individuals have no satisfying emotional connections with one another. There is no way by which sociologists and marital counselors can locate a reliable sample of such cases, although a few will turn up in almost any family study. This brief section, then, can present only a few unsystematic observations on this type of family dissolution, not a series of firm conclusions drawn from research studies.

As noted earlier, most families that divorce pass through a state—sometimes *after* the divorce—in which husband and wife no longer feel bound to each other, cease to cooperate or share with each other, and look on one another as almost a stranger. The "empty shell" family is in such a state. Its members no longer feel any strong commitment to many of the mutual role obligations, but for various reasons the husband and wife do not separate or divorce.[37]

Violent, open quarrels are not common in this family, but the atmosphere is without laughter or fun. Members do not discuss their problems or experiences with each other, and communication is kept to a minimum. Parents and children fulfill their *instrumental* obligations but not their *expressive* ones. The husband holds a job and provides for the family. The wife takes care of the house, prepares meals, and nurses those who become ill. The children go to school and do their chores at home. But any spontaneous expression of affection, or even of delight in a personal experience, is rebuffed by the others. Each tells the others whatever is necessary to integrate their instrumental activities—when one will be home for a meal, how much school supplies cost, or what chore needs to be done.

Usually one or both of the spouses are strong personalities, at least passively. The rationalizations, on the part of one or both, for avoiding divorce include "sacrifice for the children," "neighborhood respectability," a belief that it will harm the husband's occupational success, and a religious conviction that divorce is morally wrong. The first two of these are factually erroneous, since children in such a family unit are usually starved for love, embarrassed when friends visit them, and ashamed to be forced to "explain" their parents' behavior to others. The neighborhood always knows about the internal dissolution

---

[37] This type of family can be profitably contrasted with the somewhat comparable types labeled "conflict-habituated," "devitalized," and "passive congenial," in John F. Cuber and Peggy B. Harroff, "Five Types of Marriage," in A. S. Skolnick and J. H. Skolnick, *Family in Transition* (Boston: Little, Brown, 1971), pp. 287–299.

of the family, for the couple engage in few activities together, show no pleasure in one another's company, and exhibit innumerable, if tiny, differences from normal families.

The repression of emotion extends, naturally, to sex as well. This type of family is usually highly conventional with respect to sex roles, and considerably less liberal in its attitudes toward sex than other families in its neighborhood. The daughters are given less freedom than other girls their age and face more restrictions upon what types of activities they may engage in, where they may go, and when they must be home. Sexual relations between husband and wife are rare and unsatisfactory. Adolescents keep their dating activities a secret, or lie about them, to escape punishment.

The hostility in such a home is great, but arguments focus on the small issues rather than the large ones. Facing the latter would, of course, lead directly to separation or divorce, and the couple has decided that staying together overrides other values, including each other's happiness and the psychological health of their children. The casual visitor may believe that the members are cold, callous, and insensitive to each other's needs, but closer observation usually discloses that at certain levels they are sensitive: They prove that they do know each other's weaknesses and guilts by the way in which they manage frequently to hurt each other.

Until an adequate study of such families is made, these observations cannot be properly assessed. The nearly unrelieved bleakness of the picture may be erroneous, in overlooking some possible rewards that members get from one another in such a unit.

THE EXTERNALLY INDUCED CRISIS

This section focuses primarily on the family's *adjustment* to crises like depression, war, separations, natural catastrophes, incarceration, and death, since in this type of marital breakup the cause of the problem lies outside the family itself. Space does not permit us to examine all of them. We shall, then, focus on only one, adjustment to the death of a spouse.

Similarities between Divorce and Bereavement

Sociologists have often noted the similarities in adjustment to divorce and the bereavement process. In both, a set of role relationships has been disrupted, requiring a profound adjustment throughout the family network. Moreover, the old habit patterns continue, making it difficult for an individual to find immediate substitutes or to fill his life with alternate satisfactions. In both events, sexual satisfaction is likely to become less easy to obtain. In both, emotional problems may be so intense that the sex drive temporarily diminishes. If the divorced or dead spouse is the husband, his initiative and leadership in the family are lacking. Economic problems may become pressing. If the missing spouse is the wife, profound adjustments in household management are necessary. In either case emotional solace, friendship, and love are absent. Children of the same sex as the missing spouse no longer have an adult model to follow and the spouse remaining with the children is likely to find controlling and supervising them difficult and wearying. In both situations there are likely to be endless discussions with friends and relatives about the former spouse as well as about the problems of adjustment.

Differences between Divorce and Bereavement

Nevertheless, the institutionalized character of death contrasts it sharply with divorce.[38] Death formally requires kinfolk and friends to attend the bereaved person, to offer their services, to give emotional support. They must be at the funeral if possible, and may offer financial help, even if it is insufficient. The bereaved person is not only permitted to express grief, but encouraged to do so. The social support at this moment makes it possible to give way completely to grief.

The rituals and observances also give the bereaved person some definite tasks to carry out. These are not difficult, and may be no more than moving from one part of the funeral parlor to another, sitting in one place rather than another at the cemetery, greeting and talking with callers and kin, and so on. The bereaved person is not permitted to grieve alone, but is forced, almost mechanically, to go through various activities that serve to keep him or her within the social network. The funeral service itself expresses the finality of death. There is nothing in the sequence of steps toward divorce that has this character or necessitates support from others.

The bereaved person does not usually feel hostility toward the wife or husband who has died; on the contrary, there is a tendency to idealize the past relationship and the person. Both sides of the kin network are encouraged to praise the dead one, whereas in the case of divorce each side tends to criticize the relative's former spouse. Wounded pride does not figure in death as it does in divorce, and of course the widower or widow is less likely to feel a sense of failure simply because the relationship has been broken.

Although the customs of mourning do not specify ways to cope with many of the serious problems of death, they do offer some few solutions. Divorce offers none, simply because the social responses to divorce are not deeply institutionalized. There is no set of agreed-upon rights and obligations concerning the divorced person. Although there is considerable similarity in the adjust-

---

[38] For a good analysis of the effects of death on the family, see F. Ivan Nye and Felix M. Berardo, *The Family* (New York: Macmillan, 1973), Ch. 23, who draw on the much earlier work of Thomas D. Eliot in the 1930s (see also Eliot's "Bereavement: Inevitable but not Insurmountable," in Howard Becker and Reuben Hill (eds.), *Family, Marriage, and Parenthood*, 2d ed. (Boston: Heath, 1957), pp. 641–668. See also the interesting observations of David Sudnow, *Passing On* (Englewood Cliffs, N.J.: Prentice-Hall, 1967). For further comparisons, see Paul Bohannon (ed.), *Divorce and After* (New York: Doubleday, 1970) and Helena Z. Lopata, *Widowhood in an American City* (Cambridge, Mass.: Schenkman, 1973).

ment patterns of divorces, these similarities are not so much results of specific social *customs* as they are of such common social *experiences* as the economic needs of a broken family unit, the loneliness of the divorced person, and the difficulty of working out an easy life adjustment outside marriage in our society.

The widow and widower, as noted, are guided more than the divorced by social customs. These customs include a period of mourning, in which the individual is supposed to avoid relations with the opposite sex. There are always some who praise the widow who so reveres her dead husband that she never remarries, and this was the ideal in both China and India. The widow is less able than the widower to find a new spouse, in part because an older man is not criticized for marrying a considerably younger woman. Twice as many widowers as widows remarry during the first five years after the death of their spouses. On the other hand, both widows and widowers are now much more likely to remarry than a generation ago.

CHILDREN IN MARITAL DISORGANIZATION

Refined statistical calculations show that children have only a small effect on marital stability.[39] Over the past decades, couples with children have formed an increasing percentage of all divorces. Approximately 1.2 million children of minor age were involved in the divorces during 1974. Something more than 30 percent of school children are *not* living with a father and a mother who are in a continuous first marriage.[40] Overlapping somewhat with this category, in 1972 there were over 3 million children who had lost one or both parents by death at some time.

It is difficult to measure exactly the impact of a family breakup on children. Without question, children are more likely to grow up to be law-abiding, healthy, and happy if they spend their entire childhood in a happy family than if the family is broken by divorce or death. On the other hand, the family can be equally split by violent disagreements between spouses *within* marriage.

The general association of broken homes with delinquency has been demonstrated by many studies. This association can be traced to two large sets of factors. One is that both divorce rates and death rates are higher in slum areas, where delinquency rates are also higher. Thus, the association may in part be a spurious one. The other large set of factors is of course the failure of parents in cases of serious marital conflict, divorce, or death to play the normal parental roles, and to carry out the usual activities of social control and socialization in the development of their children. Consequently, even after the possibly spurious factor of class has been controlled, the delinquency rate of children is higher for broken than for unbroken homes. In a parallel way, delinquency

---

[39] For data once more supporting the notion that the effect of childlessness on the divorce rate is largely spurious, see Robert Chester, "Is There a Relationship between Childlessness and Marriage Breakdown?" *Journal of Bio-Social Science* (October 1972), pp. 443–454.

[40] Glick, *op. cit.*, p. 10.

rates are higher for those whose parents are separated or divorced than for those who lose a parent through death.

Unfortunately for those who seek easy solutions, it also seems likely that families in which there is continued marital conflict are more likely to produce children with problems of personal adjustment or juvenile delinquency than families in which there is a divorce.[41] These comparisons prove that it is the quality of the childhood experience, not the mere fact of divorce, that is crucial, and it is the conflict leading to divorce, rather than the broken home that follows it, that has the greater impact on children.

Almost all people—75 to 90 percent, depending on age, sex, and class—who divorce or lose their spouses during the marriageable ages will remarry, and thus most of their children will eventually enter a new family relationship. The problems of adjustment in that new state have not been sufficiently explored. There is some evidence that children's adjustment is likely to be better with a stepfather than with a stepmother. After all, it is usually the stepmother who will shoulder the daily household burdens. It is easier for a man to adjust to a set of children not his own than it is for the woman.[42]

In any event, the few solid data we have suggest that children do by and large negotiate this adjustment, and profit by it, since the reconstituted two-parent home is likely to be more satisfying to children than the broken one-parent household.

PARENT-YOUTH CONFLICT

Some kind of parent-youth conflict begins with the first strong assertion of the infant's will. The term, however, more commonly refers to the adolescent period, when several social factors converge to create a qualitatively different type of conflict. First, the child simply begins to be more competent at resisting authority. He or she is physically larger and often stronger than the mother—and sometimes the father as well. The adolescent child is fully as capable of reasoning well as the parent is, and thus can often win an argument. In factual matters, the adolescent may be reasonably well informed. Of greater social importance is that people in their teens spend much of their time outside the family, and thus cannot be easily supervised. In addition, as their sexual development proceeds, they not only enjoy a greater amount of energy and quick-

---

[41] For summary data on this point, see Nye and Berardo, *op. cit.*, pp. 514ff., esp. Table 20.1. Earlier, both Nye and Landis had proved this difference: see F. Ivan Nye, "Child Adjustment in Broken and Unhappy Broken Homes," *Journal of Marriage and Family Living*, Vol. 19 (November 1957), pp. 356–361; and Judson T. Landis, "A Comparison of Children from Divorced and Non-divorced Unhappy Marriages," *Family Life Coordinator*, Vol. 11 (July 1962), pp. 61–65.

[42] For data on these hypotheses, including support for the notion that stepfathers have better relations with their stepchildren than do stepmothers, see Lucille Duberman, "Stepkin Relationships," *Journal of Marriage and the Family* (May 1973), pp. 283–292. For an earlier study of stepchildren, see William C. Smith, *The Stepchild* (Chicago: University of Chicago Press, 1953).

ness of recovery than the exhausted parent; they also begin to feel internal pushes and stresses that cause them to seek their own goals with greater persistence.

The parent-youth conflict most widely discussed relates to what might be called philosophical and political matters. That is, young people begin to acquire different values and attitudes and different preferences about future and present life styles—in short, to reject values their parents have been trying for years to inculcate. Thus, when public leaders and parents complain about fights with the younger generation, they focus not so much on ordinary juvenile crime, or the unwillingness of adolescents to engage in household chores, but on more fundamental problems. Even when arguments focus on sexual behavior, the adolescent causes less concern to his or her parents by "yielding to temptation," and more by arguing that it is his or her *right* to do whatever he or she pleases.

In explaining these changes, analysts point to such factors as the rise of competing philosophies, the mass media, or the importance of the peer group, but a more fundamental factor is simply the *speed of social change* in modern societies. This can be best understood by reference to the life cycle. In traditional societies, children typically went through experiences that were similar to the ones their parents had at the same age. This situation no longer occurs. The present parental generation simply did not grow up in the kind of world the contemporary adolescent inhabits. They did not know, for example, the easy availability of drugs, the contraceptive pill, a continuing, enormous military complex, and the threat of war and world destruction through the hydrogen bomb.

The new conflicts are more akin to those that occur during a revolution. Both in revolutions and in the modern form of rapid social change, young people not only affirm the irrelevance of their parents' philosophies and political attitudes and urge that they give up their authority; typically they also *organize*, or at least attempt to create a social life that is isolated from the control of their parents. In communist China, the Soviet revolution, revolutionary Cuba, and Nazi Germany, young people organized themselves, or were organized by the new leaders, into clubs, troops, voluntary associations, or disciplined cadres, to maximize the attainment of specific objectives for the society. Many such organizations have been created in the United States as well, both with and without a revolutionary aim, but even without formal organization much of adolescent social life attempts to avoid the surveillance of adults, and to assert the autonomy of youth.

In Western nations, the "new generation" is a large segment of the population, forms a large part of the economic market, and is thus also the target for numerous adult advisors, commentators, and prophets, who seek partly to express these new strivings and philosophy, and partly to guide them. Perhaps at no prior time in the history of the Western world have young people from the ages of, say, 14 to 22 played so large a role in national life from literature to politics.

However, in any given battle between a set of parents and their nearly grown children, it is difficult to separate the differences between generations from the ordinary difficulties that parents and their offspring have in any generation, in any historical epoch. If adolescents are trying to reject the authority of their parents, they do have a handy weapon in the new ideologies, new leaders, and new data that support their position. The conflict, nevertheless, is real, and hurtful to the members of the family.

In the past decade, tens of thousands of families have split apart because of this kind of warfare between the generations. It seems certain that more young people have simply left their homes and cut off all contact with their parents, for months or years, than at any previous time in the history of this country. Doubtless the publicity in the past decade has been greater, because a very high proportion of these young people were members of middle-class families who expected their children to follow a normal progression through school and career.

Conflicts between generations are, as noted, not new. There were rebellious young adults in classical China and Japan, as there were on the U.S. frontier.

Perhaps the hurt is more intense in our generation, because both parents and children feel that they ought to "love one another."

It is obvious that any major *policy* to reduce parent-youth conflict is not likely to be successful. Both the sets of major variables, intrafamilial and societal, are not very amenable to intervention. Few policies could conceivably affect the socialization processes of individual parents in any reasonable length of time; and our ability to alter the massive, slow forces of social change in the nation as a whole seems quite limited.

In any event, most cases of parent-youth conflict are not "solved." Adolescents and young adults simply move out and drift away for a while. The problem is glossed over and avoided, and parents and children avoid seeing one another except for an occasional swift meal in silence or awkwardness. When young adults begin to take independent jobs, marry, or have children, some of the old conflicts seem to lessen and areas of basic agreement once again emerge. At this phase in their lives many young adults begin to have mild twinges of sympathy for the problems their own parents had some years before.

For all the bitterness and ferocity of parent-youth conflict, the destinies of parents and children remain indissolubly linked in all but a few cases. Their lives and emotions remain intertwined not merely during the parents' lifetime, but for years after they have died. The battles lose their intensity, and parents and children do not typically stay apart. Every study of visiting patterns among young parents and *their* parents the world over shows frequent visiting, telephoning, and exchanging or giving of gifts.

WOMEN'S LIBERATION: NEW ROLES IN THE FAMILY?

The period since World War II has witnessed a period of political revolt throughout the world. The downtrodden have been restive or rebellious against their masters. At the present time, in perhaps most countries of the world, some women have begun to express their demands for liberation.[43]

We need not apply the extreme term "revolution" to this movement, but let us at least note some of its characteristics that parallel other, more radical, revolts. They may be summarized as follows:

1. The rulers—in this case, men—are surprised to learn that the people they had controlled (i.e., the women) are not mainly contented with their lot.
2. Men find it difficult to understand what women want, because they can-

[43] Among the books that elucidate one or another aspects of this topic, see Cynthia Fuchs Epstein, *Woman's Place* (Berkeley: University of California Press, 1970); Betty Friedan, *The Feminine Mystique* (New York: Norton, 1963); William L. O'Neil, *Everyone was Brave: The Rise and Fall of Feminism in America* (Chicago: Quadrangle, 1968); Jo Freeman, *The Politics of Women's Liberation: A Case Study of an Emerging Social Movement & Its Relation to the Policy Process* (New York: McKay, 1975); Judith Hole and Ellen Levine, *Rebirth of Feminism* (New York: Quadrangle, 1971), Anne Koedt, Ellen Levine, and Anita Rapone (eds.), *Radical Feminism* (New York: Quadrangle Books, 1973).

not easily face the fact that women desire a fundamental change in all of their rights and obligations.

3. Fewer women are willing to tolerate small slights or social restrictions they once had accepted.

4. Men become angry at being viewed as oppressors.

5. Women leaders are usually of a higher educational and social rank, but the movement attracts converts (of varying commitments) from all ranks and races.

6. Those who become adherents experience a great access of energy, a feeling they can accomplish tasks they would not have tackled before.

Judged by the egalitarian canons of our official ideology, women can make an excellent case that they are not given equal rights. In all societies whatever tasks are defined as exciting, interesting, and challenging are labeled as appropriate for men only. Men in every society typically maintain a philosophy that asserts the excluded segments of the population are simply not *capable* of doing high-level tasks—and they also erect rules to insure that result. All societies attempt to prevent the awkward situation that would arise if many of the excluded people proved they could indeed do the work.

It is especially within the family that the burden on women is great. In this and other societies (including all the communist nations), it is assumed that women should permit men to make the final decisions about important matters relating even to the home, such as where the family will reside, who is to work, or which job opportunities will be accepted. In general, it is assumed that men's needs should be taken care of first, since what they do is more important.

If the women's liberation movement gains momentum, family relations will be transformed and many of the existing role patterns will be dissolved or weakened. Women will acquire full rights not merely to sexual enjoyment, but to sexual exploration outside of marriage. They will have the right to take the initiative in all matters relating to their occupation and family, and will enjoy as much authority in family relations as men do. Laws will distinguish less between men and women than they now do. The division of labor within the family will not be based on sex, and there will be considerably greater conflict as to who will do what. If, as now seems clear, all of us are mixtures of both "male" and "female" traits, then some liberated women will be able to find mates who complement their personalities well, but others may not. In any event, decisions as to who will do the housekeeping or take care of the children will not be based on sex.

These changes will have some repercussion in the occupational world. The movement to establish comprehensive day care centers has taken very few and hesitant steps over the last decade, and at present there are few facilities for handling the problems that will be created by women's assertions of full equality. It seems unlikely that U.S. society will move toward any collective responsibility for child care, as in the Israeli kibbutz. Perhaps under the new dispensation, *both* men and women might ask themselves the question, "Do I want to take a job or stay home and take care of the children?" Perhaps, too, some husbands and wives will turn away from the idea of intensive and total dedication to a single career, in which (at present) a housewife is used as a support staff that permits a man to devote himself wholeheartedly to his occupation.

Although the safest prediction about such matters is that things will go on for a long while very much as they do now, it seems likely that women will not ever again accept the domination they once tolerated, and this trend is visible in other parts of the world as well. Of course, the older generation has always shown great cleverness and tenacity in holding on to traditional family and sex role arrangements, but the young do have an advantage that is hard to match: They will eventually replace their elders. People also change as they assume new statuses and roles, and many young women who now seek liberation will doubtless adjust to, and be relatively contented in, traditional housekeeping roles. Nevertheless, it seems likely that this social movement will continue to gain momentum, and will certainly have a large impact on role relations within the family.

SUMMARY

1   In the life of the individual, family events are likely to be a major cause of unhappiness or pleasure. They are likely to be experienced as unique events, different from those other people go through. The analyst of family disorganization must examine those processes in part through the eyes of the participants, but also adopt the broader perspective of considering them as a normal part of the larger social structure. In that broader view, we examine differences in rates of conflict or marital dissolution over time, in different countries, or among different classes and groups.

2   Family disorganization may be defined as the inability or unwillingness of one or more family members to carry out their role obligations as other members define them. A basic classification of different types of disorganization processes includes: (1) the uncompleted family, or illegitimacy; (2) voluntary departure of one or both spouses; (3) changes in role definitions, resulting from cultural changes (e.g., the women's liberation movement, parent-youth conflict); ·(4) the "empty shell" family; (5) the crisis caused by "external" events like death or imprisonment; and (6) internal catastrophes that cause involuntary role failures. This classification reminds us that everyone will at some time experience one or more of these kinds of events and processes.

3   Although a family that does not begin cannot be said to be "disorganized," illegitimacy is properly to be included among the disorganization processes because it involves failure in role obligations—on the part of the potential father-husband and on the part of the parents of the young mother and father. Moreover, the social processes that produce illegitimacy or help people adjust to it are important foundations of the family system itself, in this and in other societies. In addition, the United States is part of the New World, in which the illegitimacy rates are especially high in the lower social classes. This social pattern is caused to a considerable extent by the failure of the larger society to give adequate opportunities to its disadvantaged groups.

4   The divorce process is especially ineresting among the forms of social disorganization, partly because it helps us to understand other aspects of family behavior.
In addition, many other types of family disorganization (separation, desertion,
mental illness of one member) are likely to end in divorce sooner or later.
Divorce is also the focus of much moral and social concern, and changes in the
divorce rate are usually an index of changes in other parts of the family system.

5   In analyzing differences in divorce rates among several countries, as well as
over time, it should be pointed out that both changes in evaluations of divorce
and differences in the *resources* of family members will affect their decision
to divorce. Divorce rates also differ among people of different religions, classes,
and races. Beyond such numerical differences, however, it is illuminating to
analyze the conflict process itself, and the contribution that each person makes
to it.

6   Children deserve special attention, both as part of the divorce process and as
participants in parent-youth conflict. That family disorganization generally has ill
effects on children is without question, but three factors—(a) class factors, (b)
the family conflicts that lead to divorce, and (c) the divorce itself—can be distinguished in their effects on the subsequent life patterns of children involved
in family disorganization. With reference to parent-youth conflict, the speed
of social change in modern societies seems to be a fundamental reason why it
seems to be greater in this century than in any previous one, both in the United
States and in other nations.

7   Almost certainly, the women's liberation movement is not a passing fad; indeed,
its impact can be seen in family systems all over the world. It calls for important
changes to be made in the role obligations that family members owe to one
another. Thus, from a larger perspective it may lead to large changes in the
family system. However, it also has important effects on the willingness of
individual family members to accept their traditional roles. Some couples have
experienced these new roles as an opportunity or as a justification for divorce.
Other families have been the scenes of serious ideological conflict about marriage
itself. The movement has thus had some effect on day-to-day conflicts and
adjustments within most U.S. families, while also having some impact on what
the family system is to become in the future.

RECOMMENDED READING

Since the processes of family disorganization are partly "caused" by family
patterns, the student may wish to widen his or her perspective by reading one
of the standard textbooks on the family, such as F. Ivan Nye and Felix M.
Berardo, *The Family* (1973) or Robert F. Winch, *The Modern Family*, 3d ed.
(1971). For basic statistical data on divorce, see Hugh Carter and Paul C.
Glick, *Marriage and Divorce: A Social and Economic Study* (1970).

For a better understanding of both integrative and disorganizing forces in the
"new" family, see Arlene Skolnick, *The Intimate Environment* (1973), as well
as Hans P. Dreitzel, *Family, Marriage, and the Struggle of the Sexes* (1972).
For data on changing sexual patterns, see Morton Hunt, *Sexual Behavior in the
1970s* (1974).

For a recent analysis of the social processes that affect illegitimacy, see

Phyllis Hartley, *Illegitimacy* (1975). The older study by Clark Vincent, *Unmarried Mothers* (1961), remains a valuable source.

An older study of divorce and adjustment to it remains one of the most complete analyses: William J. Goode, *Women in Divorce* (1965). A broader perspective is that of Paul Bohannon, *Divorce and After* (1970). For a study of widowhood, see Helen Z. Lopata, *Widowhood in an American City* (1973), as well as Samuel E. Wallace, *After Suicide* (1973).

A special area of family disorganization is that of violence: see Suzanne K. Steinmetz and Murray A. Strauss (eds.), *Violence in the Family* (1974).

For some of the problems of family processes in black families, see Carol B. Stack, *All Our Kin* (1974), and Joyce Aschenbrenner, *Lifelines* (1975). For comparison with lower-class whites, see Joseph T. Howell, *Hard Living on Clay Street* (1973).

Processes of generational conflict are analyzed in many current works that focus mainly on political processes. See especially Richard Flacks, *Youth and Society* (1971), and K. Keniston, *Youth and Dissent: The Rise of a New Opposition* (1971). Arlene Skolnick (see above, Ch. 10) offers a wise analysis of parent-youth interaction in different cultures. See as well E. E. LeMasters, *Parents in Modern America* (1970).

The literature on the women's movement is large, and only a few works can be noted here. For comments on the movement itself, see Jo Freeman, *The Politics of Women's Liberation* (1975). The impassioned work of Betty Friedan, *The Feminine Mystique* (1963), states the issues powerfully, and the more analytic work of Cynthia F. Epstein, *Woman's Place* (1970), offers a sociological perspective on the changing family roles of women.

For alternative family styles, see the discussion in Hans Peter Dreitzel (see above, esp. Chs. 4, 5); R. D. Laing, *Politics of the Family* (1971); and C. Rogers, *Becoming Partners: Marriage and Its Alternatives* (1972); as well as Rosabeth Kanter, *Commitment and Community: Communes and Utopias in Sociological Perspective* (1972).

12

Community Disorganization and Urban Problems

JAMES S. COLEMAN

he term "community" concerns things held in common. They may be tangible, like the common property of a family or the common pasture lands held by a tribe. Or they may be intangible: common ideas, beliefs, and values; common customs and norms; and common or joint action of a group as a whole. Furthermore, when we speak of a community we ordinarily mean a set of people who have not just one element in common, but many.

WHAT MAKES A COMMUNITY?

In the past, the principal "communities" have been groups that were geographically or residentially defined. Sometimes the term is still used in that graphic sense. But there are numerous kinds of communities in the larger society—the adolescent community, the black community, and the academic community, to name three at random—and modern society may currently be undergoing changes from geographic to other bases for community. Thus it is important to examine in general both the processes that create a community and the contemporary conditions that lead to the disorganization of geographically based communities: neighborhoods, villages, towns, cities, suburbs, farming communities, any clustering of families in one locality. Some of these clusters, in fact, show hardly enough organization, hardly enough "commonness" among their members to be called communities. This is precisely part of our inquiry. The geographic clustering that constitutes a village, town, or city ordinarily sets in motion certain processes that tend to make a community. But sometimes these natural processes are unsuccessful or are blocked, and a community either fails to develop or falls apart.

This failure is of particular importance in large cities, where the processes that create a community are most problematic. Increasingly, the United States is a country of urban dwellers. About 67 percent of Americans live within metropolitan areas. A major problem of modern society, then, is the problem of the city: Can it be made a rewarding place to live, its costs diminished below its benefits—and if not, what is to be its future? This chapter cannot answer those questions, but it can examine the issues on which answers depend.

Common Activities

One of the elements of commonness composing a community is similarity of activities. In any community where people are engaged in similar activities and are subject to the same or similar events, the very similarity generates topics for conversation, leads people to enjoy one another's company, and creates bonds of mutual understanding. This is evident in such disparate situations as those indicated below.

1. In Harlem:
All the Muslins now felt as though 125th Street was theirs. It used to belong to the hustlers and the slicksters. They're still there, but Seventh Avenue belongs to the Muslins. I think everybody knows this now. This group just came down

and claimed it. They started setting up their stands and giving speeches. People started listening, and it just became known that if you wanted to hear a good antiwhite sermon on Saturday night, all you had to do was go to 125th Street and Seventh Avenue.

It made everybody feel as though they had something. I suppose there were many people who had been mistreated by the white boss during the day. They could come out on Seventh Avenue and hear something that would be consoling . . . hear some of the "Buy Black" slogans and "hate the white devils" speeches.[1]

2. In a London slum:

"My Mum comes around at about 3:15—she comes round regularly at that time to spend the afternoon"; "Mum's always popping in here—12 times a day I should say"; "Then my Mum and I collect Stephen from the school and go back to her place for tea"; "We usually have dinner round at her place"; "She's always popping in here"; "We've got four keys—one for each of us, one for Mum, and one for Mary. That's so they can come in any time they like." "Popping in" for a chat and a cup of tea is the routine of normal life.[2]

3. In a small southern community:

The drug stores serve as social centers and are rarely empty. People come, not merely to buy a toothbrush or a cake of soap, but to linger over the Coca-Colas, which they take in small, leisurely sips interspersed with long drafts of gossip. The proprietor is always at hand and always ready with conversation. The habitués are mainly young women, clerks and stenographers from the courthouse, and "men about town," which may mean a lawyer, a county official, a planter from the country. Upon inquiring for the owner of a plantation ten or twelve miles away, one is told that he can be found any day at his favorite drug store.[3]

The similar activities and experiences of these people in their respective communities are important elements in the development of a sense of community. They shape similar attitudes and behavior, and they create among people the sympathy, or mutual identification, that pulls them together. Though these in themselves give no cause for social organization, they do provide a basis from which organization may spring, and their absence takes this basis away.

There is more than mere similarity of activities and problems, of course, to the development of a locality into a community. Consider crime prevention, for example. Almost everyone in society has the same interest in protecting himself from robbery, murder, and other criminal actions. But a resident of Los Angeles and a resident of Portland, Maine, have few *common* interests

---

[1] Claude Brown, *Manchild in the Promised Land* (New York: Macmillan, 1965), p. 332.

[2] Michael Young and Peter Wilmott, *Family and Kinship in East London* (New York: Free Press, 1957), p. 31.

[3] Hortense Powdermaker, *After Freedom* (New York: Viking, 1939), p. 10.

in crime prevention. Different criminals operate in the two places. Most actions that Portland residents might take to prevent crime would have no effect on criminal activity in Los Angeles.[4]

The matter is different, however, within a city and is even more striking within a neighborhood. *Similar* interests in self-protection become *common* interests, since safety is dependent upon the same events. A crime wave may set off neighborhood meetings, formation of vigilante groups, decisions of the city council to hire more policemen, grouping of neighbors when venturing out in the evening, and other such activities. A crime wave constitutes a common problem for those living close together, and by the very problem it creates, it spawns social organization.

Crime is but one of many matters in which similar interests become common interests for people who are in the same geographic locality. Air pollution is another example. All persons have similar interests in protecting themselves and their possessions from pollution, but within a neighborhood this becomes a common interest. Individuals can hardly protect themselves from polluted air as well as neighbors can protect themselves jointly by means of concerted action. Thus air pollution, like crime, is a problem that requires and sometimes generates community organization.

Although the existence of common problems creates common interests in organization, it does not create organization itself. This comment on the difficulties of attacking air pollution shows some typical reasons for an inability to organize for action.

In a large city in the Middle West . . . a nationally respected air pollution official concluded a disquisition on the nation's mounting smog problem by abruptly sweeping aside his sliderule, charts and tabulations and exclaiming:

"That's the official story. Now do you want to hear the truth?

"The truth is that the critical ingredient in smog simply is politics. By that I mean people and their instruments of government, and their attitudes about a community problem.

"We know how to cure smog. It's not unduly difficult or expensive. The problem is getting the people in the community to support a cleanup program . . . ."

"Politically," the candid official continued, "air pollution is a far tougher can of worms than water pollution. With water pollution, the blame goes mainly to collective sources—municipalities and industries—and cleanup costs fall on them.

"A lot of air pollution goes back to individuals—their cars, their furnaces, their incinerators. When a cleanup program threatens to hit them directly, and change the way they're doing things, and cost a little bit, they back off."[5]

---

[4] Certain types of crime, of course, have nationwide networks, so that certain kinds of crime prevention (e.g., that of drug traffic) in one city have important repercussions for other cities.

[5] J. K. Hadden et al. (eds.), *Metropolis in Crisis* (Itasca, Ill.: Peacock, 1967), pp. 346–347.

Interdependence of Dissimilar Activities

Many of a community's activities are complementary, involving an exchange of goods or services. The merchants in a city ghetto make their living from its residents; the merchants in a suburb are sustained by the commuters. A public schoolteacher is engaged in activities very different from those of a steelworker, but the schoolteacher must be paid from taxes, and the steelworker's children must be educated. That is, any geographic community in modern society contains specialists engaged in activities that are not similar but that do depend upon one another.

The question can be posed as before: How do these interdependent activities help create a community, and under what circumstances do they lead instead to conflict?

The matter is somewhat more complex here than in the case of similar activities with common dependence. *Similar* activities and problems, carried out in physical contiguity, often generate common dependence on the same events, and thus common interests. But interrelated and *different* activities generate interests that are sometimes common, sometimes conflicting. Such an alternation is typical of these interdependent activities. In contrast to the similar activities that share a joint dependence, they cannot build up a strong bond of mutual identification. The common interests are soon supplanted by conflicting ones, and the initial impulses to identify with the other person are stifled. Hostility may develop when the activities generate conflicting interests over a period of time.

Within a geographic locality, these interdependent interests may often lead to community action. For example, in a city, political leaders, business people, and ghetto residents all have a common interest in increasing the number of resident black merchants in the ghetto—political leaders and business people because of an anticipated reduction in anti-merchant rioting, and thus a more peaceful city; ghetto residents because of the greater recycling of money within the ghetto itself. For some, as shopkeepers, it would mean direct money gains; for others, as customers, money gains would only be indirect. In either case, though, the increased racial identity would be a direct psychological gain.

Yet this is but one type of activity. Much of the time, in other activities, worker and manager, customer and shopkeeper, politician and constituent have conflicting interests. These conflicting interests do not lead to "common action," but to inaction or to community conflicts. Thus, the same interdependence of activities that upon occasion creates common goals and thus community action also upon occasion creates conflicting goals and thus community conflict or a failure to act.

There are two very different mechanisms that can insure motivation to common action. They are outlined by Ferdinand Tönnies in his concepts of *Gemeinschaft* and *Gesellschaft,* and by Émile Durkheim in his distinction between repressive and restitutive law.[6] The first of these mechanisms depends on common activities, and the second on interdependent ones. The mechanism of *Gemeinschaft* operates through a strong identification of each person with all others. If each in the chain of action is strongly identified with the others, if he feels their fates as *his,* then he will carry out action to insure their well-being. Such a situation most nearly obtains in small, close communities, where all the members have known each other for a long time, and close bonds of identification with one another and with the institutions of the community have grown up. Even in large cities, such identification is present in some degree. But in a modern, large, mobile society, such identification is slight indeed, and can hardly be counted on as sufficient motive power for action.

The second mechanism that may furnish the force for action is that of the *Gesellschaft*—the interdependence of self-interests. If my acting or failing to

[6] Durkheim's major concern was the difference between the kind of solidarity that develops through mutual identification and that which develops through self-interests. His discussion of repressive law (resulting from community solidarity) and restitutive law (resulting from a network of self-interests) shows an important consequence of these different forms of organization. See his *Division of Labor* (New York: Free Press, 1947), Chs. 1-4; see also Ferdinand Tönnies, *Community and Society,* C. P. Loomis, trans. and ed. (East Lansing, Mich.: Michigan State University Press, 1957).

act can be made to have consequences for *me*, then I will act, and the same holds for the other participants in this chain of action. The genius of social organization in a *Gesellschaft* (where mutual identification is attenuated and is no longer a sufficient motive for community action) is the existence of such mechanisms. In factories, one example of such a mechanism is the suggestion box, with rewards for accepted suggestions. The large factory is not, generally, a *Gemeinschaft*, in which there is mutual identification and sympathy between worker and manager; thus the worker has little or no motivation to make suggestions that will aid the manager. But if he is paid for accepted suggestions, there is potential benefit to him, not through the *Gemeinschaft* mechanism of identification with company goals, but through the self-interest mechanism of *Gesellschaft*. (The desire of some managers to operate their business like a "big happy family" shows their awareness that the self-interest mechanism of *Gesellschaft* is often not as efficient in insuring that the organization's interest is met as is the kind of identification involved in *Gemeinschaft*.)

Most complex actions in society depend upon both these mechanisms. Some institutions, however, depend more on one than on the other. The formally organized rational bureaucracy depends most fully upon relations involving self-interest, such as the reward-for-suggestion scheme mentioned above. Communities have traditionally included a higher component of sympathetic identification. But even a community often depends greatly upon actions that derive from pure self-interest.

Identification, Hostility, and Community Organization as a Residuum of Past Action

Action toward community problems requires organization. Sometimes appropriate organization is not forthcoming, as in the example of air pollution cited earlier. Sometimes no organization of effort can solve the problem. This was the case, for example, in the dust storms of the 1930s for which farmers had no immediate solution, individual or collective. But when collective action does take place, two types of residue are left. One is a residue of sentiments—either identification or hostility (or, in many cases, both).

Collective action makes it possible for each person to identify with the other, to feel the other's problems as if they were his own. Examples of this are abundant in times of stress. For example, a young man from Watts who had become a Rhodes scholar after being an All-American football player experienced the Watts riot this way:

> At the height of the violence, he found himself joyously speaking the nitty-gritty Negro argot he hadn't used since junior high school, and despite the horrors of the night, this morning he felt a strange pride in Watts. As a riot, he told me, "It was a masterful performance. I sense a change there now, a buzz, and it tickles. For the first time people in Watts feel a pride in being black. I remember, when

I first went to Whittier, I worried that if I didn't make it there, if I was rejected, I wouldn't have a place to go back to. Now I can say 'I'm from Watts.' "[7]

This young man was experiencing the same events as others in Watts, and it allowed him to feel identified with them. He was drawn close to them by the experience, and a sense of identity emerged. Through this kind of mutual identification, each person in a sense invests a part of himself in the others, creating a solidarity unit. Common interests leave a residuum, binding the community together, so that later events affecting one may be sympathetically felt and reacted to by all.

It is important to emphasize that such solidarity, which perhaps expresses the concept of community in its purest form, does not develop automatically. It develops through time, as a consequence of accumulated shared activities and experiences of the members of the community.

One community where such mutual identification grows is the military service, particularly during wartime. Soldiers share a multitude of experiences over a long, continuous stretch of time. They "go through hell together," as they are fond of saying. The bonds of mutual identity that grow among them are recorded in innumerable war stories. Paradoxically, a group of students occupying a college building in an anti-war demonstration generates similar bonds of mutual identity. Participants in such collective actions give reports of their experiences that sound strikingly similar to those of wartime comradeship and mutual bonds among soldiers.

However, when activities are interdependent but dissimilar, mutual identification is not the only sentiment that develops. Hostility can develop as well. Close, continued contact, even when voluntary, can create strong hostility as well as strong solidarity. Murder, the most violent of crimes, is the one most characteristic of small, stable communities. In the United States, murder rates are as high in rural areas as in urban areas, while most other crimes are far more frequent in urban areas.

How can the close association of small communities generate such intense hostility? Communities take action as communities, and whether the action is the result of a town meeting, the city council vote, the city manager's decision, or a popular vote, it will seldom be favored by all. For example, an action may be decided upon forbidding parking on one side of a street. The merchants on that side of the street feel that it will hurt their trade, as indeed it may. They cannot prevent the action, nor can they easily leave the community, but they can build up hostility toward those who are in favor of the action, or toward the community as a whole. As another example, a study carried out by the Kerner Commission showed that the most frequently expressed grievance of blacks in the cities surveyed concerned the police force.[8] This hostility may be generalized to include the city as a whole.

[7] *Life,* August 27, 1965.
[8] *Report of the National Advisory Commission on Civil Disorders* (Washington, D.C.: Government Printing Office, 1968), p. 83.

Such frustrations, stored up as unexpressed hostility, can create community disorganization in two ways: by building up to the point where the hostility becomes a basis for conflict in the community, and by preventing common action when the need for it arises. The latter is probably more important. Organization is necessary to carry out any community action. If there are barriers of hostility between the segments of the community that must cooperate, no action will be taken. Roads will not be built, school bonds will not pass, parks. will not be cared for, simply because the hostility arising from frustrated goals erects a barrier to community action. The drift of responsibility for social action from towns and cities to the state and federal governments may be partly the result of such community paralysis-through-hostility, itself a product of the social and economic polarities in the community.

Thus interdependent activities may produce not only identification of community members with one another—and thus the basis for community action—but also hostility and the basis for barriers to action.

In addition to a residue of sentiments, past actions in a community may leave an organizational residue. The organization of effort that resulted in solution of the problem continues. Organizations, once in existence, tend to perpetuate themselves, as many sociologists have pointed out.[9] Even when these are informal organizations, as in the case of many community groups, the bonds between the members keep them in place.

One example illustrates this well. A new community was constructed during World War II for shipyard workers. Because of the contractor's malfeasance and wartime problems, the community was beset by problem after problem: Sidewalks caved in, electricity did not work, and so on. Because these problems involved similar interests, because they could only be solved by joint action, and because they were important and repetitive problems, they generated an extremely strong nucleus of community organization. After the problems were solved, the organizations became engaged in various social, civic, and other activities on which voluntary community groups subsist. Like a volunteer fire department, however, the groups also constituted standby organizations that could mobilize to meet problems as they arose. Merton and associates, studying this community at a later time, found that its rich community organization contrasted strikingly with the unorganized state of another development that had not been faced with such problems. The latter development had been well-constructed, was well-managed, and offered no difficulties to be overcome. Its management, in fact, provided few opportunities for organizational activity to develop. Government was administered from above, not generated from below.[10]

A second example is even more striking, because it concerns a community

[9] An interesting example at the societal level is the National Foundation for Infantile Paralysis, which sponsors the March of Dimes. When polio vaccine was proved successful (in part through this organization's efforts), the foundation did not go out of existence, but searched about for a new goal. A part of that search included a survey of its facilities, reported by David L. Sills, *The Volunteers* (New York: Free Press, 1958).
[10] Robert K. Merton et al., *Patterns of Social Life: Explorations in the Sociology of Housing,* 1948 (hectographed).

in the heart of a large city. This community's struggles in rebuilding itself were examined in detail by Rossi and Dentler.[11] Hyde Park, in Chicago, found itself faced with sharp change: rapid decay of many of its buildings and a sudden influx of blacks. The prospect was one of quick transformation of a university community into a lower-class black ghetto, similar to much of the rest of Chicago's south side. But there existed in this community a high level of organization. This was true in part because people worked and lived in the same community. More than 90 percent of the faculty of the University of Chicago lived in the Hyde Park area or in areas immediately surrounding, and thus many of their interests were localized within the community. The community also subsisted on the talents and experience of many of its members in organized community activity. For these and other reasons, the grass-roots organization, which took the form of block groups and a larger "community conference," as well as churches, neighborhood recreation centers, and other associations, played an important part in rebuilding the community, stabilizing the population, and preventing further decay. The community has achieved that extremely rare condition in modern America: a stable (for over 20 years) racially integrated neighborhood. A most important factor in this achievement has been, as Rossi and Dentler show, the extremely high degree of community organization.

An important caveat must be added here: Despite the importance of organization, it can sometimes impede action and prevent a community from carrying out any positive plan. For instance, a legislature subject to highly organized pressure groups may find itself immobilized by them. Organization must exist if an acting unit is to cope with its problems; yet it must not be so strong, so rigid, that it cannot meet a change in the problems created by its environment.

It may seem paradoxical that problems create community organization, but such is nevertheless the case. A community without common problems, like many modern "bedroom suburbs" today, has little cause for community organization; neither does a community that has been largely subject to the administration of persons outside the community. When community problems subsequently arise, there is no latent structure of organization, no "fire brigade" that can be activated to meet them. A new town, a budding community, is much like a child. If it faces no problems, if it is not challenged, it cannot grow. Each problem successfully met leaves its residue of sentiments and organizations. Without them, future problems could not be solved.

Social Processes and Their Consequences for Community Disorganization

The processes described above provide the basis for either concerted community action or inaction and conflict—the basis for organization or for disorganization. They all stem from the activities in which people engage, and

---

[11] Peter Rossi and Robert Dentler, *Rebuilding the City* (New York: Free Press, 1960).

the events that may befall them. Table 12-1 summarizes these processes, showing how they lead to certain types of actions that in turn leave psychological and social residues to influence the subsequent path of the community.

The motives or springs for individuals to act in concert, in conflict, or separately lie in *interests* and *sentiments*; the residual *organization* (or lack of it) provides a further structuring of sentiments and interests to influence the community's future.

Either community action or inaction may result from the distribution of these processes over time and also through the structure of the community.

Table 12–1 The Processes Leading to Organization and Disorganization: Summary of Preceding Sections

Intersection of activities	Effects of activities	Present interests	Resulting action	Residues: sentiments and organization
Similar activities dependent on same events	→ Action which benefits A benefits B	→ Common interests	→ Collective action	→ Identification and community organization
Dissimilar interdependent activities →	Action which benefits A benefits B	→ Common interests	→ Collective action	→ Identification and community organization
			Conflict	
	Action which benefits A hurts B	→ Opposed interests →	Unilateral action →	→ Hostility and organized cleavage
			Inaction	
Independent activities	→ Action which benefits A does not affect B	→ Independent interests	→ Individual action	→ Indifference and mass

It is easy to see that these simple forces, operating with differing frequencies and in different social structures, can produce the most diverse forms of activity: mob action, violent conflict, dictatorial rule, apathy, states of tense inaction, and so on. Community disorganization in its various forms results from the recurrent operation of certain of the above processes to the exclusion of others. These processes are found in the smallest commune and in the largest cities. The outcomes of these processes, in conjunction with changing events, may be found in many of the problems of urban life today. It is to some of those problems that we now turn.

PROBLEMS OF THE URBAN COMMUNITY

The residential patterns in America have changed radically in this century. The progression has been a curious one: first a migration from rural areas and small towns into cities, creating a largely urban nation from what had been a largely rural one; then a movement from cities into suburbs, creating the concept of a "metropolitan area" of which the central city was only the focal point, declining in population; and finally, since 1970, the beginning of a movement away from metropolitan areas back into towns and smaller cities.[12] Community organization and disorganization have been greatly affected by these changes; in turn, certain problems of community disorganization have been partly responsible for the changes.

Briefly, the matter can be put this way: The great move to the cities, first by native whites and immigrants, and since World War II by blacks, was a migration in pursuit of economic opportunity. Industry was in the cities, and with industry lay jobs. In the process of relocation, a high degree of informal community organization, including the extensive set of norms that act as social controls, was left behind in the search for economic opportunity (and in some cases, in the search for freedom from those social controls). The migration out of the city, and now even out of the larger metropolitan area, is in part an escape from the problems of community disorganization that abound in cities, and are most pronounced in the largest ones. Moreover, two factors have disconnected economic opportunity from urban residence: the ease of transportation in the era of the automobile and the relocation of industry to suburban industrial parks, or even to rural areas.

Thus there was first a movement away from the informal community organization of the small town and rural area, and then a movement away from the community disorganization of the city. Although this second movement, radiating out from the centers of population density, does not disregard economic opportunity, it is not motivated by that opportunity as was the move to the cities. It is a move of the middle classes, who have solved the pressing economic problems, and search instead for a higher quality of life than they feel able to find in the city.

Current Problems of Urban Life

In June 1975, a national sample of city dwellers were asked, "What do you regard as your community's worst problem?" By far the greatest proportion (21%) mentioned crime. Then came unemployment (11%), followed by transportation problems (including traffic congestion), education, housing, and high taxes. These are the obstacles to a satisfactory quality of life as seen by city dwellers. Except for unemployment, they are the problems that families

[12] See U.S. Bureau of the Census, *Current Population Survey Mobility Estimates, 1970 to 1973*, Report P-20, No. 262 (Washington, D.C.: Government Printing Office, 1974).

attempt to solve by leaving the cities. We will examine two of the issues that are of most concern to city dwellers, crime and school-related problems.

These two social problems of the cities, crime and education, are important barriers to the further development of urban life in America. Attempts to re-constitute cities by drawing middle-class whites back into them have been largely unsuccessful, in some part for these two reasons. As those efforts toward revitalization were occurring in the 1960s and 1970s, disparity in crime (espe-cially robberies, which involve the threat of personal harm) and in schools between city and suburbs was increasing. These were hardly propitious circum-stances for a rebirth of the cities.

Crime Crime, a direct manifestation of community disorganization, is the most severe problem faced by urban residents. And crime is much more exten-sive in the cities than anywhere else. In the six cities in the United States with populations over 1 million, the rate of reported robberies per hundred thousand people was 756.2 in 1973. This rate declines sharply with city size, to 60.9 in cities of 10,000 to 25,000 population, less than one-tenth the big-city rate.[13]

Crime also has been increasing rapidly in recent years. Two national popu-lation surveys that asked about victimization by crime showed that in 1966 about 32 out of every thousand households had been burglarized, and in 1973, 94 out of every thousand, an increase of 197 percent in this seven-year period.[14] These statistics lead immediately to two questions: What is the cause of crime in the cities? What can be done about it?

One cause of high crime in the cities is the absence of informal community organization such as exists where population density is less and populations are more stable. The recent formation of vigilante forces for neighborhood protection is an attempt to reinstate that social control. But informal social control, coming from within the community itself, cannot survive in unstable communities with shifting populations and high population densities. What is necessary is a form of social organization that for dense and shifting popula-tions is equivalent, in its control of crime, to the small community's informal norms.

The formal system of criminal justice, consisting of police, courts, and prisons, is a functional equivalent of the informal controls of a small com-munity. This system of justice is effective at some times and places but not at others, and it is growing less effective in large American cities. A recent study suggests that the source of its declining effectiveness lies very simply in a

---

[13] Federal Bureau of Investigation, *Uniform Crime Reports* (Washington, D.C.: Govern-ment Printing Office, 1973), pp. 104–105. Burglaries declined from 1850.4 in the largest to 965.5 in the smallest cities, that is, to half the big-city rate. Burglaries, however, are of less concern to victims, because they do not involve a personal confrontation and threat of physical harm.

[14] James Q. Wilson and Barbara Boland, "Crime," in William Gorham and Nathan Glazer (eds.), *The Urban Situation* [tentative title] (Washington, D.C.: The Urban Insti-tute, 1976).

decreasing rate of arrest when crimes are committed, and a decreasing rate of conviction and imprisonment when arrests are made.[15] In 1960, there were 24 arrests for every 100 crimes reported in the FBI Uniform Crime Reports, and about 35 persons were sent to prison or jail for every 100 arrests. This means about 8 persons imprisoned for every 100 reported crimes (.24 $\times$ .35 = .08). In 1970, there were only 16 arrests for every 100 reported crimes, and only about 19 persons sent to jail for every 100 arrests. This results in only about 3 persons imprisoned for every 100 crimes (.16 $\times$ .19 = .03). If a probability of .08 of serving a sentence after committing a felony seems low, then a probability of .03 is low indeed. One result of this dramatic reduction is that there were fewer persons in prison at the end of 1970 (196,429) than at the end of 1960 (212,957), despite the population increase and despite the very great increase in crime.[16]

The impact of such a decline in effectiveness on the increase in crime is very great, even if imprisonment has no deterrent effect on persons who might commit crimes. For example, if each criminal commits 10 felonies per year, and, if convicted, serves a sentence of one year, an increase from a zero conviction rate to a 5-percent rate means a 33-percent reduction in total crime; if the conviction rate is 10 percent, the reduction in total crime is an additional 17 percent, or 50 percent.[17] These reductions arise merely from keeping the criminal out of circulation, even if the imprisonments have no deterrent effect on others at all. That is, they arise because the criminal is in jail at the time he would otherwise be committing a crime. The reduction in effectiveness of the criminal justice system between 1960 and 1970 would mean, if there were no changes whatsoever in the number of persons who commit crime or in their rate of committing crime while out of prison, an increase of over 40 percent in crime from 1960 to 1970, simply because the criminals spent more time on the streets, free to commit crime.[18] Although these increases in crime are only illustrative, since they are based on the assumption that each criminal commits 10 felonies per year and is imprisoned for one year if convicted, they show how much effect on crime observed changes in the effectiveness of the criminal justice system can have. (If each criminal committed 20 felonies per year instead of 10, the increase in crime due to the reduced effectiveness from 8 percent to 3 percent would be about 85 percent; if 5 per year, the increase would be about 22 percent.)

A more effective criminal justice system is not, of course, a complete solution to the problem of crime in cities. What is important is that as a community

[15] Wilson and Boland, *op. cit.*, pp. 43, 44.

[16] U.S. Bureau of the Census, *Statistical Abstract of the United States, 1971* (Washington, D.C.: Government Printing Office, 1971), p. 160.

[17] Wilson and Boland, *op. cit.*, p. 47.

[18] 3 percent conviction represents a 22 percent reduction in crime relative to zero conviction. 8 percent conviction represents a 45 percent reduction relative to zero conviction. The increase of "over 40 percent in crime rate" is calculated by (1 − .22)/(1 − .45) −1, or .42.

grows in size, and as its rate of population turnover increases, the informal social controls become less effective and the formal system must take over its functions. If neighborhoods in cities were tight, self-contained units with stable populations, informal community organization could continue to operate. Because they often are not, the burden falls on the city's formal agencies, which in contemporary America appear unable to cope with it.

Problems in education   Unlike crime, the problems of education in American cities are not direct manifestations of community disorganization. But they are related to community organization and disorganization in important ways. The issues related to education in recent years show this well.[19] First, there has developed in the last few years a crisis of authority and control in the schools. Superintendents were once in control of school policy, and principals in full authority over their buildings. With increasing frequency since the middle 1960s, however, control of school policies has been contested by the federal and state governments and by the courts. Authority over school activities is contested by teachers, with new power through unionization, and by parents, sometimes with new power through community school boards covering a segment of the total school district. Secondary school students have challenged the schools' authority with increasing success through student "bills of rights" and through court suits on haircuts, dress, and suspensions. The resulting state is an unstable one; it is a transition stage between a past form of organization with its accompanying legitimate realms of authority and a new form of organization that will differ in substantial ways from the old. The new form is not yet evident but it will clearly involve a greater degree of autonomy and self-determination on the part of high-school students and a greater voice in school policy by teachers' organizations, as well as, very likely, a greater voice by state and federal government.

Apart from this crisis of authority in schools, two major issues threaten to create chaos in urban schools. One is school finance, and the other school desegregation.

Costs of public schools rose 164 percent between 1964 and 1974 throughout the United States. At the same time, public confidence in the schools declined precipitously, as can be seen by comparing Gallup polls or other surveys over a period of years. One consequence of this loss of confidence is an increasing rejection of school bond issues and tax increases. In 1964, 72.4 percent of all bond issue elections were approved by voters. The percentage continually declined to a low of 46.7 percent in 1971 (though in 1974 it increased to 56.2 percent). It is not at all clear just what the outcome of this collision course will be for public education, though an increase in federal financing of schools (which has already increased sharply from 4.4 percent of total school expenditures in 1963–1964 to 8.7 percent in 1972–1973) constitutes one avenue of

---

[19] These issues are discussed at greater length in James S. Coleman and S. D. Kelly, "Education," in Gorham and Glazer, *op. cit.*

escape. The greatest component of the increased cost is an increase in teaching costs, through salary increases and workload decreases.

Racial desegregation of schools has created the greatest violence and disorder of any educational issue in many years, from Little Rock to Boston and Louisville. In the early years after the Supreme Court decision, some disorder occurred in small towns, but in recent years violent responses to school desegregation have been confined to cities, though not to the South.

The initial goal in school desegregation was the elimination of "dual" school systems in the South, where black and white children were assigned by law to different schools. This was outlawed by a 1954 Supreme Court decision, but not completely eliminated until a 1969 Supreme Court decision, backed by a threatened cutoff of federal aid, ordered immediate compliance with the law by the fall of 1970.

In the 1960s a second, more ambitious goal in school desegregation arose— the creation of "racial balance" in the schools through affirmative integration. This goal was supported by social science research, but the issues were fought primarily in the courts.[20] Racial balance was implemented by school board decision in some smaller northern districts (for example, Berkeley and Evanston), but only in larger cities after court orders or HEW "desegregation plans" backed by threats of federal aid withdrawal. It is this goal of racial balance, which in large cities can be implemented only by extensive bussing of children into unfamiliar neighborhoods, that has met enormous opposition by whites. Numerous surveys have shown overwhelming opposition to bussing among whites, as well as opposition by a majority of blacks (though a much smaller majority than among whites). In Charlotte, North Carolina, in Boston, in Louisville, and in other cities, bussing orders have been met with boycotts, street demonstrations, violence in the streets, and violence in the schools. The organized resistance has been strongest in ethnically homogeneous, working-class white communities within the cities, such as South Boston, where community organization was high before the desegregation order. In such communities, many residents see bussing as a threat not merely to their children, but to the very community to which they belong. Among other whites, primarily middle-class, with higher incomes and a lower identification with their residential community, one response to central-city desegregation is moving out of the district or transferring their children to private schools, or "white flight." This response is especially pronounced in the largest cities, and in cities with a high proportion of blacks. It has added to the flow of whites out of central cities, resulting in the residential pattern of an increasingly black central city sur-

---

[20] See Gerald Grant, "Shaping Social Policy: The Politics of the Coleman Report," *Teachers College Record*, Vol. 75, No. 1 (September 1975), pp. 17–54. The legal issues are complicated ones, which cannot be dealt with here except to say that plaintiffs argue that whenever unequal treatment of black and white children in a school district is found, the proper remedy is the elimination of all segregation in the district through racial balancing of the schools to within 5 or 10 percent of the racial composition of the district. Plaintiffs have succeeded in this argument, and the remedy has been imposed in several federal courts. However, there is widespread disagreement on the issue among jurists.

Boston, 1975

rounded by predominantly white suburbs.[21] This pattern, of course, is destructive of the goal of integrated schools, of residential integration, and of community organization.

There are many sources of the opposition by white parents to bussing. One, of course, is racial prejudice against blacks. But the fact that the opposition is primarily in the largest cities, where bussing is most extensive (it has occurred peacefully in many rural counties of the South with long histories of racial prejudice), the fact that the flight of whites is greatest among the middle classes (which show less racial prejudice than the lower classes), and the fact that a majority of blacks oppose bussing indicates that there are other motives as well. An excerpt from a statement by one white parent expresses clearly one source of opposition.

I grew up in a poor white neighborhood in what is now called Milwaukee's inner city. I attended a white grade school (with a few blacks) and attended West

[21] For an extensive examination of this developing pattern, see James Coleman, Sara Kelly, and John Moore, *Trends in School Segregation, 1968–73* (Washington, D.C.: The Urban Institute, 1975).

Division High School, which was about 40 per cent black. The few prejudices I was aware of as an elementary school student increased considerably during high school. That was primarily due to racial fights, etc. . . .

I am against forcing my children into high crime neighborhoods that I worked so damn hard to get out of as fast as I could. I used to be responsible for some of those crimes, gang fights, etc. I don't want my children taken from me and transported into slums with the dangers and defeatism that thrives there. I don't care if that slum neighborhood is black, latin or like the white section I lived in while a youth. . . .

I would not mind if the children from the kind of slum neighborhoods that I left behind were transported to the schools which my children attended in the neighborhood I found safe enough to live in. But the courts and government leaders don't seem to care about that. . . .

My major point here is that if my decision shows a trend, the cities and immediate communities are in for even worse decline. As do many young professionals in their fields, I plan to be among the best in my profession. I must make up for poor education in elementary and high school years, but I will do it—I know I can do it. And if more and more of us stay away from the urban areas, and if others flee those same areas because of the bussing issue, the decline of the older American cities will happen in one or two decades."[22]

Federal Actions and Community Disorganization

A third source of urban problems leading to community disorganization has been the transition from local decision making to national decision making in many areas, the loss of self-determination of local government, and the rise of federal intervention. In most of their actions, city governments aim to preserve and strengthen the community, sometimes at the cost of other values. While some of their actions may have disorganizing side effects, mayors, city councils, and local businessmen are far more sensitive to the possibility of such side effects than are policy makers at a national level. There are a number of examples of federal actions that have undermined local community organization for the sake of other values. One was expressway construction to facilitate commuting from suburbs outside the cities. These expressways would seldom have been initiated and paid for by the city. Another was a set of Supreme Court decisions that protected the rights of persons accused of criminal offenses, at the cost of the rights of victims and potential victims, and at some cost in effectiveness of law enforcement. The consequences of federal school desegregation policies in the direction of racial balance were discussed above. Still other examples were the FHA and GI housing loan policies and, with mixed consequences, the community action programs of the Office of Economic Opportunity. There are many others, but two will be discussed below to show the effects that federal intervention can have.

[22] Personal communication to the author (1975).

Government financing policy   It is ordinarily true that buying a house requires a rather large sum of money, a considerable fraction of the total cost of the house, as a down payment. After World War II, however, the federal government initiated two loan programs, FHA and GI, that made the purchase of a new house very easy. These programs did not similarly increase the ease of purchasing an older house, and it has been even more difficult to secure government-insured loans for extensive renewal of such older properties as apartment buildings.

The result has been a remarkable stimulus to new home construction, but at the same time it has speeded up the deterioration of older neighborhoods. A house that would have been sold or rented as a single-family dwelling were it not for the discrepancy between the ease of purchasing it and that of buying a new suburban house, can no longer be thus sold or rented. It can, however, be a good real-estate investment if converted for multiple-family use—that is, converted into a tenement.

Because most new home construction lies outside city limits, this old–new disparity accelerated the exodus from the city to the suburbs. The city has thus deteriorated, while the construction industry and the suburbs have been favored by the government policy. To be sure, prospective homeowners have benefited as well, but no more (certainly less, in fact) than if the policy had made it as easy to purchase or renovate older housing as to purchase a new house.

This is not to say that the policy has been "bad," for community disorganization is not in itself necessarily "bad." The policy has had different consequences for different social entities, and the city is one entity for which the consequences have been bad.

Maximum feasible participation   In the mid-1960s a new orientation to the social problems of urban poverty areas evolved. It is based on community organization and community action. Its advocates are professionals whose careers are tied to services for the poor or research on poverty. Its resources are federal funds or foundation grants, and its goals entail upsetting the power structure of the city. This new orientation has strong advocates[23] and just as strong opponents;[24] it excites intense passions. The views of its opponents are often expressed in the pages of a journal entitled *The Public Interest*; those of its advocates appear in the pages of the journal *Social Policy*.

The primary vehicles of this approach in the 1960s were the federal Office of Economic Opportunity, some community action programs of OEO, Mobilization for Youth in New York, and a Ford-Foundation-sponsored experiment in community control of some New York schools. These programs set up

---

[23] Richard Cloward and Frances Fox Piven, "A Strategy to End Poverty," in Hadden et al., *op. cit.*, pp. 433–447.

[24] Daniel P. Moynihan, *Maximum Feasible Misunderstanding* (New York: Free Press, 1969).

organizations that challenged local authorities by attempting to organize the poor against public and private services: welfare, housing, garbage services, schools, merchants. The ideological root of this challenge rests in political control by the poor of those resources and activities that impinge upon them—a kind of reversal of the welfare-state conception of benevolent paternalism.

These attempts by social service professionals to develop community organization using federal funds can fairly be said to have successfully challenged official authority structures, municipal governments, but they have been almost uniformly unsuccessful in establishing ongoing community organization with long-term benefits. In the words of a political scientist who has studied these programs in some detail.

> A recipe for violence: Promise a lot; deliver a little. Lead people to believe they will be much better off, but let there be no dramatic improvement. Try a variety of small programs, each interesting but marginal in impact and severely underfinanced. Avoid any attempted solution remotely comparable in size to the dimensions of the problem you are trying to solve. Have middle-class civil servants hire upper-class student radicals to use lower-class Negroes as a battering ram against the existing local political systems; then complain that people are going around disrupting things and chastise local politicians for not cooperating with those out to do them in. Get some poor people involved in local decision-making, only to discover that there is not enough at stake to be worth bothering about. Feel guilty about what has happened to black people; tell them you are surprised they have not revolted before; express shock and dismay when they follow your advice. Go in for a little force, just enough to anger, not enough to discourage. Feel guilty again; say you are surprised that worse has not happened. Alternate with a little suppression. Mix well, apply a match, and run. . . .[25]

It is clear that the idea of community organization of the poor to control their own futures has not been given a valid trial in the programs referred to above. The particular ingredients that made up Mobilization for Youth and similar activities did not create effective community organization. But some other attempts have been successful. Saul Alinsky, a former trade-union organizer, has implemented effective community organization in the Back of the Yards district and other areas of Chicago, in Rochester, and elsewhere, but he has done so with a different combination of elements. He does not expect to be supported by existing authority after he begins, and therefore obtains the necessary money from authorities beforehand. He creates an indigenous grassroots organization that is soon able to subsist independent of external financial support and of his own organizing skills. It is an old formula, long used in organizing trade unions and other conflict groups.

The growth of unions after the National Labor Relations Act of 1935 suggests that favorable federal legislation can change the rules of the game enough to spur the growth of effective continuing organization focused on

---

[25] Aaron Wildavsky, in Moynihan, *op. cit.*, p. ii.

services such as welfare and public housing. But there are two fundamental policy questions: Will community organization in poverty areas really augment the value of services designed to aid the poor? And if so, how can such organization be developed? A careful study of the developments of the late 1960s and early 1970s could help in answering these questions.

LONG-TERM TRENDS AFFECTING COMMUNITY ORGANIZATION

Locality Specialization

There has long been a trend in society toward functional specialization of localities. As German sociologist Georg Simmel noted more than 50 years ago:

> At first the individual sees himself in an environment which is relatively indifferent to his individuality, but which has implicated him in a web of circumstances. These circumstances impose on him a close coexistence with those whom the accident of birth has placed next to him. . . . However, as the development of society progresses, each individual establishes for himself contacts with persons who stand outside this original group-affiliation, but who are "related" to him by virtue of an actual similarity of talents, inclinations, activities, and so on.[26]

This tendency of society to be less and less organized around communities in which one was born and more inclined toward specialized groups has produced a qualitative change in the structure of society, as Simmel goes on to note.[27] In the Middle Ages an individual was surrounded by a series of concentric groups, all based on the particular position into which he had been born. The development of specialized voluntary associations, each containing only a "part" of an individual, came about only slowly, and with difficulty. Earlier, the whole person was specialized (a soldier could not even marry, but was totally a soldier). The fragmentation of men into many roles, some dependent on purposive desires, was not common in the Middle Ages.

Such fragmentation, the result of affiliation with multiple groups transcending locality, has important implications for the organization of a community. Obviously, if all of a person's activities were contained within one community, the processes discussed earlier could operate without inhibition. Common, joint, and opposed interests would arise in abundance; mutual identification and hostility could grow unabated. Only when man broke out of this set of concentric circles did he become an individual through his particular combination of group affiliations. As this happened, a person's common activities and common interests were spread over a more and more diverse range of groups. Those persons with whom one activity was shared were not the same ones with whom

---

[26] Georg Simmel, *Conflict* (New York: Free Press, 1955), pp. 127–128.
[27] *Ibid.*, p. 148.

another was shared. Thus, the processes that tend to make a *community* out of a *geographic locality* are interrupted and diverted.

The most recent development in this fragmentation into multiple-group affiliations is physical mobility in and out of one's living place. Modern transportation has made possible part-time residence in several localities. Not only is the community no longer a rigid circle confining people's activities totally within it, it is increasingly a less important and less permanent one of several circles of which the individual is a part. At the same time, as geographic mobility becomes more frequent, communities more and more take on the character of purposive associations. Many people are now able to choose with a considerable amount of freedom where they want to live and how much of themselves they invest in their living place.

Kinds of Communities in Modern Society

As a consequence of mobility and fragmentation, communities have come to be specialized according to the kinds of activities they contain for their members.[28]

Independent towns and cities   The most complete community is a type that is slowly vanishing in industrial society except in its larger forms: the community that contains most of its members' activities—work, lesiure, education, trade, and services. It was once true, when transportation was less developed, that all cities and towns were by necessity independent, with permanent residents spending full time in the community. But now only large metropolitan areas and geographically isolated towns are even in part like this.

The very independence and isolation of such towns and cities create common problems. They must have police and fire protection; they must have water and sewage systems; they must educate their children, provide jobs for their members, regulate their drunkards, mend their roads, tend their sick, and bury their dead. If these communities were not physically set apart, isolated from other towns or cities, many such problems would not be community problems but problems of the larger aggregate. But in independent towns, each of these ordinary everyday activities of living creates problems that can usually

[28] There are, of course, many ways of classifying communities. The classification here is based upon the problem at hand: community disorganization. Because community organization depends intrinsically upon the activities of which the community consists, as indicated in earlier sections, the classification must be in terms of these activities. For other classifications, see Albert J. Reiss, Jr., "Functional Specialization of Cities," in A. J. Reiss and Paul K. Hatt, *Cities in Society*, 2nd ed. (New York: Free Press, 1957), pp. 555–575. Also, Otis Dudley Duncan and Albert J. Reiss, Jr., *Social Characteristics of Urban and Rural Communities* (New York: Wiley, 1956), p. 217; Chauncy D. Harris, "A Functional Classification of Cities in the United States," *Geographical Review*, Vol. 33 (January 1943), pp. 86–96. Duncan and Reiss provide one important element used in the classification: the economic exports of goods and services from the community. Many people in the community make their living off their neighbors, but there must be some segment that provides the income of the community. This segment differs radically in different communities, as the classification below will indicate.

be best solved jointly, within this community. Recent controversies in many communities, large and small, over fluoridation of the water supply suggest one such problem. Independent towns (unlike city suburbs) have their own water systems, so fluoridation is a matter that must be decided by the community. It thus poses a problem in these independent towns, and in some cases there is sufficient organization to solve it. In some cases, however, there is not, and an examination of such cases in a later section will suggest some of the causes.

Another problem of independent towns and cities, in contrast to new forms of communities, is providing for the economic sustenance of their members. In one study of a community, the struggle toward this end occupied much of the attention of the community members during the period of the study. The community was faced with a prospective loss of its steel mills, a prospect it resisted at every turn. The mills finally did leave, but the high degree of organized effort resulted in new industries moving into town and old ones expanding. The community was thus able to survive in spite of an apparent death sentence.[29]

The major point, then, about independent towns is that their physical isolation and the consequent fact that they contain a large part of their members' activities create many community problems of importance to the members. These problems often generate a high degree of formal and informal community organization, through the processes discussed earlier. These communities need more organization than many others, and they tend to have more. If the town is small, the organization largely takes the form of informal norms, customs, and mores, and of loosely organized volunteer groups; if it is a large city, organization takes the form of laws, offices, and other aspects of bureaucracy.

All the remaining types of localities to be examined incorporate only some part of the life which is contained in an independent town or city. Although these localities are themselves sometimes parts of a larger metropolitan community, they may nevertheless face local community problems. It is thus important to examine them as communities in themselves, and not merely as parts of a metropolitan area community.

Urban centers that import workers daily   Central cities today are becoming more and more specialized, as places of work. Central cities are becoming less and less places to *live*, less and less places for retail trade, more and more places where people work—in manufacturing, wholesale trade, service, and governmental activities.[30] Though low-income families continue to live close to the center of the city (many of them in their purely residential housing

---

[29] Charles Walker, *Steeltown* (New York: Harper & Row, 1950).

[30] See Duncan and Reiss, *op. cit.*, p. 299, for a tabulation of amount of wholesale and retail trade by size of place. Though there is no variation in mean per capita *retail* trade, *wholesale* trade in 1950 varied from a low of $667 per capita in the smallest urban places (10,000–25,000) to $3,450 in the largest (500,000 or more).

projects), middle- and high-income families live farther and farther from the center, in suburbs. The difficulties in organization that this creates for the residential suburbs were mentioned above; the difficulties it creates for the city are somewhat different. As the residences of upper-income families have moved outside the city, so have their interests and money. Their interest in and support of education and the physical improvement of the community are localized where they live. New York's or Chicago's northern suburbs, for example, have a concentration of business leaders and professionals whose absence from the city's educational and political affairs leaves a real vacuum. Similarly, school boards in suburbs of major cities include impressive arrays of legal and administrative talent, devoting their efforts to the small problems of a simple school system, while the far more complex problems of the city schools await solution.

Though the city has the formal organization for addressing its problems, much of its informal support has been lost to the suburbs. It becomes more and more a purely economic center. It imports workers, and by so doing engages some of their interest on which organization can subsist; yet some of that interest remains in the residential communities that daily export these people to their jobs.

Residential communities that export workers daily   City residential neighborhoods and suburbs outside a city have a very different character from independent towns and cities. They are living places, where people live who work elsewhere. In the economy of these communities, the major export is *people*—a daily export into factories or businesses outside the community. Such communities still contain a number of activities for their members, but many of these are tied to the central city, or to another community.[31] Police and fire protection are partly local, partly centralized in city or county departments. Water, sewage disposal, and other utilities are ordinarily provided by the central city. Roads are repaired by county, state, or city. Such communities have thus lost many of the activities that formerly bound their members together. The processes making for mutual identification and hostility have vanished with the common and interdependent activities on which they were based. Different segments of the community experience this process in varying degrees, and sometimes this variation creates further community disorganization.

In many suburban towns, there are two very different groups of people: the commuters, who are daily exported to their places of work, and the local tradespeople, who provide the goods and services of living. The relative numbers of these two groups vary greatly, because suburbs take on quite different forms. Some have industries of their own, with consequent internal economic life. In recent years, many industrial firms have left the city, along with their

[31] Chauncy Harris long ago pointed to two major types of modern suburbs: living places and working places. Thus some of the people who live in one suburb are commuters not to the central city, but to a neighboring suburb containing outlying industries. See Duncan and Reiss, *op. cit.*, p. 7, and Chauncy D. Harris, "Suburbs," *American Journal of Sociology*, Vol. 49 (July 1943), pp. 1–13.

middle-class employees. But they have often moved to industrial parks or un-incorporated areas and have seldom become integral parts of the life of a suburb or other town.

In general, older suburbs tend to have a larger component of local trades-people, and even some manufacturing or other concerns. Many of these suburbs began as independent towns, before transportation made feasible, and city growth made necessary, the daily mass movements into and out of the city. In such suburbs, with their own partial economic life, the bases for strife and conflict exist in abundance. Many activities and interests of the commuters are no longer interdependent with those of fellow community members, but are located in the larger metropolitan area. But the people whose economic and social life is bound up in the town have community problems that must be solved. When the commuters *do* become involved in some such problem, there are few bases of mutual identification, and often there is no mechanism for expression of their desires in order that divergent positions might be brought together.

For example, Yonkers, New York was in its early years largely made up of lower-middle-class Catholics, many of them employed in local industries. Later developments in East Yonkers have brought in white-collar commuters, mostly Jewish. The resulting problems in community organization (largely centering about the schools) became great. The line dividing the "old nesters" on the West and the new "carpetbaggers" on the East became as difficult to cross as the superhighway that separates the two halves of the town.[32]

Some young suburbs have, in part by design, little or no internal economic life and are almost purely residential. Even local goods and services are provided by a few large shopping centers whose owners and employees live elsewhere, keeping the suburb solely a living place for commuters. This pure case represents a new type of wholly residential community, homogeneous in age, income level, and life style. Disorganization in such communities takes the form of community disintegration, in the absence of common problems and common activities.

Such purely residential communities are not confined to suburban developments. New housing projects that have replaced slums in the center of many cities have often become solely places to live for their residents. One observer of such housing projects in New York City reports:

> Before East Harlem began to resound to the deadly plong of the wreckers' ball and the tattoo of new steel work it was a slum. But it had many institutions that gave stability. There were the Neapolitan blocks, the street fiestas, the inter-woven relationship of stores and neighbors. Out it all went. In came the gangs.
>
> The new project may permit a church to survive on a small island like St. Edward's. But an absence of churches and an absence of religious influence is

[32] Harrison Salisbury's series of articles in *The New York Times* on Yonkers' problems shows well the organizational difficulties of some of these communities. See Harrison E. Salisbury, Four Articles on Yonkers, N.Y., *The New York Times*, April 18–21, 1955.

notable among project youngsters. The Negro children seldom go to church. The same is true of the Puerto Ricans. The Irish and Italian gang youngsters are usually described by their priests as "bad Catholics," irregular in church observance.

The projects are political deserts. The precinct bosses have been wiped out with the slum. They do not seem to come back. No one cares whether the new residents vote or not. There is no basket at Thanksgiving. No boss to fix it up when Jerry gets into trouble with the police. The residents have no organization of their own and are discouraged from having any.

"We don't want none of them organizers in here," one manager of a project told me. "All they do is stir up trouble. Used to be some organizers around here. But we cleaned them out good. Lotsa Communists. That's what they were."[33]

In these ways, at least, the urban housing project and the suburban development are alike. They have become segmented, specialized parts of the adults' lives, devoid of many of the institutions that could make them complete communities. Though these dormitories may be in part the consequence of ill-conceived planning by developers, they also represent an advanced stage in the organizational structure of society—a movement away from total institutions in which a person is embedded, toward voluntary, specialized, segmental associations.

Communities that import people seasonally for leisure or education

Resort communities and college towns differ from all the communities described above. They contain two sets of people: those who *live* there and carry out most of their activities within the community; and those who *come* there for a special purpose: education, relaxation, or entertainment. As leisure becomes more important in our society, more and more communities are coming to have tourism or entertainment as their major export.[34] Whole states (for example, New Hampshire and Vermont) are undergoing a transition from an economy of subsistence farms and small manufacturing to one of resort and vacation communities.

The communities to which people come for leisure, education, or other activities have certain characteristic problems of organization. They contain both people whose activities are bound up within the community and those for whom the community is a temporary abode, fulfilling for them only one kind of function. This bifurcation of interests tends to split the community into two parts and has given rise to many conflicts: "town versus gown" fights in college towns, and "native versus resorter" disputes in resort towns. There are usually few bases for community between these two groups, and many bases of cleavage. It is significant that after the Peekskill riots (between the natives

[33] Harrison E. Salisbury, *The Shook-Up Generation* (New York: Great Books, 1959), p. 67.

[34] The term "export" used to describe tourism does not, of course, mean that these activities are physically exported. It means instead that this is the commodity that the community sells to the outside. It is the commodity that provides the income for the community.

and the resorters) of some years ago, a measure of community integration was restored by one of the few interests both groups had in common. The volunteer fire department, which had previously included only natives, added resorters to its ranks.[35]

Age-specialized communities   Some communities are tending toward a different functional character from those discussed above. They are becoming age-specific. In one type of community the matter works somewhat as follows: A couple with young children has no money for a substantial down payment on a house but can buy an inexpensive house with little or no down payment, and monthly payments lower than rent. Some new suburbs come to be filled with such people. After a few years their income is higher and they have an equity in their house with which they can buy a more expensive one. They leave, and their place is taken by another couple with young children. Such communities have a continual influx and outflow of residents, tending to maintain their special character as communities of young families.

This age specialization of communities is not confined to the example cited above. Dormitory suburbs in general are not places for young unmarried persons or for retired persons. At the same time, other communities are becoming primarily retired persons' communities. Florida and California have a large number of such communities. These, in contrast to the dormitory suburb, contain a *large* part of their members' lives, but over a *short* period of time. They have their special problems of community organization, though little is known systematically about these problems. Such communities are a relatively new occurrence, and represent another element in the vast reorganization that society is presently undergoing.

If we look at the family's life cycle, there seems to be developing a three- or four-stage pattern, with important implications for the age specialization of localities. The cycle is this: (1) early married life in a rented apartment in the central city; (2) the young-children stage in a suburb of inexpensive houses; (3) an optional third move, depending on the accumulation of capital, to a more expensive suburb; and (4) after children leave home, the return of the couple to the central city or the move to a community of retired people.[36]

The commune as a reaction to specialization   The springing up of communes, both urban and rural, among youth in the 1960s and early 1970s is a movement directly opposed to locality specialization. These communes were spawned as part of the youth movement of the 1960s by a variety of motives, one of which was clearly a search for community and a rejection of the segmentation of life into distinct roles performed in different places with different

[35] James Rorty and Winifred Raushenbusch, "The Lessons of the Peekskill Riots," *Commentary*, Vol. 10 (October 1950), pp. 309–323.

[36] For further discussion, see Philip M. Hauser, *Population Perspective* (New Brunswick, N.J.: Rutgers University Press, 1961), Ch. 4.

persons.[37] Many of these communes were short-lived, and it appears unlikely that such intentionally created communities will provide serious competition for the increasing locality specialization. They arose in enough numbers, however, to demonstrate the unfulfilled desire for community that exists among some people. And it may be that some variant upon these communities may evolve to constitute a satisfactory way of life for a number of persons. They provide certain rewards that a loosely organized or disorganized community does not, but at the same time extract certain costs (for example, a subordination of one's will to that of the collective) that do not arise in the absence of a close community. Their contrast with the open, anonymous city shows the polar opposites in community organization, with costs and benefits for each.

Disorganizing Consequences of Locality Specialization

The consequence of locality specialization that is of major interest to us is the weakening of bonds to a particular community, with all the difficulties this creates for community organization. The problem is not due to any "evil" that can be exorcised; it is an historical process that must be recognized. Localities may ultimately cease to be political entities and no longer have any form of organization involving the residents. As mobility becomes even greater and competition between communities increases, it is possible that the essential functions of a community will become incorporated as a business, whose "product" must be sold on the open market, and whose owner profits from their sales. Perhaps, in contrast, there will be an ever increasing transfer of functions from the local level to a central authority, so that community organization will become almost totally unnecessary.

Both these tendencies are evident today. The first occurs in large-scale suburban developments, in which the developer sells a "package" that includes not only a house but also roads, sewage disposal, water, a community swimming pool, a country club, a shopping center, and sometimes even a school. The difficulty, of course, is that subsequent actions must be taken by the community. The developer is gone and the community members are left holding the bag of problems, so to speak, without any structure for solving them. An interesting variation upon this is the planning by a single developer of small satellite cities, from 50,000 to 100,000 in population, containing industry as well as the institutions found in suburbs. In this variation, exemplified by Columbia, Maryland and Reston, Virginia, there is an attempt on the part of the developer to create both formal and informal community organization. As these new cities grow, it will be important to observe the kind and degree of community organization that develops within them.

The tendency toward central authority is evident in the increasing number of city and state functions taken on by the federal government. It is also evident

---

[37] See Rosabeth Kanter, *Commitment and Community* (Cambridge, Mass.: Harvard University Press, 1972), for an examination of the commune movement.

in city housing projects. Many constitute large communities, in numbers (Fort Greene project, in New York City, has about 17,000 residents), but have no community organization other than the project administrator. This is little more organization than the even larger suburban developments whose developers have sold their packages and left.

Through both tendencies, entrepreneurial activity and administration, community organization withers away. Local activity is still far from dead, but there is no sign that the historical trend away from deep involvement in a geographically-defined community is diminishing.

Children and parents One special set of problems created by this historical trend toward community specialization has to do with children. Though suburban residential communities are only living places for parents, they are total communities for their children. Thus there is a proliferation of community among the children,[38] as community among parents disintegrates.[39]

One outcome of the highly developed community among children and the minimal adult community is a relative powerlessness of adults to control their children. Because there is little communication among adults, there are not strong norms about hours for being in at night, frequency of dates, and use of cars. Adolescents have a powerful weapon when they say, "All the other kids do it; why can't I?" The parent simply does not know whether all the other kids do it or not. The "pluralistic ignorance" arising from absence of an adult community often results in the children having their own way. Many observers have viewed the greater freedom enjoyed by children as a consequence of greater permissiveness of modern parents.[40] While this may be so, it is also true that this greater permissiveness probably comes from a lack of strong community oganization. Such organization would give norms to the parents to reinforce their otherwise solitary and bewildered struggle in socializing their children.[41]

[38] For example, in a study of 10 high schools (two were suburban schools and the remainder were in independent towns and cities), the students in the upper-middle-class suburban school showed higher sensitivity to the adolescent social system and their position within it than those in any of the other nine schools. In answer to a question about whether they would like to be in the "leading crowd" of adolescents (asked of all those who said they were not in the leading crowd), a higher proportion said "yes" in this school than in any of the other nine. Reported in James S. Coleman, "The Competition for Adolescent Energies," *Phi Delta Kappan*, Vol. 42, No. 6 (March 1961), pp. 231–236. The sensitivity of adolescents to peer evaluation has grown, rather than diminished, since that study was done.

[39] Even mass-circulation newsmagazines have begun to recognize the effects of community disintegration on the ability of parents to govern children. The cover article of *Newsweek* (September 22, 1975) under the heading "Who's Raising the Kids," examines these effects.

[40] See, for example, David Riesman, *The Lonely Crowd* (New Haven: Yale University Press, 1952). Many of Riesman's observations about the current scene in modern society are undoubtedly consequences of the historical trends in social organization discussed here, rather than the consequence of personality changes.

[41] A few suburban communities have attempted to replace the now-vanished norms of the community by a rational procedure: a formal code to govern teenagers' behavior drawn up after a public-opinion poll of parents and teenagers.

The formation of gangs in cities, and most recently in suburbs, is facilitated by the same lack of community among parents. The parents do not know what their children are doing, for two reasons: First, much of the parents' lives occurs outside the local community, while the children's lives take place almost totally within it; second, in a fully developed community, the network of relations gives every parent, in a sense, a community of sentries who can keep him informed of his child's activities. In modern living places (city or suburban), where such a network is attenuated, there no longer are such sentries. Parents are lone agents facing a highly organized community of children and youth.

In the area of child raising, community disorganization and family disorganization feed each other in a vicious circle. Parents, in a well-developed community, have the support of many surrogate parents who provide extensive help in rearing children through exchange of services, through aiding in control and discipline, and through increasing the interest and attention devoted to children. Growing community disorganization removes this support from parents. Increasing family disorganization, in turn (in 1974, there were about half as many divorces as marriages), robs the community of stable families around which community organization and community activities for children can develop. Thus the family's deficiencies in child rearing cannot be offset by a well-developed community, nor are the community's deficiencies for children countered by strong families in which parents invest time and attention to their children.

One may ask what kinds of social changes might bring strength and direction back into the raising of children, apart from attempts to strengthen and stabilize both families and communities. The immediate answer to these questions, which would involve greater dependence on schools, leads to discouragement when one sees the problems and difficulties of schools. They are hardly in a position to take over responsibilities that have traditionally been those of parents and neighborhoods, as earlier sections of this chapter have indicated. Also, schools have often constituted less a *support* for family socialization (as have strong neighborhoods) than a *competitor* to it. Of greatest value would be an institution that strengthened the family's capability for raising its children, in addition to supplementing the family's activities.

It may be necessary, as problems of child rearing increase, to consider more fundamental changes in the structure of society than are ordinarily envisioned. For example, the involvement of fathers and, increasingly, mothers in formal work organizations away from home suggest a radical change that would reduce the separation between youth and adults.[42] This is the introduction of children and youth of all ages, from infancy through high school, into the organizations where parents spend their working days. The children would

---

[42] These issues, and the proposal discussed here, are examined in greater detail in *Youth: Transition to Adulthood*, Report of the President's Science Advisory Committee (Chicago: University of Chicago Press, 1974).

spend part of their time as they currently do, in classrooms (partly under the instruction of professional teachers, but partly taught by regular employees on released time from their usual jobs), and part of their time in responsible activities in the organization. In the latter activities they would learn not only skills, but also responsibility and the capacity to work with others. Most important, they would be part of a stable organization, a new form of age-heterogeneous community that was neither wholly like the neighborhood community nor wholly like the bureaucratic work organization that it replaced.[43]

Such a fundamental change in the structure of society is not easily achieved. Yet the locality specialization that has eroded neighborhood-based community organization, together with the reduced strength of the family, imply that new bases of community must be found if the family is to obtain the support it needs in raising its children. One approach is to find the organizations where the attention and interest and time of adults are currently spent, and to modify them to accommodate children and youth. In modern society, those organizations are the workplaces of adults.[44]

Geographic mobility, self-realization, and social isolation The consequences of the historical trend toward free choice of community and toward locality specialization exhibit peculiar twists. It is not easy to be "for" or "against" such changes when one examines their consequences. For example, a tightly knit community, which captures all an individual's activities over his whole life, severely restricts freedom. A person is born into a particular position in the community and finds it difficult ever to change this position. This was most pronounced in the closed communities of the Middle Ages, where life was wholly determined by one's birth; it also exists to a lesser degree in independent towns in American society. Some analysts of social stratification in American communities have pointed out that a working-class boy's or girl's chances for status mobility lie almost wholly in leaving the community.[45]

---

[43] Because work places are more integrated by race and social class than neighborhoods and schools, such a change would have as a side effect greater race and class integration among children, with less parental fear, than current school integration.

[44] Obviously, organizations competing in a market would have to be subsidized to provide these schooling and socialization functions. The funds for that subsidy already exist, in the $1,100 per year (1974) per-pupil expenditure currently paid for public schooling.

[45] This is well illustrated by A. B. Hollingshead's study of social classes and education in a midwestern town. See his *Elmtown's Youth* (New York: Wiley, 1949). A possibility of breaking out of one's position in the structure sometimes comes about through the local high school. For boys, athletics provide an avenue for mobility in the adolescent status system, and in the larger community as well. Such possibilities are not so great for girls, and probably as a consequence, girls are more anxious to leave the community than boys, and in fact do leave more frequently. For a documentation of the intent, see James S. Coleman, *The Adolescent Society* (New York: Free Press, 1961), p. 124. For a documentation of the different sex distribution of youth in cities and towns, see Duncan and Reiss, *op. cit.*, Ch. 3. The tendency of working-class young people to shed the tight organization of the high school community and the status they had in it is vividly illustrated in Ralph Keyes, *Is There Life after High School?* (Boston: Little, Brown, 1976).

Modern dormitory communities, on the other hand, do not entrap their residents by their social structure, for the structure is almost absent. And the freedom of choice of one's living place means that any ensnarement that develops while one is young, in the highly organized adolescent community, can be easily shed.

Thus the historical trend brings freedom and a greater measure of democracy than could otherwise exist. The other side of the coin, however, is not so bright. Freedom and mobility cut away the bonds of mutual identification and solidarity before they can fully develop. The psychological sustenance provided by such bonds is withdrawn. The result is social isolation and anomie, with their attendant discomforts and debilitating effects.

The structural changes in society leading toward freedom and isolation are reinforced by an ethic or value that is increasingly strong in modern society. This is the value of "self-realization," a value that has been nurtured by cherished American ideals of unlimited opportunity for each individual. Such self-oriented ideals stand in direct opposition to community, particularly small, intense community such as in a religious order or the family. These communities (and to a lesser extent the broader institutions to which they are related, as churches are related to religious communities) foster ideals of self-sacrifice, service to the community, investments of time and energy in others with no expectation of return. It is no accident that close, intense communities foster such norms. The strength of a community often requires stability when the maximization of personal opportunity would dictate a move, and requires spending time and attention on others' physical or psychological needs (especially those of children) when the maximization of personal opportunity would require that time and attention for one's own development. (For example, both parents may regard custody of children in a divorce as a burden, interfering with their own realization of self. In the 1970s there have come to be, for the first time with any frequency in America, divorce cases in which neither parent wants custody of the children.)

The strength of community in society is not determined only by technological and structural changes such as the locality specialization discussed earlier. It is affected as well by the balance between opposing values such as self-realization versus self-sacrifice for a larger cause.

The Difference Between Social and Community Disorganization

The historical trend toward locality specialization has undermined community organization in all the ways suggested above. Yet in doing so it has not necessarily undermined social organization of the larger society. A deterioration of consensus and a weakening of the norms of society (which many have seen as constituting social disorganization) are not the necessary consequences of locality specialization. To be sure, the consequences noted above involve a reduction of consensus and undermining of norms in the *local* community—but consensus and norms may be simultaneously strengthened, through this very locality specialization, in other associations within society.

There was at one time confusion among students of society between personality disorganization and social disorganization. As long as society was composed of concentric circles surrounding its members, as in the Middle Ages, personalities were little more than reflections of these concentric circles. Thus, personality disorganization and social disorganization were not distinct, even in principle. Their separation came about only with the development of multiple-group affiliations in place of the concentric ones. Because such a highly articulated structure necessarily had points of inconsistency and strain, there could be personality disorganization in the face of strong social organization; conversely, there could be a highly disorganized society filled with persons not especially afflicted with personality disorganization.[46]

In the same way today, locality specialization is beginning to separate community disorganization from social disorganization. Communities are becoming less and less the "building blocks" of which society is composed. So long as they were so, a deterioration of those building blocks meant a deterioration in the structure of society. But the present changes are of a different sort; they are changes to different kinds of building blocks for society. The new society emerging in the twentieth century may well have social organization without local community organization.

There has been much debate among social philosophers on precisely this point. Throughout American history, many intellectuals have held to the image of the rural community, or continuously interacting groups of neighbors, as the ideal building block of society. Thomas Jefferson, Alexis de Tocqueville, John Dewey, and many others viewed the new social structure developing in cities with alarm, because it was not based on the strong organization of small residential communities or neighborhoods.[47] They argued that the geographic community *is* the only building block for strong social organization. However, some authors regard the functional specialization of local areas developing in American cities as beneficial, even when these areas do not support the rich substructure of informal activities that makes for community life. This debate over the need for diffuse residential communities that serve a broad range of functions versus functionally specialized localities focuses on a fundamental question about future societies.

---

[46] As a number of authors have pointed out, from W. I. Thomas and Florian Znaniecki in *The Polish Peasant in Europe and America* (New York: Dover, reissued 1958) to Albert Cohen in "The Study of Social Disorganization and Deviant Behavior," in Robert K. Merton et al. (eds.), *Sociology Today* (New York: Basic Books, 1959), social disorganization is distinct from personal disorganization, just as psychological conflict within an individual is distinct from social conflict. Similarly, societal disorganization is distinct from community disorganization, though in the past there has been empirical connection.

[47] This anti-urban perspective is discussed by Morton and Lucia White in *The Intellectual vs. The City: From Jefferson to Frank Lloyd Wright* (Cambridge: Harvard University Press, 1962).

Community organization in future societies may not mean residential communities at all, but occupational groups, age groups, religious groups, ethnic and racial groups, even deviant minorities such as homosexual groups. To what degree can these groups, most of them voluntary associations, constitute the building blocks of society, in place of residential communities? Certainly, their lack of geographic contiguity creates important differences in certain functions, such as the control of crime and fire and other services that must be geographically local. But many services that are now organized around cities and towns—welfare, education, health services—could be organized around these non-geographic communities. There are many examples of this in current and past organization of society: schools, camps, hospitals, and welfare services organized by religious groups; apprentice schools, adult education, employment agencies, and mutual-insurance societies organized by occupational groups, trade unions, or professional societies; and others. Will these nonresidential communities develop further organization in the future? Can their community functions replace those of geographic communities? It is difficult to predict just what the structure of community organization will come to be, in part because it is too soon to know just what technical and social developments will come about in transportation and communication.

Invasion of the Community: Mass Communication

The historical trend examined above exhibits a greater and greater freeing of individuals from community bonds. They can choose their residences, and their residences, once chosen, contain only one segment of their lives. But there is yet another special development in modern society that results in an invasion of the community by the larger society. This development is mass communication, which has culminated in television. With movies, radio, and television, communication has come to be used as mass entertainment and mass leisure activity. Into the community's life comes daily entertainment from without—entertainment unrelated to the life of the community and by its very existence supplanting that life. The ultimate effects of television and other mass media on individuals and on communities have yet to be assessed, but it is indisputable that the time spent consuming this entertainment is time subtracted from the potential life of the community.

Mass communication has a second effect as well, an effect upon the content of norms in the community. Norms in a community have always derived from the structure of activities in the community and have been of such a character as to maintain these activities. For example, women have ordinarily been the upholders of norms governing sexual relationships and family responsibility in the community. Why? Georg Simmel explains it this way: Women, as the physically weaker sex, have always been subject to the exploitations and aggressions of men. Unable to protect themselves individually and unable to separate themselves into a distinct society, they have depended upon the customs and norms of the community for their protection. They have upheld these norms because it is in their interest to do so. They have most to lose by a disintegration of norms.[48]

Similarly, the laws governing protection of property in a community derive directly from the community's activities. They are made into laws through the efforts of those who have property and are most staunchly upheld by these same property owners. Most laws or norms in a community can be understood in the same way: as serving the interests either of all community members or of some faction having enough power to put them into effect. Norms about childbearing have been handed down by mothers of mothers—both by virtue of their authority in the family and by virtue of their experience. The norms they transmit are designed to uphold the existing structure of the community— they are essentially conservative.

Now, however, in an age of mass communication, norms can derive from the movies or the television set, rather than from the local community. Authority no longer rests with age, because of the rapidity of change. Mothers, fathers, and children receive, through mass communication, images of moral acceptability that may be very different from the existing norms of their community. Sometimes these norms are commensurate with those in the larger society, but sometimes they derive from the special needs of the medium of communication. Movies that feature sex and violence do so not because these attributes reflect norms of the larger society but because they sell movies. The frequency with which social drinking and requests for "bourbon and water" occur in a movie may reflect the normative structure of society less than the success of the bourbon manufacturers' trade association in persuading the producer to help them sell bourbon. The prevalence in films of such ceremonial religions as Catholicism and Episcopalianism does not reflect their position in society; they simply make better subjects for visual presentation than do nonceremonial religions, in which a minister dresses like everyone else.

Although these things do not reflect the present structure of society, they do have an effect upon the future structure. They tend to set into operation norms, attitudes, and behavior in an irresponsible way. The community and the larger society have so little control over them that normative patterns can establish themselves in full opposition to the community's previous standards.

There have, of course, always been changes in the basic activities in society that have produced changes in the norms of the society (often after rigid resistence). But there is a fundamental difference between those changes and the ones cited above. Previously, norms have developed (as they still do to a great extent) through interactions of people with one another. They thus bore a close relation to the basic activities of which society was composed, and supported

---

[48] Simmel, *op. cit.*, pp. 95, 96. As Simmel points out, the emancipation of women in modern society may tend to invalidate this relationship.

that structure of activities. But with mass communication, norms may be created in a very different and highly irrelevant way, depending, for example, on the incentives that exist in the television community.

Rapidity of Change and the Irrelevance of Existing Constraints

In a stable society, the authority of the elders in a community is well grounded. They have had more experience in life, and that experience can be a valuable aid to those younger than they. Part of that experience has been codified into customs, norms, mores, and laws. These guides and constraints are of utmost relevance to the problems that daily face members of a community.

In a rapidly changing society, the change itself makes many of these guides and constraints irrelevant. They were relevant to the society in which they developed, and they helped preserve that society. But as that society undergoes change of any sort, they become irrelevant. New guides for action are needed, and these residua of past experience are of little help.

Such a reduction in the authority of elders is likely to occur whenever society is undergoing any kind of change. The old norms are no longer good guides for action, but before new ones can grow up, the old ones must be cut away. Before new community organization can develop that is appropriate to changes in technology or in population size, for example, the old organization must give way. Thus it seems inevitable that change in the community must be accompanied by a certain amount of community disorganization, until new norms and new organization for action can become established.

Considerations like these are particularly relevant to the present. Society seems to be undergoing more than sporadic changes followed by periods of stability; since the industrial revolution, new changes have followed quickly upon previous ones. Such continual change tends to keep community organization at a low level, for the existing norms, customs, and authority structure are undergoing continual erosion as they become irrelevant for the new conditions.

SPECIAL CONDITIONS LEADING TO CONFLICT

We have discussed the conditions leading to disorganization primarily through disintegration of norms and consensus, and only secondarily through conflict. Beyond these conditions there are others that lead especially to conflict within a community. Some of these are discussed below.[49]

[49] For a more extended examination of community conflict and its dynamics, see James S. Coleman, *Community Conflict* (New York: Free Press, 1957). For a number of theoretical points in the sociology of conflict, see Simmel. *op. cit.*, and Lewis Coser, *The Functions of Social Conflict* (New York: Free Press, 1964). Further development of conflict theory occurs in Anthony Oberschall, *Social Conflict and Social Movements* (Englewood Cliffs, N.J.: Prentice-Hall, 1973). The present examination will be limited to certain conditions that lead to conflict.

Internally Generated and Externally Generated Conflict

The interdependent activities of which a community is composed sometimes generate joint action and develop community norms, but they often do just the opposite, as discussed in earlier sections. Probably the best example of interdependent activities that often lead to opposed action are economic activities. Workers and managers have some common interests (for example, high import tariffs for substitutable goods), but many that are opposed (for example, wages per unit of goods produced). Since these interests are crucial ones to both parties, they sometimes lead to open conflict such as a strike. At other times they generate mutual hostility, which may remain temporarily unexpressed, but later provides the dynamics for industrial conflict.

In another quite different way, the system of interdependent activities may lead to conflict. When one person or group has control over an activity in which another is interested as well, antagonism is likely to build up in the other, who cannot express his interests in modifying the activity to his taste. This has been a partial source of some public school fights in the past. In Pasadena, a school superintendent was unresponsive to community pressures from groups that had been heeded by the previous superintendent. Hostility built up in these groups and was fanned by nationalistic persons who had developed special hostility toward innovations in education. The final result was the removal of the superintendent and a return to the old system of easy accessibility to the administration by interested groups.[50]

Perhaps the best example of a power differential generating hostility and finally community conflict is that between blacks and whites in the South. Black citizens' lack of control over their destiny in the South has generated the latent hostility that can lead to conflict once the opportunity arises.

In general, community members' lack of control over activities that are of central interest to them creates hostility, which sometimes obtains its outlet through conflict. In any highly differentiated community, there are control differentials of this sort. Lower classes and newcomers to the community tend to be without control, in contrast to old, established families. Thus the potential for conflict exists in the very structure of activities, giving some persons control over parts of others' lives and creating situations of opposing interests. Conflicts from such sources need no external event to set them in motion, for they are generated by the activities of the community itself.

Racial conflicts are produced largely by hostilities generated through the interdependent activities of the community itself. The example below illustrates how these hostilities may be responsible for conflict.

A young mathematician from England was at the University of Chicago for a short period of study and research. When he was walking across the Midway, he was accosted by several Negro boys who demanded his wallet. He objected, one of them produced a knife, and they led him over toward bushes beside the walk.

[50] See David Hurlburd, *This Happened in Pasadena* (New York: Macmillan, 1950).

The ensuing conversation went something like this, according to his later account: One boy said, "Come on, now, give us your wallet, or we'll have to get tough with you." He replied, "Look here, I don't want to give up my wallet to you. Besides, I've just arrived here from England, and I don't think this is the way to treat someone who's a visitor here." The boys looked at one another and then one said, "Oh. We thought you were one of those white guys," and they quickly went away.

To these black boys, "white guys" had nothing to do with skin color per se, for the English mathematician was white. "White guys" were their fellow community members, the whites from whom they felt alienated because there had been no processes to create common identity between them, only those creating hostility. The Englishman was not a "white guy" against whom a reserve force of hostility had been built up.

The incident illustrates more than a peculiar, localized abnormality. There was no less integration of blacks into the local community in the Hyde Park area of Chicago, where this incident occurred, than in other large cities. The absence of integration, the absence of any processes that produce a common bond of identity, is very likely an important source not only of conflict, but also of the black crime that occurs in such areas. The flow of blacks and Puerto Ricans into large cities has been great, and the migrants initially have no stake in the city, no reason for not committing crime other than the fear of getting caught. The existence of such a flow of migrants makes especially important those processes that generate identification of the new residents with the community.

Such processes are all too few in modern cities, but they are not totally absent. More important, they need not be left to fate, but can consciously be instituted to combat the disorganizing tendencies of migration and other "natural processes" in society.

Controversies involving racial or ethnic divisions ordinarily build up through internal processes of the sort implied above. But they also usually include components that are not developed within the community itself: different backgrounds, cultural values, and norms; and differences due to time of movement into the community (classical examples of migrations inducing conflict are Irish Catholics moving into East Coast cities and New England towns in the nineteenth century; "Okies" moving into Southern California during the 1930s; ex-city dwellers moving into established suburbs in the 1950s, often with a different age and income distribution from that of the existing population; rural southerners, mostly black, moving into the center of cities in the 1950s and 1960s); and Spanish-speaking immigrants moving into some cities in the 1970s.

Some community conflicts are precipitated by purely external events. A new highway coming through a town may cause social cleavage where no trace had existed before, between those whose homes will be demolished and those who will profit by increased business. Another external source of conflict exists in some modern suburbs: continuing value differences due to the residential character of the community. In a suburb of New York City, there were school controversies in the 1950s between two groups with opposite political values. The persons concerned were employed in New York in activities supporting, respectively, their left-wing and right-wing views. Without this external support, grounded in national organizations for which these people worked, such extremes could not have maintained themselves in the same community. But grounded in New York City as they were, these differences continued to provoke violent school conflicts for a long period of time.[51]

As this example indicates, modern dormitory suburbs allow a great diversity of values to be maintained, held in place by diverse jobs and associations in the city. This value diversity can then become, as it has in numerous instances of school controversies, the basis for an explosive conflict.

To summarize, conflict can arise from the activities of the community itself, from purely external sources, or from some conjunction of the two. The internally induced conflict depends on the structure of interdependent activities in the community, which can operate over time to generate cleavage between two groups or to cause alienation of one group that has little control over these interdependent activities.

Locality Specialization, the Mass Community, and Conflict

As we have seen, locality specialization has taken out of the hands of the local community many of its former activities, resulting, for example, in modern bedroom suburbs. In doing so, it has removed many of the interests of its residents into associations that cut across community bounds. Their interests and activities have become extensive, over a wide range of associations. Most of these associations have a special organizational structure: a large mass of members, who are only tangentially interested in the activities of the organization; and a small corps of officers, whose major interests and activities are bound up in the association and for whom the organization may even be a livelihood. Voluntary associations of all sorts are like this. Unions are probably the best example; professional associations such as the American Medical Association, political groups such as the Americans for Democratic Action or the League of Women Voters, P.T.A.'s, consumer cooperatives, conservation leagues, and other similar groups are other examples.[52]

The local community, fast becoming a specialized living place, has begun

---

[51] See Louis Engel, "Port Washington, N.Y.," in "The Public School Crisis," *Saturday Review*, September 8, 1951, pp. 6–20.

[52] For a general discussion of the "mass society" structure of such organizations, see Bernard Barber, "Participation and Mass Apathy in Associations," in Alvin W. Gouldner (ed.), *Studies in Leadership* (New York: Harper, 1950). For an examination of the organizational structure of a mass society, see William Kornhauser, *The Politics of Mass Society* (New York: Free Press, 1959), and for modifications in the conception of modern society as a "mass society," see Maurice Pinard, *The Rise of a Third Party* (Englewood Cliffs, N.J.: Prentice-Hall, 1971).

to take on a form similar to that of these voluntary associations. It holds only a small part of the interests of most of its members, whose other interests have become fractionated into many parts, most of them outside the community. Only those few merchants and others whose livelihood is within the community, or who are part of its government, are centrally involved.

The community thus tends toward a "mass society," with a small organized elite and a large unorganized, undifferentiated mass. This is not, of course, to say that its members are a "mass" from the viewpoint of the larger society. They are members of many groups—occupational, recreational, political, professional, and other interest groups. But many of these are not local. Some have their locus in the central city; some spread over the nation. So long as they are not within the local community, they contribute nothing to its organization. Their members are therefore *in effect* a mass, not organized into interest groups and associations that play a role in community decisions. There are special consequences of such a structure, which have much to do with conflict.

It is interesting to note that such a mass society structure can come about through two exactly opposite societal forms: the members' having no important associations outside the family and close friends, so that no interest groups mediate between individual and government; and the members' having all their ties in large associations that go beyond the bounds of the governmental unit (in this case, the community), and thus playing no role in its decision making. Though these associations can and do play a mediating role at the metropolitan, state, or national level, protecting and furthering their members' interests, they cannot do so at the community level.

The first of these two forms of mass society is exemplified by traditional societies like those of Central America, where the large mass of the populace is tied only to family and friends. The second is exemplified by modern suburban communities. Despite the apparent polar extremes that these two social entities exemplify, their mass-society form gives rise to similar types of conflicts, as will be evident below.

Consequences for Conflict of the Mass Community

Both trade unions and Latin-American countries having the elite mass structure described above show a characteristic political cycle: long periods of apathy and violent revolts. The administrative elite goes on for a long time making decisions that are unchallenged by the mass, but then at some point the mass does rise up and attempt to "throw the rascals out." This cyclical pattern of authority seems to be a quality of many voluntary associations that engage only a small part of their members' interest and attention. Until some special issue or a special leader comes along to capture a major part of their attention, they are inactive and let the "authorities" administer the affairs of the association. But then there are no regular political channels through which the members' intentions may be expressed, and the "normal" processes of government give way to conflict in which the outsiders use any means to gain their ends.

As communities come more and more to take on the form of mass communites, with a small interested elite and an uninterested (though often educated) mass, one might expect that their political processes would take on this apathy–revolt pattern. There are no systematic data to document this, but two kinds of controversies exhibit precisely the form of a "revolt of the masses." These are controversies centering around school desegregation and controversies over whether the water supply should or should not be fluoridated.

Some fluoridation controversies show the pattern perfectly:[53] a town or city council will have considered the question of fluoridation and passed favorably upon it, voting the small sum necessary to install it. Before the action is taken, only a few voices have been raised in opposition through letters to the editor of the local newspaper; no real opposition to the plan is evident. All organizations in town—business, labor, professional associations of doctors and dentists, and others—and all members of the interested elite, favor it.

But after the action, sentiment begins to build up against the plan, based partly on the charge that fluoridation is dangerous, but partly also on the belief that this was not something for the council to decide alone, but a matter for a decision of the community as a whole. Fluoridation is then put to a vote and the revolt is accomplished, resulting (in a majority of cases that have so far come to a popular vote) in defeat of the plan.

The normal procedure of decision making in these communities is one in which the uninterested mass plays no part at all, since the community is only a segmental part of their lives. Thus the council makes this decision as it does others. But the mass membership, aroused by a few dedicated opponents of fluoridation, does not consider this assumption of authority legitimate in this case, and arises to revolt against the decision makers. There are no organizational channels through which these beliefs could be transmitted as political pressures *before* the decision; the normal process of decision making does not include the mass of community membership. Only by using new channels, that is, popular revolt, spread by word of mouth and letters to the editor, do the community members take part. By this time, their antagonism is directed against the "high-handed behavior" of the city council, so that the vote against fluoridation is in part a vote against the council itself.

In short, the mass-society form of local community that is arising through locality specialization generates a special kind of community conflict, a "revolt of the masses" against the administrative elite who have been making decisions. These revolts sometimes explode into real conflicts, because the intermediary associations, through which opinions are both expressed and compromised, are largely missing. This particular form of community conflict is especially prevalent today and is particularly interesting, since it seems to be a consequence of social changes (which promise to become even more widespread) toward locality specialization.

[53] See Coleman, *Community Conflict,* for a more detailed discussion of the pattern of fluoridation controversies.

In this, as in other processes of community disorganization, it is only possible to point to overall tendencies. The details of these processes, some given in references above, most of them yet to be found, provide the means by which community disorganization, and social organization as a whole, can be understood and in some cases altered.

SUMMARY

1   Common activities and common dependence on the same events provide one basis for community organization, in part through creating common bonds of sentiment. They do not, however, in and of themselves, bring about organization.

2   Interdependent activities of persons engaged in different activities, as in a modern differentiated city, provide a second basis for community organization, through interests that are sometimes allied. They also, however, provide the basis for conflict, because these activities often generate conflicting interests. The two forms of relationship, common activities and interdependent activities, have long been noted as two fundamentally different bases for social organization.

3   Past actions in a community leave a residue of two kinds: a residue of sentiments and a residue of organization. Thus the history of a community—the history of its successful solution of community problems and the history of its conflicts— shapes its future through these two residues.

4   Community disorganization manifests itself in contemporary problems of cities. These problems are evidenced by the movement of middle classes, who no longer need the city for economic opportunity, out of cities to suburbs and even out of metropolitan areas.

5   Crime is perhaps the most intensively felt problem in contemporary large cities, and it is far greater there than in other types of localities. It also has been increasing in large cities at a rapid rate.

6   The formal system of criminal justice is the attempt, in cities, to bring about the same kind of control that informal social organization exerts in rural areas. Statistics show, however, its decreasing effectiveness, at least since 1960.

7   Education is a second important problem area in cities. The problems are several: an unstable and changing pattern of authority over school policies; financial crises created by increasing costs and decreasing confidence of the public in their schools; and the impact of school desegregation on community organization in the city. These problems, like crime, have increased the exodus of middle-class families from cities.

8   The transition from local decision making, attentive to problems of community organization, to central decisions that are less attentive to those problems, has led to a number of policies that are destructive of community organization in their pursuit of other values. This is very likely a trend that will continue, decreasing the capability of cities to develop stable community organization. Examples are policies in housing, education, transportation, and crime prevention.

9   There are other long-term trends affecting community organization. Probably the most important of these is specialization of localities around certain activities. Such specialization has transformed American localities from independent towns and cities into a number of locality types: central cities (which are increasingly

specialized as workplaces rather than living places), residential suburbs (specialized as living places), seasonal communities (vacation communities and college towns), and age-specialized communities. The newest development, however, the urban or rural commune, is a reaction to such separation of activities.

10   Locality specialization provides many fewer supports for community organization than earlier patterns. This in turn removes some of the supports for the raising of children. Community disorganization and family disorganization feed on each other in a vicious circle.

11   It is important not to confuse community disorganization with social disorganization in the larger society. Although locality specialization and other trends may lead to the disorganization of geographic communities, there may be sufficient reorganization around other bases that no overall disorganization results. The development of alternative bases of community is an interesting topic for speculation. Nevertheless, there remain problems that are geographically localized, such as crime control and raising of children, for which disorganization of geographic communities creates serious difficulties.

12   Another long-term trend destructive of community organization is the growth of mass media and the consequent invasion of the community by values, norms, and attractions from outside.

13   There are special conditions in communities that lead to a particular form of disorganization: conflict. One of these is the very interdependence of activities that under some conditions generate cohesive organization. Another is the "mass community," which leads to alienation and sporadic but sometimes violent mass outbursts against the authority structure of the community.

RECOMMENDED READING

Classic treatises on different forms of community organization may be found in Ferdinand Tönnies, *Community and Society* (1957), and Emile Durkheim, *The Division of Labor in Society* (1947). Two of the best case studies which show organization and disorganization in cities, at the neighborhood level, are Ronald Dore, *City Life in Japan* (1958), and Michael Young and Peter Wilmott, *Family and Kinship in East London* (1957).

Contemporary urban problems in America, and alternative policies that address those problems, are examined in detail in William Gorham and Nathan Glazer (eds.), *The Urban Situation* [tentative title] (1976). In this book, the problems of crime, education, transportation, housing, and fiscal problems of cities are examined in detail.

Opposing orientations to social programs aimed at aiding the disadvantaged in urban areas may be found in William Ryan, *Blaming the Victim* (1972), and Daniel P. Moynihan, *Maximum Feasible Misunderstanding* (1969). Those with interest in pursuing the mathematics of crime control may examine Benjamine Avi-Itzhak and Reuel Shinnar, "Quantitative Models in Crime Control," *Journal of Criminal Justice* (1973). For further study of invasion of the community by mass communication, a good case study (of a city in the English Midlands) is Richard Hoggart's *Uses of Literacy* (1970).

The development of the commune movement of the 1960s is examined by

Rosabeth Kanter in *Commitment and Community* (1972), and the mode of organization in a commune is studied by Benjamin Zablocki in *The Joyful Community* (1972).

Analysis of a particular form of community disorganization, community conflict, may be found in Anthony Oberschall, *Social Conflict* and *Social Movements* (1973).

13

The World of Work

ROBERT S. WEISS
EDWIN HARWOOD
DAVID RIESMAN

This is a paradoxical time in the history of the American economy. In the words of *The New York Times*, "For the first time since public opinion research began measuring such attitudes in 1959, Americans believe they have lost substantial ground in their standard of living, and there has been a significant decline in their own expectations of what the future will bring."[1] The level of measured unemployment in the country reached its highest point since the Depression in the spring of 1975 (over 9 percent), and now stands at about 8 percent. Yet in 1974 a larger proportion of our population was employed than ever before, including increasing numbers of married women with young children, and our current level of employment (55%) is above the average for the post-World War II period.[2] Most Americans, especially those who are well educated and well paid, continue to believe (though perhaps with less conviction than in the past) that they will be economically better off in the near future.[3] And while the job market overall has tightened, we still import legal and illegal immigrants from Spanish America and elsewhere to fill such low-level jobs as picking crops. (Native Americans define the work as too demeaning and too ill-paid.) This is a recession whose hardships are distributed unevenly, so that many individuals in middle-income occupations feel economically secure despite the erosion of their real income through inflation, while many individuals lower on the socio-economic scale feel their lives painfully burdened by the problem of making ends meet.[4] Many young people have difficulty finding jobs they are willing to accept, while older people who have been laid off and lack the adaptibility needed to enter a new line of work or to move to a new part of the country may find no jobs at all.

We begin this chapter with a brief overview of the problems inherent in the current economic situation. We then consider issues associated with the American labor force—what work means to Americans, changes in the labor market over the years, and sexual and racial inequalities in the distribution of jobs and wages. The next section of the chapter examines unemployment in light of what we have said about the economy and the American worker. We then consider the jobs themselves. What makes work satisfying? What are the rewards and frustrations of blue-collar, middle-management and white-collar, professional and executive jobs? In the last section of the chapter we summarize the problems and prospects in the world of work today. Our primary concern throughout is with persisting issues relating to work and employment in America—namely, the problems of maintaining full employment without inflation; creating equal opportunity at work; and providing jobs, particularly for blue-collar workers, that adequately meet reasonable aspirations for self-realization.

The authors want to thank Professors William Form, Melvin Kohn, and Harry Brill for their comments on an earlier draft of this chapter.
[1] Robert Lindsey, *The New York Times*, October 26, 1975, p. 1.
[2] Irwin L. Kellner, "Counting the Employed, Not the Unemployed," *The New York Times*, October 26, 1975, Section F, p. 12.
[3] Lindsey, *op. cit.*
[4] *Ibid.*

THE CURRENT ECONOMIC SITUATION

Until the economic downturn of 1972, many observers of the American scene believed that it was possible to avoid the booms and busts of past business cycles by managing our economy. The economic dissipation of over-investment, over-production, and inflation could be restrained by reductions in the money supply and in government spending; the economic hangover of business slow-down and unemployment could be avoided or, if it should nevertheless occur, be combatted by tax rebates, low interest rates, and increased government spending on subsidies to industry, defense production (sometimes the same thing), and social services.

However, the experience of the past few years has brought Americans to the unaccustomed recognition that the United States is a member of a world economy in which its competitive position is increasingly precarious. Many American factories are outmoded and inefficient in comparison with the more recently built plants of Japan and Germany (an ironic benefit of the punishing mass bombings these countries suffered in World War II). In addition the United States is dependent for many essential raw materials (of which oil is only one) on countries that are beginning to organize cartels to control the prices the United States and other customer nations must pay. The "affluent decades" led American workers to expect better wages and benefits, and managers, raises and stock options—in each case quite apart from gains in productivity. As a result, some American products have become too expensive to compete effectively in world markets.

The initial problems of industrialization—dismally low wages and sweat-shop exploitation—have receded significantly within some sectors of the economy, thanks to union action, government regulation, and greater managerial concern. But we are like other industrial countries in having a two-level economy in which highly unionized workers, in both white-collar and blue-collar occupations, receive relatively high wages, considerable fringe benefits, and some protection against health hazards and layoffs, while workers in small nonunion enterprises (such as laundries and small restaurants) and on large almost industrialized farms receive little in any way. Even in the unionized sector of our economy, plant safety leaves much to be desired: without concerted pressure from either union or government, managements tend to feel responsible for limiting costs rather than accidents. Moreover, while it looked for a time as if we had put the violence that accompanied the unionization of workers behind us, a recent wave of strikes exhibited some quite old-fashioned violence, as when striking *Washington Post* pressmen wrecked equipment and assaulted those who crossed their picket lines. Despite the hope for increased harmony in industrial relations and the development of techniques for arbitrating disputes (indeed, the rise of professional arbitrators), it is apparent that we live in a society in which potentially violent conflict between workers and managers lies just beneath the surface.

Our economy and society are suffering from the unforeseen consequences of efforts to solve earlier problems in the industrial order. For example, minimum wage legislation was passed largely at the behest of labor unions, with the support of intellectuals who were determined that laborers should not be asked to work for "sweatshop wages." Yet one result of the minimum wage laws has been that unskilled young and elderly people, and others who might be employed at a low wage, are not employed at all. Moreover, the minimum wage laws have provided the incentive for many Southern farmers to mechanize and hence send thousands of unskilled, often black, farm workers to our larger metropolitan areas to make their way however they can.

Constant changes in what people want, both as producers and as consumers, make it difficult to plan production and distribution in advance. Jobs may be lost and whole areas depopulated as fashions change. Consider that Danbury, Connecticut, was once a great center of hat making in a hat-wearing society. But how many male (or female) readers of this chapter wear hats? Many New England towns once maintained themselves by manufacturing shoes, textiles, and other items that are now produced in Southern communities which offer lower taxes and a not-yet-unionized labor force. The same sort of competition that goes on among nations goes on among regions of the United States.

Just over the horizon lie a host of problems stemming from declining resources. If either energy or critical raw materials have to be rationed or become terribly costly, marginal firms, or firms lacking political allies, are likely to suffer. This will mean not only a loss of jobs, but also fewer material goods to be distributed among our work force. Already groups worried by the escalating pollution of our air, soil, and seas are demanding a modification of the industrial processes by which we extract, transport, and modify the substances of our world. We can, of course, be less wasteful, but after a certain point we can only protect our environment at cost to our comfort and, perhaps, to our security. For example, sooner or later one consequence of the banning of nuclear power must be colder homes; another consequence may be fewer jobs or lower wages. As a society, we have yet to come to terms with these issues.[5]

THE AMERICAN LABOR FORCE

Not everyone in America "works," if "work" is defined as paid employment. Full-time housewives, although they may work as hard as anyone else, are in the same category for census purposes as the retired and unemployed, and as

[5] For pessimistic appraisals of the American future, see Donella H. Meadows, Dennis L. Meadows et al., *The Limits to Growth* (New York: Universe, 1972), and Robert Heilbroner, *An Inquiry into the Human Prospect* (New York: Norton, 1974). For criticism of the methods and the conclusions of the pessimists, see Christopher Freeman, "The Luxury of Despair: A Reply to Robert Heilbroner's *Human Prospect*," *Futures*, Vol. 6 (December 1974), pp. 450–462, and Stanley Aronowitz, "Is the Enemy Really Us?" *Social Policy*, Vol. 5 (December 1974).

young people still in school—who may also work hard; all are "not in the labor force." Those who are within the labor force hold a wide variety of jobs that differ greatly in the satisfactions they provide and the social standing they support. Perhaps surprisingly, most are in the labor force not only because they have to (to earn a living), but also because they want to.

The Meaning of Work

Nearly all observers agree that work, in and of itself, is emotionally as well as economically necessary for most of our adult male population: it structures their time, provides a basis for relations with others, and sustains their sense of worth.[6] Describing the importance of work to automobile assemblers, one investigator writes, it "provides organizational cement to their lives."[7]

Though many claim that the Germans and Swiss work harder than Americans, it is doubtful that there are any other people on earth for whom work plays as great a role in establishing an individual's sense of worth as it does among Americans. Ethel Shanas found in a comparison of men 65 and over living in Denmark, Britain, and the United States that although aged Americans were as likely to retire as were aged citizens of the other two countries, retired Americans were much more likely to say that they missed some aspect of their work.[8] They missed the sense of feeling useful their jobs had provided, the people they had met at work, and the money they had earned more than the Danes or British did (but not the work itself). This study suggests that Americans consider work a primary source of feelings of worth, of being a member of the community deserving of respect. Americans have a greater tendency to rely on the work community to provide engagement and sociability. After retirement they miss the money work had provided not only because their drop in income may have been more severe than was true for the British or the Danes, but also because the ability to support oneself and one's family at a level adequate to maintain one's place among friends and neighbors is of special importance to Americans.

The special importance we attach to earning a respectable living in part explains the observation that American workers have always preferred to take their share of increased productivity in the form of increased income rather

---

[6] Daniel Yankelovich, on the basis of survey studies, writes that a majority of the adult population in the mid-1960's associated four ideas with work: (1) that to be a man in our society meant being a good provider for a family; (2) that work earns one freedom and independence; (3) that hard work leads to success; and (4) that a man's worth is reflected in the act of working. See his "The meaning of work" in Jerome M. Rosow (ed.), *The Worker and the Job* (Englewood Cliffs, N.J.: Prentice-Hall, 1974), pp. 19–47.

[7] William H. Form, "Auto workers and their machines, a study of work, factory, and job satisfaction in four countries," *Social Forces*, Vol. 52 (September 1973), pp. 1–15.

[8] Ethel Shanas, "The Meaning of Work," in Ethel Shanas et al. (eds.), *Old People in Three Industrial Societies* (New York: Atherton, 1968), pp. 320–345. See especially p. 334.

than increased leisure. (Over the past 20 years, 90 percent of the gain in productivity has been taken in the form of increased income, rather than in increased leisure.)[9] In the 1950s, many people believed that once the "affluent society" became established, large numbers of middle-class Americans would approach satiation in their demand for goods. Since then it has been demonstrated repeatedly that reasonably well-paid blue-collar workers can easily enlarge their schedule of wants to include better housing in a more pleasant neighborhood, a better car and then a second car, costlier dental and medical services, and more and better education for their children—even before they join the middle class in a desire for swimming pools, boats, and other leisure equipment. The American belief that upward mobility is always possible insures that few are satisfied with what they have. And even those who want only to keep their relative place often discover that the package of goods and services they feel to be appropriate to that place stretches their budget to its limits.

No other activity competes with work in attractiveness. Leisure time for family and fun may be high on most Americans' schedule of wants, but it cannot by itself make a life. In a study conducted 20 years ago, and since replicated several times, a representative sample of American men were asked, "If by some chance you inherited enough money to live comfortably without working do you think you would work anyway or not?" About 80 percent replied that they would work anyway. Their motives for wanting to continue work were often unclear to themselves; such vague explanations as "In order to keep occupied" or "I'd be nervous otherwise" were common. They might not want to continue working at their particular job, but money aside, they could not think how they would fill their time except by work.[10] Whether work is equally as important for women as a group is as yet unclear. Many better-educated women feel that work and career are essential to their sense of self-worth, but among the less well educated, many continue to seek satisfaction and self-esteem within their roles as wives, mothers, and homemakers.[11]

In any event it is clear that for most men and for many women the value of working at a paid job remains, even if it pays little more than might be obtained from Unemployment Benefits or Welfare. Because work means so much

[9] Howard R. Bowen and Garth L. Mangum, *Automation and Economic Progress* (Englewood Cliffs, N.J.: Prentice-Hall, 1966), p. 60.

[10] Nancy C. Morse and Robert S. Weiss, "The Function and Meaning of Work and the Job," *American Sociological Review,* Vol. 20, No. 2 (April 1965), pp. 191–198. See also Curt Tausky, "Meanings of Work among Blue-Collar Men," *Pacific Sociological Review,* Vol. 12 (Spring 1969), pp. 49–55; Form, *op. cit.;* George Strauss, "Workers: Attitudes and Adjustments," in Rosow, *op. cit.,* pp. 73–98; and the testimony of James O'Toole to the Mondale Committee's hearings on the influence of government policies on family life, *American Families: Trends and Pressures,* 1973 (Washington, D.C.: Government Printing Office, 1974), p. 99.

[11] See Robert S. Weiss and Nancy M. Samelson, "Social Roles of American Women: Their Contribution to a Feeling of Usefulness and Importance," *Marriage and Family Living,* Vol. 20 (1958), pp. 358–366. Yankelovitch has found that "the majority of women continue to feel that homemaking is more satisfying than a job" (*op. cit.,* p. 29).

to Americans, unemployment poses a threat not only to people's livelihoods but to their social identities.[12]

The Composition of the Labor Force

From the Current Population Survey (CPS), a monthly survey of approximately 50,000 American households, the Bureau of Labor Statistics is able to tell us how many Americans hold jobs and how many do not, how many have full-time or part-time jobs, and whether those working part-time do so by choice or because their employers are unable to keep them fully employed. This survey provides much additional data, including breakdowns on the distribution of workers by type of job and industry.[13]

Table 13-1   Persons in the Civilian Labor Force, August 1975

	Men		Women	
Age	No. in thousands	Percentage of total population in this age and sex category	No. in thousands	Percentage of total population in this age and sex category
16–17	2,498	59.5%	1,959	47.6%
18–19	3,134	81.0	2,668	64.8
20–24	7,809	88.9	6,327	66.6
25–34	13,958	95.5	8,306	53.3
35–44	10,294	95.8	6,335	54.4
45–54	10,455	92.4	6,558	53.7
55–64	6,980	75.6	4,161	40.1
65+	1,890	21.5	977	7.8
Total 16 and over	57,018	80.4%	37,290	46.6%

Source: U.S. Department of Labor, Bureau of Labor Statistics, *Employment and Earnings*, Vol. 22, No. 3 (September 1975), Table 4-A, pp. 22–23. The civilian labor force does not include members of the Armed Forces.

Table 13-1 presents the percentage of men and women of different ages in our labor force in August, 1975. We see that in the age groups that are clearly beyond the point of preparing for work and not yet within the shadow of retirement—between 25 and 55—well over 90 percent of all American men are working. Only a little more than half of the women within this age span are in the labor force. Presumably the remainder are engaged within their household by the tasks of managing a family and bringing up children.

Participation in the labor force drops off precipitously after age 65. This is the customary age for retirement in our society; it is an arbitrary figure, one that may come too late for some and too early for others, but one that is

[12] See Leonard Goodwin, *Do the Poor Want to Work?* (Washington, D.C.: Brookings, 1972), p. 112.

[13] Findings appear in the monthly U.S. Bureau of Labor Statistics publication, *Employment and Earnings* (Washington, D.C.: Government Printing Office).

nevertheless assumed to be an appropriate age for retirement by both private and government employers.

Trends in Jobs

The American occupational structure has changed radically over the past 100 years as the nation has moved from a predominantly agrarian society to an industrial one. Close to 40 percent of the working population worked on farms in 1900, but by 1974 only 3.5 percent of the labor force were farmers or farm laborers, and the percentage is declining.[14] This is an astonishing development: just 4 percent of American workers produce food for the entire population as a whole and, at the moment, a surplus to boot. The mechanization of farms (the installation of machinery for ploughing, harvesting, and handling crops), scientific soil analysis, and the use of intensive fertilizers and scientific breeding made it possible to produce crops with ever fewer workers. As a result, a great part of the working population was no longer needed on the farm and turned to the industries of the cities. But there, too, change has taken place. Mechanization in factories has increased the productivity of workers, thus allowing a larger proportion of the labor force to enter occupations other than manufacturing. By 1956, a majority of American workers were no longer in manufacturing, and by 1974 white-collar and service workers constituted almost two-thirds of the American labor force.

In 1900 only 20 percent of all women worked; by 1974, 46 percent of American women were holding jobs. As the proportion of women in the labor force has doubled, the proportion of men in the labor force has gradually declined. More men now stay in school into their twenties and, until very recently, increasing numbers of men were retiring before age 65. Between 1963 and 1974, the labor force participation rate of men aged 55 to 64 had declined from 86 to 77 percent. This is partly attributable to improved pension plans and new retirement rules. Perhaps more important has been the government-sponsored pension plan, Social Security, and Medicaid, which makes it easier for older workers with chronic health problems to remain at home.[15]

Some social analysts have spoken of the post-industrial society in which high living standards will allow more workers to spend more of their income on a variety of personal and professional services, as distinguished from the necessities of life (food, clothing, and shelter). And indeed, service industries —such as health, education, insurance, banking, and government—were the fastest growing sector of our economy in the 1960s. As a result, professional, clerical, and personal service jobs were growing at a faster rate than occupations associated with manufacturing until very recently. However, historical

---

[14] Irene B. Taeuber, *Population Trends in the U.S., 1900–1960,* Technical paper No. 10, U.S. Bureau of the Census (Washington, D.C.: Government Printing Office, 1964), p. 375; and *Manpower Report of the President, April 1974,* p. 268.

[15] See *Manpower Report of the President, April 1974,* p. 31.

trends are subject to fits and starts. The shortages of fuel and raw materials in the past several years have led to renewed mining and mineral exploration, with the result that Appalachian whites who left for Detroit and Chicago in the sixties in pursuit of jobs in manufacturing are returning home to the mines. And, despite the current recession and large-scale unemployment, there are still shortages of skilled workers in certain industries: diesel mechanics and drilling rig operators, for example. At the same time, the reduction in national purchasing power caused by rapid inflation has halted the expansion of the service industries (notably education and the governmentally financed service industry of social welfare, but also, in lesser measure, recreation). Indeed, some sectors within these industries have begun to contract, with all the dislocations of lives that this implies.

Quite apart from the current recession, the appraisal of our society as "post-industrial" was premature. Even before the current recession, the growth rates of both the white-collar and service sectors had slowed, whereas the percentage of blue-collar workers actually registered a slight increase. In addition, the long-term unemployment rate of professional and technical workers has increased since the late 1960s—in sharp contrast to earlier trends.[16] Our

Table 13-2   Employed Persons (16 years of age and over) by Major Occupation Group and Sex
(1974 annual averages)

	Percentage of labor force	
	Males	Females
Professional and technical workers (accountants, authors, clergymen, engineers, lawyers, physicians, schoolteachers)	14.0%	14.9%
Managers and administrators, excepting farm (government officials, corporation executives, retail tradesmen)	13.9	4.9
Sales workers (insurance brokers, sales clerks)	6.0	6.8
Clerical workers (bookkeepers, cashiers, secretaries, telephone operators)	6.4	34.9
Craft and kindred workers (carpenters, machinists, plumbers, tool and die makers)	20.9	1.5
Operatives (factory assemblers, bus drivers, deliverymen, textile spinners)	18.3	13.0
Nonfarm laborers (fishermen, stevedores, lumbermen)	7.7	1.1
Private household workers (cooks, servants, chauffeurs)	*	3.6
Other service workers (janitors, hairdressers, waiters, policemen)	8.0	17.8
Farmers and farm managers	2.9	0.3
Farm laborers and supervisors	1.9	1.2
Total:	100.0	100.0

Source: U.S. Dept. of Labor, Bureau of Labor Statistics, *Employment and Earnings,* Vol. 21, No. 7 (January 1975), Table 19, p. 149.
* Less than 0.05 percent of the male work force were in private household service.

[16] *Ibid.,* p. 282, Table A-23.

economy is still far from concentrating its efforts on the provision of services. More of our national income, as measured by our gross national product, comes from the industrial sector of our economy than from the service sector. We remain an industrial nation, even as we adopt the luxury of post-industrial disparagement of ungratifying work.

Sexual and Racial Inequities

We see in Table 13-2 that about 60 percent of female workers compared to about 40 percent of the men in the labor force work in the so-called white-collar occupations: the professions, technical work, sales, and office work. But most of those women hold clerical positions, which pay much less than do other kinds of white-collar work. Women at work tend to be order-takers rather than order-givers, secretaries rather than executives.

Throughout the economy jobs that are seen as "men's work" tend to receive higher pay than those seen as "women's work": durable goods assembly and auto repair pay more than clerical jobs in the front office.[17] Although, as Table 13-2 shows, a relatively high proportion of women are in the male-dominated job category of "operatives," they are more likely than men to be working in laundry and dry-cleaning establishments or in the food processing, textile, and apparel industries, which pay less than do automobile and appliance manufacturers. Even when women are formally in the same position as men—in social work, teaching, or management roles, and in many blue-collar fields as well—they tend to be given less responsibility and less pay. There have been attempts to defend this situation on the grounds that women in general are less able physically or socially (in the sense of being less likely to command the respect of subordinates) or on the grounds that women are likely to interrupt their careers for mothering. But those who have spoken for women's rights movements have insisted that these are self-serving arguments, designed to protect a system under which men are advantaged, and that while they may be valid in isolated cases they hardly justify systematic discrimination.

Well before the situation of women had become a matter for national debate, there had been widespread recognition that black Americans as a group did not acquire the same levels of prestige, responsibility, income, and security others did through their jobs.[18] A much larger proportion of blacks than of whites were in service work—an indication of segregation in the job world. While less than 2 percent of whites were employed in private household work in 1960, fully 14 percent of nonwhites were employed in private

---

[17] See Victor R. Fuchs, "Women's Earnings: Recent Trends and Long-run Prospects," *Monthly Labor Review* (May 1974), pp. 23–26.

[18] See Albert Wohlstetter and Sinclair Coleman, "Race Differences in Income," in Anthony H. Pascal (ed.), *Racial Discrimination in Economic Life* (Lexington, Mass.: Lexington Books, 1972), pp. 3–81.

household work.[19] By 1973 this difference had diminished greatly, as Table 13-3 shows.

Table 13-3 Employed Persons (16 Years of Age and Older) by Major Occupation Group and Race*
(1960 and 1973 annual averages)

	Percentage in labor force				
	Whites		% change	Blacks and other races		% change
	1960	1973		1960	1973	
White collar						
Professional and technical	12.1	14.4	+19.0	4.8	9.9	+106.3
Managers and administrators	11.7	11.0	+ 6.3	2.6	4.1	+ 57.7
Sales workers	7.0	6.9	− 1.4	1.5	2.3	+ 53.3
Clerical workers	15.7	17.5	+11.5	7.3	14.9	+104.1
Subtotal	46.6	49.9	+ 7.1	16.1	31.1	+ 93.2
Blue collar						
Craft and kindred workers	13.8	13.9	+ 0	6.0	8.9	+ 48.3
Operatives	17.9	16.3	− 8.9	20.4	22.2	+ 8.8
Nonfarm laborers	4.4	4.6	+ 4.5	13.7	9.7	− 29.2
Subtotal	36.2	34.7	− 4.1	40.1	40.8	+ 1.7
Service workers						
Private household	1.7	1.1	−35.3	14.2	5.7	− 59.9
Other service workers	8.2	10.6	+29.3	17.5	19.6	+ 12.0
Subtotal	9.9	11.7	+18.2	31.7	25.3	− 20.2
Farmworkers						
Farmers and farm managers	4.3	2.1	−51.2	3.2	0.7	− 78.1
Farm laborers and supervisors	3.0	1.6	−46.7	9.0	2.1	− 76.7
Subtotal	7.4	3.7	−50.1	12.1	2.8	− 76.9
Total	100.0	100.0		100.0	100.0	

Source: *Manpower Report of the President, April 1974,* adapted from Table A-12, p. 269.
* Because of changes in the Bureau of Census occupational classifications in 1971 the percentage changes registered between 1960 and 1973 must be interpreted with caution. They are included to provide a yardstick for measuring black occupational gains in relation to whites over the 13-year period. Subtotals have been rounded off.

There could be no question that much of the disadvantage blacks experienced in the job market was due to discrimination against them simply because they were black. Legislative attempts to prohibit racial discrimination go back at least to the Unemployment Relief Act of 1933, which prohibited discrimination on account of "race, color, or creed" in employment and training created through federal funds.[20] This regulation against discrimination

[19] Estimated from data on labor force participation in the 1950s in U.S. Bureau of the Census, *Historical Statistics of the United States,* Series D 26-35 and Series 72-122 (Washington, D.C.: Government Printing Office, 1960), pp. 72 and 74, together with data presented in Table 13-3.

[20] See *The Equal Employment Opportunity Act of 1972,* The Bureau of National Affairs (Washington, D.C.: Government Printing Office, 1973), p. 14.

(applicable, like other federal legislation against discrimination, only when federal funds were involved) continued in force as defense industries burgeoned in 1939, 1940, and 1941 to meet the country's urgent need for weaponry, but generally was not observed in practice. After a threat of a black march on Washington, President Roosevelt set up a surveillance committee to insure adherence to the law. But this committee, and the committees that followed it, functioned primarily by moral persuasion; they had little power of enforcement.[21] In 1961 the Kennedy administration issued an Executive Order prohibiting government contractors from discriminating that did provide for Justice Department suits against offenders, and in addition required that government contractors take "affirmative action" to ensure members of minority groups equal opportunity for employment.[22]

In 1964, after President Kennedy's assassination, his Executive Order was included in a package of civil rights regulations that President Johnson requested Congress to enact. The requirement that government contractors not only avoid discrimination but also take action against discrimination in hiring became law. A commission was set up to investigate possible violations, although responsibility for enforcement remained with the Justice Department. (In 1972 stronger enforcement powers were made available to the commission, so that the commission can itself take violators to court.) At the very last moment, possibly to make the bill as unpalatable as possible, a leading opponent of the bill (Howard Smith, Democratic Congressman from Virginia) proposed that discrimination for reasons of sex be added to the list of unlawful employment practices. This amendment was passed, along with the rest of the bill.[23]

Since the passage of the Civil Rights Act of 1964 women have made remarkable gains in a few of the more glamorous professional and business fields. In the past few years women with new Ph.D.'s from the most prestigious schools have received more job offers at better salaries than men from these schools.[24] In addition, the number of female bank officers and financial managers increased from 24,000 in 1960 to 310,000 in 1970 and of female computer specialists from 12,000 to 255,000 in the same period. But in the aggregate, the gains of women appear to have been small. Between 1960 and 1970 the proportion of women working in the professional and technical job category increased less than 2 percent, although this was the fastest growing occupational category in the labor force. And, while the gains made by women in several traditionally male blue-collar occupations such as boiler makers, die setters, millwrights, and fork lift operators have been striking, it is still unusual to

---

[21] *Ibid.*, pp. 15–17.

[22] *Ibid.*, pp. 16–17.

[23] *Ibid.*, pp. 25–27. See also Butler D. Shaffer and J. Brad Chapman, "Hiring Quotas— Will They Work?" *Labor Law Journal*, Vol. 26 (March 1975), pp. 152–162.

[24] This is corroborated by a study conducted by Cartter and Rohrter of the UCLA Center for Studies in Higher Education.

find a woman in these lines of work.[25] Whether more women would choose these occupations if they were identified less strongly as "men's work" is as yet unclear.

The efforts to achieve more nearly equal opportunity for black Americans seem to have met with more success. If we compare the occupational distributions for 1960 and 1973 (Table 13-3), we see that although blacks still trail whites in the better-paying jobs (professional, managerial, and skilled blue-collar), they have nonetheless made remarkable gains. They are no longer so heavily concentrated in the less esteemed and lower-paying job categories of nonfarm labor, private household work, and farm work.

Limited as they are, these gains by women and minorities have not been without attendant problems. The requirement that there be "affirmative action" against discrimination is based on the idea that systems of recruitment and employment could disadvantage women and minorities, even though no one intended or displayed overt discrimination. This would be the case, for example, if preference in hiring for a job were given to friends or family of those currently employed in the company. But the only way of *establishing* that a company is not practicing discrimination, other than a time-consuming and costly study of its recruitment procedures, is if there are the same proportion of women and minorities employed in every job classification as there are women and minorities available to be employed. Employers have therefore been required to strive for a certain proportion of women and minorities in every job classification. Quite apart from the imposition of new constraints (and new costs) on employers' hiring procedures, this "quota system" strikes many people as a violation of the belief that merit should always be rewarded, no matter what.[26] Indeed, a quota system contradicts the demand of the law itself—that employers not discriminate by race, color, religion, sex, or national origin.

One sore point in many industries is the clash between the desire to undo systematic discrimination and the seniority system. Many unions have fought long and hard for a rule that if layoffs are necessary, the last hired will be the first to go. Because the laws against discrimination are recent, women and blacks are often among the last to have been hired. This may well mean that women and minorities take the brunt of a layoff. Is this not an unfair relic of past discrimination? Women and minorities involved may think so. But the white male worker who would have to give up his job so that a woman or black with less seniority could stay on is likely to say he wasn't responsible for discrimination in the first place: Why should he have to make up for it?

It is entirely understandable and defensible for those who speak for women and minorities to press for change; without such pressure in the past, change would have been much, much, slower. Yet we should be aware not only of the rights of those who have been discriminated against, but also of the rights

---

[25] Constance B. Dicesare, "Changes in the Occupational Structure of U.S. Jobs," *Monthly Labor Review* (March 1975), pp. 24–30.

[26] See Shaffer and Chapman, *op. cit.*

of those who have a stake in our present social order—for example, members of craft unions who feel that perhaps the one thing they can give their sons to start them in life is preference for entry into the union. The challenge is to move to equality of opportunity without creating new injustices in which the victims might be those white males whose own job situations are precarious or whose ability to find new employment is marginal.

UNEMPLOYMENT

The monthly Current Population Survey, referred to above, is our best source of current information on unemployment. If a person is in the labor force, he or she is classified by the CPS as either (1) holding a job during the week preceding the week of interview, in which case he or she is classified as "employed"; or (2) having made specific efforts to find work during the four weeks preceding the week of the interview, and being available to work during that week, in which case he or she is classified as "unemployed." This system of classification is far from ideal. The middle-class housewife who is looking for just the right part-time secretarial job, one not too far from home and with hours that will allow her to drive her children to and from school, will be counted unemployed until she finds the job or gives up looking. By contrast, a discouraged mother on Welfare who could not find work that would pay her a living wage after she deducts the costs of child care, and therefore has not made an effort to look for a job, will not be counted among the unemployed. Nor will a steelworker, laid off from his regular job, who has become a part-time cab driver. Everything considered, the CPS figure understates the *potential* work force.

Table 13-4 presents the differential incidence of official unemployment by

Table 13-4   Percent Unemployed by Age, Sex, and Race (1974)

Age	Men		Women	
	White	Black	White	Black
16–17	16.2%	39.0%	16.4%	36.2%
18–19	11.5	26.6	13.0	33.7
20–24	7.8	15.4	8.2	18.0
25–34	3.5	7.2	5.7	8.6
35–44	2.4	4.1	4.3	6.7
45–54	2.2	4.0	3.6	4.3
55–64	2.5	3.6	3.2	3.3
65+	3.0	5.6	3.9	1.5
Total average	4.3%	9.1%	6.1%	10.7%

Source: U.S. Dept. of Labor, Bureau of Labor Statistics, *Employment and Earnings*, Vol. 21. No. 7 (January 1975), Table 1, pp. 136–137.

age, sex, and race for 1974. We see that the young are much more likely to be unemployed than those farther along in their work careers; that nonwhites are much more likely to be unemployed than whites; and that women are somewhat more likely to be unemployed than men. The group with the highest level of unemployment is young black women, closely followed by young black men. The difference between adults who are established in the labor force and young people who are just seeking entrance is very great, and this is especially true for nonwhites.

Beginning in 1972, with the downturn of the economy (and possibly exacerbated by the fuel shortages of 1973), the rate of unemployment in the United States began to rise. It continued to rise through 1974, and by March 1975 peaked at 9.1 percent, almost double the 4.9 percent unemployed in 1973. By the middle of 1975 the United States had the highest unemployment rate of the nine major industrialized countries outside the socialist bloc.[27] In addition,

[27] See Catherine C. Defina, "Labor and the Economy in 1974," *Monthly Labor Review*, Vol. 98 (January 1975), pp. 3–16, and Joyanna Moy and Constance Sorrentino, "Unemployment in Nine Industrial Nations, 1973–75," *Monthly Labor Review*, Vol. 98 (June 1975), pp. 9–18.

there almost certainly was a sizable increase in the number of "discouraged workers," the men and women who were not counted as unemployed because they were no longer looking for work, although they would have accepted work if jobs were available.[28]

In 1973, an unusually large proportion of our population was employed, and it may have been expecting too much to have wanted all the many new jobs to continue; perhaps we should accept that the 1973 level of employment was somehow extraordinary. But *why* could it not be sustained? Several reasons have been offered. These include: (1) it was normal for increased use of credit to lead to an interval in which warehouses were full and potential buyers were already too deeply in debt to deplete them; (2) the fuel and petroleum shortage of 1973 had disrupted production, and the subsequent increase in cost had burdened it; (3) there was a decline in consumer confidence caused by high and continuing inflation, which led to declining purchases of goods at a time when corporations, fearing yet further increases in raw material prices, had overstocked their inventory; and (4) the Federal Reserve, in its desire to combat inflation, had slowed the growth of the money supply and so reduced the capacity to purchase.

In any event, in 1974 as 40 years earlier (although not on nearly so large a scale), a significant proportion of our labor force faced unemployment. The young and unskilled, who have always been marginal employees everywhere except in the Armed Forces, and, despite the Civil Rights Act, members of minority groups, were the most vulnerable. The jobless rate for black workers reached nearly 12 percent in November 1974, while the rate for white workers was not quite 6 percent.[29]

The Meaning of Unemployment

The meaning of unemployment, of course, differs greatly depending on the individual's sex, age, and expectations. The young may worry that they will never find a niche in the society, or at least not one that commands their own respect and that of others.[30] But so long as they retain links to a community of other young people not fully engaged by work, they are not devastated.[31] Their elders, however, are likely to feel that they are losing ground in a society they had mistakenly trusted. They are expected to hold a job—by themselves and others. Their families' economic fate depends on their doing so. Given the American belief that what happens in an individual's life is for the most part his own doing, they may well see unemployment as personal failure. Even

[28] Moy and Sorrentino, *op. cit.*
[29] Defina, *op. cit.*, p. 6.
[30] See *Work in America* (Cambridge, Mass.: M.I.T., 1973), p. 89.
[31] See Richard C. Wilcock and Walter H. Franke, *Unwanted Workers* (New York: Free Press, 1963.).

during the Depression of the 1930s many unemployed men blamed themselves for a situation that clearly was not of their own making. They became self-doubting and withdrawn. Often unemployment brought still other problems: to the extent that a man's position in his family was dependent on his role as breadwinner, his homelife, too, was threatened.[32]

A 1960 study of the consequences of long-term unemployment for men found little change since the 1930s.[33] Despite severance pay (now written into many union contracts) and Unemployment Insurance benefits (first introduced in the late 1930s), a single year of unemployment brought men to financial desperation. Their severance pay was spent early, for the most part on debts already incurred; Unemployment Insurance brought in less than they needed and ended abruptly after twenty-six weeks.[34] The men felt stigmatized by their lack of work and, out of embarrassment as well as lack of money, withdrew from friends and social groups, including their church and union. Since they had already lost the community of men with whom they worked, their lives became increasingly empty. As time went on, and their helplessness turned to hostility, they directed their anger toward the system, the company, their families, and themselves.

It has long been recognized that loss of a job can affect not only a man's morale, but also his health. Current research supports this. Problems associated with work, including unemployment, have been associated with hospitalizable depression.[35] A longitudinal study of the health of workers who had been notified that their company was shutting down permanently found significant increases in physical complaints immediately after the news was received, immediately after the plants shut down, and again after protracted unemployment. Overall, men who did not have a supportive community suffered most. Younger men were more threatened at first, but recovered sooner, although men of every age group varied in resilience, with some doing much better than others.[36]

---

[32] Mirra Komarovsky, *The Unemployed Man and His Family* (New York: Dryden, 1940). See also Robert C. Angell, *The American Family Encounters the Depression* (New York: Scribner, 1936).

[33] Wilcock and Franke, *op. cit.*

[34] Although the unemployment insurance program is federally funded and administered, its specific provisions are decided by the States, and so vary from State to State. At present most States provide 26 weeks of benefits, the maximum benefit being no more than about $190, or half the average weekly wage of the previous year, whichever is the less. In some States an allowance for dependent children can be added. Recently the duration of benefits has been extended in 9 States particularly hard hit by unemployment so that some claimants in these States can continue to receive benefits for as long as 65 weeks.

[35] Eugene S. Paykel, "Life Stress and Psychiatric Disorder: Applications of the Clinical Approach," in Barbara Snell Dohrenwend and Bruce P. Dohrenwend, (eds.), *Stressful Life Events: Their Nature and Effects* (New York: Wiley-Interscience, 1974), pp. 135–150.

[36] Stanislav V. Kasl, Susan Gore, and Sidney Cobb, "The Experience of Losing a Job: Reported Changes in Health Symptoms and Illness Behavior, *Psychosomatic Medicine,* Vol. 37 (March–April 1975), pp. 106–122.

Acceptable Levels of Unemployment

Clearly, job loss exacts a cost in well-being that cannot be compensated for by increased Unemployment Insurance benefits. One might suppose that our country would therefore maintain a policy of "full employment" and make every effort to have work available for all who want it. Surprisingly, this is not so. Indeed, few other industrial countries tolerate anywhere near the level of unemployment the current U.S. government considers acceptable—4 to 5 percent. Perhaps in our defense it can be noted that the highly industrialized countries of Western and Northern Europe can manage unemployment by importing so-called "guest laborers" from Southern Europe when short of labor and sending them back home again when jobs are scarce. (In 1975 the governments of West Germany and Austria began reducing the number of work permits available to foreigners as a way of meeting their unemployment problems.) Although at times of labor shortage we fill a relatively small proportion of jobs with legal and illegal immigrants, we do not later send them home.

The reason our present governmental policy is one of striving for "an acceptable level of unemployment" rather than full employment—in which still and all there might be enough individuals between jobs to amount to 2 percent or so of the labor force—has to do with the highly controversial concept of a *Phillips curve*. The Phillips curve is a presumed relationship between inflation and unemployment, such that as inflation rises unemployment is reduced, and vice versa. In addition, when the unemployment rate becomes quite low, its further reduction results in a sharp increase in inflation, and when the inflation rate is equally low, *its* further reduction results in a sharp increase in unemployment. Thus there is an optimum point at which unemployment rate and inflation are each fairly low. Movement from this point will result either in unemployment or in inflation rising precipitously. The theory associated with the Phillips curve has it that the point of optimal level of unemployment and inflation is different for different countries, yet stable for a given country over time.[37]

The validity of the Phillips curve was brought into question most sharply by the experience of 1974, when high rates of unemployment and inflation occurred simultaneously. Nevertheless, there does appear to be an association between the percentage of people employed and the rate of inflation. As a financial commentator for *The New York Times* put it, "When the employment rate remains above normal for a considerable length of time, the inflation rate jumps above its long-term norm . . . too."[38] In other words, it may be high

[37] The Phillips curve was displayed first in A. W. Phillips, "The Relation Between Unemployment and the Rate of Change of Money Wage Rates in the United Kingdom, 1861–1957," *Economica*, Vol. 25 (November 1958), pp. 283–299. The discussion in the text is based largely on Charles C. Holt et al., *The Unemployment–Inflation Dilemma: A Manpower Solution* (Washington, D.C.: Urban Institute, 1971). See also *Work in America*, pp. 159–160.

[38] Kellner, *op. cit.*

employment levels rather than low unemployment levels that encourage inflation. Either way, however, the implication for government policy would seem
to be that the provision of jobs fuels inflation. And, by the same token, government policies that combat inflation by, for example, reducing the amount of
money in consumers' pockets by increasing taxes or by making credit more
difficult to obtain, raise unemployment levels.

How might we change the system to minimize the employment–inflation
trade-off? One move in this direction might be a program to increase productivity, which would increase the supply of goods as well as the employment
rate, thus satisfying rising consumer demands. From this standpoint, training
programs, profit sharing, and work redesign programs, so long as they increase
productivity, are desirable.[39]

A quite different approach would be to attempt to limit inflation by taxing
those who are able to afford luxury goods, at the same time imposing price
controls on the necessities of life. The aim of this policy would be to permit all
to purchase necessities by keeping their prices down, while limiting the demand for luxuries by reducing the purchasing power of those who would otherwise buy them. In theory this would stimulate the production of necessities so
long as the controlled price permitted industry to make even the smallest profit.
But here we enter a controversial area. Whenever one group is to be selectively injured to benefit the society as a whole, there will be those who insist
that the plan is morally wrong—in this case, the advantaged group, which may
feel it has earned its privileges, might protest their being taxed away. And there
are many who would say that any interference with a free market system, no
matter its insensitivity to distress, inevitably results in misallocations of resources just because planners cannot be omniscient.

THE JOB

Jobs vary greatly in their potential for satisfaction and the degree of commitment they elicit. A substantial minority of people wind up in jobs they dislike:
in tedious, mind-numbing jobs such as those on a food-processing line; in dirty
and dangerous jobs, such as many of those in steel plants; or in jobs that make
it difficult to believe one is contributing to the society such as work in
advertising.[40]

Job Satisfaction

What makes a job desirable? Job satisfaction depends on a number of factors,
of which the relationship between the job-holder and the boss is among the
most important. The Survey Research Center of the University of Michigan

[39] See *Work in America*, pp. 158–171.
[40] For an account of work on a food-processing line see Barbara Garson, "Tunafish,"
Liberation, Vol. 19, No. 5 (July–August 1975), pp. 9–24; in a steel mill see Studs Terkel,
Working (New York: Random House, 1974); in an advertising firm see Ian Lewis (pseudo-
nym), in Peter Berger (ed.), *The Human Shape of Work* (Chicago: Regnery, 1973).

found in a 1969 study that people were most satisfied with their jobs when the supervisor was helpful and supportive, fair, technically competent, and willing to permit the worker autonomy.[41] Desirable hours, adequate levels of safety and cleanliness, and accessibility of the workplace also played a role in job satisfaction, as did the nature of the work itself. But the nature of relationships with managerial figures was at least as important to workers as the type of work they performed. Similar findings emerged from a more recent study by Melvin L. Kohn and Carmi Schooler. On the basis of interviews with a sample of over 3,000 men representative of all those employed in civilian occupations in the United States, the investigators report that job satisfaction was most likely when men were permitted adequate freedom to do their work as they thought best and treated fairly (in the sense of not being held responsible for things outside their control), and when their jobs were secure, clean, free from undue pressure, and presented adequate challenge. Not surprisingly, jobs of relatively high prestige, such as management, teaching, and accounting, were most likely to have such attributes; jobs of lesser prestige, such as handling materials or cleaning, least likely.[42]

Although few jobs are "perfect," jobs that are desirable in one respect are often desirable in others. This holds when jobs are separated by their prestige level. Despite an occasional job in the blue-collar category that seems to give workers autonomy and some level of challenge, most blue-collar jobs offer neither. The upper-middle-class jobs of manager or professional not only are better paid; they are better jobs quite aside from pay. This is, of course, not always the case; positions that look attractive to an outsider can subject those who occupy them to cruel pressures. But in the aggregate, better paid jobs tend to be better in every way.

For the most part, desirable jobs are available only to those with college training. But noncollege youth, like college youth, have been affected by the increasingly widespread belief that a job should be more than just a source of livelihood—that it should be an aid to self-realization as well. In the words of Daniel Yankelovitch, "Their new values and folkways inevitably clash with the built-in rigidities and limited responses at the workplace."[43]

Despite a generally agreed-upon hierarchy of desirability among jobs, there are wide individual differences in the ways individuals react to differences in work requirements. What is to one person challenge is to another unmanageable pressure; what is to one person an easy, undemanding job is to another

---

[41] Quoted by George Strauss, "Workers: Attitudes and Adjustments," in Rosow, *op. cit.*, pp. 73–98.

[42] Melvin L. Kohn and Carmi Schooler, "Occupational Experience and Psychological Functioning: An Assessment of Reciprocal Effects," *American Sociological Review*, Vol. 38 (February 1973), pp. 97–118. The income derived from a job is so critical to the maintenance of an acceptable quality of life that it needs little emphasis. But for a vivid picture of the problems imposed by income insufficient for needs see Robert Coles' testimony to the Mondale Committee's hearings, *American Families, op. cit.*, pp. 109–119.

[43] Yankelovitch, *op. cit.* Many managers are aware of young people's desires for satisfying work, as is clear from the frequent articles on the topic in the *Harvard Business Review* and other journals directed to managers.

mind-numbing monotony. Ross Stagner has concluded, on the basis of his research and the research of others, that "Both physiological and psychological data indicate there are wide individual differences in the way human beings react to paced constrained jobs."[44]

In the pages that follow we will consider the problems of workers in three different occupational strata: the blue-collar and service worker, with special attention to the machine operators who make up so large a part of the work force within manufacturing; the lower white-collar worker, as exemplified by the insurance clerk and the department store salesperson, whose jobs pay little yet demand the sort of responsible job-identified behavior that is symbolized by business clothes; and the professional and executive, individuals at the top of our job hierarchy, for whom advancement in their career may be as important as the quality of their present job.

The Blue-Collar Job

There is much controversy as to whether blue-collar workers, taken as a group, can be said to be dissatisfied with their work. On the one hand, when asked whether they are satisfied with their jobs, most workers say that they are. They are happy to be working both because they need the money and because it is not clear what else there is to do. Given the alternative jobs available to them, the jobs they have seem good enough. Should the alternative to their jobs be unemployment, they may be delighted to have the jobs, no matter what they entail.[45]

On the other hand, there is much evidence that blue-collar work is not intrinsically desirable. The study by Morse and Weiss, referred to earlier, shows that although the great majority of men would continue to work even if work were not economically required of them, only in the middle-class occupations would the majority remain in the same type of work.[46] (See Table 13-5.)

In a survey conducted among members of the Pennsylvania AFL–CIO, about half of those whose jobs were "most negative" in variety, autonomy, and responsibility were "discontented." They felt that they were less well off than they had hoped they would be when they finished school, and that they seemed to be stuck.[47] Reports by participant observers who have worked with men on automobile assembly lines or as members of labor gangs in steel plants bring this discontent to life. These reports describe the smoldering resentments of

---

[44] Ross Stagner, "Boredom on the Assembly Line: Age and Personality Variables," *Industrial Gerontology,* Vol. 2, No. 1 (Winter 1975), pp. 23–44.

[45] See William H. Form, *op. cit.* See also Harold Wool, "What's Wrong with Work in America?—A Review Essay," *Monthly Labor Review,* Vol. 96, No. 3 (March 1973), pp. 38–44.

[46] See also the similar findings for particular occupational groups reported in *Work in America,* p. 16.

[47] Harold L. Sheppard and Neal Q. Herrick, *Where Have All the Robots Gone?* (New York: Free Press, 1972), calculated from data they present on pages 19 and 29.

Table 13-5   Percentage of Respondents Who Would Continue to Work and Percentage Who Would Continue on the Same Job

	Would continue to work	Would continue in the same type of work
Middle Class		
Professional	86	68
Manager	82	55
Sales	91	59
Working Class		
Trades	79	40
Operatives	78	32
Unskilled	58	16
Service	71	33

Source: Nancy C. Morse and Robert S. Weiss, "The Function and Meaning of Work and the Job" *American Sociological Review*, Vol. 20, No. 2 (April 1955)

people required to perform work that seems meaningless, their general disregard—indeed, antagonism—toward the goals of management, and the use of soft drugs to make the day go faster. Workers were often absent on Mondays and Fridays, and appeared almost indifferent to the threat of being laid off.[48]

One observer, however, concludes that active rejection of work is not typical, even for those whose work seems valueless. George Strauss believes that adaptation based on resignation and apathy is more common, as illustrated by a worker who described his job as follows.

> "Don't get me wrong. I didn't say it is a *good* job. It's an OK job—about as good a job as a guy like me might expect. The foreman leaves me alone and it pays well. But I would never call it a *good* job. It doesn't amount to much, but it's not bad."[49]

In recent years there have been a good many attempts to make industrial jobs more rewarding psychologically. Approaches have included: enlarging the tasks required of a single worker and giving that worker the right to decide how to perform them; giving task responsibilities to autonomous work groups; rotating workers through the plant so that no worker is stuck in any particular job; making it possible for all workers to advance to positions as supervisors or technicians; providing immediate rewards for increased productivity; giving workers responsibility for designing jobs; establishing worker task forces to recommend solutions for specific plant problems; allowing workers to schedule their own hours so long as they worked a full work-week; paying workers weekly salaries rather than hourly wages; paying workers according to the number of skills they have mastered, irrespective of the work they happened to be doing that week.[50]

A notable example of the problems, as well as the value, of attempting to redesign work was the reorganization of jobs within the Gaines pet food plant. Workers there were organized into groups which then were given the right to establish productivity goals, to decide how they should attempt to meet them, to set their working hours, and even to hire new workers to replace those who left. The result of this reorganization seemed to include both increased productivity and higher worker morale. However, some employees felt that they were not adequately compensated for the new skills they had developed in order to meet their new job responsibilities.[51] And undoubtedly at Gaines, as

---

[48] See Bennet Kreman, "No Pride in this Dust," in Irving Howe (ed.), *The World of the Blue-Collar Worker* (New York: Quadrangle, 1972), pp. 11–22. Absenteeism was reported to reach 10 percent in some auto plants in the late 1960s. See Agis Salpukis, "Unions: New Role?" in Rosow, *op. cit.*, pp. 99–117.

[49] George Strauss, "Workers: Attitudes and Adjustments," in Rosow, *op. cit.*, p. 86.

[50] See "Appendix—Case Studies in the Humanization of Work," in *Work in America, op. cit.*, pp. 188–201. See also Richard E. Walton, "Innovative Restructuring of Work," Rosow, *op. cit.*, pp. 145–176.

[51] For a generally positive, although judicious, evaluation of the Gaines experiment, see Robert Schrank, "On Ending Worker Alienation: The Gaines Pet Food Plant," in Roy P. Fairfield (ed.), *Humanizing the Workplace* (Buffalo, N.Y.: Prometheus, 1974).

elsewhere, there were some workers who would have preferred to work by themselves at a job they had learned to do effortlessly.[52]

Critics of work redesign accept that morale and perhaps productivity as well can be increased by such programs. But they wonder if work redesign is what workers really want. If given a choice between jobs with greater "intrinsic interest" and higher pay, wouldn't workers choose the latter? The critics of work redesign suggest that managements should devote less energy to redesigning work and more to devising more efficient systems for production, providing workers with a fair share of the profits. They are not opposed to interesting jobs for blue-collar workers, but they *are* opposed to workers being cozened into acceptance of less than their fair share of a company's earnings.[53]

A quite different issue is that some workers prefer that their jobs *not* be redesigned. They may want their superiors to assume the responsibility of deciding how their work is to be performed, to be able to occupy their thoughts and energies with matters other than work, or to pass the time with small talk with their fellows.[54] The job enlargement that would make work meaningful for most workers might be an unwanted burden to some.

In any event, workers are rarely helpless cogs in a system, no matter how authoritarian the atmosphere of a workplace. They often find ways of controlling their work pace and introducing variety into the day's routine. For example, when an assembly-line is sped up, workers can always "get even" with management by judicious industrial sabotage.[55] Automobiles that come off the line with bolts misapplied or missing are, among other things, a message to management.

A strike is another way of delivering a message to management. The number of strikes has increased sharply in recent years, from 3,333 in 1960 to 5,010 in 1972 (although there were fewer industry-wide strikes that involved a great many workers). Most strikes are over issues of wages and fringe benefits, but a slightly larger proportion of strikes in recent years has involved issues such as work environments, job assignments, and work loads.[56]

Even in plants without formal union leadership, factory workers manage to organize informally in work groups and cliques, both to humanize the bleak impersonality of the plant and to mitigate the impact of managerial directives on their work. Management tends to see these informal work groups as implacably hostile to company aims, and often enough management is right. Informal social groups can reduce the efficiency of a factory's operation. They

[52] See Salpukas, *op. cit.*, p. 113.

[53] See Wool, *op. cit.*

[54] See Sheppard and Herrick, *op. cit.*, pp. 65–67, and Georges Friedmann, *Industrial Society* (New York: Free Press, 1955), especially the chapters on problems of monotony, rhythm of work, and assembly-line work. See also Donald Roy, "Quota Restrictions and Goldbricking in a Machine Shop," *American Journal of Sociology* (March 1952, pp. 427–442), and "Banana Time," in Warren G. Bennis et al. (eds.), *Interpersonal Dynamics* (Homewood, Ill.: Dorsey, 1964), pp. 583–599.

[55] See *Work in America, op. cit.*, pp. 88–89.

[56] Peter Henle, "Economic Effects: Reviewing the Evidence," in Rosow, *op. cit.*, pp. 119–144.

may hoard work secrets and refuse them to newcomers until the newcomers are accepted into the group; insist that certain jobs be given only to people with high seniority and refuse to allow management to assign a new worker to these jobs, no matter how extensive his or her experience outside the plant; use social pressure to force inspectors or foremen to modify their insistence on a particular level of quality. Yet some studies have shown that even though informal work groups are likely to restrict output to a level below that which management would consider optimal, they nevertheless tend to keep output *up* to a level that seems fair to them, and may in fact set quite high levels of productivity where management is favorably regarded.[57]

As noted, not all blue-collar jobs are like the closely supervised, wearing, sometimes dangerous, often dirty, manufacturing jobs we have just been considering. Milk route salesmen, telephone linemen, truckers, maintenance workers, and individuals in public service often have a degree of autonomy sufficient to make them similar to the cab driver who, though he is employed by a fleet, *can* feel that because he can stop for coffee whenever he wants to, he is his own boss. These blue-collar occupations often provide satisfaction and self-esteem. Yet one of the problems these jobs share with factory jobs is that they are working-class in a society that measures a man by "how far he has gotten." Despite the pieties uttered periodically about the dignity of labor, the blue-collar or service workers know that they have not gotten very far. Many blue-collar workers, even those who feel they are satisfied with their work when all things are taken into consideration, hope for more for their children.[58]

Middle-Management and White-Collar Jobs

Although only a small proportion of sales workers and managers earn more than skilled blue-collar workers, they are much more likely to say that they would continue working at the jobs they now have even if they no longer needed the money. The white-collar jobs, including technical and clerical work, drafting, accounting, selling, and administration on a third or fourth level, seem to provide enough support to an individual's sense of worth so that the job itself, and not just the fact of working, can be of value to a person. It is difficult to say just why this is, for often the work is not especially challenging. Perhaps the white-collar worker can identify more easily with the enterprise of which he or she is a member; perhaps white-collar work provides greater opportunity for autonomous activity; perhaps white-collar work, because it involves work with symbols and with people, is more interesting and carries more

[57] See Stanley Seashore, *Group Cohesiveness and Industrial Work Group,* Publication No. 14 (Ann Arbor: University of Michigan, Institute for Social Research, 1955).

[58] See Theodore V. Purcell, S. J., "The Hopes of Negro Workers for their Children," in Arthur B. Shostak and William Gomberg (eds.), *Blue-Collar World* (Englewood Cliffs, N.J.: Prentice-Hall, 1964), pp. 144–153. See also Richard Sennett and Jonathan Cobb, *The Hidden Injuries of Class* (New York: Knopf, 1972).

prestige than "thing-focussed" or "activity-focussed" blue-collar work. For whatever reason, white-collar work apparently provides psychic benefits that offset its frequently low remuneration.

Yet there is a set of difficulties that seems peculiar to white-collar work. To begin with, white-collar workers, even more than foremen, tend to be "people in the middle." They are often in *boundary roles* that require them to represent the organization to others, yet they have no authority to make policy or, indeed, to affect what the organization is or does. And they are more constrained than others in the work force: they have neither the freedom of the top executives to determine for themselves how and when they will do their work, a freedom that comes with authority, nor the very different freedom of blue-collar workers to suit themselves in dress and demeanor, a freedom that is one of the few benefits of being defined as a "hired hand" rather than as a true member of the firm.

Often those in middle-level jobs must sell not so much their time or their skills as their personality. C. Wright Mills has vividly described the self-alienation that can develop from this marketing of self:

> In many strata of white-collar employment, such traits as courtesy, helpfulness, and kindness, once intimate, are now part of the impersonal means of livelihood. Self-alienation is thus an accompaniment of . . . alienated labor. . . . When white-collar people get jobs they sell not only their time and energy, but their personalities as well.[59]

However, Mills fails to recognize how greatly the climate of organization varies from firm to firm. One department store may demand a submissive conformity and amiability from its employees, while another may welcome aggressive selling. Some oil companies value managers who display adaptability and loyalty to the firm, whereas high-technology firms tend instead to demand cool competence and ability to get a job done. One extremely successful firm, though it rarely fires anyone, may demote an executive who fails to deliver.[60]

In almost every firm, many middle-level employees are in positions that demand no special skill except, perhaps, an amorphous administrative "knowhow." They are hired not to provide a specific service dependent on specialized knowledge, but rather to advance the interests of the firm in whatever way they can. They are therefore expected to be loyal to the firm, even when the firm's policies strike them as socially malicious or unjustifiable. "Whistle-blowing" (exposing policies that may be not simply reprehensible but actually criminal) is a sure way for an employee to encounter trouble on the job—at

---

[59] C. Wright Mills, *White Collar* (New York: Oxford, 1951), p. xvii.

[60] On the oil companies, see Alan Harrington, *Life in the Crystal Palace* (New York: Knopf, 1959); on the high-technology organization, Fred H. Goldner, "Demotion in Industrial Management," *American Sociological Review*, Vol. 30 (October 1965), pp. 714–725.

least with those on whom the whistle is blown, if not with the firm as a whole.[61] This can produce excruciating conflict, in which continued loyalty to the firm requires one to become an accessory to dishonesty.

There are other forms of contradictory pressures on lower ranking white-collar workers. Members of organizations may be required to display initiative while following rules; to rely on others in the organization while maintaining independence; to contribute to the success of the organization as a whole while ensuring that their group or department and they themselves do not lose out in the distribution of recognition and other rewards. Constant need for co-ordination with others is almost certain to create tensions and conflicts. But a good organization member is expected to be able to get along and so must learn to repress hostility and maintain the outward appearance of friendliness, no matter how he or she feels. Even so, those who work in "the office" are much more likely than those who work on the shop floor to say that they would remain, even if they did not have to work.

Professionals and Executives

Professionals and higher level executives have problems substantially different from those of an industrial worker, whose day is spent at a disliked task in a subordinate position, or a lower level manager or white-collar worker, whose horizons are severely limited. Those in the top level of our occupational strata tend to make a *personal* commitment to their tasks because their self-esteem depends on accomplishment and recognition. In addition, there is strong pressure on them to evaluate their success not only in terms of the job they hold at the moment but also in terms of their career—that is, in terms of where they are in an anticipated sequence of ever-increasing accomplishment and recognition.

There is some logic in discussing the executive positions and professional occupations together, beyond the fact that they carry about the same social rank and that members of each are equally likely to be concerned with the rise and fall of their careers. Executives are becoming more and more professionalized. Such distinctively professional institutions as the graduate school and the professional journal have found their place in the business world. Modern executives rarely built the business they are running; they may own a small number of shares in their company, but they are more nearly a paid employee than an owner, although stock option plans may give them a speculative stake in the profits. While executives may receive a handsome salary and be surrounded by the trappings of high rank, they can seldom afford to be autocratic; they must exercise power with restraint and tact.[62] By the same token, more and more professionals are members of organizations. Everett Hughes

---

[61] See Ralph Nader et al. (eds.), *Whistle Blowing: Report of the Conference on Professional Responsibility, Washington, 1971* (New York: Grossman, 1972).

[62] Wilbert E. Moore, *The Conduct of the Corporation* (New York: Random House, 1962), especially Ch. 1.

has noted that both law and medicine, the model professions, are "far along the road to practice in organizations," and that other professions—teaching, for example—are nearly always practiced within organizations.[63] Professionals within organizations have some problems they do not share with executives, often stemming from conflicting responsibilities to firm and to clients. But in their desire for achievement and recognition they are apt to be indistinguishable from executives.

Both executives and professionals often pay for their freedom and prestige by working 70-hour weeks (if one takes into account job-related reading and job-necessitated entertaining). Asked their hobby, many executives and professionals would respond, "work," and would insist that not only do they work constantly, but it is only at work that they truly enjoy themselves.[64] Harold L. Wilensky reports that only one-fifth of all lawyers and one-quarter of all professors work *fewer* than forty-five hours per week.[65] When such individuals are forced to retire, they may have more than adequate financial resources, but they may be bereft of psychological ones. And should they have the misfortune to lose their jobs, as has happened to some executives in the current recession, the emotional consequences may be severe.[66]

Self-employed professionals can often work as long as they care to, since they do not belong to a bureaucracy that forces them to retire at a certain age and can keep their job so long as patients or clients continue to come to them. But America values youth and vigor more than age and wisdom, and lawyers may well find themselves losing clients before they begin losing cases. In fact, the dependence of professionals on customers or clients always produces tension, no matter how much it may be glossed over by friendliness and tact on both sides. The clients judge the professional's competence without understanding how they work, and the professional, though he or she may reject their conclusion, will prosper or fail according to it.

The fact that the professions are freely chosen is by no means as advantageous as it might at first appear. Just as in one's choice of husband or wife, one's choice of profession is sometimes misguided, and this is the more likely since the choice of profession, unlike that of future spouse, ordinarily is made without a "getting acquainted" period and requires a near-final decision mainly on the basis of public image. Public image frequently proves false: medicine, for example, seems to provide unrivaled opportunity for service, but in their course of training medical students must learn to see their patients as problems rather than persons, and themselves as people with a function rather

---

[63] Everett C. Hughes, "Professions," in *Daedalus*, Vol. 92, No. 4 (1963), pp. 655–658.

[64] See William H. Whyte, Jr., "How Hard Do Executives Work?" in Gerald D. Bell (ed.), *Organizations and Human Behavior* (Englewood Cliffs, N.J.: Prentice-Hall, 1967), pp. 272–281.

[65] Harold L. Wilensky, "The Uneven Distribution of Leisure: The Impact of Economic Growth on 'Free Time,'" in Erwin O. Smigel (ed.), *Work and Leisure* (New Haven: College and University Press, 1963), pp. 107–145.

[66] See, for example, Thomas J. Murray, "The Plight of the Fired Executives," *Dun's*, Vol. 97, No. 2 (February 1971), pp. 43–45.

than a mission.[67] Often the problems that will be met in the course of a professional career are not visible to its aspirants, whose models may be furnished by the most prominent "stars" of the career. Thus Lawrence Kubie, the late psychiatrist, argued that the scientific career and its hazards are little understood by the young people who are attracted to it: in particular, they underestimate the possibility that they may devote themselves to science without ever being able to make a noteworthy contribution to their field.[68]

To be sure, in some professions it is possible to shift one's actual activities without going back to school for another lengthy and expensive course of training. For example, a physician who doesn't really like dealing directly with patients can become an anesthesiologist who only deals with patients when they are "out" or find a new career as a hospital administrator or editor of a medical journal. But these shifts always require finding new colleagues and new positions, and thus risking one's reputation and security. As a person gets older, shifting becomes increasingly difficult.

Each occupation within the executive and professional category has its own distinct career line, and some of these are more likely to permit the realization of hopes for success than are others. Some career lines are marked by early rises and high plateaus, as is the case in many areas of government service. Others provide a relatively steady increase in responsibilities and rewards and a degree of advancement for all those who overcome the hurdles of entry, as in some parts of the academic profession in which there is a steady progression from a fairly elevated entry level to a moderate ceiling. The academic profession also illustrates the divergence that exists even within what might appear to be a single occupation to an outsider. In the sciences an unusually able and successful person can become a full professor, running an enormous operation, while in his or her early thirties; an equally able and equally well-regarded professor of Greek may be unable to advance from a junior rank until an already occupied position is vacated by the death or retirement of the incumbent.

Executives and professionals tend to assess the progress of their careers by comparing how far they have come with the distance achieved by others of the same age or length of time in the field. In addition there may be some absolute standards: executives, for example, sometimes say that a person who has not entered top management by the age of forty will never enter it at all, and both physicists and mathematicians believe that if one is first-class, he or she will have made a significant contribution to the field by age thirty. As people age, their aspirations often shrink to meet the "reality" they have come to perceive. (This is true of industrial workers as well.) As a result, they may redefine success in terms of their personal relations with clients or their ability to support their family and lead a pleasant life away from work. Whether this

[67] See Howard S. Becker and Blanche Geer, "The Fate of Idealism in Medical School," *American Sociological Review*, Vol. 23, No. 1 (February 1958), pp. 50–56.

[68] Lawrence S. Kubie, "Psychoneurotic Problems of the American Scientist," *Chicago Review*, Vol. 8, No. 3 (1954), pp. 65–80.

maneuver brings satisfaction we cannot say: there has been little systematic attention given to the problems, if they exist, of the executive or professional with only modest achievement.[69]

Since we tend to know a good deal about the frustrations of the literate and articulate, it is sometimes believed that the lure of opportunities for achievement causes people in professional and executive occupations to lead lives that are particularly harried and full of tension. But research clearly indicates that the chances for contentment and self-realization are on the whole greater in these prestigious occupations than in less demanding lines of work. Those whose work brings them material reward are apt to report that it brings them other satisfactions as well.[70]

PROBLEMS AND PROSPECTS

As we review what seem to be the critical problems in the work sector of our society today, and compare them with the problems that existed fifty or a hundred years ago, it appears that much has been gained. Increased productivity and affluence, together with the activities of unions and the introduction of protective laws, has improved the lot of ordinary working people. (Indeed, the increased wealth and productivity of our society has raised the standard of living of almost everyone.) In response to the effects on families of the Great Depression of the thirties, the government introduced the Unemployment Insurance program to tide individuals over intervals between jobs. The Social Security program, though inadequate in itself, is at any rate a help to the retired, as is Medicare. This is not to say that pockets of poverty no longer exist, or that families may not still be destitute; poverty does remain, and much more needs to be done to help those who are poor.

Some of the apparent problems of the recent past no longer trouble us; they turned out not to be real. Fifteen years ago intellectuals were concerned about the development of a "leisure society" and wondered what people would do when they no longer needed to work full-time. It turned out that there is still plenty of work to be done in our society—although it is still unclear just how to match individuals to jobs, and how to pay for work that would benefit the public but no particular private firm. Fifteen years ago we were concerned about automation and the possibility that much of our work force would be replaced by computer-guided machines. This threat proved exaggerated. Hiring humans provides an employer with more capability and flexibility at a lower cost in capital investment than does automation. Perhaps we will some day find that machines have taken over, but that day will not be soon.

---

[69] For evidence that the pursuit of the usual notion of intellectual success may produce heartbreak see the account of failures along the tenure trail in Benn Morreale, "Tales of Academe," *Encounter*, Vol. 33 (August 1969), pp. 35–42.

[70] See, for example, the data quoted by Gerald Gurin et al. in *America Looks at Its Mental Health* (New York: Basic Books, 1960), especially Ch. 6.

At present it appears that our main problems have to do with limits on our continued prosperity and with our ability to realize our social aims under conditions of stable, or even decreasing, gross national product. We want to move toward a more equal, more just, society, and also toward a society that accepts ultimate responsibility for each of its members. But there is some possibility that we may have to accept a decreased aggregate standard of living as a result of increased costs of materials and energy. If this should indeed occur, it will no longer be possible to "equalize up"—that is, to give more to those at the disadvantaged end of our distribution curve without taking something from those better situated. Increased equality will have to be achieved through redistribution, through taking away from those who have more whatever we make available to those who have less. Because it hurts one group to benefit another, redistribution is a policy with great potential for inducing conflict, no matter how committed we are, as a society, to the ideology of equality.

If our gross national product declines, or merely stops increasing, can we move toward a more just society without engendering tremendous and perhaps irreconcilable conflicts in our midst? This remains to be seen.

SUMMARY

1   Our current economy presents a paradoxical picture, combining high levels of employment with high levels of unemployment. The hardships of our current recession seem to be distributed unevenly.

2   Work and earning a respectable income appear to be of critical emotional importance to Americans. This may explain their tendency to choose increased income over increased leisure. Many better-educated women feel, as most men do, that work and career are essential to their sense of self, but many less well-educated women continue to seek satisfaction and self-esteem in their roles as wives and mothers.

3   Until recently, many economists believed that the American economy could be maintained in a continuing healthy state. Recently this optimism has been lessened by increasing recognition of the economy's vulnerability to developments abroad and to conditions affecting the availability of raw materials and energy and to difficult-to-control internal dynamics.

4   The exploitation of workers associated with early industrialization has receded significantly, thanks in part to unionization. But there remain the problems of worker exploitation within the nonunion sector, sporadic industrial strife, and inadequate plant safety.

5   Solutions to one set of problems often give rise to a new set. Minimum-wage laws, for example, reduce the jobs available for individuals marginal to the labor force. And laws intended to prevent exploitation of women and children may "protect" these groups to their disadvantage.

6   The American labor force includes nearly all men aged 25 to 55, and slightly more than half of women within that age range. The proportion of women in the labor force has been rising steadily throughout this century, and there has

been a narrowing of the years during which virtually all men are in the labor force. The result is a labor force in which women are more prominent than they have ever been except in time of war.

7   The belief that our economy was moving toward a "post-industrial" form, in which only a small proportion of the work force would produce has led to a desire for emphasis on the services and the professions in our job-training plans. This may well be premature, since, as recent events have reminded us, we are still primarily an industrial nation.

8   Men in the United States have always held more prestigious and better-paid jobs than women, and whites than nonwhites. Prejudice has been one of many reasons for the differences. Federal attempts to outlaw discrimination have resulted in substantial gains for blacks and in the beginning of changes affecting women. But government requirements for "affirmative action" have led to new problems, like forced consideration of race or sex in hiring and clashes with established rules of seniority.

9   Unemployment measures tend to misclassify both those who prefer not working at all to a less desirable job, and those who are so discouraged by the absence of job prospects that they do not look for work. The latter is probably the more serious problem in terms of numbers, since it results in an underestimation of the the the actual level of employment.

10   Possible reasons for the present high level of unemployment are: that more members of our potential work force, women as well as men, are searching for employment so that there are no longer enough jobs to go around; the vicissitudes of the business cycle; the failure of government to limit wages and prices, leading to higher costs, reduced demand, and fewer jobs; and the impact on the economy of the energy shortage of 1973.

11   Despite the emotional and material hardships caused by unemployment for individuals and families, our government is not committed to a policy of "full employment" out of fear that it would fuel inflation. It has been shown that over many years there has existed between inflation and unemployment a relationship, described by the Phillips curve, such that increase in the one accompanies decrease in the other. Although recently unemployment and inflation have risen simultaneously, there may still be reason to fear that government financing of jobs would be inflationary unless accompanied by some combination of higher productivity, increased taxation, and wage and price controls.

12   A number of factors seem to contribute to whether a job is considered desirable, including employee–supervisor relations, hours, levels of safety and cleanliness, accessibility of the workplace, and the challenge of the work.

13   Although few jobs are desirable in all respects, jobs that are desirable in one respect tend to be desirable in others as well. In particular, jobs higher in prestige ranking tend to provide greater opportunity for autonomy, more challenge, and higher pay.

14   There is controversy regarding blue-collar workers' dissatisfaction with their jobs. When asked, most blue-collar workers say that they are satisfied, but only a minority would continue in the same work if they had alternatives, and many, if not most, hope for more for their children.

15   Work redesign is an attempt to give blue-collar workers more recognition and more control over their own work. The success of such efforts is still a matter of debate, although some seem to have largely succeeded in their own terms.

16   Workers can make dissatisfaction known through strikes, which have increased sharply in recent years, or by opposing management efforts through informal organization.

17   People in white-collar jobs, even jobs that are not especially challenging or well-paid, often seem relatively satisfied with their work. There frequently are, however, pressures on them for adaptability, loyalty, and acceptance of the particular company's norms.

18   Those on a higher level, in jobs that most in our society would consider unusually good, tend to make great personal commitment to their tasks. They may pay for the stimulation their responsibilities give them by working long hours and bringing home tensions, if not tasks, left over from the workday.

19   Professionals and managers may evaluate themselves in terms of their movement within a career, a sequence of jobs whose ultimate goal may be an office or level of recognition obtainable by only a few. Some measure of disappointment may be the fate of most of those who aspire to be company president or a leader in their field, but professionals and managers tend to be satisfied with the opportunities for self-realization their work provides them.

20   One critical problem of the future will be how to move toward a more equal, more just society that accepts ultimate responsibility for each of its members, in the event that such a society requires a redistribution of income. If our gross national product declines, or merely stops increasing, can we move toward a more just society without engendering tremendous and perhaps irreconcilable conflicts?

RECOMMENDED READING

The best single introduction to problems in the world of work may be the collection of essays edited by Jerome M. Rosow, *The Worker and the Job: Coping with Change* (1974). The initial chapter, by Daniel Yankelovich, describes trends in the way Americans view work, based largely on surveys conducted by a research organization of which he is head. In the next essay Eli Ginzberg describes the changing American work force, with special attention to blacks, women, and youth. Then George Strauss examines the attitudes of workers toward their jobs, relying largely on already-published materials to evaluate the jobs the American economy makes available. In other articles, the history and present status of unionization is described, a variety of indicators of job dissatisfaction are appraised, and a variety of experiments in job enlargement are described and evaluated.

A book that has been the subject of some controversy, and that covers nearly the same ground, is *Work in America,* prepared by James O'Toole et al. (1973). It is the first half of this book, in which jobs available to American workers are criticized as offering too little scope for self-realization and, in some instances, imposing too much pressure and insecurity, that has come under criticism as over-drawn. The second half, in which an economic argument for a "full-employment" strategy is developed, has encountered less questioning.

A number of books and articles deal with the importance of work. In addition to the article by George Strauss referred to above, well worth consulting is the study by Leonard Goodwin, *Do the Poor Want to Work?* (1972). On the value of specific jobs, two articles should be consulted: William H. Form, "Auto Workers and Their Machines, a Study of Work, Factory, and Job Satisfaction in

Four Countries," *Social Forces,* Vol. 52 (September 1973); and Melvin L. Kohn and Carmi Schooler, "Occupational Experience and Psychological Functioning: An Assessment of Reciprocal Effects," *American Sociological Review,* Vol. 38 (February 1973).

On the redesign of jobs, the best single source may be Chapter 4 of *Work in America,* together with the case studies in "The Humanization of Work," included as an appendix to that book. There are many specific studies cited as footnotes in this appendix. Another direction in changing the nature of jobs is to extend the scope of worker control, perhaps to the point where workers participate in decisions regarding production processes or even the direction a firm is to take. A collection of papers on participatory democracy in the workplace has been edited by Gerry Hunnius, G. David Garson, and John Case: *Workers' Control: A Reader on Labor and Social Change* (1973).

There are a few books and articles that provide one or more ethnographies of occupations. Notable among them are the following: Peter Berger (ed.), *The Human Shape of Work* (1973); Studs Terkel, *Working* (1974); Barbara Garson, *All the Livelong Day: The Meaning and Demeaning of Routine Work* (1975). The articles in the Berger book are written by sociologists from a sociological standpoint. The Terkel book reprints interviews with individuals who follow a great many different occupations. The Garson book reports the author's firsthand experiences as well as her observations of workers and interviews with not only workers but also members of management. It is passionately critical.

14

Poverty and Proletariat

DAVID MATZA
HENRY MILLER

E ver since the claim to basic life necessities became a function of wages, poverty has been directly and intimately linked to the vicissitudes of employment. The connection between wages and life has been a feature of Western society for some six hundred years; when human labor became a marketable commodity, the possibility of becoming poor—in the sense we mean it today—became a reality. This is not to say that in manorial times there was no misery. It would be a gross distortion to argue a romanticized portrait of the feudal social economy; disease, unhappiness, and famine were endemic. But there was *no* unemployment and, hence, there was no requirement of living that was absent by virtue of a loss of wage income.

The sacrifice of labor to the working whim of the market was a momentous transformation in the organization of society, polity, and economy.[2] It was not perceived as harmonious with the natural order of things—the nobility, the church, and probably most serfs were bitterly opposed to such a novel and inhuman construction of labor. Indeed, it took several centuries before the equation between work and wages was commonly accepted—not until the Industrial Revolution was well under way did it become a commonplace.[3] Even today in the most industrialized and capitalized nation of the globe there exist pockets of outrageous resistance to what was once a notion in itself deemed outrageous.

Nonetheless, we must deal with realities and, like it or not, the U.S. economy is predicated on a wage-based labor force, and contemporary poverty must be considered from that vantage point. This is not a trivial point: What should be obvious—that poverty is related to economy—is not at all the dominant line of analysis.[4] Rather, the most vocal and articulate analysts have been inclined to treat poverty as an attribute of individual character; when put kindly, it is said that the poor are victims of their own deficit; when put more harshly, of their own perversity.[5] Such a distorted analysis is not surprising when it is realized that industrial capitalism was required to produce not only tangible commodi-

The authors wish to thank Connie Philipp and Judith Gunton for their assistance.

[1] Julia Vinograd, "Hard Times," in *Street Feet* (Berkeley, Calif.: Thorp Springs Press, 1974).

[2] Karl Polanyi, *The Great Transformation* (New York: Rinehart, 1944).

[3] E. P. Thompson, *The Making of the English Working Class* (New York: Random House, 1964).

[4] For a recent statement of this classical view, see Frances Piven and Richard Cloward, *Regulating the Poor* (New York: Pantheon, 1971). For a more general framework that illuminates the relation between labor and capital, see Harry Braverman, *Labor and Monopoly Capital* (New York: Monthly Review Press, 1974). Representative of the voluminous and complicated classical Marxian view are Friedrich Engels, *The Condition of the Working Class in England;* Karl Kautsky, *The Class Struggle;* and Daniel DeLeon, *Two Pages from Roman History.*

[5] Exemplary of this conservative mode is Josephine Shaw Lowell, *Public Relief and Private Charity* (New York: Putnam, 1884). A less elegant rendition of the same view appears in Edward Banfield, *The Unheavenly City* (Boston: Little, Brown, 1968).

ties but also an ideology: the advertisement or promise of a cornucopic good life with unbounded economic possibility. In such a world of overflowing potential those who have not may be piously regarded as blameworthy; fault is deflected from the limitless or miraculous market of free enterprise.

A more important insight into the nature of poverty based on the equation between income deficit and wages is the *variable* character of poverty and the *variable* quality of employment. Thus we will see that poverty is not easily defined in terms of any absolute dollar standard—there are gradations of poverty and this must be so simply because there are gradations of labor compensation. The scale has a wide range; its beginning is, of course, zero because there is some labor for which there is no wage. The upper reaches of poverty blend with the lower reaches of nonpoverty—an ambiguous line to which most people claim a sometime proximity. Further, employment—or wage-compensated labor —is not a discrete category; it can range from "non" to "full" with intervening gradations specified by such ambiguities as "sub" or "under" or "partial."

To the extent that the vast majority of Americans, at some point in their life cycle, are wage earners they are peculiarly vulnerable to the hazards of poverty. Unless there is another nonwage source of income, the loss of employment results in an immediate encounter with the boundaries of poverty—and, if the unemployment continues, the condition evolves into real poverty. Modern industrial nations have developed a series of cushions to ease an individual's fall into the domain of poverty: unemployment compensation, an expedient that it is hoped will tide one through a temporary phase of nonwork; workmen's compensation, for the disabled; old age insurance, for the "retired" who are defined as no longer useful to the labor force; Aid to Families with Dependent Children (AFDC), for children who are dependent and not yet able to join the ranks of wage earners; and a variety of other welfare and/or insurance programs for miscellaneous categories of people who are not working, not working enough, or not working for wages sufficient to sustain their existence.

These devices, so proudly heralded as the humane response of enlightened capitalism to the uncontrolled vagaries of the labor market and of human character, do not keep people from being poor. Rather, they maintain existence at a subsistence level and—as such—the programs serve to define certain important categories of the poor. Welfare and unsupplemented Old Age and Survivors Insurance (OASI) recipients are among the poorest of America's poor and they represent, for the most part, the two temporal extremes of wage earners: those not yet employed but who ordinarily will be and those who were but are no longer. In between is the active labor force, but it should not be assumed that membership in this entity provides a certain respite from poverty or its potential. Not all labor provides a wage that is beyond marginal subsistence; and not all labor is immune to recession or depression. In short, the labor force—potential, actual, and retired—represents those who are either poor or at risk of being poor. Thus we conceive of poverty as a phenomenon produced by disturbances in a political economy that are inflicted on wage labor. It is a perspective most congruent with the operation of the U.S. economy—one that is fairly described as an industrial capitalism (including pre- and post-industrial sectors) tempered by a welfare system that more or less assures existence to those victimized by a nonliving wage. Such a conception suggests a dual focus: first, we portray the layers of poverty based on the obvious notion that some poor are poorer than others; second, we show that poverty is embedded in the life cycles of working people.[6] Any given age cohort will have its own peculiar incidence of poverty—and this, again, follows inexorably from the fact that for all but a privileged few, income derives from paid work and wages do not accrue to all who labor.

A DELINEATION OF POVERTY

In an earlier version of the chapter, the varieties of poverty were conceived as occupying concentric circles: the widest circle comprising all the poor; an intermediary circle comprising the welfare poor; and an innermost "hard core" comprising the disreputable, who suffer the stigma of immorality. This schema provided a picture that was useful to a point for the clarification of disrepute and its subjectively defined nature. From the vantage point of objective poverty, however—poverty conceived in terms of dollar income—something like the chemist's graduated cylinder may be more instructive. Within the cylinder are particles immersed in a liquid of variable viscosities. Let particles stand for people and fluid represent conditions or context. Viscosity means the internal resistance of the fluid, that which makes it resist a tendency to flow. The heaviest or most sluggish fluids are at the bottom, the lighter ones at the top. Bottom and top represent low to high dollar incomes and the associated life chances. The particles move up and down but the lower they fall the harder to rise. There are no clear boundaries, one layer blends into another, and a constant turbulence allows for shift of suspended particles within the limited strata of the cylinder. Needless to say, many particles float magically out of the cylinder altogether, lifted by the turbulence, perhaps to higher horizons. Thus mobility is assumed in the model—and out of it. What is the scale of current incomes at which the various lines of poverty may be reasonably drawn? Such a delineation would provide a description of the various layers and the basis for considering whether proportions have changed over time.

---

[6] Our outlook is well summarized by S. M. Miller and Pamela Roby: "In casting many of the issues of poverty in terms of stratification, we do not wish to imply that the poor are a fixed, homogeneous group that shares a common outlook. Rather, we see the poor as those who lag behind the rest of society in terms of one or more dimensions of life. There may be considerable turnover in these bottom groups. Although we lack data showing what proportion of persons in the bottom groups move in and out of poverty, we do know that a life cycle pattern is of some importance for the risk of being at the bottom is much greater for the older individuals." "Poverty: Changing Social Stratification," in Peter Townsend (ed.), *Concepts of Poverty* (New York: American Elsevier, 1970). For a definitive discussion of the life cycle perspective, see Leonard Cain, Jr., "Life Course and Social Structure," in Robert E. Faris (ed.), *Handbook of Modern Sociology* (Chicago: Rand McNally, 1964).

A concise and universally agreed-on definition of poverty is very unlikely. As in the case of defining employment, each definition is charged with political implication.[7] Obvious enough to the poor themselves, the matter of definition remains problematic for specialists. However, disagreement among writers on details should not be allowed to obscure the fact that general agreement on some matters seems accomplished.

Absolute and Relative Poverty

The basic division of expertise is between an absolute and relative definition of poverty.

> The most prevalent absolute definition was the Orshansky Social Security Administration definition . . . [1965]. This . . . defined and priced a minimum food budget and multiplied that amount by a factor of three to estimate the poverty floor. Two principal relative definitions began to attract attention: The income share of the bottom decile or quintile of the income distribution; or a measure first proposed by Victor Fuchs [1965]—the percentage of families earning half the national median family income. Many revisions of the absolute definitions were also proposed.[8]

A serious shortcoming of a relative conception of poverty—one, say, that considers the lowest one-fifth poor—is that it obscures the proportion of the population who share the lot of being poor; more important, however, according to critics of the relative definition, it fixes the proportion irrespective of the average overall improvements in income over time. The measure proposed by Victor Fuchs—the percentage of families earning half the national median family income—helps some in answering this objection but not a great deal. Conversely, the advantage of the absolute definition is that, paradoxically, it is useful in focusing on the relative deprivation experienced by various segments of the society. Subjectively, living in a family of four whose earnings were below $5,038 in 1974, the official poverty threshold as defined by Orshansky, may mean one thing when most others make no more and quite another when a small minority earn so little.

A fixed or absolute conception of poverty also has shortcomings. One difficulty is that it ignores shifts in customary definitions of an acceptable minimal standard of life. Rising aspirations, which are hardly limited to underdeveloped economies, not only refer to the highest possibilities; they also affect the minimal standards of life acceptable in a society. Moreover, absolute standards may ignore or minimize "the increasingly expensive requisites for daily 'subsistence' in urbanizing, technologically more complicated societies. Telephones and auto-

---

[7] Townsend, *op. cit.;* and the excellent discussion: Stanley Moses, "Labor Supply Concepts: The Political Economy of Conceptual Change," *Annals* (March 1975), pp. 26–44.

[8] David Gordon, *Theories of Poverty and Underemployment* (Lexington, Mass.: Heath, 1972), p. 139.

mobiles become more indispensable in the United States . . . even for the poor."[9]

Finally, the absolute definition is less absolute than it appears. Nutritional need, the key component of the Orshansky measure, is somewhat idiosyncratic, varying by age, sex, weight, and energy expenditures. A further complication is the fact that consumers purchase marketed foods—not calories. Consequently, dietary habit, custom, and availability will affect whether $5,038 in 1974 would actually constitute a minimum subsistence budget. The same difficulty, of course, obtains in multiplying food cost by three to determine minimum subsistence.

Despite their difficulties, both measures provide useful, objective estimates regarding different but important matters. The relative conception contends quite plausibly that those in the bottom fifth of the income distribution will

Table 14-1 Ratio of the Mean Income of Each Fifth of Families to the Mean Income of All Families: 1947–1971 (Families Ranked by Size of Income)

	Lowest fifth	Second fifth	Middle fifth	Fourth fifth	Highest fifth	Top 5 percent
1947	0.25	0.59	0.85	1.16	2.16	3.50
1948	0.25	0.60	0.87	1.16	2.13	3.42
1949	0.23	0.59	0.86	1.17	2.14	3.38
1950	0.22	0.59	0.87	1.17	2.14	3.46
1951	0.25	0.62	0.88	1.17	2.08	3.36
1952	0.24	0.61	0.87	1.16	2.11	3.54
1953	0.23	0.62	0.90	1.20	2.06	3.16
1954	0.23	0.60	0.89	1.19	2.10	3.28
1955	0.24	0.61	0.89	1.19	2.08	3.36
1956	0.25	0.62	0.89	1.19	2.06	3.28
1957	0.25	0.63	0.91	1.19	2.03	3.16
1958	0.25	0.62	0.89	1.18	2.04	3.16
1959	0.25	0.60	0.88	1.19	2.07	3.26
1960	0.24	0.60	0.88	1.18	2.10	3.36
1961	0.24	0.59	0.87	1.18	2.13	3.42
1962	0.25	0.60	0.88	1.19	2.08	3.26
1963	0.25	0.60	0.88	1.19	2.07	3.20
1964	0.26	0.60	0.89	1.20	2.06	3.16
1965	0.26	0.61	0.88	1.19	2.07	3.16
1966	0.29	0.64	0.88	1.17	2.02	3.02
1967	0.27	0.61	0.87	1.17	2.08	3.08
1968	0.29	0.62	0.88	1.18	2.04	2.82
1969	0.28	0.62	0.88	1.18	2.05	2.80
1970	0.28	0.60	0.87	1.17	2.08	2.88
1971	0.28	0.59	0.87	1.18	2.08	3.24

Source: U.S. Bureau of the Census, *Social Indicators, 1973* (Washington, D.C.: Government Printing Office, 1973), Table 5/9, p. 179.

[9] *Ibid.,* p. 4.

feel deprived irrespective of their level of income. A key question when using this conception is whether important shifts have occurred in the percentage of aggregate income going to the poorest one-fifth. A doubling of the share of aggregate income going to the poorest one-fifth over a 25-year period would represent a major improvement in the relative position of the poorest category of the population. However, no such shift has occurred in recent American history. As indicated in Table 14-1, the ratio of the mean income of the poorest one-fifth to the mean of all families hardly changed between 1947 and 1971.

More substantial improvements are detectable when the absolute conception of poverty is adopted, but a serious consideration of recent trends must proceed cautiously because of the problems of measuring the extent of poverty and of determining whether the trends are secular or merely cyclical. The first problem may be resolved relatively simply, at least with regard to exposition; several estimates of the extent of poverty will be provided with their respective definitions and assumptions.

The question of whether the approximately 15-year overall improvement will survive the current depression cannot be answered. The answer to questions regarding future extent and level of poverty depend mainly on the direction and health of the national and world economy. Only soothsayers and futurologists claim expertise in such matters. Perhaps the answer will be known to the reader by the time of publication. More likely, given the propensity of Americans to think big, indecision and uncertainty will still be rampant since the unemployment rate may still be "only" 8 or 9 percent. By the gargantuan reckoning of many portions of the educated American public, the Great Depression presumably only lasted from 1932 to 1935, the period when the rate of unemployment was between 20 and 25 percent. In 1930, the year after the crash of the stock market, unemployment was 9 percent. In 1931 and in the period from 1936 to 1941, the rate was between 10 and 19 percent. Thus it can be seen that only about four of the 12 depression years were actually Great; the rest were just ordinary. The period as a whole produced "one-third of a nation" in poverty.

The Constraints of Poverty

A more tangible and perhaps understandable way of defining poverty is to describe what it is like to be poor. Such a task is difficult since it is not the same for everyone below the poverty level; children experience the condition differently from their mothers and these mothers, in turn, construct a life that is different from the aged man or woman who is unattached and living in a hotel room. Beyond this simplistic observation there is the notable fact that individuals have idiosyncratic biographies; they bring unique understanding and meaning and coping patterns to their daily lives.[10]

[10] See Robert Coles, *Migrants, Sharecroppers, Mountaineers* (Boston: Little, Brown, 1971); *The South Goes North* (Boston: Little, Brown, 1971).

We cannot, then, convey to the reader what it *feels* like to be poor; there is a rich body of sensitive literature that has attended to that. What we can do, however, is to show the inevitable limitations imposed by poverty and trust that an imaginative and empathic reader will be able to sense how it would feel to be forced to live under such constraints. Thus we turn to a portrait of what is essentially a set of possibilities: to exceed what is possible is to leave poverty; that is to say, the reader can imagine doing better only by cheating on the rules.

As of December, 1974 the poverty threshold for a nonfarm family of four was $5,302[11] per year. The logic of the threshold requires that one-third of this sum be expended for food purchases under the "economy" food plan—which was intended only for *emergency* and *temporary* use (it being 75% of the "low-cost plan" or minimum diet). The allocation of the remaining two-thirds is nonspecific according to the threshold criteria, but some guidelines as to how this fraction *ought* to be spent is available from the very specific budgets of welfare departments.

Thus the state of California—a relatively generous welfare state—in the fall of 1974 allowed a maximum monthly standard of $311 per month for an AFDC family of four.[12] One-third of this is allocated for food, another third for rent and utilities, and the remaining third for clothing, recreation, personal incidentals, transportation, education, and household operations. If the California AFDC budget is distributed *by percentage* across the $5,302 poverty level for December, 1974—as shown in Table 14-2—the reader can gain an approximate

Table 14-2   Poverty Budget for Family of Four

	Percentage allocated	Per year	Per month
Food	33	$1,749	$145.80
Rent	28	1,484	123.71
Utilities	5	265	22.09
Clothing	12	636	53.02
Recreation and education	4	212	17.67
Transportation	2	107	8.83
Household operation	6	318	26.50
Personals and incidentals	10	530	44.18
Total	100	$5,302	$441.83

Source: These percentage distributions are calculated from the most recent revisions of the California State Department of Social Welfare Manual, Regulation 44–115 to 44–265. See also *Poverty Amid Plenty,* President's Commission on Income Maintenance Programs (November 1969), pp. 14, 117.

[11] This threshold differs from the previously cited figure of $5,038, which is an average for all of 1974; it is obtained by simply adjusting that sum by the December, 1974 Consumer Price Index.

[12] This standard brings the AFDC family up to an annual income of $3,732—some $1,600 below the national poverty level. The $3,732 can, however, be supplemented by specific special needs—for example, occasional furniture replacement—although it is doubtful if the sum of such special needs would equal $1,600.

idea of what is concretely possible on such a budget. This distribution of expenditures should not be treated too literally; $8.83 per month for transportation needs for a family of four reduces to 7¢ per person per day. If the budget were to be strictly adhered to, the use of a public bus would be a rather important event—not to be undertaken too lightly or too frequently.

So, too, with rent. The average rental for working-class families in metropolitan areas was $1,879 per year—some $400 more than what is "permitted" in the budget.[13] Some families below the poverty level undoubtedly pay less than the budgeted amount for rent and, hence, have the luxury of spending the surplus for other matters; but many more families have rentals in excess of the budgeted amount and must then reduce other areas of expenditure.

The food budget of $145.80 per month for a four-person family comes to 40¢ per person per meal. By conscious intent and by practical necessity the budget does not allow for the cost of any meals eaten away from home (although it does not preclude the preparation of a carried bag lunch), but it does presume a very skillful marketing and kitchen management talent. Shopping must be astute and calculating; food preparation allows for waste of less than 5 percent.[14] The organization of the budget insists that menus be planned at least a week in advance.

> The economy food plan was designed as a nutritionally adequate diet for use when the cost of food must be lower than the average food expenditures of low income families. It is essentially for emergency use. It deviates further from average food habits than the other plans and relies heavily on dry beans and peas, potatoes, and grain products—foods that are inexpensive sources of many nutrients.[15]

And it is cut by 25 percent.

The economy food plan allows for *only* the diet, based on 1964 prices, shown in Table 14-3. Since then, such prices have increased by 75 percent whereas the overall Consumer Price Index (CPI) has gone up only 59 percent —which means that the food part of a poverty budget has not increased commensurately with the total budget. Nonetheless, it is apparent that the food expenditures of people below the poverty level must be judicious and can only result in a rather monotonous diet. And, by definition, in the long run it must be inadequate.

In fact, the diet of any given individual below the poverty line varies considerably. If AFDC families are any guide, the data show that before check day, food supplies are very low, if not nonexistent. At any time few mothers

---

[13] Obtained by adjusting the 1971 low-level housing expenditure by the average increase in the CPI; U.S. Department of Labor, *Handbook of Labor Statistics, 1973,* Table 136.

[14] Alan Haber, "Poverty Budgets: How Much Is Enough." *Poverty and Human Resources Abstracts* (1966), Table 1.

[15] U.S. Department of Agriculture, *Family Food Plans and Food Costs,* Report No. 20 (November 1962), p. 25.

Table 14-3 Economy Food Plan

	Individual daily quantities
Milk products	½ qt.
Meat, poultry, fish	¼ lb.
Eggs	less than 1
Dry beans and peas	1.1 oz.
Grains	½ lb.
Fruits	¼ lb.
Vegetables	2 oz.
Potatoes	½ lb.
Other vegetables and fruits	½ lb.
Fats and oils	1.4 oz.
Sugars and sweets	1.7 oz.

Source: Adapted from Alan Haber, "Poverty Budgets: How Much Is Enough," *Poverty and Human Resources Abstracts* (1966), Table 1.

have as much as half a gallon of milk on hand. And there is a universal complaint—"no fruit" and "no vegetables either."[16]

A further recitation of how poor families manage to eat would be somewhat redundant and essentially *misleading*. The fact is that they do eat—but not adequately; they eat by making incursions into other budgetary allotments and, when that is not possible, by the time-honored devices of borrowing, scrounging, foregoing rent payments—postponing, cutting here and there, and browbeating welfare functionaries for "special allotments."

The Reality of Poverty

Here is the heart of the matter. To be poor in America does not mean to literally starve. What it means, rather is to live in an unending state of fiscal desperation and degradation:

> . . . skipping a rent payment or a utility bill—sometimes being evicted saves a month's rent; "borrowing" food from friends and relatives; and reliance on credit. "We don't pay the full price for food" one witness said, explaining, "we get credit on food and pay once a month. But we don't pay all of it, we just pay a portion of it." Who pays the rest? "He [the grocer] just carries it over to the next month." . . . "We sold our home and sold everything we had. Had to."[17]

When AFDC recipients were asked during the course of Lebeaux's inquiry

---

[16] For one of the few inquiries that attempts to ascertain what it is really like to live on welfare, see Charles Lebeaux, "Life on ADC: Budgets of Despair," in Louis Ferman et al., *Poverty in America* (Ann Arbor: University of Michigan Press, 1965). See also G. Bonem and P. Rino, "By Bread Alone: Life on AFDC," *Social Work*, 13 (October 1968).

[17] *Poverty Amid Plenty*, Report of the President's Commission on Income Maintenance Programs (1969), p. 16.

what they did about running out of money, two-thirds said they borrowed and one-third said they just "stayed run out."[18] And that means letting the bills go, cashing in returnable bottles, pawning the toaster (although 55% of AFDC families do *not* own a toaster[19]), or borrowing food.

To be poor means making impossible decisions as to which item of necessity is less necessary, whether to splurge on a movie (and it is a splurge when one $2 movie ticket represents 11 percent of the total monthly family recreational budget); it means a chronic hassle with the day-to-day exigencies of life; it

[18] Lebeaux, *op. cit.*, p. 409.
[19] Bonem and Rino, *op. cit.*, Table 1.

means never being able to discard creditors, bureaucrats, well-meaning and not so well-meaning functionaries, landlords, police, grocers—it is a status not to be desired.

RECENT TRENDS IN ABSOLUTE POVERTY

The inherent difficulty with a conception of absolute poverty lies in the very assumption that poverty can be conceived of in a fixed, certain, or absolute way. Poverty means living at or about subsistence. The trouble is that even so simple a statement contains a substantial zone of ambiguity. Drastically or durably below subsistence is death. But intermittently over long periods, or entirely for a short period, the zone below subsistence includes morbidity, malnutrition, apathy, and even what is sometimes called laziness by laymen and inefficiency by employers. Thus a latitude exists in any "absolute" conception of poverty. Consequently, several competing measures have appeared.

The widely used poverty standard in this country was developed by Molly Orshansky in 1965, based on the U.S. Department of Agriculture "economy" food plan for "temporary or emergency use when funds are low." The economy plan was based on Department of Agriculture "Recommended Dietary Allowances," which were then reduced by 25 percent to yield the "emergency" base, a figure more consonant with the actual welfare allotments to needy families though still higher than levels provided by most states.

The nutritional estimates form the basis of the measure. After adjusting food budget for family size and for urban or rural locations, a coefficient is used (sometimes called the Engels factor) to yield a full budget on the reasonable assumption that shelter, transportation, and other costs are necessities. The size of this coefficient is of obvious importance in calculating the poverty line: the higher the Engels factor, the higher the poverty line.[20] The factor varies according to the age of the household head, the number of persons in the household, and the place of residence. The basic family of four is endowed an Engels factor of three, which means that a full monthly budget is assumed to require three times the cost of food. The factors utilized are based on survey data on consumer expenditures. Through samples of low-income families, such surveys attempt to find the proportion of income typically devoted to consumables other than food, and the variations in this proportion according to family size, location, and other factors.

Moreover, a final adjustment has been made since 1969. The mechanical multiplication of the food budget is corrected for changes in an overall Consumer Price Index instead of being based solely on changes in the cost of food.

Table 14-4 gives the dollar threshold, the number of people below the threshold, and the percentage of the total population they represent for the

---

[20] See Martin Rein, "Problems in the Definition and Measurement of Poverty," in Townsend, *op. cit.*, pp. 46–64.

Table 14-4   Poverty Thresholds, Number of People Below the Threshold, and Percentage of Total Population (1959–1974)

	Threshold in dollars	Number of persons (in thousands)	Percentage of population
1959	2,973	39,490	22.4
1960	3,022	39,851	22.2
1961	3,054	39,628	21.9
1962	3,089	38,625	21.0
1963	3,128	36,436	19.5
1964	3,169	36,055	19.0
1965	3,223	33,185	17.3
1966	3,317	30,424	15.7
1967	3,410	27,769	14.2
1968	3,553	25,389	12.8
1969	3,743	24,147	12.1
1970	3,968	25,420	12.6
1971	4,137	25,559	12.5
1972	4,275	24,460	11.9
1973	4,540	22,973	11.1
1974	5,038	24,260	11.6

Source: U.S. Bureau of the Census, "Characteristics of the Low-Income Population," Series P-60, No. 98; *Social Indicators, 1973;* and "Money Income and Poverty Status of Families and Persons in the U.S., 1974," Series P-60, No. 99 (Washington, D.C.: Government Printing Office).

years 1959 through 1974. Between 1959 and 1974 the percentage of all persons below the poverty line decreased from 22.4 to 11.6; in essence the proportion of poor people was nearly halved in the course of 15 years. By far, the largest part of this decline occurred in the six years between 1962 and 1968; since 1968 the rate of "poverty reduction" has leveled off and, in fact, the absolute number of poor was slightly higher in 1974 than it was in 1969. Given the economic difficulty that has affected the American economy in 1975, both the number of poor people and the rate may have increased substantially.

The distribution of poverty is not uniform across all segments of the population. Thus, persons in families without a male head of household and unrelated individuals are especially vulnerable to being below the threshold even though the "intact" male-headed family is still the largest single family form (in 1973, some 44% of all poor families were of this sort).[21]

There is the expected maldistribution of poverty in regard to race: about 8.4 percent of the white population and 31.4 percent of the black population were below the poverty level in 1973; in terms of the total population of poor, however, the proportions are 66 percent white, 32 percent black, and 2 percent other.

In about one-half of low-income families the family head worked at some time during 1973, and of this group 35 percent worked year-round full time.

[21] All data for 1973 are from the U.S. Bureau of the Census, "Characteristics of the Low Income Population," Series P-60, No. 98. These data were gathered in March, 1974 and thus reflect annual statistics that are, as of this writing, slightly more than a year old.

Of the low-income family heads who did not work at all during 1973, three-fifths were women with family responsibilities or retired persons.

In male-headed families, 62 percent of the heads were formally in the labor force, with an unemployment rate of 9.6 percent; some 53 percent of the remainder were ill or disabled. In female-headed households, 39 percent of the heads had worked during the year; of the 60 percent remaining, 97 percent were either keeping house—that is, caring for their children—or were ill or disabled.

Thus poor families are primarily working families; unattached individuals below the poverty line are predominantly aged people over 65 years who by and large were once labor-force participants. The kinds of occupations held by poor workers are those one would expect—they work in marginal, erratic, and low-paying jobs.

The Orshansky threshold has long been seen by some analysts as rather miserly; a family of four subsisting on an *emergency* food intake for any length of time is not only poor, it is flirting with nonsubsistence. Thus an arbitrary increase by 25 percent of the official standard is seen as a more reasonable threshold, but by no means a generous one.

When the poverty level is increased by 25 percent, the numbers of poor obviously increase. Table 14-5 gives the trends from 1959 through 1974 of this 125 percent poverty level. In 1973 the increment was by 10,000,000 people—fully one-half more: 69 percent of these families are white, and 31 percent nonwhite—a slightly higher white to nonwhite ratio than is found at the lower poverty line.

Table 14-5   Poverty Thresholds (125% Level), Number of People Below the Threshold, and Percentage of Total Population (1959–1974)

	Threshold in dollars	Number of persons (in thousands)	Percentage of population
1959	3,716	54,942	31.1
1960	3,777	54,560	30.4
1961	3,817	54,280	30.0
1962	3,861	53,119	28.2
1963	3,910	50,778	27.1
1964	3,961	49,819	26.3
1965	4,028	46,163	24.1
1966	4,146	40,617	21.0
1967	4,262	39,206	20.0
1968	4,441	35,905	18.2
1969	4,678	34,665	17.4
1970	4,960	35,624	17.6
1971	5,171	36,501	17.8
1972	5,343	34,653	16.8
1973	5,675	32,828	15.8
1974	6,297	34,615	16.5

Source: See Table 14-4.

As Table 14-6 shows, the increment in numbers of poor people at the 125 percent level comes mainly from "intact" male-headed families. The more obviously working-class part of the population makes up a larger part of the "upper" strata of poor.

Table 14-6   Composition of the Poor, at the Two Poverty Levels, by Household Status (1973)

	100% level	125% level	Percentage increase
Male headed families	10,121,000	16,461,000	62.5
Female headed families	8,178,000	10,048,000	22.9
Unrelated individuals	4,674,000	6,318,000	35.2
Total	22,973,000	32,827,000	42.9

Source: U.S. Bureau of the Census, "Characteristics of the Low-Income Population," Series P-60, No. 98 (Washington, D.C.: Government Printing Office, 1975).

As we move further up in the chemist's cylinder of income, more and more people are embraced—but there must be a limit beyond which no reasonable student would be willing to go in defining a level of poverty. That limit is most likely the Department of Labor's "low-level" budget—the most stringent of three budgets devised by the department (the higher two are called, informatively, "intermediate" and "high"). The estimates derive from two kinds of data: nutritional and health standards (but far more reasonable ones than those used by the SSA) and analytic studies of consumer expenditures.

In the first quarter of 1975, the low standard-of-living budget was $9,200 per year for an urban family of four (the Orshansky threshold was approximately $5,302) and although the data are not available to us, this level would encompass some 60,000,000 people, or approximately 30 percent of American families with a household head over 25 years.[22]

THE WELFARE POOR

The bottommost level of the poor consists of those who are welfare recipients. By far, most of these are people below the official or Orshansky poverty level—in December, 1974 when that index was $5,302 per year for a nonfarm family of four no state allowed more for a comparable AFDC family. (Wisconsin, the most generous of the states, allowed a maximum grant of $4,836 per year.) In earlier years, however, before the great acceleration of the CPI, some states allowed for some families with special needs a grant that did exceed the official poverty level. Receiving public assistance thus practically assures being poor—but it does not exhaust the poor population.

[22] The estimate is minimal; it is simply the number and percentage who fell below the 1971 Department of Labor level in 1971—and thus does not take into account the effects of the depression.

Table 14-7   Number of Recipients and Average Payments per Recipient
in the Various Categorical Assistance Programs (Fall, 1974)

	Aged[b]	SSI Blind[b]	Disabled[b]	State Program AFDCU[c]	GA[c]
Number of recipients	2,270,394	74,918	1,617,980	10,755,000	708,000
Average payment per recipient (per month)	$94.00[a]	$142.22[a]	$144.60[a]	$58.90	$90.52

Source: Supplemental Security Income data: U.S. Department of Health, Education and Welfare, *Monthly Benefit Statistics* (March 1975), Table 3; AFDCU and General Assistance data: U.S. Department of Health, Education and Welfare, *Public Assistance Statistics* (September 1974).
[a] Includes state supplementation.
[b] Data for November, 1974.
[c] Data for September, 1974.

The numbers of persons receiving assistance under the various categorical programs is given in Table 14-7. Thus some 15,425,000 people were in the fall of 1974 recipients of what used to be called "welfare"—two-thirds of whom were AFDC families. This total represents not more than 67 percent of the officially defined poor—in 1973 an additional 7,000,000 people whose annual income fell below the poverty standard were not welfare recipients.

Unlike the trends found for other "indicators" of poverty, the AFDC rolls have shown a consistent rise over the years—with a leveling off occurring in late 1971.[23] The rise, indeed, had been dramatic (Table 14-8).

There are various explanations for the marked increase in AFDC recipients during the decade of the 1960s and the subsequent leveling off of the increment. The most popular argument holds that two factors were operative during the decade: a general relaxation of eligibility requirements and an expansion of

Table 14-8   AFDC Recipients (1962–1974)

Year	Number of recipients
1962	3,658,000
1964	4,126,000
1966	4,472,000
1968	5,609,000
1970	8,292,000
1972	10,500,000
1974 (December)	11,004,283
1975 (March)	11,346,994

Source: U.S. Department of Health, Education and Welfare, *Trend Report, 1971* (for 1962–1970 data), and *Public Assistance Statistics* (for 1972 through 1975).

[23] The current recession may have prompted a new rise in AFDCU caseloads. In California there was an 11.2 percent increase in December, 1974 over November and a 9.1 percent increase in January, 1975 over December. Further, the number of people receiving food stamps increased in January, 1975 by 59,690, or 4 percent.

benefits that coincided with attitudinal changes on the part of potential recipients that made the application for assistance less opprobrious. Thus a large number of previously eligible families began to enter the program. By the early 1970s, this pool of eligible people was primarily exhausted—hence, the leveling off.

The AFDC program is intended to provide assistance to dependent children; the image, on the program's passage in 1936, was of the orphaned child being attentively raised by a struggling and widowed mother. Assistance to female-headed households still predominates: in 1973 three-fourths of all AFDC households were headed by women. The "reason" for this, however, departs from the initial image—divorce, separation, and illegitimacy are the ordinary precipitants of dependency. Thus of the nearly 3 million AFDC families in 1973, 18 percent had children whose parents were divorced, 28 percent separated, and 43 percent were illegitimate.[24] Ethnically, minority groups are overrepresented in the AFDC population but whites still predominate as the largest single racial entity among the poor, constituting in 1973 47 percent of the recipient families with blacks constituting 46 percent.

Of the 379,048 families with the natural or adoptive father in the home, 39.3 percent of these fathers were in the labor force—although three-quarters of them were unemployed. Of those not in the labor force, 88 percent were incapacitated for employment. Thus the rate of disengagement of male-headed AFDC families from the labor force is extremely small—only 15 percent of the potential labor force pool of fathers.[25]

The mothers in female-headed families are, likewise, more connected with the labor market than commonly supposed; 27.6 percent were formally in the labor force, 8.1 percent were incapacitated, and 46.9 percent were needed as full-time homemakers.

Finally, a brief note on the food stamp and food distribution programs of the Department of Agriculture. These programs are independent of categorical welfare assistance; although most welfare recipients are eligible for food stamp assistance, many others are also eligible. The food stamp program has grown significantly since its inception in the 1960s: 633,000 recipients in 1965 to 12,227,000 in 1973, with an additional 2,441,000 receiving aid through the federal commodities program.[26] In January, 1975 the department estimated that 18.1 million people were getting food aid—a rise of 20 percent in one year and a tangible indicator of the serious economic crisis that existed in the first quarter of 1975.

The welfare rolls become the most extreme measure of economic distress

---

[24] There is some overlap among the categories since 25 percent of the families had more than one father of the children in the household. See U.S. Department of Health, Education and Welfare, Social and Rehabilitation Service, *Findings of the 1973 AFDC Study*, Part I (June 1974).

[25] *Ibid.* See Tables 33 and 44 for a more detailed breakdown of the employment status of AFDC heads.

[26] *Statistical Abstract of the United States, 1974*, Table 150.

and the most stringent indicator of the extent of poverty within the country. Recession—and its most telling human consequence, unemployment—does not appear in welfare departments until other protective devices are exhausted. The most important such device is unemployment compensation; when that runs out, when savings are exhausted, and other assets are depleted, the dole becomes the measure of last resort. Further, we have seen that—recession aside —welfare recipients are among the lowest of the poor. In spite of some loosening of eligibility (a liberalization much undone during the Nixon years and the rather frantic outcry against welfare chiselers), the requirements for aid are still quite stringent and the level of aid is well below the official poverty line.[27] Welfare poverty is the deepest poverty.

In sum, poverty in the United States is a substantial phenomenon by even the most stringent standard. By the most generous standard of the Department of Labor nearly one-third of the population lives in a rather precarious state— many have enough to eat and are housed, clothed, and recreated at a "low level"—but any negative change in the economic conditions of the country is a serious threat to their financial adjustment. The data in Table 14-9 summarize

Table 14-9 Levels of Poverty

	Number of people	Percentage
The welfare "load" level[b]	15,425,000	7.3
The SSA poverty level (100%)[a]	25,559,000	12.5
The SSA poverty level (125%)[a]	36,501,000	17.8
The DOL "low level"[a]	60,000,000	30.0

[a] Data are for 1971 (U.S. Bureau of the Census, *Current Population Statistics*, Series P-60, No. 98; and U.S. Department of Labor, *Handbook of Labor Statistics, 1973*).
[b] Data are for 1974 (see Table 14-7).

the more obvious strata of the poor. One-third of the people hang by a thread; they are, for the most part, working people who maintain a delicate equilibrium. From the outside it may appear to be the capitalist dream come true—a comfortable and well-stocked proletariat; from the inside it is a precarious hold on economic well-being.

The large increase in AFDC families that occurred during the 1960s was accompanied, as could be expected, by a resurgence in anti-welfare attitudes among the general public. Such antipathy was always directed against the poor —especially against those who had the temerity to ask for assistance—hence the chronic concern with welfare chiselers and the allegedly demoralizing consequences of the welfare state.

Welfare chiseling is often imputed to the poor. This understandable—one might even say reasonable—response to being on the dole received considerable

[27] In September, 1974 Massachusetts had the highest average family grant of $362.14 and Puerto Rico the lowest with $46.15 per month.

attention as a result of the "Newburgh affair"[28] and subsequently achieved some prominence in the ill-fated Goldwater campaign of 1964. A recrudescence of this always dormant attitude could only be exacerbated by the current economic crisis and, indeed, it has.

Welfare chiseling may be defined as the receipt of assistance despite ineligibility or the receipt of more assistance than is legitimately warranted, given prevailing rules and rates. Needless to say, such illicit receipt should be *intentional* if it is to be regarded as chiseling. The beneficiaries of modest windfalls in an inefficient welfare system can hardly be regarded as chiselers unless they knowingly contrived toward that end.

There is little adequate knowledge of the number or proportion of chiselers among those who are assisted—no more, say, than exists for wealthy tax chiselers. What little research does exist has been limited to recipients of AFDC, and it is handicapped by the obvious fact that if welfare investigators can be defrauded so can researchers.[29]

POVERTY, THE LIFE CYCLE, AND SUBEMPLOYMENT

In 1970 there were approximately 76,000,000 young people in the United States under the age of 20 years. At least 10 percent of these children were on the welfare rolls as recipients of AFDC. Of black children, at least 36 percent were welfare recipients. Welfare poverty, as we have said, is the deepest poverty: by the standards of the Orshansky indicator the proportion of children rises to 14 percent;[30] at the 125 percent level it increases to 17.5 percent; and by the Department of Labor "low standard of living" level, it would rise to perhaps one-third, or some 25,000,000 children.[31]

We must remind the reader that these data refer to the poor at a given moment in time; they do not begin to reflect the number of children who *at any point in their childhood may have been poor*. Thus between 20 and 25 percent of AFDC families have been receiving aid for less than six months; 41 percent

[28] For a good review of the Newburgh affair, see Edgar May, *The Wasted Americans* (New York: Harper & Row, 1964), Ch. 2.

[29] Studies dealing with this and related questions have included Greenleigh Associates, *Facts, Fallacies, and Future,* A Study of the Aid to Dependent Children Program of Cook County, Illinois (New York: 1960); a national study requested by the United States Senate Appropriations Committee, *Eligibility of Families Receiving Aid to Families with Dependent Children* (Department of Health, Education and Welfare, July, 1963); and Scott Briar, "Welfare from Below," *California Law Review,* Vol. 54, No. 2 (May, 1966), pp. 370–385.

[30] In 1974, the number of related children under the age of 18 years who were in families below the poverty level increased to 10.2 million, or 15.5 percent. U.S. Department of Commerce, "Money Income and Poverty Status of Families and Persons in the U.S.: 1974." Series P-60, No. 99.

[31] These estimates are approximate and derived from taking the published data as to the number of children at the various levels and dividing by the base of 76,000,000. In some cases the age categories were not cut at 20 years; our inclination was to err on the side of *underestimation*.

for less than 18 months.[32] For children, welfare assistance is time limited as we might have expected from the knowledge that their parents are in and out of the labor force. In short, there is *turnover* within the ranks of child poverty and although welfare children are prone to "recidivism"—about one-third of current recipients have had a prior experience on the dole—most are newcomers to the depths of poverty. The point is that although "only" 10 percent of children will be on welfare at any given moment, a much larger percentage will have had this dubious honor at some point in their childhood.

By definition, childhood is a peculiarly vulnerable life stage for the poverty prone—children are formally excluded from the labor force. So, too, are the aged—those who, by and large, have served some 45 years in the work force. Of the 20,000,000 men and women aged 65 or over in 1970, approximately 10 percent were on the active roles of welfare (Old Age Assistance) and an additional 80 percent were receiving OASI benefits.[33] By the Orshansky standard, 25 percent of aged people were poor; most of the remainder were not far from the threshold. The median family income of family heads aged 65 and over was $5,270 per year—the lowest income-age category in the population.[34] And over the years their plight has worsened. Thus the ratio of the median income of those 65 and over to the median income of all ages decreased from 0.60 in 1947 to 0.51 in 1970.[35] The plight of the aged is too well known to belabor in this essay—it is an end to lives of labor bitter in its commentary. The poverty of the aged is a condition that awaits many if not most of us; we may have escaped the poverty of childhood, but the odds are rather worse when we approach old age.

Even the ripe years of active labor-force participation, however, yield little certainty or decent income, once we distinguish between incidence and prevalence. In May, 1975 the unemployment rate was 9.2 percent; in April it had been 8.9 percent. During May, some of the 8.9 percent were re-employed and, hence, for the two months of April and May the total percentage of unemployment must have been larger than 9.2. If a span of three or six or 12 months were the base, the rate would be larger still.

But the prevalence of unemployment is not the only reason to see poverty as a more ordinary experience than is usually indicated in official measures or commonly imagined in the public mind. The official unemployment rate is a very precise and conceptually clear measure: the proportion of those people in the labor force who are not working and who are actively looking for work. The problem, long recognized, is that it does not distinguish among different segments of the employed: the part-time labor force and the underpaid labor force and those out of the labor force who "should" be in—the discouraged.

---

[32] U.S. Department of Health, Education and Welfare, *op. cit.*

[33] U.S. Department of Health, Education and Welfare, *Trend Report, 1971.*

[34] U.S. Bureau of the Census, Current Population Survey, Series P-60, No. 80 (Washington, D.C.: Government Printing Office).

[35] U.S. Department of Commerce, *Social Indicators, 1973.*

The employed are all those who work for *any* amount of time and for *any* remuneration; the unemployed are all those who actively seek work.

A subemployment conception attempts to develop a measure of the extent, value, and opportunity for employment. Such a measure has been devised by, first, counting the subemployed; second, excluding all those subemployed in households with a more than "adequate" income (i.e., an income above the poverty level); and, finally, dividing this total by the number of labor-force participants and discouraged workers to yield a single index. The subemployed consist of the following:

1. unemployed individuals who are willing, able and currently available for work, and who have taken definite steps in the last month to find a job;
2. discouraged workers who want jobs but are not looking because they think no work is available, lack the necessary experience or schooling, are too young or too old, or have other personal handicaps making them unattractive to employers;
3. currently employed family heads and unrelated individuals whose earnings in the previous 12 months were inadequate to lift their households above the poverty threshold;
4. other currently employed household heads earning less than a poverty income during the preceding year because of intermittent employment, less than full-time work and/or low wages;
5. workers employed part-time during the survey week not included in the previous category, who want full-time jobs but cannot find them, have been laid off during the survey week, or have some other economic impediment requiring part-time employment.[36]

Excluded from the subemployed are all people, working or not, who are over 65 years of age and all youths 16 to 21 whose major activity is going to school. Such an index, called the Employment and Earnings Inadequacy Index (EEI), gives the proportion of people "working, seeking work, or discouraged from seeking work who are unable to provide a minimum income and are also not fortunate enough to have other working family members or other sources of income which ameliorate the consequences of their own labor market problems."[37]

The EEI, still in the process of being refined, is not yet an official governmental index, but it has been computed by Levitan and Taggart for the years 1968 through 1972. During those years the rate rose from 10.4 percent in 1968 to 11.5 percent in 1972. (The formal unemployment rate rose from 3.8 to 6.1 percent and whereas there is a relationship between oscillations in unemployment and oscillations in the EEI, the latter, as one might expect, is a much more stable index.) The 11.5 percent reported for 1972 is the index for *all* segments of the potential labor force and a more revealing breakdown is shown in Table 14-10.

[36] Sar A. Levitan and Robert Taggart III, *Employment and Earnings Inadequacy: A New Social Indicator* (Baltimore: Johns Hopkins Press, 1974), p. 34.
[37] *Ibid.*, p. 35.

Table 14-10 Employment and Earnings Inadequacy Index (1972)

All	11.5
Black Males	24.7
Black Females	25.8
White Males	9.9
White Females	10.0

Source: Compiled from Sar A. Levitan and Robert Taggart III, *Employment and Earnings Inadequacy* (Baltimore: Johns Hopkins Press, 1974), Table 13.

It should be remembered that the index excludes young people 16 to 21 years who are ostensibly students and people over 65 years—and the table above does not show a geographic breakdown of the rate.[38] Nonetheless, a 25 percent EEI for blacks and 10 percent for whites is a rather telling commentary of the extent of marginal labor-force status in this country. In 1975, the EEI must reach ominous proportions.

The rewards of employment must be reckoned as well as the fact of employment; part-time workers or erratically employed workers who may want full-time work are not as employed as the more stable and completely employed—and, if a series of five observations can constitute a trend (1968–1972), there appeared to be a slight growth in the proportion of the subemployed.

SUBEMPLOYMENT AND DISREPUTE

Subemployment is the key to an understanding of contemporary industrial and public poverty. It enlightens us with regard to the basic causes of poverty by drawing attention to economic facts related to the underpayment or under-utilization of human capacity and talent. Subjected to economies, the poor are first of all the objects of poverty being ground and degraded by it. Their subjectivity develops nonetheless but takes form within that reality. Several "neo-marxian" formulations have been emphasized in recent years locating unemployment and thus poverty in specific sectors of the economy. David Gordon stresses a dual labor market in which the second or bottom tier features irregular and badly paid work of relatively low skill level. The same general point is made by James O'Connor in reference to work and payment in the "competitive sector" of the economy in contrast to the more monopolistic sector and/or the public sector.[39]

Poverty thus is caused by economy and not by the poor. Subemployment is also enlightening for a second reason: the concept mediates and links the objective facts of underpayment and underutilization with the subjective realm.

---

[38] Such a breakdown would undoubtedly yield startling rates as the "subemployment" study of 1967 showed—rates approaching 50 percent in some metropolitan neighborhoods.

[39] See Gordon, *op. cit.*; and James O'Connor, *The Fiscal Crisis of the State* (New York: St. Martin's Press, 1973).

The subemployment of people—whether in the form of coerced leisure, of sweated labor, or of involuntary receipt of socially degraded wages—yields a contrast with the lot of the typical member of the working class. The employment of the working class has been connected with citizenship and participation, exemplified in individual families through social mobility and collectively through the social movement of the trades-union or the class party. For that reason, though in variable measure, the subjective side of the working class is captured in a concept that above all stresses *activity*. The working class is proletariat. Poverty subjects people to the condition of subemployment and thus facilitates a tendency somewhat different from the reconstructive project inherent in the idea—and reality—of proletariat. Subemployment breeds apathy, provides an isolated context that promotes inactivity, and in a variety of ways seems connected with *pathology*. A basic idea that summarizes this latter tendency is disrepute. Disrepute is the pathology of poverty. Above all it is a *social* pathology, which is to say that disrepute is the imputation or stigma that goes along with being subemployed. The subjective side of poverty, disrepute is fostered in the sentiments of the employed and the surveillance of the subemployed, so much so that over the centuries a case is gradually constructed that the poor are in fact and not just in reputation disreputable. Their humanity systematically reduced, the poor sometimes respond with a greater interest perhaps in the enticements of such phenomena as delinquency, alcoholism, illegitimacy, or mental illness. It is this plausible though unprovable assertion that suggests the link between poverty and "pathology."

In stressing the subjective side of poverty for the remainder of the essay, we wish to make clear that the category of disrepute is not a sociological invention of the authors. It is the social category of the good citizen foisted on those suffering the misfortune of subemployment. Only illness and aging have served effectively to deflect the negative social judgment connecting poverty with disrepute. The so-called deserving poor have had constantly to prove and reprove their daily worth.

An element of indecision and ambiguity must remain in the serious consideration of whether poverty, or subemployment, necessarily yields a subjective category of disrepute. This is because the category itself, and the basic meaning conveyed, is deeply interactional: disreputable is how the able-bodied poor ordinarily appear to the good citizens engaged in their strained project of maintaining piety. The shift in terminology from *disrepute*—which clearly lies in the eyes of the beholder of the interaction between the poor and the well-to-do—to *disreputable* reflects the key shift in the stigmatic process by which the complicated interaction is reified and invested in the subordinate party, or status. To be found disreputable is the unanswerable charge, which like that of being "uneducable" or "ungovernable" yields demoralization and helps to fulfill the prophecy through the obvious communication that the mind of the accuser is clearly made up and the mind of the accused accordingly boggled. "I cannot teach you," a statement regarding the reality of relations that would receive

the overwhelming agreement of most poor (and many well-to-do) children having had the misfortune of direct observation of education, undergoes a magical transformation: "You are uneducable." As in teaching, so in morality. Teachers make a claim with surface legitimacy regarding expertise over education. The clergy and afterwards social work and currently the welfare official claim knowledge over morality and reputation. In summary, being disreputable is to be referred to one of several extant categories in which language and a reflective practice prejudge the entire matter at issue.

Of all conceptions, pauperism comes closest to what is conveyed by the term *disreputable poverty*. Though there are differences,[40] many of the features of disreputable poverty are implicit in the conception of pauperism. It conveys the same ideas of disaffiliation and immobilization that, taken together, indicate the outcasting from modern society suggested by Thomas and Znaniecki. Pauperism, like vice, "declasses a man definitely, puts him outside both the old and new hierarchy. Beggars, tramps, criminals, prostitutes, have no place in the class hierarchy."[41]

To understand disreputable poverty, and to appreciate its complexity, one must distinguish among the various components of its milieu. Disreputable poverty and the tradition it sustains are a compote, blending together the distinctive contributions of each ingredient. Together these ingredients constitute the *situation* of disreputable poverty.

Dregs

The core of disreputable poor consists of *dregs*—persons spawned in poverty and belonging to families who have been left behind by otherwise mobile ethnic populations. In these families there is at least the beginning of some tradition of disreputable poverty. In America, the primary examples include immobile descendants of Italian and Polish immigrants and of the remnants of even earlier arrivals—Germans, Irish, and Yankees and blacks who have already become habituated to the regions in which disreputable poverty flourishes.

Rural immigrants to urban areas in the United States and other nations usually entered the system at the very bottom, but in the course of a few generations—depending on the availability of new ethnic or regional replacements and numerous other factors—their descendants achieved conventional, reputable positions in society. But some proportion of each cohort, the majority of which advances to the reputable working class or the lower rungs of the middle class, remains behind. Each experience of ethnic mobility leaves a sediment that appears to be trapped in slum life, whether because some of those who come insist on maintaining traditional peasant values or as a result of family disorganization, limited opportunities for steady employment, or just plain misfortune. These are the dregs who settle into the milieu of disreputable poverty and perpetuate its distinctive characteristics.

Dregs are the key components of the milieu of disreputable poverty also because they link new groups entering the lowest level of society and the old ones leaving it. In the conflict between new and old ethnic arrivals, the unseemly traditions of disreputable poverty are transmitted from one to the other. These traditions are manifested in a style of life distinctive to disreputable poverty and apparently similar in different parts of the world.

[40] For instance, a pauper, strictly speaking, depends on public or private charity for sustenance, while in conception, the disreputable poor are sometimes recipients of welfare. They also work casually or irregularly and occasionally engage in petty crime and other forms of hustling.

[41] William I. Thomas and Florian Znaniecki, *The Polish Peasant in America* (New York: Dover, reissued 1958), p. 136.

What are the main features of this style?[42] Income in this stratum is obviously low, but "more important even than the size of income is its regularity."[43] Unemployment and underemployment are common. When work can be found it is unskilled or at best semiskilled. Jobs are available for relatively short periods; hiring is frequently on a day-to-day basis. Child labor lingers on,[44] and in many families the wage earner, if there is one, is frequently ill and only intermittently employed. Savings, even for a very short time, is virtually unknown, and, as a result, small quantities of food may be bought many times a day as the need arises. Also evident is "the pawning of personal possessions, borrowing from local money lenders at usurious rates, and the use of second-hand clothing and furniture."[45]

The disreputable poor "react to their economic situation and to their degradation in the eyes of respectable people by becoming fatalistic; they feel that they are down and out, and that there is no point in trying to improve. . . ."[46] Their life is provincial and locally oriented. "Its members are only partly integrated into national institutions and are a marginal people even when they live in the heart of a great city."[47] Typically, they neither belong to trade unions nor support any political party.[48] They are immobilized in that they do not participate in the two responses to discontent characteristic of Western working classes—collective mobilization culminating in trade unions, ethnic federations, or political action, and familial mobilization culminating in individual mobility.

Thus the style of disreputable poverty apparently transcends national boundaries, though it is perhaps most noticeable in nations with strong puritan traditions. To point to such similarities some writers have referred to the phenomenon as a "culture of poverty," Oscar Lewis being the foremost.[49]

---

[42] It should be reiterated that these characteristics pertain mostly to the disreputable poor and considerably less to the welfare poor or the lower class, two broader categories that include the disreputable poor as a small segment. If one appreciates these distinctions, the skeptical and critical discussion of the thesis positing a close relationship between poverty and pathology by Barbara Wooten will not seem inconsistent with the view taken here. See the excellent summary of studies bearing on the presumed general relationship between poverty and pathology in Barbara Wooten, *Social Science and Social Pathology* (New York: Macmillan, 1959), Ch. 2, "Social Pathology and Social Hierarchy." For a more recent and more limited consideration, guided by the same skeptical spirit, see Henry Miller, "Characteristics of AFDC Families," *Social Service Review* (December, 1965), pp. 399–409.

[43] Tom Stephens (ed.), *Problem Families* (London: Victor Gollancz, 1946), p. 3. The coincidence between the nature of work and style of life was succinctly and classically summarized by Charles Booth in 1896. He said: "The character of the men matched well with the character of the work and that of its remuneration. All alike were low and irregular."

[44] Oscar Lewis, *The Children of Sanchez* (New York: Random House, 1961), p. xxvi.

[45] *Ibid.*

[46] Joseph A. Kahl, *The American Class Structure* (New York: Rinehart, 1953), p. 211.

[47] Lewis, *op. cit.*, p. xxvi.

[48] Genevieve Knupfer, "Portrait of the Underdog," *Public Opinion Quarterly* (Spring, 1947), pp. 103–114.

[49] For a critique of this viewpoint, see Charles Valentine, *Culture and Poverty: Critique and Counter-Proposals* (Chicago: University of Chicago Press, 1968). For a response to Valentine by several authors allegedly associated with the idea of a culture of poverty, see *Current Anthropology*, Vol. 10, No. 3 (April–June, 1969).

Newcomers

Recent arrivals are the second component of the disreputable poor. Not all *newcomers* gravitate to the slums or ghettos—mostly, those who come are without marketable skills or financial resources. Irish newcomers escaping to America, even before the great famine, settled in neighborhoods already infamous and disreputable.

Numerically, newcomers are probably the largest component of the disreputable poor, but it is important to recall that except for a small proportion their collective destiny is eventually to enter reputable society. Thus the new ethnics do not fully exhibit the features of disreputable poverty described above, nor do they manifest the embittered sense of defeat and resignation characteristic of dregs.[50] They are more apt to express a sort of naive optimism, especially since their new urban standard of life is, if anything, higher than the standard they previously experienced. Newcomers contribute an exotic element, whether they are European, Latin, native Americans from the reservation, or long-standing Americans as in the case of southern blacks. They season the melting pot of the streets with the spice of peasant tradition. It is this element that has excited the imagination of Bohemians and other intellectuals and led to the persistent romanticizing of life among the disreputable poor. Unfortunately, however, this exotic quality is double-edged, and one of the edges is considerably sharper than the other. Admiration from intellectuals was of little consequence for newly arrived ethnics compared with the persistent humiliation and degradation they underwent at the hands of resident ethnics. A negative degrading conception of newcomers seems a general feature of the attitude of older, established members of the community.

In the folklore of slum tradition and, to a considerable degree, in reality, the newcomers are untutored in the ways of slum sophistication. "Greenhorns," "banana boaters," whatever they are called, they learn the style of disreputable poverty primarily through being victims of it. They learn not by doing but, initially, by "being had." This traditional pattern is neatly summarized in an older description of the environment of newcomers in American slums, a description refreshingly free of the contrived relativism that currently misleads some anthropologists and sociologists.

> The moral surroundings are . . . bad for them. In tenement districts the unsophisticated Italian peasant or the quiet, inoffensive Hebrew is thrown into contact with the degenerate remnants of former immigrant populations, who bring influence to bear to rob, persecute, and corrupt the newcomers.[51]

[50] For a discussion contrasting the ambition and optimism of new European migrants with the resignation and apathy of old Americans of Scotch-Irish descent, see Herman Lantz, "Resignation, Industrialization and the Problem of Social Change," in Arthur Shostak and William Gomberg (eds.), *Blue-Collar World* (Englewood Cliffs, N.J.: Prentice-Hall, 1964), pp. 258–270. Also see Herman Lantz, *People of Coal Town* (New York: Columbia University Press, 1958).

[51] *United States Industrial Commission on Immigration,* Volume 15 of the Commission's Report (Washington, D.C.: U.S. Government Printing Office, 1901), p. xlvii.

Why have the newly arrived ethnics been so persistently humiliated and degraded by the old ethnic remnants? At one level, the answer seems simple. Despite all their failings, those who were left behind could lord it over the new arrivals, for they at least were somewhat Americanized, though not sufficiently so to be confident. Embittered and resentful on the one hand, and anxious and uncertain about their Americanism on the other, the ethnic dregs suffered from the classic conditions that make groups seek out scapegoats.

Exposure to the life style of disreputable poverty in the context of humiliation and victimization helped to dampen the optimism that newcomers frequently felt and thus facilitated the adoption of a similar life style by a segment of them. Optimism and other cultural resistances were never completely obliterated, however, and only a small proportion were actually reduced to disreputable poverty. Ethnic groups entering America and other nations have varied considerably in their vulnerability to slum pressures, but in each one at least a few families became dregs.

Skidders

Skidders are a third component in the milieu of disreputable poverty. These are men and women who have fallen from higher social niches. They include alcoholics, addicts, perverts, and otherwise disturbed individuals who come, after a long history of skidding, to live in the run-down section of the metropolis.[52] To a slight extent, low-cost public housing has concealed skidders from immediate view, but it still serves only a small proportion of the poor and at any rate tends to be reserved for the deserving poor. Among the disreputable poor, the visibility of skidders remains high.

Occasionally, along with the skidders, one finds some especially hardy Bohemians, who take their ideology seriously enough to live among their folk. But it is the skidders, rather than the Bohemians, who contribute importantly to the culture of disreputable poverty. Even when they live in these sections, Bohemians tends to be insulated, partially by their clannishness but primarily because they are ungratefully rejected by the authentic outsiders they romanticize.

Skidders contribute a tone of neuroticism and flagrant degradation to the life style of the slums. They are pathetic and dramatic symbols of the ultimate in disreputable poverty. Perhaps more important, they are visible evidence of the flimsy foundations of success and standing in society; they, as such, furnish yet another argument against sustained and conscientious effort. These are the fallen; they have achieved at least modest success and found it somehow lacking in worth. Skidders are important not because they are very numerous among the disreputable poor, but because they dramatically exemplify the

[52] See Donald Bogue, *Skid Row in American Cities* (Chicago: Community and Family Study Center, 1963).

worthlessness of effort. While their degradation may sometimes goad others, particularly the new ethnic, to conscientious efforts to escape a similar fate, the old ethnic dregs take the skidder's fall as additional evidence of the meanness of social life and the whimsy of destiny. Such a view of life makes it almost impossible to maintain either ambition or morality.

The Infirm

The *infirm* are the fourth element in the milieu of disreputable poverty. Before age, injury, or illness made them infirm, these people belonged to other strata—especially in the reputable sections of the working class. Their downward shift may take the form of physically moving from a reputable to a disreputable neighborhood, but more frequently perhaps, the infirm stay put, and the neighborhood moves out from under them. Frequently, they belong to old ethnic groups, but not to the dregs, since they did achieve reputable status. They slipped because of some misfortune: aging being the most common.[53] Their contribution is, in part, similar to the skidders', but without the blatant elements of neuroticism and degradation. Like the skidders, they testify to the flimsy foundations of respectability, the worthlessness of sustained effort, and the whimsical nature of fate, or destiny. Like the skidders—even more so because they have done less to provoke their fate—they symbolize the "beat" conception of life among the disreputable poor.

But the infirm have a distinctive contribution to make. In a completely ineffective way, they oppose the tradition of disreputable poverty. Their cantankerous complaints and what is perceived as their nosy interference frequently precipitate a flagrant and vengeful show of license and sin. The infirm become a captive and powerless audience before whom the youth who inhabit this world can flaunt their freedom from restraint. Intruders in this world because they are of different stock, because they claim reputability, or because of both these reasons, they are simultaneously powerless and rejected. Those who claim reputability in a disreputable milieu inevitably give the appearance of taking on airs and are thus vulnerable to ridicule and sarcasm—the typical sanctions for that minor vice. Furthermore, their opposition is weakened because before long the law-enforcement agencies begin to view them as pests; the police cannot, after all, bother with their complaints if they are to attend to the serious violations that abound in these areas. The infirm are the one indigenous source of opposition, but their marginal status makes them powerless to effect change. Thus, their distinctive contribution is to demonstrate the pettiness of character and the incredible impotence of those who oppose disreputable poverty.

---

[53] For good reviews of the economic situation of the aged, see Charles Linninger, "Some Aspects of the Economic Situation of the Aged," and Lenore Epstein, "The Income Position of the Aged," both in Harold Orbach and Clark Tibbits (eds.), *Aging and the Economy* (Ann Arbor: University of Michigan Press, 1963), pp. 71–90 and 91–102.

Functionaries

Functionaries occupy a special and persistent place in the lives of the disreputable poor. The regions these poor inhabit are inundated by a variety of agents and officials whose conventional purposes include regulation, control, and moral restoration.[54] "Branch Street," which may be regarded as typical of such regions, is notable for the fact that "social workers of all kinds are in and out of [the] houses continually."[55] Not only are the disreputable poor dependent—a feature they share with others—but they have deviated from conventional standards. For both reasons, their habits are seen as a suitable topic for inquiry, their paths as warranting redirection, and their lives as requiring intervention. The direct responsibility for these tasks falls to welfare functionaries.

Part of the job of welfare functionaries is to oversee the conduct of those who require assistance. Consequently, they are appropriately placed to pass judgment on the moral character of the welfare poor. The distinction between deserving and undeserving poor and the moral classification of persons as one or the other originate in the functionary perspective and continue to be a matter of special moment among those who share that perspective. Though welfare functionaries possess no monopoly either in making the distinction between reputable and disreputable poverty or in morally classifying persons within these categories, they claim and are accorded special competence in these endeavors. For welfare functionaries, these are not matters of idle gossip or spirited indignation but rather the substance of their profession. They are the duly authorized overseers of the assisted. Though they may think it, it is hard for recipients to utter the phrase, "It's none of your business," to welfare functionaries—a phrase regarded as legitimate when directed to those for whom moral judgment is a mere avocation. For welfare functionaries, moral classification is a vocation. In the strictest possible sense, it *is* their business.[56]

Moral classification is implicit in the work of functionaries because it is, first, necessary in determining eligibility for assistance, and, subsequently, part of what is taken into account in reviewing the advisability of continued assistance. Such classification must be based on systematic scrutiny. As a condition of assistance, the modern state (like private charities before it) requires that its

---

[54] For a general discussion of the relations between the poor and officials, see Warren C. Haggstrom, "The Power of the Poor," in Frank Riessman et al. (eds.), *Mental Health and the Poor* (New York: Free Press, 1964), pp. 212–213.

[55] Josephine Klein, *Samples from English Cultures* (London: Routledge, 1965), pp. 4–5.

[56] The observation that psychiatric or casework "diagnosis" frequently harbors moral judgments has been made many times. For a discussion of the transition from the explicit moral classification of the Charity Organization Societies to the implicit moral judgments of "casework diagnosis," see Roy Lubove, *The Professional Altruist* (Cambridge, Mass.: Harvard University Press, 1965). For more general discussions of the persistence of moral classification in "scientific" disciplines, see Kingsley Davis, "Mental Hygiene and the Class Structure," *Psychiatry*, Vol. 1 (February, 1938); C. W. Mills, "The Professional Ideology of Social Pathologists," *American Journal of Sociology* (September, 1943); and Erving Goffman, *Asylums* (New York: Doubleday [Anchor], 1961).

agents become privy to matters that are otherwise regarded as private. Welfare functionaries possess a license to scrutinize. Many writers have suggested the stigmatizing consequences of such scrutiny. It is because the recipients of aid are subjected to extraordinary scrutiny and regulation that Lewis Coser goes so far as to suggest that public assistance is forthcoming "only at the price of . . . degradation."[57]

Though Coser's comments apply to the welfare poor generally, they have special meaning for the disreputable poor. Coser attributes the degradation of being assisted to the fact that recipients are obliged, as a condition of assistance, to partly forfeit their privacy and partly surrender key symbols of maturity. With regard to the partial forfeiture of privacy, he says:

> Members of nearly all status groups in society can make use of a variety of legitimate mechanisms to shield their behavior from observability by others; society recognizes a right to privacy, that is, the right to conceal parts of his role behavior from public observation. But this right is denied to the poor. At least in principle, facets of his behavior which ordinarily are not public are . . . under public control and are open to scrutiny by social workers and other investigators.[58]

And in connection with the partial surrender of key symbols of maturity, he observes:

> When money is allocated to members of any other status group in society, they have the freedom to dispose of it in almost any way they see fit. Here again, the treatment of the poor differs sharply. When monies are allocated to them, they do not have free disposition over their use. They must account to the donors for their expenses and the donors decide whether the money is spent "wisely" or "foolishly." . . . The poor are treated in this respect much like children who have to account to their parents for the wise use of their pocket money; the poor are infantilized through such procedures.[59]

Thus Coser argues that degradation is implicit in the situation of assistance since the ordinarily conceived rights of privacy and maturity are partly abrogated. This applies generally to the welfare poor. For the disreputable poor, however, an additional degradation is implicit in the official scrutiny to which they are subjected. They are reminded of their undeserving character; their disrepute is noted, commented on, and filed away. Irrespective of whether sanc-

---

[57] Lewis Coser, "The Sociology of Poverty," *Social Problems,* Vol. 13, No. 2 (Fall, 1965), p. 144.

[58] *Ibid.,* p. 145.

[59] *Ibid.* Also on the point of "infantilizing," see Charles Silberman, *Crisis in Black and White* (New York: Random House, 1964), pp. 313–315. For a detailed and documented discussion of the special legal status and special penalties of the assisted that bears directly on the partial forfeitures of privacy and maturity, see Jacobus TenBroek, "California's Dual System of Family Law: Its Origin, Development, and Present Status," *Stanford Law Review,* Vol. 16 (March, 1964), pp. 257–317; (July, 1964), pp. 900–981; and Vol. 17 (April, 1965), pp. 614–882.

tions are taken—the main sanction being the "holding of checks"—the negative moral judgments of officials and the wider society they represent are subtly implied, cued, or loudly proclaimed.[60] In either case, the common conception of the disreputable poor as something less than human is apt to be confirmed and reinforced. It is in this light, perhaps, that the piercing cry of a nameless black welfare recipient is best understood. "I'm human! I'm human! I'm human! You dirty son of a bitch, can't you see I'm human!"[61] And it is in their encounters with functionaries that the disreputable poor are most apt to be reminded of their dismal moral condition and of their basic differences from the rest of humanity. Perhaps that is why, as Julius Horwitz observed, "the cry of being human was the most commonplace cry in the service. I heard it daily."[62]

CONCLUSION

How conceive poverty during the year of economic depression? That was the question before us when faced with the difficult matter of collaboratively revising a chapter first written uncollaboratively during the recession of the early sixties in which the deviance or the disrepute of poverty was emphasized. The criticism, self-criticism, and revision may be simply summarized: the deviance of poverty that grounds the concept of disrepute is the surface truth and not the inner nature or "law." Such a surface is most apparent during an era of recession, for in such periods poverty is easily mistaken for a layer. When poverty is perceived as a layer or mass lodged at the bottom of the class hierarchy, as an "underclass" or *Lumpenproletariat*, the concept of disrepute emerges. When, however, there is a more plentiful economic generation of poverty, as during a year of depression, another surface becomes socially apparent and comes to light. Poverty may then be conceived periodically or in life-cycle terms as a typical condition of working people subjected to political economy and thus to oscillations of subemployment and full employment.

Both aspects are true to the surface of poverty. But the inner law, being the deeper point, reveals the essential feature: the contradiction between the surfaces. Objectively, poverty belongs to working-class life; subjectively it is cast out. The unity or the synthesis of that contradiction *is* the proletariat. The failure to evoke the unity and to make the synthesis in theory and practice yields the duplication of the present: a mass of poverty in disrepute and a workforce organized in business unions. False consciousness resides in the alienation by which the lived reality of life-cycle unity of workers and poor people is mystified and lost from view. That mental division in the minds of ordinary people is today the germ of false consciousness, and not the older point stressed by

[60] For a journalistic description of checkholding and other matters relating to the treatment of disreputable clients by welfare caseworkers, see Joseph P. Mullen, *Room 103* (Philadelphia: Dorrance, 1963).

[61] Julius Horwitz, *The Inhabitants* (Cleveland: World, 1960), p. 104.

[62] *Ibid.*

Lukacs,[63] regarding the mystification of surplus value. To evoke the unity of the proletariat is the clear task of social movement during the depression—if not always.

SUMMARY

1   Poverty is related to economy. The U.S. economy is predicated on a wage-based labor force; thus poverty must be considered from that vantage point.

2   Poverty is not, as thought by some analysts, an attribute of individual character. Some poor are poorer than others; these gradations of poverty exist because gradations of labor compensation exist.

3   While there is no universally agreed-on definition of poverty, many definitions—both absolute and relative—have been proposed. An absolute definition fixes the poverty threshold at a specified income (e.g., arrived at through an analysis of minimum nutritional needs and other factors). A relative definition places a certain percentage of the population in the poor category (e.g., the percentage of families earning half the national median family income). Both definitions have advantages and shortcomings.

4   In the United States, the Orshansky plan is the most widely used poverty standard: after adjusting the food budget for family size and location, a co-efficient (the Engels factor) is used to yield a full budget for housing, transportation, and other necessities.

5   The constraints of poverty are many: an inadequate and monotonous diet; severely limited opportunities for recreation; a chronic hassle with the day-to-day exigencies of life. To be poor in the United States does not mean literally to starve, but to live in an unending state of fiscal desperation and degradation.

6   Welfare recipients are the bottommost level of the poor—mostly those whose income falls below the official poverty level. The various programs to aid the poor—AFDC, OASI, and so on—merely maintain them at a subsistence level.

7   Welfare chiseling is often imputed to the poor, but the extent of its actual occurrence, like that of tax evasion, has not been determined.

8   Poverty in the United States is a substantial phenomenon—nearly one-third of the population lives in a rather precarious state. The poor, however, are not a fixed group; they are those who are poor at a given moment in time—for example, data on current AFDC recipients do not reflect the number of children who have been poor at any point in their childhood.

9   The official unemployment rate is a precise measure: those in the labor force who are not working and who are actively seeking work. Among those employed, the amount of work for the amount of money is not taken into account.

10   Thus, a subemployment conception attempts to measure the extent, value, and opportunity for employment. Among the subemployed are: unemployed individuals who are actively seeking work; discouraged workers who are not looking because they lack experience or schooling, or are too young or too old; and employed individuals and heads of households whose earnings are below the poverty level.

11   The label "disreputable" is given to the subemployed by the employed. The

[63] George Lukacs, *History and Class Consciousness* (Cambridge, Mass.: MIT Press, 1972).

core of disreputable poor are the dregs (those spawned in poverty who have never left it), followed by newcomers (those without marketable skills or financial resources who gravitate to slums), skidders (those who have fallen from higher niches), and the infirm (those who have moved downward because of age, injury, or illness).

12 The job of welfare functionaries is to assist the poor; it is also to oversee their conduct, to pass judgment on their moral character.

13 Objectively, poverty can be seen as a periodic condition in the life cycle of working people subjected to fluctuating employment levels. The view of the poor as a layer at the bottom of the class hierarchy is a subjective one, and it is the basis for the concept of disrepute. The two views together make it possible to see the essential unity of the proletariat.

RECOMMENDED READING

The great War on Poverty that occurred under the Johnson administration produced a rather large literature on the poor. Two of the better anthologies, containing a series of uneven papers, are Margaret Gordon (ed.), *Poverty in America* (1965), and Louis Ferman, Joyce Kornbluh, and Alan Haber (eds.), *Poverty in America* (1965).

The literature on the culture of poverty and, indeed, the phenomenology of poverty is also quite extensive. The student is referred to the classic works by Oscar Lewis, *The Children of Sanchez* (1961) and Robert Coles, *Migrants, Sharecroppers, Mountaineers* (1971). A more critical view of the culture-of-poverty viewpoint is found in Charles Valentine's *Culture and Poverty: Critique and Counter-Proposals* (1968).

The welfare poor provide for a distinctive literature; an old but still pertinent discussion is that of Elaine Burgess and Daniel Price, *An American Dependency Challenge* (1963). A more recent analysis, in keeping with the spirit of this chapter, can be found in Richard Cloward and Francis Piven, *Regulating the Poor* (1971).

A full discussion of disrepute is located in the third edition of *Contemporary Social Problems* (1971)—the chapter on "Poverty and Disrepute" by David Matza treats of this surface in some detail. The economist's version of disrepute is seen in the dual labor market theory and is well stated by David Gordon, *Theories of Poverty and Underemployment* (1972).

Finally, the serious student is referred to the detailed and readily available data on poverty in the United States that can be found in the annual publications of the U.S. Bureau of the Census. These data are based on recurrent population surveys and are located in Series P-60, under the title: "Characteristics of the Low-Income Population." These easily obtained annuals contain a mass of straightforward, tabular data out of which the reader can devise his own conclusions as to the magnitude of poverty.

15 Collective Violence

AMITAI ETZIONI

K illing, maiming, and the willful destruction of property have occurred throughout history and in all societies. Violence is not only common during wars but is part of everyday life. One American is murdered every 27 minutes; forcibly raped every 10 minutes; subject to aggravated assault evry 76 seconds; and robbed every 82 seconds.[1] 17 percent more crimes were reported for 1974 than for 1973, and the national crime rate has risen by 32 percent since 1967. While much daily violence is the result of deviant acts by criminals or the mentally ill, some is collective, resulting from conflicts among social groups, such as blacks and whites, or between the government and groups of citizens—for instance, when demonstrations are violent or are suppressed. And collective conditions, such as the legitimation of authority and the availability of opportunities, affect the level of personal violence.

In contrast to such "routine" violence, there have been periods throughout history (and in a number of contemporary societies as well) during which the scope and intensity of violence has risen to the point of threatening the very organization of society. In Northern Ireland, for example, from 1969 to 1975 violent political conflict was responsible for more than 1,200 deaths (civilian and military), as well as for more than 20,000 shootings, more than 4,000 explosions, and millions of dollars' worth of property damage.[2] Since August, 1969, except for a few short periods of cease-fire, bomb explosions in Northern Ireland have averaged two a day. As *Time* magazine reported: "Ulstermen have had to accustom themselves to the surrealistic world of urban guerrilla warfare; violence has become almost as common as shepherd's pie and assassination squads move through Belfast with ease."[3] Urban life is said to "stutter along but only barely." City residents are often called out of the cinema three times a showing because of bomb scares. Women go shopping with first-aid kits in their bags. People lock themselves into their respective ghettos as the sun sets. Each enclave has its own rigid rules and enforcers who man the barricades around the clock. No one is secure from a random bullet let alone a plotted revenge.

In still other periods a threat to social organization is perceived, not necessarily because violence has reached the point of posing an explicit challenge to established political authority, as in Northern Ireland, but (1) because violence, or particular forms of violence, are perceived as rising to higher levels than previously, or (2) because the society seeks actively, as a matter of policy, to reduce the level of violence it is experiencing. Thus in the 1960s the rates of all major forms of violence in the United States rose steadily and were perceived by many as threatening the social fabric. The rising level of both collec-

The author is grateful to Pamela Doty for editorial suggestions on a previous draft and to Steve Cohen and Sherry Brandt for research assistance.
[1] Federal Bureau of Investigation, *Uniform Crime Reports for the United States* (Washington, D.C.: U.S. Department of Justice, 1973), Chart 1, p. ix.
[2] Alvin Shuster, "The Torment of Ulster," *The New York Times Magazine,* February 2, 1975, pp. 8–9ff, and Paul Harrison, "The Dark Ages of Ulster," *Human Behavior,* Vol. 4 (October 1975), pp. 17–23.
[3] *Time,* September 11, 1972.

tive and personal violence was regarded by many as a kind of "fever chart" for the society, symptomatic of underlying social maladies in need of attention. Riots in cities were common; campus unrest was unprecedentedly frequent; 588,840 violent crimes were reported in one year, 1968; serious crime was up about 100 percent from 1958. President John F. Kennedy, the Reverend Martin Luther King, Jr., and Senator Robert F. Kennedy were victims of political assassination. The United States was involved in a war in Southeast Asia. By 1975, 56,400 American servicemen had been killed, in addition to the 184,500 South Vietnamese and 927,000 North Vietnamese and Vietcong who were dead by 1974 (these figures do not include civilians). Within the United States itself the rate of deaths by homicide was exceptionally high in comparison with other industrialized societies.

By the mid-seventies personal violence took a divergent course from collective violence. Personal violence continued to rise at a high rate and to be perceived as socially threatening despite continual, intensive efforts to reduce it. Since 1961, the incidence of all serious crimes has more than doubled. From 1973 to 1974 the rate rose 17 percent, the largest rise in 44 years of keeping national records. At the same time, the incidence of most forms of collective violence subsided substantially to the point where collective violence was no longer perceived as a significant issue. Thus riots in ghettos became very rare; violent student demonstrations became very infrequent; and the U.S. involvement in the war in Southeast Asia was phased out. The shift was accorded considerable attention by the media, which first gave extensive coverage to riots, demonstrations, and other acts of collective violence, then dramatized the new pacificity of the ghetto residents, the return of "student demonstrators back to study," and the "cooling of America." Thus, while in the sixties incidents of collective violence made front-page news (and thus may have helped to encourage other incidents), in the mid-seventies whatever incidents did occur were accorded comparatively little attention, as the media were preoccupied with the energy crisis, economic troubles, and other matters. Indeed, a major rise in one type of collective violence during this period received relatively little attention and even less interpretation. It took the form of *waves* of vandalism, arson, and interracial fights in schools. According to one report, "crime and violence, in varying degrees, have become the norm in schools throughout the country. Many officials have become so anesthetized to the scope of the problem that they now consider a certain number of serious incidents inevitable."[4] About 70,000 teachers are injured each year by assaults. No exact figures on the number of students injured each year are available. Annual property damage exceeds $500 million. A form of collective violence which received much attention was the rise in terrorism—the use of extreme violence against individuals for political gains. Thus the level of violence a society experiences, and how problematic it considers it to be, is a matter of both the

---

[4] *The New York Times*, June 14, 1975.

number of actual incidents and the degree of attention they receive from the media, policy makers, and citizens.

The reasons the rate of violence, especially collective violence, may rise or fall are explored below. It should be mentioned in the context of this brief historical note that there is no reason to rest assured that collective violence will not have a resurgence in the near future. If collective violence has subsided in recent years, it is apparently not because minorities, young people, *and* other alienated citizens (55 percent of all adult Americans, according to Harris poll in 1973[5]) have become positively committed to American values and institutions or to their own place in the social structure. The relative tranquility of the mid-seventies seems to be more the result of retreatism than renewed commitment to widely shared goals and means. This retreatism could reflect an intensified search for *personal* solutions—or a despair of any. A low level of involvement may set the stage for a new mobilization for societal change, renewed conflict, and possibly mass violence. Thus, while the course of collective violence cannot be predicted, a new upsurge certainly cannot be ruled out just because the violent sixties (and early seventies) gave way to the subdued mid-seventies. After all, the violent sixties followed the silent fifties.

THE CONCEPT OF VIOLENCE

The 1970s began with widespread debate over the moral concepts and authority structures of the society. In 1974 a national sample of Americans was given a list of thirty domestic problems and asked to rank them by degree of worry or concern; "the amount of violence in American life" and "crime in this country" were ranked in second and third place respectively.[6] (Inflation ranked highest.) One segment of the citizenry and their leaders felt it was a question of law and order; they viewed parents, police, judges, and other authorities as having become "too permissive." A smaller number of Americans viewed the unresponsiveness of the societal structure to the needs and demands of the minorities, the young, and ultimately most Americans as inviting violent uprisings and crime.

Social thinkers and political philosophers tend to view violence as a social evil. Even when it is argued that violence is "justified"—for example, that the oppressed have a right to rise up against their violent oppressors—what is usually meant is that people are willing to condone the human sacrifice entailed

---

[5] Louis Harris and Associates, " 'Alienated' Americans Now a Majority," December 9, 1973. On the sociological meaning and significance of these terms, see Chapter 6, "Social Structure and Anomie," in Robert K. Merton, *Social Theory and Social Structure* (New York: Free Press, 1968), esp. pp. 207–211.

[6] William Watts and Lloyd A. Free, *State of the Nation 1974* (Washington, D.C.: Potomac Association, 1974), p. 20.

in an uprising if it promises to prevent further violence and advance other values such as social justice and freedom. The "justified" violence is viewed in itself as demeaning, to both the victims and the executioners. To make a human being an object of violence brutalizes not only him but also the violent actor. Concentration camp guards, hangmen, or totalitarian elites are not free, happy people. Only a very few writers have depicted violent acts as indicating positive attributes such as virility or toughness, or being therapeutic and releasing inhibitions. Most students of violence ask how it can be minimized and how other means of advancing one's goals can be followed instead.

Without entering into a lengthy expansion of conceptual differences of definitions we should note two distinctions in the concept of violence because the terms used technically here differ significantly from some common usages.

First, we are dealing in this chapter with physical violence, not with economic or psychic coercion. Some people argue that in forcing a person to take a line he does not wish to pursue there is no difference between pointing a gun at him, threatening the loss of his job, or manipulating his symbols, such as those involved in excommunication. This view is especially argued by those who justify their acts of physical violence by the economic and psychic coercion of others. Social scientists must note the difference: While economic and psychic pressures can be very powerful indeed, except in limited conditions they leave the ultimate decision to the subject—the pressures reduce but do not eliminate his freedom. When physical force is used, however—when a person is jailed, gagged, or shot—under most conditions he has no choice left in the matter. This difference may account for a corollary one. Most people find physical violence more alienating than psychic or economic pressures; they would rather be scolded or have their pay reduced than be beaten.[7] Hence it does matter to those subject to pressure which means of social control are employed, and it is not useful to cloud the issue semantically by referring to all acts of coercion as violence.

Second, violence and aggression are not to be confused. Violence is an act that causes damage, often to a person, sometimes only to property. Aggression involves the entire range of "assertive, intrusive, and attacking behaviors. Aggression thus includes both overt and covert attacks, such defamatory acts as sarcasm, self-directed attacks, and dominance behavior."[8]

Aggression may lead to violence, but it may also find an outlet in business competition, legal debate, and sports—all legitimate modes of conduct. Those who seek peace do not want a world, a society, or even a family free of aggressive feelings or conflicts—which may well be impossible and even undesirable. Peace does not mean the tranquility of inaction; it requires the advancement of one's positions and the solution or curbing of conflict by nonviolent means. Actually, developing and maintaining a nonviolent system way well require

[7] For some evidence, see Amitai Etzioni, *A Comparative Analysis of Complex Organizations,* rev. ed. (New York: Free Press, 1975), p. 7.

[8] Marshall F. Gilula and David N. Daniels, "Violence and Man's Struggle to Adapt," *Science,* April 25, 1969, p. 396.

providing sufficient room for legitimate forms of conflict, just as keeping a bicycle upright requires pushing the pedals. Standing still, passivity, is not a prerequisite of a nonviolent world.

Violence takes many forms: the assassination of presidents; the murder of mafiosi; riots in which city blocks are burned down and shops looted; bombs planted in mail boxes, police headquarters, and department stores; lynching of blacks by whites; police or National Guardsmen using excessive force in their legal capacity or running beserk; war; genocide. For the social scientist, behind this plethora of concrete forms are a few analytic dimensions that allow an order to emerge from the chaos. Violence may be defined according to the specific actors involved—whether individuals, small groups, or collectivities, such as classes or regions; how organized it is—whether spontaneous or planned; and its legitimacy—whether it is authorized by the society's institutions and sanctioned by its values or is condemned for seeking to evade these controls and values, or whether it is revolutionary, seeking to redefine society, in which case the use of violence may be considered legitimate.

These distinctions express a general concern with consequences rather than with motives. Thus individual or small-group deviant violence does not tend to have societal consequences unless it rises to very high levels or is hysterically perceived, whereas violence by collectivities seeking to redefine the society tends to alter history, as civil wars and revolutions indicate. The form of violence, though, does not determine the consequences. These are primarily affected by the sources of violence and the ways they are faced.

Few other areas studied by social scientists are as pervaded with normative issues and overtones as the discussion of the sources and dynamics of violence. To some, it brings to mind the violence done by the establishment to people in general and disadvantaged persons in particular. These researchers therefore focus either on specific features of the regime or on generic attributes of "establishments" which are responsible for the lack of responsiveness. Studies of the correlation between police brutality, merchants' exploitative practices, and black ghetto riots are illustrative of the former.[9] Studies investigating the relationships between high crime rates and low income, low social prestige, poor housing, and high population density belong to the generic category.[10] They, in effect, assert and attempt to document that "it's society's fault."

Closer examination, often by the same researchers, has revealed, however, that such background variables explain violence only in part. Thus, while there are more incidents of crime in poor neighborhoods than in better-off ones, many people who grow up in poor neighborhoods do not become criminals. Clearly other variables must be at work. And according to Rossi and Berk,

[9] Peter H. Rossi and Richard A. Berk, "Local Political Leadership and Popular Discontent in the Ghetto," in James F. Short, Jr., and Marvin E. Wolfgang (eds.), *Collective Violence* (Chicago: Aldine, 1972), pp. 292–308.

[10] President's Commission on Law Enforcement and Administration of Justice, *The Challenge of Crime in a Free Society* (Washington, D.C.: Government Printing Office, 1967), p. 35.

while merchants' exploitation has changed little over time, attention drawn to it by militants makes the rank and file more aware of it and triggers their protest.[11]

At the opposite end are those researchers who see violence as generated by agitators who dupe the naive, the young, uneducated minorities, and the working class into rebelling against a society in which economic opportunities and the respect for personal rights are greater than in any other. The conspirators or agitators are seen as motivated by envy that "failures" feel toward those who have been "successful." Instead of recognizing that they themselves are to blame for their circumstances, these people seek to evade their personal responsibility by unfairly accusing society. Thus various government commissions sought to find the "foreign" elements in the black and youth rebellions, but found no conspiracy. For instance, the National Commission on the Causes and Prevention of Violence concluded:

> Strife in the United States and other European countries is quite likely to mobilize members of both the working class and the middle classes but rarely members of the political establishment such as military officers, civil servants, and disaffected political leaders. Strife also is likely to occur within or on the periphery of the normal and open political processes in Western nations, rather than being organized by clandestine revolutionary movements or cells of plotters within the political and military hierarchy.[12]

The Kerner Commission, which studied race riots, concluded:

> On the basis of all the information collected the Commission concludes that the urban disorders of the summer of 1967 were not caused by, nor were they the consequences of, any organized plan or "conspiracy." Specifically, the Commission has found no evidence that all or any of the disorders or the incidents that led to them were planned or directed by any organization or group, international, national or local.[13]

These conclusions should *not* be interpreted to suggest that members of a disaffected race, class, or subculture rise up wholly spontaneously. Leaders, organizers, and intellectuals do play a role in mobilizing protest behavior. They can do so, however, only because they have tapped a genuine need felt by their followers. Moreover, leaders arise through an interaction with the group they mobilize. They are not imported from the outside as full-fledged leaders in a sealed car, as some would have it.

---

[11] Rossi and Berk, *op. cit.*, p. 300.

[12] Progress Report of the National Commission on the Causes and Prevention of Violence to President Lyndon B. Johnson (Washington, D.C.: Government Printing Office, 1969), p. A-7.

[13] *Report of the National Advisory Commission on Civil Disorders* (New York: Bantam, 1968), p. 202.

QUANTITATIVE PROFILES

Several students of violence have interested themselves in the frequency of various forms of violence, generating the data necessary for drawing both practical and theoretical conclusions. Among the first to proceed in this manner were Lewis Richardson and Quincy Wright.

Richardson reports that historically wars have remained "stable" as a social phenomenon, neither rising nor falling in frequency, although at least since 1820 large wars have been more frequent, and small wars, less so. That is, the number of wars has not increased with the rise of capitalism, communism, or even nationalism, although the scope of individual wars has expanded. Moreover, contrary to a widely held belief, daily murders were responsible for fewer deaths than wars, which were found to be the main cause of lives lost through deliberate killing.[14]

Finally, though it is often alleged that a "latent function" of war is birth control and that accelerated population growth therefore creates a climate favorable to war, population increases from 1820 to 1949 (the period studied by Richardson) have *not* resulted in heightened belligerency. Richardson lists scores of other such pieces of data. Wright's list runs literally into the thousands.[15]

According to a study by J. David Singer and Melvin Small[16] over the approximately 150-year period from 1816 until 1965, there were neither any increases nor decreases in the frequency, magnitude, severity, or intensity of war. While there were more battle deaths in the twentieth century than in the nineteenth, when the figures are "corrected" to take into account the number of nations (which also rose), the differential disappears. While the introduction of nuclear weapons may have made world wars between superpowers "impossible" or "unthinkable," it surely did not stop wars between many other nations, including those closely allied with the superpowers, or even between the superpowers themselves and countries not possessing nuclear weapons.

Singer and Small found, however, that not all nations have been equally aggressive or war-prone. The list is dominated by the superpowers of the particular era in which the wars occurred. Leading this dubious honor list are France and England (19 wars each), Turkey (17), Russia (15), Italy (11), Spain (9), and the United States (6). No major power of its day escaped being on the list, and Singer and Small wonder if being war-prone was not either a prerequisite or a consequence of being a mighty nation. In contrast, smaller states, especially outside of Europe, enjoyed long periods of peace (although some did experience high levels of civil strife).

[14] Lewis Richardson, *Statistics of Deadly Quarrels* (Pittsburgh: Boxwood Press, 1960).

[15] Quincy Wright, *A Study of War*, 2nd ed. (Chicago: University of Chicago Press, 1965).

[16] J. David Singer and Melvin Small, *The Wages of War, 1816–1965* (New York: Wiley, 1972).

These and similar studies do not claim to provide definitive answers on the causes of collective violence. They do indicate, however, that quantitative tools can be applied to the study of violence, and they serve to warn against the acceptance of such simplistic generalizations as "War is on the rise" or "Population excesses are corrected by wars."

TOWARD A THEORY OF COLLECTIVE VIOLENCE

The single most significant insight for a sociopolitical theory of collective violence is, to paraphrase a famous saying, that violence is the continuation of normal societal processes by "other" means. To illustrate, workers may have grievances (a sign of social tension) and go on strike (in itself a legitimate, nonviolent form of conflict); but a peaceful strike may turn into a violent confrontation if demands are continually ignored, if attempts are made to suppress the overt expression of the conflict (by use of police or strikebreakers), or if the workers are egged on by agitators.

It is difficult to account fully for the level of conflict in society and the conditions under which it escalates into collective violence without going into considerable detail concerning the structure and processes of societies.[17] Three central concepts, however, can be briefly introduced and their relationship to violence explored. These are *societal bonds*, which are indicative of the extent to which a society is cohesive or integrated; *societal structures*, which refer to the shapes or patterns of the relationships among those bound together into one societal group (e.g., whether one subgroup subjugates the others or whether there is a more egalitarian distribution of opportunities); and *societal processes*, which are the mechanisms through which both societal bonds and societal structures can be maintained and changed. The processes may be effective and make structures and bonds responsive to the societal membership; or they may be ineffective and allow for great or growing discrepancies between the desires of the members and what the society provides for them. The societal sources and dynamics of collective violence lie in these three concepts.

Societal Bonds (or Systems): The Extent of Societal Integration

The intricate webs of societal bonds that tie individuals and groups to each other are of three major kinds. One is the values that people share, which they acquire at home, in school, from peers, and in church. For instance, they may share a belief in the "American way of life" or in "individualism." Shared beliefs allow groups with conflicting interests and viewpoints to work together and

---

[17] A theory on which we draw here is presented in detail in Amitai Etzioni, *The Active Society: A Theory of Societal and Political Processes* (New York: Free Press, 1968), and is applied to social problems in Amitai Etzioni, *Social Problems* (Englewood Cliffs, N.J.: Prentice-Hall, 1976).

hence to curb conflict, limiting it to nonviolent means. It is as if each participant says to himself, "Well, I don't really like this"—"this" being whatever the conflict is all about—"but there is something more important that I and my adversary share; so I will give in, at least part of the way, to keep the shared enterprise alive." When basic values are not shared by members of a society— as, for instance, among the Christian and Moslem citizens of Lebanon, the Turkish and Greek Cypriots, or Southerners and Northerners in the United States before the Civil War—intergroup violence is more likely. This violence may take the form of tribal warfare, civil war, urban riot, or, among societies, international war.

The second major societal bond is the economic exchanges that tie people and groups to each other not out of commitment but out of necessity. They trade with each other or use each other's facilities (e.g., ports) or own joint facilities (e.g., interstate railroads). The more exchanges occur, all other things being equal, the more people or groups are bound to each other and the less likely they are to come into violent conflict. Thus the more integrated the United States became after the Civil War, especially after the 1890s, the more trade evolved among the various regions, which in turn bound them more deeply into one society.

A third societal bond, frequently not recognized as such, is the ability of an authority to speak for the unit (whatever unit is encompassed by the bonds) to keep the subunits "in line" (i.e., to continue within the system and not to threaten it) by disarming them, or at least by keeping their capacity to fight at clearly lower levels. It is something like a schoolyard: One reason the fourth graders do not fight each other, at least not much, is that some eighth graders (or teachers) are appointed to see that they do not. Both the superior power and the legitimacy of the "law and order" force are relevant. If the "peacekeeping" force is weak, it will invite a revolution; if it is itself unjust, not duly appointed, or discriminatory in its enforcement of nonviolence, it will encourage the "subjects" to seek means to rebel. In the process of nation building, in which societal bonds are intensified, often the right to bear arms is shifted from individuals and local groups to a national authority such as the police or the army.

A brief look at the development of societal bonds in the United States is useful. Having grown out of colonies that were fairly separate entities, the United States only slowly evolved nationwide integrative forces of all three kinds, and this largely after the Civil War. Even today no nationwide school system teaches all children the same "civics" or otherwise introduces them to the same set of ultimate values, as in France or Israel. Even today segments of the country, especially the poorest ones, are left out of many economic exchanges. Even today the United States, unlike most Western countries, has no nationwide police force. These factors are a major reason the United States is more violent than most Western nations. They also help to explain why in many underdeveloped nations, much less integrated than the United States, intergroup violence is considerably higher.

The three kinds of bonds are weakest *among* nations; hence conflicts which arise among these entities are most likely to turn to violence that, once it erupts, is most difficult to curb. If we view a nation divided by a civil war or large-scale intergroup violence, along racial or class lines, for example, as two or more "nations" not deeply bound together, we see how the same conception of bonds applies to both intra- and international conflicts.

So far, we have asked a "static" question: What bonds tie persons together? Dynamically, we ask next: Under what conditions may groups heretofore not sufficiently tied to make a community that rules out large-scale intergroup violence come to fashion such bonds? We shall illustrate our answer by examples from situations in which bonds are weakest, among nations, but the same points apply to *intra*national systems.

System Building: An International Example

Encapsulation, not conflict resolution   Bonds provide a "capsule" that contains conflicts and prevents them from turning into violence. *Encapsulation* refers to the process by which conflicts are modified so that they become limited by rules (the "capsule"). The rules exclude some earlier modes of conflict, while they legitimate other modes. Encapsulated conflicts are not solved in the sense that the parties necessarily become pacified. But the use of arms, or at least some usage of some arms, is effectively ruled out. Where some observers may see only two alternatives—powers are basically either hostile or friendly— encapsulation points to a third kind of relationship. Here, some differences of belief or interests, even a mutually aggressive orientation, might well continue. But states agree to rule out some means and some modes of conflict—namely, armed ones—and to set up the machinery necessary to enforce this agreement. Encapsulation is thus less demanding than pacification, since it does not require that the conflict be resolved or extinguished, only that the range of its expression be curbed.

Propelling forces, the limits of communication   How may bonds be built up to curb intergroup violence? Robert Ezra Park points out that conflict generates interaction between its parties (e.g., races); as the parties come to know each other and communicate with each other, they evolve shared perspectives and relations—until the conflict turns into competition. (Park and many other sociologists use the term *competition* to refer to a conflict limited by a set of rules.)[18] Daniel Lerner reports that French businessmen who travel, read foreign magazines, and meet foreign visitors are more likely to favor the formation of a European community than those less exposed to foreigners. Among businessmen with much exposure, sentiment in favor of such a community is about six to one, while those who have had little contact with foreigners favor the community only by a ratio of two to one. The difference

[18] Robert E. Park, *Human Communities* (New York: Free Press, 1952).

between these two groups might be related to factors other than exposure, but Lerner shows that variables such as age, birthplace, socioeconomic status, size of firm, and location of firm do not explain the differences.[19]

The theorem that increased communication between parties is the mechanism through which conflicts are encapsulated, and violence thus reduced, seems to hold more for parties with similar values and sentiments to begin with. Communication may make the participants aware of a latent consensus upon which they may draw to build agreed-upon procedures that will further limit conflicts and legitimate accommodation. But when the basic values, sentiments, and interests of the parties are not compatible, increased communication may only stir this incompatibility into conflict, make the parties more conscious of the deep cleavages that separate them, and increase the likelihood of violence. The larger the differences between the parties to a conflict, the smaller the degree of encapsulation that can be attained through increased communication.

The effect of power constellations   Among hostile parties who lack shared values, encapsulation of conflicts seems to depend less on communication than on the number of members in the system and the distribution of power among them. The balance-of-power system seems to require at least four or five participants.[20] Systems with three participants tend to lead to coalitions, in which two gang up against the third.[21] Bipolar systems (i.e., with two participants) have been shown to be particularly difficult to pacify. Encapsulation seems to be enhanced by the transition from a relatively duopolistic (two-party) system to a more pluralistic one.

International relations approximated a state of duopoly between 1946 and 1956. In this period, the height of the cold war, there were two fairly monolithic camps, one directed from Moscow, the other from Washington. A number of countries were not aligned with either camp, but their military and political weight was small. Such a duopolistic situation was highly unfavorable to encapsulation. The sides focused their attention on keeping their respective blocs integrated and trying to keep nonaligned countries from swelling the ranks of the opposite camp. Each bloc eyed the other, hoping for an opportunity to expand its respective area of influence while waiting for the other's collapse.

Between 1956 and 1964 a secondary power rebelled in each of the two major camps. Both France and China had been weak powers, forced to follow a foreign policy formulated in foreign capitals. Under reawakening nationalism and augmented national power, both, however, increasingly followed an inde-

[19] Daniel Lerner, "French Business Leaders Look at EDC: A Preliminary Report," *Public Opinion Quarterly*, Vol. 20 (1965), pp. 212–221.
[20] See Morton A. Kaplan, *System and Process in International Politics* (New York: Wiley, 1957), pp. 27, 34ff.
[21] Georg Simmel, *Conflict* (New York: Free Press, 1955).

pendent foreign policy. The rebellion of the secondary powers in both camps pushed the two superpowers closer to each other. Seeking to maintain their superior status and fearing the consequences of conflicts generated by their rebelling client-states, the superpowers set out to formulate some rules binding on all parties. The treaty of the partial cessation of nuclear tests, which the United States and the Soviet Union tried to make binding on France and China as well, was a case in point. American-Russian efforts to stem proliferation of nuclear weapons was another. In this period Russia stopped whatever technical aid it was giving to Chinese nuclear research and development,[22] and the United States refused to help France develop its nuclear force. American-Soviet negotiations to agree on inspection of atomic plants, aimed mainly at insuring the use of atomic research for nonmilitary purposes in third countries, pointed in the same direction. The 1963–1964 détente, which isolated Communist China and France, and the Geneva disarmament negotiations in the same years, in which these two countries did not participate, were further reflections of this trend.

These measures have in common the important characteristic that they serve the more "narrow" needs of the superpowers while they advance the "general welfare" of the world, they can therefore be presented as universal values and implemented through world institutions (i.e., extend the "capsule"). For instance, the prime superpower motivation for the 1963 test-ban treaty might well have been the desire of the United States and Russia to remain the only two great nuclear powers, but the treaty also indirectly reduced the danger of nuclear war. It was presented as if the prime motive were to advance peace and disarmament and reduce fallout to protect human health. It is a familiar strategy of political interest groups to work out solutions among themselves and then clothe them in the values of the community at large. Indirectly, these values affect the course of action an interest group chooses to follow from among available alternatives, and they provide a common basis upon which similar or compatible interests of divergent powers can be harmonized and the shared community broadened.

Consensus formation and "intermediary" bodies Sociopolitical processes that reduce differences of interest and viewpoint and build ties are conflict-reducing, violence-curbing processes, as well as community-building processes. Communities, especially if they have a government, require some means of developing political consensus. To build an effective consensus-forming structure, it is essential to divide the processes into several levels of representation. Rather than attempting to reach consensus among all parties in one general assembly, the parties are best divided into subgroups that are more homogeneous than the community as a whole. These subgroups work out a compromise and are represented as if they were a single unit on the next level of the

---

[22] G. F. Hudson et al., *The Sino-Soviet Dispute* (New York: Praeger, 1961).

structure in which consensus is formed. To be effective, such divisions may have to be repeated several times.[23]

Regional organizations, communities, and blocs might serve as "intermediary bodies" for the international community. It would, however, be a mistake to view every regional organization as a step toward a world community. Regional organizations that have only socially marginal roles, such as the European research organization on peaceful uses of nuclear energy (CERN), tend to have much less impact than those that pool the sovereignties of several nations, as the European Economic Community (EEC) has begun to do. Regional bodies intended to countervail other regional bodies, especially military alliances such as NATO and the Warsaw Treaty Organization, often retard rather than advance encapsulation of conflict; they tend to reflect, on a large scale, the features of nationalism. Regional bodies aimed at internal improvement, such as "welfare" communities (a foundation of the EEC) or development associations (e.g., in Central America) that stress rapid economic growth, are more likely to serve as intermediary layers in the process of building a world community.

Above all, only regional bodies that allow the process of "upward transfer" of loyalties are helpful in building a world community. Studies of social structures as different as the American federal government and the Southern Baptist Association have shown that once a center of authority is established, it tends to acquire the power, rights, and command of loyalties earlier commanded by the units (as when states' rights declined and those of the federal government grew).[24] But a social unit can, by the use of ideological and political mechanisms, advance or retard this process. Only those units that encourage or at least allow the process to occur provide a sociopolitical foundation on which a world community might be erected.

Rules and enforcement Another major process of community building is the evolution of rules and of agencies for their enforcement. Here is much room for the application and further development of the sociology of law, which warns against relying excessively on legislation when there is only a narrow sociopolitical base. A premature and ineffectual world law might be worse than no law at all. Laws that are not backed by effective enforcement

---

[23] In the American political system the primaries and the national conventions and, to a degree, post-election negotiations over participation in the cabinet provide such a multi-layer consensus-formation structure. Thus, for instance, the struggle over the presidential and vice-presidential candidates is also a struggle over what policy the party is to face the electorate with. Once the candidates are chosen, most segments of the party—liberal and conservative—tend, as a rule, to support the candidates and the policy. In the negotiations on participation in the cabinet, the party that lost the election is often given some indirect representation to enhance national support for what is a one-party administration.

[24] Paul M. Harrison, *Authority and Power in the Free Church Tradition* (Princeton, N.J.: Princeton University Press, 1959), especially the chapter on power and authority in the church.

and adequate consensus, as illustrated by the abortive attempt to institute prohibition in the United States, breed contempt for laws and their makers and nurture a whole range of previously unknown criminal interests. A premature world law on disarmament might well generate clandestine production of weapons and large profits to arms smugglers, and thereby lead to repeal of the law rather than to lasting disarmament.

The concern in the study of encapsulation is not so much with protecting the existing mechanism from erosion as with accelerating its extension and growth. Hence the importance of formalizing implicit and "understood" rules into explicit and enforced international laws becomes clear. This principle is neither obvious nor widely agreed upon. Many stress the value of implicit, unnegotiated understandings. For instance, after the Soviet Union removed its missiles from Cuba late in 1962, the United States removed its Thor and Jupiter missiles from Turkey and Italy in 1963, without such reciprocation ever being publicly discussed, let alone negotiated. (Even today it is not clear that this was a deliberate act of reciprocation.)

There are several disadvantages in reaching agreement in this particular way, especially for community-building efforts. The danger of misunderstanding is larger, especially when matters are complex. When misunderstandings occur, they generate bitter feelings of betrayal and mistrust, which in turn stand in the way of future exchanges. Further, the community's institutions do not gain in experience and responsibility unless implicit understandings are codified and enforced. This is not to suggest that the path of implicit understanding should not be traveled, but only that unless an enlarging flow of such traffic is directed through world institutions, they will remain the dirt roads rather than the highways of international relations.

When rules are formalized, effective verification and response machinery is necessary. The 1954 agreements to neutralize Laos and limit arms supplies for Vietnam were supervised by an understaffed, underfinanced, ill-equipped, and above all politically deadlocked commission. (Its members were India, Poland, and Canada.) In 1959 East and West accused each other of violating these agreements; the enforcement machinery provided neither a clear picture of who was the first to violate the agreements nor an appropriate response.

We have examined the ways societal bonds may be built up among previously less integrated societal units. We illustrated the factors by drawing upon the relations among nations; but similar statements about the role of increased communication, varying power constellations, the functions of intermediary bodies (or subgroups) in building consensus, and the role of developing shared laws all apply to the relations among the parts of an underdeveloped country or the races in one society. In all these systems, the more favorable these factors are, the more and stronger societal bonds we expect; and the more powerful these bonds—for reasons discussed earlier—the less intergroup violence is to be expected. But the potency of the societal bonds is not the only factor in determining the level of violence; the particular way members bound together relate to each other is another major factor in accounting for both group and personal violence.

Violence-Prone Structures

Each society can be viewed as a set of asset distributions. Society has economic assets, annual income, educational opportunities, prestige, and power—but who gets what? Sociologists ask this question not in terms of individuals but in terms of large groups of people. While the distributions of various assets are not the same, and while all change over time, those groups at the top of one distribution tend to get a very disproportionate share of what is to be had. And those at the bottom of one distribution tend to be at the bottom of most other distributions. For instance, the annual income of the United States is divided in such a way that the 13 percent of the population at the "lowest" end of the income distribution receives 2 percent of the total national income, while the "highest" 10 percent receives 29 percent.[25] With regard to higher education in the United States, among those families whose income is $15,000 or more, 53.7 percent have members enrolled full time in college, compared with 12.7 percent among those earning less than $3,000 a year.[26]

Having a disproportionately low share of society's assets does not by itself cause much violence; it is a universal condition in which some groups in most, if not all, societies find themselves (although there are significant differences in degree). However, once a group—a class, a race, an age category—has become aware of its deprived status and is mobilized to act on it, intergroup tension and conflicts mount. (Mobilization is frequently initiated by intellectuals and leaders who are not themselves members of the group, but anger soon is internalized and the conflict is taken over by those who are members.) The rise in tensions and conflicts may cause no violence if reallocation follows, or if some project is advanced in which all groups will share equally, such as opening up new territories or stimulating the economy into rapid growth.

But if the structure is rigid, and no reallocations occur after the society is faced with rising demands, tensions and conflicts are likely to escalate to a level where violence is highly probable. This does not mean that the demanded reallocations or, more generally, social justice, will follow. Those who have most of what there is may, despite the violence, use their power to keep the new demands at bay. Or some accommodations may be made to reduce, perhaps only temporarily and partially, the new violence (say, riots in slums). Or those in power may be ousted in a revolution and a new disproportionate allocative pattern set up. Whatever the final accommodation, a rise in violence is the price of undue rigidity.

---

[25] Paul A. Samuelson, *Economics: An Introductory Analysis,* 8th ed. (New York: McGraw-Hill, 1970), p. 109.

[26] U.S. Bureau of the Census, *Characteristics of American Youth, 1974,* Series P-23, No. 51 (Washington, D.C.: Government Printing Office, 1974), Table 15, p. 13.

The theorem of relative deprivation   What are the characteristics of those most likely to join in an uprising? At what point in sociohistory do they rise? A number of studies suggest that participants are rarely from groups so oppressed that "they have nothing to lose but their chains." Rather, they tend to come from groups whose life situation has been improving but who then experience feelings of "relative deprivation" when their gains are threatened by periods of economic setback or when the rate of further improvement fails to keep pace with their expectations.

James C. Davies studied the fit between the theory of relative deprivation and the patterns discernible in a variety of instances of revolution or rebellion, widely separated historically and geographically, including the French Revolution, the American Civil War, the rise of the Nazis in Germany, and the black and student rebellions of the 1960s in the United States.[27]

A discussion of the black militancy of the 1960s illustrates the way the other cases are analyzed. First, Davies explains why he considers the black uprising "revolutionary" even though it did not lead to the kind of holistic change that the French and Nazi revolutions brought about. For Davies, the difference is chiefly quantitative. Like other revolutionary groups, Negroes sought a fundamental change throughout the nation and within specific sectors of society— not only in economic or cultural or political matters. Moreover, the black confrontation with white society involved the violence that is, according to Davies, a universal element of revolution.

Specifically, what Davies sees as having triggered the black as well as the other uprisings studied was a set of expectations "at first gratified, then frustrated." Thus, typically, black people were better off, or perhaps one should say less outrageously disadvantaged, in the 1960s than in the 1930s or 1860s. Rebellion came at this point because revolt is a product not of total despair but of frustrated hope.

According to Davies, at the end of the Civil War Negroes were as close to minimal survival as they had been since their transportation from Africa. Moreover, they had lost even the security of food, clothing, shelter, and physical safety that their status as slaves had provided. Post-Civil War segregation did not spark a rebellion among the former slaves because those who must concentrate only on survival usually do not rebel: They are too hungry. This preoccupation with survival continued through the next decades. Between 1882 and 1941 lynchings averaged 78 per year. While there was some improvement over the years in the condition of the Negroes, progress was very slow until the beginning of World War II. The war brought an executive order prohibiting discrimination and establishing the Fair Employment Practices Commission. By 1945, 2 million blacks had industrial jobs. In 1946 the CIO and the AFL both initiated drives to organize Negroes. Major sports became open to blacks in 1947; public housing in 1956. A few blacks gained access to

---

[27] James C. Davies, "The J-Curve of Rising and Declining Satisfactions as a Cause of Some Great Revolutions and a Contained Rebellion," in Hugh Davis Graham and Ted Robert Gurr (eds.), *Violence in America* (New York: Bantam, 1969), pp. 690–730, 716–725.

public office. Progress was taking place simultaneously with respect to the economic, the political, and the "symbolic" (i.e., matters dealing with status symbols and hence dignity). Lynching also declined. There was one case in 1947, two in 1948.

Demonstrations by blacks to further the cause of racial equality and integration became common in the late fifties and frequently erupted in violent confrontations, most of which, at least at first, was fomented by white counterdemonstrators or police. The level of violence reached a peak in 1965–1967 with a wave of black ghetto riots. Davies suggests that the reason for the turn toward violence on the part of blacks was not a sudden drop or even slowdown in jobs or other material goods available to them; rather, it was a perceived decrease in personal safety and dignity, following the use of police dogs against blacks in May, 1963 in Birmingham, Alabama and the murders of several civil rights activists. The violent opposition of some whites to integration, Davies suggests, put an abrupt stop to the dream of peaceful progress toward an integrated, egalitarian, brotherly society.

Correlation between alienation and strife   The issue here is not whether we agree with Davies' recounting of civil rights history or with his interpretation of it. The important point is that his analysis illustrates the hypothesis that the subjective perception of *relative* deprivation is as important a cause of rebellion as objective forces in society. A similar theoretical perspective can be found in the studies of revolution and rebellion carried out by Ted Gurr.[28] Gurr drew together a sample of incidents in which alienated (i.e., discontented) groups expressed their disenchantment by resorting to violent uprising, excluding violence perpetrated by the state against its members. His focus was on discontent resulting not from objective wants but from perceived discrepancies between human needs and opportunities to satisfy those needs. Using as his sample 1,100 occurrences of strife in 114 nations (during the period 1961–1965), he found that 93 percent originated in such discontent.[29] Examples of strife in 21 Western nations (during the same period) were subjected to additional analysis. The magnitude of the strife was measured (using men-days of strife per 100,000 persons as well as death rates, thereby avoiding the less precise measure of casualties). Incidents of strife were next categorized as either examples of "turmoil"—that is, relatively spontaneous armed or unarmed rebellion—or examples of more organized forms of collective protest. In addition, violent and nonviolent instances of strife were discriminated. Gurr found that the magnitude of all four types of strife was less in the 21 Western nations than in the sample of 114 nations over the same period. Particularly rare, comparatively, was rebellious, nonviolent strife. If one holds to the view that during the early sixties (the time period of the analysis), the Western nations

---

[28] Ted Robert Gurr, *The Conditions of Civil Violence* (Princeton, N.J.: Princeton University Press, 1967); *Why Men Rebel* (Princeton, N.J.: Princeton University Press, 1970).
[29] Ted Robert Gurr, "Sources of Rebellion in Western Societies: Some Quantitative Evidence," in Short and Wolfgang, *op. cit.*, p. 134.

were by and large more advantaged not only in terms of economic well-being but in terms of the subjective perceptions of the citizens as well, the findings lend support to the hypothesis that the degree of alienation and magnitude of strife vary directly. On the other hand, factors such as differences in cultural values or political institutions rather than in psychology might also account for the result.

Differences *among* Western nations from the viewpoint of their alienating features and associated strife were correlated, but not too strongly. Short-term political deprivation correlated quite strongly with strife (.50) as well as persisting deprivation (.39), but only weakly with economic discontent (.06). Turmoil was not found to correlate at all; however, rebellion correlated quite strongly with deprivation.

Studies such as those by Davies and Gurr are particularly significant in that they offer an illustration of how sociological analysis can produce insights that are far from self-evident and that indeed may go directly counter to what most people would expect on the basis of "common sense" alone. Few people unacquainted with the findings from relative-deprivation studies would predict that it is not the most downtrodden and oppressed who typically rebel, but those who in fact have "something to lose" and who rebel (1) because they perceive their hard-won gains (material or symbolic) to be in danger; (2) because they view their gains in one area as incommensurate with their gains in another (e.g., they see their political power as less than their economic achievements warrant); or (3) because their actual gains have not kept pace with the rate of progress they had come to expect. In all these instances, however, it is not the objective character of deprivation but the subjective perception of it that is the prime source of rebellion and revolution.

The military-industrial complex   Sociologists have also turned an analytical eye toward the role that internal structure of societies plays in international violence. One explanation often given for international strife—an explanation that has been advanced by persons as different as C. Wright Mills and Dwight D. Eisenhower—is that war derives not from imbalances of power among nations or from the megalomania or other psychological propensities of leaders, but from economic and power relations within the warring nations.[30] The essence of this analysis is that arms buildups are promoted by business interests who reap profits directly or indirectly from weapons production. These interests include not only the arms manufacturers and those who supply them with parts and raw materials, but also America's millions of stockholders— for whenever preparations for war decline, it is said that the entire American economy (and with it the economies of many industrial Western countries) suffers a recession. The Great Depression was not really overcome, it is said, until the arms buildup for World War II started. The postwar recession ended

---

[30] C. Wright Mills, *The Causes of World War III* (New York: Simon and Schuster, 1958); Dwight D. Eisenhower, "Farewell Address," January 16, 1971.

only when rearmament for the Korean War spurred the American economy. Subsequent smaller ups and downs in the economy have been related to ups and downs in the tensions of the cold war. For instance, the American stock market experienced hearty rallies after the breakdown of the 1960 summit conference in Paris, the 1961 Berlin crisis, and the 1965 escalation of the war in Vietnam. The rallies were led by "defense" stocks, but other stocks benefited as well.

Workers also benefit from the arms race. The close association between employment and international tension, unemployment and relaxation of this tension, is reflected in the following figures. In 1939, 17.2 percent of the American labor force was unemployed. The war reduced unemployment to 1.2 percent in 1944. Unemployment rose after the war in 1946 to 3.9 percent, was reduced by the Korean War to 2.5 percent, rose after this war ended to 5 percent by 1954, and continued to rise to 7 percent in 1961. In the same year, between 6.5 million and 7.5 million American jobs depended on defense spending. Had these jobs been abolished and no others created, the United States would have had the same percentage of unemployed as in 1939—about 17 percent. As the war in Vietnam ended, unemployment was again on the rise.

No less important in explaining many international actions by the United States and its overall strategy, it is suggested, are business investments abroad. U.S. foreign investments amounted to 44.8 billion in 1959. Earnings from these investments are comparatively 60 percent higher than earnings from investments in the United States (13.8 percent versus 8.5 percent); moreover, most foreign investments are held by the powerful 100 top American corporations. It is common among followers of this line of analysis to explain specific U.S. foreign policy acts by reference to big-business interests abroad. For example, intervention in Guatemala in 1954 is explained by the interests of the United Fruit Company, whose property was nationalized by the Arbenz government; intervention in Cuba in 1961, by the interests of the sugar industry, whose property was confiscated by Castro;[31] and intervention in the Middle East to pressure Israel to make concessions to the Arabs, by the new power of the oil-producing countries.

Two groups other than owners and workers also have vested interests in the arms race. One is composed of generals and admirals and other senior officers. It is said that such men would, for obvious reasons, object to disarmament, which would leave them unemployed and, so to speak, disinvested. The second interest group is composed of thousands of scientists and technicians who are directly employed by the military services or who have received large military research grants. With the diminution of defense expenditures, many of them would lose income and prestige. These professionals are sometimes accused of supplying the antidisarmament business and military groups with ideologies to cover up their naked self-interest. The RAND Corporation, subsidized by the U.S. Air Force, is one of many examples. C. Wright Mills'

---

[31] Samuel Shapiro, *Invisible Latin America* (Boston: Beacon Press, 1963), pp. 84ff.

book *The Causes of World War III* stressed the role of the "military meta-physics" in what seemed to many of the left as a "drift toward nuclear disaster":

> Technologists and scientists readily develop new weapons; preachers and rabbis and priests bless the great endeavor; newsmen disseminate the official definitions of world reality, labeling for their publics the shifting line-up of friends and enemies; publicists elaborate the "reasons" for the coming war and the "necessity" for the causes of it. They do not set forth alternative policies; they do not po-litically oppose and politically debate the thrust toward war. . . . They have generally become the Swiss Guard of the power elite. . . .[32]

Alleviating pressures toward war What can be done to counter these pressures toward war? Most radical analysts doubt that anything constructive can be done within the framework of a capitalist society, in particular, that of the United States; they believe that changing international relations must begin with a revolutionary change at home. Only when public ownership of the means of production abolishes the profit motive will the true incentive for armaments production and the arms race disappear. Only when employment is controlled by the government, and not by the business cycle, will the socio-economic prerequisites of disarmament be met. To work for peace, radicals say, therefore requires working for a socialist revolution.[33]

Among sociologists, Marc Pilisuk has put forth a somewhat moderated version of the radical position that the entire structure of American society is ultimately responsible for the high level of international tension and the nation's frequent involvement in war in the mid-twentieth century. He asks "Is there a military-industrial complex which prevents peace?" and concludes:

> The answer is inextricably embedded in American institutions and mores. Our concept is not that American society contains a ruling military-industrial complex. It is more nearly that American society *is* a military-industrial complex. The complex can accommodate a wide range of factional interests, from those concerned with the production or use of a particular weapon to those enraptured with the mys-tique of optimal global strategies. It can accommodate those who rabidly desire to advance toward the brink and into limitless intensification of the arms race. It can even accommodate those who wish either to prevent war or to limit the destructiveness of war through the gradual achievement of arms control and dis-armament agreements. What it cannot accommodate is the type of radical de-parture needed to produce enduring peace.[34]

Liberal economists have proposed several schemes for alleviating pressures toward armament within the framework of a capitalist society. For instance, various peaceful functions are suggested for ex-armament industries; programs

---

[32] Mills, *op. cit.*, p. 85.

[33] This is, roughly, the position taken by publications such as *The Monthly Review* and *The Guardian*, both on the extreme left.

[34] Marc Pilisuk, *International Conflict and Social Policy* (Englewood Cliffs, N.J.: Prentice-Hall, 1972), p. 132.

are recommended to keep the economy running at full speed by spending the funds saved by cuts in the military budget. Increased investment in schools, medicine, and underdeveloped countries are the favorite recommendations. In addition, as economist Kenneth E. Boulding points out, disarmament may require as much investment as the arms race, if not more, because of the cost of inspection, monitors, international armies, and international organizations.[35] It is estimated that about 40,000 militarily trained personnel will be required to staff disarmament inspection programs alone. Programs have been suggested to retrain army officers for peaceful vocations while maintaining their salary, status, and security. For instance, military staff members might, in some circumstances, make good college teachers; and medical researchers developing nerve gas and bacteriological weapons could be used to fight cancer and mental illness. In short, disarmament, the liberal economists suggest, can be brought into line with the economic self-interests of members of the society.

An accurate assessment of the economic forces that serve to perpetuate the arms race is extremely difficult. It would require a book at least the size of this one to disentangle truth from half-truth and to analyze the various complications involved. It may be true, for instance, that officers have a vested interest in a military career. On the other hand, many officers are truly devoted to their country and might willingly expose themselves to the hardships of retraining for civil careers, to serve the country's best interests, if they were convinced that disarmament was possible. Moreover, the American government did make sharp reductions in its military budget after World War II and the Korean War, though economists warned that such reductions were likely to bring about recession or depression.

The details of various programs advocated to break down the anticipated resistance to disarmament by businessmen, officers, and scientists are sometimes naive, but they indicate that the situation is not beyond remedy. It is somewhat unlikely that SAC pilots would be welcome in the civilian airlines, which are already overstaffed as a consequence of the introduction of jets. It is also questionable whether army colonels would relish teaching college freshmen, even if the salary were satisfactory. Yet it is true that locating alternative employment and subsidizing retraining when necessary will ease the transition. If it is true that enforcing disarmament will, at least initially, require considerable personnel and considerable equipment for which ex-military assembly lines can be used (e.g., observation towers, satellites, and monitors), then the economic crisis caused by disarmament would be less severe. It seems safe to conclude that if we investigate the problems involved and plan ahead for them, the transition to a peacetime economy can be eased, the anxiety of vested-interest groups can be alleviated, and with it resistance to disarmament can be reduced, though not eliminated.

Limitations of space do not allow discussion here of the role occupied by

---

[35] Kenneth E. Boulding and Emile Benoit, *Disarmament and the Economy* (New York: Harper & Row, 1963).

military institutions in other societies. The role of the military in Soviet society and its relative weight compared to the Communist party is of paramount interest. The military in developing nations, often viewed as a major obstacle to development, is in fact sometimes the only effective force for development. Nor can we study here the effects of outside armed intervention on internal processes or social change. The number of countries in which such intervention has taken place, either on the side of the status quo or on that of social change, or both, is so large that it is almost impossible to study social change anywhere—in Tanzania, Tibet, Brazil, Vietnam, Cuba, or the Gabonese Republic—without studying the role of outside forces. This is another subject unto itself.

Societal Processes: The Mechanisms of Change

The strength of the societal bonds and the "slant" of the societal structure affect the level of violence. So does the flexibility of the processes that allows for adaptation to changes in the environment and in the relations among the members constituting a society. Each society has a set of procedures and processes whose function is to keep adjusting the societal bonds and structure to the changing relations among the group members. These are mainly political processes, such as lobbying, legislation, and presidential action. Those processes differ in two ways: (1) their efficacy in keeping the societal bonds and structure responsive to new mobilized demands, even if the adjustment entails far-reaching transformation of both, and (2) the extent to which they themselves—by the way they operate—encourage or discourage escalation of conflicts to a violent level. For instance, in some Latin American societies the armed forces act like interest groups and the government is adjusted to reflect the changing relations among the army, navy, and air force, and the social groups they are allied with. The procedures in such adjustments are the renegotiation of cabinet membership and the marshaling of divisions by each service. Often this is very peaceful; at one point, it is told, the president of a Latin American republic sent a telegram to each of six commanders who were marching on the capital to ask whom they favored, and the future composition of the government was reflected in their answers. But violent clashes among the armed services occasionally do erupt. The ballot box is a less violence-prone mechanism, aside from the fact that it is much more participatory.

But voting, petitions, and the other means of democratic adjustment may not suffice for the vast social changes contemporary society must respond to. To illustrate response-producing processes and their effects on the level of violence, the author reports briefly one of his own studies of the newest one—that of demonstrations.

Demonstration democracy: an example   *Webster's* defines a demonstration as "the act of making known or evident by visible or tangible means . . . a public display of group feeling." Demonstrations are thus public acts designed to express or call attention to a position. The specific features of demonstrations—from carrying placards to obstructionist acts—are intimately tied to the wish to make a position "visible or tangible," and this characteristic distinguishes demonstrations from more routine forms of expression, such as participation in a town meeting or party convention. In this sense demonstrations are still an extraordinary, not entirely institutionalized means of political expression.

Each generation of Americans evolves its own procedures to sustain and reinforce democracy. Our generation is characterized by the evolution of new means of mass communication, notably television; by an increased political mobilization of underprivileged groups; and by increasingly complex bureaucratic structures in government, education, religion, and other areas. Demonstrations are a particularly effective means of political expression, in an age of television, for underprivileged groups to advance their interests and, more generally, to prod stalemated bureaucracies into taking necessary actions. Indeed, demonstrations are becoming part of the daily routine of contemporary democracy and may be its most distinctive mark.

Today's American citizen has available a number of alternative methods for taking political action during the long periods between elections and for dealing with the numerous "private governments" not directly responsible to the electorate, such as universities, hospitals, and churches. In addition to writing letters to his representatives, submitting petitions, advertising in the press, and supporting organized pressure groups, a citizen may demonstrate to make known his views when expression through other means has brought no, or only inadequate, redress. In this sense, demonstrations are becoming for the citizen the avenue that strikes have become for the worker. Like strikes, demonstrations—especially in this early stage of their evolution—entail a danger: They may escalate into obstructionism or violence. For a democracy to function effectively, it is essential that the modes of political expression be both nonviolent and effective. That is, the inevitable differences of viewpoint, interest, and belief must be worked out peacefully, and the legitimate needs of all the member groups of the society must be taken into account. To suppress all demonstrations because they are a volatile means of expression would be both impossible under our present form of government and inconsistent with the basic tenets of the democratic system, for suppression would deprive the citizens—especially disadvantaged ones—of a political tool.

The number of participants in demonstrations seems to be growing and includes an increasingly large proportion of the members of society. In one month chosen at random, 216 demonstrations were reported in the United States, or about 7 per day. This figure is an understatement of the actual number. It is very likely that many cases went unreported. Anti-war demonstrations in the United States, for example, grew almost continuously in the late 1960s, from approximately 100,000 participants in the spring of 1965 to about 280,000 at their highest point.[36] Students produced at least 221 demon-

---

[36] Jerome H. Skolnick, *The Politics of Protest* (New York: Ballantine, 1969), p. 32.

strations in 101 colleges between January 1 and June 15, 1968, involving 38,911 participants, according to a study conducted by the National Student Association.

In more recent years students have demonstrated much less often, but other social groups have become more active. Demonstrations are often viewed as the political tool of only a few dissenting groups, such as students and blacks. Actually, the number and variety of social groups resorting to demonstrations, as least on occasion, seem to be increasing. This is not to suggest that all social groups demonstrate with equal frequency. Blacks and students do demonstrate much more often than other groups. But such professional groups as teachers and social workers, who rarely took part in demonstrations a decade ago, now do so fairly frequently. A very large number of the demonstrators are white, middle-class citizens, as well as "respectable" professionals. Thus in the fall of 1974 parent groups in West Virginia conducted school boycotts and held demonstrations to protest the use of school textbooks which they saw as reflecting values other than their own; parents in Boston used the same tactics to protest school desegregation. Even the staffs of law enforcement agencies have not refrained from demonstrating. In the summer of 1974, 500 policemen in Baltimore walked off their jobs for higher wages; and in July, 1975 prison guards, angry at having been laid off, picketed and blocked the entrance to the Rikers Island prison in New York City. In November, 1974 union workers, housewives, and apartment dwellers in New York City joined in organizing marches and rallies to protest inflation.

There are basically three kinds of demonstrations: (1) nonviolent and legal demonstrations, such as marches following the issuance of legal permits and carried out in accordance with their restrictions; (2) obstructionist demonstrations, which entail some act of obstruction—for example, blocking the traffic on a street, the entrance to a school, or the movement of construction equipment— and, as a rule, some degree of civil disobedience; and (3) violent demonstrations, which may include the throwing of missiles, fist fights, beatings, arson, and even shooting—clearly illegal acts.

Contrary to a widely held belief, the majority of demonstrations begin, are carried out, and end peacefully. Of 216 incidents examined, 134 (or 62%) were reported to be peaceful; 7 (3%) involved an act of obstruction; and 75 (35%) were violent. Of the 75 incidents that included violence, the reporting of 11 incidents was not clear enough on this point to allow the initiator of the violence to be specified. In 26 of the demonstrations the violence was initiated not by the demonstrators but by other groups—either those opposed to the demonstrators or their cause (in 17 incidents) or the police (in 9 cases). In only 38 cases—17.5 percent of the total number of demonstrations—did the violence appear to have been started by the demonstrators.

Wide segments of the public do not distinguish between peaceful demonstrations—which are a legal and constitutional means of political expression— and violent demonstrations or riots. And these segments of the public condemn demonstrations indiscriminately. For instance, 74 percent of the adults questioned in a poll in California expressed disapproval of the student demonstrations at Berkeley in 1964, although they were nonviolent up to that point. Asked explicitly about the right to engage in peaceful demonstrations "against the war in Vietnam," 40 percent of the people sampled in both December, 1966 and July, 1967 felt that the citizenry had no such right. Fifty-eight percent were prepared to "accept" such demonstrations "as long as they are peaceful," showing a majority of the public to be unaware that such demonstrations have the same legal status as writing a letter to a congressman or participating in a town meeting.

The situation is somewhat similar to the first appearances of organized, peaceful labor strikes at the beginning of the century. At first, not only the owners and managers of industrial plants but also broad segments of the public did not recognize the rights of workers to strike if their grievances were unheeded and to picket factories peacefully if such actions did not violate the rights of others (e.g., occupying the plant or physically preventing people from coming or going). Strikes are widely accepted now. According to a Harris poll of March 27, 1967, the majority (77 percent of those sampled) feels that the refusal to work is the ultimate and legitimate recourse for union members engaged in the process of collective bargaining. Gradually the public is likely to accept the legitimacy of peaceful demonstrations more completely.

It should be noted in this context that as more of the public learned to accept strikes, violent strikes became less frequent. Of course, other factors are in part responsible for the decrease in labor-management violence, the most important of which seems to be the increased readiness to respond to the issues raised by the strikers rather than responding merely to the act of striking. It is to be expected that reactions to peaceful demonstrations will undergo similar transformations both in the public mind and in the relevant institutions. Thus demonstrations, especially peaceful ones, are one major new way societal structures and bonds may be made more responsive or kept responsive.

The function of demonstrations is *not* to "cool it," to provide an inauthentic solution, but to make the needed changes that will result in a reduction of tension. If the poor are rebelling because they are unable to earn a living, because welfare payments have been cut, because their schools do not educate, and because their houses are falling apart, measures such as setting up television sets in public squares on hot nights and sending baseball heroes to tour the community do not constitute adaptive mechanisms. These measures may only postpone the explosion, which may well be more violent when it finally erupts. Negotiating with the neighborhood about the construction of a housing project, which will employ men from the community and provide opportunities for on-the-job training as well as an immediate rise in income and prestige, constitutes a much more meaningful and effective way of dealing with the tensions.

Signaling   Albert O. Hirschman's study of underdeveloped nations looks on the function of violence as similar to that of the red light that flashes on an automobile dashboard when something is wrong with the lubrication.[37] One way of conceptualizing the problem is to view the normal channels of "upward" communication (from the rank and file to the elite) as inadequate (e.g., there is no effective representative structure) or as having been interrupted (e.g., the elite closes off such channels as a free press or the right to hold public meetings). Communicative violence then serves as an *ab*normal channel. Alternatively, violence may in fact be the routine communication channel between the rank and file and the elite when the development of nonviolent channels has been seriously hindered or deteriorated.

In either case, because the resulting violence is meant to communicate grievances rather than to serve as a means for seizing political power, it is relatively small in scale and short-lived—as when farmers block a road to protest low prices or when, under feudal social structures, the peasants burned their lord's property to protest his failure to perform the duties the feudal relationship required of him in return for exacting rights and privileges from them. Violence under these circumstances has primarily symbolic significance; it is meant to trigger reform or redress of a grievance. Unlike some other forms of collective violence, it is not in and of itself transformative of structure.

Hirschman expects that such signaling violence will more often than not be effective, perhaps because it evokes the fear of massive violence if the grievances being signaled are ignored. Thus he points out that when violent protest took place in Chile in the 1950s over inflation, and in the United States in the 1930s over unemployment, these issues became subject to large-scale government policy intervention; during those same years poor health care, which was also a serious problem in both nations, was not protested and was largely ignored by government. Similarly, the looting of food stores in Brazil is said to have "reminded" government officials to pay greater heed to undoing the snarls that were slowing delivery of food to flooded areas; violence by squatters in Colombia allegedly accelerated land reform.

Aside from distinguishing those acts of violence whose function is limited to signaling dissatisfaction from those whose function is structure-changing or revolutionary, Hirschman notes that some acts of violence can be considered *direct*, albeit limited, efforts at problem solving. Thus the squatters in Colombia who actually took over pieces of land previously belonging to landlords not only achieved some success in persuading the elite to undertake the reforms they desired, but in part carried out the reforms themselves by their actions.

Finally, Hirschman holds, violence often serves to encourage change by peaceful means: As violence intensifies, the reformers are more likely to coalesce and work for effective policies, while the supporters of the status quo are more likely to heed them so as to avoid further violence. Thus, because of violence

---

[37] Albert O. Hirschman, *Journeys Toward Progress: Studies of Economic Policy-Making in Latin America* (Garden City, N.Y.: Anchor Books, 1965), pp. 302, 318, 335–336.

from refugee peasants, a development agency was created in northeastern Brazil in 1958. The administrative powers of this agency were increasingly strengthened because the threat of continued violence in this area was high. The agency claimed that only through heightened reform efforts could violence be averted. According to Hirschman, this sort of violence "is compatible with reform and frequently appears to be part and parcel of it," but it "is not the kind of decisive clash . . . which is usually associated with revolutionary violence."

Violence as a limited political tool Numerous social movements and political organizations—from labor unions to student groups, from civil rights organizations to the Ku Klux Klan—have faced the problem of deciding whether they should limit their political action to legitimate means or resort to various kinds and levels of violence (e.g., against property or people; occasionally or continuously; overtly or covertly). The issue is often debated in moral terms ("The end justifies the means"; "You have to crack eggs to make omelettes"; vs. "Violence defiles the goals of the movement"; "People should be treated as ends in themselves"). It is also discussed from the viewpoint of practicality ("You'll end up in jail"; "The country is not ripe for revolution"; "You'll alienate your liberal allies, public opinion, your potential followers").

William Gamson has put the question "What are the fruits of violence?" to an empirical test by drawing a sample of "challenging groups" from American history from 1800 to 1945 and evaluating their success in terms of their tactics.[38] A challenging group is defined as one that mobilizes its members to make claims on the government, and a successful group is one that wins acceptance and/or gains the desired advantages for its members.

In the period studied, 64 such groups were found. Of these, 53 were studied. Thirty-eight percent of the groups studied succeeded on both counts; 11 percent gained advantages but not acceptance; 9 percent gained acceptance but not advantages; 44 percent gained neither.

Gamson then compared the political instruments the groups used. The result:

> In the case of violence, it appears better to give than to receive if you want to succeed in American politics. The activist groups that fought back, or, in some cases, initiated violence, had a higher than average success rate; six of the eight won . . . advantages and five [violent challenging groups] were eventually accepted as well. . . . [In contrast, nonviolent groups] lost out completely. None of them met their goals, although one, the Dairyman's League, was coopted.[39]

Gamson points out that violence is particularly effective when the group's aim is not to replace the antagonists (i.e., revolutionary) but to coexist with them (i.e., reformist or reallocative). When revolutionary groups are dropped

---

[38] William A. Gamson, "The Meek Don't Make It," *Psychology Today*, July 1974, pp. 35–41, and *The Strategy of Social Protest* (New York: Dover, forthcoming) as well as *Power and Discontent* (Homewood, Ill.: Dorsey, 1968), an important book.

[39] Gamson, "The Meek Don't Make It," p. 37.

from the list under study, Gamson judges all users of violence to have been effective and all pacifists to have failed. The least effective strategy was to *talk* about violence and *act* pacifically—strategies followed by the Communist Labor party, the Revolutionary Workers League, and the German-American Bund. These groups, according to Gamson, soon found themselves "easy targets for repression." However, if violence was effective, more violence was not necessarily more effective. Thus "unruly strategies" such as boycotting and demonstrating were found to be as effective as outright use of force.

A somewhat different view of the fruits of violence was espoused by the U.S. Task Force on Historical and Comparative Perspectives, which was part of a Presidential commission studying the causes and prevention of violence. This task force was interested in the question of whether group violence, though illegal, is an effective tactic for either bringing about or preventing some significant change:[40]

> History provides no ready answer to this question. There have been a great many protest movements marked by violence which eventually achieved some of their aims. But whether offensive violence by the protesting group helped or hindered the subsequent achievement remains a matter of conjecture, as does the question of whether defensive violence by the threatened group hindered or helped the eventual change. In the history of the American labor movement, for example, violence persistently accompanied the struggle of workingmen to gain decent working conditions and recognition for their unions; both ends were eventually achieved, but there are differences of opinion whether pro-labor violence helped the cause or whether anti-labor violence hindered it. Labor leaders themselves doubted the effectiveness of violence, and no major labor organization in American history advocated violence as a policy. Typically, pro-labor violence was a response to the use of excessive force by militia or private police or strikebreakers. While violence proved to be a better short-run weapon for employers than for workers, the escalation of counterviolence it produced was a factor in the passage of the laws that eventually established the rights of labor.

The task force saw less of a question about the long-run effects of the use of violence:

> If the lessons of history are ambiguous on the short-term effectiveness of violence as a political tactic, they are clear on its long-term dangers. As we noted in our Statement on Campus Disorder, violence tends to feed on itself, with one power group imposing its will on another until repressive elements succeed in reestablishing order. The violent cycles of the French and Russian Revolutions and the decade resulting in the Third Reich are dark abysses of history to ponder. Violence tends to become a style, with many eager followers.

In other words, if you shoot, you must expect to be shot at.

[40] National Commission on the Causes and Prevention of Violence, Task Force Report on Historical and Comparative Perspectives (Washington, D.C.: Government Printing Office, 1969), pp. 5, 6.

September 6, 1973: Palestinian Fedayans, with French and Arab hostages taken from the Saudi Arabian embassy in Paris, board a Syrian plane bound for Algiers.

Terrorism   Extreme violence (slaughter of innocent civilians; assassination of political figures for political gains) has been used throughout human history, both against government and by governments; by the extreme left and extreme right and by anarchists; by members of one nationality or ethnic group against another (Arabs vs. Israelis) or against its own members (Irish); in the country-side and in the cities. Nevertheless, as Walter Laqueur points out in a masterful essay,[41] relatively little can be said sociologically about terrorism, precisely because it is so divergent in its origin, setting, and nature. It is certainly not always or even usually Marxist or leftist. Neither is it a simple indication of deprivation. For instance, guerrilla war broke out in Cuba despite the fact that Cubans were better off than most Latin Americans. It is not, by a long shot, always or even commonly successful; guerrilla movements that failed include post-World War II drives in Greece, Malaya, and the Philippines. One of the

[41] Walter Laqueur, "In Dubious Battle," *Times Literary Supplement*, August 1, 1975. For an earlier scholarly study, see Eugene V. Walter, *Terror and Resistance* (New York: Oxford, 1969).

few generalizations which hold is that terrorism "works" best against pluralistic societies and authoritarian governments but is not effective in totalitarian societies, where governments find it much easier to take massive repressive action. Indeed, Laqueur chides the counterinsurgency experts in democratic nations for advocating means, such as counterterrorist tactics, suited only to dictatorships. What a democracy is to do to effectively combat terrorism remains a largely unanswered question.

In contrast to Laqueur, Michael Waltzer sees the recent international wave of terrorism as *not* part of "terror-as-usual."[42] He points out that historically acts of terror tended to set off political persons (Tsarist officials, British ministers) from the rest of the civilian population, a kind of terrorist line to separate combatants from noncombatants. Recently this line has eroded and all members of the target group (Catholics or Protestants in Ireland; Israelis for some Palestinian groups) have become the subjects of violence. Despite this serious escalation in the scope of violence and in its boundless unethicality, the new terrorism thrives, Waltzer writes, because of the new permissiveness: "Statesmen rush about to make bargains with them; journalists construct elaborate apologies on their behalf." Thus Waltzer's conclusion is rather similar to that of Laqueur: pluralistic societies are the likely setting for terror and its lack of punishment.

Violence—clash at the societal entry points Drawing on detailed analyses of historical cases, Charles Tilly offers a theory of the conditions under which conflict intensifies, violence escalates, and revolution erupts.[43] Unlike most students of political conflict and collective violence, Tilly seeks a theoretical framework that will incorporate premodern forms of violence as well as the revolutions and rebellions of the era since the French Revolution. In particular, his aim is to uncover changes in the goals and organization of political violence and to relate these changes to the processes of modernization. For our present purposes, we may set aside most of Tilly's data and conceptual comments and focus on a few essential points.

As Tilly sees it, the principal actors in the drama of collective violence are not aggregates of dissatisfied individuals (as the relative-deprivation theory would appear to imply) but politically mobilized groups. Whereas in the premodern era the bases of mobilization were "communal" ties (i.e., status bonds such as kinship or locality), in the modern era mobilization is based primarily on "associational" bonds (i.e., the creation of associations such as labor unions or political organizations which act on behalf of persons united by common interests or shared normative commitments as opposed to nonrational affective bonds). The mobilized groups "lay claims" on the state to increase their share of whatever the society allots, from wealth to prestige to political power. Often

---

[42] Michael Waltzer, "The New Terrorists," *The New Republic,* August 30, 1975, pp. 12–14.

[43] See his most recent and complete work, Charles Tilly et al., *The Rebellious Century* (Cambridge, Mass.: Harvard University Press, 1975). See also his frequently cited article in Graham and Gurr, *op. cit.,* p. 4.

what the group seeks is membership in the "polity" that the government represents and is responsive to (e.g., the struggle at various historical periods in the United States of women, blacks, and others for the right to vote and the social recognition it entails). Or the group may seek to have an economic right recognized as legitimately theirs (e.g., the struggle of organized labor for legal recognition of the right to collective bargaining). Alternatively, the claim to legitimacy may center on the recognition of human worth and dignity of a group (e.g., "Black is beautiful"). In many instances, more than one type of claim is at issue.

Tilly is at great pains to separate his line of analysis from that of other researchers.[44] He sees his work as highly "structural," as dealing with macro-factors such as "states," "polities," and social groups and their power relations. He characterizes the work of James C. Davies and Ted Gurr as "social psychological" because these analysts tie the rise of violence to changes in the psychic state of individuals whose rebelliousness arises from alienation or from a sense of "relative deprivation" resulting from a discrepancy between the actual rate of allocation of increased assets and the expected rate. In contrast, Tilly sees violence as the result of a particular type of relationship between macroscopic entities (i.e., a claiming group whose claims are resisted as illegitimate by a government representing groups with established membership in the polity).

Tilly reserves his heaviest criticism for Samuel P. Huntington, whose perspective on political violence is in many ways close to his own.[45] Like Tilly, Huntington deals with collective actors and with the dynamic relationship between new, mobilizing groups seeking a place in the existing political community (a demand for "participation") and existing structures, communities, and governments, which must either accommodate the new members, employ violence to suppress their claims, or risk facing violence on the part of those who insist that their demands be met. The potential for political violence is viewed as greatest where the state or established members of the polity who feel their positions to be particularly threatened persist in regarding the group's claims as illegitimate, since once legitimacy is granted "normal" political processes—either already existing or newly established ones—can be utilized for negotiating the extent of the reallocation. Revolution is an extreme case in which the competing groups cannot concede legitimacy, cannot coexist within the same polity, and thus become locked in a struggle for control over the core allocating mechanism of the society, the apparatus of state. Often the success of one group in capturing and holding on to governmental power is bound up with a transformation of the societal structure.

Tilly's disagreement with Huntington centers on Huntington's assertion that rapid modernization—in particular, the urbanization this process entails—produces conditions particularly conducive to political violence. As Huntington

---

[44] Charles Tilly, "Does Modernization Breed Revolution?" *Comparative Politics* (April 1973), pp. 425–447; also Graham and Gurr, *op. cit.*, pp. 4–45.

[45] See Samuel P. Huntington, *Political Order in Changing Societies* (New Haven: Yale University Press, 1968).

sees it, the masses who flock from the country to the city in search of work during the early phases of modernization have been set free from the usual restraint on impulse imposed by culture and social structure—for example, the social control exerted by tradition, family loyalties, community approval and disapproval. Having few societal bonds of any type, this uprooted population is thus said to be especially volatile, prone to participation in violent crowd behavior via a process of sociological "spontaneous combustion." According to Tilly, however, the data on collective violence in the early industrial era in Europe contradict this proposition:

> The experience of France challenges the plausible presumption that rapid urbanization produces disruptions of social life that in turn generate protest. There is, if anything, a negative correlation over time and space between the pace of urban growth and the intensity of collective violence. The extreme example is the contrast between the 1840's with slow urban growth plus enormous violence and the decade after 1851 with very fast growth and extensive peace.[46]

Moreover, during much of the early industrial period rural collective violence was quite common, taking the form of tax rebellions, food riots, and movements against conscription. Tilly concedes, however, that urbanization was probably responsible for some of this rural protest—as when the development of a national grain market and abolition of traditional price restraints incited food riots, or when the shift of textiles and other industries from the country to the city provoked workers in the cottage industry to rebel against the loss of their livelihood.

Finally, Tilly points out that newcomers to the city rarely participated in incidents of urban collective violence:

> The initial fragmentation of the work force into small groups of diverse origins, the slow development of mutual awareness and confidence, the lack of organizational experience among the new workers and the obstacles thrown up by employers and governments all combined to make the development of the means and the will for collective action a faltering, time-consuming process. Collective violence did not begin in earnest until the new industrial workers began forming or joining associations—trade unions, mutual-aid societies, political clubs, conspiratorial groups—devoted to the collective pursuit of their interests.

Thus Tilly concludes that urbanization and industrialization produced, not a rise in the level of collective violence, but a change in its character. In contrast to premodern forms of collective violence, modern protest tends to be associationally rather than communally based; particular instances tend to involve more people; and the aims of the protest are generally more "forward looking" (i.e., modern groups tend to demand societal recognition of new and

---

[46] Charles Tilly, "Collective Violence in European Perspective," in Graham and Gurr, *op. cit.*, pp. 33–34.

more egalitarian rights for members of the group rather than to demand that their superiors honor traditional obligations toward "subjects").

VIOLENCE AND THE MEDIA

Does the display of violence on TV and in films, especially as a form of entertainment, encourage violent behavior? Or, on the contrary, does media violence provide a catharsis, a means of harmlessly releasing pent-up aggressions which might otherwise come out in street gang wars, rising crime statistics, vandalism, dangerous pranks, rioting, or other acts of violence? Or are the effects of violence in the media largely *neutral,* having little or no independent effects, the level of violence being determined chiefly by other factors?

Studies on the Role of Media Violence

These questions have been the subject of numerous studies by individual social scientists, by the National Commission on the Causes and Prevention of Violence (findings released in 1969), and by a special study group set up by the Department of Health, Education, and Welfare (findings released in 1972).[47] We shall trace here the course of one major research effort, that of the National Commission on Violence, in order to illustrate the problems, payoffs, and pitfalls of such research. The reader is forewarned to focus on the "trip"—the research process—because the destination is still unknown; that is, the conclusion regarding the role of media in generating mass violence is still unclear and in dispute.

The Commission on the Causes and Prevention of Violence stated its views on the role of the media in promoting violence as follows:

1. The weight of social science stands in opposition to the conclusion that mass media portrayals of violence have no effect upon individuals, groups, and society.
2. To the extent that mass media portrayals of violence have effects upon individuals, groups, and society, it is a variety that most persons would deem costly and harmful to individuals and society.
3. The direction of effects of mass media portrayals of violence is to extend the behavioral and attitudinal boundaries of acceptable violence beyond legal and social norms currently espoused by a majority of Americans.[48]

One must read these sentences carefully. The first statement is worded awkwardly because, as we shall see, the data do not permit the flat statement

---

[47] David L. Lange et al., *Mass Media and Violence,* A Report to the National Commission on the Causes and Prevention of Violence, Vol. 11 (Washington, D.C.: Government Printing Office, November 1969). For an additional discussion of the 1972 survey see Monica D. Blumenthal, "Predicting Attitudes toward Violence," Science, Vol. 176 (June 23, 1972), pp. 1296–1303.

[48] Lange et al., *op. cit.,* p. 375.

that exposure to violence in the media significantly encourages violence in society. The second statement serves to shore up the first one but is basically hypothetical ("To the extent . . ."). The third statement was based, not on what effects researchers found TV to actually have on violence, but on public opinion surveys of how Americans perceived its effects or likely effects as well as their self-reported data on feelings about violence, experience with it, and TV watching habits. The commission reported, for example, that according to one survey the majority of adult Americans agreed with the conclusions just summarized. For example, 75 percent felt it was "likely" or "possible" that TV "plays a part in making America a violent society"; 86 percent agreed that TV violence triggers violent acts from people who are "unstable"; and 60 percent felt that it makes people "insensitive to real acts of violence." However, 62 percent subscribed to the view that TV violence "provides entertainment and relaxation without harmful or bad effects." The commission itself then added that such public opinion surveys lend no scientific support to conclusions concerning the actual effects of TV violence.

The commission based its views on the following data. First, researchers monitoring TV programs found numerous episodes involving violence, and in many of these violence was central to the plot. Of all the programs studied in 1967 and 1968, 86 percent and 80 percent respectively contained violence. Next, the commission polled a national sample of 1,176 adults and 496 teenagers concerning their views on violence, their involvement with violence, and their media habits and preferences. With respect to norms relating to violence, the study found that adult Americans disapproved of *severe* acts of violence in all relationships studied—with two exceptions: policemen dealing with male adults and judges dealing with citizens. Thus 93 percent approved of parents spanking a healthy child at least a year old (classified as nonsevere violence), but only 8 percent approved of parental beatings (classified as severe violence). Twenty-two percent would let a wife slap her husband's face, but only 4 percent would defend her right to shoot him under any circumstances. Fifty-three percent upheld a judge's authority to pronounce a sentence of death, and 71 pecent said circumstances could make it legitimate for a cop to shoot a male adult. The responses of teenagers were very similar to those of the adults just cited.

The next step was to uncover respondents' experiences with violence: as assailants, victims, or observers. While the researchers themselves alert us to the dangers of placing much stock in self-reported data, the findings were as follows: The majority of Americans reported no personal experience with violence. Those who had experienced violence in one role had often experienced it in the other two as well; in other words, they alternated among the roles of violent actor, victim of violence, and bystander to a violent incident. Those subgroups most often involved in violence were disproportionately young adult males (aged 18 to 35), blacks, and those with less than a college education.

Now to the connecting link: The three subgroups that reported the greatest

ture of what is here called "aggression." As I have already suggested, I think that what the experiments call "aggression" is so distant from violence that the one has virtually no bearing on the other. . . .[52]

Otto Larsen, a sociologist who specializes in the study of violence, started from the same point, criticism of the studies, but reached a rather different conclusion:

. . . Survey research produces no evidence that mass media-depicted violence is a prime mover in producing violence or aggressive behavior, and laboratory studies merely suggest short-range possibilities along this line. As a result, media spokesmen are prone to conclude that their instruments by portraying models of violence, do not create violent action, but merely tend to reinforce those behavioral and attitude tendencies born of family, peer, and other influences in the community. . . .

It is my contention that the conception of the role of mass media with respect to violence as implied both in the remarks of concerned citizens and defensive communicators, as well as in the research response of social scientists, has been much too narrow. It has been too narrow by its focus on the media as a source of models for direct imitative behavior by individuals. We must enlarge our concern to take in the possible contributions of the media to the arena of social norms, where all acts, including acts of violence, ultimately mature and take hold in society. What could the mass media portrayal of violence possibly do?

Implicit in most of the research thus far is the assumption that the major effect is to induce persons to engage in violent acts pretty much in the form that they see depicted in the mass media. But are there other messages in the plethora of beatings, knifings and shootings that daily may be seen on various scenes? I believe that there are. And those messages could shape the norms, both the formal and the informal rules, which set the conditions for the appropriate use of violence in society.[53]

Leo Bogart, of the American Newspaper Publishers Association, further questioned the commission's conclusions about the role of TV:

It seems to me that in the discussion of media violence a disproportionate amount of attention has been given to the matter of direct imitation, in which the child learns specific aggressive techniques which he sees portrayed by media personalities, or learns the broader lesson that aggressive behavior represents a widely accepted form of social expression. The learning experience reflected in much of the experimental evidence represents a specific response to a specific message: I see a man shoot; I reach for a gun myself. But there is another kind of learning which may be much more important and which has had, I think, less of a place in the discussion, and that is whether the child is learning the lesson that the world is a wicked and hostile place in which one must aggressively protect oneself. This kind of learning effect is much harder to measure either in the

[52] Baker and Ball, *op. cit.*, pp. 17–18.
[53] *Ibid.*, p. 66.

laboratory or in the field, because it arises not out of exposure to any one com-munication—any one scene in the TV or movies or story in the newspaper, how-ever provocative it might be of anger or anxiety—but out of cumulative exposure to many, many communications, each of which may leave only the most modest and unmeasurable residual trace.

The really great impact of media violence on our culture may arise mainly from this diffuse raising of the general public level of anxiety, rather than from individual acts of behavior in response to individual media episodes or instances. This broader range of effects is at the very least difficult, and perhaps even im-possible, to measure.

Our areas of ignorance are in an understanding of the comparative orders of mag-nitude. What proportion of the emotional charge produced by a motion picture in a psychological laboratory is reproduced under normal conditions, in the cinema and on television? How do the tension-producing effects of fictionalized violence experienced through the mass media compare with the tensions aroused by re-ports of actual news events, or with the frustrations and irritations which peo-ple experience personally in the daily strain of coping with life in our crowded society?

The answers to these rhetorical questions are not independent of each other. The fantasy of fictional violence may be a solace and a release for those who have no direct means of coping with the demands of the boss or with the threat of racial strife or nuclear war. On the other hand, drama, even in the attenuated form it takes within the popular culture, is designed to produce an emotional effect, and dramatic violence may, therefore, arouse greater levels of tension than real by episodically presented scenes of war, rioting or disaster as they occur in the news.[54]

In the years since this 1969 study was made public the demand for a clearer answer to the question of the media's role in stimulating violent conduct or approval of such conduct has intensified. Another major study was completed in 1972, but it too had inconclusive findings quite similar to those of previous studies. The investigators noted:

It is sometimes asked if the fact that children watch a steady fare of violent ma-terial on television many hours a day from early childhood through adolescence causes our society to be more violent. Presumably the answer is, to some de-gree, "yes," but we consider the question misleading. We know that children imitate and learn from everything they see—parents, fellow children, schools, the media; it would be extraordinary, indeed, if they did not imitate and learn from what they see on television. We have some limited data that conform to our pre-sumption. We have noted in the studies at hand a modest association between viewing of violence and aggression among at least some children, and we have noted some data which are consonant with the interpretation that violence view-ing produces the aggression; this evidence is not conclusive, however, and some of the data are also consonant with other interpretations.

Yet, as we have said, the real issue is once again quantitative: how much

---

[54] *Ibid.,* p. 104.

contribution to the violence of our society is made by extensive violent television viewing by our youth? The evidence (or more accurately, the difficulty of finding evidence) suggests that the effect is small compared with many other possible causes, such as parental attitudes or knowledge of and experience with the real violence of our society. . . .

All of the studies inquired into the relationship between exposure to television violence and aggressive tendencies. Most of the relationships observed were positive, but most were also of low magnitude, ranging from null relationships to correlation coefficients of about .20. A few of the observed correlation coefficients, however, reached .30 or just above.[55]

The 1972 study again fueled rather than dampened the controversy. Among its participants were several representatives of the television industry (which on the whole is interested in playing down both the role of violence in TV and its possible effects); notably absent were several leading social scientists specializing in the study of violence. In order to document and publicize the high levels of TV violence, the investigators decided to monitor programs and create an index. The evidence of the index and public attention to it would then hopefully prod the television industry to impose some voluntary self-restraint. Setting up the profile, however, posed serious technical difficulties and smacked of government censorship to some; consequently, no results have been issued to date. Other evidence suggests that until 1974 TV violence stayed at approximately the same level; since then some reduction is believed to have been achieved, not because of government action but largely because other kinds of programs (e.g., family comedies, game shows) got higher audience ratings.

THE TECHNOLOGY OF VIOLENCE: CAUSE OR SYMPTOM?

Arms and National Insecurity

Human nature permits violence, and as we have seen some theories of collective violence lay primary stress on its psychological sources. One theory holds aggression is rooted in man's animal nature, and motivations such as greed, envy, and frustration serve to unleash it. Other theories see collective violence as "politics by other means," emphasizing its role as a means of communicating grievances or reallocating societal assets. The focus is on the relationship of groups to the structure of power and the eruption of violence as associated with shifts or attempted shifts in this alignment. Still other theories underscore the relation of collective violence to economic processes, either as a response to changes in the economic structure of society—that is, as rising to especially high levels with industrialization and urbanization—or, alternatively,

---

[55] *Television and Growing Up: The Impact of Televised Violence,* Report to the Surgeon General, Public Health Service (Washington, D.C.: Government Printing Office, 1972), pp. 7, 13.

as an ongoing fuel required to maintain the economic growth of advanced industrial societies. Radical theoreticians of war emphasize the profits that are to be made from supplying war materials and from engaging in "peacetime" international competition over ever bigger and more devastating weapons. Others, however, look at the proliferation of arms and see behind it not self-serving "merchants of death" but a Frankenstein's monster of uncontrolled technological development that has gone from being humankind's servant to becoming its master.

Some people see the main source of danger in the very existence of arms, especially the new thermonuclear weapons. In this view, man can regain control of his fate by reasserting his control over the development of weapons. Arms races follow their own "logic." "The increase of armaments that is intended in each nation to produce consciousness of strength and a sense of security does not produce these effects. On the contrary, it produces a consciousness of the strength of other nations and a sense of fear," wrote the British foreign secretary Sir Edward Grey at the outbreak of World War I.[56] Every nation that arms for its own security is simultaneously the "other nation." Arming for security often leads to arming for defense by the "other nation." The first nation rarely regards the arms buildup by the other nation as defensive; rather it sees in the other's new arms evidence of its hostile intent. Often the first nation then sees no alternative but a new rush of armaments—for security. Hence one major approach to the prevention of war is to reduce armaments. If the nuclear genie were somehow to be returned to the bottle, the main new

[56] Quoted in Lewis Richardson, *Arms and Insecurity* (Pittsburgh: Boxwood, 1960), p. 15. For a good review article of various approaches to the "symptoms and disease" question, see Philip Green, "Alternatives to Overkill: Dream and Reality," *Bulletin of the Atomic Scientists,* November 1963, pp. 23–27.

danger of war would be erased. If military arms could be entirely eliminated, it is argued, there would be no war.

An opposing view suggests that arms are chiefly the symptoms of deep-seated conflicts. If there were no hostile motivations, people would not produce arms; even if there were triggers, they would not pull them. The people of Canada do not fear American nuclear bombardment. "War starts in the minds of men," says the charter of UNESCO. Curbing arms, it is said, is like treating only the symptoms of disease, without identifying and treating the illness. The treatment is unlikely to be successful, and even if it is successful other symptoms will soon break out elsewhere. Disarmament, if ever achieved, will be followed not by peace, but by rearmament. What is needed is a treatment for the underlying conflicts of ideology and interest, the clash of powers.

A third position seems more tenable. This one conceives of arms as both a symptom and a contributory cause that must be treated. The malaise that results in the arms race and war is a deep one; basically, it expresses people's willingness to treat others as objects rather than as ends in themselves, to the point of turning them into perishable utensils. The complete cure of this malaise requires providing the social foundations for a world community, since only members of a community treat each other as goals as well as means. If such a global community can be built at all, it will surely be a long process; meanwhile, mankind might destroy itself. The world society in the nuclear age is like a patient running a high fever: Until we determine and treat the sources of this fever, some measures must be taken to reduce the fever itself if the patient is to survive. But obviously the treatment of the symptoms must be accompanied and followed by treatment of the disease itself.

Furthermore, while the main causes of war seem to lie outside the propelling force and spell of armaments, the pressures of the military establishment are more than a symptom; they are a contributory cause. The military services, as a rule, demand larger defense budgets, not their curtailment;[57] the military's power, prestige, and—to a degree—income are affected by the size of these budgets. Most industries set up or extended to serve the military can turn elsewhere for their business, but the shift involves, at the least, the costs and pains of transition. Congressmen are known to lobby against closing military bases in their districts, and since each district has a congressman—and many at least one military installation—it is hard to sustain a broad reduction of arms without evoking some political resistance. This holds true not simply for missile sites or naval yards. The production of nuclear warheads in the United States was continued beyond the point of need, as estimated by most military experts, in part because congressmen whose states had employment problems feared deeper unemployment.[58] Added to these extrinsic interests in the production of arms are the intrinsic pressures to expand the

---

[57] This holds for the Soviet Union as well. See, for instance, Colonel S. Kozlov, "Armed Forces Communist," *Survival* (July–August 1961), p. 160.

[58] James Reston, *The New York Times*, December 18, 1963, p. 40.

military system continually, for building one component generates a call for others. Bombers are of little use without runways. Runways are of little value if they are not protected from bombardment. The commanders of the bomber fleets have to be sheltered. Thus armed systems tend to produce both extrinsic and intrinsic pressures for their expansion. When a point is reached where the original reason for building up armaments might have declined or disappeared, special efforts are still required if arms are to be reduced. Simply treating the original causes will not suffice.

Finally, armaments contribute to the potential of war through psychological consequences. Arms buildups express and magnify hostilities; arms reductions tend to indicate efforts to move toward an accommodation. Russia's abrupt resumption of the testing of thermonuclear bombs in 1961, after a three-year moratorium, was taken by the United States as a hostile and aggressive act. The 1963 Soviet-American agreement on partial cessation of thermonuclear tests, though of limited disarmament value, was hailed as heralding a new period in East-West relations. The 1974 Soviet-American agreements to limit strategic nuclear arms, known as the SALT agreements, although tentative, were lauded as "fundamentally reshaping American-Soviet relations on the basis of peaceful coexistence and equal security."[59] In other words, arms reductions can be used to create an atmosphere in which the "treatment" of the deeper causes of war can be better achieved, in much the way that reducing the fever of the patient enables him to survive long enough for antibiotics to take effect.

Gun Control

A surprisingly similar issue exists in domestic politics. On the one hand, there are those who hold that the prevalence of guns, pistols, and other arms—there are an estimated 100 million in the nation—is a major reason that the United States has a higher rate of homicides, suicides, and fatal firearms accidents than most other industrialized countries. There were 10,340 murders by hand guns in the United States in 1973, nearly twice as many as in 1967. Also in 1973, 279,169 gun-related crimes were committed—a rate of one crime every two minutes.[60] In England, with a population of about 50 million, there were only 35 homicides by firearms in 1971. In the United States, with a population of roughly 207 million in that year, the number was 12,243! Japan, with 107 million people, had 28 murders by handguns in 1972 (and a total of 1,927 murders). On the other hand, there are those who hold that arms are only a symptom, that individuals intent on murder or suicide will simply adopt other means if guns are not available. Most specialists disinterested in the area are in the first category. The National Rifle Association, gun collectors, sportsmen,

[59] Joint Soviet-American Communiqué, *The New York Times,* November 25, 1974, p. 14.
[60] "Big New Drive for Gun Controls," *U.S. News and World Report,* February 10, 1975, p. 25.

and gun manufacturers tend to be in the second group. Illustrating his view that there is no relationship between the availability of firearms and the occurrence of homicides, the NRA's president told a visiting reporter that "there are twenty weapons in this office that I could use to kill you, and you won't find a single gun in the room. This dictating machine. The telephone. That picture frame—I could kill you with any of them if I wanted to badly enough."[61]

Much of the evidence suggests that effective domestic disarmament would save thousands of lives. A comparison of homicides committed by the use of guns in states with strong gun laws and those with weak ones supports the point. There are weak laws in Mississippi, Texas, and Florida; in these states guns were used, respectively, in 71, 69, and 66 percent of all murders during the four years ending in 1965. In three states with strong laws—New Jersey, Massachusetts, and New York—the comparable rates were 38, 35, and 32 percent. The same point holds in cross-national comparisons. Firearms control is strict in other nations. Britain requires a certificate from local police before a long gun can be purchased. There, guns account for 10 percent of all homicides, compared to 60 percent in the United States. France requires police permits for handguns and military rifle purchases; Canada requires registration of all handguns; in Sweden a need must be proved before gun ownership is allowed. In these nations homicide with handguns or long guns seldom occurs as against the high rates in the United States. As a very high proportion of homicides in the United States involves guns, their elimination would sharply reduce the total homicide rate. Much of the killing is done "in hot blood." Of the 13,650 homicides committed in 1968 in the United States, roughly 65 percent were relatives and acquaintances.

The National Commission on the Causes and Prevention of Violence concluded on the basis of its studies that homicide and assault, unlike robbery, "usually occur between relatives, friends, or acquaintances (about two-thirds to three-fourths of the cases in which the relationship is known). They occur in the home or other indoor locations about 50–60 percent of the time."[62] Were weapons not so readily available, people would have more chance to calm down. When a knife is used, studies show that in four out of five instances the wound is not fatal.

Domestic disarmament is blocked in the United States by the gun lobby, which is one of the most powerful, well-organized, and highly mobilized political pressure groups in the nation. The gun lobby appeals to the sentiments and values of millions of Americans who truly believe that if private citizens are disarmed, the nation will be left defenseless against foreign invaders; that the Constitution guarantees their right to bear arms; that guns in the home are the ultimate defense of life, property, and freedom; and that guns in the hands of law-abiding citizens such as themselves are harmless. A rather

---

[61] *The New York Times,* June 8, 1968.

[62] National Commission on the Causes and Prevention of Violence, Statement on Violent Crime, Homicide, Assault, Rape, Robbery, Milton S. Eisenhower (ed.) (Washington, D.C.: Government Printing Office, 1969), p. 5.

moderate statement by Congressman Robert L. F. Sikes of Florida, who opposes gun control, reads: "Firearms are used by American citizens to protect their lives, families and property. The need to possess them for self-defense today is as great if not greater than in earlier periods of our nation's history."[63] More expressive are two bumper stickers which read: "Register criminals, not guns," and "I will give up my gun when they peel my cold, dead fingers from around it." Despite the prevalence of such sentiments, the vast majority of Americans favor some form of gun control. In November, 1974, for example, a Gallup poll found that 71 percent of Americans surveyed would vote for gun registration if such a proposition were to appear on the ballot in the forthcoming election. A July, 1975 Gallup poll found that 44 percent of American households had at least one gun (either short guns or rifles or handguns). The majority of both nonowners (76%) and owners (55%) favored gun registration. For the past 40 years, in fact, Gallup polls have found high support for gun registration and more stringent forms of gun control. The opposed minority is, however, much more adamant and activist than the supportive majority, as those members of Congress to come out in favor of gun control soon discovered. The sharp contrast in mobilized strength on opposing sides of the issue becomes clear when one compares the membership size of the major pro- and anti-gun-control organizations. In 1968, when several assassinations of public figures had brought the percentage of Gallup poll respondents favoring gun registration to 85 percent, the National Rifle Association, the most powerful anti-gun-control group, had 900,000 members, while the chief organization on the pro side of the gun-control issue, the Council for a Responsible Firearms Policy, had only about 75. As a consequence, the various gun-control measures which have been enacted or are being seriously considered will not disarm the nation and only place a few restrictions on actual availability of firearms. Thus, for instance, suggestions to reduce the number of gun dealers from 156,000 to 40,000 though far from being implemented, could not significantly reduce Americans' firepower. Similarly, the 1974 drive of the Baltimore police, whose offer to pay $50 for each gun turned in netted 13,000 guns within six weeks, did reduce shooting for a while; but the effect can hardly be expected to last as long as guns are freely available in and around Baltimore, and often for less than $50. How ineffectual existing laws are is illustrated by the report that in New York City, believed to have the "strictest" gun-control laws in the United States, only 28,000 of the city's estimated 1.3 million handguns are registered.[64]

The enormous costs of major societal reforms have encouraged social planners to look for technological shortcuts or "fixes"—that is, quick, low-cost, but effective procedures for attaining the desired reforms through nonsocial and nonpsychic means. Examples of such "fixes" include the administration of drugs that terminate the desire for heroin, alcohol, or cigarettes and the use

[63] *The New York Times,* April 8, 1975, p. 16.
[64] "Big New Drive for Gun Controls," p. 25.

of teaching machines to promote learning. In light of these applications, the question arises: Can violent crime also be treated in this way?

The answer depends in part on a more precise formulation of the question. If "treated" is taken to mean "eliminated," the answer is definitely negative. However, the answer is quite likely to be affirmative if the question is reformulated to ask: Can violent crime be reduced very significantly, say by more than one-half? The level of violent crime depends on a complex interaction among personal and societal pressures and on the tools that are available. Curbing the available instruments will reduce the fatalities caused by criminals, even if the motivational and the structured predispositions to engage in crime will remain untouched by these efforts.

SUMMARY

1 Violence is a common social problem. Like other social problems, its scope is in part a matter of number of incidents and in part a matter of public concern with the incidents; concern may rise or fall independent of changes in incidents. There was much collective violence in America in the 1960s. The 1970s have been more peaceful, though personal violence is rising, and one form of collective violence, centering on schools, is also rising.

2 The focus of this chapter is on physical violence, not other forms of coercion or aggression.

3 Physical violence is an area full of normative suppositions. Some researchers focus on the role of establishments in fostering conditions that lead to violence or in using violence to suppress "the people"; others see violence as generated by agitators who dupe people into incoherent rebellion. The role of social science is to obtain a more objective view of violence.

4 One orientation of sociologists is toward quantitative analysis of certain forms of violence. Several studies conclude that wars kill more people than murder does; wars have remained "stable" as a social phenomenon for 150 years, though in recent years large wars have been more frequent; there is no change in the frequency, magnitude, severity, or intensity of wars; and major powers of the day are more war-prone than other countries.

5 One theory of collective violence is that violence is the continuation of normal societal processes by "other" means. Thus it is necessary to understand the forces that cause strains and conflicts within a society in order to account for the level of violence and the ways it is dealt with. Three sociological concepts are useful in exploring the relationship between the structure and processes of society and its level of violence. These are *societal bonds*, which indicate the degree of social integration and are seen in shared values, necessary economic exchanges, and the ability of a central authority to speak for the unit; *societal structures*, which are the patterns of relationships among social groups; and *societal processes*, which are the mechanisms through which the bonds and structures are maintained and changed. Societal processes may be responsive to members, or they may allow discrepancies between the desires of members and the provisions of society to grow. The greater the discrepancy, the greater the violence potential.

6   Social bonds are weakest *among* nations. But there are ways of reducing conflicts at this level that are part of the notion of *system building. Encapsulation*
is the method whereby conflicts are modified and come to be limited by rules.
This can take place in a variety of ways: *Increased communication* can lead to
shared perspectives and understanding, though if deep cleavages exist, more
communication may bring them to the fore and escalate conflict. *Power constellations* may develop, bringing about a balance of power. *Consensus formation* can create intermediary groups with shared ideologies within the international community. And the development of *international rules and enforcement
agencies* can help to preserve peace.

7   Within social systems there are various asset distributions (economic, educational, prestige, power). Unequal distribution and a rigid structure unamenable
to demands for change set the stage for escalation of violence.

8   According to the concept of *relative deprivation,* it is not usually those with the
least who rebel, but rather those whose situation has improved somewhat and
who then fear that they will slip back into their old status or that the rate of
improvement is not keeping pace with their expectations. Davies shows in his
history of black emancipation in the United States that a pattern of gratified
expectations which are subsequently frustrated is a prime trigger for violence.
Here subjective perception is as important as objective forces within society. Gurr
shows that a perceived discrepancy between needs and opportunities to satisfy
these needs is a major cause of strife.

9   Both Mills and Eisenhower see war as resulting from economic and power relations *within* the warring nations. The *military-industrial complex* promotes
arms buildups as manufacturers profit from weapons production, scientists and
technicians extend their research, and military personnel seek to keep their
positions. Thus disarmament is politically hard to achieve, and it appears that
the whole economy picks up in such situations, with full employment and a
rising stock market. Radicals say the framework of capitalism must change, while
liberals argue that disarmament itself would be economically sound.

10   *Political processes* function to adjust social bonds and structure to the changing
relations among group members. Such processes include lobbying, legislation,
and presidential action. They vary in the degree to which they keep the bonds
and structures responsive to new demands and the extent to which they themselves encourage or discourage the escalation of conflict to violent levels. An
illustration is the use of demonstrations—public acts to express or call attention to a position. Contrary to public opinion, the majority of demonstrations
begin and end peacefully. They are increasingly used by a variety of social
groups but are still not viewed by most Americans as a "right" within the
political process. As with strikes, their legitimacy has to be proved. They attempt to effect needed change, whereas violent forms of protest, such as looting and destroying property, are often more symbolic. According to Hirschman,
violence may either signal the fact that communication channels are blocked or
serve in itself as the normal manner of communication. Violence is rarely an
attempt to seize power and transform society; rather, it is usually meant to trigger reform, which it does by evoking fear and prompting others to act.

11   The success of violence in bringing about reform is debatable. Gamson's study
of challenging groups in American history shows that violent groups attain their

goals; the *Violence in America* report, however, notes the escalation of counter-violence.

12 *Terrorism* is a new form of violence in which, Walter says, everyone is a "combatant." Lacquer says situational analyses are necessary, but terror seems to work best in pluralist, authoritarian societies, not in totalitarian ones, where massive repressive action would be taken.

13 Tilly stresses that participants in collective violence are politically mobilized groups trying to force claims against an established government; they are not just collections of dissatisfied people (as the relative-deprivation theory would have). Huntington says the potential for violence is greatest when claims are seen as "illegitimate," for if they were legitimate the "normal" political processes could be used to deal with them. In his view, the most volatile groups are the masses who move to the cities in the early phases of modernization, as they are free of many normal constraints. Tilly criticizes this position and says that associations are necessary before activity can take place.

14 There has been much research on the role of the media regarding violence, but the results are inconclusive. It seems as though those most often involved in violence are disproportionately young adult males, blacks, and those with less than a college education. These groups express the greatest degree of approval of violent conduct and also a taste for TV programs featuring violence. But statistical correlations do not show causal links, so it is still unclear whether TV incites a person to violence or whether being prone to violent behavior leads a person to prefer violent TV shows. The controversy continues.

15 The same kind of debate surrounds the technology of violence—the question of whether existing armaments promote not security but fear, which results in further arms buildups and war. Some say that if military arms were eliminated there would be no war. Others say that the conflicts are much deeper, and that arms are merely the symbol. Probably a combination of both views is most tenable. The social malaise reveals a willingness to treat people as objects, as expendable, rather than as ends in themselves. A global community could solve such a problem, for only in a community do members treat each other as goals as well as means.

16 There is a tendency to view social reforms as technological "fixes." That is, by curbing the available instruments of violent crime, society can reduce the number of fatalities. As with armaments, the initial effect may be so, but the motivational and structural predispositions to violent crime will remain.

RECOMMENDED READING

Some general discussion on the nature of violence can be found in Ernst Nolte, *Three Faces of Fascism* (1966), which examines the masculine view of violence. Georges Sorel attributes mystic rejuvenating power to mass violence in *Reflections on Violence* (1915). Franz Fanon sees in violence a personal therapeutic potential in *Wretched of the Earth* (1965).

James F. Short and Marvin W. Wolfgang have a useful anthology, *Collective Violence* (1972), and for a specifically American focus, see Hugh Davis Graham and Ted Robert Gurr (eds.), *Violence in America* (1969).

For studies on the frequency and extent of war, see Lewis Richardson, *Statistics of Deadly Quarrels* (1960); Quincy Wright, *A Study of War* (1965); J. David Singer and Melvin Small, *The Wages of War, 1816–1965* (1972); Michael Stohl, "War and Domestic Political Violence: The Case of the United States, 1890–1970," *Journal of Conflict Revolution*, Vol. 19, No. 3 (September 1975), pp. 379–415.

The relative-deprivation theory is examined in Ted Robert Gurr, *The Conditions of Civil Violence* (1967) and *Why Men Rebel* (1970). See also the article by James C. Davies in the *Violence in America*.

On terrorism, see Eugene V. Walter, *Terror and Resistance* (1969); a masterful article by Walter Lacquer, "In Dubious Battle," *Times Literary Supplement*, August 1, 1975. For an analysis of the new mode of terrorism, see Michael Walter, "The New Terrorists," *New Republic*, August 30, 1975.

Historical perspectives are provided by Charles Tilly et al., *The Rebellious Century* (1975); Tilly's article in the *Violence in America* anthology; and his article "Does Modernization Breed Revolution?" in *Comparative Politics*, April 1973. He does battle with the theory espoused by Samuel Huntington in *Political Order in Changing Societies* (1968).

For discussions of violence and the communications media, see David L. Lange, Robert K. Baker, and Sandra J. Ball, *Mass Media and Violence*, A Report to the National Commission on the Causes and Prevention of Violence, Vol. 11 (1969); Robert K. Baker and Sandra J. Ball, *Violence and the Media*, Vol. 9A of the same report (1969); and *Television and Growing Up: The Impact of Televised Violence*, Report to the Surgeon General, U.S. Public Health Service (1972).

On international armaments and violence, see Lewis Richardson, *Arms and Insecurity* (1960); John Burton, *Peace Theory* (1962); Herbert Kelman (ed.), *International Behavior* (1965); Evan Luard, *Peace and Opinion* (1962); and Walter Millis, *An End to Arms* (1965). For a discussion of the military-industrial complex and its push toward arms buildups, see C. Wright Mills, *The Causes of World War III* (1958); Dwight D. Eisenhower, "Farewell Address," January 16, 1971; Marc Pilisuk, *International Conflict and Social Policy* (1972); and Kenneth Boulding and Emile Benoit, *Disarmament and the Economy* (1969). For a good review article of various approaches to the "symptoms and disease" question, see Philip Green, "Alternatives to Overkill: Dream and Reality," in *Bulletin of the Atomic Scientists* (November 1963).

Finally, analysis of gun control, crime, and violence in the United States can be found in *Uniform Crime Reports for the United States*, U.S. Department of Justice (1973); various articles in the *Violence in America* anthology; *The Challenge of Crime in a Free Society*, U.S. Government Printing Office (1967); Report of the National Advisory Commission on Civil Disorders (1968); and the National Commission on the Causes and Prevention of Violence, Task Force Report on Historical and Comparative Perspectives (1969).

Epilogue **The Future
and
Social
Problems**

ROBERT NISBET

I t is almost impossible to read the preceding chapters of this book without giving thought to the future. We live in an age that is increasingly occupied by systematic reflection on what lies ahead. Such words as "futurology," "futurism," and "future shock" suggest, by their prevalence, the attraction the future holds for us. The imminence of the year 2000 only quickens interest. Human beings have long been interested in the beginnings and endings of thousand-year periods. (The Greek word *chiloi*—the source of our own word "chiliastic," which refers to a more or less blissful future—means literally "thousand.") Most of us do not attach the same significance to a millennium that our forebears did, but it is instructive, all the same, to note the great increase in specific attention to the year 2000. In this country there is the Commission on the Year 2000, chaired by sociologist Daniel Bell and sponsored by the American Academy of Arts and Sciences. The Hudson Institute, directed by the physicist Herman Kahn, has an ongoing Study of Future Alternatives. For some years the Rand Corporation has conducted what it calls the Delphi Prediction Studies. In France there is the *Prospectives* study group originated by Gaston Berger and Bertrand de Jouvenel's *Futuribles*. The British Social Science Research Council has created The Committee for the Next Thirty Years. These are but a few of the enterprises, public and private, which are concerned with the best possible means of gaining insight into the future and identifying the present trends that show highest probability of extending into the years ahead. Beyond count are the programs in government and industry that are concerned with forecasting, whether in the short run or long.[1]

In this chapter we shall examine several aspects of study of the future, all of which are germane to any consideration of the future of social problems and their contexts. I shall begin with a brief account of the oldest visualizations of the future we find in Western thought. We shall then turn to contemporary approaches to the study of the future, the principal means employed in the social sciences, the limits of future forecasting, and the social function of the future in present-day thought. Finally, we shall look at certain economic, social, and political trends in the present which seem likely to extend into, and shape, the future, and thus provide the key contexts of the social problems Western man faces in the decades ahead.

THREE IMAGES OF THE FUTURE

Systematic concern with the shape of the future is very old in Western thought, and is as evocative today as at any time in the past.[2] The three distinct visions

---

[1] See Daniel Bell, *The Coming of Post-Industrial Society: A Venture in Social Forecasting* (New York: Basic Books, 1973); Herman Kahn and Anthony J. Wiener, *The Year 2000* (New York: Macmillan Company, 1967); *Daedalus,* Journal of the American Academy of Arts and Sciences (Summer 1967); and Albert Somit (ed.), *Political Science and the Study of the Future* (Hinsdale, Illinois: Dryden Press, 1974).

[2] See J. B. Bury, *The Idea of Progress* (London: Macmillan, 1920) and Robert Nisbet, *Social Change and History* (New York: Oxford University Press, 1969).

of the future that dominate contemporary thought have deep roots in the past.

The most popular view at the present time is the *cyclical* conception of human history, which was widespread among ancient Greek and Roman philosophers. Each great civilization, it was asserted, has its birth, its development, maturity, decline, and eventual death—often by catastrophe. Moreover this cycle of genesis and decay repeats itself in endless series throughout all time. Plato thought the duration of each cycle to be approximately 70,000 years. A Golden Age of happiness and virtue marks the beginning of each cycle. Gradually, however, human vices come into being, often as byproducts of the development of culture, the arts, technology, and government. In the end these vices, manifest in rising incidence of social problems, bring destruction. This view accounts for the strain of pessimism in so much classical Greek and Roman thought. Plato and Aristotle, and later Lucretius and Seneca, lived in a period that conceived the future in terms of constantly increasing disorganization, conflict, and breakdown, with nothing in man's powers capable of offsetting this trend. However, the Greeks generally believed that the end of one cycle was the genesis of another, with a fresh Golden Age to begin it.

The rise of Christianity brought a somewhat different forecast of the future, which can be found in the writings of the greatest of the ancient Christian philosophers, St. Augustine. There human existence is pictured as a single cycle that commenced a few thousand years earlier when God created man, as described in the Book of Genesis. The Christians, too, had the idea of the Golden Age, that of the Garden of Eden, from which Adam and Eve were expelled for sinning in God's eyes. Ever since, man has suffered continuing moral degradation (though Augustine was careful to point out the material and cultural progress that had taken place). The coming of Christ, declares Augustine in approved Christian fashion, restored man's hope, but only for the eternity that will follow this world, not for the world itself. Augustine foresaw intensification of conflict, disorder, torment, and pain—a process that will eventually terminate forever in an immense holocaust. Such is the Christian future.

The third perspective, the modern philosophy of secular progress, arose in the seventeenth century. For reasons too numerous and complex to go into here, the essential pessimism of the Christian view (so far as life on earth is concerned) was replaced in philosophy and science by a vision of never-ending progress in the arts and sciences and increasing happiness for mankind. By the eighteenth century this conception of progressive change was sufficiently widespread among thinkers to become the basis of the modern social sciences. Skeptics may be found here and there during the Enlightenment. But for the most part it was taken for granted that, with or without God's original creative act, mankind had come into existence at some remote point in the past; that from the most primitive of origins, culture and institutions slowly developed and improved; and that this development, this progress, which had been accelerating rapidly during more recent centuries, would continue indefinitely into the most distant future. The critical rationalists of the Enlightenment declared the Christian philosophy of rise followed by inevitable decline and destruction mere superstition. Turgot, Condorcet, Herder, Price, Godwin: these are only a handful of the names in the period we associate with belief in a golden future on earth, a future made inevitable by developmental processes at work from the very beginning.

Condorcet, in the final section of his famous *Outline of Human Progress,* foretold a future, not more than a century distant, free of all the social problems rooted in poverty, inequality, and ignorance. The spread of reason and the knowledge drawn from reason would succeed in banishing the ecclesiastical superstitions under which mankind had suffered for so many millennia. In his *Inquiry into Political Justice* William Godwin went so far as to predict a future free of not merely superstition and tyranny, but also of human disease and, eventually, of death itself. (It was this work that stimulated Thomas Malthus to write his *Essay on Population,* which warned that the abolition of the diseases and deprivations that lead to ordinary death could only result in the horrors of unending increases in population imposed upon a limited food supply.)

The French Revolution gave this school of thought dramatic substance. The leaders of the Revolution did not doubt that in toppling the monarchy and other traditional institutions in France they were clearing the way for a benign future that would in time include all of human society. In 1794 Robespierre declared: "We wish, in a word, to fulfill the course of nature, to accomplish the destiny of mankind . . . ; and in sealing our work with our blood may we ourselves see at least the dawn of universal felicity gleam before us. That is our ambition; that is our aim."[3]

The idea of progress, with its implicit vision of mankind gradually perfecting itself, flourished in the nineteenth century. In part this was the result of a significant improvement in living standards for large numbers of people, but in larger part it was the result of the dramatic eruption of technology in the forms of railroads, steam-powered ships, increasingly automatic modes of factory production, and other machines and devices that seemed to promise liberation from age-old torments and privations. Whatever the reasons, the idea of progress was assured a role in social philosophy, judging from its central place in the works of such leading thinkers as Auguste Comte, Herbert Spencer, and Karl Marx. Whether the future was envisaged in Comte's terms of a stable-progressive society governed by scientists; in Spencer's evolutionary declaration of man's ever more perfect adaptation to environment, which would abolish the contexts of social problems; or in Marx's and Engels' laws of motion leading to a classless society freed of private property and profit, the prevailing view of the future was overwhelmingly optimistic.

Utopianism (from the Greek words for an imaginary place) also flourished in the nineteenth century. Old as a theme in literature in philosophy, it now produced large numbers of actual as well as written "utopias": that is, experimen-

---

[3] Cited in Robert R. Palmer, *Twelve Who Ruled* (Princeton: Princeton University Press, 1941, 1969), pp. 275–276.

tal communities of individuals removed from the main centers of Western society. As we know from the letters and testaments of their founders, these "communities in the wilderness" had an unwavering confidence in the future. Members of such utopias as the famous Oneida and New Harmony, both in the United States, regarded their communities as forerunners of a kind of ideal society that would in due time include the whole of mankind. Very strong was their belief in the outmoded character of private property and profit and in the necessity of subordination of the self to community.[4]

Present-day communes (responsibly estimated to have reached 10,000 in number) draw on the models provided by the utopian communities of the nineteenth and early twentieth centuries and on a tradition of philosophical utopianism that goes back to Plato's *Republic*. Many contemporary communes—perhaps all in some degree—maintain the belief that a beneficent future, one freed from most of the social problems now plaguing us, is possible if only human impulses to egoism and greed are abolished or moderated through communal action.[5]

However, the generally optimistic view of the future that reached its heyday in the nineteenth century has diminished in our own century. Reigning social philosophies reveal a high degree of pessimism.[6] War, internal conflict and terror, famine, economic crisis, social disorganization and individual alienation are expected to increase, even over present intensity. Liberal democracy—two centuries old and until recently the unambiguous, unqualified, American dream—is increasingly perceived as moribund. If we are to believe the polls and surveys, which are virtually unanimous in their testimony, majorities in America and other Western countries believe its potential for freedom and creativity is choked by ever more tortuous structures of bureaucracy. Lack of confidence in democratic government has replaced what was, in effect, a civil religion not many decades ago.

World order, once a widespread hope given structure first in the League of Nations, then in the United Nations, seems to many an empty dream, what with the increase in the number of military governments of the right and the left. If the possibility of war on the scale of World Wars I and II has been lessened by the existence of weapons capable of massive destruction, the incidence of small wars and organized terror can easily be seen as on the increase.

The spirit of utopianism has not died in the twentieth century, but the best known description of the future, such as Aldous Huxley's *Brave New World* and George Orwell's *1984*, tend to be inverted or negative in character—dystopias (from the Greek words for bad places). Some of the social problems that confront us today, and are analyzed in the chapters of this book, are absent in

---

[4] See especially Frank E. Manuel, *Utopias and Utopian Thought* (Boston: Beacon Press, 1966); the articles on utopianism by George Kateb and B. F. Skinner in *The International Encyclopedia of the Social Sciences*, Vol. 16 (New York: Macmillan, 1968), pp. 267–275; and Martin Buber, *Paths in Utopia* (New York: Macmillan, 1950).

[5] See Benjamin Zablocki, *The Joyful Community* (New York: Penguin Books, 1971).

[6] Nisbet, *op. cit.*

Huxley's and Orwell's imagined societies of the future, but they have been replaced by other, perhaps worse problems. Huxley presents us with the tyranny possible in a society where technology is unchecked, unguided by humanistic values. If force and violence have disappeared in Huxley's projected world of the future, it is not because the norms of freedom, reason, and humanity have triumphed. It is because through psychological conditioning and drugs, human beings have been sterilized of any impulses which might affect the homogeneity and uniformity of the scene around them. Orwell's *1984* has become a byword for absolute power, buttressed by a combination of war, terror, and unremitting propaganda, that finds its way into the very recesses of the human mind. What gives both Huxley and Orwell their peculiar fascination, however morbid, is the degree to which each dystopia is made to seem an inevitable development of forces already present in Western society.

I am referring here to the West. Matters may be very different in other civilizations at the present time—Marxist and Muslim, for example. No matter what the historical motivations of Marxism were, what it has become for hundreds of millions of people is a kind of spiritual faith in the continuing progress of mankind. Karl Marx wrote when the idea of progress was in its heyday in the West, and although he himself was loath to provide detailed pictures of the communist future, his thought, taken in the large, is nothing less than an effort to demonstrate that mankind's progress to a benign future is necessary, according to the laws of development Marx deduced from his study of society. How deeply Marxist faith permeates the minds of the masses in countries such as Russia, China, Yugoslavia, and Albania, we cannot know for certain. What we do know is that Marxism is the official philosophy of these countries, as it is for social movements in almost every country on earth at the present time, and a faith in progress is the essence of this philosophy.

The world of Islam must also be given special place when we think of contemporary visions of the future. From the beginning the Muslim religion has been a dynamic, aggressive, proselytising force in the world. Even if the highest rewards promised are, unlike those of Marxism, supernatural, those of an eternal hereafter, its shaping impact upon nations, cultures, and belief systems in this world is not to be denied. The confidence in eventual Islamic supremacy is at least the equal of what we find in Marxist conviction.

LOOKING INTO THE FUTURE

Social problems are inseparable from *contexts*, as Robert Merton emphasizes in his opening chapter. If we seek to preview possible types and incidences of social problems in the decades ahead, we must examine the means through which we acquire ideas about the social, political, economic and contexts of the future. How, it must first be asked, do we make our way to the future, that is, to the crucial contexts of social problems that the future would appear to hold? The first point to be stressed here is that all forecasting or prophecy or prediction—call it what we will—is at bottom nothing more than *a uniting of imagi-nation with what may be perceived in the surrounding present.* Imagination may be buttressed by any number of aids to reason, including the most sophisti-cated of techniques and computers, but it is human imagination that remains sovereign. It is tempting to suppose that just as our technology has launched man's observation millions of miles into extraterrestrial space, what with the use of complex unmanned projectiles reaching the outskirts of other planets, so will technology in due course be able to transport us into the time dimension we call the future. The "time machine" that H. G. Wells described in a memo-rable short story many years ago, a machine that could quite literally transport one backward and forward in time, still makes for excellent reading, but it remains now what it was then—pure fantasy. Technology notwithstanding, there is no way in which we can literally peer into the future. We are confined to the present; at best we can attempt to identify those aspects of the present which give highest probability of projecting themselves into the future.

Not that the artist, the science fiction writer, is without value to us in our efforts to prophesy. There are scores of instances in which present reality in the world of technology, and also social organization, approximates predictions in the pages of novels and stories. The remarkable prophecies of Jules Verne made in the last century are an example. *Twenty Thousand Leagues Under the Sea* illustrates as well as any what a powerful imagination linked to detailed awareness of surrounding world can effect. There were no submarines in Verne's day; but there were machine-driven surface vessels, there were under-water observation devices, and people were beginning to understand electric power. For a gifted mind, it was not difficult to put these pieces together in a novel way, creating Captain Nemo's wondrous submarine. Similarly, H. G. Wells let his imagination play with reports of Ernest Rutherford's and Frederick Soddy's pioneering studies of radium and, early in the century, predicted the invention of atomic bombs.

It is no different with those science fiction writers of our own day who, like the talented Arthur C. Clarke, unite very real knowledge of present realities and possibilities in the world of science with imagination capable of lifting us forward in time, and with a high degree of plausibility. Few if any scientists take the visions of the very best of the science fiction writers lightly. I am not suggesting that the methods of science are those of science-fiction writers; only that in science and art alike the role of imagination is fundamental.[7]

So do professional forecasters in the social and physical sciences work with imagination, analytical reason, and logic on the one hand, and detailed under-standing of the present on the other. Basically, all the forecasts and prophecies we find in the scientific literature are projections, extrapolations (that is, conjec-tures), or complex extensions of what are discerned as trends, rates, movements,

---

[7] It should be emphasized that quite apart from their fascinating visions of the future, the stories and novels of such writers as H. G. Wells, Arthur C. Clarke and Ray Bradbury are impressive works of literature. It is nevertheless the extraordinary fertility of insight into possible futures that gives these works their greatest importance.

or serial relationships in the present, or from past to present. How perilous forecasting can be is evident in the number of prophecies that prove to be false within very short periods of time. On the other hand, some succeed, though never with sustained success except when they have been couched in such general or ambiguous terms as to defy genuine verification. Nevertheless, the fact remains that some kind of forecasting is an inescapable part not only of planning for the future, but of life itself. As someone has correctly said, the first futurologist was that primitive man who, looking ahead to the winter, stored up provisions in the autumn.

The number and diversity of forecasts is very great, but for our purposes they can be reduced to three general kinds: *projections, models,* and *panel-judgments.*[8]

Projections

Projections may be qualitative or quantitative in character, unilinear or multilinear, straight-line or cyclical. What they all have in common is the short-term or long-term projection of some aspect of the present into the future. It may be a dominant structure such as technology or the political state, or a process such as conflict or cooperation; or it may be price or wage levels, employment and unemployment, school attendances, crimes, number of automobiles sold, highways built, jet miles traveled, and so on. The objective is to discern, so far as possible, some trend or tendency that, with suitable qualifications and premises, can then be extended into the future. Obviously, all that one has to build on is what can be found in the present and in the past that leads up to the present. Rates of change and their directions over a ten year period can look secure indeed so far as projection into the future is concerned, only to reverse themselves or in other respects become significantly modified within a year or two after prophecy has been made. One need think only of stock-market forecasting. There is probably no area with a greater abundance of highly quantified data, carefully recorded over long periods, than this one. Yet projections based on past and present trends in the market only occasionally prove true. Nevertheless concern with future is inevitable—a necessary part of planning—the search for reliable indicators as the basis of increasingly reliable projections will undoubtedly continue.

Models

In his chapter on population Kingsley Davis describes one of the best known models of the future, that created by a group of scientists at the Massachusetts Institute of Technology who were inspired by preliminary work of an industrial

---

[8] I am indebted in what follows to Denis F. Johnston, "Forecasting Methods in the Social Sciences," in Albert Somit, *op. cit.,* pp. 68–88; Daniel Bell, "Introduction," *op. cit.;* and Fred Charles Iklé, "Can Social Predictions be Evaluated?" *Daedalus* (Summer 1967), pp. 733–758.

engineer, Jay W. Forrester. This group (which worked under the sponsorship of an organization of business and professional people called The Club of Rome) created models of possible developments during the next 130 years, dealing with such vital areas as population growth, industrialization, food production, non-renewable resources, and pollution. Like projections, models involve conjecture. However models allow scientists to deal with a great number of alternatives and to make continuing readjustments.

We can applaud serious efforts to discern the social problems of the future through use of models, whether by the Forrester group or any other. But it is necessary to remain alert to the questionable inferences found in such models and to the limits inherent in any model-building. Despite the abundance of computer-controlled data and the relative sophistication of techniques employed, the model-builder is as dependent as any science fiction writer on imagination united to perceptions of the present.

Panels

Here we are dealing with judgments made by panels of experts on a given issue. If we are trying to gain insight into probable rates of crime, urban blight, population increase in a given area, mental illness, or any other social problem during the years and decades ahead, we may establish a panel, composed of experts on the particular problem being considered, drawing from them as individuals and also as a group reasoned forecasts based upon apparent trends in all the spheres affecting that problem. Perhaps the best-known example of the panel technique is the Rand Corporation's Delphi Prediction Studies. Even with the best possible light put on the Delphi predictions, it has to be said that they suffer from the same inherent limitations found in all modes of forecasting. There is simply no way in which we can in fact put ourselves across time into the future as we do across interplanetary space. Whether through projections and extrapolations, through models, or through consultations with groups of experts, the present is all we have to work with. What emerges is inevitably the product of observation of this present coupled with guesswork, however sophisticated. Experience teaches us that some predictions made in the past have been borne out, and it is useful to study these carefully for whatever insight we can gain for making our own predictions. But the past is strewn with predictions that seemed eminently plausible to learned and imaginative minds at the time, but never came even close to fulfillment. In all matters of forecasting and prophecy, wariness on the part of expert and public alike is essential.

SOME LARGE-SCALE PREDICTIONS

Among minds of the past engaged in predictions of the future, two stand out: Karl Marx and Alexis de Tocqueville.[9] A great deal of current writing attests to the high esteem, the admiration, in which we hold both of these men for prophecies made well over a century ago. Marx and Tocqueville were primarily concerned with the *contexts* which they believed were forming in their own time and which would dominate the future. But they were also concerned, often presciently, with specific social problems. Marx foresaw an intensification of poverty, class conflict, unemployment, and all the social ills associated with these conditions as capitalism reached its final stages prior to the revolutionary onset of socialism. Tocqueville, who was primarily concerned with political rather than economic conditions, foresaw increasing centralization, militarization, and repression in the ages ahead. Both minds worked from profoundly held philosophies of history—theories of social development in which present and future alike could be seen emerging inexorably from the past.

For Marx the course of history operates from slave society through feudalism and capitalist to eventual socialism. The socialist future, which Marx regarded as certain for all mankind in due time, would rest upon people's ownership of the means of production and, with this, the abolition of private property, profit, and social classes. Inasmuch as social problems of crime, poverty, alcoholism, war, ethnic conflict, and even individual alienation are, for Marx, inescapable consequences of private property set in class conflict, he did not doubt that such problems would end, or would certainly become significantly lessened, once the socialist order came into being.

Looking out on the world today, with its large and apparently growing number of socialist—or self-designated socialist—societies (Soviet Russia, China, Albania, Cuba, and others), it is tempting to regard Marx as an impressive prophet. The conspicuous fact is that noncapitalist, officially socialist or communist nations exist in vast areas today where none existed at the beginning of the present century. True, the socialisms which we see in our age carry with them a degree of authoritarianism, a consecration to military values, strata of power and privilege not unlike social classes, and a near-absence of democratic procedures that might well lead Marx or Engels, returned to earth, to deny the label socialist to any of them. There is also the fact that none of the socialisms has come into being in the countries Marx's doctrine declared most probable for this transformation—that is, countries of advanced capitalism such as England and France. Moreover, where socialism has come into being it has been through the operation of processes and events which have little in common with those that are central in Marxian thought. Without exception the socialist states of the world have made their appearance in societies more nearly agrarian–feudal than capitalist and through international wars as well as class

---

[9] See Karl Marx, *The Communist Manifesto*, and *Critique of the Gotha Program*. For Tocqueville's prophecies, see especially *Democracy in America* (2 vols.), (New York: Alfred A. Knopf, 1945).

conflict. All of this is true. But the socialist societies do exist, and even so conservative and critical an economist as the late Joseph Schumpeter was quite willing to accord Marx high honors as a prophet.[10]

Marx is by no means alone as a more or less successful prophet in the past. Alexis de Tocqueville's *Democracy in America* (especially the second volume, published in 1840) also contains chapters which seem nothing short of prescient in their descriptions of the kind of social, psychological, and political *problems* the democracies would face in the future. Tocqueville foresaw, along with the levelling of social strata that democracy would bring, a rise in problems of individual alienation, widespread boredom, increasingly frenetic pursuit of material pleasures, breakdown or erosion of the smaller communities in society, and the vast growth of centralized political power. He correctly stated that in the United States the next great revolution, if it ever took place, would arise from the oppressed condition in which the blacks lived. The recent and ongoing civil rights revolution in this country is some validation of this prophecy.

At about the same time that Tocqueville and Marx were writing, Jacob Burckhardt was describing the future of the West in terms of the rise of great military superpowers, with more and more social, economic, and political authority passing into the hands of what Burckhardt called "military commandos," and with military regimentation gradually replacing all the diversities European societies had once known.[11] Max Weber, as every sociologist knows, foresaw the future in the light of an increasing "rationalization" of function and power in the West, with bureaucracy taking command of the governing process not only in the state but also in industry, the professions, education, and culture generally. Weber thought "bureaucratization of the spirit" inherent in the future of the West.[12] And Emile Durkheim, though less positively and categorically, believed that unless certain major and reconstitutive changes were made in Western societies, anomie would overtake Western man on a constantly widening scale.[13]

These few examples illustrate the fact that by looking back into the writings of the past we can occasionally come upon prophetic utterances which to our eyes are remarkable. Who can doubt that in our own day there are individuals whose forecasts will prove equally remarkable to readers of the next century—just as there are prophets whose equally plausible visions will prove faulty in every respect?

Yet, striking as the prophecies of a Marx or Tocqueville are, we must stress once again that they were based, not upon any real cognitive leap into the

---

[10] Joseph Schumpeter, *Capitalism, Socialism and Democracy* (New York: Harper, 1942), especially the first three chapters.

[11] Cited in Albert Salomon, *The Tyranny of Progress* (New York: The Noonday Press, 1955), pp. 6–7.

[12] See the concluding pages of *Politics as Vocation* and also those of *The Protestant Ethic and the Spirit of Capitalism*.

[13] Durkheim's views are to be found in *Moral Education*, especially pp. 40 and 101, and *Suicide*, p. 370 and the final section of the work.

future, not upon the kind of anticipation, or attempted anticipation, of the future that we associate with fortune-tellers, but rather upon close analytical observation of the present coupled with a willingness to select and project into the future certain aspects of the present. The conditions making for the eventual breakdown of capitalism and its replacement by socialism were, for Marx, already apparent, even though they were still relatively small in scope and intensity. In the same way, Tocqueville's famous prediction of the future represented his selection (and intensifying and heightening) of tendencies which, even in the 1830s, he believed he could see at work in modern democracies. Conceivably he could have chosen other aspects of the present to project into the future. Indeed, some of his contemporaries did, prophesying virtually unlimited freedom, prosperity, and happiness in decades to come. Even at the present time we cannot be sure that either Marx's or Tocqueville's predictions will prove accurate in the long run. The important point here, however, is that such predictions, right or wrong, sprang from imaginative observation of what could be seen, however dimly, in the present.

THE LIMITS OF SOCIAL PREDICTION

It is often said that the test of any science is its power to predict. This is true, but we must be careful about what is meant by the word "predict." Prediction in science has nothing whatever in common with the kinds of flights into the future we associate with astrology, "consciousness-raising," or even philosophies of history. Indeed, in the strict sense, scientific prediction is only very incidentally concerned with the domain of the future. What the scientist seeks are statements of functional or causal relationships among data. Thus if it is discovered that whenever and wherever A, B, and C are present, D will also be present, or will shortly manifest itself, we have a scientific statement that can be properly interpreted as a "prediction." Scientific prediction, as distinguished from prophecy or forecasting the future, is basically an *explanation:* We are making a causal or explanatory statement about a certain set of variables.[14] When our astronomers confidently and accurately predict that at a given hour on a specified day of the week in, say, 1986 there will be a solar eclipse, they are in no way predicting a unique event in the future, as we would be doing if we prophesized which party or which individual would be elected to the White House in some future year. The astronomers' prediction of solar eclipse rests upon discovery of certain invariable movements of the earth in

[14] On the nature of prediction and its relation to explanation in science see E. Nagel, *The Structure of Science* (New York: Harcourt Brace Jovanovich, 1961); C. H. Hempel, *Aspects of Scientific Explanation* (New York: The Free Press, 1965); and R. B. Braithwaite, *Scientific Explanation* (Cambridge: Cambridge University Press, 1953). For treatment of the relation between social theory and scientific prediction see Robert K. Merton, *Social Theory and Social Structure* (New York: The Free Press, 1968), especially pp. 149–153.

relation to the moon, requiring a certain number of years in our reckoning of time to complete themselves, which results in a temporary obscuration of the sun's light on our own planet. Although from the layman's point of view predicting an eclipse is more complex and more remarkable than declaring in advance when the "sun will rise" on a given day in the future, the two intellectual operations are basically identical.

The earth sciences present us with examples perhaps closer in kind to what the social sciences seek in the way of predictions. The theory of plate tectonics, described as a scientific revolution a few years ago, has enabled earth scientists to make predictions which would not have been possible a decade or two ago. As Professor Peter Wyllie writes, "Whereas the geological creed for more than 100 years has been that 'the present is the key to the past,' the new theory permits predictions on the grounds that 'the past and present are a guide to the future'."

Within a hundred years, Professor Wyllie declares, "at least one densely populated city in the western U.S.A. will be devastated by a major earthquake." The oil and natural gas "produced within the earth during the past 300 million years, will be completely used up." Further, "continued shifting of global climatic belts will cause drought and famine as deserts extend their ranges." Such predictions have been lengthened into thousand-year periods. "Within thousands of years sea level will rise through tens of feet as the ice sheets melt, flooding world ports and many square miles of arable land; later, the ice sheets will spread from the polar regions toward the Equator causing sea level to fall and thus strand world ports inland and curtail the area of land suitable for habitation; a large meteorite will blast the earth with sufficient force to generate a crater with diameter measured in kilometers."[15]

Such predictions are interesting and, given their impressive intellectual source, have to be taken seriously. Even so, it is important for us to be wary of all predictions where extension of *present processes and rates* are concerned. The role of the contingent, the fortuitous, and unique is simply too great in both nature and society for us to adopt a passive attitude toward even the most plausible and well-grounded prophecies. This is particularly true of human history and of the apparent processes and rates to be found in the society around us. Think how polluted our cities would be today if the rate of increase in the number of horses found in 1850 had continued to the present. We should without doubt be buried in horse droppings. But in fact the automobile—hailed at the time as the blessed solution to the pollution problem—appeared. To be sure, the automobile brought problems of a different nature. And today we hear predictions of the blanket of pollution we shall live under a few decades hence as the result of mechanized transport. But before we extend present rates uncritically into the future, we should reflect upon the power history seemingly has of occasionally wiping out problems in unforeseeable ways.

[15] Peter Wyllie, "Future Developments and Events in Earth Sciences," a lecture given in Chicago, September 30, 1974 and printed by *Encyclopedia Britannica,* 1975.

Even the generalized predictions regarding the earth and what is in and on it are but probability statements: high-probability in certain cases, but probability nonetheless. The possibility of geological changes of sufficient scale to counteract movements and processes presently to be seen, or of some breakthrough or discovery, fresh knowledge that offsets what was previously taken for granted, remains.

In sum, the limits of prediction in any field are set by what we know or can discover about the present, its structures, processes, relationships, and trends reaching from past to present. Any prediction of the future involves assumptions of the continuation of present processes. *If* oil and gas are used worldwide at present rates, no deposits of these will be left a century hence. *If* present rates of population increase in certain parts of the world continue, and *if* present rates of increases in food supply become no greater, then widespread famine may be predicted in these areas—*unless* better-endowed countries take countervailing measures or supplies of food of a variety now unknown become available. *If* urban conditions in the United States remain what they are at present, with the affluent fleeing the central cities, their places taken by the increasingly restless poor, then present rates of increase in crime, violence, and the varied indices of poverty will continue. There is a substantial measure of precariousness in all scientific predictions; but that measure is bound to increase the farther we stray from the realm of the fixed, the regular, and the recurrent, and the closer we come to the world of the unique, the individual, and the random event.

We cannot be as precise in the social sciences—where we are dealing with far more complex variables, starting with man's brain, his purposeful, goal-oriented behavior, and his immensely adaptive relationship to environment—as we are in the physical sciences. Even so, we have gradually reached the point, in a few areas at least, where we can offer explanatory or causal propositions which have a substantial measure of validity, and in these areas it is possible to offer predictions in the scientific sense of the term. True, we will always be limited to probability statements, but these are in no way antithetical to either science itself or to scientific prediction.

All genuine scientific prediction deals with contexts in one form or other. If we are predicting rates of armed robbery, rape, murder, or other kind of crime for next year, or the next decade, we are obliged to make certain assumptions which are in effect contexts. What we say, if we are speaking as social scientists and not as visionaries or prophets, is that *assuming the continuation of some existing contexts* and adjusting for probable changes in other contexts, such as population, rates of crime will be thus and such. We can, with some confidence, predict, in the same light, the contingent incidences of alcoholism, of marriage breakdown, schizophrenia, and other social problems. Given certain contexts, many of which are not easily specifiable, problem-behavior can be predicted with a reasonably high degree of probability.

Social science lends itself to another type of prediction, as Durkheim's notable proposition on the functional necessity of crime illustrates. Given the fact, Durkheim tells us, that all social organization is built around certain moral values, and given the unalterable statistical variety of human behavior, there will always be variations in degrees of adaptation or adherence to these moral values. The result will be conduct described by a social order as "good" *and* conduct described as "bad" or deviant. It is possible, in sum, to predict that there will always be crime in human society, even though what is called crime and its rates will vary substantially from age to age, society to society. What Durkheim states is that the very nature of social organization, no matter what its dominant theme may be or however well socialized its members may be from childhood on, creates an inevitable context for behavior that will be pronounced, in some degree, deviant or criminal.[16] Such a statement, emerging as it does from a theoretical proposition, is at once explanatory and predictive.

THE FUNCTION OF THE FUTURE

Leaving science, prophecy, and forecasting to one side for a moment, what accounts for the concern with the future that has for so long been a part of human belief and thought? More precisely, what is the *function* of the future in human behavior and thought as we find it in past and present, from one human group to another?[17]

It was earliest man's confrontation with *problems*, those of the social as well as the physical world, that stirred interest in the future. The problems of food supply, shelter, safety, disease, and death may have come first; but there were also problems of a social and psychological nature which demanded not only immediate adaptations of kinship and other types of social structure but also planning for the future. Given man's "time-binding" mental capacity, it is beyond dispute that thought of the future exerted profound influence upon his ways of dealing with the present. From the beginning, therefore, the future served a distinct function in responses to social problems.

Second, concern with the future has an integrative value in human life. How an individual regards the future is bound to influence his daily existence; and how whole cultures regard the future is bound to affect central intellectual and moral themes in their religions, philosophies, and traditions. A social order convinced of the imminence of catastrophe or of inexorable degeneration is certain to be a different kind of social order from one in which the idea of unlimited progress is dominant. Studies of the classical, medieval, and modern periods in the history of Western civilization make sufficiently evident the effect visions of the future had upon their respective patterns of culture. Much religious ritual integrates time-dimensions.

---

[16] Emile Durkheim, *The Rules of Sociological Method*, tr. by E. Solvay (New York: The Free Press, 1950), pp. 68–69.

[17] See Bertrand de Jouvenel, *The Art of Conjecture* (New York: Basic Books, 1967); Daniel Bell, "Introduction," *op. cit.;* and Donald A. Schon, "Forecasting and Technological Forecasting" *Daedalus* (Summer 1967), pp. 759–770.

Third, experience suggests that one good way of seeking to understand the present, of becoming aware of what are central, dominant forces in the present, is to concern one's self with the probable future. Much important insight into man's behavior, into the nature of society and of the processes of history, has come from the works of scholars and scientists whose eyes have been fixed on the future. No one reading either Marx or Tocqueville, for example, can doubt that a powerful sense of the future guided their respective analyses of economic and political currents in the present. If it is true, as noted above, that their value as prophets lies in their intensive studies of what was going on around them, it is equally true that their interest in surrounding matters would not have been as great had they not been preoccupied by the future.

Fourth, planning, at whatever level, would of course be impossible if there were no concern with, no effort to foretell, the future. Indeed, planning is inescapable, whether in our individual or collective existences. The most inflamed antagonist of "planned economy" would not deny that at some level, in whatever sphere, planning is imperative. This is as true of the business world as of the educational, the religious, the recreational, or any other. When budgets are set up in governments and corporations, when schools are ordered built by school boards, fund-raising drives for churches inaugurated, and great stadiums planned, they are based on an attempted reading of the future, on forecasts of probable income and outgo, of enrollments several years hence, of size of parish, number of spectators, and so on. In short, planning in some form is a requisite of society, and there can be no planning without assessments of the future.

Finally, concern with the future has positive value in our efforts to shape the future. No group could have been more determined to create, to engineer the future than the signers of this country's Constitution at the end of the eighteenth century. The care with which that document was written is indication of the extent to which the Founding Fathers believed themselves to be architects of the future. But their efforts to shape the future were based on definite views as to the probable course of the future, given the nature of man and society as they saw it. The same was true of the revolutionary leaders in France a decade later and in Russia in 1917 when the Bolsheviks won control. The extensive legislation that went into both the French and the Russian Revolutions, the detailed planning of economy and society, is incomprehensible except in the light of a very confident sense of what the future would be. This remains true today. Nowhere is there more committed, even devout, conviction about the character of the future, about the inexorable course of history, than in those countries, or among those groups in the world which strive in organized fashion, to create the future. The great strength of Marxism and Islam, as noted above, proceeds from firm convictions among their leaders and followers in the present world as to what the future should be and what it *will* be. We may lack that intense conviction in the West, but the very existence of five-, ten-, and even fifty-year plans in all spheres of our society is strong testimony to our desire and need to chart, as well as shape, the future.

THE NEW SOCIETY

Much recent interest in the future and its contexts and social problems rises directly from the distinctive character of the society we find ourselves living in at the present time in Western nations. This late-twentieth-century society has been variously referred to as managerial, post-capitalist, consumer-service, technetronic, and, most widely now, post-industrial. Its dominant characteristics have been described by James Burnham, Colin Clark, Bertrand de Jouvenel, Jacques Ellul, C. Wright Mills, Herman Kahn, Zbigniew Brzezinski, and Daniel Bell—to name but a few of those who have sought to identify the new society during the past several decades.[18]

New Trends

What are the characteristics which have seemed to warrant a change from the historic labels of "capitalist" or "industrial" for Western society?

The service economy   In the economic sector there is a change from the predominance of either agriculture or industry to service occupations. Over 30 years ago the Australian Colin Clark distinguished among three sectors of the economy: the primary (agricultural), the secondary (industrial), and the tertiary (the whole proliferating sphere of professions, businesses, occupations, and skills whose primary purpose is rendering services rather than extracting or processing natural resources). In a statement that has since earned wide, if modified, acceptance, Clark pointed out that the tertiary sector—which includes lawyers, physicians, scientists, teachers, and civil servants, as well as professional athletes, beauty parlor operators, and security guards—has gradually assumed ascendancy over the other two sectors of the economy in terms of number of people involved in and financial or economic values associated with this type of work. At the moment, there is no reason to assume that this trend will decline in the decades immediately ahead.[19]

The professional-technical class   Accompanying the rise of the services sector of the modern economy is the increasing importance, indeed the preeminence of the professional and technical groups in the social order. Much of the authority and prestige once enjoyed by great landowners and businessmen in Western society now falls to scientists, technologists, teachers, lawyers, and others who are notable not for ownership or possession of things, but rather

---

[18] See James Burnham, *The Managerial Revolution* (New York, 1941); Colin Clark, *Conditions of Economic Progress* (London, 1940); Bertrand de Jouvenel, *The Ethics of Redistribution* (Cambridge: Cambridge University Press, 1951); Jacques Ellul, *The Technological Society* (Paris, 1954); C. Wright Mills, *White Collar Society* (New York, 1951); Herman Kahn, *op. cit.;* Zbigniew Brzezinski, *Between Two Ages* (New York: 1970); and Daniel Bell, *op. cit.*

[19] Clark, *op. cit.*

for valuable skills and organizational, inventive, or managerial talents. One of the most striking statistical facts of the present century is that the growth rate of this whole professional-technical sphere, as Daniel Bell writes, has been "twice that of the average labor force, the growth rate of scientists and engineers has been triple that of the working population." Admittedly, unemployment in these areas has been on the upswing for some time—possibly the result of temporary oversupply during the past quarter of a century, possibly the result of inflation and recession striking all parts of the economy. But nothing can take away from the extraordinary increase of the technical-professional sector in societies all over the world during the present century, or from the social status and political influence of this sector at the present time and in the foreseeable future.[20]

The "knowledge industry" The influence of knowledge—that is, what William James once referred to as "knowledge about" in contrast to the "knowledge of" that is in some degree an element of every craft or mode of life, however primitive—has increased. When we refer to "knowledge about" we have in mind scholarship, science, and other forms of organized research. We need only compare the role of the professional seeker of knowledge, the scientist foremost, in government and industry today with what prevailed a mere half-century ago, when scholars were confined almost entirely to the university or the then-rare research laboratory in the industrial world. Once it was unlikely, to say the least, that a chemist or engineer, as such, would hold high and responsible business or government office. It no longer is. Add to this the widespread acceptance (and not infrequent hostility) the public accords what has come to be called "the knowledge industry." Research into physical ailments, the diverse problems of pollution, military technology, economic growth, communications, and, most pertinent to this book, the whole gamut of social problems, has changed from the occasional pursuit of a relatively few academic scholars at the beginning of the century to what is nothing less than a multibillion dollar industry. This is true in communist as well as in Western countries. Here again we are dealing with something that clearly recommends itself, in varying intensities, to all other parts of the world where modernization is occurring.[21]

These are the three most obvious and essential aspects of the new society. These trends—the increase of service occupations, the ascendancy of the technical-professional class, and the rise of the "knowledge industry"—are by no means confined to the Western democracies. We find them in the so-called "mixed" societies, such as Sweden and Great Britain, where nationalization of

[20] Thorstein Veblen, *The Engineers and the Price System* (1919), was one of the first to call attention to this class and its tenuous relation to the capitalist system. Later, Adolph Berle and Gardiner Means, *The Modern Corporation and Private Property* (1933) and still later Burnham, *op. cit.*, dealt in even greater detail with this class.

[21] See Fritz Machlup, *The Production and Distribution of Knowledge in the United States* (Princeton; Princeton University Press, 1962).

industry and the professions has taken place without significant loss of traditional democratic freedoms. We also find them in an all-out socialist or communist state such as Soviet Russia, and in Maoist China (albeit with wholly different aim as to their relation to the masses).

Making all allowance for the possibility of radical change—for the rise of prophets committed to a very different kind of society, one rooted, say, in a form of religion or agrarianism that could, in theory at least, wipe out the new society and its motivations—ordinary reason suggests that there is high probability of post-industrial society remaining in existence for a long time ahead. Such probability is rooted in the often-observed tendency of social structures and social values that have reached a high degree of diffusion and of popular acceptance to persist over the long run. Whether the social problems now associated with the contexts they generate will also persist, even if in modified intensity, is more difficult to prophesy. As almost every chapter in this book makes clear, the element of social perception, of social definition, is vital in the identification of social problems, and in a variety of ways. The recent history of such "problems" as marijuana, abortion, homosexuality, and the economically subordinated place of women (to name but a few), has given us an opportunity to observe how quickly significant changes can take place, especially in a society where the role of knowledge is as great and as widely accepted as it is in ours.

Persistent Values

It will be useful now to turn to certain other, historically older, characteristics of Western society which also seem likely to influence the future. Far from restricting the values and structures just described, these tendencies appear to be congruent, even functionally related.

Egalitarianism   As Tocqueville pointed out, the egalitarian ethic has been a powerful influence in the West for two centuries or more.[22] Beginning primarily as a political doctrine, leading to the theory of the modern democratic state, the ethic has spread, as Tocqueville specifically noted, from the political to the economic, social, and moral spheres. We need only look back on the struggle during the past century by group after group—religious, economic, ethnic, and other—for increased equality of position in the social order to see how firmly rooted egalitarianism is in the contemporary world. All revolutions, Tocqueville declared, are generated by perceptions of inequality that has come to seem illegitimate to a given class. The chapters in this book on ethnic relations; the struggle for upward mobility of blacks, Chicanos, and other groups; the drive toward equalization of sex roles; and the efforts to deal with poverty are evidence of the present intensity of this force and its background in

---

[22] See especially Tocqueville, "Introduction," *Democracy in America*, Vol. 1. Nearly all of Vol. 2 is concerned with the present and future implications of equalitarianism.

history. It is unlikely that so powerful and durable an ethic will erode during the latter part of this century.[23] Far more likely, as Seymour Lipset notes in his chapter, is the extension of the ethic to ever-new contexts.

Achievement Side by side with equality, reinforcing and in turn being reinforced by it, is the desire for achievement. One of the major characteristics of modern society, and of those occupations and professions that are central to the new society, is the continuing reduction in social importance of ascribed roles—sex, ethnicity, family, chiefly—and the gradual increase in importance of achieved roles. Much of the momentum of the various civil rights movements comes from desire on the part of blacks, women, and others heretofore limited by tradition or law in the occupations and other achievements to which they could realistically aspire to be granted *equal possibility of achievement*.[24]

As indicated in Lipset's chapter, however, a significant tension exists, or can exist, between the equalitarian and the achievement norms.[25] Basically, the desire for open achievement rests upon attainment of equality of *opportunity*, with no one prevented by accident of ascribed status from competing on equal terms for occupational and other rewards in society. But given existing inequalities of family-position, education, social status, motivation, and intelligence, rewards based solely on achievement can only create fresh degrees of inequality. Hence the increased emphasis in very recent times upon, not equality of opportunity, but what is called equality of condition or result. There is much evidence to suggest that this emphasis will continue for a long time. For, it is argued, there cannot be genuine equality of opportunity until all persons have been brought into sufficient equality of status to give reality to equality of opportunity. Hence the great, and increasing, variety of programs for income redistribution, equalizing of admissions to education and to jobs and professions, and other specific objectives related to an equalizing of individual positions in the social order.

Mobility As many of the chapters in this book have pointed out, people today move about, laterally and vertically, in striking degree. In America especially (but hardly exceptionally), it is increasingly rare for human beings to remain in the locality where they are born or to follow the careers and patterns of life of their parents and forebears. Rootedness, whether in neighborhood, locality, family, or other associations, is hardly a dominant characteristic of the social life of our time. The automobile, railroad, and jet are technological symbols of a mass mobility that extends to a great many sectors of our society.

[23] The popularity and apparent influence of such recent works as John Rawls, *Theory of Justice* (Boston: Harvard University Press, 1971); Christopher Jencks, *Inequality* (New York: Basic Books, 1972); and Herbert Gans, *More Equality* (New York: Random House, 1974) suggests the strength of the idea of equality of condition or result at the present time among intellectuals.

[24] See Seymour M. Lipset, *America: The First New Nation* (New York: Basic Books, 1963).

[25] See also David Potter, *People of Plenty* (Chicago: University of Chicago Press, 1963), and David Riesman, *The Lonely Crowd* (New Haven: Yale University Press, 1969).

There is no reason at present to suppose that the mobility we find in contemporary society will diminish in the future. The desire for advanced means of transportation in modernizing nations, and the rise and spread of international political, economic, professional, and recreational organizations suggests that the scope of mobility can only increase. Tourism draws millions of people from country to country each year. The mounting importance of multi-national economic corporations, with executives and workers now being sent from country to country as once they might be sent from state to state in America, indicates still another massive context of built-in mobility.

Bureaucracy Max Weber is the sociologist who first gave systematic attention to the role of bureaucracy in modern society. What he wrote remains to this day vital and illuminating. However, Weber did not live long enough to see the degree to which prophecy could become reality, not only in Western society but in other parts of the world as well. Bureaucracy is, like other central elements of the new society, common to the capitalist and the socialist countries. More and more functions and controls, once diffused to family, village, occupation, church, and neighborhood (which possessed a high degree of autonomy), have been taken over by large bureaucracies. Even the pursuit of knowledge, central, as we have seen, to contemporary society, has become bureaucratized to a degree once undreamed of.

For a long time we were more aware of the benefits which flow from bureaucratic rationalization of basic social functions—those, for example, of welfare, public order or security, education, and the care of the aged—than we were of problems or dysfunctions bureaucratization created. However, recently there has been a sharp rise in public perceptions of *failure* of bureaucracy, and of *new problems* of disorder, alienation, anomie, previously rare forms of crime, and corruption. Bureaucracy's double face, which Max Weber so prophetically emphasized at the beginning of the century has become reality in the minds of many millions of people.[26]

Central planning and management It becomes more and more evident that centralization of planning and control is an overriding, possibly irreversible, trend in all modern states, "capitalist" included. We need only compare the number of central-national agencies in the United States today (created by both major parties) with what existed three or four decades ago. The dependence of almost every major sector of our society upon the federal government increases decade by decade, even year by year. Our economy, educational system, transportation and communications networks, cities, housing developments, social welfare, family life, even organized sports, are affected by federal legislation, regulatory agencies, and commissions. Granted that the public and

---

[26] See Robert Nisbet, *Twilight of Authority* (New York: Oxford University Press, 1975), especially Chaps. 1 and 4 for a review of contemporary reactions to government and bureaucracy. The Louis Harris polls over the past five years have been recurrently concerned with Americans' perceptions of their large scale, especially political, institutions.

private sectors remain differentiated in Western democracies, and that especially in the United States, a constitutional division of powers checks centralization of political authority. Even so, the degree of direct influence the central government exercises upon the social order could hardly have been foreseen a half-century ago. Ideologies react in diverse ways to the increased influence of the central government in the spheres of planning and operation, but short of a very substantial change of national orientation not yet in view, the role of central government is likely to increase in the years ahead rather than diminish.

AN EXCURSUS ON SOCIALISM

"I have seen the future and it works." These now famous words were the reaction of Lincoln Steffens, a politically-sensitive American journalist, to the changes which had already been effected in Soviet Russia when he visited it shortly after the Revolution. Obviously, Steffens' sentence was designed not only to express approval of what he saw in Russia, but also to suggest that the social order there would in time become universal. He was, in effect, endorsing the Marxian philosophy of history, set forth militantly in *The Communist Manifesto* by Marx and Engels in 1848. This document predicts the future collapse of capitalism everywhere, followed by socialism for all human beings.

By now Soviet Russia is more than a half-century old, and it has been joined in its avowed socialism by other countries, including China, the largest nation in the world. The presence of socialism as fact rather than as the dream it was for so long raises an interesting question: What relation, if any, exists between socialism as a structure of society, and the incidence of the kind of social problems dealt with in this book?

Fundamental to the Marxist doctrine from the beginning has been the proposition that social problems such as crime, poverty, ethnic conflict, worker alienation, over-population, and role inequalities are only the negative side effects of private ownership, private profit, and the existence of social classes. Throughout the world, including Western societies not committed to socialism in practice, there are people whose faith in the reconstructive, even redemptive, mission of socialism is intense, the equal of the kind of faith we ordinarily associate with religion. As noted above, Marxism is today a repository of optimism regarding the future, with little parallel in the history of secular belief.

As long as we are dealing with socialism strictly as a utopian ideal, one not yet properly realized in any existing country, there is, of course, no feasible way any genuinely sociological proposition relating to socialism and social problems can be verified. We are left in the realm of faith, hope, and militance. But for more than half a century now we have had in the world one large and powerful nation that is officially committed to socialism, and as students of social problems we cannot help but be interested in Soviet Russia. Of course not all socialists are willing to accord a Soviet Russia true socialist, much less communist status. But the fact remains that for over 50 years the

Russian government has nationalized the means of production, outlawed private profit, and abolished social classes as these are known in capitalist countries. We have, in short, a body of data to which we may go with our question about the relation between socialism and such social problems as alcoholism, ethnic discrimination, worker alienation, narcotics addiction, crime and delinquency, and violence.

I say "we have a body of data," but there is more to be said on that point. As we have emphasized throughout this book, conclusions regarding the existence and intensity of social problems are never anchored solely in what we like to think of as external, objective data. Always there are contexts formed by norms, established social perceptions, and expectations. It is difficult if not impossible to separate our ways of perceiving social problems, abroad or in our own country, from the influence of the social order in which we live. The expectations we have acquired of what constitutes a good or acceptable society inevitably influence our thinking. If such expectations have been significantly raised by a people's history, perceptions of problems, of flaws and imperfections, are likely to be more acute.

Add to these considerations the sheer problem of finding adequate data. The United States is probably one of the more thoroughly recorded and reported countries in the world. A great variety of agencies, public and private, exists for the sole purpose of gathering and reporting data about social life. Even so, it would be hard to find a social scientist in this country who is entirely satisfied with either the quantity or quality of the records we work with.

Nevertheless data on social problems do exist; they have been made public in some degree and studied by Soviet and non-Soviet social scientists alike. With a single exception, *all the social problems* considered in this book do indeed exist in Soviet Russia in the sense of being both recorded and *defined* as problems, although their exact incidence and intensity are matters of much controversy. The exception is poverty, which is not officially recognized as a social problem in Soviet Russia. That large numbers of people in Russia exist in material circumstances which would be officially declared those of poverty in this country, Sweden, or other nations does not really affect the matter, for as we have seen, social problems are bound up with normative and other contexts.[27]

The whole problem of comparison of two types of societies—of seeking through comparative data some kind of answer to the question of the relative contributions of "capitalism" and "socialism" to the contexts of social problems —is further complicated by the immense difference between the two political systems. Freedom of speech, of press, of political party, of secret ballot, are not recognized in Soviet Russia as constitutional rights or practices anymore than are the autonomies, privacies, immunities, and civil rights which we asso-

[27] See Paul Hollander, *Soviet and American Society: A Comparison* (New York: Oxford University Press, 1973), especially Chap. 8; and Walter D. Connor, *Deviance in Soviet Society* (New York: Columbia University Press, 1972).

ciate with the law in this country. Other and superior forms of freedom, it is declared, exist in the place of these "bourgeois" liberties. The most serious kind of crime in Russia is political crime—officially crimes against the people, in substance ideological dissidence—and it is this kind of crime that accounts for by far the largest number of those in the detention system Solzenhitsyn calls "the Gulag Archipelago."

Finally, no man lives by socialism or capitalism alone, whether in Russia, in China, or in the United States. That is, a condition found in a given socialist or capitalist country may be the result of extraneous factors, of historical traditions that have nothing to do directly with the economic system as such. As such students as Max Weber and Joseph Schumpeter pointed out, types of behavior such as marriage ties, property inheritance, and higher education which are to be found in capitalist societies, which indeed are crucial as bulwarks to such societies, are often "precapitalist" in nature, going back in time to contexts which are not capitalist at all. Many of the essential motivations of capitalism, both Weber and Schumpeter argued, proceed from contexts which are not even economic, much less capitalist.[28]

Precisely the same may be said of Russian behavior under socialism. If urban violence, alcoholism, divorce, certain types of crime, and other problems are less common in Russian cities than in American, the reason might reside in conditions which, although Russian, have little or nothing to do with socialism. After all, Tokyo is an eminently capitalist city, and one of the most highly congested in the world, possessed of large sectors of poverty and subject to substantial rates of unemployment. Nevertheless Tokyo has one of the lowest rates of urban crime (and other social problems) in the world.

In sum, if we can manage to put propaganda and ideological preferences to one side, social scientists can say little with any assurance about the discrepant effects of socialism and capitalism upon the kinds of social problems dealt with in this book. Ideological claims abound; sound, serious comparative investigations cannot yet be developed, owing, in no small part, to the absence of real comparable sociological evidence. A pity, but a fact.

THE FUTURE AND SOCIAL PROBLEMS

That social problems in one form or other will continue into the future is evident enough. Everything we have learned about the nature of social problems and their contexts in this book makes clear that as long as there are social norms with unequal or otherwise diverse means of achieving these norms, deviance, often perceived as a social problem by significant numbers of people, will exist. In addition, some of the central features of the new society—notably the preeminent role of organized knowledge and of the professional-technical sector—will make for heightened, not lowered, recognition of social problems.

[28] See Schumpeter, *op. cit.*, pp. 131–165.

The last point is worth stressing. The recognition and study of social problems, as represented by this book, derive from eighteenth century rationalism, secularism, and humanitarianism. I am not suggesting that prior to the eighteenth century social thinkers were insensitive to the privations and torments of human life. However there was, as Robert Merton notes in his chapter, a greater fatalism about these conditions. We don't have to read long or deeply in the whole philosophical tradition that stretches from the ancient world to our own to realize the extent to which even the most humane minds regarded the great majority of these privations and torments as inescapable elements of the human condition. This explains the function of religion, particularly of such a religion as Christianity, which views this world as only preparation for the next, where relief from earthly miseries could be found. It was not necessarily contempt that inspired Marx to refer to religion as "the opium of the people." What Marx the atheist writes just before that famous phrase is instructive: "Religious distress is at the same time the expression of real distress and the protest against real distress. Religion is the sigh of the oppressed creature, the heart of a heartless world, just as it is the spirit of an unspiritual situation."[29]

Beginning, as has been noted, in the eighteenth century, gaining immense momentum in the nineteenth, this fatalism was replaced by the view that it is not necessary to wait for heavenly redemption; that intelligence united with reform or revolution can solve the problems of this world *in* this world. This view, as is evident enough, has become part of the texture of the twentieth century, passing from the West to almost all other parts of the world. Nothing in this view—which in the large contains the spirit of the *study* of social problems as well as that of their removal through reform or revolution—suggests that concern with social problems is likely to disappear in the near future. Conceivably a mood of generalized apathy could come over populations made cynical by repeated failures to solve social problems and by the spreading view that in the very act of trying to solve problems we make them worse or create new ones. Such a state of mind is not impossible, but neither is it probable. It is the very nature of contemporary society, as we have seen, to give priority to the technical-professional class, to organized knowledge, and to the combined ethics of equalitarianism and achievement.[30]

A strong awareness of social problems is therefore likely to remain, even to grow and spread in the world, and with this awareness a concerted desire to do whatever can be done to solve them or to moderate their effects. In some instances, social problems, like other kinds of problems, are "solved" by their disappearance from consciousness *as problems.* Few things agitated more minds in the fifteenth and sixteenth centuries in Western Europe and on into the seventeenth century in certain areas, than witchcraft. Societies invented all manner of techniques to deal with witchcraft—including formal and intensive

---

[29] *Toward the Critique of Hegel's Philosophy of Right,* in Lewis Feuer (ed.), *Marx and Engels: Basic Writings on Politics and Philosophy* (Garden City: Doubleday Anchor Books, 1959), p. 263.

[30] See Bell, *op. cit.,* Chaps. 3 and 5 and the Coda.

investigations of the "facts," solemn trials, tortures, and executions. It can scarcely be said that these techniques eliminated the "problem" of witchcraft. But in terms of history the problem was solved simply by its disappearance, a disappearance almost as sudden as its appearance several centuries earlier (current fads of interest in exorcism notwithstanding).

How many of the problems dealt with in whole or part in this book will have analogous solutions? That is, how many will be obliterated as problems by changing tides of human belief? The question cannot be answered with confidence, and in any event answers would have to be mixed. In our own time certain problems have shown signs of being "solved" by substantial decline in public concern. We need think only of the fast-changing attitudes toward the use of marijuana, homosexuality, and public display of sexually explicit words and scenes which only a decade or two ago were still widely considered to be social problems. (On the other hand, some problems such as poverty and ethnic discrimination quite obviously cannot be dealt with in this manner.)

Sometimes, though, problems effaced by history reappear in new contexts. Tobacco is an example. Regarded at the beginning of the century as a moral and social problem by members of the Anti-Tobacco League and others, it became a staple of gracious living in the 1920s. But when the historic Surgeon General's Report linked tobacco with cancer and heart disease, smoking once again became a social problem, requiring, in the minds of many persons, extreme prohibitory action by the government.

Not all social problems can be erased by changing attitudes, by altered contexts of definition. It is difficult to think of any form of society in which murder, assault, and robbery, for example, could become assimilated into the norms of that society as marijuana, pornography, and divorce have in significant degree. What is much more probable is change in the ways in which social orders perceive such behavior—as forms of disease, say, rather than as manifestations of evil. Samuel Butler's *Erewhon* describes an imaginary society in which people are jailed for pneumonia and other ailments but hospitalized for offences we define as felonies and misdemeanors. Change along the latter (if not the former) line has taken place in the West and other parts of the world during recent decades.

Without doubt, most if not all of the problems dealt with in this book could be solved *if*, as problems, they were given high national priority. But that of course leads to the question, *which* problem or problems deserve the highest priority? Some would certainly list the problem of violence, of law and order, as highest. But others believe that in the long run control of population in relation to foreseeable food supply, sharp limitation of human uses of the world's energy supply, arresting environmental pollution, race relations, the care of the aged, and the education of the young, rank higher.

No doubt, some problems (crime among them) *could* be reduced sharply and fairly quickly if we were willing to abandon some of the liberties contained in the Bill of Rights and our several legal codes, liberties such as due process, the right to a jury trial, and so on. Robert Merton's discussion of this in his chapter is highly pertinent here. Most of us, however, would regard the loss of civil liberties as worse than the problem it would be designed to solve. We prefer other approaches to the problem of crime.

As every chapter in this book has, in one way or other, stressed, social problems are inseparable from social and value *contexts*. The "tumor" image of a social problem—that is, something only needing direct excision through one means or other—is false. In so many instances the ways of behavior we pronounce problems are only extensions or ramifications of ways of behavior we pronounce acceptable, right, proper, or "civilized." Thus the problem of overpopulation is set in, indeed caused by, traditions honoring fertility; the problem of old age is inseparable from the large and growing number of the elderly and the environmental means by which we have prolonged human life; narcotics addiction exists in social framework that approves of the widespread use of legal drugs, which often serve the same function as illegal ones; alcoholism is backed by a complex of social sanctioned uses of alcohol; crimes against property, particularly those of white-collar type found in the higher social-economic strata, exist in a strongly gain-motivated, property-based, and achievement-driven society in which success is commonly measured in economic terms; the line between "legitimate" and "illegitimate" economic activity often seems a blurred one; eruptions of violence occur in a century that has seen organized violence in the form of international and revolutionary war increase by quantum jumps; the urgency of the problem of sex and gender roles in our age is incomprehensible apart from tides of equalitarian change in law and economy. So it goes. Social problems, as we have repeatedly seen in this book, have their contexts.

Yet it would be a mistake to distort the argument of contexts into deterministic patterns. Contexts may continue, but it does not follow that they are beyond shaping, that their impact cannot be changed or lessened. We must not fall into the trap of confusing contexts with "roots," which inevitably create certain types of problems. Those of deeply religious persuasion who argue that social problems are expressions of the evil rooted in man's original sin are not very different from those who argue that social problems are rooted in a given type of total economic order and that complete abolition of that order is the only possible way to solve them. Socialists have argued in the latter fashion, but there is no evidence that socialist economies are immune to many of the problems that beset capitalist economies.

Moreover, as a number of social scientists and other professionals have shown (among them Alvin Weinberg and, recently, Amitai Etzioni and Richard Remp in their *Technological Shortcuts to Social Change*), it is possible to reduce the intensity of at least a few social problems through the strategic use of technological means. One thinks of improved coverage of crime- or delinquency-infested areas by police or other professionals; the widened use of easily-distributed, low-cost, highly-nutritious foods among the poor; the use of certain drugs for the control, if not cure, of alcoholism and narcotics addiction. Such techniques do not of course remove the problems, but they can improve circumstances while efforts of a broader, more far-reaching and socio-logical nature continue.

Complacency is to be avoided at all costs, but it is easy sometimes to forget that genuine gains have been made during the past few decades. As Thomas Pettigrew's chapter on race relations suggests, the future is at least less grim in this sphere than it once was, a fact that should encourage scholars and policy-makers most closely associated with this sphere. As Amitai Etzioni indi-cates in his chapter on violence, however pressing this problem may be or seem, there is generally less violence in American cities and towns today than there was at other times in American history. And with all that remains to be done in reversing environmental pollution, the experiences of the last two or three decades demonstrate that Americans have at least become aware that pollution is a major social problem.

However, one of the prime characteristics of our age is that *expectations* keep rising. Tocqueville thought that this increase in expectations—with re-spect to equality, prosperity, or any other aspect of human existence—was the secret of the rising unhappiness he believed he could see among democratic or mass societies.[31] Both Durkheim and Freud, to name two seminal thinkers early in the present century, thought that there is a direct ratio between ad-vance of civilization and rise in unhappiness.[32] Whether this is really the case, we do not, cannot, know for sure. The late distinguished psychologist, Abraham Maslow, arranged human needs in hierarchical fashion, with the need for self-preservative or physical survival at the base and increasingly social, ethical, and psychological needs at the higher levels. Only when needs of the "lower" order are met in some degree, Maslow suggested, do those of the "higher" order begin to be perceived. The individual for whom food and shelter are daily problems is less likely to be agitated by problems of, say, ego-identity or aliena-tion than the individual whose food and shelter are assured.[33]

Perhaps there is something along this line to be seen in the behavior of human groups, including whole societies. It is at least possible that what we call progress may consist in no small measure in the substituting of a constantly "higher" set of social problems for those of "lower" order, relating to sheer survival.

SUMMARY

1 The approach of the year 2000 has increased efforts to forecast the future and its problems, but concern with the future is a very old theme in Western thought.

[31] Tocqueville, *op. cit.*, Vol. 2, Bk. 2, Ch. 13, "Why the Americans are so Restless in the Midst of their Prosperity."

[32] Emile Durkheim, *Division of Labor,* tr. George Simpson (New York: Macmillan, 1933), p. 250. Sigmund Freud, *Civilization and its Discontents,* in *The Standard Edition of the Complete Psychological Works of Sigmund Freud,* Vol. 22 (London: Hogarth), pp. 64–148.

[33] Abraham Maslow, *Motivation and Personality* (New York: Harper & Row, 1954).

2   At the present time three major images or conceptions of the future, all of them coming out of the past, are to be found in Western writing: the idea of cycles, with its thesis of decline followed by the birth of a new civilization; the idea of impending, final destruction of civilization on earth; and the idea of progress, with the implication of more or less constant improvement in the ages ahead.

3   All efforts to forecast the future are rooted in close analysis of the *present,* with the aim of seeking those trends or tendencies which are likely to continue into the future. Use of imaginative understanding of the present coupled with a keen sense of probabilities for the future is vital. We cannot transport ourselves into the future in the way we catapult ourselves through space.

4   Among the most famous of prophecies of the future are those of Karl Marx and Alexis de Tocqueville, both nineteenth century minds with great continuing influence: the first optimistic in his view that all civilization will become eventually socialist, putting an end to all or most of present social problems; the second pessimistic, envisaging the future as one of increasing totalitarianism.

5   Although certainty is impossible, more and more social scientists believe we are now at the beginning of what is commonly called "post-industrial" society, characterized by increasing predominance of service over goods-producing occupations, of the professional-technical sector, of organized, systematic knowledge, and of central planning agencies, and by widening acceptance of egalitarianism, the achievement ethic, and upward mobility for all groups in the social order.

6   Socialism, which millions regard as the shape of the future for all mankind, is found (in Soviet Russia at least) to contain most of the social problems we are acquainted with in Western countries, although in different intensities in some cases. There is no scientific evidence that socialism in itself will lead to eradication of the problems dealt with in this book.

7   All indications at the present suggest that while our more extreme social problems will be reduced during the decades ahead, as the result of spread of knowledge and of the humanitarian ethic, other problems will undoubtedly take their place, given the nature of human dependence upon social norms and the differential responses of individuals to these norms.

RECOMMENDED READING

Perhaps the liveliest and most diversely oriented treatment of the future and its possible range of problems in all spheres is the Summer 1967 issue of the journal *Daedalus,* by now almost a collector's item. The entire issue is devoted to the thoughts, prophecies, and insights of some of the most notable of living scholars and scientists on the subject of the future and our means of forecasting it. Bertrand de Jouvenel, *The Art of Conjecture* (1967) is a wise, lucid, and extremely penetrating discussion of the issues involved in any attempt to deal with the future. Albert Somit (ed.), *Political Science and the Study of the Future* (1974) is by no means limited to political science and has a wide range of essays on the future, including several concerned with existing methods of forecasting the future. Also to be recommended is Michael Young, *Forecasting and the Social Sciences* (1968), which covers in comprehensive and lucid fashion the place of forecasting in contemporary social science. Herman Kahn and Anthony Wiener, *The Year 2000* (1967) contains interesting trends and links of events reaching from the early part of the twentieth century to the end. The authors are admirably candid on the asumptions and subjective judgments which must necessarily go into such efforts. The best, if somewhat long and at times confusingly organized, of the books dealing with "post-industrial" society is Daniel Bell, *The Coming of Post-Industrial Society: A Venture in Social Forecasting* (1973). The revival of interest in utopianism at the present time makes Frank Manuel, *Utopias and Utopian Thought* (1966) useful for background material. For those interested in the contemporary commune movement as possible harbinger of the future, Benjamin Zablocki, *The Joyful Community* (1971) will be useful for its careful analytical treatment. The views of Marx, Tocqueville, Weber and other major early sociologists regarding the future of Western society are dealt with in Robert Nisbet, *The Sociological Tradition* (1967).

NAME INDEX

SUBJECT INDEX

aberrant behavior, vs. nonconformity, 29–31
abortion, 240; and family, 450–451; macroscopic vs. microscopic viewpoint, 11–12; public attitude on, 520; as social problem, 11–12
abstinence syndrome, 147
achievement, as persistent value, 747
activism, and social problems, 18–19
affirmative action, on discrimination, 615, 616
Africa, industrialization and illegitimacy, 519
age (*see also* age inequality; aging): community specialized by, 584; and crime and delinquency, 59–61; and disabilities, 362–363; and drinking customs, 189; and education, 361; family income by, 368; and heroin use, 157; and infirm among disreputable poor, 668; labor force participation by, 367; and marital roles, 369; and mental disorders, 111; of population, and political instability, 274–275; and poverty, 642, 653; psychiatric patient care episodes by, 115–116; and redistribution of work, education, and leisure, 400–402; and role allocation, 399–400; segregation vs. integration of strata, 377–379; stratification, 359, 362–364; subemployment, poverty, and, 659; and success opportunities, 366–369
age dynamics, 358–360
age inequality (*see also* age; aging): and cross-age linkages, 379; and deviance, 372–374; and quality of life, 374–377; and age stratification, 366–372
Agency for International Development (AID), 292
aggression vs. violence, 680–681
aging (*see also* age; age inequality): and age dynamics, 358–360; and cohort flow, 358–360; constraints on intervention, 406–407; and death, 392–393; individual reactions to, 393–395; myths and misperceptions about, 396–399; and role structure modification, 399–402; and role transitions, 379–385; and social change, 402–406; and societal dynamics, 360–362; societal view of, 395–396; stereotypes, 397–399; strains and imbalances, 364–365; and transition to devalued role, 389–392; and transition to valued role, 385–389
agriculture, energy, and food, 290–292
Aid to Families of Dependent Children, 642, 647; and welfare poor, 655–658

alcohol (*see also* alcoholism and problem drinking; drugs; drug use): and automobile, 206–209; combination with drugs, 187; and drinking customs, 187–189; as drug, 146; and family, 210–211; identifying problems of, 183–184; institutional dependence, plateau effect, and, 198–199; lowering of drinking age, 205; physiological effects of, 185–186; psychological effects, 186–187; social policy and normative behavior, 214–215; as social problem, 10–11; social responses to problems of, 212–215; and social systems, 212–214; and work, 211; and youth, 203–206
alcoholic, 193
Alcoholics Anonymous, 212
alcoholism and problem drinking, 183, 190–193 (*see also* alcohol, drugs; drug use): causation theories, 199–200; costs, 209–210; cultural factors, 200–202; dependence in, 193–198; effect of drinking customs, 187–188; and heredity, 202–203
alienation and strife, 693–694
American Bar Association, 431
An American Dilemma (Myrdal), 339
American G.I. Forum, 496
American Management Association, 431–432
American Medical Association, 12, 596
Americans for Democratic Action, 596
American Telephone and Telegraph Co., 420, 428
amphetamines, 151
anomie, and premarital sexual conflict, 236–238
anomie-and-opportunity-structure theory of deviance, 31, 32, 34
anomie theory, 6, 73–74; distortion of, 35
annulment, and family disorganization, 515
anticipatory socialization, and role transition, 385–386
antiwar demonstrations, 699–700
apathy, collective, as social problem, 19
apprenticeship problems, and sex typing, 428–429
Arab Algeria, divorce rates, 514
arms race: and economy, 694–696, 697; national insecurity, violence, and, 715–718
Army-McCarthy hearings, 17
arrests and convictions for drug use, 170
assassination, 678
Association of Cell Biologists, 431
Association of Women Geographers, 432

associations, legitimate, crime in, 82–85
attitudes, and laws, 485
authoritarian personality, 486–487
authority relationships, and inequality, 315
automobile, and alcohol, 206–209

barbiturates, 151–152
Barrows v. *Jackson*, 471n
behavior (*see also* deviant behavior; homosexual behavior): aberrant vs. nonconforming, 29–31; as adaptive problem solving, 70–71; alcohol's effect on, 186–187; effect of criminal justice system on, 52–53; and moral status of law, 52; normative, and social policy, 214–215; political, and sex roles, 432–436; social, drug use as, 158–159
Benjamin Rush parable, 5, 6, 31, 32
bereavement, vs. divorce, 544–545
Berger Court, 472
biological theories of criminology, 68–69
birth rate and population control, 297–298
Black Nationalists, stand on abortion and contraceptives, 520
blacks: desertion and divorce rates, 534–535; economic trends, 478–480; educational trends, 480–482; and id stereotype, 489; illegitimacy among, 519–521; migration to cities, 473–474; and mobility, 324–329; "Negro" role, 491; political trends, 474–475; unrest, and relative deprivation, 492–493, 692–693
black women: changes in lives of, 442–443; work and social condition, 441–442
blue-collar job, 624–628
bonds, societal, and violence, 684–686
boundary roles, white collar workers, 629
brain syndromes, organic, 110
Brave New World (Huxley), 732
British Social Science Research Council, 729
Brown v. *Board of Education,* 471
Buchanan v. *Warley,* 470n
bureaucracy, as persistent value, 748
business, crimes within, 82–83
bussing: and community disorganization, 573–574; and school desegregation, 472, 473

California: AFDC, 647; population and resources, 283
cancer, cervical, and sexual intercourse, 242
Capital (Marx), 314
Cassell v. *Texas,* 471n
categoric risks, 59
Catholics: and abortion, 451; discrimination against, 463; and marriage dissolution, 535–536; mobility, 323
The Causes of World War III (Mills), 696
celibacy, as Catholic ideal, 225
cerebral arteriosclerosis, psychosis with, 111

change (*see also* social change): institutional, 30; mechanisms of, 698–709; rapid, and irrelevance of constraints, 593
Chicano movement, 505
children: conflict with parents, 547–550; illegitimate, and extramarital coitus, 238–240; and locality specialization, 586–588; in marital disorganization, 545–546; and poverty, 658–659
Chile, sexual norms in, 229–230
China: marriage system, 522–523; position on population control, 298
Chinese Americans, discrimination against, 462
city (*see also* community; urbanization): black mayors, 476; black migration to, 473–474; crime in, 569–572; education in, 572–575; independent, 579–580; problems, 569–575; societies and mental illness, 118–120; that imports workers daily, 580–581
civil commitment of drug addicts, 175
civil rights, and social control, 93–94, 95–96
Civil Rights Act (1964), 325, 331, 420, 428, 472, 480, 488, 615
Civil Rights Cases, 470n
civil rights laws, 471–472
classified ads, sex-segregated, 428
classroom, sexism in, 439
Club of Rome, 284
cocaine, 151; use of, 156–157
coffee, as drug, 146
cohabitation, 235–236
cohort analysis, in anticipating social change, 403–406
cohort flow: and aging, 358–360; and balancing people and roles, 402–403
cold war, 687–688
Coleman Report on Educational Opportunities, 23–24, 481
collective action: residuum of, 564–567; and social problems, 19–21
college students, drug use, 163
Commission on Population Growth and the American Future, 292, 296
Commission on the Year 2000, 729
commitment to mental hospital, 132–133
communes: and extramarital sex relations, 244; as reaction to specialization, 584–585
communication: limits, and system building, 686–687; social, and social disorganization, 27
Communist Labor party, 704
Communist Manifesto (Marx and Engels), 749
communist world: efforts to redefine equality, 344–346; equality and inequality in, 339–344; heightened awareness of status in, 346–347; pressures toward deviation, 348–349
community (*see also* city; community disor-

B
C
D
E
F
G
H
I
J